MARKET
SHARE
REPORTER

ISSN 1052-9578

MARKET SHARE REPORTER

AN ANNUAL COMPILATION

OF REPORTED MARKET SHARE

DATA ON COMPANIES,

PRODUCTS, AND SERVICES

2006

Volume 1

ROBERT S. LAZICH, Editor

THOMSON

GALE

Detroit • New York • San Francisco • San Diego • New Haven, Conn. • Waterville, Maine • London • Munich

Market Share Reporter 2006
Robert S. Lazich

Project Editor
Virgil L. Burton III

Editorial
Joyce P. Simkin, Susan M. Turner

Manufacturing
Rita Wimberley

ISBN 0-7876-8608-5 (2 vol. set)
ISBN 0-7876-9460-6 (Vol. 1)
ISBN 0-7876-9461-4 (Vol. 2)
ISSN 1052-9578

Printed in the United States of America
10 9 8 7 6 5 4 3 2 1

TABLE OF CONTENTS

TABLE OF TOPICS

The *Table of Topics* lists all topics used in *Market Share Reporter* in alphabetical order. One or more page references follow each topic; the page references identify the starting point where the topic is shown. The same topic name may be used under different SICs; therefore, in some cases, more than one page reference is provided. Roman numerals indicate volume number.

INTRODUCTION

Market Share Reporter (MSR) is a compilation of market share reports from periodical literature. As shown by reviews of previous editions plus correspondence and telephone contact with many users, this is a unique resource for competitive analysis, diversification planning, marketing research, and other forms of economic and policy analysis.

This is the sixteenth edition of *Market Share Reporter*. In previous editions, *Market Share Reporter* presented market share data on the North American market. In 1997, *World Market Share Reporter* was first published, which provided international coverage -- market shares on global industries or markets in countries other than the United States, Canada and Mexico.

The editorial staff of *Market Share Reporter* decided that the needs of the users of *Market Share Reporter* would best be served by combining the two titles into one two-volume set. Previously, users would need to consult two separate books to gather research on market shares. The 2006 edition of *MSR* now provides market share information on domestic and international markets in one volume. A user seeking market share information on the automobile market, for example, will find entries covering the United States as well as foreign countries and the entire global industry. Having such data together in one chapter should be both entertaining and informative to readers.

However, little has changed from previous editions of *Market Share Reporter.* Frequent users will find that the book is still primarily arranged around the *Standard Industrial Classification* (SIC) code. Features of the 2006 edition include—

- More than 3,600 entries, all new or updated.
- Entries arranged under both SIC and NAICS codes.
- Corporate, brand, product, service and commodity market shares.
- Coverage of private and public sector activities.
- Comprehensive indexes, including products, companies, brands, places, sources, NAICS, ISIC, Harmonized and SIC codes.
- Table of Topics showing topical subdivisions of chapters with page references.
- Graphics.
- Annotated source listing—provides publishers' information for journals cited in this edition of *MSR.*
- *MSR* is a one-of-a-kind resource for ready reference, marketing research, economic analysis, planning, and a host of other disciplines.

Categories of Market Shares

Entries in *Market Share Reporter* fall into four broad categories. Items were included if they showed the relative strengths of participants in a market or provided subdivisions of economic activity in some manner that could assist the analyst.

- *Corporate market shares* show the names of companies that participate in an industry, produce a product, or provide a service. Each company's market share is shown as a percent of total industry or product sales for a defined period, usually a year. In some cases, the company's share represents the share of the sales of the companies shown (group total)—because shares of the total market were not cited in the source or were not relevant. In some corporate share tables, brand information appears behind company names in parentheses. In these cases, the tables can be located using either the company or the brand index.

- *Institutional shares* are like corporate shares but show the shares of other kinds of organizations. The most common institutional entries in *MSR* display the shares of states, provinces, or regions in an activity. The shares of not-for-profit organizations in some economic or service functions fall under this heading.

- *Brand market shares* are similar to corporate shares with the difference that brand names are shown. Brand names include equivalent categories such as the names of television programs, magazines, publishers' imprints, etc. In some cases, the names of corporations appear in parentheses behind the brand name; in these cases, tables can be located using either the brand or the company index.

- *Product, commodity, service, and facility shares* feature a broad category (e.g. household appliances) and show how the category is subdivided into components (e.g. refrigerators, ranges, washing machines, dryers, and dishwashers). Entries under this category cover products (autos, lawnmowers, polyethylene, etc.), commodities (cattle, grains, crops), services (telephone, child care), and facilities (port berths, hotel suites, etc.). Subdivisions may be products, categories of services (long-distance telephone, residential phone service, 800-service), types of commodities (varieties of grain), size categories (e.g., horsepower ranges), modes (rail, air, barge), types of facilities (categories of hospitals, ports, and the like), or other subdivisions.

- *Other shares.* MSR includes a number of entries that show subdivisions, breakdowns, and shares that do not fit neatly into the above categorizations but properly belong in such a book because they shed light on public policy, foreign trade, and other subjects of general interest. These items include, for instance, subdivisions of governmental expenditures, environmental issues, and the like.

Coverage

MSR reports on *published* market shares rather than attempting exhaustive coverage of the market shares, say, of all major corporations and of all products and services. Despite this limitation, *MSR* holds share information on more than 6,100 companies, more than 3,000 brands, and more than 2,300 product, commodity, service, and facility categories. Several entries are usually available for each industry group in the SIC classification; omitted groups are those that do not play a conventional role in the market, e.g., Private Households (SIC 88).

As pointed out in previous editions, *MSR* tends to reflect the current concerns of the business press. In addition to being a source of market share data, it mirrors journalistic preoccupations, issues in the business community, and events abroad. Important and controversial industries and activities get most of the ink. Heavy coverage is provided in those areas that are—

- large, important, basic (autos, chemicals)
- on the leading edge of technological change (computers, electronics, software)
- very competitive (toiletries, beer, soft drinks)
- in the news because of product recalls, new product introductions, mergers and acquisitions, lawsuits, and for other reasons
- relate to popular issues (environment, crime), or have excellent coverage in their respective trade press.

Variation in coverage from previous editions is due in part to publication cycles of sources and a different mix of brokerage house reports for the period covered (due to shifting interests within the investment community).

How Entries Are Prepared

In many cases, several entries are provided on a subject each citing the same companies. No attempt was made to eliminate such seeming duplication if the publishing and/or original sources were different and the market shares were not identical. Those who work with such data know that market share reports are often little more than the "best guesses" of knowledgeable observers rather than precise measurements. To the planner or analyst, variant reports about an industry's market shares are useful for interpreting the data.

Publications appearing in the January 2004 to July 2005 period were used in preparing *MSR*. Market shares were gathered from newspapers, magazines, newsletters, government reports and press releases.

As a rule, material on market share data for 2005 were used by preference; in response to reader requests, we have included historical data when available. In some instances, information for earlier years was included if the category was unique or if the earlier year was necessary for context. In a number of cases, projections for 2006 and later years were also included.

Some of the entries covering the global marketplace may be deemed "old" by the user. However, it is important to note that when analyzing the international marketplace the most recent data available may indeed be several years old. Such data are kept to a minimum and are used only if the share provides coverage of an unusual market or a popular, competitive one (diapers or toiletries, for example).

Entry titles. Because *Market Share Reporter* now holds entries on domestic and international markets, titles have become more descriptive than in previous editions. Each entry will indicate in the title if it is for a particular country, state, city or region. An entry may address a global market (Top Computer Makers Worldwide).

In such entries, the title will feature "worldwide" or "global" so that the reader understands the market being discussed.

Many entries do not feature any geographical reference in the title. In these instances, the entries are referring to the market in the United States. Market data on the United States make up well over half the entries in this book, so such an editorial decision seemed reasonable to the staff of *MSR*.

It is important to note that some sources do not explicitly state whether the market shares they publish are for the domestic or international market. Often, it is obvious by some measure in the article—dollar sales or unit shipments, for example—if the shares describe the United States or some global industry. However, in a handful of entries the staff of *MSR* has had to use their best judgment. As stated earlier, market share data is often best guesses of knowledgeable observers. The staff of *MSR* feels that its own best guesses have been sufficient.

SIC and NAICS

The United States has used the *Standard Industrial Classification* code for roughly 60 years. It became clear, however, that the SIC code had its limitations. It was difficult to address the new technologies and ways of selling that had come to the global marketplace, such as warehouse clubs, office supply stores, and Internet businesses and technology. The *North American Industrial Classification System (NAICS)* is intended to serve as a more comprehensive method to classify industries.

The transition between SIC and NAICS was implemented for the 1997 Economic Census. The new NAICS coding—which is used in the United States, Canada and Mexico—is a major revamping of the industrial classification system. *NAICS* coding includes new sectors and a more detailed study of the "services" category (industries that would fall under the 5300 and higher section of the SIC code).

Under *NAICS* coding, a 6-digit industry code replaces the old 4-digit SIC code. The first two digits indicate the sector, the third the subsector, the fourth designates the industry group, the fifth the NAICS industry and the sixth the national industry. There are 20 sectors in *NAICS* and 1,170 industries in *NAICS*.

Because the SIC code is still the more popular classification system, *Market Share Reporter* is organized around its coding. However, each entry now contains *NAICS* codes appropriate to the industry being discussed. Most entries will have only one *NAICS* code. However, some entries will have more than one code (three is the maximum). As stated, *NAICS* codes are more detailed than *SIC* classifications. Because of this, more than one *NAICS* code was sometimes necessary to provide the most accurate description of the industry being analyzed.

More information about *NAICS* is available through the U.S. Department of Commerce web site at http://www.ntis.gov/naics.

"Unusual" Market Shares

Some reviewers of the first edition questioned—sometimes tongue-in-cheek, sometimes seriously—the inclusion of tables on such topics as computer crime, the pet population, children's allowances, governmental budgets, and weapons system stockpiles. Indeed, some of these categories do not fit the sober meaning of "market share." A few tables on such subjects are present in every edition—because they provide market information, albeit indirectly, or because they are the "market share equivalents" in an industrial classification which is in the public sector or dominated by the public sector's purchasing power.

Organization of Chapters

Market Share Reporter is organized into chapters by 2-digit SIC categories (industry groups). The exception is the first chapter, entitled *General Interest and Broad Topics*; this chapter holds all entries that bridge two or more 2-digit SIC industry codes (e.g. retailing in general, beverage containers, building materials, etc.) and cannot, therefore, be classified using the SIC system without distortion. Please note, however, that a topic in this chapter will often have one or more additional entries later—where the table could be assigned to a detailed industry. Thus, in addition to tables on packaging in the first chapter, numerous tables appear later on glass containers, metal cans, etc.

Within each chapter, entries are shown by 4-digit SIC (industry level). Within blocks of 4-digit SIC entries, entries are sorted alphabetically by topic, then alphabetically by title.

SIC and Topic Assignments

MSR's SIC classifications are based on the coding as defined in the *Standard Industrial Classification Manual* for 1987, issued by the Bureau of the Census, Department of Commerce. This 1987 classification system introduced significant revisions to the 1972 classification (as slightly modified in 1977); the 1972 system is still in widespread use (even by the Federal government); care should be used in comparing data classified in the new and in the old way.

The closest appropriate 4-digit SIC was assigned to each table. In many cases, a 3-digit SIC had to be used because the substance of the table was broader than the nearest 4-digit SIC category. Such SICs always end with a zero. In yet other cases, the closest classification possible was at the 2-digit level; these SICs terminate with double-zero. If the content of the table did not fit the 2-digit level, it was assigned to the first chapter of *MSR* and classified by topic only.

Topic assignments are based on terminology for commodities, products, industries, and services in the SIC Manual; however, in many cases phrasing has been simplified, shortened, or updated; in general, journalistically succinct rather than bureaucratically exhaustive phraseology was used throughout.

Organization of Entries

Entries are organized in a uniform manner. A sample entry is provided below. Explanations for each part of an entry, shown in boxes, are provided below the sample.

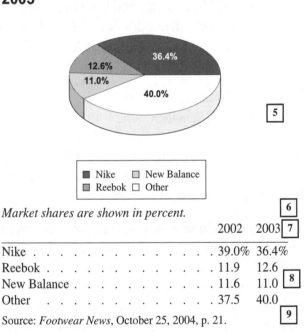

★ 1503 ★ [1]
Footwear [2]
SIC: 3149; NAICS: 316211 [3]
Sports Shoe Market Worldwide, 2002- [4]
2003

[5]

Market shares are shown in percent. [6]

	2002	2003 [7]
Nike	39.0%	36.4%
Reebok	11.9	12.6
New Balance	11.6	11.0 [8]
Other	37.5	40.0

Source: *Footwear News*, October 25, 2004, p. 21. [9]

[1] *Entry Number.* A numeral between star symbols. Used for locating an entry from the index.

[2] *Topic.* Second line, small type. Gives the broad or general product or service category of the entry. The topic for Sports Shoe Market Worldwide, 2002-2003 is Footwear.

[3] *SIC and NAICS Code.* Second line, small type, follows the topic. General entries in the first chapter do not have an SIC code.

[4] *Title.* Third line, large type. Describes the entry with a headline.

[5] *Graphic.* When a graphic is present, it follows the title. Some entries will be illustrated with a pie or bar chart. The information used to create the graphic is always shown below the pie or bar chart.

[6] *Note Block.* When present, follows the title and is in italic type. The note provides contextual information about the entry to make the data more understandable. Special notes about the data, information about time periods covered, market totals, and other comments are provided. Self-explanatory entries do not have a note block.

[7] *Column headers.* Follow the note block. Some entries have more than one column or the single column requires a header. In these cases, column headers are used to describe information covered in the column. In most cases, column headers are years (2005) or indicators of type and magnitude ($ mil.). Column headers are shown only when necessary for clarity of presentation.

[8] *Body.* Follows the note block or the column header and shows the actual data in two or more columns. In most cases, individual rows of data in the body are arranged in descending order, with the largest market share holder heading the list. Collective shares, usually labeled "Others" are placed last.

[9] *Source.* Follows the body. All entries cite the source of the table, the date of publication, and the page number (if given). In many cases, the publisher obtained the

information from another source (original source); in all such cases, the original source is also shown.

Continued entries. Entries that extend over two adjacent columns on the same page are not marked to indicate continuation with *continue* in the second column. Entries that extend over two pages are marked *Continued on the next page.* Entries carried over from the previous page repeat the entry number, topic (followed by the word *continued*), title, and column header (if any).

Use of Names

Company Names. The editors reproduced company names as they appeared in the source unless it was clearly evident from the name and the context that a name had been misspelled in the original. Large companies, of course, tend to appear in a large number of entries and in variant renditions. General Electric Corporation may appear as GE, General Electric, General Electric Corp., GE Corp., and other variants. No attempt was made to enforce a uniform rendition of names in the entries. In the Company Index, variant renditions were reduced to a single version or cross-referenced.

Use of Numbers

Throughout *MSR*, tables showing percentage breakdowns may add to less than 100 or fractionally more than 100 due to rounding. In those cases where only a few leading participants in a market are shown, the total of the shares may be substantially less than 100.

Numbers in the note block showing the total size of the market are provided with as many significant digits as possible in order to permit the user to calculate the sales of a particular company by multiplying the market total by the market share.

In a relatively small number of entries, actual unit or dollar information is provided rather than share information in percent. In such cases, the denomination of the unit (tons, gallons, $) and its magnitude (000 indicates multiply by 1,000; mil., multiply by 1,000,000) are mentioned in the note block or shown in the column header.

Data in some entries are based on different kinds of currencies and different weight and liquid measures. Where necessary, the unit is identified in the note block or in the column header. Examples are long tons, short tons, metric tons or Canadian dollars, etc.

Graphics

Pie and bar charts are used to illustrate some of the entries. This edition of *MSR* features more sophisticated looking pie and bar charts than in previous editions. The editors of *Market Share Reporter* hope that regular users of the book enjoy these changes.

The graphics show the names of companies, products, and services when they fit on the charts. When room is insufficient to accommodate the label, the first word of a full name is used followed by three periods (...) to indicate omission of the rest of the label.

Pie charts include a key to indicate the name that corresponds to each "pie slice" in the graphic. Bar charts now include a scale on the bottom axis with a denomination such as "million dollars" or "billion units." The largest share sets the width of the column, and smaller shares are drawn in proportion.

Sources

The majority of entries were extracted from newspapers and from general purpose, trade, and technical periodicals normally available in larger public, special, or university libraries. All told, 2,018 sources were used; of these, 1,004 were primary print sources. Many more sources were reviewed but lacked coverage of the subject. These primary sources, in turn, used 1,014 original sources.

In many cases, the primary source in which the entry was published cites another source for the data, the original source. Original sources include other publications, brokerage houses, consultancies and research organizations, associations, government agencies, special surveys, and the like.

Many sources have also been used from the World Wide Web. The citation includes the Web address, the date the article was retrieved, and, if possible, the title of the article or report. In many cases Web pages have no title or author name. As well, it is not uncommon for Web pages to be moved or temporarily out of operation.

Since many primary sources appear as original sources elsewhere, and vice-versa, primary and original sources are shown in a single Source Index under two headings. Primary sources included in *MSR* almost always used the market share data as illustrative material for narratives covering many aspects of the subject. We hope that this book will also serve as a guide to those articles.

Indexes

Market Share Reporter features five indexes and two appendices.

- **Source Index**. This index holds 2,018 references in two groupings. *Primary sources* (1,004) are publications where the data were found. *Original sources* (1,014) are sources cited in the primary sources. Each item in the index is followed by one or more entry numbers arranged sequentially, beginning with the first mention of the source.

- **Place Names Index**. This index provides references to cities, states, parks and regions in North America. Five hundred sixty three place name citations are included. References are to entry numbers.

- **Products, Services, Names and Issues Index**. This index holds more than 2,300 references to products, personal names and services in alphabetical order. The index also lists subject categories that do not fit the definition of a product or service but properly belong in the index. Examples include *aquariums, consumer spending, crime, defense spending, economies, lotteries*, and the like. Some listings are abbreviations for chemical substances, computer software, etc. which may not be meaningful to those unfamiliar with the industries. Wherever possible, the full name is also provided for abbreviations commonly in use. Each listing is followed by one or more references to entry numbers.

- **Company Index**. This index shows references to more than 6,100 company names by entry number. Companies are arranged in alphabetical order. In some cases, the market share table from which the company name was derived showed the share for a combination of two or more companies; these combinations are reproduced in the index.

- **Brand Index**. The Brand Index shows references to nearly 3,000 brands by entry number. The arrangement is alphabetical. Brands include names of publications, computer software, operating systems, etc., as well as the more conventional brand names (Coca Cola, Maxwell House, Budweiser, etc.)

Appendix I

- **SIC Coverage**. The first appendix shows SICs covered by *Market Share Reporter*. The listing shows major SIC groupings at the 2-digit level as bold-face headings followed by 4-digit SIC numbers, the names of the SIC, and a *page* reference (rather than a reference to an entry number, as in the indexes). The page shows the first occurrence of the SIC in the book. *MSR*'s SIC coverage is quite comprehensive, as shown in the appendix. However, many 4-digit SIC categories are further divided into major product groupings. Not all of these have corresponding entries in the book.

- **NAICS Coverage**. This section of the appendix contains a listing of the *North American Industrial Classification System* codes that appear in *Market Share Reporter*. *NAICS* is a six digit classification system that covers 20 sectors and 1,170 industries. The page shows the first occurrence of the *NAICS* code in the book.

- **ISIC Coverage**. This section of the appendix provides a listing of the Industrial Standard Industrial Classification (ISIC) codes that appear in *Market Share Reporter*. ISIC codes, as with Harmonized Codes, are coding systems similar to NAICS. If features broader classifications and is less widely used. The ISIC listing shows the 4-digit level along with name of the industries. References to entries are not included.

- **HC Coverage**. This section provides a listing of the Harmonized Commodity classifications that appear in *MSR*. The listing shows industrial groups at the 2-digit, or chapter, level along with the names of the industries. Reference entries are not included. Both the Harmonized Code and the ISIC code sections are included in *MSR* because while they are older classification systems they are still of interest to some readers.

Appendix II

- **Annotated Source List**. The second appendix provides publisher names, addresses, telephone and fax numbers, and publication frequency of primary sources cited in *Market Share Reporter*, 16th Edition.

What's New

As stated, this edition of *MSR* includes more sophisticated graphics. The book includes pie graphs, vertical bar graphs and new horizontal bar graphs.

Also, the editors have redesigned the indexes, from two to three columns. The geographic index has also been better organized. For countries and regions that have a large number of entries, subheadings have now been included. In previous editions, for example, the United States was followed by a long list of entries in which the country appears. Now these entries have been organized by industry subheadings such as "apparel", "building materials", "chemicals".

Available in Electronic Formats

Licensing. *Market Share Reporter* is available for licensing. The complete database is provided in a fielded format and is deliverable on such media as disk, CD-ROM or tape. For more information, contact Gale's Business Development Group at (800) 877-GALE or visit us on our web site at www.galegroup.com/bizdev.

Online. *Market Share Reporter* is accessible online as File MKTSHR through LEXIS-NEXIS and as part of the MarkIntel service offered by Thomson Financial Securities Data. For more information, contact LEXIS-NEXIS, P.O. Box 933, Dayton, OH 45401-0933, phone (937) 865-6800, toll-free (800) 227-4908, website: http://www.lexis-nexis.com; or Thomson Financial Securities Data, Two Gateway Center, Newark, NJ 07102, phone: (973) 622-3100, toll-free: (888) 989-8373, website: www.tfsd.com.

Acknowledgements

Market Share Reporter is something of a collective enterprise which involves not only the editorial team but also many users who share comments, criticisms, and suggestions over the telephone. Their help and encouragement is very much appreciated. *MSR* could not have been produced without the help of many people in and outside of The Gale Group. The editors would like to express their special appreciation to Virgil Burton (Coordinating Editor, Gale Group) and to the staff of Editorial Code and Data, Inc.

Comments and Suggestions

Comments on *MSR* or suggestions for improvement of its usefulness, format, and coverage are always welcome. Although every effort is made to maintain accuracy, errors may occasionally occur; the editors will be grateful if these are called to their attention. Please contact:

Editors
Market Share Reporter
Thomson Gale
27500 Drake Road
Farmington Hills, MI 48331-3535
Phone: (248) 699-GALE
or (800) 347-GALE
Fax: (248) 699-8069

General Interest and Broad Topics

★ 1 ★
Auctions

Auction Sales by Year

Auction sales are shown in billions of dollars.

2002	$ 190
2003	203
2004	217

Source: *USA TODAY*, February 23, 2005, p. B1, from National Auctioneers Association.

★ 2 ★
Auctions

Popular Auction Categories, 2004

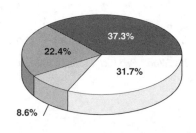

■ Autos □ Agricultural equipment
■ Real estate □ Other

Total auction sales were $217 billion, a sharp increase over $203.2 billion in 2003. Real estate was the most active category with land and agricultural real estate up 14.7%. Residential real estate grew 14.1%. The automotive category was the slowest grower, up just 1%.

	($ bil.)	Share
Autos	$ 79.8	37.29%
Real estate	48.0	22.43
Agricultural equipment	18.4	8.60
Other	67.8	31.68

Source: ''Live Auction Industry Sales Hit Record $217.2B Pace in 2004.'' [online] from http://www.auctioneers.org [Press release January 13, 2005], p. B1, from National Auctioneers Association.

★ 3 ★
Christmas Trees

Christmas Tree Sales, 2003

More consumers still purchase real trees than fake ones, but the lead is narrowing. Consumers purchased 23.4 million real trees, up 5% over the previous year, while 9.6 million households purchased fake trees, up 30% for the same period.

Real	$ 791
Fake	600

Source: *Knight Ridder/Tribune Business News*, December 3, 2004, p. NA, from National Christmas Tree Association.

★ 4 ★
Consumer Spending

Holiday Spending

Spending is shown in billions of dollars.

Christmas/Hanukkah/Kwanza	$ 219.90
Valentine's Day	12.79
Easter	10.47
Mother's Day	10.43
Father's Day	8.04

Source: *America's Intelligence Wire*, October 4, 2004, p. NA, from National Retail Foundation.

★ 5 ★
Consumer Spending

How Consumers Pay for Goods

The use of debit cards has been on the increase. 40 million checks are transported each year.

	1999	2003
Cash	39.0%	32.0%
Credit cards	22.0	21.0
Debit cards	21.0	31.0
Checks	18.0	15.0
Prepaid cards	0.0	1.0

Source: *USA TODAY*, October 12, 2004, p. B4, from American Bankers Association.

★ 6 ★
Corporate Sponsors

Leading Industries for Corporate Sponsorship Worldwide, 2004

There were 1,382 new deals during the year, up from 1,353 in 2003. The value of the deals was up to $6.9 billion from $5.8 billion in 2003. Sports remains the volume leader, much of this coming from naming rights from the National Football League.

Sports	78.0%
Arts and culture	9.0
Broadcasting	8.0
Other	5.0

Source: *Brandweek*, February 14, 2005, p. 20, from *World Sponsorship Monitor*.

★ 7 ★
Countertops

Bathroom Countertop Market

The table shows the preferred brands of residential remodeling and new home construction.

	Re-Modeling	New Homes
Laminates	27.0%	26.0%
Cultured marble	22.0	54.0
Solid surface	20.0	6.0
Ceramic tile	8.0	7.0

Source: *Kitchen & Bath Design News*, June 2004, p. NA, from National Kitchen & Bath Association 2003 research.

★ 8 ★
Countertops

Kitchen and Bath Countertop Demand, 2002 and 2007

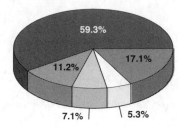

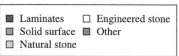

Demand is expected to increase more than 2 percent each year to 467 million square feet in 2007. Kitchen and bath remodeling willl also help drive expenditures. Figures are shown in millions of square feet.

	2002	2007	Share
Laminates	259.1	277.0	59.31%
Solid surface	46.5	52.1	11.16
Natural stone	24.4	33.1	7.09
Engineered stone	15.9	25.0	5.35
Other	74.1	79.8	17.09

Source: *Wood & Wood Products*, March 2004, p. 57, from Freedonia Group.

★ 9 ★
Countertops

Kitchen Countertop Market

The table shows the preferred brands of residential remodeling and new home construction.

	Re-Modeling	New Homes
Laminates	58.0%	50.0%
Solid surface	15.0	16.0
Granite	14.0	14.0
Ceramic tile	7.0	8.0

Source: *Kitchen & Bath Design News*, June 2004, p. NA, from National Kitchen & Bath Association 2003 research.

★ 10 ★
Flooring

Flooring Industry in the U.K., 2003

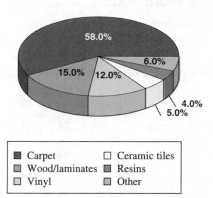

The industry is valued at 887 million pounds sterling. Offices represent about 20% of the total, with leisure second at 19%.

	(mil.)	Share
Carpet	£ 512	58.0%
Wood/laminates	132	15.0
Vinyl	103	12.0
Ceramic tiles	47	5.0
Resins	37	4.0
Other	56	6.0

Source: *Contract Flooring Journal*, September 2004, p. 46, from AMA Research estimates.

★ 11 ★
Flooring

Flooring Market Shares, 2003

Shares are shown based on volume.

Carpets	67.8%
Vinyl	13.8
Ceramic tiles	11.2
Laminates	3.7
Rubber	0.2
Other	4.3

Source: *Floor Covering Weekly*, Annual 2004, p. NA.

★ 12 ★
Licensed Merchandise

Largest Licensing Categories in the U.K., 2004

Categories are ranked by character revenue sales in millions of pounds for the first six months of the year.

Toys	£ 279
Clothing	169
Video/DVD	119
School equipment	94
Publishing	94

Source: *Brand Strategy*, December 2004 - January 2005, p. 47, from Eurotoys.

★ 13 ★
Licensed Merchandise

Licensing Revenues, 2003-2004

Total licensing revenue grew less than 1% during this period, up from $5,805 million in 2003 to $5,845 million in 2004. The industry benefits from hit movies like Spider-Man and Shrek. Music increased 8%, the largest increase in the group. Publishing fell 4.7% (the other category fell 31.8%).

	2003	2004	Share
Entertainment, TV, movie characters	$ 2,502	$ 2,565	43.88%
Trademarks/brands	1,060	1,081	18.49
Fashion	848	814	13.93
Sports	807	795	13.60
Collegiate	203	201	3.44
Art	167	170	2.91
Music	113	122	2.09
Publishing	43	41	0.70
Museums, charitable and non-profits	40	41	0.70
Other	22	15	0.26

Source: *USA TODAY*, June 21, 2005, p. 4B, from International Licensing Industry Merchandising Merchandisers Association.

★ 14 ★
Licensed Merchandise

Richest Fictional Characters, 2003

Fictional characters are ranked by gross revenues in millions of dollars.

Mickey Mouse & friends	$ 5,800
Winnie the Pooh & friends	5,600
Frodo Baggins (Lord of the Rings)	2,900
Harry Potter	2,800
Nemo	2,000
Yu-gi-oh	1,600
SpongeBob SquarePants	1,500
Spider-Man	1,300
Wolverine (X-Men)	900
Pokemon	825

Source: *Forbes*, November 1, 2004, p. 58.

★ 15 ★
Luxury

Luxury Industry, 2004

Total spending on luxury items stood at $525 billion in 2004. Luxury travel includes hotels, cruises, airlines and international travel.

	($ bil.)	Share
Luxury travel	$ 130	24.30%
Homes and luxury home renovations	100	18.69
Luxury cars, SUVs, light trucks	80	14.95
Luxury home goods and electronics	60	11.21
Dining out	60	11.21
Food, coffee, wine	50	9.35
Fashion	30	5.61
Spas, cosmetic survery and dentistry	25	4.67

Source: *PR Newswire*, January 20, 2005, p. NA, from Boston Consulting Group.

★ 16 ★
Nanotechnology

Nanomagnetic Materials and Devices Industry Worldwide

Nanotechnology is thought to potentially offer serious benefits to energy efficiency, storage, and production. It also has implications for the environmental industry. The industry is forecasted to grow to $12 billion by 2009.

	2004	2009	Share
Information storage	$ 4,070	$ 11,480.9	96.01%
Biotechnology	158	310.0	2.59
Industrial products	93	167.1	1.40

Source: *Research Studies - Business Communications Inc.*, October 14, 2004, p. NA, from BCC Inc.

★ 17 ★
Nanotechnology

Nanotechnology Tool Market, 2008 and 2013

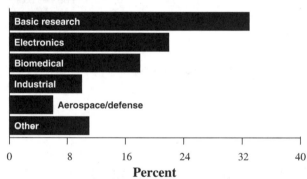

Nanotechnology tools represent a significant portion of the nanotechnology industry. Demand is forecasted to increase from $900 million in 2008 to $2.7 billion in 2013. As the technology improves, spending will move from general research to specific applications.

	2008	2013	Share
Basic research	$ 500	$ 900	32.73%
Electronics	150	600	21.82
Biomedical	75	500	18.18
Industrial	50	275	10.00
Aerospace/defense	50	175	6.36
Other	75	300	10.91

Source: *American Ceramic Society Bulletin*, November 2004, p. 5, from Freedonia Group.

★ 18 ★

Packaging

Beverage Container Industry, 2007

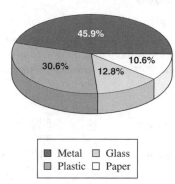

Metal ☐ Glass
Plastic ☐ Paper

Demand increased 1.7% from 205 billion units in 2002 to 223.5 billion units to 2007. Plastic grew 4.9% during this period, far greater than metal (1.7%) or glass (1.1%). Soft drinks are primarily packaged in plastic containers. By 2007, they will represent 30.5 billion of the 68.5 billion unit market, according to the source. Water is increasingly popular too, however, representing 17.5 billion of the total.

	(bil.)	Share
Metal	$ 102.6	45.91%
Plastic	68.5	30.65
Glass	28.7	12.84
Paper	23.7	10.60

Source: *Beverage Industry*, April 2004, p. 36, from Freedonia Group.

★ 19 ★

Packaging

Closure Market by Segment

Demand for caps and closures will increase to $6.8 billion in 2008. Leaders in the industry include Alcoa, AptarGroup, Berry Plastics, Erie Plastics, Owens-Illinois, Portola Packaging and Saint Gobain-Calmar. The top five firms account for about 33% of the domestic market.

Beverages	.35.0%
Food	.20.0
Personal care	.15.0
Household chemicals	8.0
Other	.24.0

Source: *Modern Plastics*, December 2004, p. 28, from Piper Jaffray.

★ 20 ★

Packaging

Fruit Drink Packaging, 2003

Pouches had a 1.5% share of the overall beverage packaging market in 2003. Worldwide, Packaging Strategies estimates that 6.5 billion pouches will be produced for fruit-flavored drinks in 2006, up from 4.1 billion in 2001.

Pouches	.34.2%
Plastics	.30.1
Aseptic boxes	.20.9
Other	.14.8

Source: *Beverage World*, January 15, 2005, p. 32, from Beverage Marketing Corp.

★ 21 ★

Packaging

Largest Beverage Packagers, 2003

Firms are ranked by revenues in millions of dollars.

Coca-Cola Co.	$ 21,044.0
Nestle SA	19,122.2
PepsiCo Inc.	16,400.0
Diageo	15,624.0
Kirin Brewery Co. Ltd.	14,356.8
Anheuser-Busch	11,998.0
Heineken	11,616.9
Kraft Foods Inc.	10,543.4
Interbrew	8,841.6
SABMiller	8,295.0

Source: *Food & Drug Packaging*, July 2004, p. 22.

★ 22 ★

Packaging

Largest Drug Packagers, 2003

Firms are ranked by revenues in millions of dollars.

Pfizer Inc.	$ 44,271.0
GlaxoSmithKline	35,163.0
Novartis	24,864.0
Merck & Co.	22,485.9
Aventis Pharmaceuticals	22,397.0
Bristol-Myers Squibb	19,543.0
Johnson & Johnson	19,517.0
AstraZeneca	18,800.0

Continued on next page.

★ 22 ★

[Continued]
Packaging

Largest Drug Packagers, 2003

Firms are ranked by revenues in millions of dollars.

Roche Group . . . . $ 17,196.8
Wyeth 15,850.6

Source: *Food & Drug Packaging*, July 2004, p. 22.

★ 23 ★

Packaging

Largest Food Packagers, 2003

Firms are ranked by revenues in millions of dollars.

Nestle SA . . . . $ 47,451.5
Tyson Foods 24,549.0
Unilever 21,355.7
Kraft Foods 20,466.6
Mars Inc. 17,000.0
ConAgra Foods 14,681.0
Groupe Danone 12,050.8
General Mills 10,506.0
Pepsico Inc. 10,500.0
Dean Foods Co. 9,184.6

Source: *Food & Drug Packaging*, July 2004, p. 22.

★ 24 ★

Packaging

Paper Packaging Demand, 2008

Sales of paper-based packaging materials (excluding boxes) are forecast to climb 2.3% a year through 2008. Demand will reach $8.4 billion. Plastic continues to steal share of the overall packaging market from paper. Paper still thrives in some sectors however - such as paper combined with foil and film in order to improve product performance.

Food 33.0%
Manufacturing 28.0
Beverages 15.0
Foodservice 14.0
Other 10.0

Source: *Converting*, March 2005, p. 14, from Freedonia Group.

★ 25 ★

Packaging

Sterile Medical Packaging Demand, 2003 and 2008

Medical packaging demand is forecast to increase 5.4% annually until it reaches $2.8 billion in 2008. Figures are in millions of dollars. Prefillable syringes grew 7.4% from 2003 to 2008 while blisterpacks and clamshells grew 6.6%.

	2003	2008	Share
Thermoformed trays	$ 370	$ 475	23.00%
Pouches	330	427	20.68
Prefillable syringes	210	300	14.53
Blisterpacks & clamshells . . .	140	193	9.35
Other	540	670	32.45

Source: *Cleanroom Technology*, March 2005, p. 3, from Freedonia Group.

★ 26 ★

Pets

Pet Industry

The fastest growing segment of the industry is in super high-end luxury items. ''Other'' includes boarding, grooming, pet sitting and other services. Spending is shown in billions of dollars.

	2001	2005	Share
Food	$ 12.8	$ 14.5	40.39%
Veterinary care	7.1	8.6	23.96
Supplies, medicine	6.2	8.8	24.51
Live animal sales	1.2	1.6	4.46
Other	1.2	2.4	6.69

Source: *USA TODAY*, February 11, 2005, p. 2A, from American Pet Products Manufacturers Association.

★ 27 ★

Pets

Pet Population

Pet ownership is currently at its highest level with 63% of all households owning a pet, which equates to 69 million households. Figures are in millions.

Freshwater fish 139
Cats 90
Dogs 73
Small animals 18
Birds 16

Continued on next page.

★ 27 ★

[Continued]
Pets

Pet Population

Pet ownership is currently at its highest level with 63% of all households owning a pet, which equates to 69 million households. Figures are in millions.

Reptiles   11
Saltwater fish   9

Source: *Business Wire*, April 27, 2005, p. NA, from American Pet Products Manufacturers Association.

★ 28 ★

Windows & Doors

Entry Door Market

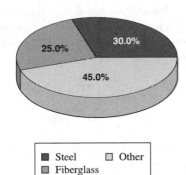

■ Steel   □ Other
■ Fiberglass

Steel took between 25-30% of the market. Fiberglass is becoming more popular but steel is still seen as the most secure.

Steel 30.0%
Fiberglass 25.0
Other 45.0

Source: *Building Products*, January - February 2005, p. 139, from Insulated Steel Door Institute.

★ 29 ★

Windows & Doors

Fire Door Sales

Data show sales by merchants over the previous 12 months.

	Internal	External
Flush doors	69.0%	87.0%
Panel doors	19.0	5.0

	Internal	External
Laminated timber cored flush doors	5.0%	3.0%
Die formed doors	5.0	2.0
Other	2.0	3.0

Source: *TTJ - The Timber Industry Magazine*, November 27, 2004, p. 23, from *Timber Fire Doors Survey*.

★ 30 ★

Windows & Doors

Global Windows & Doors Demand, 2007

Total demand is projected to rise to $146.5 billion in 2007. Global demand for vinyl, fiberglass and other plastic door products will grow faster than the demand for other types of products.

Asia/Pacific . . . .$ 58.6
North America 36.2
Other 5.2

Source: *Wood & Wood Products*, May 2004, p. 18, from Freedonia Group.

★ 31 ★

Windows & Doors

Leading Window and Door Makers in North America

Masonite recently agreed to take over Kohlberg, Kravis & Roberts. With this merger, Masonite may also soon be able to claim to be the largest manufacturer in the window & door industry. Andersen reports making 5 million doors and windows each year. Firms are ranked by estimated sales in millions of dollars.

Jeld-Wen Inc. . . . .$ 2,190
Anderson Corp. 2,150
Masonite International Corp. 1,780
Pella Corp. 1,060
Atrium Windows & Doors 800
MI Windows & Doors 700

Source: *Window & Door*, May 2005, p. NA, from *Forbes* and local sources and *Window & Door Top 100*.

★ 32 ★
Windows & Doors

Nonresidential Entry Door Market, 2003 and 2007

The industry is based on 3.1 million units in 2003 and 3.4 million units in 2007. Steel remains the dominant material in both residential and nonresidential markets.

	2003	2007
Aluminum	33.0%	31.0%
Wood	6.0	9.0
Steel	55.0	5.0
Other	6.0	55.0

Source: *Wood & Wood Products*, February 2005, p. 32, from Ducker Research.

★ 33 ★
Windows & Doors

Window & Door Demand, 1997 and 2012

According to the source, the household hardware business is one of the few manufacturing industries that maintains a strong domestic presence. The cabinet, door and window industry consolidated through the 1990s. The top four firms in the $25 billion window and door industry — Andersen Corp., Jeld-Wen, Masonite and Pella Corp — represent about 20% of sales. Figures are in millions of dollars.

	2007	2012	Share
Metal	$ 12,950	$ 16,610	43.14%
Wood	11,900	13,820	35.90
Plastic	6,200	8,070	20.96

Source: *Assembly*, June 2004, p. 52, from Freedonia Group.

★ 34 ★
Windows & Doors

Window Industry in Western Europe, 2003

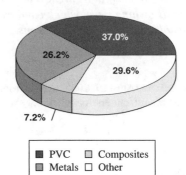

The industry is expected to see positive growth in 2004 after a steady market for the last three years. PVC has the largest market share in the U.K., Ireland, and the DACH area (Germany, Austria and Switzerland) with more than 50% share. Metal has an 80% market share in Spain and Portugal.

PVC	37.0%
Metals	26.2
Composites	7.2
Other	29.6

Source: *Glass Age*, October 31, 2004, p. 16, from Interconnection Consulting Group.

SIC 01 - Agricultural Production - Crops

★ 35 ★
Crops
SIC: 0110; NAICS: 11114, 11115

Crops Industry

Distribution is shown based on a market size of $7.5 billion.

Professional products	.27.0%
Corn	.22.0
Fruits and nuts	9.0
Cotton	9.0
Vegetables	8.0
Soybeans	8.0
Cereals	5.0
Other	.12.0

Source: "Crop Protection Regional and Country Detail." [online] from http://www.syngenta.com [Published March 30, 2005], from Syngenta estimates.

★ 36 ★
Crops
SIC: 0110; NAICS: 11114, 11115

Crops Industry in Eastern Europe

Distribution is shown based on a market size of $1.5 billion.

Cereals	.37.0%
Corn	.14.0
Oilseeds	.12.0
Beets	.12.0
Vegetables	9.0
Fruit & nuts	8.0
Other	9.0

Source: "Crop Protection Regional and Country Detail." [online] from http://www.syngenta.com [Published March 30, 2005], from Syngenta estimates.

★ 37 ★
Crops
SIC: 0110; NAICS: 11114, 11115

Crops Industry in France

Distribution is shown based on a market size of $2.2 billion.

Cereals	.38.0%
Fruit and nuts	.18.0
Corn	.10.0
Oilseeds	8.0
Vegetables	5.0
Beets	5.0
Other	.16.0

Source: "Crop Protection Regional and Country Detail." [online] from http://www.syngenta.com [Published March 30, 2005], from Syngenta estimates.

★ 38 ★
Wheat
SIC: 0111; NAICS: 11114

Wheat Production by State, 2005

Production is forecasted in thousands of bushels as of May 1, 2005.

	(000)	Share
Kansas	422,400	26.55%
Oklahoma	146,200	9.19
Washington	125,800	7.91
Texas	105,000	6.60
Colorado	85,750	5.39
Montana	84,050	5.28
Nebraska	76,500	4.81
Idaho	65,700	4.13
South Dakota	63,000	3.96
Ohio	53,460	3.36
Other	363,002	22.82

Source: *Crop Production*, May 2005, p. 4, from National Agricultural Statistics Service, U.S. Department of Agriculture.

★ 39 ★
Corn
SIC: 0115; NAICS: 11115

Corn Seed Market

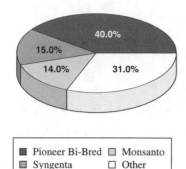

Market shares are shown in percent.

Pioneer Bi-Bred 40.0%
Syngenta 15.0
Monsanto 14.0
Other 31.0

Source: *Farm Industry News*, July 1, 2004, p. NA.

★ 40 ★
Soybeans
SIC: 0116; NAICS: 11111

Largest Soybean Producers, 2004

Data are in millions of bushels for the year through November 2004.

	(mil.)	Share
Iowa	497.4	15.54%
Illinois	492.5	15.39
Indiana	287.8	8.99
Minnesota	244.8	7.65
Nebraska	228.0	7.12
Missouri	227.2	7.10
Ohio	207.7	6.49
South Dakota	139.1	4.35
Arkansas	126.0	3.94
Kansas	110.7	3.46
Other	638.8	19.96

Source: *USA TODAY*, November 29, 2004, p. 2B.

★ 41 ★
Soybeans
SIC: 0116; NAICS: 11111

Leading Soybean Seed Makers in Argentina

The local industry is valued at $70 million.

Nidera 55.0%
Don Mario 25.0
Other 20.0

Source: *America's Intelligence Wire*, July 8, 2004, p. NA.

★ 42 ★
Cotton
SIC: 0131; NAICS: 11192

Largest Cotton Producers

Total production was 22.43 million tons.

	(mil.)	Share
China	5.42	24.36%
United States	4.39	19.73
India	3.12	14.02
Pakistan	1.73	7.78
Brazil	1.38	6.20
Uzbekistan	1.01	4.54
Turkey	0.99	4.45
Greece	0.35	1.57
Australia	0.34	1.53
Mali	0.29	1.30
Other	3.23	14.52

Source: *New York Times*, June 29, 2004, p. W1, from International Cotton Advisory Committee.

★ 43 ★
Cotton
SIC: 0131; NAICS: 11192

Leading Cotton Producing States, 2004

Data are in millions of bales.

Texas 7.5
Mississippi 2.4
California 2.4
Arkansas 2.1
Georgia 1.8
North Carolina 1.4
Tennessee 1.0
Louisiana 0.9
Missouri 0.8
Alabama 0.8

Source: *USA TODAY*, February 2, 2005, p. 2B, from U.S. Department of Agriculture.

★ 44 ★
Tobacco
SIC: 0132; NAICS: 11191
Tobacco Production by State

Production is shown in thousands of dollars.

	($ 000)	Share
North Carolina	$ 650,104	37.20%
Kentucky	481,708	27.56
Tennessee	139,762	8.00
Virginia	125,517	7.18
South Carolina	109,472	6.26
Georgia	85,676	4.90
Ohio	21,842	1.25
Florida	18,120	1.04
Indiana	17,065	0.98
Other	98,348	5.63

Source: *Crop Production*, May 2005, p. 4, from National Agricultural Statistics Service, U.S. Department of Agriculture.

★ 45 ★
Potatoes
SIC: 0134; NAICS: 111211
Potato Market Shares, 2004

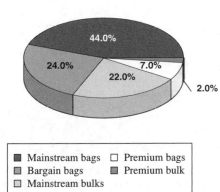

Potato sales averaged $1,714 per week per store, according to the source. Dollar shares of packaging are shown for October 2003 - September 2004.

Mainstream bags	.44.0%
Bargain bags	.24.0
Mainstream bulks	.22.0
Premium bags	. 7.0
Premium bulk	. 2.0

Source: *Produce Merchandising*, February 2005, p. 1, from ACNielsen and Persishables Group.

★ 46 ★
Vegetables
SIC: 0161; NAICS: 111219
Fresh-Cut Vegetable Sales

Fresh-cut vegetables are number two in the fresh produce category.

Packaged salads	.54.3%
Baby carrots	.17.7
Spinach	. 5.5
Broccoli-based	. 3.3
Vegetable slaws	. 2.4
Other	. 5.5

Source: *Food Processing*, April 2005, p. 33, from Packaging Strategies, International Fresh Produce Association, Information Resources Inc., and ACNielsen.

★ 47 ★
Vegetables
SIC: 0161; NAICS: 111219
Fresh Produce Sales, 2004

Fresh-cut produce sales totaled $4 billion for the 52 weeks ended December 31, 2004.

Packaged salads	.63.0%
Fresh-cut vegetables	.31.0
Fresh-cut fruit	. 6.0

Source: *Grocery Headquarters*, March 2005, p. 50, from Information Resources Inc.

★ 48 ★
Vegetables
SIC: 0161; NAICS: 111219
Largest Vegetable Growers in the North

Companies are ranked by total acreage devoted to vegetable production.

R.D. Offutt Co.	65,000
Bird's Eye Foods	40,904
Hartung Brothers Inc.	17,968
Black Gold Farms	12,395
Heartland Farms Inc.	12,313
Paramount Farms Inc.	10,137
Walther Farms	9,375
Wysocki Produce Farm Inc.	8,606
Torrey Farms Inc.	7,486
Okray Farms Inc.	7,006

Source: *AVG*, October 2004, p. 15.

★ 49 ★
Vegetables
SIC: 0161; NAICS: 111219

Largest Vegetable Growers in the Southeast

Companies are ranked by total acreage devoted to vegetable production.

Thomas Produce Co.	16,850
Pacific Tomato Growers Ltd./Triple E Produce Corp.	16,142
Hundley Farms Inc.	14,623
Six L's Packing Co. Inc.	12,500
Pero Family Farms Inc.	9,738
Garglulo Inc.	9,500
Suwannee Farms/Eagle Island Farms	7,434
Nash Produce Company	6,230
Barnes Farming Crp.	5,735
A. Duda & Sons Inc.	1,926

Source: *AVG*, October 2004, p. 15.

★ 50 ★
Vegetables
SIC: 0161; NAICS: 111219

Largest Vegetable Growers in the Southwest

Companies are ranked by total acreage devoted to vegetable production.

Navajo Agricultural Products Industry	16,134
Martori Farms	12,200
Amigo Farms Inc.	7,398
Pasquinelli Produce Co.	7,109
Greer Farms	5,500
Rousseau Farming Co.	5,492
Wyatt Hidalgo Farms Inc.	5,426
Del Monte Fresh Produce	5,255
J & D Produce Inc.	4,800
Nakasawa Farms	4,541

Source: *AVG*, October 2004, p. 15.

★ 51 ★
Vegetables
SIC: 0161; NAICS: 111219

Largest Vegetable Growers in the West

Companies are ranked by total acreage devoted to vegetable production.

Tanimura & Antle	50,347
Grimmway Farms	44,750

D'Arrigo Bros. Co. of California Inc.	34,100
J.G. Boswell Co.	23,120
Larsen Farms	21,744
Mission Ranches	21,463
Ocean Mist Farms/Boutonnet Farms	19,625
Rio Farms	15,260
Nunes Vegetables Inc.	15,244
Betteravia Farms	13,477

Source: *AVG*, October 2004, p. 15.

★ 52 ★
Vegetables
SIC: 0161; NAICS: 111219

Onion Stocks by State

Market shares are shown in percent.

Idaho/Oregon	44.0%
Washington	27.0
Central Oregon	8.0
Other	21.0

Source: *Food Institute Report*, March 21, 2005, p. 14.

★ 53 ★
Vegetables
SIC: 0161; NAICS: 111219

Romaine Lettuce Production Worldwide

Market shares are shown in percent.

China	48.0%
United States	21.0
Spain	3.0
Other	21.0

Source: *Food Institute Report*, March 21, 2005, p. 14.

★ 54 ★
Fruit
SIC: 0170; NAICS: 111332, 111333, 111334

Fresh Fruit Market, 2003

The volume of fresh-cut fruit is expected to increase 20-30% annually over the next four years. By 2008, the market may stand at $1-2 billion. Leaders in the market are Ready Pac with a 23% share, Del Monte 13%, Country Fresh 7%, Club Fresh 3%, Fresh Express 1% and private label with 31%.

Fruit mixes	31.0%
Pineapple	16.0
Watermelon	14.0

Continued on next page.

★ 54 ★
[Continued]
Fruit
SIC: 0170; NAICS: 111332, 111333, 111334
Fresh Fruit Market, 2003

The volume of fresh-cut fruit is expected to increase 20-30% annually over the next four years. By 2008, the market may stand at $1-2 billion. Leaders in the market are Ready Pac with a 23% share, Del Monte 13%, Country Fresh 7%, Club Fresh 3%, Fresh Express 1% and private label with 31%.

Melon mixes	13.0%
Cantaloupe	7.0
Other	19.0

Source: "Opportunities in the Fresh Cut Fruit." [online] from http://www.agecon.purdue.edu.ventures [Accessed April 25, 2005], from *Fresh Cut 2003*.

★ 55 ★
Fruit
SIC: 0172; NAICS: 111332
Grapevine Nursery Industry

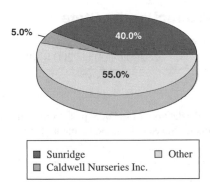

- Sunridge
- Caldwell Nurseries Inc.
- Other

Sunridge Nurseries recently purchased Caldwell Nurseries. Market shares are estimated.

Sunridge	40.0%
Caldwell Nurseries Inc.	5.0
Other	55.0

Source: *The Bakersfield Californian*, December 7, 2004, p. NA, from Sunridge.

★ 56 ★
Fruit
SIC: 0172; NAICS: 111332
Largest Grape Growers

Firms are ranked by total acreage owned or leased by one company that is responsible for maintaining it.

Bronco Wine Company	25,000
E&J Gallo Winery	23,000
Beringer Wine Estates	10,254
Delicato Vineyards	8,500
Vino Farms	7,353
Monterey Pacific	6,986
Gerawan Farming	6,227
John Kautz Farms	5,550
Trinchero Family Estates	5,454

Source: *American/Western Fruit Grower*, June 2004, p. 42.

★ 57 ★
Nuts
SIC: 0173; NAICS: 111335
Top Walnut Producers Worldwide, 2003

Data are in thousands of metric tons.

	(000)	Share
China	360	25.0%
United States	285	20.0
Iran	160	11.0
Turkey	136	10.0

Source: *Food Institute Report*, May 10, 2004, p. 21, from Food and Agriculture Organization.

★ 58 ★
Fruit
SIC: 0174; NAICS: 11132
Citrus Industry in Israel, 2004

Citrus production for the metric year is forecast to be 575,000 metric tons, a 15% increase over 2003. The Central parts of the state represent 60% of all plantings.

	2003-04	2004-05
Grapefruit	235	239
Oranges	133	165
Easy peeler	100	130

Continued on next page.

★ 58 ★
[Continued]
Fruit
SIC: 0174; NAICS: 11132
Citrus Industry in Israel, 2004

Citrus production for the metric year is forecast to be 575,000 metric tons, a 15% increase over 2003. The Central parts of the state represent 60% of all plantings.

	2003-04	2004-05
Lemon & lime	22	25
Other citrus	10	16

Source: "Israel Citrus Annual 2004." [online] from http://ffas.usda.gov [Published January 25, 2005], from Foreign Agricultural Service, U.S. Department of Agriculture and Plants Production and Marketing Board.

★ 59 ★
Fruit
SIC: 0174; NAICS: 11132
Citrus Market Shares, 2004

Citrus sales peak during the winter, boosted by holidays at the end of the year. December sales averaged $2,013 for the period shown, compared to the national average of $1,365 per week. Dollar shares are shown for July 2003 - June 2004.

Oranges	52.0%
Lemons	15.0
Tangerines	13.0
Grapefruit	11.0
Limes	8.0
Tangelos	1.0

Source: *Produce Merchandising*, February 2005, from Efficient Marketing Services and ACNielsen.

★ 60 ★
Fruit
SIC: 0174; NAICS: 11132
Lemon Market Shares

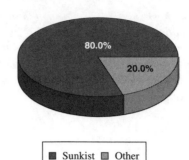

■ Sunkist ■ Other

Sunkist also has 55% of the entire citrus market.

Sunkist	80.0%
Other	20.0

Source: *Mail Tribune*, September 19, 2004, p. NA.

★ 61 ★
Fruit
SIC: 0174; NAICS: 11132
Lemon Production by State

Production is forecasted in thousands of tons.

	2002-2003	2004-2005	Share
California	912	741	89.06%
Arizona	114	91	10.94

Source: *Crop Production*, May 2005, p. 4, from National Agricultural Statistics Service, U.S. Department of Agriculture.

★ 62 ★
Fruit
SIC: 0175; NAICS: 111331
Apple Production by State, 2004

The crop size increased from 2003 levels, but it is at its lowest level in five years. Data are in thousands of 42-lb. units.

	(000)	Share
Washington	123,810	55.88%
New York	26,000	11.74
Michigan	20,000	9.03
Pennsylvania	9,250	4.18
California	9,000	4.06
Virginia	5,800	2.62
North Carolina	3,750	1.69

Continued on next page.

★ 62 ★
[Continued]
Fruit
SIC: 0175; NAICS: 111331
Apple Production by State, 2004

The crop size increased from 2003 levels, but it is at its lowest level in five years. Data are in thousands of 42-lb. units.

	(000)	Share
Oregon	3,500	1.58%
Ohio	2,500	1.13
West Virginia	1,800	0.81
Other	16,141	7.29

Source: *American/Western Fruit Grower*, September/October 2004, p. 11, from United States Department of Agriculture and U.S. Apple Association.

★ 63 ★
Fruit
SIC: 0175; NAICS: 111339
Global Pear Production, 2003-2004

Pear production increased for the eighth consecutive season to 15.1 million metric tons.

China	65.2%
United States	5.6
European Union	3.0
Argentina	3.0
Chile	1.6
Other	10.2

Source: *Food Institute Report*, May 24, 2004, p. 21.

★ 64 ★
Fruit
SIC: 0175; NAICS: 111339
Largest Banana Companies Worldwide

Market shares are shown in percent.

Dole	25.0%
Chiquita	25.0
Del Monte	15.0
Noboa	11.0
Fyffes	8.0
Other	16.0

Source: "Access to Market by Small Holder Producers." [online] from http://www.north-south.nl/files/Agrofood/La_Cruz.ppt [Accessed April 21, 2005].

★ 65 ★
Fruit
SIC: 0175; NAICS: 111339
Pear Market Shares, 2004

Pears generally enjoy their greatest sales during the final quarter of the year. Dollar shares are shown for July 2003 - June 2004.

Anjou	37.0%
Bartlett	36.0
Bosc	16.0
Packham	3.0
Asian	3.0
Comice	2.0
Forelle	1.0
Other	2.0

Source: *Produce Merchandising*, February 2005, from Efficient Marketing Services and ACNielsen.

★ 66 ★
Fruit
SIC: 0175; NAICS: 111339
Stone Fruit Sales, 2004

Summer fruit sales account for an average of 31.2% of produce sales. Sales are shown for June - August 2004.

Cherries	34.7%
Peaches	30.4
Nectarines	21.4
Plums	11.6
Apricots	1.9

Source: *Produce Merchandising*, May 2005, p. 72, from ACNielsen and Perishables Group.

★ 67 ★
Fruit
SIC: 0175; NAICS: 111339
Top Stone Fruit Growers

Companies are ranked by apple/pear acreage. Shares are shown based on the top 25 companies.

	Acreage	Share
Gerawan Farming	5,858	10.23%
Fowler Packing	4,095	7.15
ITO Packing	3,586	6.26
Taylor Orchards	3,500	6.11
Southern Orchard	3,200	5.59
California Prune Packing	3,097	5.41
Thiera Brothers Orchards	2,650	4.63
Titan Peach Farms	2,300	4.02
Simonian Fruit Co.	2,130	3.72

Continued on next page.

★ 67 ★

[Continued]
Fruit
SIC: 0175; NAICS: 111339

Top Stone Fruit Growers

Companies are ranked by apple/pear acreage. Shares are shown based on the top 25 companies.

	Acreage	Share
Cherry Ke Inc.	2,100	3.67%
Other	24,767	43.24

Source: *American Fruit Grower*, September/October 2004, p. NA.

★ 68 ★

Fruit
SIC: 0179; NAICS: 111336

Avocado Industry in South Africa

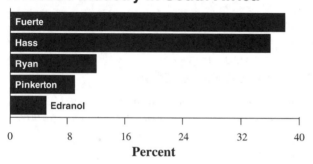

Percent

Average annual production is between 85,000 - 100,000 metric tons. Plantings for the Haas variety are increasing.

Fuerte	38.0%
Hass	36.0
Ryan	11.8
Pinkerton	9.0
Edranol	5.2

Source: "South Africa, Republic of Avocado Annual 2004." [online] from http://ffas.usda.gov [Published November 16, 2004], from Foreign Agricultural Service, U.S. Department of Agriculture.

★ 69 ★

Fruit
SIC: 0179; NAICS: 111336

Largest Pineapple Sellers Worldwide

Market shares are estimated in percent.

Del Monte	50.0%
Other	50.0

Source: *Seattle Post Intelligencer*, February 15, 2005, p. NA.

★ 70 ★

Fruit
SIC: 0179; NAICS: 111336

Pomegranate Industry

Market shares are estimated in percent.

POM Wonderful	60.0%
Other	40.0

Source: *PR Week*, October 25, 2004, p. 2.

★ 71 ★

Floriculture
SIC: 0181; NAICS: 111421, 111422

Flower Production

Figures are in thousands of stems. Glads are measured in spikes and mums are in bunches.

Roses	1,826,442
Carnations - standard	748,898
Alstroemeria	215,523
Lilies	211,492
Chrysanthmums	198,787
Tulips	156,286
Asters	156,286
Gerbera	149,275
Glads	137,558
Mums - pompon	110,731

Source: *Supermarket News*, October 11, 2004, p. 76, from Society of American Florists and *Floriculture Crops Summary*.

★ 72 ★

Floriculture
SIC: 0181; NAICS: 111421, 111422

Green Good Sales, 2004

Green goods sales represented 46% (or $47.7 billion) out of the $103.6 billion lawn & garden industry.

Bedding plants	32.3%
Shrubs	15.5
Flower plants	10.4
Evergreens	10.4
Flowering trees	6.5
Decorative trees	6.5
Foliage	6.3
Roses	5.9
Bulbs	3.9
Fruit & nut trees	2.3

Source: *Nursery Retailer*, January/February 2005, p. 60, from *Nursery Retailer's MarketShare Report*.

★ 73 ★

Floriculture

SIC: 0181; NAICS: 111421, 111422

Leading Flower/Auction Firms in the Netherlands

Netherlands and Belgium export more than $19 billion a year in horticultural products. Auction systems are the main link between growers and traders of flowers and plants. Firms are ranked by turnover sales in millions of dollars.

FloraHolland	$ 1,988
Aalsmeer	1,796
Oost-Nederlands	71
Vleuten	26

Source: "Benelux Horticulture Market." [online] from http://www.ffas.usda.gov [Published February 22, 2005], from annual reports.

★ 74 ★

Floriculture

SIC: 0181; NAICS: 111421, 111422

Nursery Product Shipments, 2003

California lead with 25% of production, with Florida and Oregon following with 16% each.

Broadleaf evergreens	21.0%
Deciduous shrubs	15.0
Deciduous shade trees	13.0
Other	51.0

Source: *Grounds Maintenance*, December 1, 2004, p. NA, from United States Department of Agriculture.

★ 75 ★

Mushrooms

SIC: 0182; NAICS: 111411

Agaricus Mushroom Sales by State

Sales are shown in thousands of dollars.

	2002-2003	2003-2004	Share
Pennsylvania	$ 365,650	$ 379,333	43.08%
California	170,234	172,683	19.61
Florida	44,426	47,519	5.40
Washington	14,497	13,525	1.54
Other	261,176	267,377	30.37

Source: *Mushrooms*, August 16, 2004, p. NA, from National Agricultural Statistics Service, U.S. Department of Commerce.

SIC 02 - Agricultural Production - Livestock

★ 76 ★

Cattle

SIC: 0211; NAICS: 112112

Cattle and Calves by State, 2004

States are ranked by number of cattle and calves in thousands of heads.

	2004	2005	Share
Texas	13,900	13,800	14.40%
Kansas	6,650	6,650	6.94
Nebraska	6,250	6,350	6.63
California	5,200	5,400	5.63
Oklahoma	5,100	5,400	5.63
Montana	4,350	4,450	4.64
South Dakota	3,650	3,750	3.91
Iowa	3,450	3,600	3.76
Wisconsin	3,350	3,350	3.50

Source: *Cattle*, April 2005, p. 4, from National Agricultural Statistics Service, U.S. Department of Agriculture.

★ 77 ★

Hogs and Pigs

SIC: 0213; NAICS: 11221

Hogs and Pigs by State, 2004-2005

States are ranked by number of hogs and pigs in thousands of heads.

	2004	2005	Share
Iowa	15,500	16,200	27.05%
North Carolina	9,900	9,700	16.19
Minnesota	6,500	6,300	10.52
Illinois	3,850	4,000	6.68
Missouri	2,900	2,850	4.76
Nebraska	2,850	2,750	4.59
Oklahoma	2,350	2,420	4.04
Kansas	1,720	1,700	2.84

Source: *Hogs and Pigs*, March 2005, p. 4, from National Agricultural Statistics Service, U.S. Department of Agriculture.

★ 78 ★

Sheep and Goats

SIC: 0214; NAICS: 11221

Sheep and Goats by State, 2004-2005

States are ranked by number of sheep and goats in thousands of heads.

	2004	2005	Share
Texas	1,100	1,070	17.44%
California	680	670	10.92
Wyoming	430	450	7.33
South Dakota	370	375	6.11
Colorado	360	365	5.95
Utah	265	270	4.40
Idaho	260	270	4.40
Iowa	250	245	3.99
New Mexico	160	145	2.36
Minnesota	140	145	2.36

Source: *Sheep and Goats*, March 2005, p. 4, from National Agricultural Statistics Service, U.S. Department of Agriculture.

★ 79 ★

Poultry

SIC: 0251; NAICS: 11232

Broiler Production by State, 2004

Production is shown in thousands of dollars for December 1, 2003 - November 30, 2004.

	($ 000)	Share
Georgia	$ 2,857,580	14.36%
Arkansas	2,731,300	13.72
Alabama	2,406,976	12.09
North Carolina	2,041,785	10.26
Mississippi	1,930,412	9.70
Texas	1,424,520	7.16
Kentucky	690,932	3.47
Delaware	686,458	3.45
Maryland	628,406	3.16
Other	4,504,092	22.63

Source: *Poultry - Production and Value 2004 Summary*, April 2005, p. 4, from National Agricultural Statistics Service, U.S. Department of Agriculture.

★ 80 ★
Poultry
SIC: 0251; NAICS: 11232

Largest Broiler Consumers Worldwide, 2003

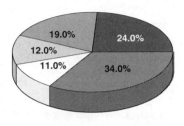

Much of the growth in the industry has come from China, Brazil, Mexico and India.

United States 24.0%
China 19.0
EU-15 . . . . .12.0
Brazil 11.0
Other 34.0

Source: *WATT PoultryUSA*, December 2004, p. 76, from U.S. Department of Agriculture.

★ 81 ★
Poultry
SIC: 0251; NAICS: 11232

Largest Broiler Firms, 2004

Companies are ranked by average weekly ready-to-cook production in millions of pounds. Figures are for the previous 12 months.

	(mil.)	Share
Tyson Foods Inc.	151.30	21.99%
Pilgrim's Pride	109.06	15.85
Gold Kist Inc.	61.79	8.98
Perdue Farms Inc.	51.32	7.46
Sanderson Farms Inc.	30.39	4.42
Wayne Farms LLC	28.95	4.21
Mountaire Farms	23.44	3.41
Foster Farms	16.51	2.40
O.K. Foods Inc.	15.80	2.30
Peco Foods Inc.	15.60	2.27
House of Raeford Farms	15.29	2.22
Other	168.64	24.51

Source: *WATT PoultryUSA*, January 2005, p. 18C.

★ 82 ★
Poultry
SIC: 0251; NAICS: 11232

Largest Broiler Producers Worldwide, 2003

Market shares are shown in percent.

United States 28.0%
China 19.0
Brazil 14.0
EU-15 . . . . .13.0
Other 26.0

Source: *WATT PoultryUSA*, December 2004, p. 76, from U.S. Department of Agriculture.

★ 83 ★
Poultry
SIC: 0251; NAICS: 11232

Leading Chicken Meat Producing Nations, 2003

Production is shown in metric tons (Mt).

	Mt	Share
United States	14,854,700	22.50%
China	9,517,580	14.42
Brazil	7,760,000	11.75
Mexico	2,156,580	3.27
India	1,440,000	2.18
United Kingdom	1,294,900	1.96
Thailand	1,227,000	1.86
Japan	1,218,000	1.85
France	1,130,000	1.71
Russian Federation	1,033,887	1.57
Other	24,381,857	36.93

Source: *World Poultry*, no. 10, 2004, p. 12, from FAOStat.

★ 84 ★
Poultry
SIC: 0251; NAICS: 11232

Leading Goose Meat Producing Nations, 2003

Production is shown in metric tons (Mt).

	Mt	Share
China	1,972,150	92.64%
Hungary	43,600	2.05
Egypt	42,210	1.98
Poland	12,000	0.56
Serbia and Montenegro	7,000	0.33
France	6,400	0.30

Continued on next page.

★ 84 ★
[Continued]
Poultry
SIC: 0251; NAICS: 11232

Leading Goose Meat Producing Nations, 2003

Production is shown in metric tons (Mt).

	Mt	Share
Israel	5,100	0.24%
Germany	4,500	0.21
Other	35,835	1.68

Source: *World Poultry*, no. 10, 2004, p. 12, from FAOStat.

★ 85 ★
Poultry
SIC: 0251; NAICS: 11232

Leading Poultry Firms in Mexico

Market shares are shown in percent.

Pilgrim's/Tyson	30.0%
Bachoco	30.0
Other	40.0

Source: *Internet Securities*, February 25, 2005, p. NA, from Mexico Analytica and National Poultry Association.

★ 86 ★
Eggs
SIC: 0252; NAICS: 11231

Egg Industry in Ireland

Retail sales are increasing 8% by volume and 12% by value. Private label has about two-thirds of both. The source points out that because of this branded labels do have an opportunity to gain share from own private label brands.

	Current	Future
Caged	69.0%	50.0%
Free range	22.0	40.0
Other	9.0	10.0

Source: *Poultry World*, November 2004, p. 19.

★ 87 ★
Eggs
SIC: 0252; NAICS: 11232

Egg Production by State, 2004

Production is shown in thousands of dollars for December 1, 2003 - November 30, 2004.

	($ 000)	Share
Iowa	$ 491,586	9.27%
Georgia	394,223	7.43
Arkansas	362,442	6.83
Pennsylvania	339,676	6.41
Ohio	334,040	6.30
Texas	306,388	5.78
Indiana	291,947	5.51
California	288,412	5.44
Alabama	287,956	5.43
North Carolina	239,590	4.52
Other	1,966,984	37.09

Source: *Poultry - Production and Value 2004 Summary*, April 2005, p. 4, from National Agricultural Statistics Service, U.S. Department of Agriculture.

★ 88 ★
Eggs
SIC: 0252; NAICS: 11231

Leading Egg Producing Nations, 2003

Production is shown in metric tons (Mt).

	Mt	Share
China	22,332,500	40.00%
United States	5,123,000	9.18
Japan	2,500,000	4.48
India	2,200,000	3.94
Russian Federation	2,040,000	3.65
Mexico	1,881,770	3.37
Brazil	1,550,000	2.78
France	919,392	1.65
Germany	843,000	1.51
Indonesia	790,304	1.42
Other	15,647,743	28.03

Source: *World Poultry*, no. 10, 2004, p. 12, from FAOStat.

★ 89 ★
Eggs
SIC: 0252; NAICS: 11231

Top Egg Firms, 2004

Firms are ranked by millions of layers as of December 31, 2004.

	(mil.)	Share
Cal-Maine Foods Inc.	20.20	8.37%
Rose Acres	17.50	7.25
Moark LLC	14.20	5.88
Michael Foods Egg Prod.	14.00	5.80
Sparboe Companies	12.50	5.18
Decoster Egg Farms	10.50	4.35
Ohio Fresh Eggs	10.00	4.14
Dutchland Farms	6.90	2.86
Daybreak Foods	6.80	2.82
Fort Recovery Equity	6.70	2.78
ISE America	6.50	2.69
Other	115.64	47.90

Source: *Egg Industry*, January 2005, p. 18.

★ 90 ★
Eggs
SIC: 0252; NAICS: 11231

Top Fresh Egg Brands, 2004

Market shares are shown based on sales at food stores, drug stores and mass merchandisers (excluding Wal-Mart) for the 52 weeks ended October 31, 2004.

Eggland's Best	5.3%
Rose Acre	2.4
Crystal Farms	1.3
Penn Dutch Farms	0.8
Hillandale Farms	0.7
Land O Lakes	0.6
California Ranch Fresh	0.5
New England Egg Farms	0.4
Private label	71.4
Other	16.6

Source: *Grocery Headquarters*, February 2005, p. 55, from Information Resources Inc.

★ 91 ★
Turkeys
SIC: 0253; NAICS: 11233

Largest Turkey Processors

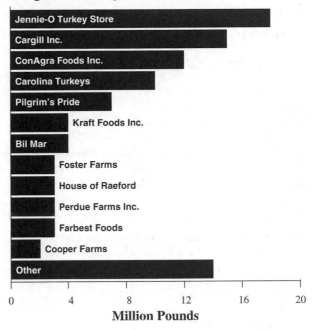

Companies are ranked by millions of live pounds processed.

	(mil.)	Share
Jennie-O Turkey Store	1,245.0	17.98%
Cargill Inc.	1,010.9	14.60
ConAgra Foods Inc.	830.0	11.99
Carolina Turkeys	725.0	10.47
Pilgrim's Pride	474.0	6.85
Kraft Foods Inc.	300.0	4.33
Bil Mar (Sara Lee)	300.0	4.33
Foster Farms	240.0	3.47
House of Raeford	239.0	3.45
Perdue Farms Inc.	236.0	3.41
Farbest Foods	186.0	2.69
Cooper Farms	170.0	2.46
Other	967.3	13.97

Source: *WATT PoultryUSA*, January 2005, p. 18C.

★ 92 ★
Turkeys
SIC: 0253; NAICS: 11233

Leading Turkey Meat Producing Nations, 2003

Production is shown in metric tons (Mt).

	Mt	Share
United States	2,562,800	47.90%
France	700,000	13.08
Germany	366,000	6.84
Italy	340,000	6.36
United Kingdom	232,000	4.34
Brazil	200,000	3.74
Canada	145,000	2.71
Israel	128,000	2.39
Hungary	90,000	1.68
Other	586,311	10.96

Source: *World Poultry*, no. 10, 2004, p. 12, from FAOStat.

★ 93 ★
Turkeys
SIC: 0253; NAICS: 11233

Turkey Production by State, 2004

Production is shown in thousands of dollars for September 1, 2003 - August 31, 2004.

	($ 000)	Share
Minnesota	$ 515,592	16.82%
North Carolina	448,812	14.64
Missouri	279,930	9.13
Arkansas	226,718	7.40
Virginia	182,855	5.97
Indiana	172,049	5.61
California	169,937	5.54
Iowa	136,080	4.44
Pennsylvania	112,320	3.66
Other	821,124	26.79

Source: *Poultry - Production and Value 2004 Summary*, April 2005, p. 4, from National Agricultural Statistics Service, U.S. Department of Agriculture.

★ 94 ★
Vicunas
SIC: 0271; NAICS: 11293

Vicuna Population Worldwide

Distribution is shown based on 255.32 thousand heads.

Peru	87.0%
Chile	14.6
Argentina	11.2%
Bolivia	5.8
Ecuador	0.2

Source: *El Comercio*, May 22, 2005, p. B1, from Copacs/Maximize.

★ 95 ★
Horses
SIC: 0272; NAICS: 11299

New Horse Registrations, 2002 and 2004

Quarterhorses lead in the transfer of ownership category as well, with 207,679 transfers in 2002 and 210,863 transfers in 2004. Figures for 2004 are projected.

	2002	2004
Quarter Horse	156,199	162,590
Paint Horse	60,000	52,000
Thoroughbred	35,600	37,200
Tennessee Walking Horse	14,865	15,000
Standardbred	11,699	11,500
Arabian	9,394	12,000
Appaloosa	9,092	9,200
Morcan Horse	3,976	3,500
Saddlebred	2,931	3,200

Source: *Equus*, November 2004, p. 44.

★ 96 ★
Dogs
SIC: 0279; NAICS: 11299

Popular Breeds of Dogs, 2004

The most popular purebred dogs are shown based on number of registrations.

Labrador retriever	146,692
Golden retriever	52,550
German shepherd	46,046
Beagle	44,555
Yorkshire terrier	43,522
Dachshund	40,770
Boxer	37,741
Poodle	32,671
Shih Tzu	28,958
Chihuahua	25,850

Source: *USA TODAY*, January 13, 2005, p. 8D, from American Kennel Co.

★ 97 ★
Farms
SIC: 0291; NAICS: 11299

Farms by Region, 2004

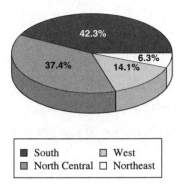

Distribution is shown in percent.

South	.42.3%
North Central	.37.4
West	.14.1
Northeast	. 6.3

Source: ''Number of Farms and Land in Farms.'' [online] from http://wwwusda.gov/nass/aggraphs/fncht5.htm [Accessed June 8, 2005], from U.S. Department of Agriculture.

SIC 07 - Agricultural Services

★ 98 ★
Oilseeds
SIC: 0722; NAICS: 115113

Oilseed Harvesting, 2004

Oilseeds are ranked by area harvested in thousands of acres.

	(000)	Share
Soybeans for beans	73,958.0	94.04%
Sunflower	1,711.0	2.18
Peanuts	1,394.0	1.77
Canola	828.0	1.05
Flaxseed	516.0	0.66
Saflower	159.0	0.20
Mustard seed	68.7	0.09
Rapeseed	7.8	0.01

Source: *Crop Production*, May 2005, p. 4, from National Agricultural Statistics Service, U.S. Department of Agriculture.

★ 99 ★
Cotton Ginning
SIC: 0724; NAICS: 115111

Cotton Ginning by State, 2004

Production is shown in running bales ginned (excluding linters). Production is up noticeably over previous years: 17.7 million in 2003, up from 16.7 million in 2002.

	Bales	Share
Texas	7,618,050	33.77%
California	2,414,850	10.71
Mississippi	2,274,250	10.08
Arizona	2,016,500	8.94
Georgia	1,749,800	7.76
Tennessee	958,550	4.25
Louisiana	888,250	3.94
Missouri	808,700	3.59
Alabama	797,350	3.54
Arizona	678,350	3.01
Other	2,350,900	10.42

Source: *Cotton Gittings 2004 Summary*, May 2005, p. 4, from National Agricultural Statistics Service, U.S. Department of Agriculture.

★ 100 ★
Veterinarians
SIC: 0740; NAICS: 54194

Veterinarians by Practice

There were 47,264 private clinical practice veterinarians as of December 31, 2004. There were 8,478 additional public and corporate employment.

	No.	Share
Small animal exclusive	29,951	63.4%
Mixed animal	3,868	8.2
Large animal predominant	2,596	5.4
Equine	2,257	4.8
Large animal exclusive	1,887	4.0
Other	1,198	2.5

Source: "U.S. Veterinarians." [online] from http://www.avma.org [Accessed June 8, 2005], from American Veterinary Medical Association.

★ 101 ★
Landscaping
SIC: 0782; NAICS: 56173

Green Industry in Wisconsin, 2002

Total receipts were $819.4 million.

Landscape installation	47.0%
Landscape/lawn/garden maintenance	15.0
Tree and shrub service	10.0
Landscape architecture, design or planning	10.0
Fertilizer/pesticide application for customers	7.0
Irrigation installation/maintenance	5.0
Interiorscape	1.0
Florist service	1.0
Other	4.0

Source: *Landscape Management*, August 2004, p. 82, from Wisconsin Landscape Federation.

★ 102 ★

Landscaping

SIC: 0782; NAICS: 56173

Largest Lawn & Garden Management Firms

Firms are ranked by revenues in millions of dollars.
Weed Man's figure is in Canadian dollars.

TruGreen Cos.	$ 1,400
ValleyCrest Co.	675
Brickman Group	380
The Davey Tree Expert Co.	370
American Civil Constructors	200
Scotts Lawn Service	150
Weed Man	95
Gothic Landscape	95
OneSource Landscape & Golf	80
Lawn Doctor	78

Source: *Landscape Management*, July 2004, p. 27.

SIC 08 - Forestry

★ 103 ★

Christmas Trees

SIC: 0811; NAICS: 111421, 11311

Christmas Tree Production by State

States are ranked by number of trees harvested in 2002. The top 5% of farms sold 61% of trees.

	No.	Share
Oregon	6,466,551	31.08%
North Carolina	2,915,507	14.01
Michigan	2,380,173	11.44
Pennsylvania	1,724,419	8.29
Wisconsin	1,605,981	7.72
Washington	1,164,139	5.59
New York	618,917	2.97
Virginia	507,791	2.44
Minnesota	463,885	2.23
California	383,940	1.85
Other	2,576,762	12.38

Source: ''Agricultural Census.'' [online] from http://www.realchristmastrees.org/04_PR4.html [Accessed July 4, 2005], from U.S. Bureau of the Census.

★ 104 ★

Forestry

SIC: 0811; NAICS: 111421, 11311

Forest Classifications in Australia

Australia has a total of 162.7 million hectares in forests and woodland areas.

Woodland forest	62.0%
Native forest	31.0
Plantation	1.0
Other	6.0

Source: ''Australia Solid Wood Products Annual 2004.'' [online] from http://ffas.usda.gov [Published January 25, 2005], from Foreign Agricultural Service, U.S. Department of Agriculture and ABARE data.

★ 105 ★

Forestry

SIC: 0831; NAICS: 111998, 11321

Forestry Products Exports in New Zealand, 2003

Exports are shown in cubic meters.

Tauranga	2,973,037
Whangarei	824,870
Nelson	573,413
Napier	553,192
Gisborne	363,032
Dunedin	258,283
Bluff	61,026
New Plymouth	20,862
Auckland	1,397

Source: *New Zealand Forest Industries Magazine*, December 2004, p. S1.

★ 106 ★

Fishing

SIC: 0910; NAICS: 114111, 114112

Fishing in South Korea, 2004

Total fish production has been falling in recent years as the industry faces the depletion of fish in local waters. Total allowable catches were 217,650 tons.

	Tons	Share
Mackerel	155,000	71.22%
Large red crab	21,000	9.65
Snow crabs	13,000	5.97
Jack mackerel	10,000	4.59
Purplish Washington clams	8,000	3.68
Sardines	5,000	2.30
Pen shells	2,500	1.15
Top shells	2,158	0.99
Other	992	0.46

Source: "Korea Revised - Fishery Products Annual, 2004." [online] from http://ffas.usda.gov [Published November 15, 2004], from Foreign Agricultural Service, U.S. Department of Agriculture and Ministry of Maritime Affairs and Fisheries.

★ 107 ★

Fishing

SIC: 0910; NAICS: 114111, 114112

Largest Fishing Nations, 2003

Countries are ranked by capture in millions of tons. Figures include fish, crustaceans and molluscs.

	(mil.)	Share
China	45.64	33.19%
Peru	6.10	4.44
India	5.90	4.29
Indonesia	5.67	4.12
United States	5.48	3.98
Japan	5.45	3.96
Thailand	3.59	2.61
Russia	3.38	2.46
Norway	3.13	2.28
Philippines	2.62	1.91

	(mil.)	Share
Vietnam	2.60	1.89%
Other	47.96	34.87

Source: "Yearbook of Fisheries Statistics." [online] from http://www.fao.org/filstatist/statist.asp [Accessed June 8, 2005], from Food and Agriculture Organization of the United Nations.

SIC 10 - Metal Mining

★ 108 ★

Mining

SIC: 1000; NAICS: 21221, 212234

Largest Metal Miners Worldwide

Market shares are shown based on production.

BHP Billiton	3.9%
Rio Tinto	3.8
Norilsk Nickel	3.1
CVRD	2.9
Codelco	2.1
Newmont Mining Corp.	2.0
Noranda	1.4
Phelps Dodge	1.3
Barrick Gold	1.3
Other	78.2

Source: *American Metal Market*, October 12, 2004, p. 6, from Raw Materials Group.

★ 109 ★

Mining

SIC: 1000; NAICS: 21221, 212234

Mining Industry in Australia

Figures show committed capital expenditures over the medium for A$21.4 billion as of April 2004. Many budgets were cut to help companies increase cash flows and provide similar boosts.

Petroleum	42.0%
Gold	11.0
Coal	10.0
Alumina	10.0
Nickel	8.0
Iron ore	7.0
Other	12.0

Source: *Financial Times*, June 17, 2004, p. 23.

★ 110 ★

Mining

SIC: 1000; NAICS: 21221, 212234

Top Mining Companies in Australia

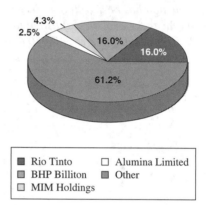

Australia is one of the world's leading mining nations. It has the world's largest resources of bauxite, lead and mineral sands.

Rio Tinto	16.0%
BHP Billiton	16.0
MIM Holdings	4.3
Alumina Limited	2.5
Other	61.2

Source: "US & FCS Market Research Reports." [online] from http://www.stat-usa.gov [Published November 2004].

★ 111 ★

Iron

SIC: 1011; NAICS: 21221

Largest Iron Ore Producing Nations, 2004

China was the world's leading producer of iron ore on a gross tonnage basis, but third in terms of iron ore content. Consumption increased strongly between 2000 and 2004. This growth will continue past 2004, but not at the same levels. Countries are ranked by estimated production in thousands of metric tons.

	(000)	Share
China	280	22.38%
Brazil	220	17.59
Australia	220	17.59
India	110	8.79
Russia	95	7.59
Ukraine	66	5.28
United States	54	4.32
South Africa	40	3.20
Canada	31	2.48
Other	135	10.79

Source: *Mineral Commodities Summaries 2005*, January 2005, p. 20, from U.S. Geological Survey, U.S. Department of the Interior.

★ 112 ★

Copper

SIC: 1021; NAICS: 212234

How Copper is Used, 2004

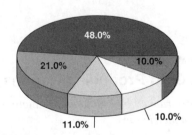

- ■ Building construction
- ▨ Electronic and electronic products
- ▥ Consumer and general products
- ▢ Transportation equipment
- ▦ Industrial machinery and equipment

Domestic mine production in 2004 rose to 1.16 million tons.

Building construction	48.0%
Electronic and electronic products	21.0
Consumer and general products	11.0%
Transportation equipment	10.0
Industrial machinery and equipment	10.0

Source: *Mineral Commodities Summaries 2005*, January 2005, p. 20, from U.S. Geological Survey, U.S. Department of the Interior.

★ 113 ★

Copper

SIC: 1021; NAICS: 212234

Largest Copper Producing Nations, 2004

Global refined production increased 560,000 tons (3.7%) in 2004 while world use grew 900,000 tons (5.7%). Chile and Peru represented about two-thirds of the increased output. Copper use is expected to increase in China as this market develops. The source points out that the production deficit of 375,000 tons in 2003 will climb to 700,000 tons in 2004. Countries are ranked by estimated production in thousands of metric tons.

	(000)	Share
Chile	5,380	37.13%
United States	1,160	8.01
Peru	1,000	6.90
Indonesia	860	5.94
Australia	850	5.87
Russia	675	4.66
China	620	4.28
Canada	560	3.86
Poland	500	3.45
Kazakhstan	485	3.35
Other	2,400	16.56

Source: *Mineral Commodities Summaries 2005*, January 2005, p. 20, from U.S. Geological Survey, U.S. Department of the Interior.

★ 114 ★

Lead

SIC: 1031; NAICS: 212231

Largest Lead Producing Nations, 2004

Countries are ranked by estimated production in thousands of metric tons.

	(000)	Share
China	950	30.14%
Australia	680	21.57
United States	440	13.96
Peru	300	9.52

Continued on next page.

★ 114 ★

[Continued]
Lead
SIC: 1031; NAICS: 212231

Largest Lead Producing Nations, 2004

Countries are ranked by estimated production in thousands of metric tons.

	(000)	Share
Mexico	150	4.76%
Canada	80	2.54
Sweden	61	1.94
Kazakhstan	44	1.40
Morocco	41	1.30
Other	406	12.88

Source: *Mineral Commodities Summaries 2005*, January 2005, p. 20, from U.S. Geological Survey, U.S. Department of the Interior.

★ 115 ★

Zinc
SIC: 1031; NAICS: 212231

How Zinc is Consumed

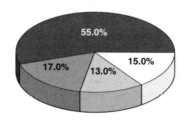

■ Galvanizing	▨ Brass and bronze
▧ Zinc-based alloys	□ Other

The value of zinc mined is $885 million. Alaska, Missouri and Montana represent 99% of mine output.

Galvanizing	55.0%
Zinc-based alloys	17.0
Brass and bronze	13.0
Other	15.0

Source: *Mineral Commodities Summaries 2005*, January 2005, p. 20, from U.S. Geological Survey, U.S. Department of the Interior.

★ 116 ★

Gold
SIC: 1041; NAICS: 212221

Gold Industry in China, 2004

Total gold production was 186.29 tons for the first 11 months of 2004.

Shandong Province	24.42%
Henan Province	14.81
Fujian Province	7.33
Shaanxi Province	6.77
Liaoning Province	5.64
Hunan Province	4.69
Gansu Province	4.47
Hebei Province	3.73
Other	28.14

Source: *Asia Pulse*, January 21, 2005, p. NA, from China Gold Association.

★ 117 ★

Gold
SIC: 1041; NAICS: 212221

How Gold is Used, 2004

A few dozen companies dominate the market for fabricated gold products.

Jewelry and arts	92.0%
Electrical and electronics	4.0
Dental	3.0
Other	1.0

Source: *Mineral Commodities Summaries 2005*, January 2005, p. 20, from U.S. Geological Survey, U.S. Department of the Interior.

★ 118 ★

Gold
SIC: 1041; NAICS: 212221

Largest Gold Producing Nations, 2004

Countries are ranked by estimated production in thousands of metric tons.

	(000)	Share
South Africa	344	14.61%
United States	247	10.49
Australia	242	10.28
China	210	8.92
Russia	180	7.65
Canada	171	7.26
Peru	160	6.80
Other	800	33.98

Source: *Mineral Commodities Summaries 2005*, January 2005, p. 20, from U.S. Geological Survey, U.S. Department of the Interior.

★ 119 ★
Gold
SIC: 1041; NAICS: 212221

Top Gold Producers, 2003

Companies are ranked by production in thousands of ounces.

	(000)	Share
Newmont Mining	2,613	29.02%
Barrick Gold	2,563	28.47
Placer Dome Inc.	1,058	11.75
Rio Tinto	869	9.65
Anglo Gold	585	6.50
Kinross Gold Corporation	424	4.71
Echo Bay Mines	381	4.23
Apollo Gold	158	1.75
Glamis Gold Inc.	128	1.42
Goldcorp	71	0.79
Coeur d'Alenes Mines	52	0.58
Other	102	1.13

Source: "Top U.S. Gold Producers." [online] from http://www.nma.org [Accessed July 3, 2005], from U.S. Geological Survey and National Mining Association.

★ 120 ★
Gold
SIC: 1041; NAICS: 212221

Top Gold Producers Worldwide, 2003

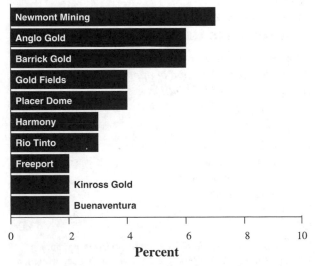

Companies are ranked by production in millions of ounces.

Newmont Mining	7.38
Anglo Gold	5.63
Barrick Gold	5.51
Gold Fields	4.20
Placer Dome	3.86

Harmony	3.33
Rio Tinto	2.73
Freeport	2.46
Kinross Gold	1.65
Buenaventura	1.53

Source: *Financial Times*, October 18, 2004, p. 1, from Thomson Datastream and World Gold.

★ 121 ★
Silver
SIC: 1044; NAICS: 212222

Largest Silver Producing Nations, 2004

Countries are ranked by estimated production in thousands of metric tons.

	(000)	Share
Mexico	2,850	14.63%
Peru	2,800	14.37
China	2,600	13.35
Australia	2,230	11.45
Canada	1,300	6.67
Chile	1,300	6.67
Poland	1,200	6.16
United States	1,200	6.16
Other	4,000	20.53

Source: *Mineral Commodities Summaries 2005*, January 2005, p. 20, from U.S. Geological Survey, U.S. Department of the Interior.

★ 122 ★
Silver
SIC: 1044; NAICS: 212222

Top Silver Producers Worldwide, 2004

Companies are ranked by output in millions of ounces. Mexico, Peru and Australia were the top silver producing countries during the year. The largest primary silver mine was in Cannington, Australia and operated by BHP Billiton. Its production was 45.91 million ounces.

BHP Billiton	49.7
Industrias Penoles	44.5
KGHM Polska Miedz	43.2
Grupo Medxico	19.4
Kazakhmys	17.7
Polymetal	17.3
Barrick Gold	17.3
Rio Tinto	14.8

Continued on next page.

★ 122 ★
[Continued]
Silver
SIC: 1044; NAICS: 212222

Top Silver Producers Worldwide, 2004

Companies are ranked by output in millions of ounces. Mexico, Peru and Australia were the top silver producing countries during the year. The largest primary silver mine was in Cannington, Australia and operated by BHP Billiton. Its production was 45.91 million ounces.

Coeur d'Alene Mines	14.1
Cia. De Minas Buenaventura	12.8

Source: "Supply and Demand Production." [online] from http://www.silverinstitute.org [Accessed July 4, 2005], from Silver Institute.

★ 123 ★
Cobalt
SIC: 1061; NAICS: 212299

Top Cobalt Producing Nations, 2004

Countries are ranked by estimated mine production in thousands of metric tons. Cobalt demand is shown by industry: superalloys 44%, cemented carbides 9%, chemicals 26% and other 21%.

	(000)	Share
Congo (Kinshasa)	11,000	23.45%
Zambia	9,000	19.19
Australia	7,000	14.93
Canada	5,200	11.09
Russia	4,800	10.23
Cuba	3,400	7.25
New Caledonia	1,500	3.20
Morocco	1,300	2.77
Brazil	1,300	2.77
Other	2,400	5.12

Source: *Mineral Commodities Summaries 2005*, January 2005, p. 20, from U.S. Geological Survey, U.S. Department of the Interior.

★ 124 ★
Manganese
SIC: 1061; NAICS: 212299

How Manganese is Used

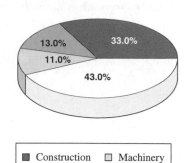

■ Construction	□ Machinery	
■ Transportation	□ Other	

Manganese ore is consumed by 8 firms. Total consumption was valued at $1.29 billion.

Construction	.33.0%
Transportation	.13.0
Machinery	.11.0
Other	.43.0

Source: *Mineral Commodities Summaries 2005*, January 2005, p. 20, from U.S. Geological Survey, U.S. Department of the Interior.

★ 125 ★
Nickel
SIC: 1061; NAICS: 212234

How Nickel is Used, 2004

No nickel mines were operating in the United States during the year. The value of apparent primary nickel consumption was $1.74 billion.

Transportation	.32.0%
Chemicals	.14.0
Electrical	.11.0
Construction	9.0
Fabricated metal products	8.0
Household appliances	7.0
Machinery	6.0
Other	.13.0

Source: *Mineral Commodities Summaries 2005*, January 2005, p. 20, from U.S. Geological Survey, U.S. Department of the Interior.

★ 126 ★
Nickel
SIC: 1061; NAICS: 212234

Largest Nickel Producers Worldwide, 2004

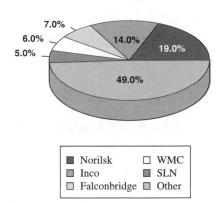

■ Norilsk	□ WMC
■ Inco	■ SLN
□ Falconbridge	■ Other

Market shares are shown in percent.

Norilsk	.19.0%
Inco	.14.0
Falconbridge	7.0
WMC	6.0
SLN	5.0
Other	.49.0

Source: *Financial Times*, February 3, 2005, p. 15, from Morgan Stanley and CS First Boston.

★ 127 ★
Nickel
SIC: 1061; NAICS: 212234

Leading Nickel Producing Nations, 2004

Countries are ranked by production in thousands of metric tons.

	(000)	Share
Russia	315,000	23.94%
Australia	210,000	15.96
Canada	180,000	13.68
Indonesia	144,000	10.94
Cuba	75,000	5.70
Colombia	72,500	5.51
China	62,000	4.71
Dominican Republic	47,000	3.57
Brazil	45,000	3.42
Other	165,200	12.56

Source: *Mineral Commodities Summaries 2005*, January 2005, p. 20, from U.S. Geological Survey, U.S. Department of the Interior.

★ 128 ★
Beryllium
SIC: 1099; NAICS: 212299

Top Beryllium Producing Nations, 2004

Beryllium saw its strongest demand in the automotive industry (particularly Europe) and the industrial and telecommunications sectors. Data show estimated mine production in thousands of metric tons.

	(000)	Share
United States	100	61.35%
Russia	40	24.54
China	15	9.20
Kazakhstan	4	2.45
Mozambique	3	1.84
Other	1	0.61

Source: *Mineral Commodities Summaries 2005*, January 2005, p. 20, from U.S. Geological Survey, U.S. Department of the Interior.

★ 129 ★
Platinum
SIC: 1099; NAICS: 212299

Leading Platinum Metal Producers Worldwide

Countries are ranked by estimated production in thousands of metric tons.

	(000)	Share
South Africa	163,000	74.67%
Russia	36,000	16.49
Canada	8,600	3.94
United States	4,200	1.92
Other	6,500	2.98

Source: *Mineral Commodities Summaries 2005*, January 2005, p. 20, from U.S. Geological Survey, U.S. Department of the Interior.

★ 130 ★
Rare Earth
SIC: 1099; NAICS: 212299

How Rare Earth is Used, 2004

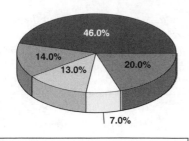

■ Automatic catalytic convertors
▨ Glass polishing for ceramics
□ Metallurgical additives and alloys
□ Petroleum refining catalysts
▨ Other

Refined rare earth consumption was valued at more than $1 billion in 2004.

Automatic catalytic convertors	.46.0%
Glass polishing for ceramics	.14.0
Metallurgical additives and alloys	.13.0
Petroleum refining catalysts	. 7.0
Other	.20.0

Source: *Mineral Commodities Summaries 2005*, January 2005, p. 20, from U.S. Geological Survey, U.S. Department of the Interior.

★ 131 ★
Tin
SIC: 1099; NAICS: 212299

How Tin is Consumed, 2004

Tin has not been mined domestically since 1993.

Cans and containers	.27.0%
Electrical	.23.0
Transportation	.10.0
Construction	.10.0
Other	.30.0

Source: *Mineral Commodities Summaries 2005*, January 2005, p. 20, from U.S. Geological Survey, U.S. Department of the Interior.

SIC 12 - Coal Mining

★ 132 ★
Coal

SIC: 1220; NAICS: 212111, 212112

Global Coal Reserves

Distribution is shown in percent.

U.S.	25.4%
Russia	13.9
China	11.6
India	8.6
Australia	8.3
Germany	6.7
Other	23.5

Source: *Financial Times*, August 17, 2004, p. 11, from Bloomberg, Thomson Datastream, BP, and Peabody.

★ 133 ★
Coal

SIC: 1220; NAICS: 212111, 212112

Top Coal Producers, 2003

Market shares are shown based on 1.07 billion short tons.

Peabody Coal Co.	14.6%
Kennecott Energy & Coal Co.	10.7
Arch Coal Inc.	10.1
RAG American Coal Holding	5.9
CONSOL Energy Inc.	5.5
Vulcan Partners	3.9
A.T. Massey Coal Co. Inc.	3.7
Horizon Natural Resources Inc.	3.1
North American Coal Corp.	3.0
Westmoreland Mining LLC	2.6
TXU Corp.	2.3
Black Beauty Coal Co.	1.9
Other	32.5

Source: "Major U.S. Coal Producers, 2003." [online] from http://www.eia.doe.gov [Accessed June 29, 2005], from COALdat.

★ 134 ★
Coal

SIC: 1220; NAICS: 212111, 212112

Top Coal Producing Nations, 2004

Figures are for the year to date 2004.

	(000)	Share
Wyoming	326,710	35.50%
West Virginia	124,261	13.50
Kentucky	94,388	10.26
Pennsylvania	54,848	5.96
Texas	35,807	3.89
Colorado	33,498	3.64
Montana	31,485	3.42
Indiana	29,511	3.21
Illinois	27,720	3.01
Virginia	27,582	3.00
Other	134,587	14.62

Source: *Coal Age*, November 2004, p. 5.

SIC 13 - Oil and Gas Extraction

★ 135 ★
Natural Gas
SIC: 1311; NAICS: 211111

Gas Demand by Region, 2020

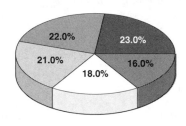

■ Mountain and West   □ Northeast
■ Midwest and Plains   ■ Southeast and Florida
□ Gulf Coast

Total demand was 29,658 billions of cubic feet.

Mountain and West	23.0%
Midwest and Plains	22.0
Gulf Coast	21.0
Northeast	18.0
Southeast and Florida	16.0

Source: *Pipline & Gas Journal*, October 2004, p. 17, from
Energy and Environmental Analysis Inc.

★ 136 ★
Natural Gas
SIC: 1311; NAICS: 211111

Largest Natural Gas Producers Worldwide, 2003

*Natural gas is expected to account for a quarter of the
world's energy supply by 2020. Companies are ranked
by output in billions of cubic feet per day.*

Gazprom	52.2
Exxon Mobil	10.1
Shell/RD	8.8
BP	8.6
Total	4.8
ChevronTexaco	4.3

Eni	3.5
ConocoPhillips	3.5
Repsol	3.0
Encana	2.4

Source: *Wall Street Journal*, April 1, 2005, p. B2, from Petroleum Intelligence and Thomson Datastream.

★ 137 ★
Natural Gas
SIC: 1311; NAICS: 211111

Leading Natural Gas Producers

*Companies are ranked by production in millions of cu-
bic feet per day.*

BP Plc	5,512
ExxonMobil Corp.	3,130
ChevronTexaco Inc.	2,846
ConocoPhillips	2,445
Shell Oil Co.	2,377

Source: *Waste News*, November 22, 2004, p. 3C, from U.S.
Energy Information Adminsitration, American Petroleum Institute, and National Petrochemical and Refiners Association.

★ 138 ★
Natural Gas
SIC: 1311; NAICS: 211111

Natural Gas Demand Worldwide

Data are in trillions of cubic feet.

	2003	2008
Conventional	90.16	95.76
Unconventional	7.68	12.78
Liquified natural gas	5.97	8.37

Source: *American Ceramic Society Bulletin*, September
2004, p. 9, from Business Communications Co.

★ 139 ★
Natural Gas
SIC: 1311; NAICS: 211111

Natural Gas Production in North America, 2020

Most analysts believe that production from traditional basins in the United States and Canada is on the decline. Therefore, production in the coming decades will have to come from previously untapped sources. Total demand is forecast to be 29,658 billion of cubic feet.

Western Canada	21.0%
Offshore Gulf	15.0
Rockies	14.0
GOL Slope	11.0
Westen Texas/Oklahoma	10.0
Alaska	10.0
Gulf of Mexico Shelf	8.0
San Juan	4.0
Eastern Canada	2.0
Mackenzie Delta	1.0
Other	4.0

Source: *Pipeline & Gas Journal*, October 2004, p. 17, from INGAA Foundation by Energy and Environmental Analysis.

★ 140 ★
Natural Gas
SIC: 1311; NAICS: 211111

Natural Gas Use, 2003

Industry is the largest consumer of natural gas.

Manufactured products like fertilizer	26.8%
Residential	23.3
Electric utilities	22.5
Commercial	14.3
Electricity and heat production	5.2
Plant fuel	5.1
Transportation	2.9

Source: *New York Times*, August 20, 2004, p. C5, from Energy Information Administration.

★ 141 ★
Oil
SIC: 1311; NAICS: 211111

How Oil is Consumed Worldwide

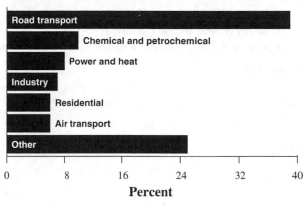

Distribution is shown in percent.

Road transport	39.0%
Chemical and petrochemical	9.7
Power and heat	7.8
Industry	6.8
Residential	6.4
Air transport	5.9
Other	24.5

Source: *Financial Times*, August 5, 2004, p. 32, from Thomson Datastream and International Energy Administration.

★ 142 ★
Oil
SIC: 1311; NAICS: 211111

Leading Oil & Gas Firms, 2004

Companies are ranked by total revenues in millions of dollars for the third quarter of 2004.

ExxonMobil Corp.	$ 76.37
ChevronTexaco Corp.	40.71
ConocoPhillips	34.74
Marathon Oil Corp.	12.31
Amerada Hess Corp.	3.93
Occidental Petroleum Corp.	3.06
Murphy Oil Corp.	2.29
Devon Energy Corp.	2.26
Unocal Corp.	1.99
Anadarko Petroleum Corp.	1.56

Source: *Oil & Gas Financial Journal*, April 2005, p. 13.

★ 143 ★

Oil

SIC: 1311; NAICS: 211111

Leading Oil Consumers, 2004

Consumption is shown in millions of barrels per day. During the first week of 2005, a barrel cost $43, down from a peak of $56 in mid October 2004.

United States	20.5
China	6.3
Japan	5.5
Former Soviet Union	3.7
Germany	2.6
India	2.5
Canada	2.3
South Korea	2.2
Brazil	2.2
Mexico	2.0

Source: *U.S. News & World Report*, January 10, 2005, p. 44, from International Energy Administration and U.S. Energy Information Administration.

★ 144 ★

Oil

SIC: 1311; NAICS: 211111

Leading Petroleum Firms Worldwide, 2003

Firms are ranked by reserves in millions of dollars.

BP	$ 235,899
Exxon Mobil Corp.	222,654
Royal Dutch/Shell	205,212
Total	119,250
ChevronTexaco Corp.	114,666
Saudi Aramco	93,100
ConocoPhillips	91,392
Eni	60,566
Pernex	55,926
Sinopec	53,533
PDV	45,000
PetroChina	36,783

Source: *Petroleum Intelligence Weekly*, December 13, 2004, p. S2.

★ 145 ★

Oil

SIC: 1311; NAICS: 211111

Oil Production by State, 2004

States are ranked by annual production in thousands of barrels.

	(000)	Share
Louisiana	522,850	26.33%
Texas	489,753	24.66
Alaska	355,582	17.91
California	270,911	13.64
Oklahoma	63,933	3.22
New Mexico	62,982	3.17
Wyoming	51,749	2.61
Kansas	33,135	1.67
North Dakota	30,381	1.53
Other	104,653	5.27

Source: *Word Oil*, February 2005, p. 42, from American Petroleum Institute and U.S. Department of Commerce.

★ 146 ★

Oil

SIC: 1311; NAICS: 211111

Oil Production in Brazil

Distribution is shown based on water depth.

> 1,500 m	5.0%
0 to 300m	17.0
300 to 1,500m	62.0
Onshore	17.0

Source: *World Oil*, October 2004, p. S7.

★ 147 ★

Oil

SIC: 1311; NAICS: 211111

U.S. Crude Oil Imports, 2005

The oil market is facing threats by terrorism, capacity challenges in the United States and little excess production. The source points out that two decades ago the United States imported oil from countries from stable regions with stable governments. Oil now comes from unstable regions (for example, from 1985-2004 oil imports increased 322% in Venezuela, were up 279% in Nigeria, 194% in Angola and 178% in Gabon. Data show the crude oil imports by region in millions of barrels per day.

	(mil.)	Share
Canada/Mexico	2.80	27.9%
Persian Gulf	2.62	26.1
Latin America	2.14	21.3

Continued on next page.

★ 147 ★

[Continued]
Oil
SIC: 1311; NAICS: 211111

U.S. Crude Oil Imports, 2005

The oil market is facing threats by terrorism, capacity challenges in the United States and little excess production. The source points out that two decades ago the United States imported oil from countries from stable regions with stable governments. Oil now comes from unstable regions (for example, from 1985-2004 oil imports increased 322% in Venezuela, were up 279% in Nigeria, 194% in Angola and 178% in Gabon. Data show the crude oil imports by region in millions of barrels per day.

	(mil.)	Share
Africa	1.68	16.7%
Other	0.81	8.1

Source: *Wall Street Journal*, April 11, 2005, p. A4, from U.S. Department of Energy.

★ 148 ★

Natural Gas Liquids
SIC: 1321; NAICS: 211112

LPG Industry in Brazil

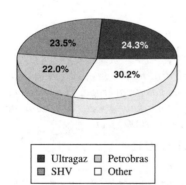

Legend: ■ Ultragaz ☐ Petrobras ▨ SHV ☐ Other

SHV's share reflects the recently acquired company Supergasbras. LPG stands for liquid petroleum gas.

Ultragaz	24.3%
SHV	23.5
Petrobras	22.0
Other	30.2

Source: *America's Intelligence Wire*, July 8, 2004, p. NA.

★ 149 ★

Horizontal Directional Drilling
SIC: 1381; NAICS: 213111

Horizontal Directional Drilling, 2004

Just under half of the fleet (49.5%) is between 5 and 10 years of age. Just over 29 percent of the fleet is 2-5 years old, 8.8% is 10 years or greater and 12.3% of the fleet is 2 years old or less.

Telecommunications	21.8%
Gas distribution	18.6
Water	13.4
Sewer	12.3
Electric	12.3
Oil/gas pipelines	11.3
Other	10.3

Source: *Underground Construction*, June 2005, p. 28, from *Underground Construction's 7th Annual HDD Survey*.

★ 150 ★

Oil & Gas Wells
SIC: 1381; NAICS: 213111

Coiled Tubing Industry

In the United States only about 25 wells are drilled each year using coiled tubing. Canada represents 90% of all coiled tubing worldwide. The coiled tube drilling industry is thought to have peaked several years ago. Companies are ranked by coiled tubing fleet.

	Units	Share
Schlumberger	200	25.81%
BJ Services	165	21.29
Halliburton	105	13.55
Superior Energy Services	38	4.90
Cudd Pressure Control	23	2.97
Precision Drilling	11	1.42
Technicoil	6	0.77
Tucker Energy Services	5	0.65
Saber Energy Services	5	0.65
Other	217	28.00

Source: *World Oil*, February 2005, p. 85, from Spears & Associates and U.S. Department of Energy.

★ 151 ★
Oil & Gas Wells
SIC: 1381; NAICS: 213111

Gas Well Production by State

States are ranked by gas wells.

	Units	Share
Texas	70,022	17.70%
Pennsylvania	44,227	11.18
West Virginia	40,400	10.21
New Mexico	37,198	9.40
Ohio	34,320	8.68
Oklahoma	33,500	8.47
Kansas	24,352	6.16
Colorado	16,718	4.23
Lousiana	16,006	4.05
Kentucky	15,532	3.93
Michigan	8,700	2.20
Montana	5,509	1.39
Other	49,079	12.41

Source: *World Oil*, February 2005, p. 42, from American Petroleum Institute and U.S. Department of Energy.

★ 152 ★
Oil & Gas Wells
SIC: 1381; NAICS: 213111

Natural Gas Wells by State

The number of wells increased from 376,036 wells in 2003 to 395,023 wells in 2004. Maryland saw the largest increase during this period, up 45.5% (from 6 to 11 wells). Kansas increased 30.6% and Kentucky increased 23.8%.

	2003	2004	Share
Texas	66,315	70,022	17.73%
Pennsylvania	43,563	44,227	11.20
West Virginia	40,186	40,400	10.23
New Mexico	36,437	37,198	9.42
Oklahoma	34,283	33,500	8.48
Ohio	33,873	34,320	8.69
Kansas	18,639	24,352	6.16
Colorado	16,250	16,718	4.23
Louisiana	15,694	16,006	4.05
Wyoming	15,250	18,291	4.63
Kentucky	12,551	15,532	3.93
Michigan	8,500	8,700	2.20

Source: *World Oil*, February 2005, p. 52, from American Petroleum Institute and U.S. Department of Energy.

★ 153 ★
Oil & Gas Wells
SIC: 1381; NAICS: 213111

Oil and Gas Well Drilling by State, 2004-2005

Total wells drilled are forecasted to increase from 37,257 wells to 39,958 wells. New York saw the largest increase (+206.5% from 92 to 282). South Dakota was next with a 92.3% increase. The biggest drop was Tennessee (14%).

	2004	2005	Share
Texas	12,168	12,768	31.95%
Wyoming	3,631	4,000	10.01
Kansas	2,500	2,757	6.90
California	2,380	2,450	6.13
Pennsylvania	2,225	2,300	5.76
Oklahoma	2,205	2,162	5.41
Colorado	1,847	2,180	5.46
New Mexico	1,670	1,816	4.54
Louisiana	1,334	1,380	3.45
Montana	712	889	2.22

Source: *World Oil*, February 2005, p. 42, from American Petroleum Institute and U.S. Department of Energy.

★ 154 ★
Oil & Gas Wells
SIC: 1381; NAICS: 213111

Oil Well Drilling Past 8,000 Feet

More rigs are drilling for gas in 2004 than in 2001 but are finding less gas on average. The two companies have half of the market for wells drilled in the United States deeper than 8,000 feet.

Nabors/Patterson-UTI	.50.0%
Other	.50.0

Source: *Petroleum Finance Week*, August 30, 2004, p. NA.

★ 155 ★
Oil & Gas Wells
SIC: 1381; NAICS: 213111

Types of Wells Drilled

	2003	2004
Gas	.48.0%	39.0%
Oil & gas	.36.0	47.0
Oil	.16.0	14.0

Source: *World Oil*, October 2004, p. 69.

★ 156 ★
Gas Gathering
SIC: 1389; NAICS: 213112
Gathering Services in Panola County, TX

Gas gathering is the pipeline transportation of natural gas from a wellhead or delivery point to a gas transmission pipeline or gas processing plant. The company's share is estimated.

Natural Gas Partners 50.0%
Other 50.0

Source: *Gas Processors Report*, December 13, 2004, p. NA.

★ 157 ★
Seismic Services
SIC: 1389; NAICS: 213112
Onshore Seismic Contracting

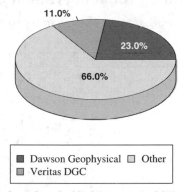

Veritas has less than half of Dawson's 23% share. Its figure is estimated.

Dawson Geophysical 23.0%
Veritas DGC 11.0
Other 66.0

Source: *Investor's Business Daily*, April 8, 2005, p. A5, from Raymond James & Associates.

SIC 14 - Nonmetallic Minerals, Except Fuels

★ 158 ★

Dimension Stone

SIC: 1411; NAICS: 212311

Largest Dimension Stone Markets, 2004

Distribution is shown based on tonnage. Indiana, Wisconsin, Georgia, Virginia and Texas represent 50% of production.

Granite	.35.0%
Limestone	.28.0
Misc. stone	.18.0
Sandstone	.13.0
Marble	.5.0
Slate	.1.0

Source: *Mineral Commodities Summaries 2005*, January 2005, p. 20, from U.S. Geological Survey, U.S. Department of the Interior.

★ 159 ★

Sand and Gravel

SIC: 1420; NAICS: 212312

How Sand and Gravel is Used, 2004

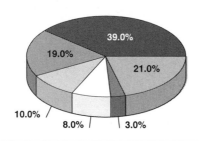

■ Glassmaking sand	□ Hydraulic fracturing sand
▨ Foundry sand	▩ Abrasive sand
□ Building products	▨ Other

California, Texas and Arizona are the top producers by tonnage. The value of consumption was $6.3 billion in 2004, with 4,000 companies operating 6,500 facilities in all 50 states.

Glassmaking sand	.39.0%
Foundry sand	.19.0
Building products	.10.0

Hydraulic fracturing sand	.8.0%
Abrasive sand	.3.0
Other	.21.0

Source: *Mineral Commodities Summaries 2005*, January 2005, p. 20, from U.S. Geological Survey, U.S. Department of the Interior.

★ 160 ★

Lime

SIC: 1422; NAICS: 212312

Largest Lime Producing Nations, 2004

Countries are ranked by production in thousands of metric tons.

	(000)	Share
France	23,500	19.35%
United States	20,400	16.80
Russia	8,000	6.59
Japan	7,400	6.09
Mexico	6,500	5.35
Germany	6,500	5.35
Brazil	6,500	5.35
Other	42,650	35.12

Source: *Mineral Commodities Summaries 2005*, January 2005, p. 20, from U.S. Geological Survey, U.S. Department of the Interior.

★ 161 ★

Clay and Shale

SIC: 1455; NAICS: 212324

How Common Clay is Used, 2004

A total of 240 companies in 41 states were involved in common clay production. The top 20 firms represented about 50% of production by tonnage and 79% of value.

Brick	.55.0%
Cement	.19.0
Lightweight aggregate	.16.0
Other	.10.0

Source: *Mineral Commodities Summaries 2005*, January 2005, p. 20, from U.S. Geological Survey, U.S. Department of the Interior.

★ 162 ★
Clay and Shale
SIC: 1455; NAICS: 212324

Largest Clay and Shale Producers

Leading end markets for clay and shale are building bricks, lightweight aggregate and portland cement clicker. Production is shown in millions of short tons.

	(mil.)	Share
North Carolina	2.60	10.20%
Alabama	2.22	8.71
Ohio	1.44	5.65
Georgia	1.44	5.65
Missouri	1.15	4.51
Oklahoma	1.13	4.43
California	1.13	4.43
South Carolina	1.12	4.39
Kentucky	1.00	3.92
Other	12.27	48.12

Source: *Mining Engineering*, June 17, 2004, p. NA, from U.S. Geological Survey.

★ 163 ★
Clay and Shale
SIC: 1455; NAICS: 212324

Leading Ball Clay End Markets

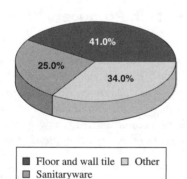

The end markets are shown in percent.

Floor and wall tile	.41.0%
Sanitaryware	.25.0
Other	.34.0

Source: *Ceramic Bulletin*, August 2004, p. 26, from U.S. Geological Survey.

★ 164 ★
Kaolin
SIC: 1455; NAICS: 212324

Top End Markets for Kaolin

Consumption dropped just over 4% to 7.68 million tons.

	Tons	Share
Oil & gas refining catalysts	209,000	53.0%
Sanitaryware	85,300	19.2
Wall and floor tile	61,900	13.9

Source: *Ceramic Industry*, January 2005, p. 13, from U.S. Geological Survey.

★ 165 ★
Feldspar
SIC: 1459; NAICS: 212325

Largest Feldspar Producing Nations, 2004

Countries are ranked by estimated production in thousands of metric tons.

	(000)	Share
Italy	2,500	22.73%
Turkey	1,900	17.27
United States	790	7.18
Thailand	780	7.09
France	670	6.09
Spain	500	4.55
Germany	500	4.55
Other	3,360	30.55

Source: *Mineral Commodities Summaries 2005*, January 2005, p. 20, from U.S. Geological Survey, U.S. Department of the Interior.

★ 166 ★
Fullers Earth
SIC: 1459; NAICS: 212325

Fuller's Earth Production Worldwide, 2004

Countries are ranked by estimated production in thousands of metric tons.

	(000)	Share
United States	3,960	77.88%
Germany	500	9.83
Mexico	155	3.05
United Kingdom	140	2.75
Italy	30	0.59
Other	300	5.90

Source: *Mineral Commodities Summaries 2005*, January 2005, p. 20, from U.S. Geological Survey, U.S. Department of the Interior.

★ 167 ★
Boron
SIC: 1474; NAICS: 212391

How Boron Compounds are Used, 2004

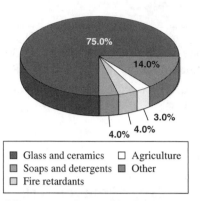

75.0%
14.0%
3.0%
4.0% 4.0%

■ Glass and ceramics   □ Agriculture
■ Soaps and detergents ■ Other
□ Fire retardants

The United States was the world's leading producer of refined boron compounds during 2004. About one half of production was exported. The estimated value of boric oxide produced was $517 million.

Glass and ceramics	75.0%
Soaps and detergents	4.0
Fire retardants	4.0
Agriculture	3.0
Other	14.0

Source: *Mineral Commodities Summaries 2005*, January 2005, p. 20, from U.S. Geological Survey, U.S. Department of the Interior.

★ 168 ★
Boron
SIC: 1474; NAICS: 212391

Leading Boron End Markets

The United States was the world's largest producer of refined boron compounds. Demand for boron is often linked to a strong housing market.

Fiberglass	69.0%
Soaps and detergents	6.0
Borosilicate glass	5.0
Frits and ceramics	4.0
Agriculture	4.0
Cellulose insulation	3.0
Other	3.0

Source: *Ceramic Bulletin*, August 2004, p. 26.

★ 169 ★
Boron
SIC: 1474; NAICS: 212391

Top Boron Producing Nations, 2004

Fiberglass takes 64%, borosilicate glass takes 6%, flame retardants and soaps/detergents each take 4%. Data show estimated mine production in thousands of metric tons.

	(000)	Share
Turkey	1,400	30.63%
United States	1,130	24.73
Russia	1,000	21.88
Argentina	550	12.04
Chile	300	6.56
China	130	2.84
Bolivia	33	0.72
Peru	7	0.15
Iran	3	0.07
Other	17	0.37

Source: *Mineral Commodities Summaries 2005*, January 2005, p. 20, from U.S. Geological Survey, U.S. Department of the Interior.

★ 170 ★
Potash
SIC: 1474; NAICS: 212391

Leading Potash Producers Worldwide, 2004

Global demand was 30 million tons, not seen since its peak in 1987 and 1988. The potash industry has to address the need for new capacity, when Belarus and Russia withdraw from the global market to address needs in their own countries. Nations are ranked by estimated production in thousands of metric tons.

	(000)	Share
Canada	9,500	31.62%
Russia	5,400	17.98
Belarus	4,650	15.48
Germany	3,670	12.22
Israel	1,940	6.46
United States	1,200	3.99
Jordan	1,130	3.76
Spain	600	2.00
United Kingdom	580	1.93
Other	1,370	4.56

Source: *Mineral Commodities Summaries 2005*, January 2005, p. 20, from U.S. Geological Survey, U.S. Department of the Interior.

★ 171 ★

Phosphate Rock

SIC: 1475; NAICS: 212392

Leading Phosphate Rock Producers Worldwide

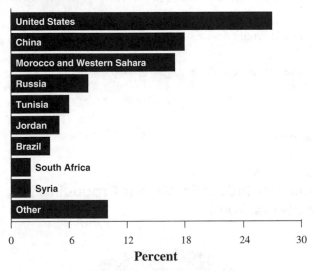

Countries are ranked by estimated production in thousands of metric tons.

	(000)	Share
United States	37,000	27.37%
China	25,000	18.49
Morocco and Western Sahara	23,000	17.01
Russia	11,000	8.14
Tunisia	8,000	5.92
Jordan	6,800	5.03
Brazil	5,650	4.18
South Africa	2,600	1.92
Syria	2,400	1.78
Other	13,750	10.17

Source: *Mineral Commodities Summaries 2005*, January 2005, p. 20, from U.S. Geological Survey, U.S. Department of the Interior.

★ 172 ★

Fluorspar

SIC: 1479; NAICS: 212393

Largest Fluorspar Producing Nations, 2004

Countries are ranked by estimated production in thousands of metric tons.

	(000)	Share
China	2,700	54.76%
Mexico	750	15.21
Mongolia	270	5.48
South Africa	235	4.77
Russia	170	3.45

	(000)	Share
Spain	130	2.64%
Kenya	120	2.43
France	105	2.13
Other	451	9.15

Source: *Mineral Commodities Summaries 2005*, January 2005, p. 20, from U.S. Geological Survey, U.S. Department of the Interior.

★ 173 ★

Asbestos

SIC: 1499; NAICS: 212399

Top Asbestos Producing Nations, 2004

Data show estimated mine production in thousands of metric tons. In the United States 60% of asbestos is used in roofing and 25% in coatings and compounds.

	(000)	Share
Russia	900	39.56%
Kazakhstan	360	15.82
China	350	15.38
Canada	250	10.99
Brazil	200	8.79
Zimbabwe	130	5.71
Other	85	3.74

Source: *Mineral Commodities Summaries 2005*, January 2005, p. 20, from U.S. Geological Survey, U.S. Department of the Interior.

★ 174 ★

Diamonds

SIC: 1499; NAICS: 212399

Largest Diamond (Industrial) Producing Nations, 2004

Countries are ranked by production in thousands of metric tons. Total production was estimated to be 250 million carats. The United States is still the leading market for industrial diamonds. More than 88% of the industrial diamond market now uses synthetic individual diamonds because of quality control and customization issues.

	(000)	Share
Congo (Kinshasa)	20.0	34.48%
Australia	19.0	32.76
Botswana	7.5	12.93
South Africa	6.0	10.34

Continued on next page.

★ 174 ★

[Continued]
Diamonds
SIC: 1499; NAICS: 212399

Largest Diamond (Industrial) Producing Nations, 2004

Countries are ranked by production in thousands of metric tons. Total production was estimated to be 250 million carats. The United States is still the leading market for industrial diamonds. More than 88% of the industrial diamond market now uses synthetic individual diamonds because of quality control and customization issues.

	(000)	Share
China	1.0	1.72%
Other	4.5	7.76

Source: Mineral Commodities Summaries 2005, January 2005, p. 20, from U.S. Geological Survey, U.S. Department of the Interior.

★ 175 ★

Diatomite
SIC: 1499; NAICS: 212399

Largest Diatomite Producing Nations, 2004

Countries are ranked by production in thousands of metric tons. Diatomite is primarily used in the filtration of beverages, oils and synthetics.

	(000)	Share
United States	635	32.33%
China	370	18.84
Denmark	232	11.81
Japan	180	9.16
CIS	80	4.07
France	75	3.82
Mexico	65	3.31
Spain	36	1.83
Peru	35	1.78
Czech Republic	35	1.78
Other	221	11.25

Source: Mineral Commodities Summaries 2005, January 2005, p. 20, from U.S. Geological Survey, U.S. Department of the Interior.

★ 176 ★

Gallium
SIC: 1499; NAICS: 212399

Leading Gallium End Markets, 2003

The end markets are shown in percent.

Integrated circuits	49.0%
Optoelectronic devices	42.0
Other	9.0

Source: Ceramic Bulletin, August 2004, p. 26, from U.S. Geological Survey.

★ 177 ★

Garnets
SIC: 1499; NAICS: 212399

Largest Industrial Garnet Producing Nations, 2004

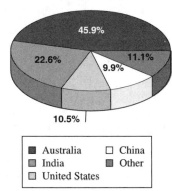

Garnet resources worldwide are large and occur in a number of rocks. In the United States the industrial garnet market by end use is abrasive blasting media 35%, waterjet cutting 30% and water filtration 15%. Countries are ranked by estimated production in thousands of metric tons.

	(000)	Share
Australia	130,000	45.90%
India	64,000	22.60
United States	29,700	10.49
China	28,000	9.89
Other	31,500	11.12

Source: Mineral Commodities Summaries 2005, January 2005, p. 20, from U.S. Geological Survey, U.S. Department of the Interior.

★ 178 ★
Gemstones
SIC: 1499; NAICS: 212399

Largest Gemstone Producing Nations, 2004

In the United States the market for unset gem-quality exceeded $12.9 billion. It represents about 35% of world demand. Countries are ranked by estimated production in thousands of metric tons.

	(000)	Share
Botswana	22,500	33.67%
Russia	12,500	18.70
Canada	11,300	16.91
Angola	5,500	8.23
South Africa	5,000	7.48
Congo (Kinshasa)	5,000	7.48
Namibia	1,700	2.54
Ghana	750	1.12
Brazil	500	0.75
Other	2,080	3.11

Source: *Mineral Commodities Summaries 2005*, January 2005, p. 20, from U.S. Geological Survey, U.S. Department of the Interior.

★ 179 ★
Graphite
SIC: 1499; NAICS: 212399

How Graphite is Used

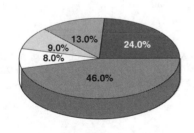
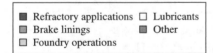

Natural graphite is not produced in the United States. Market share leaders are China with 37%, Mexico 23% and Canada 19%.

Refractory applications	24.0%
Brake linings	13.0
Foundry operations	9.0

Lubricants 8.0%
Other 46.0

Source: *Mineral Commodities Summaries 2005*, January 2005, p. 20, from U.S. Geological Survey, U.S. Department of the Interior.

★ 180 ★
Gypsum
SIC: 1499; NAICS: 212399

Largest Gypsum Producing Nations, 2004

Demand for gypsum is related to the construction industry, as 95% of gypsum is used in wallboard production, cement and building plasters. Countries are ranked by estimated production in thousands of metric tons.

	(000)	Share
United States	18,000	20.10%
Iran	11,500	12.84
Canada	9,000	10.05
Spain	7,500	8.38
China	6,900	7.71
Mexico	6,800	7.60
Thailand	6,500	7.26
Japan	5,700	6.37
Australia	4,000	4.47
Other	13,630	15.22

Source: *Mineral Commodities Summaries 2005*, January 2005, p. 20, from U.S. Geological Survey, U.S. Department of the Interior.

★ 181 ★
Perlite
SIC: 1499; NAICS: 212399

How Perlite is Used, 2004

The estimated value of processed perlite was $18 million.

Building construction products	62.0%
Horticultural aggregate	13.0
Fillers	10.0
Filter aid	9.0
Other	6.0

Source: *Mineral Commodities Summaries 2005*, January 2005, p. 20, from U.S. Geological Survey, U.S. Department of the Interior.

SIC 15 - General Building Contractors

★ 182 ★
Construction
SIC: 1500; NAICS: 23321, 23331, 23332
Construction Spending, 2004

Almost all markets saw growth in 2004, with the overall market up 9%. Spending is shown in millions of dollars.

	($ mil.)	Share
Single-family housing	$ 242,289	41.38%
Educational buildings	43,934	7.50
Highways and bridges	42,466	7.25
Multifamily housing	40,798	6.97
Stores and shopping centers	20,220	3.45
Sewers and water supply	18,889	3.23
Office buildings	18,396	3.14
Health care facilities	15,719	2.68
Electric utilities	8,868	1.51
Manufacturing	6,423	1.10
Hotels and motels	5,246	0.90
Other	122,277	20.88

Source: *ENR*, November 15, 2004, p. 26, from McGraw-Hill Construction and U.S. Department of Commerce.

★ 183 ★
Construction
SIC: 1500; NAICS: 23321, 23331, 23332
Top Construction Firms Worldwide, 2003

The top 100 firms had combined revenues of $519.6 billion. European firms are a major presence in the market with 50 firms on the list. Firms are ranked by sales in millions of dollars. Shares are shown based on the top 30 firms.

	($ mil.)	Share
Vinci	$ 23,147	7.37%
Skanska Group	18,624	5.93
Kajima Corporation	17,654	5.62
Bouygues Construction division	17,062	5.43
Bechtel	16,337	5.20
Taisei Corporation	15,486	4.93
Hochtief	14,693	4.68

	($ mil.)	Share
Shimizu Corporation	$ 13,229	4.21%
Obayashi Corporation	12,627	4.02
Sekisui House	12,486	3.98
Other	152,652	48.62

Source: *International Construction*, July/August 2004, p. 14.

★ 184 ★
Construction
SIC: 1520; NAICS: 23321, 23322
Building Construction in South Korea

In 2002, there were 6,079 construction companies registered as general builders. Total value of construction was 95,053 KrW billion.

Apartments	34.9%
Plants	8.3
Office-residential hybrids	8.0
Commercial (retailing) buildings	7.2
Schools	6.9
Office buildings	5.2
Hotels, lodging facilities	2.8
Houses	2.5
Other	24.2

Source: "US & FCS Market Research Reports." [online] from http://www.stat-usa.gov [Published October 28, 2004], from National Statistical Office, Republic of Korea.

★ 185 ★
Construction
SIC: 1520; NAICS: 23321, 23332
Top Builders in the U.K.

Contractors are ranked by revenues in millions of pounds.

Skanksa	£ 2,973
Balfour Beatty	2,918
Laing O'Rourke	1,661
Carillion	1,613
Amec	1,193
Mowlem	1,192

Continued on next page.

★ 185 ★
[Continued]
Construction
SIC: 1520; NAICS: 23321, 23332

Top Builders in the U.K.

Contractors are ranked by revenues in millions of pounds.

Jarvis	£ 1,167
Bovis Lend Lease	922
Sir Robert McAlpine	895
AWG	877

Source: *Contract Journal*, May 6, 2004, p. 16.

★ 186 ★
Construction
SIC: 1520; NAICS: 23321, 23332

Top Builders Worldwide

Firms are ranked by revenue in millions of dollars. The top 400 generated a total of $193.5 billion in 2003. Domestically, there was a drop in revenues. The opportunities in the heavy and highway sector kept the slide from being even steeper.

Centex	$ 8,493.7
The Turner Corp.	4,904.8
Skanska USA Inc.	2,917.1
Bovis Lend Lease	2,781.9
The Clark Construction Group Inc.	2,056.7
Gilbane Building Co.	1,679.7
Swinerton Inc.	1,597.0
Structure Tone Inc.	1,540.0
Hensel Phelps Construction Co.	1,529.2
The Whiting-Turner Contracting Co.	1,489.0

Source: *ENR*, May 17, 2004, p. 44, from *ENR's Top 400 Contractors* list.

★ 187 ★
Residential Construction
SIC: 1521; NAICS: 23321

Top Home Builders

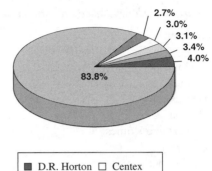

■ D.R. Horton □ Centex
■ Pulte ▨ KB Home
□ Lennar ▨ Other

Market shares are shown in percent.

D.R. Horton	4.0%
Pulte	3.4
Lennar	3.1
Centex	3.0
KB Home	2.7
Other	83.8

Source: *Investor's Business Daily*, May 5, 2005, p. B3, from U.S. Bureau of the Census and A.G. Edwards.

★ 188 ★
Residential Construction
SIC: 1521; NAICS: 23321

Top Home Builders in Atlanta, GA

Market shares are shown based on number of closings.

Pulte Homes	2.6%
D.R. Horton/Torrey Homes	2.3
KB Home/Colony Homes	2.1
MDC Homes	2.0
Ryland Homes	1.8
Bowen Builders Group	1.8
John Wieland Homes & Neighborhoods	1.7
Centex Homes	1.5
Other	84.2

Source: *Builder*, May 2004, p. 220.

★ 189 ★
Residential Construction
SIC: 1521; NAICS: 23321

Top Home Builders in Columbus, OH

Market shares are shown based on number of closings.

Dominion Homes	22.7%
M/I Homes	18.0
Rockford Homes	4.1
Centex Homes	2.4
Beazer Homes USA	2.1
Diyanni Homes	1.7
American Heritage Homes	1.5
Joshua Homes	1.1
Bob Webb Builders	1.1
Other	45.3

Source: *Builder*, May 2004, p. 220.

★ 190 ★
Residential Construction
SIC: 1521; NAICS: 23321

Top Home Builders in Daytona Beach, FL

Market shares are shown based on number of closings.

Holiday Builders	6.2%
ICI Homes	5.8
Maronda Homes	4.9
Mercedes Homes	4.3
Seagate Homes	3.4
Centex Homes	2.4
Today Homes	1.8
The Johnson Group	1.8
Other	69.4

Source: *Builder*, May 2004, p. 220.

★ 191 ★
Residential Construction
SIC: 1521; NAICS: 23321

Top Home Builders in Denver, CO

Market shares are shown based on number of closings.

D.R. Horton/Continental Homes/Trimark Homes/Melody Homes	19.4%
Lennar Corp./U.S. Home Corp.	14.8
M.D.C. Holdings/Richmond American Homes	11.3
KB Home	7.7
Oakwood Homes	6.4
Shea Homes	5.3
Ryland Homes	5.3
Village Homes of Colorado	3.7
Other	26.1

Source: *Builder*, May 2004, p. 220.

★ 192 ★
Residential Construction
SIC: 1521; NAICS: 23321

Top Home Builders in Detroit, MI

Market shares are shown based on number of closings.

Pulte Homes	9.4%
MJC Cos.	5.2
S.R. Jacobson Development Corp./Tadian Homes	3.7
Centex Homes	2.9
Crosswinds Communities	2.8
Toll Brothers	2.0
Lombardo Cos.	1.7
Ivanhoe-Huntley	1.7
R. Lockwood Construction	1.4
Other	69.2

Source: *Builder*, May 2004, p. 220.

★ 193 ★

Residential Construction
SIC: 1521; NAICS: 23321

Top Home Builders in Fort Myers/Cape Coral, FL

Market shares are shown based on number of closings.

Lennar Corp./U.S. Home Corp.	.16.3%
First Home Builders of Florida	.11.6
Transeastern Homes	5.6
Centex Homes	4.3
Holiday Builders	4.0
Pulte Homes	3.8
WCI Communities	3.7
Beazer Homes USA	3.7
Lowder New Homes/Colonial Homes	2.7
Other	.44.3

Source: *Builder*, May 2004, p. 220.

★ 194 ★

Residential Construction
SIC: 1521; NAICS: 23321

Top Home Builders in Houston, TX

Market shares are shown based on number of closings.

Lennar Corp./U.S. Home Corp/Village Builders	.11.5%
KB Home	7.1
Perry Homes	6.0
MHI/McGuyer Homebuilders	5.8
D.R. Horton/Emerald/Dietz-Crane Homes	5.3
Royce Homes	4.2
Hovnanian Enterprises/Brighton Homes/ Parkwood Builders/Parkside Homes	3.6
Pulte Homes	3.5
David Weekley Homes	3.3
Other	.49.7

Source: *Builder*, May 2004, p. 220.

★ 195 ★

Residential Construction
SIC: 1521; NAICS: 23321

Top Home Builders in Indianapolis, IN

Market shares are shown based on number of closings.

C.P. Morgan	.18.5%
Beazer Homes USA	.12.5
Davis Homes	7.7
American West Homes/Arbor Homes	5.9
Ryland Homes	5.8

Centex Homes	4.3%
Dura Builders	4.0
The Estridge Cos.	3.6
Other	.37.7

Source: *Builder*, May 2004, p. 220.

★ 196 ★

Residential Construction
SIC: 1521; NAICS: 23321

Top Home Builders in Jacksonville, FL

Market shares are shown in percent.

D.R. Horton	.10.0%
KB Home	5.3
Other	.84.7

Source: *Business Journal of Jacksonville*, August 2, 2004, p. NA, from Real Estate Strategy Center.

★ 197 ★

Residential Construction
SIC: 1521; NAICS: 23321

Top Home Builders in Kansas City, MO/KS

Market shares are shown based on number of closings.

Pulte Homes	2.1%
Rob Washam Homes	1.1
Duggan Homes	1.1
Wiley Enterprises	0.9
J.S. Robinson Construction	0.9
Don Bell Homes	0.8
Brown-Midwest	0.7
Other	.92.4

Source: *Builder*, May 2004, p. 220.

★ 198 ★

Residential Construction
SIC: 1521; NAICS: 23321

Top Home Builders in Las Vegas, NV

Market shares are shown based on number of closings.

KB Home	.11.1%
Pulte Homes/Del Webb	9.0
M.D.C. Holdings/Richmond American Homes	6.8
D.R. Horton	5.9
Weyerhaeuser Real Estate Co/Pardee Homes	3.7
Beazer Homes USA	3.6

Continued on next page.

★ 198 ★

[Continued]
Residential Construction
SIC: 1521; NAICS: 23321

Top Home Builders in Las Vegas, NV

Market shares are shown based on number of closings.

Centex Homes	2.8%
Other	57.1

Source: *Builder*, May 2004, p. 220.

★ 199 ★

Residential Construction
SIC: 1521; NAICS: 23321

Top Home Builders in Los Angeles/ Long Beach, CA

Market shares are shown based on number of closings.

Centex Homes	5.5%
Beazer Homes USA	4.6
KB Home	4.3
D.R. Horton/Western Pacific Housing	4.1
Hovnanian Enterprises/Richmond American Homes	3.3
Lennar Corp./Greystone Homes	3.1
Standard Pacific Corp.	3.0
John Laing Homes	3.0
Other	69.1

Source: *Builder*, May 2004, p. 220.

★ 200 ★

Residential Construction
SIC: 1521; NAICS: 23321

Top Home Builders in Memphis, TN/ AK/MS

Market shares are shown based on number of closings.

Kalian Cos./Reeves-Williams	7.8%
Bowden Homes	5.3
Matthews Brothers Builders	3.9
Lenox Homes/Bronze-Christian	2.2
Summit Homes	2.0
Buehler Affordable Homes	1.9
Chamberlain & McCreery	1.8
Beazer Homes USA	1.4
Other	73.7

Source: *Builder*, May 2004, p. 220.

★ 201 ★

Residential Construction
SIC: 1521; NAICS: 23321

Top Home Builders in Minneapolis/St. Paul, MN

Market shares are shown based on number of closings.

Centex Homes	5.1%
Rottlund Homes	4.8
Lennar Corp/.Lundgren Bros./Orrin Thompson Homes	3.9
D.R. Horton	3.4
Ryland Homes	2.9
Pulte Homes	2.9
M.W. Johnson Construction	2.6
Wensmann Homes	2.2
Town & Country Homes	2.2
Other	70.0

Source: *Builder*, May 2004, p. 220.

★ 202 ★

Residential Construction
SIC: 1521; NAICS: 23321

Top Home Builders in Nashville, TN

Market shares are shown based on number of closings.

Ole South Properties	6.5%
Beazer Homes USA	4.7
The Jones Co. of Tennessee	2.3
Greenvale Construction	2.1
Centex Homes	1.6
Pulte Homes	1.4
The Drees Co.	1.3
Technical Olympic USA/Newark Homes	1.3
Other	78.8

Source: *Builder*, May 2004, p. 220.

★ 203 ★

Residential Construction
SIC: 1521; NAICS: 23321

Top Home Builders in Orlando, FL

Market shares are shown based on number of closings.

The Villages	14.9%
Lennar Corp./U.S. Home Corp.	6.0
Avatar Holdings/Brookman-Fels	4.7
Ryland Homes	4.2
Centex Homes	3.8
Maronda Homes	3.5

Continued on next page.

★ 203 ★

[Continued]
Residential Construction
SIC: 1521; NAICS: 23321

Top Home Builders in Orlando, FL

Market shares are shown based on number of closings.

Pulte Homes 3.4%
Technical Olympic USA/Engle Homes 3.2
Other 57.3

Source: *Builder*, May 2004, p. 220.

★ 204 ★

Residential Construction
SIC: 1521; NAICS: 23321

Top Home Builders in Philadelphia, PA

Market shares are shown based on number of closings.

Pulte Homes 6.0%
Orleans Homebuilders 5.6
NVR/Ryan Homes 5.1
Toll Brothers 4.4
D.R. Horton/SGS Communities 4.3
T.H. Properties 3.8
Hovnanian Enterprises 3.5
David Culter Group 2.7
Other 68.9

Source: *Builder*, May 2004, p. 220.

★ 205 ★

Residential Construction
SIC: 1521; NAICS: 23321

Top Home Builders in Phoenix/Mesa, AZ

Market shares are shown based on number of closings.

DR Horton/Continental Homes/Dietz-Homes/
  Schuler Homes 9.8%
Pulte Homes/Sivage-Thomas Homes 8.7
M.D.C. Holdings/Richmond American Homes . 4.8
Shea Homes 4.1
KB Home 3.4
Standard Pacific Corp. 3.3
Fulton Homes 3.0
Beazer Homes USA 2.9
Other 60.0

Source: *Builder*, May 2004, p. 220.

★ 206 ★

Residential Construction
SIC: 1521; NAICS: 23321

Top Home Builders in Portland, OR/ Vancouver, WA

Market shares are shown based on number of closings.

D.R. Horton 5.0%
Arbor Homes 4.4
Hayden Homes 4.0
Centex Homes 3.2
New Tradition Homes 3.0
Legend Homes Corp. 2.8
Sun Country Homes 2.4
Polygon Northwest 2.4
Don Morrissette Homes 2.2
Other 70.6

Source: *Builder*, May 2004, p. 220.

★ 207 ★

Residential Construction
SIC: 1521; NAICS: 23321

Top Home Builders in Salt Lake City/ Ogden, UT

Market shares are shown based on number of closings.

Ivory Homes 7.2%
Salisbury Homes 4.3
Woodside Group/Woodside Homes 3.6
Hamlet Homes 3.2
M.D.C. Holdings/Richmond American Homes . 3.0
Fieldstone Homes 2.5
D.R. Horton 2.3
Liberty Homes 2.2
Perry Homes 2.1
Other 69.6

Source: *Builder*, May 2004, p. 220.

★ 208 ★

Residential Construction
SIC: 1521; NAICS: 23321

Top Home Builders in San Diego, CA, 2003

Companies are ranked by number of homes closed. Shares are shown for the top 20 firms.

	Units	Share
D.R. Horton Inc.	2,011	27.86%
Centex Homes	635	8.80
Shea Homes San Diego	628	8.70

Continued on next page.

★ 208 ★

[Continued]
Residential Construction
SIC: 1521; NAICS: 23321

Top Home Builders in San Diego, CA, 2003

Companies are ranked by number of homes closed.
Shares are shown for the top 20 firms.

	Units	Share
Barratt	598	8.28%
Standard Pacific Homes	463	6.41
William Lyon Homes	438	6.07
Pardee Homes	433	6.00
Other	2,013	27.88

Source: *San Diego Business Journal*, October 25, 2004, p. 18.

★ 209 ★

Residential Construction
SIC: 1521; NAICS: 23321

Top Home Builders in Tampa Bay, FL

Market shares are shown based on number of closings.

Lennar Corp./U.S. Home Corp.	.11.2%
Ryland Homes	5.5
Maronda Homes	4.9
Standard Pacific Corp./Westfield Homes	4.3
Pulte Homes	3.7
Inland Homes	3.5
Hovnanian Enterprises/Woodward Homes . . .	3.5
M/I Homes	2.7
Suarez Housing Corp.	2.3
Other	.58.4

Source: *Builder*, May 2004, p. 220.

★ 210 ★

Apartments
SIC: 1522; NAICS: 23322

Largest Apartment Markets, 2004

Data show the number of permits issued in the largest construction markets (5 or more units). Shares are shown based on the top 40 markets.

	Units	Share
New York/Northern New Jersey/ Long Island NY-NJ-PA	22,754	9.45%
Miami-Ft. Lauderdale-Miami Beach, FL	20,011	8.31
Los Angeles-Long Beach-Santa Ana, CA	18,369	7.63

	Units	Share
Atlanta-Sandy Springs-Marietta GA	16,179	6.72%
Houston-Baytown-Sugar Land, TX .	10,427	4.33
Washington-Arlington-Alexandria DC-VA-MD-WV	9,785	4.06
Chicago-Naperville-Joliet IL-IN-WI	8,758	3.64
Dallas-Fort Worth-Arlinton, TX . .	7,686	3.19
Riverside-San Bernadino-Ontario, CA	7,235	3.00
San Francisco-Oakland-Fremont, CA	6,873	2.85
Other	112,696	46.81

Source: *Units*, March 2005, p. 73, from U.S. Department of Commerce & Labor and Regis J. Sheehan & Associates.

★ 211 ★

Condominiums
SIC: 1531; NAICS: 23321

Leading Condominium Makers in Japan, 2003

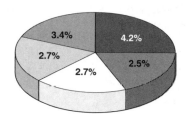

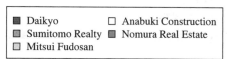

Market shares are estimated based on domestic sales of 154,951 units.

Daikyo	.4.2%
Sumitomo Realty	.3.4
Mitsui Fudosan	.2.7
Anabuki Construction	.2.7
Nomura Real Estate	.2.5

Source: "Market Share Survey Report 2003." [online] from http://www.nni.nikkei.co.jp [Published July 26, 2004], from Real Estate Economic Institute.

★ 212 ★
Retail Construction
SIC: 1542; NAICS: 23332

Retail Construction Starts, 2004

Data are in thousands of feet for the first nine months of the year.

	(000)	Share
South	96,103	31.99%
Midwest	53,204	17.71
West	48,043	15.99
Pacific Southwest	39,312	13.09
East North Central	34,924	11.63
West South Central	28,787	9.58

Source: *Display & Design Ideas*, December 2004, p. 11, from McGraw Hill Construction.

SIC 16 - Heavy Construction, Except Building

★ 213 ★
Contracting Work
SIC: 1600; NAICS: 23321, 23331, 23332
Leading Contractors

Firms are ranked by revenues in millions of dollars.

Bechtel	$ 13,212.0
Centex	8,985.9
KBR	8,030.4
Fluor Corp.	6,703.0
The Turner Corp.	5,876.2
Skanska USA Inc.	5,625.2
Peter Kiewit Sons Inc.	3,558.1
Bovis Lend Lease	3,153.1
Foster Wheeler	2,723.0
The Shaw Group Inc.	2,678.4

Source: *ENR*, October 2004, p. 10, from *ENR* survey.

★ 214 ★
Contracting Work - Highways
SIC: 1611; NAICS: 23411
Leading Highway Contractors

Contractors are ranked by awards in millions of dollars.

APAC Inc.	$ 508.87
Peter Kiewit Sons Inc.	393.47
Granite Construction Co.	344.24
Edward Kraemer & Sons Inc.	323.10
Williams Bros. Construction	298.43
The Walsh Group Inc.	279.59
Balfour Beatty Const.	251.59
W.W. Webber Inc.	231.31
American Bridge Co.	177.92
Tully Construction	177.78

Source: *Asphalt Contractor*, February 2005, p. 88, from American Road & Transportation Builders Association.

★ 215 ★
Contracting Work - Highways
SIC: 1611; NAICS: 23411
Leading Highway Contractors in the Southwest, 2003

Firms are ranked by contract awards from January 1, 2003 - December 31, 2003. The Southwest refers to Arkansas, Louisiana, New Mexico, Oklahoma and Texas.

Williams Bros. Construction Inc.	$ 298.40
W.W. Webber Inc.	231.31
Balfour Beatty Constr. (Div. Of Balfour Beatty)	170.30
Abrams, J.D. Inc.	158.50
Zachry, H.B. Constr. Co.	156.95
Archer-Western Contractor (Div. Of Walsh)	103.01
Hunter Industries Inc.	69.92
Austin Bridge & Road Inc.	63.56
McCarthy Building Co.	50.83
Gilchrist Const. Co.	47.92

Source: *TransportationBuilder*, November - December 2004, p. 23.

★ 216 ★
Contracting Work - Bridges
SIC: 1622; NAICS: 23412
Leading Bridge Contractors

Firms are ranked by revenues in millions of dollars.

Peter Kiewit Sons Inc.	$ 549.9
Skanska USA Inc.	541.6
Flatiron Construction Corp.	318.3
The Walsh Group	306.6
Edward Kraemer & Sons Inc.	251.0
American Bridge Co.	219.1
Lunda Construction Co.	196.1
PCL Construction Enterprises Inc.	143.0
AMEC	132.0
MCM Construction Inc.	120.0

Source: *ENR*, October 2004, p. 45, from *ENR* survey.

★ 217 ★

Contracting Work - Sewers

SIC: 1623; NAICS: 23491

Leading Sanitary/Storm Sewer Contractors

Firms are ranked by revenues in millions of dollars.

Traylor Bros. Inc.	$ 62.0
Reynolds Inc.	46.7
American Infrastructure Inc.	45.2
Kokosing Construction Co. Inc.	31.4
Peter Kiewit Sons Inc.	28.3
Balfour Beatty Inc.	25.9
Modern Continental Cos. Inc.	18.3
Sundt Continental Inc.	17.9
MWH	17.2
Garney Holding Co.	15.4

Source: *ENR*, October 2004, p. 45, from *ENR* survey.

SIC 17 - Special Trade Contractors

★ 218 ★
Contracting Work - Electrical
SIC: 1731; NAICS: 23531

Largest Electrical Contractors

Companies are ranked by sales in millions of dollars.

Integrated Electrical Services Inc.	$ 1,449.0
EMCOR Group Inc.	1,265.0
Quanta Services Inc.	1,028.0
Henkels & McCoy	516.0
MYR Group Inc.	437.8
Utility Services Inc.	434.2
Mass. Electric Construction Co.	371.2
Fisk Corp.	363.1
Infrasource Services Inc.	330.0
Sasco	301.0

Source: *EC&M*, September 1, 2004, p. NA, from *EC&M 2004 Top 50 survey.*

★ 219 ★
Contracting Work - Masonry
SIC: 1741; NAICS: 23541

Top Masonry Contractors

The 77 companies that responded to the source's survey generated slightly more than $1 billion with commercial/industrial work taking 72% of volume, residential taking 15% and repair/construction taking 13%. Firms are ranked by masonry revenue in millions of dollars.

McGee Brothers Co. Inc.	$ 78.4
The Western Group	47.5
Dee Brown Inc.	43.4
J.D. Long Masonry Inc.	41.6
Sun Valley Masonry Inc.	39.3
Leonard Masonry Inc.	28.5
D'Agostino Associates	28.0
Mid-Continental Restoration Co.	27.0
Design Masonry	27.0
B.W. Dexter	26.8

Source: *Masonry Construction*, September 2004, p. 22.

★ 220 ★
Contracting Work - Roofing
SIC: 1761; NAICS: 23561

Leading Roofing Contractors, 2003

Companies are ranked by annual volume in millions of dollars.

generalRoofing	$ 312.00
Centimark Corporation	251.00
TECTA America Corp.	219.00
Latite Roofing & Sheet Metal Co.	69.89
Baker Roofing Co.	59.44
Westurn Roofing & Siding Inc.	59.00
ABLE Roofing	51.27
Beldon Enterprises	45.63
Best Roofing & Waterproofing Inc.	42.90
Silktown Roofing Inc.	41.76

Source: *RSI*, October 2004, p. 30.

★ 221 ★
Roofing
SIC: 1761; NAICS: 23561

Commercial Roofing Market in the Western States

The industry is shown by segment. BUR stands for built-up roofing. APP stands for atatic polypropylene. SBS stands for styrene butadiene styrene. EPDM stands for etylene propylene diene monomer. TPO stands for thermoplastic polyolefin. PVC stands for polyvinyl chloride.

	($ bil.)	Share
BUR	$ 1.82	28.2%
APP modified	1.06	15.1
SBS modified	0.86	14.2
TPO	0.54	9.1
EPDM	0.53	8.6
PVC	0.39	5.9
Metal/architectural	0.20	4.1
Fiberglass shingles	0.19	2.8
Liquid applied	0.17	3.1

Source: "Growing Western Roofing Market." [online] from http://www.westernroofing.com/western_market.htm [Accessed March 17, 2005].

★ 222 ★
Roofing
SIC: 1761; NAICS: 23561

Residential Roofing Market in the Western States

The industry is shown by segment. BUR stands for built-up roofing. APP stands for atatic polypropylene. SBS stands for styrene butadiene styrene.

	($ bil.)	Share
Fiberglass shingles	$ 1.80	47.9%
Concrete/tile	0.57	14.5
Clay tile	0.47	12.4
Metal/arch.	0.26	7.0
Slate	0.19	4.9
Wood shingles/shakes	0.17	3.6
SBS modified	0.08	1.9
APP modified	0.07	1.6

Source: "Growing Western Roofing Market." [online] from http://www.westernroofing.com/western_market.htm [Accessed March 17, 2005].

★ 223 ★
Roofing
SIC: 1761; NAICS: 23561

Roofing Demand Worldwide, 2003 and 2008

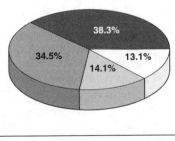

- ■ North America
- ■ Asia/Pacific
- □ Western Europe
- □ Other

The market is forecast to climb to $48 billion by 2008. The industry will benefit from residential and nonresidential building construction in Asia and Eastern Europe. Demand is shown in millions of square meters.

	2003	2008	Share
North America	2,473	2,665	38.26%
Asia/Pacific	1,905	2,405	34.53
Western Europe	920	985	14.14
Other	786	910	13.07

Source: *RSI*, October 2004, p. 2, from Freedonia Group and McGraw-Hill Construction.

★ 224 ★
Roofing
SIC: 1761; NAICS: 23561

Roofing Industry, 2004

Figures compare the new roof and reroofing segments based on a survey. EPDM stands for etylene propylene diene monomer. TPO stands for thermoplastic polyolefin. PVC stands for polyvinyl chloride.

	New	Re-Roof
EPDM	30.0%	28.0%
Hot BUR	15.0	18.0
TPOs	12.0	9.0
SBS	10.0	12.0
Metal	10.0	9.0
PVC	9.0	8.0
APP	6.0	7.0
SPF	4.0	4.0
Cold	4.0	5.0

Source: *RSI*, December 2004, p. 2, from Freedonia Group.

★ 225 ★
Roofing
SIC: 1761; NAICS: 23561

Roofing Industry in China, 2004

There are 2,000 waterproofing/roofing material makers in the country.

Asphalt sheet with composite reinforcement	40.85%
SBS and APP modified bitumen	17.97
Waterproofing	13.07
Polymer sheet	11.44
Organic felt	10.95
Other	5.72

Source: *Professional Roofing*, February 2005, p. NA, from *2004 Report on the Chinese Waterproofing Industry.*

★ 226 ★
Contracting Work - Concrete
SIC: 1771; NAICS: 23542, 23571

Top Concrete Contractors

Firms are ranked by concrete revenue in millions of dollars.

Baker Concrete Construction	$ 384.0
Miller & Long	264.7
S&F Concrete Construction	175.0
Webcor Concrete	151.0
Suncoast Post-Tension	127.0
Capform	113.0
Keystone Concrete Placement	111.6

Continued on next page.

★ 226 ★
[Continued]
Contracting Work - Concrete
SIC: 1771; NAICS: 23542, 23571

Top Concrete Contractors

Firms are ranked by concrete revenue in millions of dollars.

T.A.S. Commercial Concrete . . . . $ 76.0
Concrete Structures of the Midwest 66.8
Southern Pan Services 56.4

Source: *Concrete Construction*, May 2004, p. 109.

★ 227 ★
Contracting Work - Concrete
SIC: 1771; NAICS: 23542, 23571

Types of Concrete Work

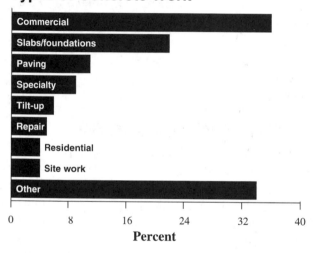

Percent

Revenues for the top 100 firms: $9.16 billion in 2001, $9.48 billion in 2002 and $10.26 billion in 2003.

Commercial 36.0%
Slabs/foundations 21.8
Paving 10.5
Specialty 8.7
Tilt-up 6.3
Repair 5.1
Residential 3.9
Site work 3.8
Other 33.9

Source: *Concrete Construction*, July 2004, p. 109, from *CC100 Contractors.*

★ 228 ★
Contracting Work - Glazing
SIC: 1793; NAICS: 23592

Leading Glazing Contractors

Firms are ranked by sales in millions of dollars.

Harmon Inc. . . . .$ 144.5
Enclos 143.0
Trainor Glass 73.0
Walters & Wolf 63.6
W&W Glass Systems 47.9
Karas & Karas Glass 45.9
Architectural Glass & Aluminum Co. 44.4
Haley-Greer Inc. 43.3
AWallS Inc. Architectural Wall Solutions . . . 36.2
TSI Exterior Wall Systems Inc. 24.1

Source: *Glass Magazine*, Top 50 List, 2004, p. NA.

★ 229 ★
Contracting Work - Swimming Pools
SIC: 1799; NAICS: 23599

Leading Pool Builders

Companies are ranked by construction revenues in millions of dollars. Shares are shown based on the top 50 firms.

	($ mil.)	Share
Blue Haven Pools & Spas	$ 221.50	17.28%
Anthony & Sylvan Pools Corp. . . .	175.00	13.65
Paddock Pools	66.30	5.17
Shasta Industries	63.50	4.95
Swan Pools	60.00	4.68
California Pools and Spas	48.00	3.74
California Pools & Spas of Arizona .	44.00	3.43
Premier Pools and Spas Inc.	43.90	3.42
Mission Pools Inc.	32.40	2.53
Pacific Pools & Spas	28.30	2.21
The Pool People Inc.	27.40	2.14
Aqua Pool & Spa	26.70	2.08
Other	445.11	34.72

Source: *Pool & Spa News*, September 17, 2004, p. 50, from *Pool & Spa News Top 50 Builders.*

★ 230 ★
Contracting Work - Swimming Pools
SIC: 1799; NAICS: 23599

Swimming Pool Sales in the U.K., 2003

An estimated 163,000 pools exist in the country in
2003, with roughly 2,000 new pools added each year.

Vinyl	.50.0%
Fiberglass	.25.0
Concrete	.25.0

Source: *Pool & Spa Marketing*, Directory 2004, p. 24.

SIC 20 - Food and Kindred Products

★ 231 ★
Food

SIC: 2000; NAICS: 311412, 311421, 311511

Food and Consumable Sales, 2004

Figures are estimated based on food statistics for the year ended May 15, 2004.

	($ bil.)	Share
Dry grocery	$ 162.63	41.46%
Health & beauty aids	50.77	12.94
Non-food grocery	46.04	11.74
Dairy	45.13	11.50
Frozen foods	34.44	8.78
Alcoholic beverages	20.30	5.17
Fresh produce	13.54	3.45
Packaged meat	12.49	3.18
Deli	5.40	1.38
Fresh meat	1.54	0.39

Source: *DSN Retailing Today*, August 2, 2004, p. 35, from ACNielsen.

★ 232 ★
Food

SIC: 2000; NAICS: 311421, 311422, 312111

Food Industry in the U.K.

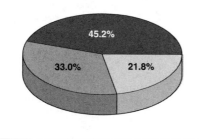

Legend	
■ Export	□ Foodservice sector
▨ Grocery wholesalers	

Market shares are shown in percent.

Export	45.2%
Grocery wholesalers	33.0
Foodservice sector	21.8

Source: *Food (UK)*, November 26, 2004, p. NA, from IBISWorld.

★ 233 ★
Food

SIC: 2000; NAICS: 311511, 311513, 311615

Largest Food Categories, 2004

Supermarket sales are shown in billions of dollars for the year ended July 11, 2004.

Milk	$ 10.45
Fresh bread	5.63
Natural cheese	5.49
Juices & drinks, refrigerated	3.81
Lunch meat	3.30
Salad and coleslaw, refrigerated	3.29
Breakfast meat	2.96
Egss, refrigerated fresh	2.93
Yogurt	2.68
Processed cheese	2.26
Frankfurters	1.63

Source: *Grocery Headquarters*, September 2004, p. S4, from Information Resources Inc.

★ 234 ★
Food

SIC: 2000; NAICS: 311615, 311812

Leading Meal/Entree Makers, 2004

Companies are ranked by sales in millions of dollars.

Nestle USA	$ 3,300
ConAgra Foods	3,000
Kraft Foods Inc.	1,900
The Schwan Food Co.	1,800
Pinnacle Foods Corp.	850
H.J. Heinz Co.	800
Luigino's Inc.	500
Kellogg Co.	460
General Mills Inc.	450
Gorton's Inc.	350
Windsor Foods Inc.	300
Ruiz Foods Inc.	300

Source: *Refrigerated & Frozen Foods*, March 2005, p. 16, from *Refrigerated & Frozen Foods Annual Top 150 Report*.

★ 235 ★

Food

SIC: 2000; NAICS: 311999

Pizza Market by Segment, 2003

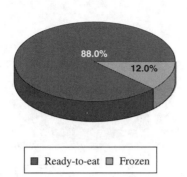

Market shares are shown in percent.

Ready-to-eat 88.0%
Frozen 12.0

Source: *Food Processing*, January 2005, p. S17.

★ 236 ★

Food

SIC: 2000; NAICS: 311423, 311823, 311999

Prepared Food Sales (Ready to Serve), 2003

Supermarket sales are shown in millions of dollars.

Beans with meat, shelf stable . . . .$ 436.22
Meat, imitation/additives 330.53
Chili, shelf stable 292.22
Lasagna, canned 217.68
Spaghetti, canned 199.61
Ravioli, canned 195.92
Chicken, shelf stable 172.52
Macaroni products, shelf stable 108.52
Vienna sausage, canned 105.98
Stew, beef, shelf stable 90.44

Source: *Progressive Grocer*, Sept. 15, 2004, p. 26, from *2004 Progressive Grocer Consumer Expenditure Survey*.

★ 237 ★

Food

SIC: 2000; NAICS: 311412, 311421, 311422

Private Label Food Goods, 2003

Private label foods have begun to gain ground on branded label foods. In the 12 weeks to mid February food companies improved sales by 1.4% but private label firms did so by 3.3%. Market shares are shown based on volume at food stores, drug stores and mass merchandisers (excluding Wal-Mart).

No. 1 brand 24.9%
No. 2 brand 11.5
Private label 31.3
Other 32.3

Source: *Financial Times*, March 11, 2005, p. 19, from Banc of America.

★ 238 ★

Food

SIC: 2000; NAICS: 311511, 311821, 312111

Top Food & Drink Firms Worldwide

North America remains the dominant region for food and beverage companies. Various low-carb diets (Atkins, South Beach) have had an effect on companies' sales, with meat processors enjoying higher sales and dairy/baked good firms seeing a slide in sales. Firms are ranked by food sales in millions of dollars.

Nestle S.A. . . . . $ 61,615
Archer Daniels Midland Co. 36,151
Kraft Foods 31,010
Unilever 29,938
Cargill 27,260
PepsiCo Inc. 26,971
Tyson Foods Inc. 24,549
Coca-Cola Co. 21,044
Mars Inc. 17,000
Groupe Danone 14,850

Source: *Food Engineering*, October 2004, p. 58.

★ 239 ★

Food

SIC: 2000; NAICS: 311422, 311511, 311513

Top Food Companies in North America, 2003

Firms are ranked by food sales in millions of dollars.

Kraft Foods . . . .$ 21,907
Tyson Foods Inc. 21,894

Continued on next page.

★ 239 ★
[Continued]
Food
SIC: 2000; NAICS: 311422, 311511, 311513

Top Food Companies in North America, 2003

Firms are ranked by food sales in millions of dollars.

Pepsico Inc.	$ 18,293
ConAgra Foods	16,927
Nestle	13,798
Anheuser-Busch	10,984
Mars Inc.	10,000
Sara Lee Corp.	9,778
General Mills	9,520
Dean Foods Co.	9,185
Swift & Co.	8,432

Source: *Food Processing*, August 2004, p. 26, from *Food Processing Top 100*.

★ 240 ★
Food
SIC: 2000; NAICS: 311615, 311812, 312111

Top Ready Made Firms in Western Europe

Market shares are for December 2004. The United Kingdom took 30% of the market in 2003, followed by Germany 24% and France 12%.

Nestle	8.7%
Unilever	7.7
Greencore	4.3
Uniq	3.6
Oetker	3.4
Heinz	3.3
Northern Foods	3.1
Sudzucker	2.6
Apetito	2.0
Other	61.3

Source: "Ready Meal Markets." [online] from http://www.fft.com [Market Synopsis dated January 2005], from *Food for Thought's 2005 West European Food & Drink Database*.

★ 241 ★
Food
SIC: 2000; NAICS: 11231, 311615

Top Refrigerated Breakfast Entrees, 2004

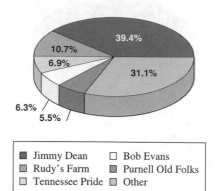

Jimmy Dean · Bob Evans
Rudy's Farm · Purnell Old Folks
Tennessee Pride · Other

Brands are ranked by sales in millions of dollars for the year ended July 11, 2004.

	($ mil.)	Share
Jimmy Dean	$ 43.15	39.38%
Rudy's Farm	11.73	10.70
Tennessee Pride	7.56	6.90
Bob Evans	6.96	6.35
Purnell Old Folks	6.06	5.53
Other	34.12	31.14

Source: *National Provisioner*, August 2004, p. 56, from Information Resources Inc.

★ 242 ★
Specialty Foods
SIC: 2000; NAICS: 311999

Convenience Food Industry Leaders Worldwide, 2002

Companies are ranked by sales in billions of dollars.

Nestle	$ 64.3
Unilever	50.1
Kraft	33.9
Tyson Foods	24.5
ConAgra Foods Inc.	19.8
General Mills Inc.	10.5

Source: *just-food.com*, September 2004, p. 32, from just-food.com, company reports and web sites.

★ 243 ★
Specialty Foods
SIC: 2000; NAICS: 311999
Convenience/Ready Food Sales in North America, 2003

Total sales in the United States and Canada increased from $13.2 billion in 2002 to $14.9 billion in 2003.

Frozen	.61.2%
Canned	.16.0
Dried	.14.9
Chilled	7.2
Other	0.7

Source: *just-food.com*, September 2004, p. 12, from just-food.com research from published sources.

★ 244 ★
Specialty Foods
SIC: 2000; NAICS: 311999
Convenience/Ready Meal Sales Worldwide, 2003

In terms of retail sales, frozen foods took 38.5% of sales, followed by chilled foods with 37% of sales.

North America	.37.2%
Asia Pacific	.28.8
Western Europe	.28.4
Eastern Europe	3.1
Africa & Middle East	1.0
Latin America & the Caribbean	0.8
Australasia	0.6

Source: *just-food.com*, September 2004, p. 7, from just-food estimates on published data.

★ 245 ★
Specialty Foods
SIC: 2000; NAICS: 311412, 311422, 311612
Ethnic Food Sales in the U.K., 2004

Ethnic snacking and light meals are outperforming the total snacking category. The Indian and Chinese categories are the main drivers of the sector. The industry was valued at 995.3 million pounds for the year ended September 12, 2004.

Chilled ready meals	.47.1%
Ethnic cooking sauces	.19.1
Chilled bitesize snacks	.10.0
Retail rice	9.6
Naan bread	5.4

Noodles	3.0%
Pita bread	2.5
Poppadoms	1.5
Soy sauce	1.0
Other	0.8

Source: *Grocer*, November 20, 2004, p. 50, from Taylor Nelson Sofres Superpanel.

★ 246 ★
Specialty Foods
SIC: 2000; NAICS: 31133, 31152, 312111
Functional Food Industry Worldwide

Sales are shown in millions of dollars.

	2003	2008
Confectionery	$ 5,656.6	$ 7,389.8
Snack bars	1,198.4	1,757.9
Biscuits, cakes and pastries	521.3	646.4
Bread	429.8	652.3

Source: *Food Engineering & Ingredients*, June 2004, p. 22, from Euromonitor.

★ 247 ★
Specialty Foods
SIC: 2000; NAICS: 311999, 325411
Functional Food Market Worldwide

According to the source, the funcctional food industry has expanded for a number of reasons: a health concious consumer base, the rise of self medication, a crowded market, and scientific research. Japan is the largest market for functional foods.

For sport or energy protection	.42.0%
Added vitamins, minerals, supplements	.19.0
Promotes intestinal health or digestion	.18.0
Added calcium	.10.0
Other	.11.0

Source: *International Food Ingredients*, October - November 2004, p. 66, from Euromonitor.

★ 248 ★
Specialty Foods
SIC: 2000; NAICS: 311422, 311511, 311513
Functional Food Sales by Year

Sales are shown in millions of dollars.

2003	$ 4,603
2004	4,966
2005	5,332
2006	5,699

Continued on next page.

★ 248 ★
[Continued]
Specialty Foods
SIC: 2000; NAICS: 311422, 311511, 311513

Functional Food Sales by Year

Sales are shown in millions of dollars.

2007	$ 6,060
2008	6,404

Source: *Dairy Foods*, January 2005, p. 40, from Mintel.

★ 249 ★

Specialty Foods
SIC: 2000; NAICS: 311412, 311421, 311615

Organic Food Sales, 2003

According to the Organic Trade Association, the industry was worth $10.4 billion in 2003. Fruits and vegetables take 42% of sales. Mass market grocers 37% and natural food independent grocers 28%. Meat, fish and poultry are forecast to grow 30.7% from 2004-2008.

	($ mil.)
Fruit & vegetables	$ 4,336
Beverages	1,581
Dairy	1,385
Packaged/prepared foods	1,326
Bread & grains	966
Snack foods	484
Sauces/condiments	229
Meat/fish/poultry	75

Source: *Beverage Industry*, June 2004, p. 36, from *Organic Trade Association's 2004 Manufacturer Survey*, *Nutrition Business Journal*, and SPINS retail data.

★ 250 ★

Specialty Foods
SIC: 2000; NAICS: 311421, 311513, 31192

Specialty Food Industry

It is difficult to estimate the size of the specialty food industry because it depends on how the category is defined. The source places the market at $22.8 billion.

Condiments	11.1%
Tea	5.1
Cheese	5.0
Coffee and cocoa	4.9
Chips and snacks	4.7
Cookies and snack bars	4.2
Cooking oil	3.8
Carbonated beverages	3.6

Seasonings	3.4%
Frozen entrees/convenience foods	3.4
Other	50.8

Source: *Grocery Headquarters*, August 2004, p. 18, from *State of the Specialty Food Industry, 2004*.

★ 251 ★

Specialty Foods
SIC: 2000; NAICS: 311511, 311513, 31192

Specialty Food Sales, 2003

By channel, mainstream stores took 67% of the market, with specialty food stores with 23.2% and natural food stores taking 9.8%. Sales increased from $19 billion in 2001 to $22.8 billion in 2003.

Condiments	$ 1,823
Teas	838
Cheese	827
Coffee, coffee substitutes and cocoa	811
Chips, pretzels, and snacks	763
Cookies and snack bars	690
Cooking oils	627
Shelf-stable pasta	615
Carbonated beverages and single-serve drinks .	596

Source: *Food Institute Report*, April 26, 2004, p. 1, from *Specialty Food Magazine*.

★ 252 ★

Specialty Foods
SIC: 2000; NAICS: 311412, 311421, 311511

Vegetarian Food Sales

It wasn't until the mid 1990s that consumers began to see vegetarian foods as a mainstream food trend rather than a small, counter-cultural segment. The vegetarian food market exceeded $1.6 billion in sales in 2003. Tofu sales include all channels, not food, drug and mass merchandisers only.

	($ mil.)	Share
Refrigerated dairy milk substitute . .	$ 301.7	37.3%
Frozen meat substitute	273.8	33.8
Shelf-stable dairy milk substitute . .	131.6	16.3
Tofu	75.1	9.3
Refrigerated meat substitute	11.2	1.4
Entrees	9.2	1.1
Canned meat substitute	6.9	0.9

Source: *Prepared Foods*, February 2005, p. 13, from Information Resources Inc. InfoScan and Mintel.

★ 253 ★
Meat Packing
SIC: 2011; NAICS: 311611, 311613
Pork Processing Operations, 2004

There were 70,130 hog processing operations in the United States as of January 1, 2004. Market share is shown by number of heads in operation. The top 159 largest firms processed 59% of all hogs in the country.

1,000-3,000	8.0%
10,000-50,000	19.0
3,000-5,000	4.0
5,000-10,000	9.0
50,000-500,000	19.0
500,000-plus	40.0
Less than 1,000	1.0

Source: *Feedstuffs*, August 23, 2004, p. 8.

★ 254 ★
Bacon
SIC: 2013; NAICS: 311612, 311613
Top Bacon Brands, 2005

Market shares are shown based on sales at food stores, drug stores and mass merchandisers (but not Wal-Mart) for the 52 weeks ended January 23, 2005.

Oscar Mayer	18.4%
Hormel Black Label	6.8
Bar-S	3.3
Farmland	3.2
Gwaltney of Smithfield	3.1
Wright	2.9
Smithfield	2.8
Louis Rich	2.6
Hormel	2.6
Private label	18.7
Other	35.6

Source: *Grocery Headquarters*, April 2005, p. 22, from Information Resources Inc.

★ 255 ★
Bacon
SIC: 2013; NAICS: 311612, 311613
Top Bacon Vendors (Refrigerated), 2004

Companies are ranked by supermarket, drug store and mass merchandiser sales (but not Wal-Mart) for the 52 weeks ended October 31, 2004.

Oscar Mayer/Kraft	$ 392.59
Hormel	212.49
Gwaltney of Smithfield	82.12
Farmland	75.45
Bar-S	75.04
ConAgra	68.24
Smithfield	66.90
Wright	66.16
John Morrell	61.29
Private label	397.14

Source: *Meat & Deli Retailer*, December 2004, p. NA, from Information Resources Inc.

★ 256 ★
Hot Dogs
SIC: 2013; NAICS: 311612, 311613
Hot Dog Industry in the Philippines

The top brand is Purefoods Tender Juicy.

Hormel	65.0%
Other	35.0

Source: *Post-Bulletin*, November 23, 2004, p. NA.

★ 257 ★
Hot Dogs
SIC: 2013; NAICS: 311612, 311613
Top Hot Dog Brands, 2005

Market shares are shown based on sales at food stores, drug stores and mass merchandisers (but not Wal-Mart) for the 52 weeks ended January 23, 2005.

Oscar Mayer	18.6%
Ball Park	15.5
Bar-S	7.2
Hebrew National	5.0
Nathan	4.0
Gwaltney	2.1
Bryan	2.1
Armour	2.1
Eckrich	1.8

Continued on next page.

★ 257 ★
[Continued]
Hot Dogs
SIC: 2013; NAICS: 311612, 311613

Top Hot Dog Brands, 2005

Market shares are shown based on sales at food stores, drug stores and mass merchandisers (but not Wal-Mart) for the 52 weeks ended January 23, 2005.

Private label	6.0%
Other	35.6

Source: *Grocery Headquarters*, April 2005, p. 22, from Information Resources Inc.

★ 258 ★
Hot Dogs
SIC: 2013; NAICS: 311612, 311613

Top Hot Dog Makers, 2005

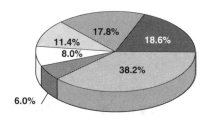

Market shares are shown based on sales at food stores, drug stores and mass merchandisers (but not Wal-Mart) for the 52 weeks ended January 23, 2005.

Kraft/Oscar Mayer	18.6%
Ball Park Brands	17.8
ConAgra Inc.	11.4
Bar-S Foods Co.	8.0
Private label	6.0
Other	38.2

Source: *Grocery Headquarters*, April 2005, p. 22, from Information Resources Inc.

★ 259 ★
Hot Dogs
SIC: 2013; NAICS: 311612, 311613

Top Hot Dogs (Frozen), 2004

Brands are ranked by supermarket sales for the 52 weeks ended December 26, 2004.

	Sales	Share
Sheiton fz frankfurters	$ 447,079	70.11%
Roger Wood fz frankfurters	114,630	17.98
Cloverdale fz frankfurters	49,488	7.76
Orientex fz frankfurters	8,140	1.28
Star-B Ranch fz frankfurters	603	0.09
Other	17,740	2.78

Source: *National Provisioner*, February 2005, p. 19, from Information Resources Inc.

★ 260 ★
Lunch Meat
SIC: 2013; NAICS: 311612, 311613

Top Lunch Meat (Refrigerated, Non-Sliced) Brands, 2004

Brands are ranked by supermarket, drug store and mass merchandiser sales (excluding Wal-Mart) for the year ended August 8, 2004.

Oscar Mayer	25.5%
Hillshire Farm Deli Select	6.9
Buddig	4.4
Butterball	4.2
Louis Rich	2.6
Bar S	2.5
Land O' Frost Premium	2.4
Hormel	2.3
Bryan	1.7
Private label	14.3
Other	33.2

Source: *Progressive Grocer*, November 1, 2004, p. 48, from Information Resources Inc.

★ 261 ★
Lunch Meat
SIC: 2013; NAICS: 311612, 311613

Top Lunch Meat (Sliced) Brands, 2005

Market shares are shown based on sales at food stores, drug stores and mass merchandisers (but not Wal-Mart) for the 52 weeks ended January 23, 2005.

Oscar Mayer	25.9%
Hillshire Farm Deli Select	7.9

Continued on next page.

★ 261 ★

[Continued]
Lunch Meat
SIC: 2013; NAICS: 311612, 311613

Top Lunch Meat (Sliced) Brands, 2005

Market shares are shown based on sales at food stores, drug stores and mass merchandisers (but not Wal-Mart) for the 52 weeks ended January 23, 2005.

Buddig	4.4%
Butterball	3.9
Louis Rich	2.5
Land O Frost Premium	2.4
Hormel	2.4
Bar S	2.4
Bryan	1.6
Private label	14.1
Other	32.5

Source: *Grocery Headquarters*, April 2005, p. 22, from Information Resources Inc.

★ 262 ★

Lunch Meat
SIC: 2013; NAICS: 311612, 311613

Top Lunch Meat (Sliced) Makers, 2005

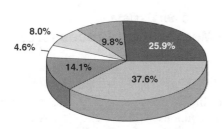

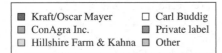

Market shares are shown based on sales at food stores, drug stores and mass merchandisers (but not Wal-Mart) for the 52 weeks ended January 23, 2005.

Kraft/Oscar Mayer	25.9%
ConAgra Inc.	9.8
Hillshire Farm & Kahna	8.0
Carl Buddig	4.6
Private label	14.1
Other	37.6

Source: *Grocery Headquarters*, April 2005, p. 22, from Information Resources Inc.

★ 263 ★

Meat
SIC: 2013; NAICS: 311612, 311613

Fresh Meat Sales, 2004

The fastest-growing segments are poultry (up 23%), beef and prepared meals, both up 19%.

Beef	52.0%
Chicken	20.0
Pork	17.0
Smoked ham	3.0
Sausage	2.0
Veal	1.0
Lamb	1.0
Other	4.0

Source: *Progressive Grocer*, March 1, 2005, p. 62, from *Progressive Grocer's 2005 Meat Operations Review*.

★ 264 ★

Meat
SIC: 2013; NAICS: 311612, 311613

Largest Beef Processors

Smithfield recently merged its cattle feedlots with ContiBeef.

Tyson	30.0%
Excel	23.0
Swift	22.0
National Beef	8.0
Smithfield	6.0
Other	11.0

Source: *Daily Press*, February 20, 2005, p. NA.

★ 265 ★

Meat

SIC: 2013; NAICS: 311612, 311613

Largest Meat Firms Worldwide, 2004

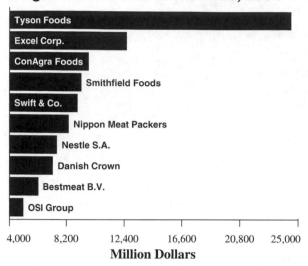

Million Dollars

The industry has done well in spite of challenges such as Mad Cow disease and Avian Influenza. Firms are ranked by sales in millions of dollars. Some companies such as GFI America do not release sales figures and could not be included.

Tyson Foods	$ 24,500
Excel Corp.	12,600
ConAgra Foods	9,810
Smithfield Foods	9,267
Swift & Co.	9,000
Nippon Meat Packers	8,364
Nestle S.A.	7,527
Danish Crown	7,238
Bestmeat B.V.	6,133
OSI Group	5,000

Source: *Meat & Poultry*, October 1, 2004, p. NA.

★ 266 ★

Meat

SIC: 2013; NAICS: 311612, 311613

Leading Beef Exporting Countries

Just as three countries are the top producers, consumption is concentrated in just a few countries as well. The industry has benefitted from diets that stress proteins over carbohydrates.

Australia	25.9%
Brazil	24.1
United States	23.5
India	9.5
EU-15	8.2

Argentina	7.9%
China	0.9

Source: *WATT PoultryUSA*, September 2004, p. 14.

★ 267 ★

Meat

SIC: 2013; NAICS: 311612, 311613

Leading Ham/Sausage Makers in Japan, 2003

Market shares are estimated based on domestic shipments.

Nippon Meat Packers	23.3%
Itoham Foods	20.3
Marudai Food	16.3
Prima Meat Packers	11.6
Yonekyu	6.3
Other	12.2

Source: "Market Share Survey Report 2003." [online] from http://www.nni.nikkei.co.jp [Published July 26, 2004], from Nikkei estimates.

★ 268 ★

Meat

SIC: 2013; NAICS: 311612, 311613

Leading Meat/Poultry Processors, 2004

Companies are ranked by sales in millions of dollars.

Tyson Foods Inc.	$ 26,400
Cargill Meat Solutions	13,000
Swift & Co.	9,900
Smithfield Foods Inc.	9,300
Pilgrim's Pride Corp.	5,300
Sara Lee Corp.	4,200
National Beef Packing Co.	3,500
OSI Group	3,300
Hormel Foods Corp.	3,300
ConAgra Foods Inc.	3,000
Perdue Farms	2,800
Keystone Foods	2,800

Source: *Refrigerated & Frozen Foods*, March 2005, p. 16, from *Refrigerated & Frozen Foods Annual Top 150 Report*.

★ 269 ★
Meat
SIC: 2013; NAICS: 311612, 311613

Private-label Meat Sales

Private-label has a 16.3% dollar share and 20.7% unit share.

Refrigerated meat/poultry	28.3%
Breakfast meats	14.9
Luncheon meats	14.5
Refrigerated seafood	13.4
Meat pies	12.4
Dinner sausage	7.9
Frankfurters	6.1
Other	2.5

Source: *National Provisioner*, June 2004, p. 10, from Information Resources Inc.

★ 270 ★
Meat
SIC: 2013; NAICS: 311612, 311613

Top Meat (No Poultry) Brands, 2004

Brands are ranked by sales for the 12 weeks ended July 11, 2004.

	Sales	Share
Moran	$ 13,453,129	6.96%
Topps	11,736,891	6.07
Philly Gourmet	10,383,255	5.37
Bubba Burger	9,319,743	4.82
Private label	41,879,376	21.67
Other	106,458,150	55.09

Source: *Frozen Food Age*, September 2004, p. 12, from Information Resources Inc.

★ 271 ★
Meat Snacks
SIC: 2013; NAICS: 311612, 311613

Top Meat Snack Brands, 2004

Brands are ranked by sales in millions of dollars for the year ended July 11, 2004.

	($ mil.)	Share
Oh Boy! Oberto	$ 69.91	23.31%
Jack Link's	49.45	16.49
Slim Jim	48.84	16.29
Pemmican	25.90	8.64
Bridgford	23.96	7.99
Other	81.83	27.29

Source: *National Provisioner*, August 2004, p. 56, from Information Resources Inc.

★ 272 ★
Refrigerated Dinners
SIC: 2013; NAICS: 311612, 311613

Top Refrigerated Dinner Brands, 2004

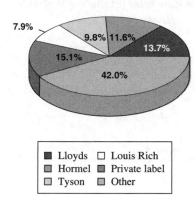

■ Lloyds □ Louis Rich
■ Hormel ■ Private label
■ Tyson   ■ Other

Brands are ranked by sales in millions of dollars for the year ended July 11, 2004.

	($ mil.)	Share
Lloyds	$ 89.30	13.73%
Hormel	75.20	11.56
Tyson	63.57	9.77
Louis Rich	51.14	7.86
Private label	97.98	15.06
Other	273.42	42.03

Source: *National Provisioner*, August 2004, p. 56, from Information Resources Inc.

★ 273 ★
Sausage
SIC: 2013; NAICS: 311612, 311613

Collagen Sausage Casing Market Worldwide

Devro's share is between 55-60% of the market. Nippi and Nittta have 11-12% market shares.

Devro	60.0%
Viscofan	22.0
Nitta	12.0
Nippi	12.0

Source: *Sunday Herald*, December 12, 2004, p. NA.

★ 274 ★
Sausage
SIC: 2013; NAICS: 311612, 311613

Top Dinner Sausage, 2004

Brands are ranked by supermarket, drug store and mass merchandiser sales (excluding Wal-Mart) for the 52 weeks ended December 26, 2004.

	($ mil.)	Share
Hillshire Farm	$ 284.96	18.64%
Johnsonville	195.40	12.78
Eckrich	103.29	6.76
Bryan	29.02	1.90
Private label	115.65	7.56
Other	800.66	52.37

Source: *National Provisioner*, February 2005, p. 19, from Information Resources Inc.

★ 275 ★
Sausage
SIC: 2013; NAICS: 311612, 311613

Top Frozen Sausage Brands, 2004

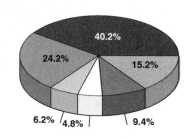

Legend:
- Swift-Premium Brown 'N Serve
- Johnsonville
- Jones Golden Brown
- Jones
- Private label
- Other

Brands are ranked by sales in millions of dollars for the year ended July 11, 2004.

	($ mil.)	Share
Swift-Premium Brown 'N Serve	$ 88.98	40.18%
Johnsonville	53.69	24.24
Jones Golden Brown	13.69	6.18
Jones	10.53	4.76
Private label	20.89	9.43
Other	33.67	15.20

Source: *National Provisioner*, August 2004, p. 56, from Information Resources Inc.

★ 276 ★
Sausage
SIC: 2013; NAICS: 311612, 311613

Top Refrigerated Breakfast Sausage/ Ham Brands, 2004

Brands are ranked by sales in millions of dollars for the year ended July 11, 2004.

	($ mil.)	Share
Jimmy Dean	$ 192.58	21.86%
Bob Evans	120.60	13.69
Jimmy Dean Fresh Taste Fast	45.07	5.12
Johnsonville	44.76	5.08
Private label	61.04	6.93
Other	416.95	47.33

Source: *National Provisioner*, August 2004, p. 56, from Information Resources Inc.

★ 277 ★
Turkeys
SIC: 2013; NAICS: 311611, 311613

Top Turkey/Turkey Substitute Brands, 2004

Sales are shown for the 12 weeks ended October 3, 2004.

	Sales	Share
Jennie-O	$ 9,998,648	26.98%
Butterball	5,808,768	15.67
Foster Farms	4,412,673	11.91
Shadybrook Farms	2,914,624	7.86
Private label	1,840,044	4.97
Other	12,085,199	32.61

Source: *Frozen Food Age*, November 2004, p. 14, from Information Resources Inc.

★ 278 ★
Egg Substitutes
SIC: 2015; NAICS: 311615

Top Egg Substitute Brands, 2004

Brands are ranked by sales in millions of dollars for the year ended October 3, 2004.

	Sales	Share
Egg Beaters	$ 28,515,676	63.69%
Papetti Foods Better N Eggs	4,532,530	10.12
Papetti Foods All Whites	4,242,230	9.47
Second Nature	995,065	2.22
Private label	5,750,658	12.84
Other	737,697	1.65

Source: *Frozen Food Age*, November 2004, p. 37, from Information Resources Inc.

★ 279 ★
Poultry
SIC: 2015; NAICS: 311615

Duck Industry

Duck consumption tood at 119 million pounds processed in 2003 (compared to chicken at 32 billion and turkey at 5.6 billion). White Pekin has 95% of the industry (not to be confused with Peking Duck).

White Pekin	.95.0%
Other	5.0

Source: *Knight Ridder/Tribune News Service*, November 2, 2004, p. NA, from Duckling Council.

★ 280 ★
Poultry
SIC: 2015; NAICS: 311615

Largest Duck Meat Producers Worldwide, 2003

Over the last two decades duck meat production increased 297.5% and 63% respectively. This is far higher than the increases of 154% and 39.5% in the overall poultry market. Countries are ranked by annual production in thousands of tons.

	(000)	Share
China	2,193,094	66.46%
France	250,000	7.58
India	159,900	4.85
Vietnam	82,800	2.51
United States	50,755	1.54
Malaysia	50,600	1.53
Germany	50,292	1.52
Hungary	45,000	1.36
United Kingdom	43,211	1.31
Korea, Republic of	42,000	1.27
Other	332,348	10.07

Source: *World Poultry*, no. 10, 2004, p. 41.

★ 281 ★
Poultry
SIC: 2015; NAICS: 311615

Top Broiler Makers in Brazil, 2003

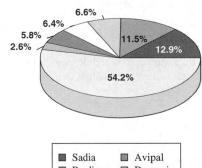

Legend: ■ Sadia ■ Avipal ■ Perdigao ■ Dagranja ■ Seara □ Other □ Frangosul

Companies are ranked by production in millions of birds.

	(mil.)	Share
Sadia	479.90	12.92%
Perdigao	427.44	11.51
Seara	246.15	6.63
Frangosul	237.80	6.40
Avipal	213.95	5.76
Dagranja	95.78	2.58
Other	2,012.66	54.20

Source: *WATT Poultry USA*, December 2004, p. 64, from Food and Agricultural Organization.

★ 282 ★
Poultry
SIC: 2015; NAICS: 311615

Top Pork Producing Nations, 2003

Total production was 87.96 million tons.

China	.51.0%
EU-15	.20.0
United States	.10.0
Brazil	3.0
Russia	2.0
Poland	2.0
Canada	2.0
Mexico	1.0
Hungary	1.0
Czech Republic	1.0
Other	7.0

Source: *WATT Poultry USA*, October 2004, p. 18.

★ 283 ★
Poultry
SIC: 2015; NAICS: 311615

Top Poultry Producers in Chile

Market shares are shown in percent.

Agrosuper/Empresas/Ariztia/Sopraval 97.0%
Other 3.0

Source: "US & FCS Market Research Reports." [online] from http://www.stat-usa.gov [Published October 2004].

★ 284 ★
Dairy Industry
SIC: 2020; NAICS: 311511, 311513, 311514

Dairy Industry in the U.K.

The retail market for milk and dairy products has been placed at 7.43 billions of pounds sterling in 2003. The industry is valued in millions of euros.

	2001	2003	Share
Liquid	4,629	4,710	42.67%
Cheese	2,473	2,687	24.35
Yogurt and chilled desserts . .	1,798	2,048	18.56
Yellow fats	1,314	1,353	12.26
Cream	230	239	2.17

Source: *Dairy Industries International*, September 2004, p. 19, from Key Note.

★ 285 ★
Dairy Industry
SIC: 2020; NAICS: 311511, 311513, 311514

Dairy Market in New Zealand, 2004

Sales are shown in millions of dollars as of March 21, 2004.

Total fresh milk & cream . . . .$ 282.0
Total butter & margarine 134.7
Total natural cheese 133.3
Total specialty cheese 50.1
Total processed cheese 24.8
Total cream cheese 9.7
Total cottage cheese 6.3

Source: *Grocer's Review*, May 2004, p. NA, from ACNielsen.

★ 286 ★
Dairy Industry
SIC: 2020; NAICS: 311511, 311513, 311514

Largest Dairy Food Categories, 2004

The top brands are ranked by sales in thousands of dollars for the 52 weeks ended December 28, 2004. Sales increased 5.1% during the year, mostly from higher prices. Unit sales, in fact, fell .8%. Milk accounts for nearly a quarter of department sales.

Private label skim/low fat milk . . . . .$ 4,128,500.9
Private label whole milk 2,079,942.1
Private label fresh eggs 1,811,098.8
Tropicana Pure Premium orange juice . . 1,114,058.4
Private label natural shredded cheese . . 834,044.5
Private label natural cheese chunks . . . 827,611.0
Dole fresh cut salad 668,038.2
Private label butter 578,757.2
Kraft natural shredded cheese 543,843.5

Source: *Frozen Food Age*, April 2005, p. 18, from Information Resources Inc.

★ 287 ★
Dairy Industry
SIC: 2020; NAICS: 311511, 311513, 311514

Leading Dairy Processors, 2004

Companies are ranked by sales in millions of dollars.

Dean Foods . . . .$ 10,800
Dairy Farmers of America 6,900
Kraft Foods Inc. 4,300
Land O'Lakes Dairy Foods Group 3,000
The Kroger Co. 2,800
H.P. Food 2,200
Schreiber Foods Co. 2,000
Leprino Foods Co. 2,000
Prairie Farms Dairy 1,400
Good-Humor-Breyers's Ice Cream 1,300

Source: *Refrigerated & Frozen Foods*, March 2005, p. 16, from *Refrigerated & Frozen Foods Annual Top 150 Report*.

★ 288 ★

Dairy Industry

SIC: 2020; NAICS: 311511, 311513, 311514

Top Dairy Firms Worldwide, 2002

The United States remains the leading market for dairy sales with $48.3 billion in 2003 and a 20.5% share.

Nestle	4.7%
Kraft Food	4.2
Danone	4.2
Parmalat Finanziana	2.7
Dean Foods	2.2
Sodiaal	1.8
Arla Foods Amba	1.4
Agro-alimentaire	1.4
Morinaga Milk Industry Co.	1.2
Other	76.2

Source: *Dairy Field*, August 2004, p. 74, from Euromonitor.

★ 289 ★

Dairy Industry

SIC: 2020; NAICS: 311511, 311513, 311514

Top Dairy Producing Nations, 2003

Global sales were $236,533.7 million in 2003, up from $207,861.4 million in 2001.

United States	20.5%
Japan	8.1
Italy	6.4
France	6.4
Germany	5.8
United Kingdom	4.4
Brazil	3.7
Mexico	3.6
Spain	2.9
China	2.2
Canada	2.2
Other	33.8

Source: *Dairy Field*, August 2004, p. 74, from Euromonitor.

★ 290 ★

Butter

SIC: 2021; NAICS: 311512

Top Butter Brands, 2004

Market shares are shown based on supermarket, drug store and mass merchandiser sales (excluding Wal-Mart) for the year ended May 16, 2004.

Land O'Lakes	30.9%
Challenge	5.1

Breakstone	2.4%
Tillamook	2.2
Crystal Farms	1.8
Keller's	1.7
Hotel bar	1.4
Cabot	1.2
Darigold	0.8
Private label	43.8
Other	8.7

Source: *Dairy Field*, May 2004, p. 14, from Information Resources Inc.

★ 291 ★

Butter

SIC: 2021; NAICS: 311512

Top Butter Vendors, 2004

Market shares are shown based on supermarket, drug store and mass merchandiser sales (excluding Wal-Mart) for the year ended May 16, 2004.

Land O'Lakes Inc.	30.9%
Keller's Creamery	5.9
Challenge Dairy Products	5.6
Tillamook County Creamery	2.2
Crystal Farms Inc.	1.9
Cabot Creamery Inc.	1.2
WestFarm Foods	0.8
Quality Chekd Dairy Products	0.6
Horizon Organic	0.6
Private label	43.8
Other	6.5

Source: *Dairy Field*, May 2004, p. 14, from Information Resources Inc.

★ 292 ★

Margarine

SIC: 2021; NAICS: 311512

Top Margarine/Spread/Butter Blend Brands, 2004

Market shares are shown based on supermarket, drug store and mass merchandiser sales (excluding Wal-Mart) for the year ended May 16, 2004.

I Can't Believe It's Not Butter	17.1%
Shedd's	15.3
Parkay	8.0
Land O'Lakes	6.7
Blue Bonnet	6.5
Imperial	4.9

Continued on next page.

★ 292 ★

[Continued]
Margarine
SIC: 2021; NAICS: 311512

Top Margarine/Spread/Butter Blend Brands, 2004

Market shares are shown based on supermarket, drug store and mass merchandiser sales (excluding Wal-Mart) for the year ended May 16, 2004.

Reischmann's	4.3%
I Can't Believe It's Not Butter Light	3.8
Brummel & Brown	3.2
Private label	8.4
Other	21.8

Source: *Dairy Field*, May 2004, p. 14, from Information Resources Inc.

★ 293 ★

Margarine
SIC: 2021; NAICS: 311512

Top Margarine/Spread/Butter Blend Makers, 2004

Market shares are shown based on supermarket, drug store and mass merchandiser sales (excluding Wal-Mart) for the year ended May 16, 2004.

Van Der Bergh Foods Co.	49.0%
ConAgra Inc.	19.4
Land O'Lakes Inc.	7.0
Great Foods of America	5.7
Lever Brothers Co.	3.6
McNeil Consumer Products	1.8
Lipton	1.8
Other	3.3

Source: *Dairy Field*, May 2004, p. 14, from Information Resources Inc.

★ 294 ★

Cheese
SIC: 2022; NAICS: 311513

Leading Natural Cubed Cheese Brands, 2004

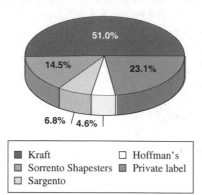

■ Kraft	□ Hoffman's
▨ Sorrento Shapesters	■ Private label
▢ Sargento	

Brands are ranked by sales for the 12 weeks ended June 13, 2004.

	Sales	Share
Kraft	$6,987,950	50.95%
Sorrento Shapesters	1,992,354	14.53
Sargento	929,248	6.78
Hoffman's	635,049	4.63
Private label	3,170,586	23.12

Source: *Frozen Food Age*, July 2004, p. 22, from Information Resources Inc.

★ 295 ★

Cheese
SIC: 2022; NAICS: 311513

Natural Cheese Sales

Natural cheese represents about 68% of all volume sales of cheese. Supermarket sales are in millions of pounds.

	(mil.)	Share
Chunk/loaf	474.5	38.94%
Shredded	425.1	34.88
Sliced	63.7	5.23
Grated	56.1	4.60
Spread	11.4	0.94
Cubed	11.4	0.94
Other	176.4	14.48

Source: *Dairy Foods*, July 2004, p. 15, from Information Resources Inc. and International Dairy Foods Association.

★ 296 ★
Cheese
SIC: 2022; NAICS: 311513

Specialty Cheese Sales, 2004

Total specialty cheese sales were $1.43 billion for the year ended May 30, 2004. Such cheese represent 17.3% of total cheese sales.

	($ mil.)	Share
Italian blends	$ 103.5	7.23%
Feta	103.0	7.19
Colby	100.3	7.00
Provolone	72.2	5.04
Queso Fresco	69.2	4.83
Blue Cheese	53.6	3.74
Muenster	49.2	3.44
Brie	38.8	2.71
Goat Cheese	36.5	2.55
Other	806.0	56.27

Source: *Dairy Field*, September 2004, p. 16, from Information Resources Inc.

★ 297 ★
Cheese
SIC: 2022; NAICS: 311513

Top Cheese Ball/Spread Brands, 2004

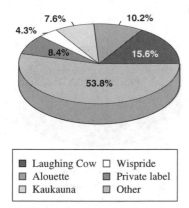

- ■ Laughing Cow □ Wispride
- ■ Alouette ■ Private label
- □ Kaukauna ■ Other

Brands are ranked by sales for the year ended October 3, 2004.

	Sales	Share
Laughing Cow	$ 10,303,944	15.65%
Alouette	6,718,036	10.21
Kaukauna	5,023,308	7.63
Wispride	2,859,436	4.34
Private label	5,512,987	8.38
Other	35,401,517	53.79

Source: *Frozen Food Age*, November 2004, p. 37, from Information Resources Inc.

★ 298 ★
Cheese
SIC: 2022; NAICS: 311513

Top Cheese Brands (Pre-Packed) in the U.K., 2004

Brands are ranked by sales in pounds sterling for the year ended October 2, 2004. The market, valued at 603 million, is a mature industry with almost no growth.

	Sales	Share
Dairylea	£ 127,296	7.04%
Cathedral City	75,162	4.16
Philadelphia	48,936	2.71
Cheestrings	48,803	2.70
McLelland	41,456	2.29
Pilgrims Choice	32,943	1.82
Baby Bel	28,862	1.60
Laughing Cow	21,943	1.21
Anchor	16,180	0.89
Other	1,366,422	75.58

Source: *Grocer*, December 11, 2004, p. 53, from ACNielsen.

★ 299 ★
Cheese
SIC: 2022; NAICS: 311513

Top Natural Cheese Brands, 2004

Market shares are shown based on supermarket, drug stores and mass merchandiser sales (excluding Wal-Mart) for the year ended December 26, 2004.

Kraft	22.5%
Sargento	6.7
Tillamook	3.4
Crystal Farms	2.3
Sorrento	1.8
Precious	1.8
Frigo	1.7
Polly-O	1.6
Borden	1.4
Private label	36.1
Other	20.7

Source: *Dairy Field*, February 2005, p. 38, from Information Resources Inc.

★ 300 ★
Cheese
SIC: 2022; NAICS: 311513

Top Natural Chunk Cheese Makers, 2004

Market shares are shown based on supermarket sales, drug stores and mass merchandisers (excluding Wal-Mart) for the year ended May 16, 2004.

Kraft Foods Inc.	19.5%
Tillamook County Creamery	6.7
Lactalis USA	3.7
Land O'Lakes Inc.	3.5
Cabot Creamery Inc.	2.7
Cacique Creamery Inc.	2.3
Heluva Good Cheese Inc.	2.0
Saputo Cheese USA	1.5
Crystal Farms Inc.	1.3
Private label	39.2
Other	17.6

Source: *Dairy Field*, August 2004, p. 32, from Information Resources Inc.

★ 301 ★
Cheese
SIC: 2022; NAICS: 311513

Top Natural Shredded Cheese Brands, 2004

Market shares are shown based on supermarket, drug stores and mass merchandiser sales (excluding Wal-Mart) for the year ended December 26, 2004.

Kraft	28.0%
Sargento	11.4
Crystal Farms	4.0
Borden	3.3
Kraft Free	1.6
Kraft Classic Melts	1.6
DioGiorno	1.2
Sorrento	0.8
Stella	0.6
Private label	42.5
Other	5.0

Source: *Dairy Field*, February 2005, p. 38, from Information Resources Inc.

★ 302 ★
Cheese
SIC: 2022; NAICS: 311513

Top Natural Shredded Cheese Makers, 2004

Market shares are shown based on supermarket sales, drug stores and mass merchandisers (excluding Wal-Mart) for the year ended May 16, 2004.

Kraft Foods Inc.	31.7%
Sargento Food Co.	12.3
Crystal Farms Inc.	3.9
American Dairy Brands	3.5
Lactalis	1.1
Saputo Cheese USA	0.9
Tillamook County Creamery	0.4
Schreiber Foods Inc.	0.3
Cabot Creamery Inc.	0.3
Other	2.7

Source: *Dairy Field*, August 2004, p. 32, from Information Resources Inc.

★ 303 ★
Evaporated Milk
SIC: 2023; NAICS: 311514

Top Evaporated Milk Brands in Thailand

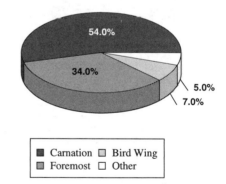

■ Carnation   □ Bird Wing
■ Foremost   □ Other

The industry is valued at 500 million baht.

Carnation	54.0%
Foremost	34.0
Bird Wing	7.0
Other	5.0

Source: *Bangkok Post*, February 16, 2005, p. NA.

★ 304 ★
Frozen Desserts
SIC: 2024; NAICS: 31152

Top Frozen Novelty Brands, 2004

Market shares are shown based on supermarket, drug stores and mass merchandiser sales (excluding Wal-Mart) for the year ended December 26, 2004.

Nestle Drumstick	5.7%
Klondike	5.5
Weight Watchers Smart Ones	4.5
Dreyer's/Edy's Whole Fruit	4.1
Silhouette	4.0
Popsicle	4.0
Klondike Carb Smart	3.0
Haagen-Dazs	2.5
Klondike Slim-A-Bear	2.3
Private label	14.8
Other	49.6

Source: *Dairy Field*, February 2005, p. 38, from Information Resources Inc.

★ 305 ★
Frozen Desserts
SIC: 2024; NAICS: 31152

Top Frozen Novelty Makers, 2005

Market shares are shown based on sales at food stores, drug stores and mass merchandisers (but not Wal-Mart) for the 52 weeks ended January 23, 2005.

Good Humor	24.7%
Dreyers Grand Ice Cream Inc.	18.2
Integrated Brands	8.2
Masterfoods USA	4.8
Private label	14.8
Other	29.3

Source: *Grocery Headquarters*, April 2005, p. 22, from Information Resources Inc.

★ 306 ★
Frozen Desserts
SIC: 2024; NAICS: 31152

Top Frozen Yogurt/Tofu Brands, 2004

Market shares are shown based on sales at food stores, drug stores and mass merchandisers (excluding Wal-Mart) for the 52 weeks ended October 31, 2004.

Dreyer's/Edy's	$ 35.8
Ben & Jerry's	35.0
Haagen-Dazs	14.4
Turkey Hill	13.6

Kemps	$ 8.1
Ben & Jerry's 2 Twisted	5.4
Tofutti	4.6
Organic Soy Delicious	4.3
Blue Bell	3.7
Private label	35.8

Source: *Dairy Field*, January 2005, p. 34, from Information Resources Inc.

★ 307 ★
Ice Cream
SIC: 2024; NAICS: 31152

Ice Cream Sales by Year

Retail sales are shown in millions of dollars.

2003	$ 20,667.0
2004	21,134.1
2005	21,613.1
2006	22,114.9
2007	22,572.6
2008	23,020.2

Source: *Convenience Store News*, February 7, 2005, p. 47, from Packaged Facts.

★ 308 ★
Ice Cream
SIC: 2024; NAICS: 31152

Popular Ice Cream Flavors

Data show the most consumed flavors of ice cream. About 1.4 billion gallons of ice cream are produced annually.

Vanilla	33.0%
Chocolate	19.0
Other	48.0

Source: *Washington Times*, August 5, 2004, p. A2, from NPD Group.

★ 309 ★

Ice Cream

SIC: 2024; NAICS: 31152

Top Ice Cream Brands, 2004

Market shares are shown based on sales at food stores, drug stores and mass merchandisers (excluding Wal-Mart) for the 52 weeks ended October 31, 2004.

	($ mil.)	Share
Breyers	$ 523.1	12.00%
Dreyer's/Edy's Grand	417.6	9.58
Blue Bell	245.2	5.62
Haagen-Dazs	208.2	4.78
Ben & Jerry's	180.3	4.14
Dreyer's/Edy's Grand Light	121.6	2.79
Wells' Blue Bunny	103.9	2.38
Turkey Hill	92.5	2.12
Dreyer's/Edy's	78.1	1.79
Other	2,389.5	54.81

Source: *Dairy Field*, January 2005, p. 34, from Information Resources Inc.

★ 310 ★

Ice Cream

SIC: 2024; NAICS: 31152

Top Ice Cream Firms, 2005

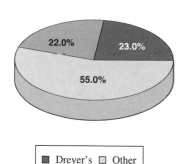

■ Dreyer's □ Other
■ Unilever

Sales of prepackaged ice cream topped food stores, convenience stores and mass merchandisers (excluding Wal-Mart) for the 52 weeks ended March 19, 2005.

Dreyer's	23.0%
Unilever	22.0
Other	55.0

Source: *Los Angeles Times*, May 25, 2005, p. NA, from ACNielsen.

★ 311 ★

Ice Cream

SIC: 2024; NAICS: 31152

Top Ice Cream Makers in Brazil

Market shares are shown for April - May 2004.

Kibon	50.0%
Nestle	25.0
Other	25.0

Source: *America's Intelligence Wire*, August 3, 2004, p. NA.

★ 312 ★

Ice Cream

SIC: 2024; NAICS: 31152

Top Ice Cream Makers in Japan, 2003

Market shares are estimated based on domestic sales.

Ezaki Glico	12.7%
Haagen-Dazs Japan	12.3
Morinaga Milk	11.9
Meiji Dairies	11.0
Lotte	10.8
Other	41.3

Source: "Market Share Survey Report 2003." [online] from http://www.nni.nikkei.co.jp [Published July 26, 2004], from Nikkei estimates.

★ 313 ★

Ice Cream

SIC: 2024; NAICS: 31152

Top Ice Cream Makers in Peru, 2004

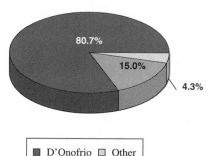

■ D'Onofrio □ Other
■ Lamorgini

Market shares are shown for December 2004.

D'Onofrio	80.7%
Lamorgini	15.0
Other	4.3

Source: *FWN Select*, February 7, 2005, p. NA.

★ 314 ★

Ice Cream

SIC: 2024; NAICS: 31152

Top Ice Cream Makers in Russia

The ice cream market grows by 4% a year, the slowest segment of the dairy industry.

Russkiy Kholod	9.0%
Inmarko	8.2
Nestle	5.4
Talosto	4.8
Ice Phili	4.5
Other	68.1

Source: *Ice Cream Reporter*, July 20, 2004, p. 7, from *St. Petersburg Times*.

★ 315 ★

Ice Cream

SIC: 2024; NAICS: 31152

Top Ice Cream Makers in Thailand

Walls 45.0% Nestle 38.0% Other 17.0%

☐ Walls ☐ Other
☐ Nestle

Wall's has 40-45% of the market. Nestle has 80% of ice cream sales through gas stations and 95% of sales through amusement parks.

Walls	45.0%
Nestle	38.0
Other	17.0

Source: *Ice Cream Reporter*, June 20, 2004, p. 3.

★ 316 ★

Ice Cream

SIC: 2024; NAICS: 31152

Top Ice Cream Makers Worldwide, 2002

Market shares are shown in percent.

Unilever	16.3%
Nestle	11.0
McDonald's	4.5

Haagen-Dazs	2.6%
Private label	6.5
Other	59.1

Source: "Food." [online] from http://www.mind-advertising.com/sectors/sector_food.htm [Accessed July 8, 2005], from Unilever.

★ 317 ★

Ice Cream

SIC: 2024; NAICS: 31152

Top Luxury Ice Cream Firms in the U.K., 2004

Suppliers are ranked by sales value in millions of pounds for the year ended March 4, 2004.

Unilever	£ 76.08
General Mills	27.25
Ben & Jerry's	22.90
Masterfoods	17.98
Fredericks Dairies	15.19
Mackie's	8.85
Richmond	6.57
J Thayer	1.42
Private label	69.90

Source: *Marketing*, May 6, 2004, p. 38, from ACNielsen.

★ 318 ★

Ice Cream

SIC: 2024; NAICS: 31152

Top Premium Ice Cream Makers in Japan

Market shares are shown in percent.

Haagen-Dazs	80.0%
Other	20.0

Source: *Japan Weekly Monitor*, January 10, 2005, p. NA.

★ 319 ★

Coffee Creamer

SIC: 2026; NAICS: 311514

Top Coffee Creamer Brands, 2004

Brands are ranked by sales in millions of dollars for the year ended October 3, 2004.

	Sales	Share
Carnation Coffee Mate	$ 93,258,864	64.58%
International Delight	36,565,328	25.32
Mocha Mix	4,683,711	3.24

Continued on next page.

★ 319 ★
[Continued]
Coffee Creamer
SIC: 2026; NAICS: 311514

Top Coffee Creamer Brands, 2004

Brands are ranked by sales in millions of dollars for the year ended October 3, 2004.

	Sales	Share
Rich's Farm Rich	$ 1,238,689	0.86%
Private label	6,191,000	4.29
Other	2,464,040	1.71

Source: *Frozen Food Age*, November 2004, p. 37, from Information Resources Inc.

★ 320 ★
Cottage Cheese
SIC: 2026; NAICS: 311514

Top Cottage Cheese Brands, 2004

Market shares are shown based on supermarket, drug stores and mass merchandiser sales (excluding Wal-Mart) for the year ended December 26, 2004.

Breakstone	9.6%
Knudsen	8.7
Friendship	3.1
Dean's	3.1
Breakstone Cottage Doubles	3.1
Hood	2.6
Prairie Farms	2.1
Light N Lively	2.1
Hiland	1.7
Private label	35.8
Other	31.2

Source: *Dairy Field*, February 2005, p. 38, from Information Resources Inc.

★ 321 ★
Dips
SIC: 2026; NAICS: 311514

Top Dip Brands, 2004

Market shares are shown based on supermarket, drug store and mass merchandiser sales (excluding Wal-Mart) for the year ended August 8, 2004. Total sales were $388.1 million.

T. Marzetti	19.0%
Dean's	12.7
Kraft	7.6
Heluva Good	7.4

Classic Guacamole	4.6%
Marie's	2.3
Bison	1.2
Yoder's	1.0
Calavo	1.0
Private label	17.1
Other	26.1

Source: *Dairy Field*, October 2004, p. 16, from Information Resources Inc.

★ 322 ★
Dips
SIC: 2026; NAICS: 311514

Top Dips in Australia

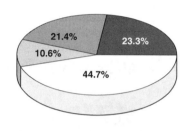

Annual turnover of dairy dips is worth $A118.7 million.

Black Swan	23.3%
Chris' Greek Dips	21.4
Kraft Dairy Dip	10.6
Other	44.7

Source: *Australasian Business Intelligence*, November 9, 2004, p. NA.

★ 323 ★
Milk
SIC: 2026; NAICS: 311511

Largest Milk Co-ops

Million Gallons

Firms are ranked by billions of pounds of milk processed. Shares are shown based on the top 50 firms.

	(bil.)	Share
Dairy Farmers of America	35.108	28.90%
California Dairies Inc.	14.639	12.05
Land O'Lakes Inc.	12.185	10.03
Northwest Dairy Association	6.400	5.27
Dairylea Cooperative	5.500	4.53
Family Dairies	5.480	4.51
Associated Milk Producers Inc.	5.200	4.28
Foremost Farms USA	5.030	4.14
Manitowoc Milk Producers	3.970	3.27
Michigan Milk Producers	3.200	2.63
Other	24.750	20.38

Source: *Dairy Field*, June 2004, p. 20, from *Dairy Field's Top 100 Processor ranking.*

★ 324 ★
Milk
SIC: 2026; NAICS: 311511

Largest Milk Producing Nations Worldwide

Production has fallen in many European countries. Production and consumption has increased in Brazil.

United States	15.3%
India	7.1
Russian Federation	6.6
Germany	5.6%
France	5.0
Brazil	4.5
United Kingdom	3.0
Ukraine	2.8
New Zealand	2.8
Other	50.1

Source: *Beverage World*, October 15, 2004, p. 18, from Beverage Marketing Corp.

★ 325 ★
Milk
SIC: 2026; NAICS: 311511

Milk Production by State

Figures are in billions of dollars.

California	$ 4.1
Wisconsin	2.6
New York	1.4
Pennsylvania	1.2
Idaho	1.0

Source: *USA TODAY*, June 16, 2004, p. A1, from California Milk Advisory Board.

★ 326 ★
Milk
SIC: 2026; NAICS: 311511

Refrigerated Soy Milk Market, 2003

The company has more than 70% of the category. Sales at supermarkets and mass merchandisers grew 20% during the year.

Silk	70.0%
Other	30.0

Source: *Dallas Morning News*, September 25, 2004, p. NA, from Information Resources Inc.

★ 327 ★
Milk
SIC: 2026; NAICS: 311511

Top Flavored Milk/Eggnog/Buttermilk Brands, 2004

Market shares are shown based on supermarket, drug stores and mass merchandiser sales (excluding Wal-Mart) for the year ended December 26, 2004.

Nestle Nesquik	14.3%
Dean's	4.1

Continued on next page.

★ 327 ★

[Continued]
Milk
SIC: 2026; NAICS: 311511

Top Flavored Milk/Eggnog/Buttermilk Brands, 2004

Market shares are shown based on supermarket, drug stores and mass merchandiser sales (excluding Wal-Mart) for the year ended December 26, 2004.

Kemps	3.6%
Hershey's-Morningstar	2.6
Mayfield	1.8
Prarie Farms	1.6
Garelick Farms	1.6
Borden	1.6
Hood	1.5
Private label	27.8
Other	39.5

Source: *Dairy Field*, February 2005, p. 38, from Information Resources Inc.

★ 328 ★

Milk
SIC: 2026; NAICS: 311511

Top Flavored Milk Firms, 2004

Market shares are shown based on sales at food stores, drug stores and mass merchandsiers (excluding Wal-Mart) for the 52 weeks ended May 16, 2004.

Nestle USA Inc.	15.2%
Dean Foods Co.	6.0
Marigold Foods Inc.	3.5
Morningstar Foods Inc.	3.1
Milk Products LP	2.0
HP Hood Inc.	1.8
Mayfield Dairy Farms Inc.	1.7
Garelick Farms Inc.	1.6
Prairie Farms Dairy	1.5
Private label	26.6
Other	37.0

Source: *Dairy Field*, August 2004, p. NA, from Information Resources Inc.

★ 329 ★

Milk
SIC: 2026; NAICS: 311511

Top Refrigerated Milk Brands, 2004

Market shares are shown based on sales at food stores, drug stores and mass merchandisers (excluding Wal-Mart) for the 52 weeks ended October 31, 2004.

Borden	1.3%
Garelick Farms	1.1
Prairie Farms	1.0
Lehigh Valley	1.0
PET	0.9
Tuscan Farms	0.8
Mayfield	0.7
Lactaid 100	0.7
Horizon Organic	0.7
Private label	64.1
Other	27.7

Source: *Grocery Headquarters*, February 2005, p. 55, from Information Resources Inc.

★ 330 ★

Milk
SIC: 2026; NAICS: 311511

Top Refrigerated Skim/Lowfat Milk Firms, 2004

Market shares are shown based on sales at food stores, drug stores and mass merchandsiers (excluding Wal Mart) for the 52 weeks ended May 16, 2004.

McNeil Consumer Products	3.0%
Dean Foods Co.	2.5
Marigold Foods Inc.	2.3
Horizon Organic	1.7
Prairie Farms Dairy	1.2
Parmalat USA Corp.	1.2
HP Hood Inc.	1.2
Garelick Farms Inc.	1.1
Mayfield Dairy Farms Inc.	1.0
Private label	62.8
Other	22.0

Source: *Dairy Field*, August 2004, p. NA, from Information Resources Inc.

★ 331 ★
Milk
SIC: 2026; NAICS: 311511

Top Skin/Low-Fat Milk Brands, 2004

Market shares are shown based on sales at food stores, drug stores and mass merchandisers (excluding Wal-Mart) for the 52 weeks ended October 31, 2004.

Lactaid 100	2.8%
Horizon Organic	1.4
Kemp's	1.3
Dean's	1.2
Prairie Farms	1.1
Garelick Farms	1.1
Mayfield	0.9
Organic Valley	0.8
Hood	0.8
Private label	62.8
Other	25.6

Source: *Grocery Headquarters*, February 2005, p. 55, from Information Resources Inc.

★ 332 ★
Milk
SIC: 2026; NAICS: 311511

Top Whole Milk Firms, 2004

Market shares are shown based on sales at food stores, drug stores and mass merchandsiers (excluding Wal-Mart) for the 52 weeks ended May 16, 2004.

Milk Products LP	1.8%
Oak Farms Dairy	1.4
Dean Foods Co.	1.3
Horizon Organix	1.2
Prairie Farms Dairy	1.0
Parmalat USA Corp.	1.0
McNeil Consumer Products	1.0
Lehigh Valley Dairies Inc.	1.0
Garelick Farms Inc.	0.9
Private label	64.9
Other	24.5

Source: *Dairy Field*, August 2004, p. NA, from Information Resources Inc.

★ 333 ★
Milkshakes
SIC: 2026; NAICS: 311511

Top Flavored Milkshakes/Milk Substitutes, 2004

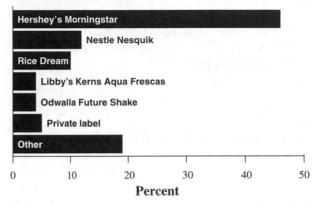

Market shares are shown based on sales at food stores, drug stores and mass merchandisers (excluding Wal-Mart) for the 52 weeks ended October 3, 2004.

Hershey's Morningstar	46.3%
Nestle Nesquik	11.9
Rice Dream	9.6
Libby's Kerns Aqua Frescas	4.2
Odwalla Future Shake	4.0
Private label	5.0
Other	19.0

Source: *Beverage Industry*, July 2004, p. 22, from Information Resources Inc.

★ 334 ★
Pudding
SIC: 2026; NAICS: 311511

Top Pudding/Mousse/Gelatin/Parfait Brands, 2004

Market shares are shown based on supermarket, drug stores and mass merchandiser sales (excluding Wal-Mart) for the year ended December 26, 2004.

Jell-O	25.4%
Jell-O Gelatin Snacks	15.1
Kozy Shack	14.6
Jell-O Free	9.9
Swiss Miss	8.5
Jell-O Smoothie	4.0
Jell-O Extreme	2.6
Private label	6.1
Other	13.8

Source: *Dairy Field*, February 2005, p. 38, from Information Resources Inc.

★ 335 ★

Smoothies

SIC: 2026; NAICS: 311511

Leading Smoothie Brands in the U.K., 2003

The smoothie industry was born in the juice markets of health food stores in the early 1990s. Sales of smoothies grew 17% in retail value to 69 million pounds sterling in 2003.

PJs	.40.0%
Innocent	.26.1
Private label	.29.1

Source: *just-drinks.com*, June 22, 2004, p. NA, from ACNielsen.

★ 336 ★

Sour Cream

SIC: 2026; NAICS: 311514

Top Sour Cream Brands, 2004

Market shares are shown based on supermarket, drug store and mass merchandiser sales (excluding Wal-Mart) for the year ended August 8, 2004.

Breakstone	.28.9%
Daisy	.15.5
Knudsen Hampshire	.11.2
Daisy Light	4.4
Friendship	2.0
Knudsen	1.6
Dean's	1.5
Tillamook	1.4
Cacique	1.4
Private label	.28.9
Other	3.2

Source: *Dairy Field*, October 2004, p. 16, from Information Resources Inc.

★ 337 ★

Whipped Toppings

SIC: 2026; NAICS: 311514

Top Whipped Topping Brands, 2004

Brands are ranked by sales for the 12 weeks ended July 11, 2004.

	Sales	Share
Cool Whip	$ 35,679,976	43.63%
Cool Whip Lite	13,083,997	16.00
Cool Whip Free	10,506,245	12.85
Real Whip	159,028	0.19

	Sales	Share
Private label	$ 22,276,662	27.24%
Other	66,316	0.08

Source: *Frozen Food Age*, September 2004, p. 12, from Information Resources Inc.

★ 338 ★

Yogurt

SIC: 2026; NAICS: 311511

Organic Yogurt Market

Market shares are shown in percent.

Stonyfield Farm	.77.0%
Other	.23.0

Source: "Stonyfield Farm Converts Best-Selling Fat Free Line." [online] from http://www.stonyfield.com [Press release April 11, 2004].

★ 339 ★

Yogurt

SIC: 2026; NAICS: 311511

Top Yogurt Makers, 2004

Market shares are shown based on supermarket sales, drug stores and mass merchandisers (excluding Wal-Mart) for the year ended May 16, 2004.

Yoplait	.34.4%
Dannon	.30.5
Stonyfield Farms	4.7
Kraft Foods Inc.	4.6
Columbo Inc.	2.2
YoFarm Corp.	1.8
Johanna Foods Inc.	1.3
Meadow Gold Dairy Inc.	1.2
Crowley Foods	1.1
Private label	.12.2
Other	6.0

Source: *Dairy Field*, August 2004, p. 32, from Information Resources Inc.

★ 340 ★

Yogurt

SIC: 2026; NAICS: 311511

Top Yogurt/Yogurt Drink Brands, 2004

Market shares are shown based on supermarket, drug stores and mass merchandiser sales (excluding Wal-Mart) for the year ended December 26, 2004.

Yoplait	.10.1%
Yoplait Light	6.2
Dannon Light 'n Fit	5.9
Yoplait Go-Gurt	4.6

Continued on next page.

★ 340 ★

[Continued]

Yogurt

SIC: 2026; NAICS: 311511

Top Yogurt/Yogurt Drink Brands, 2004

Market shares are shown based on supermarket, drug stores and mass merchandiser sales (excluding Wal-Mart) for the year ended December 26, 2004.

Dannon Danimals	3.4%
Toplait Trix	3.3
Yoplait Whips	3.1
Stonyfield Farm	3.0
Dannon Fruit on the Bottom	2.8
Private label	11.8
Other	45.6

Source: *Dairy Field*, February 2005, p. 38, from Information Resources Inc.

★ 341 ★

Baby Food

SIC: 2032; NAICS: 311422

Top Baby Electrolyte Brands, 2004

Brands are ranked by sales at supermarkets, drug stores and discount stores (but not Wal-Mart) for the year ended September 5, 2004.

	($ mil.)	Share
Pedialyte	$ 68.5	68.43%
Gerber	5.7	5.69
Revital	0.8	0.80
Revital Ice	0.6	0.60
Nutra Max	0.6	0.60
Gerber Liquilytes	0.6	0.60
Revital Jel	0.5	0.50
Oralyte	0.3	0.30
Naturalyte	0.3	0.30
Private label	21.7	21.68
Other	0.5	0.50

Source: *MMR*, November 29, 2004, p. 21, from Information Resources Inc.

★ 342 ★

Baby Food

SIC: 2032; NAICS: 311422

Top Baby Food Makers, 2004

Companies are ranked by food store, drug store and mass merchandiser sales (excluding Wal-Mart) for the year ended May 16, 2004.

	($ mil.)	Share
Gerber Products Co.	$ 626.8	80.57%
Beech-Nut Corp.	77.0	9.90
Del Monte Foods	39.5	5.08

	($ mil.)	Share
Heinz USA	$ 13.0	1.67%
The Hain Celestial Group Inc.	9.3	1.20
Kraft/Nabisco	8.1	1.04
Private label	2.4	0.31
Other	1.9	0.24

Source: *Grocery Headquarters*, August 2004, p. 30, from Information Resources Inc.

★ 343 ★

Baby Food

SIC: 2032; NAICS: 311422

Top Baby Food Makers in the U.K., 2002 and 2004

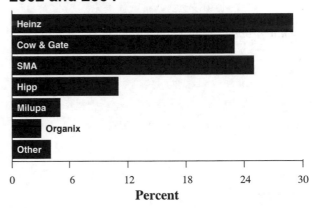

The baby food industry followed certain trends: BSE (Mad Cow disease) affected the market just as it did the larger food and beverage industry. Also a new campaign stressed breast milk over formula. Total spending increased from 288.2 million pounds in 2002 to 314.5 million pounds in 2004.

	2002	2004
Heinz	31.3%	29.1%
Cow & Gate	23.2	22.8
SMA	22.9	25.3
Hipp	9.8	10.5
Milupa (Nutricia)	4.8	4.8
Organix	3.3	3.4
Other	4.7	4.1

Source: *Marketing*, November 24, 2004, p. 30, from Mintel.

★ 344 ★
Baby Food
SIC: 2032; NAICS: 311422

Top Baby Food Makers (Organic) in the U.K.

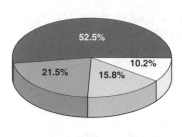

| ■ Heinz | □ Cow and Gate |
| ■ Hipp | □ Other |

Organic products represent nearly half of the market.

Heinz 52.5%
Hipp 21.5
Cow and Gate 15.8
Other 10.2

Source: *just-food.com*, February 9, 2005, p. NA.

★ 345 ★
Baby Food
SIC: 2032; NAICS: 311422

Top Baby Food/Snack Brands, 2004

Brands are ranked by food store, drug store and mass merchandiser sales (excluding Wal-Mart) for the year ended May 16, 2004.

	($ mil.)	Share
Gerber 2nd Foods	$ 216.1	27.78%
Gerber Baby	98.3	12.63
Gerber Graduates	95.7	12.30
Gerber 3rd Foods	72.3	9.29
Gerber 1st Foods	56.4	7.25
Other	239.2	30.75

Source: *Grocery Headquarters*, August 2004, p. 30, from Information Resources Inc.

★ 346 ★
Baby Food
SIC: 2032; NAICS: 311422

Top Baby Formula (Liquid Concentrate) Brands, 2005

Market shares are shown based on drug store sales for the 52 weeks ended February 20, 2005.

Similac Advanced 23.8%
Similac 16.3
Enfamil 11.8
Enfamil Lipil. 11.7
Isomil Advanced 11.2
Isomil 6.9
Prosobee 4.2
Similac Lactose-free Advanced 3.9
Enfamil Prosobee Lipil. 3.3
Other 6.9

Source: *Chain Drug Review*, May 23, 2005, p. 69, from Information Resources Inc.

★ 347 ★
Canned Food
SIC: 2032; NAICS: 311422

Baked Beans Market

Market shares are shown in percent.

Bush Brothers 80.0%
Other 20.0

Source: "Bush Brothers Profile." [online] from http://www.northharvestbean.org/html/news.cfm?ID854 [Published April 14, 2005].

★ 348 ★
Canned Food
SIC: 2032; NAICS: 311422

Baked Beans Market in New Zealand

Sales are shown as of April 18, 2004.

Wattie's Baked Beans 67.3%
Other 32.7

Source: *Grocer's Review*, June 2004, p. NA, from ACNielsen.

★ 349 ★
Canned Food
SIC: 2032; NAICS: 311422
Canned Pasta Market

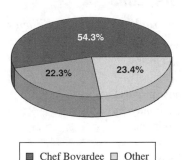

■ Chef Boyardee □ Other
■ SpaghettiOs

The annual canned pasta market was worth $543 million.

	($ mil.)	Share
Chef Boyardee	$ 295	54.33%
SpaghettiOs	121	22.28
Other	127	23.39

Source: *USA TODAY*, November 18, 2004, p. NA, from Campbell Soup.

★ 350 ★
Canned Food
SIC: 2032; NAICS: 311422
Leading Canned Good Brands, 2004

Data show respondent answers to this survey question: "If you were shopping for canned foods in a discount store or superstore, which brand would you want?"

Del Monte	16.0%
Campbell's	12.0
Kraft	5.0
Libby's	4.0
Green Giant	4.0
General Mills	4.0
Wonder Bread	3.0
Progresso	3.0
Kellogg's	3.0
Dole	3.0

Source: *DSN Retailing Today*, October 25, 2004, p. 48, from Leo J. Shapiro for *DSN Retailing Today*.

★ 351 ★
Canned Food
SIC: 2032; NAICS: 311422
Shelf-Stable Olive Sales

Supermarket sales are shown in millions of dollars for shelf stable olives.

2000	$ 385.7
2001	397.5
2002	410.0
2003	399.5
2004	396.1

Source: *Food Institute Report*, January 31, 2005, p. 18, from Information Resources Inc. InfoScan.

★ 352 ★
Canned Food
SIC: 2032; NAICS: 311422
Top Canned Food Firms in Western Europe

Market shares are for August 2004. Germany took 23% of the market in 2003, followed by France 20% and the United Kingdom 13%.

Mars	8.5%
Nestle	7.9
Heinz	7.8
Unilever	3.7
Bolton	3.6
Stockmeyer	3.2
Bonduelle	3.2
Orkla	2.6
Cirio Del Monte	2.4
Other	57.1

Source: "Canned Product Markets." [online] from http://www.fft.com [Market Synopsis dated September 2004], from *Food for Thought's 2004 West European Food & Drink Database*.

★ 353 ★
Canned Food
SIC: 2033; NAICS: 311421
Best-Selling Canned Vegetables (Private-label), 2004

Sales are shown for the year ended June 19, 2004.

Pickles	$ 173.1
Corn	145.6
Green beans	141.5
Mushrooms	85.5
Beans, other	59.4

Continued on next page.

★ 353 ★

[Continued]
Canned Food
SIC: 2033; NAICS: 311421

Best-Selling Canned Vegetables (Private-label), 2004

Sales are shown for the year ended June 19, 2004.

Beans, kidney/red	$ 39.7
Relishes	39.1
Beets	29.9
Asparagus	23.9

Source: *Food Institute Report*, December 6, 2004, p. 14, from *ACNielsen 2004 Private Label Report*.

★ 354 ★

Canned Food
SIC: 2033; NAICS: 311421

Canned Fruit Sales, 2003

Supermarket sales are shown in millions of dollars.

Pineapple	$ 229.77
Peaches, cling	226.57
Apples	183.21
Fruit cocktail	98.61
Cranberries, shelf stable	98.46
Oranges	91.72
Mixes & salad fruits	69.35
Pumpkin, canned	50.30

Source: *Progressive Grocer*, September 15, 2004, p. 26, from *2004 Progressive Grocer Consumer Expenditure Survey*.

★ 355 ★

Condiments
SIC: 2033; NAICS: 311421

Private Label Condiments

Condiments are ranked by private label sales. Shares are of overall category sales.

	($ mil.)	Share
Olives	$ 185.40	46.1%
Pickles	157.90	29.1
Mayonnaise	96.80	9.0
Ketchup	76.52	16.7
Mustard	52.90	18.1
Relish	36.20	33.9
Peppers/pimentos	19.90	7.5

Source: *Private Label Buyer*, September 2004, p. 25, from Information Resources Inc.

★ 356 ★

Fruits and Vegetables
SIC: 2033; NAICS: 311421

Leading Fruit/Vegetable/Juice Processors, 2003

Companies are ranked by sales in millions of dollars.

ConAgra Foodservice	$ 1,500
Simplot Food Group	1,300
Fresh Express	933
McCain Foods (potato business)	900
Dole Food Company Inc.	800
Birds Eye Foods Inc.	625
H.J. Heinz Co.	500
General Mills Inc.	420
Ready Pac Produce Inc.	350
Norpac Foods Inc.	275
A. Duda & Sons Inc.	250
Hanover Foods Corp.	240

Source: *Refrigerated & Frozen Foods*, February 2004, p. 32.

★ 357 ★

Fruits and Vegetables
SIC: 2033; NAICS: 311421

Top Fruit Product Marketers, 2003

Data are estimated based on sales at supermarkets, drug stores and mass merchandisers (but not Wal-Mart).

PepsiCo	13.7%
Coca-Cola Co.	11.2
Altria Group/Kraft Foods Inc.	8.0
Ocean Spray Cranberries	4.6
Cadbury Schweppes	4.4
Welch Foods	3.4
Other	54.7

Source: *Souvenirs, Gifts & Novelties*, September - October 2004, p. 156, from Information Resources Inc.

★ 358 ★
Jams and Jellies
SIC: 2033; NAICS: 311421

Jam and Jelly Market

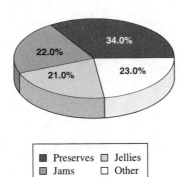

Market shares are shown in percent.

Preserves 34.0%
Jams 22.0
Jellies 21.0
Other 23.0

Source: *Arizona Central*, April 25, 2005, p. NA.

★ 359 ★
Jams and Jellies
SIC: 2033; NAICS: 311421

Jams/Jelly/Spread Sales, 2003

Supermarket sales are shown in millions of dollars.

Peanut butter . . . .$ 829.81
Preserves 225.52
Honey 199.66
Jams 143.96
Jelly 134.53
Fruit spreads 110.36
Marmalade 34.77
Butter, fruit & honey 21.89
Garlic spreads 4.99

Source: *Progressive Grocer*, Sept. 15, 2004, p. 26, from *2004 Progressive Grocer Consumer Expenditure Survey*.

★ 360 ★
Juices
SIC: 2033; NAICS: 311421

Cranberry Juice Industry Worldwide

Market shares are shown in percent.

Ocean Spray 70.0%
Other 30.0

Source: *Australasian Business Intelligence*, September 21, 2004, p. NA.

★ 361 ★
Juices
SIC: 2033; NAICS: 311421

Frozen Juice Sales, 2004

Sales are shown for the year ended June 13, 2004 at food stores, drug stores and mass merchandisers (excluding Wal-Mart).

	($ mil.)	Share
Frozen orange juice concentrates . .	$ 227.04	41.83%
Frozen drink/cocktail drink concentrates	72.32	13.32
Frozen lemonade/limeade concentrate	65.06	11.99
Frozen fruit juice concentrate . . .	40.49	7.46
Frozen cocktail mixes	35.61	6.56
Frozen grape juice concentrate . . .	32.92	6.07
Frozen apple juice concentrate . . .	32.59	6.00
Frozen cranberry/cranberry juice blends concentrate	20.24	3.73
Frozen grapefruit juice concentrate .	4.35	0.80
Other	12.14	2.24

Source: *Supermarket News*, August 9, 2004, p. 69, from Information Resources Inc.

★ 362 ★
Juices
SIC: 2033; NAICS: 311421
Fruit Juice Market in Thailand

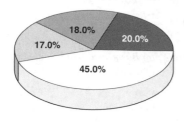

Market shares are shown in percent.

Tipco.	.20.0%
Uni-President.	.18.0
Malee	.17.0
Other.	.45.0

Source: *Asia Africa Intelligence Wire*, February 16, 2005, p. NA.

★ 363 ★
Juices
SIC: 2033; NAICS: 311421
Juice Market in Russia

The market reached volume of more than 2 billion litres.

Lebedyanskiy	.27.4%
Multon	.25.5
Vimm-Bill-Dann	.25.4
Other	.21.7

Source: *Kommersant*, April 1, 2005, p. NA.

★ 364 ★
Juices
SIC: 2033; NAICS: 311421
Leading Cranberry Juice Makers

Market shares are shown in percent.

Ocean Spray	.65.0%
Northland	.12.0
Other	.13.0

Source: *Milwaukee Journal Sentinel*, February 23, 2005, p. NA.

★ 365 ★
Juices
SIC: 2033; NAICS: 311421
Leading Fresh Juice Brands in the U.K., 2002

Total sales were 834 million British pounds.

Own label	.46.0%
Sunny D	.10.0
Ribena	. 8.0
Ocean Spray	. 8.0
Robinson	. 6.0
Other	.21.0

Source: *Marketing*, September 15, 2004, p. 20, from Mintel.

★ 366 ★
Juices
SIC: 2033; NAICS: 311421
Top Bottled Fruit Beverage Brands, 2004

Brands are ranked by supermarket, drug store and mass merchandiser sales (excluding Wal-Mart) for the year ended January 23, 2004.

Ocean Spray Cranberry Cocktail/Juice Drink	. $ 323.53
Priavate label apple juice	. 197.91
Libby's Juicy Juice SS Bottled Fruit Juice	. . 177.17
Welch's Grape Juice	. 146.18
Private label cranberry cocktail/juice drink	. . 125.88
V8 SS Bottled Tomato/Vegetable Juice/ Cocktail	. 120.88
Hawaiian Punch	. 111.68
Tropicana Twister	. 79.67
Ocean Spray Light Cranberry Cocktail/Jucie Drink	. 69.50
Mott's Apple Juice	. 66.25

Source: *Progressive Grocer*, April 1, 2005, p. 34, from Beverage Marketing Corp.

★ 367 ★
Juices
SIC: 2033; NAICS: 311421
Top Juice Brands (Shelf Stable), 2004

Brands are ranked by sales at supermarkets, drug stores and discount stores (but not Wal-Mart) for the year ended September 5, 2004.

	($ mil.)	Share
Ocean Spray	$ 334.1	8.78%
Libby's Juicy	172.2	4.53

Continued on next page.

★ 367 ★

[Continued]

Juices

SIC: 2033; NAICS: 311421

Top Juice Brands (Shelf Stable), 2004

Brands are ranked by sales at supermarkets, drug stores and discount stores (but not Wal-Mart) for the year ended September 5, 2004.

	($ mil.)	Share
Welch's	$ 155.9	4.10%
V8	121.9	3.20
Hawaiian Punch	116.1	3.05
Tropicana Twister	84.3	2.22
Ocean Spray Twister	66.8	1.76
Motts	66.4	1.75
V8 Splash	64.3	1.69
Tree Top	59.4	1.56
Private label	324.1	8.52
Other	2,239.5	58.86

Source: *MMR*, November 29, 2004, p. 21, from Information Resources Inc.

★ 368 ★

Juices

SIC: 2033; NAICS: 311421

Top Juice Makers in Mexico, 2003

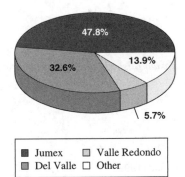

■ Jumex	□ Valle Redondo
■ Del Valle	□ Other

In 2003, juice sales were $1.15 billion.

Jumex	47.8%
Del Valle	32.6
Valle Redondo	5.7
Other	13.9

Source: *America's Intelligence Wire*, January 11, 2005, p. NA, from ACNielsen.

★ 369 ★

Juices

SIC: 2033; NAICS: 311421

Top Orange Juice (Refrigerated) Brands, 2005

Market shares are shown based on sales at food stores, drug stores and mass merchandisers (but not Wal-Mart) for the 52 weeks ended January 23, 2005.

Tropicana Pure Premium	43.6%
Minute Maid Premium	15.3
Florida's Natural	9.0
Simply Orange	6.0
Minute Maid Premium Heart Wise	0.9
Citrus World Donald Duck	0.7
Tropicana Healthy Heart	0.7
Minute Maid Premium For Kids	0.6
Dole	0.5
Private label	15.4
Other	7.3

Source: *Grocery Headquarters*, April 2005, p. 22, from Information Resources Inc.

★ 370 ★

Juices

SIC: 2033; NAICS: 311421

Top Orange Juice (Refrigerated) Makers, 2005

Market shares are shown based on sales at food stores, drug stores and mass merchandisers (but not Wal-Mart) for the 52 weeks ended January 23, 2005.

Tropicana Dole Beverages	44.9%
Minute Maid Co.	23.1
Citrus World Inc.	10.1
Dean Foods Co.	0.7
Private label	15.4
Other	5.8

Source: *Grocery Headquarters*, April 2005, p. 22, from Information Resources Inc.

★ 371 ★
Ketchup
SIC: 2033; NAICS: 311421

Ketchup Market in India, 2004

Market shares are for the first nine months of the year.

Maggi	39.7%
HLL's Kissan	25.0
Heinz	3.6
Other	31.7

Source: *Economic Times*, December 10, 2004, p. NA.

★ 372 ★
Ketchup
SIC: 2033; NAICS: 311421

Ketchup Market in Russia

Market shares are shown in percent.

Baltimor	50.0%
Other	50.0

Source: "News Service." [online] from http://www.akm.ru/eng/news/2005/February/18/ns1405836.htm [Published February 18, 2005].

★ 373 ★
Raisins
SIC: 2033; NAICS: 311421

Raisin Market

California raisins also represents 88% of the Japan raisin market and 85% of Sweden's market.

California	95.0%
Other	5.0

Source: *Fresno Bee*, December 5, 2004, p. B1, from Sun-Maid.

★ 374 ★
Dried Fruit
SIC: 2034; NAICS: 311423

Leading Specialty Dried Fruit Makers, 2004

Companies are ranked by food store sales in millions of dollars for the year ended June 13, 2004.

	($ mil.)	Share
Sun-Maid Growers	$ 136.13	30.87%
Sunsweet Growers	68.99	15.64
Corporate Brands	64.91	14.72
Ocean Spray Cranberries Inc.	29.72	6.74
Mariani Packing Co.	28.86	6.54

	($ mil.)	Share
Dole Packaged Foods	$ 21.71	4.92%
Seneca Foods Corp.	7.71	1.75
Valley Fig Growers	6.29	1.43
Del Monte Foods	6.11	1.39
Great Lakes Intl.	3.30	0.75
Other	67.27	15.25

Source: *Grocery Headquarters*, August 2004, p. 35, from Information Resources Inc.

★ 375 ★
Soup
SIC: 2034; NAICS: 311999

Dehydrated Soup Sales in Australia

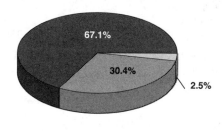

The soup market is worth A$250 million.

Unilever	67.1%
Uncle Toby's	30.4
Other	2.5

Source: *Australasian Business Intelligence*, February 25, 2005, p. NA.

★ 376 ★
Soup
SIC: 2034; NAICS: 311999

Leading Soup Makers in Japan, 2003

Market shares are estimated based on domestic sales.

Nissin Food	41.0%
Toyo Suisan	17.7
Sanyo Foods	14.0
Myojo Foods	9.8
Ace Cook	6.1
Other	11.4

Source: "Market Share Survey Report 2003." [online] from http://www.nni.nikkei.co.jp [Published July 26, 2004], from Nikkei estimates.

★ 377 ★
Soup
SIC: 2034; NAICS: 311423

Top Soup Brands, 2004

Brands are ranked by sales at supermarkets, drug stores and discount stores (but not Wal-Mart) for the year ended September 5, 2004.

	($ mil.)	Share
Campbell's	$ 934.4	25.53%
Campbell's Chunky	468.8	12.81
Progresso	394.4	10.78
Campbell's Select	196.0	5.36
Swanson	139.4	3.81
Maruchan	99.1	2.71
Campbell's Soup At Hand	97.7	2.67
Maruchan Instant	86.8	2.37
Campbell's Healthy Request	80.4	2.20
Healthy Choice	59.9	1.64
Private label	257.4	7.03
Other	845.7	23.11

Source: *MMR*, November 29, 2004, p. 21, from Information Resources Inc.

★ 378 ★
Soup
SIC: 2034; NAICS: 311423

Top Soup Brands in the U.K., 2003

The market is valued at 544 million in 2004. Wet/ ambient soup takes a 65% share of the industry. However, the market's growth comes from chilled soup. According to the source, 80% of soup purchases take place from November through February.

Heinz	32.3%
Batchelors	10.7
Baxters	8.1
New Covent Garden	6.2
Campbell's	3.4
Knorr	2.7
Seeds of Change	0.3
Soup Sensations	0.2
Homepride	0.2
Other	35.9

Source: *Marketing*, April 6, 2005, p. 36, from Euromonitor.

★ 379 ★
Soup
SIC: 2034; NAICS: 311999

Top Soup Brands (Ready-to-Serve), 2005

Market shares are shown based on sales at food stores, drug stores and mass merchandisers (but not Wal-Mart) for the 52 weeks ended January 23, 2005.

Campbell's Chunky Soup	27.4%
Progresso	22.6
Campbell's Select	10.0
Swanson	8.5
Campbell's Soup At Hand	5.2
Healthy Choice	3.3
Campbell's Kitchen Classics	3.1
College Inn	3.0
Wolfgang Puck's	1.9
Private label	5.9
Other	9.1

Source: *Grocery Headquarters*, April 2005, p. 22, from Information Resources Inc.

★ 380 ★
Soup
SIC: 2034; NAICS: 311999

Top Soup Makers (Condensed Wet), 2005

Market shares are shown based on sales at food stores, drug stores and mass merchandisers (but not Wal-Mart) for the 52 weeks ended January 23, 2005.

Campbell Soup Co.	84.5%
Snow's/Doxsee Inc.	0.5
Del Monte Foods	0.3
Hormel Foods	0.2
Private label	13.1
Other	1.4

Source: *Grocery Headquarters*, April 2005, p. 22, from Information Resources Inc.

★ 381 ★
Condiments
SIC: 2035; NAICS: 311421, 311941

Condiment Sales, 2003

Supermarket sales are shown in millions of dollars.

Spaghetti/marinara sauces	$ 1,348.32
Mexican sauces	886.66

Continued on next page.

★ 381 ★
[Continued]
Condiments
SIC: 2035; NAICS: 311421, 311941

Condiment Sales, 2003

Supermarket sales are shown in millions of dollars.

Catsup	$ 466.09
Barbecue sauces	353.59
Mustard	299.29
Vinegar	221.09
Meat sauces	204.23
Gravy, canned	190.42
Gravy mixes, packaged	161.98
Cooking sauces	151.16

Source: *Progressive Grocer*, Sept. 15, 2004, p. 26, from *2004 Progressive Grocer Consumer Expenditure Survey*.

★ 382 ★
Mustard
SIC: 2035; NAICS: 311421, 311941

Top Mustard Brands, 2004

Market shares are shown based on supermarket sales for the year ended December 26, 2004.

French's	32.1%
Grey Poupon	14.2
Guldens	6.6
Plochman's	4.3
Maille	2.0
Hellman's Dijonnaise	1.8
Inglehoffer	1.4
Hellman's	1.3
Jack Daniel's	1.1
Private label	18.3
Other	16.9

Source: *Food Processing*, February 2005, p. 45, from Information Resources Inc.

★ 383 ★
Mustard
SIC: 2035; NAICS: 311421, 311941

Top Mustard Vendors, 2004

Market shares are shown based on supermarket sales for the year ended December 26, 2004.

Reckitt Benckiser	32.1%
Kraft Foods	14.9
ConAgra Inc.	6.8
Plochman Inc.	4.6
Bestfoods	3.8
Beaverton Foods	2.3

Moutardes Maille Societe	2.0%
Romanoff Foods Inc.	1.1
Woeber Mustard Mfg.	0.9
Private label	18.3
Other	13.2

Source: *Food Processing*, February 2005, p. 45, from Information Resources Inc.

★ 384 ★
Pickles
SIC: 2035; NAICS: 311421, 311941

Pickles/Olives/Relish Sales, 2003

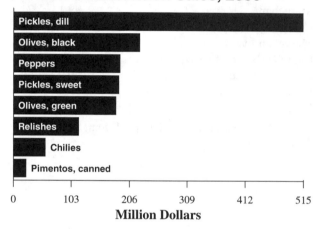

Million Dollars

Supermarket sales are shown in millions of dollars.

Pickles, dill	$ 514.49
Olives, black	224.48
Peppers	189.34
Pickles, sweet	186.67
Olives, green	182.14
Relishes	116.20
Chilies	57.02
Pimentos, canned	23.46

Source: *Progressive Grocer*, September 15, 2004, p. 26, from *2004 Progressive Grocer Consumer Expenditure Survey*.

★ 385 ★
Pickles
SIC: 2035; NAICS: 311421, 311941

Top Pickle Brands, 2004

Brands are ranked by sales for the 12 weeks ended September 9, 2004.

	Sales	Share
Claussen	$ 27,716,136	86.43%
Ba Tampte	1,756,422	5.48

Continued on next page.

★ 385 ★

[Continued]
Pickles
SIC: 2035; NAICS: 311421, 311941

Top Pickle Brands, 2004

Brands are ranked by sales for the 12 weeks ended September 9, 2004.

	Sales	Share
Bubbies	$ 455,943	1.42%
Vlasic	287,544	0.90
Private label	463,609	1.45
Other	1,389,724	4.33

Source: *Frozen Food Age*, October 2004, p. 39, from Information Resources Inc.

★ 386 ★

Salad Dressings
SIC: 2035; NAICS: 311421, 311941

Core Dressing Sales, 2004

The West generates the most in weekly sales of salad dressings ($275 per store). Market shares are shown in percent.

Blue cheese	49.0%
Ranch	19.0
Caesar	10.0
1000 Island	7.0
Coleslaw	5.0
Honey mustard	4.0
Poppyseed	2.0
Italian	1.0
Honey french	1.0
French	1.0

Source: *Produce Merchandising*, April 2005, p. 34, from ACNielsen and Perishables Group.

★ 387 ★

Salad Dressings
SIC: 2035; NAICS: 311421, 311941

Top Salad Dressing Brands, 2005

Market shares are shown based on sales at food stores, drug stores and mass merchandisers (but not Wal-Mart) for the 52 weeks ended January 23, 2005.

Kraft	18.6%
Wishbone	12.1
Ken's Steak House	8.9
Hidden Valley Ranch	8.0
Hidden Valley	6.3
Kraft Free	4.5

Newman's Own	3.8%
Wishbone Just 2 Good	3.0
Kraft Light Done Right	3.0
Kraft Special Collections	2.4
Girard's	1.5
Private label	8.6
Other	19.3

Source: *Grocery Headquarters*, April 2005, p. 22, from Information Resources Inc.

★ 388 ★

Salad Dressings
SIC: 2035; NAICS: 311421, 311941

Top Salad Dressing Makers, 2005

Market shares are shown based on sales at food stores, drug stores and mass merchandisers (but not Wal-Mart) for the 52 weeks ended January 23, 2005.

Kraft Foods Inc.	30.9%
Lipton	16.9
Clorox Co.	14.3
Ken's Foods Inc.	8.9
Newman's Own Inc.	5.2
T. Marzetti Co.	1.7
Girard's Fine Foods Inc.	1.5
Del Sol Food Co.	1.3
Birds Eye Foods Inc.	1.2
B&G Foods Inc.	1.2
Private label	5.2
Other	11.7

Source: *Grocery Headquarters*, April 2005, p. 22, from Information Resources Inc.

★ 389 ★

Salsa
SIC: 2035; NAICS: 311421, 311941

Top Salsa Brands, 2005

Sales of salsa totaled $646 million for the 12 months ended April 16, 2005. Unit shares are shown in percent.

Tostitos Salsa	30.8%
Pace	10.9
Private label	14.0
Other	44.3

Source: *San Antonio Express-News*, June 1, 2005, p. NA, from Information Resources Inc.

★ 390 ★
Sauces
SIC: 2035; NAICS: 311941

Marinades and Tenderizer Sales

Sales at shown at food stores in millions of dollars for the year ended May 15, 2004.

	2002	2003	2004
Meat marinades	$ 153.21	$ 164.96	$ 174.51
Meat tenderizers	23.28	23.11	21.82

Source: *Progressive Grocer*, August 1, 2004, p. 55, from ACNielsen Strategic Planner.

★ 391 ★
Sauces
SIC: 2035; NAICS: 311941

Sauce Sales in the U.K., 2003

Salt, pepper, vinegar and mustard all have 2.9 - 4.9% shares.

Table sauces, salad accompaniments, pickles, chutney	75.0%
Dish-specific sauces	9.5
Vinegar	4.9
Salt	4.9
Pepper	4.9
Mustard	4.9
Marinades	1.1

Source: *Fish & Chips and Fast Food*, December 2004, p. 23, from *Condiments and Sauces Market Report 2004*.

★ 392 ★
Sauces
SIC: 2035; NAICS: 311421

Soy Sauce Market in Brazil

Market shares are shown in percent.

Sakura	80.0%
Other	20.0

Source: *America's Intelligence Wire*, September 27, 2004, p. NA, from SABI.

★ 393 ★
Sauces
SIC: 2035; NAICS: 311941

Top Pasta/Italian Sauce Brands, 2005

Market shares are shown based on sales at food stores, drug stores and mass merchandisers (excluding Wal-Mart) for the 52 weeks ended January 23, 2005.

Prego	18.2%
Classico	10.5
Ragu	10.2
Hunt's	6.9
Ragu Chunky Gardenstyle	6.0
Five Brothers Bertolli Lucca	5.3
Ragu Old World Style	4.4
Barilla	4.1
Ragu Hearty	3.2
Private label	4.7
Other	26.5

Source: *Grocery Headquarters*, April 2005, p. 22, from Information Resources Inc.

★ 394 ★
Sauces
SIC: 2035; NAICS: 311941

Top Pasta/Italian Sauce Makers, 2005

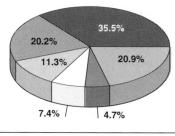

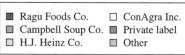

Market shares are shown based on sales at food stores, drug stores and mass merchandisers (excluding Wal-Mart) for the 52 weeks ended January 23, 2005.

Ragu Foods Co.	35.5%
Campbell Soup Co.	20.2
H.J. Heinz Co.	11.3
ConAgra Inc.	7.4
Private label	4.7
Other	20.9

Source: *Grocery Headquarters*, April 2005, p. 22, from Information Resources Inc.

★ 395 ★
Sauces

SIC: 2035; NAICS: 311941

Top Pasta Sauce Brands in the U.K.

Total sales were 229 million pounds. The wet/ambient sauce market was 238 million pounds.

	(mil.)	Share
Masterfoods (Dolmio)	92	40.0%
Unilever Bestfoods (Ragu, Bertoli)	39	17.0
Own label	34	15.0
Premier Foods (Loyd Grossman)	23	10.0
Sacla	18	8.0
Campbell's (Homepride)	16	7.0
Other brands	7	3.0

Source: *Marketing*, February 9, 2005, p. 40, from Mintel.

★ 396 ★
Sauerkraut

SIC: 2035; NAICS: 311421

Sauerkraut Market in Canada

Market shares are estimated in percent.

Great Lakes Kraut Co.	90.0%
Other	10.0

Source: *The Post-Crescent*, August 4, 2004, p. NA.

★ 397 ★
Spreads

SIC: 2035; NAICS: 311941

Flavored Spread Market, 2004

The top brands of refrigerated flavored spreads are ranked by sales for 52 weeks ended December 26, 2004.

	($ mil.)	Share
Athenos	$ 33.86	31.64%
Rite Tribe of the Two Sheiks	22.45	20.98
Cedar's	14.89	13.92
Rite	5.62	5.25
Joseph's	3.90	3.64
Sabra	3.84	3.59
Brummel & Brown	2.47	2.31
Cantare	2.46	2.30
Meza	1.76	1.64
Private label	1.91	1.79
Other	13.84	12.93

Source: *Frozen Food Age*, February 2005, p. 21, from Information Resources Inc.

★ 398 ★
Frozen Desserts

SIC: 2038; NAICS: 311412

Frozen Desserts and the Foodservice Industry, 2003

Total foodservice sales were $11.57 billion for the year.

	($ mil.)	Share
Ice cream	$ 7,398	63.90%
Frozen novelties	2,505	21.64
Frozen yogurt	1,116	9.64
Sherbert/sorbet/water ice	558	4.82

Source: *Refrigerated & Frozen Foods*, October 2004, p. 32, from Packaged Facts.

★ 399 ★
Frozen Desserts

SIC: 2038; NAICS: 311412

Top Frozen Dessert Brands in the U.K., 2004

Brands are ranked by sales in pounds sterling for the year ended October 2, 2004.

	Sales	Share
Viennetta	£ 21,050	8.68%
Heinz Weight Watchers Dessert	10,180	4.20
Sara Lee Gateau	8,722	3.60
Heinz Weight Watchers	5,556	2.29
Heinz Cheesecakes	4,720	1.95
Heinz Devonshire Cheesecake	4,236	1.75
Other	188,120	77.55

Source: *Grocer*, December 11, 2004, p. 53, from ACNielsen.

★ 400 ★
Frozen Dinners

SIC: 2038; NAICS: 311412

Top Frozen Dinner Brands, 2005

Market shares are shown based on sales at food stores, drug stores and mass merchandisers (excluding Wal-Mart) for the 52 weeks ended January 23, 2005.

Banquet Select Menu	14.6%
Healthy Choice	13.0
Marie Callender's Complete Dinners	11.7
Swanson Hungry Man	10.6
Banquet Value Menu	9.7
Kid Cuisine	9.3
Swanson American Recipes	6.4
Stouffer's Homestyle Dinners	5.2

Continued on next page.

★ 400 ★
[Continued]
Frozen Dinners
SIC: 2038; NAICS: 311412
Top Frozen Dinner Brands, 2005

Market shares are shown based on sales at food stores, drug stores and mass merchandisers (excluding Wal-Mart) for the 52 weeks ended January 23, 2005.

Stouffer's Lean Cuisine Café Classics	3.6%
Stouffer's Lean Cuisine Dinnertime Selects . . .	2.7
Other	13.2

Source: *Grocery Headquarters*, April 2005, p. 22, from Information Resources Inc.

★ 401 ★
Frozen Dinners
SIC: 2038; NAICS: 311412
Top Frozen Dinner Makers, 2005

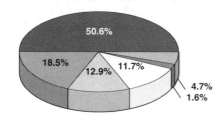

■ ConAgra Inc.
■ Pinnacle Foods Products Inc.
□ Nestle USA Inc.
□ Marie Callender's
■ Heinz Frozen Foods
□ Other

Market shares are shown based on sales at food stores, drug stores and mass merchandisers (excluding Wal-Mart) for the 52 weeks ended January 23, 2005.

ConAgra Inc.	50.6%
Pinnacle Foods Products Inc.	18.5
Nestle USA Inc.	12.9
Marie Callender's	11.7
Heinz Frozen Foods	1.6
Other	4.7

Source: *Grocery Headquarters*, April 2005, p. 22, from Information Resources Inc.

★ 402 ★
Frozen Dinners
SIC: 2038; NAICS: 311412
Top Frozen Entree Brands, 2004

Brands are ranked by supermarket, drug store and mass merchandiser sales (excluding Wal-Mart) for the year ended August 8, 2004.

	($ mil.)	Share
Stouffer's	$ 343.7	10.54%
Lean Cuisine Cafe Classics	324.0	9.94
Lean Cuisine Everyday Favorites . .	246.5	7.56
Stouffer's Family Style	240.5	7.38
Weight Watchers Smart Ones . . .	208.6	6.40
Other	1,896.6	58.18

Source: *Refrigerated & Frozen Foods*, October 2004, p. 40, from Information Resources Inc. Infoscan.

★ 403 ★
Frozen Dinners
SIC: 2038; NAICS: 311412
Top Frozen Entree Makers, 2005

Market shares are shown based on sales at food stores, drug stores and mass merchandisers (but not Wal-Mart) for the 52 weeks ended January 23, 2005.

Nestle USA Inc.	46.3%
ConAgra Inc.	11.0
Weight Watchers Co.	9.2
Luigino's Inc.	7.3
Marie Callender's	2.8
Other	23.4

Source: *Grocery Headquarters*, April 2005, p. 22, from Information Resources Inc.

★ 404 ★
Frozen Dinners
SIC: 2038; NAICS: 311412

Top Frozen Meal Makers

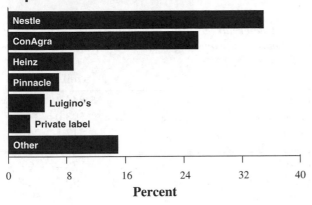

Percent

Market shares are shown in percent.

Nestle	.35.0%
ConAgra	.26.0
Heinz	9.0
Pinnacle	7.0
Luigino's	5.0
Private label	3.0
Other	.15.0

Source: *Prepared Foods*, April 2005, p. 21.

★ 405 ★
Frozen Foods
SIC: 2038; NAICS: 311412

Frozen Food Market in Europe

Consumption is shown in millions of euros.

	(mil.)	Share
Germany	15,234.5	23.64%
United Kingdom	10,249.3	15.90
France	8,096.8	12.56
Italy	6,938.7	10.77
Spain	6,122.2	9.50
Sweden	2,334.5	3.62
Netherlands	2,248.1	3.49
Belgium/Luxembourg	1,754.4	2.72
Norway	1,719.8	2.67
Austria	1,369.8	2.13
Other	8,382.3	13.01

Source: *Quick Frozen Foods International*, October 2004, p. 88, from Food for Thought.

★ 406 ★
Frozen Foods
SIC: 2038; NAICS: 311412

Frozen Pasta Sales, 2004

Sales are shown in millions of dollars for the 52 weeks ended December 26, 2004.

	($ mil.)	Share
Ravioli	$ 92.80	43.31%
Pierogi	51.30	23.94
Tortellini/tortelloni	30.50	14.23
Stuffed pasta shell	7.22	3.37
Manicotti	4.68	2.18
Gnocchi	3.65	1.70
Other	24.14	11.27

Source: *Frozen Food Age*, February 2005, p. 11, from Information Resources Inc.

★ 407 ★
Frozen Foods
SIC: 2038; NAICS: 311412

Largest Frozen Food Categories, 2004

Categories are ranked by sales in millions of dollars for the 52 weeks ended December 28, 2004. Sales rose only .7% during the year and this increase came mostly from price hikes.

	($ mil.)	Share
Ice cream	$ 3,852.62	14.19%
Entrees	3,227.96	11.89
Pizza	2,544.05	9.37
Frozen novelties	2,176.80	8.02
Chicken/chicken substitutes . . .	2,001.56	7.37
Seafood	1,563.12	5.76
Dinners	1,134.03	4.18
Hand-held entrees (non-breakfast) .	1,014.37	3.74
Appetizers/snack rolls	789.41	2.91
Meat (no poultry)	687.75	2.53
Waffles	485.18	1.79
Other	7,673.96	28.26

Source: *Frozen Food Age*, April 2005, p. 18, from Information Resources Inc.

★ 408 ★
Frozen Foods
SIC: 2038; NAICS: 311412

Leading Frozen Food Makers in Japan, 2003

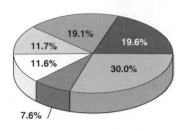

Market shares are estimated based on domestic shipments.

Nichirei	.19.6%
Katokichi	.19.1
Ajinomoto Frozen Foods	.11.7
Nichiro	.11.6
Nippon Suisan Kaisha	7.6
Other	.30.0

Source: "Market Share Survey Report 2003." [online] from http://www.nni.nikkei.co.jp [Published July 26, 2004], from Nikkei estimates.

★ 409 ★
Frozen Foods
SIC: 2038; NAICS: 311412

Leading Snack/Appetizer/Side Dish Processors, 2004

Companies are ranked by sales in millions of dollars.

McCain Snack Foods	$ 725
H.J. Heinz Co.	525
Reser's Fine Foods	410
Windsor Foods	385
Kraft Foods	375
Orval Kent Foods	350
ConAgra Foods	300
J&J Snack Foods Corp.	270
General Mills	221
Kozy Shack Enterprises	200

Source: *Refrigerated & Frozen Foods*, March 2005, p. 16, from *Refrigerated & Frozen Foods Annual Top 150 Report*.

★ 410 ★
Frozen Foods
SIC: 2038; NAICS: 311412

Private Label Frozen Food Sales, 2004

The top selling store label products are ranked by sales at supermarkets, drug stores and mass merchandisers (excluding Wal-Mart) for the year ended May 16, 2004.

	($ mil.)	Share
Ice cream	$ 844.4	21.6%
Fish/seafood	593.0	38.1
Chicken	517.5	26.7
Fries/hash browns	264.6	32.6
Pizza	175.4	6.8
Meal entrees	90.7	2.8
Misc. plain vegetables	78.1	50.9
Pies/pie shells	34.3	30.7
Appetizers/snacks	32.7	4.2

Source: *Quick Frozen Foods International*, October 2004, p. 156, from Information Resources Inc.

★ 411 ★
Frozen Foods
SIC: 2038; NAICS: 311412

Top Frozen Breakfast Brands, 2004

Market shares are shown based on supermarket, drug store and mass merchandiser unit sales for the year ended February 29, 2004. Figures exclude Wal-Mart.

Kelloggs Eggos	.25.57%
Pillsbury Hungry Jack	7.46
Lenders Bagels	5.59
Aunt Jemima Waffles	5.40
Aunt Jemima (Other)	5.03
Swanson Great Starts	3.38
Pillsbury Hungry Jack	3.17
Other	.44.27

Source: *Baking Business*, August 15, 2004, pp. SI-23, from Information Resources Inc.

★ 412 ★
Frozen Foods
SIC: 2038; NAICS: 311412

Top Frozen Breakfast Foods, 2004

Brands are ranked by sales in millions of dollars for the year ended July 11, 2004.

	($ mil.)	Share
Swanson Great Starts	$ 55.90	13.29%
Aunt Jemima	48.27	11.48
Jimmy Dean	44.22	10.52

Continued on next page.

★ 412 ★

[Continued]
Frozen Foods
SIC: 2038; NAICS: 311412

Top Frozen Breakfast Foods, 2004

Brands are ranked by sales in millions of dollars for the year ended July 11, 2004.

	($ mil.)	Share
Hot Pockets	$ 34.61	8.23%
Pillsbury Toaster Scrambles	28.99	6.89
Other	208.48	49.58

Source: *National Provisioner*, August 2004, p. 56, from Information Resources Inc.

★ 413 ★

Frozen Foods
SIC: 2038; NAICS: 311412

Top Frozen Food Firms in Western Europe

Market shares are for September 2004. Germany took 23% of the market in 2003, followed by France 20% and the United Kingdom 13%.

Unilever	17.7%
Nestle	8.8
Artisanal	2.6
McCain	2.4
Investor/EQT	2.4
Frosta	2.0
Pescanova	1.8
Oetker	1.6
Bonduelle	1.5
Other	59.2

Source: "Canned Product Markets." [online] from http://www.fft.com [Market Synopsis dated September 2004], from *Food for Thought's 2004 West European Food & Drink Database.*

★ 414 ★

Frozen Foods
SIC: 2038; NAICS: 311412

Top Frozen Meat Processors

Companies are ranked by sales in millions of dollars. The red meat category was worth $44.5 billion, according to Mintel. The industry grew 18% between 2002 and 2004. Data exclude poultry.

Moran Frozen Meats	$ 46.67
Bubba Burger	30.13
Philly Gourmet	27.22

Topps	$ 26.75
Steak-Umm	22.95
Armour Homestyle	22.93
Flander	20.61
Excel	18.55

Source: *Food Processing*, December 2004, p. 27.

★ 415 ★

Frozen Foods
SIC: 2038; NAICS: 311412

Top Frozen Pizza Brands, 2005

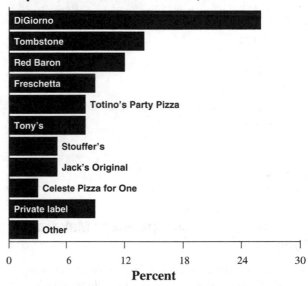

Brands are ranked by sales in millions of dollars for the 52 weeks ended February 23, 2005.

	($ mil.)	Share
DiGiorno	$ 515.6	25.53%
Tombstone	282.3	13.98
Red Baron	234.4	11.61
Freschetta	184.4	9.13
Totino's Party Pizza	159.1	7.88
Tony's	151.5	7.50
Stouffer's	91.9	4.55
Jack's Original	91.0	4.51
Celeste Pizza for One	66.3	3.28
Private label	178.4	8.83
Other	64.9	3.21

Source: *Baking & Snack*, April 2005, p. 48, from Information Resources Inc.

★ 416 ★
Frozen Foods
SIC: 2038; NAICS: 311412

Top Frozen Pizza Makers, 2005

Companies are ranked by sales in millions of dollars for the 52 weeks ended February 23, 2005.

	($ mil.)	Share
Kraft Foods	$ 856.1	32.88%
Schwan's Consumer Brands	699.4	26.86
General Mills	216.0	8.30
Nestle USA	170.4	6.54
Jack's Frozen Pizza	155.3	5.96
Aurora Foods	67.3	2.58
McCain Ellio's Foods	32.8	1.26
Home Run Inn	30.3	1.16
Bud's Pizza	29.2	1.12
Private label	178.4	6.85
Other	168.7	6.48

Source: *Baking & Snack*, April 2005, p. 48, from Information Resources Inc.

★ 417 ★
Frozen Foods
SIC: 2038; NAICS: 311412

Top Frozen Snack/Appetizer Makers, 2004

Market shares are shown based on supermarket, drug store and mass merchandiser sales (excluding Wal-Mart) for the year ended August 8, 2004.

H.J. Heinz	30.0%
General Mills	20.9
Specialty Brands	6.4
Schwan Foods Co.	5.7
Ruiz Foods	5.1
Other	31.9

Source: *Refrigerated & Frozen Foods*, October 2004, p. 40, from Information Resources Inc. Infoscan.

★ 418 ★
Frozen Foods
SIC: 2038; NAICS: 311412

Top Frozen Snack/Appetizers, 2004

Brands are ranked by supermarket, drug store and mass merchandiser sales (excluding Wal-Mart) for the year ended August 8, 2004.

	($ mil.)	Share
Totinos Pizza Rolls	$ 175.4	20.75%
TGI Friday's	101.1	11.96

	($ mil.)	Share
Bagel Bites	$ 61.1	7.23%
Delimex	36.1	4.27
El Monterey	35.3	4.18
Other	436.4	51.62

Source: *Refrigerated & Frozen Foods*, October 2004, p. 40, from Information Resources Inc. Infoscan.

★ 419 ★
Frozen Foods
SIC: 2038; NAICS: 311412

Top Frozen Waffle Brands, 2004

Brands are ranked by supermarket sales for the year ended October 3, 2004.

	($ mil.)	Share
Kellogg's Eggo	$ 249.2	51.01%
Pillsbury Hungry Jack	34.1	6.98
Aunt Jemima	32.7	6.69
Kellogg's Nutri-Grain	28.2	5.77
Private label	65.7	13.45
Other	78.6	16.09

Source: *Baking & Snack*, November 2004, p. 44, from Information Resources Inc.

★ 420 ★
Frozen Foods
SIC: 2038; NAICS: 311412

Top Frozen Waffle Makers

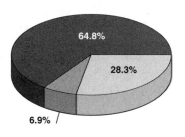

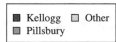

The market is flat at $487 million.

Kellogg	64.8%
Pillsbury	6.9
Other	28.3

Source: *Brandweek*, December 13, 2004, p. 6.

★ 421 ★
Frozen Foods
SIC: 2038; NAICS: 311412

Top Handheld Entrees (Non-Breakfast), 2004

Brands are ranked by supermarket, drug store and mass merchandiser sales (excluding Wal-Mart) for the year ended August 8, 2004.

	($ mil.)	Share
Hot Pockets	$ 276.5	27.01%
Lean Pockets	146.8	14.34
Croissant Pockets	78.6	7.68
El Monterey	59.3	5.79
State Fair	56.6	5.53
Other	405.8	39.64

Source: *Refrigerated & Frozen Foods*, October 2004, p. 40, from Information Resources Inc. Infoscan.

★ 422 ★
Frozen Foods
SIC: 2038; NAICS: 311412

Top Meatless Entrees, 2004

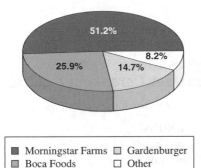

Morningstar Farms ■ Gardenburger □
Boca Foods ■ Other □

Brands are ranked by supermarket, drug store and mass merchandiser sales (excluding Wal-Mart) for the year ended August 8, 2004.

	($ mil.)	Share
Morningstar Farms	$ 107.0	51.17%
Boca Foods	54.2	25.92
Gardenburger	30.8	14.73
Other	17.1	8.18

Source: *Refrigerated & Frozen Foods*, October 2004, p. 40, from Information Resources Inc. Infoscan.

★ 423 ★
Frozen Foods
SIC: 2038; NAICS: 311412

Top Pierogi Brands, 2004

Brands are ranked by sales for the 12 weeks ended July 11, 2004.

	Sales	Share
Mrs. T's	$ 7,733,805	72.85%
Mrs. T's Rogies	800,463	7.54
Poppy's Pierogi's	478,130	4.50
Kasia's	313,485	2.95
Private label	334,406	3.15
Other	956,201	9.01

Source: *Frozen Food Age*, September 2004, p. 12, from Information Resources Inc.

★ 424 ★
Frozen Foods
SIC: 2038; NAICS: 311412

Top Pot Pie Brands, 2004

Brands are ranked by sales for the 12 weeks ended July 11, 2004.

	Sales	Share
Marie Callender's	$ 19,848,518	38.59%
Banquet	11,379,996	22.12
Swanson	6,487,722	12.61
Hot Pockets Pot Pie Express	4,701,770	9.14
Stouffer's	4,335,955	8.43
Other	4,683,961	9.11

Source: *Frozen Food Age*, September 2004, p. 12, from Information Resources Inc.

★ 425 ★
Frozen Foods
SIC: 2038; NAICS: 311412

Top Ready Meal Brands in the U.K., 2004

Brands are ranked by sales in pounds sterling for the year ended October 2, 2004.

	Sales	Share
Birds Eye	£ 67,909	5.74%
Weight Watchers	62,456	5.28
Menu Mast	50,177	4.24
Oriental Express	19,987	1.69
Findus	16,584	1.40
Other	966,418	81.66

Source: *Grocer*, December 11, 2004, p. 53, from ACNielsen.

★ 426 ★
Flour
SIC: 2041; NAICS: 311211
Corn Flour Market in Mexico

Market shares are shown in percent.

GRUMA 71.0%
Other 29.0

Source: "Investor Relations Company Overview." [online] from http://www.gruma [April 19, 2005].

★ 427 ★
Flour
SIC: 2041; NAICS: 311211
Flour Sales, 2003

Supermarket sales are shown in millions of dollars.

White wheat, all purpose . . . . $ 263.05
Cornmeal 78.61
Single purpose 25.30
All purpose remaining 23.92

Source: *Progressive Grocer*, Sept. 15, 2004, p. 26, from *2004 Progressive Grocer Consumer Expenditure Survey.*

★ 428 ★
Cereal
SIC: 2043; NAICS: 31123
Cereal Market in Ireland

The ready-to-eat cereal category is worth 136 million Irish pounds.

Kellogg's 60.0%
Other 40.0

Source: *Checkout*, September 2004, p. NA, from ACNielsen.

★ 429 ★
Cereal
SIC: 2043; NAICS: 31123
Cereal Market in Venezuela

Venezuela is the third largest breakfast market, by consumption, in Latin America. Kellog's Corn Flakes takes 70% of both volume and value.

Kellogg's 70.0%
Other 30.0

Source: *South American Business Information*, December 1, 2004, p. NA.

★ 430 ★
Cereal
SIC: 2043; NAICS: 31123
Sugar Coated Wheat Cereal Leaders

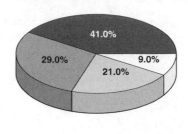

■ Golden Puffs □ Golden Crisps
■ Smacks □ Other

In the overall ready-to-eat cereal market, Kellogg leads with a 31.2% market share. Producers are shown in parentheses.

Golden Puffs (Malt O Meal) 41.0%
Smacks (Kellogg) 29.0
Golden Crisps (Post) 21.0
Other 9.0

Source: *Saint Paul Pioneer Press*, March 10, 2005, p. NA.

★ 431 ★
Cereal
SIC: 2043; NAICS: 31123
Top Breakfast Cereals in Australia

Market shares are shown in percent.

Sanitarium Weet-Bix 17.5%
Kellogg's Nutri-Grain 7.9
Kellogg's Corn Flakes 6.6
Kellogg's Just Right 6.4
Uncle Toby's Vita Brits 5.6
Kellogg's Coco Pops 5.2
Uncle Toby's Flakes Plus 4.4
Kellogg's Sultana Bran 3.7
Kellogg's Special K 3.1
Other 39.6

Source: *Choice*, March 2005, p. 8, from *Retail World's Australasian Grocery Guide 2004.*

★ 432 ★
Cereal
SIC: 2043; NAICS: 31123

Top Cereal Brands, 2004

Brands are ranked by sales at supermarkets, drug stores and discount stores (but not Wal-Mart) for the year ended September 5, 2004.

	($ mil.)	Share
General Mills Cheerios	$ 290.0	4.76%
Kellogg's Froster Flakes	237.3	3.90
General Mills Honey Nut Cheerios .	235.1	3.86
Post Honey Bunches of Oats . . .	212.2	3.48
General Mills Cinnamon Taste Crunch	164.7	2.70
Kellogg's Frosted Mini Wheats . .	147.1	2.42
Kellogg's Froot Loops	137.1	2.25
General Mills Lucky Charms . . .	135.4	2.22
Kellogg's Corn Flakes	127.9	2.10
Kellogg's Special K	125.6	2.06
Private label	503.5	8.27
Other	3,774.1	61.97

Source: *MMR*, November 29, 2004, p. 21, from Information Resources Inc.

★ 433 ★
Cereal
SIC: 2043; NAICS: 31123

Top Cereal Brands in the U.K., 2003

Market shares are shown in percent.

Weetabix	7.0%
Corn Flakes	6.6
Crunchy Nut Corn Flakes	4.1
Frosties	3.7
Rice Krispies	3.2
Coco Pops	3.2
Special K	3.0
Shreddies	2.7
Sugar Puffs	2.6
Shredded Wheat	2.5
Other	61.4

Source: *Marketing*, May 12, 2004, p. 40, from Mintel.

★ 434 ★
Cereal
SIC: 2043; NAICS: 31123

Top Cereal Vendors, 2004

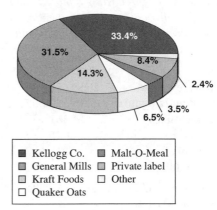

- ■ Kellogg Co.
- ■ General Mills
- ■ Kraft Foods
- □ Quaker Oats
- ■ Malt-O-Meal
- ■ Private label
- □ Other

Market shares of ready-to-eat cereal makers are shown for the year ended November 8, 2004.

Kellogg Co.	33.4%
General Mills	31.5
Kraft Foods	14.3
Quaker Oats	6.5
Malt-O-Meal	3.5
Private label	8.4
Other	2.4

Source: *Star Tribune*, January 8, 2005, p. 1D, from Information Resources Inc.

★ 435 ★
Baking Mixes
SIC: 2045; NAICS: 311822

Baking Mix Sales, 2003

Supermarket sales are shown in millions of dollars.

Cakes/layer, over 10 oz.	$ 310.02
Brownies	215.55
Pancakes	176.88
Muffins	173.87
Rolls & biscuits	117.19
Bread	86.65
Cookies	60.65
Pie crust	6.79
Gingerbread	5.02

Source: *Progressive Grocer*, September 15, 2004, p. 26, from *2004 Progressive Grocer Consumer Expenditure Survey*.

★ 436 ★
Baking Mixes
SIC: 2045; NAICS: 311822

Dessert Mix Sales, 2004

Analysts have been forecasting a plateau and gradual decline in the carb-counting phenomenon. Sales are from food stores with sales of at least $2 million.

	Q1	Q2
Cake mixes over 10 oz	$ 70,902,994	$ 74,872,088
Total brownie mixes	53,412,139	55,046,290
Total swted pudding mix	35,650,605	36,575,256
Total cookie mixes	14,381,537	14,567,711
CC brownie mixes	926,937	1,082,831
CC cookie mixes	216,678	206,074
CC swted pudding mix	27,057	16,853

Source: *Progressive Grocer*, October 15, 2004, p. 43, from ACNielsen LabelTrends.

★ 437 ★
Dough
SIC: 2045; NAICS: 311822

Top Pizza Crust/Dough Brands, 2005

Brands are ranked by supermarket sales for the 12 weeks ended February 20, 2005.

	Sales	Share
Pillsbury	$ 4,126,482	43.21%
Mama Mary's	2,906,964	30.44
Wenner	121,293	1.27
Bernadino's	73,698	0.77
Private label	1,683,444	17.63
Other	637,799	6.68

Source: *Frozen Food Age*, May 2005, p. 28, from Information Resources Inc.

★ 438 ★
Pet Food
SIC: 2047; NAICS: 311111

Dog Food Sales, 2004

Sales are shown in millions of dollars. Over 2003, wet mid-priced dog food fell 7.2%. The biggest gain was in the wet premium segment, up 5.3%.

	($ mil.)	Share
Dry premium	$ 2,692.0	38.34%
Dry mid-priced	2,188.0	31.16
Dry economy	738.0	10.51
Wet premium	543.1	7.73
Wet mid-priced	$ 442.5	6.30%
Wet economy	418.2	5.96

Source: *Pet Product News*, February 2005, p. 8, from Euromonitor International's *Pet Food and Pet Care in the USA*.

★ 439 ★
Pet Food
SIC: 2047; NAICS: 311111

Pet Food Market in Australia, 2004

The country has 12 million people associated with pets, one of the highest incidences of pet ownership in the world. There are 3.6 million dogs, 2.3 million cats, 7.5 birds and 13.2 million fish.

Uncle Ben's/Friskies	75.0%
Other	25.0

Source: "Pet Industry in Australia." [online] from http://www.export.gov [Published February 2005].

★ 440 ★
Pet Food
SIC: 2047; NAICS: 311111

Pet Food Market in Germany, 2004

The country's pet population: 5.3 million dogs, 7.3 million cats, 5.9 million small animals, 4.6 million birds and 1.9 aquarium creatures and 1.2 million garden ponds with fish.

	($ mil.)	Share
Cat food, wet	$ 757	34.10%
Dog food, dry	346	15.59
Dog food, wet	333	15.00
Dog snacks	249	11.22
Cat food, dry	195	8.78
Cat food snacks	93	4.19
Bird food	89	4.01
Ornamental fish food	63	2.84
Other	95	4.28

Source: "German Pet Market." [online] from http://www.export.gov [Published February 2005].

★ 441 ★
Pet Food
SIC: 2047; NAICS: 311111

Pet Food Market in the Caribbean Basin

Sales are shown by segment.

Dry dog	43.0%
Wet dog	32.0
Dry cat	13.0
Wet cat	10.0
Dog/cat treats	2.0

Source: "Caribbean Bain Pet Food Market Report." [online] from http://www.export.gov [accessed October 21, 2004], from U.S. Department of Agriculture.

★ 442 ★
Pet Food
SIC: 2047; NAICS: 311111

Top Cat Food Firms in Brazil

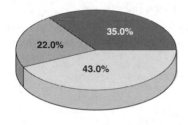
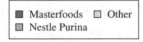

The overall pet food industry is valued at $1.2 billion.

Masterfoods	35.0%
Nestle Purina	22.0
Other	43.0

Source: *America's Intelligence Wire*, July 26, 2004, p. NA.

★ 443 ★
Pet Food
SIC: 2047; NAICS: 311111

Top Dog Food (Frozen) Brands, 2004

Brands are ranked by sales for the 12 weeks ended November 28, 2004.

	Sales	Share
Frosty Paws	$ 2,364,812	70.30%
Bil Jac	645,221	19.18
Dogsters	349,212	10.38

	Sales	Share
Bone Ice Petit	$ 3,161	0.09%
Doggy Pops	1,369	0.04

Source: *Frozen Food Age*, January 2005, p. 16, from Information Resources Inc.

★ 444 ★
Pet Food
SIC: 2047; NAICS: 311111

Top Pet Food Makers, 2003

Market shares are shown in percent.

Nestle Purina	31.0%
Proceter & Gamble (Iams)	12.0
Mars Inc.	11.0
Colgate-Palmolive	11.0
Delmonte	8.0
Other	27.0

Source: "Petcare." [online] from http://www.mind-advertising.com/sectors/sector_pets.htm [Accessed May 24, 2005].

★ 445 ★
Pet Food
SIC: 2047; NAICS: 311111

Top Pet Food Makers in Chile, 2002

Market shares are shown in percent.

Nestle/Masterfoods Chile	60.0%
Champion S.A./Nutrpro S.A.	30.0
Other	10.0

Source: *AgExporter*, October 2004, p. 12.

★ 446 ★
Bakery Products
SIC: 2051; NAICS: 311812

Baked Industry in Germany, 2003

Figures are in thousands of metric tons.

	(000)	Share
Chocolate-coated biscuits/wafers	298.9	44.39%
Gingerbreads	114.4	16.99
Crisp breads	30.2	4.48
Rusks, toasted bread	21.8	3.24
Fresh wafers	11.6	1.72
Other sweet biscuits	142.4	21.15
Other sweet wafers	54.1	8.03

Source: *The Manufacturing Confectioner*, September 2004, p. 28.

★ 447 ★
Bakery Products
SIC: 2051; NAICS: 311812

Bakery Industry in Italy

Italy is the world's fifth largest consumer market and leads Western Europe in the sale of bakery products.

Bread	.74.0%
Pastries	9.0
Biscuits	9.0
Cakes	7.0
Breakfast cereal	1.0
Other	0.7

Source: *Baking & Snack International*, Special Issue 2004, p. NA, from Euromonitor International.

★ 448 ★
Bakery Products
SIC: 2051; NAICS: 311812

Bakery Product Sales

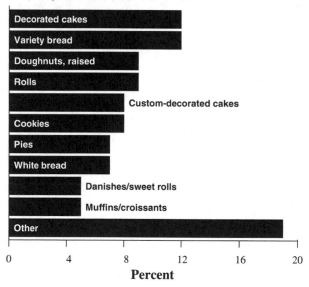

The fastest-growing categories: cakes (34%), bread (21%) and cookies (9%). In-store fresh bakery department sales saw sales of $9.05 billion.

Decorated cakes	.11.8%
Variety bread	.11.6
Doughnuts, raised	9.2
Rolls	8.8
Custom-decorated cakes	8.4
Cookies	7.5
Pies	7.4
White bread	6.7
Danishes/sweet rolls	4.8

Muffins/croissants	4.7%
Other	.19.1

Source: *Progressive Grocer*, March 1, 2005, p. 74, from *Progressive Grocer 2005 Bakery Operations Review.*

★ 449 ★
Bakery Products
SIC: 2051; NAICS: 311812

Leading Bakery Processors, 2004

Companies are ranked by sales in millions of dollars.

General Mills	$ 3,000
Sara Lee Corp.	700
Rich Products Corp.	650
Schwan's Bakery	550
Otis Spunkmeyer	300
Dawn Foods Products	300
Maplehurst Bakeries	285
Ralcorp Holdings	280
Pepperidge Farm Inc.	220
The Bama Companies	200
Maple Leaf Frozen Bakery	170

Source: *Refrigerated & Frozen Foods*, March 2005, p. 16, from *Refrigerated & Frozen Foods Annual Top 150 Report.*

★ 450 ★
Bakery Products
SIC: 2051; NAICS: 311812

Top Baked Goods Makers in the U.K.

George Weston has 15-20% of the market, Simplot (15-20%), Burns, Philip & Co. and Patties Foods have 5-10% each.

Simplot	.20.0%
George Weston	.20.0
Patties Foods	.10.0
Burns, Philip & Co.	.10.0
Other	.40.0

Source: *Food*, April 1, 2005, p. NA, from IBIS World.

★ 451 ★
Bakery Products
SIC: 2051; NAICS: 311812
Top Cake Brands in the U.K., 2004

Brands are ranked by sales in thousands of pounds for the 52 weeks ended October 2, 2004.

	(000)	Share
Cadbury Mini Rolls	£ 36,813	4.51%
Mr. Kipling Fruit Pies	23,367	2.86
Mr. Kipling Bakewell Tarts	14,009	1.72
Mr. Kipling Viennese Whirls	10,566	1.29
Mr. Kipling French Fancies	9,862	1.21
Mr. Kipling Lemon Slices	8,852	1.08
McVitie's Jamica Ginger Cake	8,555	1.05
Soreen Malt Loaf	8,366	1.03
Other	695,687	85.25

Source: *The Manufacturing Confectioner*, February 2005, p. 22, from ACNielsen and *The Grocer*.

★ 452 ★
Bakery Products
SIC: 2051; NAICS: 311812
Top Cheesecake Makers, 2004

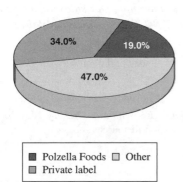

Market shares are shown in percent.

Polzella Foods	19.0%
Private label	34.0
Other	47.0

Source: *Milwaukee Journal Sentinel*, May 21, 2005, p. NA.

★ 453 ★
Bakery Products
SIC: 2051; NAICS: 311812
Top Fresh Coffee Cake Brands, 2004

Market shares are shown based on supermarket, drug store and mass merchandiser unit sales for the year ended February 29, 2004. Figures exclude Wal-Mart.

Entenmann's	45.1%
Drake	7.9
Little Debbie	7.1
Tastykake	5.7
Private label	23.8
Other	10.4

Source: *Snack Food & Wholesale Bakery*, May 2004, pp. SI-23, from Information Resources Inc.

★ 454 ★
Bakery Products
SIC: 2051; NAICS: 311812
Top Fresh Danish Brands, 2004

Market shares are shown based on supermarket, drug store and mass merchandiser unit sales for the year ended February 29, 2004. Figures exclude Wal-Mart.

Entenmanns	28.2%
Svenhards	20.3
CloverHill	6.7
Otis Spunkmeyer	4.3
Dolly Madison	3.3
Metz Brands	2.2
Café Valley	1.7
Nickles	1.4
Private label	22.2
Other	9.7

Source: *Baking Business*, August 15, 2004, pp. SI-23, from Information Resources Inc.

★ 455 ★
Bakery Products
SIC: 2051; NAICS: 311812
Top Fresh Donut Brands, 2004

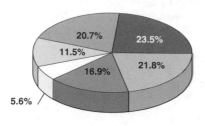

Market shares are shown based on supermarket, drug store and mass merchandiser unit sales for the year ended February 29, 2004. Figures exclude Wal-Mart.

Krispy Kreme	. . . . .23.5%
Entenmann's	. . . . .20.7
Hostess	. . . . .11.5
Dolly Madison	. . . . 5.6
Private label	. . . . .16.9
Other	. . . . .21.8

Source: *Snack Food & Wholesale Bakery*, May 2004, pp. SI-23, from Information Resources Inc.

★ 456 ★
Bakery Products
SIC: 2051; NAICS: 311812
Top Snack Cake Brands, 2004

Market shares are shown based on supermarket, drug store and mass merchandiser sales for the year ended February 29, 2004. Figures exclude Wal-Mart.

Little Debbie	. . . . .52.7%
Hostess	. . . . .19.9
Tastykake	. . . . 7.7
Drake	. . . . 4.3
Private label	. . . . 7.3
Other	. . . . 8.1

Source: *Snack Food & Wholesale Bakery*, May 2004, pp. SI-23, from Information Resources Inc.

★ 457 ★
Bakery Products
SIC: 2051; NAICS: 311812
Top Toaster Pastries (Shelf Stable), 2004

Brands are ranked by supermarket sales for the year ended October 3, 2004.

	($ mil.)	Share
Kellogg's Pop Tarts	$ 317.8	73.65%
Quaker Fruit & Oatmeal	16.1	3.73
Thomas	12.3	2.85
Kellogg's SpongeBob SquarePants		
Pop-Tarts	7.7	1.78
Private label	51.3	11.89
Other	26.3	6.10

Source: *Baking & Snack*, November 2004, p. 44, from Information Resources Inc.

★ 458 ★
Bakery Products
SIC: 2051; NAICS: 311812
Top Toaster Pastry Brands, 2004

Market shares are shown based on supermarket, drug store and mass merchandiser sales for the year ended February 29, 2004. Figures exclude Wal-Mart.

Kellogg's PopTart	. . . . .69.16%
Quaker Fruit & Oatmeal Toastables	. . . . . 5.29
Private label	. . . . .12.17
Other	. . . . .13.38

Source: *Snack Food & Wholesale Bakery*, May 2004, pp. SI-23, from Information Resources Inc.

★ 459 ★
Bread
SIC: 2051; NAICS: 311812
Bread Market in Hong Kong, 2003

According to the source, Hong Kong represents the second largest per capita consumption rate for bread in Asia at 8 kg (Singapore is number one).

Garden Co Ltd.	. . . . .64.0%
Other	. . . . .36.0

Source: *just-food.com*, December 21, 2004, p. NA, from Euromonitor.

★ 460 ★
Bread
SIC: 2051; NAICS: 311812

Bread Sales by Type, 2004

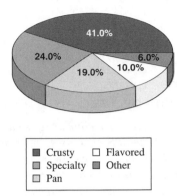

Fresh bread sales registered an average of $1,077 per week per store in 2004. In the specialty category, rye led with 25% of sales followed by sourdough with 23%.

Crusty	.41.0%
Specialty	.24.0
Pan	.19.0
Flavored	.10.0
Other	6.0

Source: *InStore Buyer*, February/March 2005, p. 66, from ACNielsen and Perishables Group.

★ 461 ★
Bread
SIC: 2051; NAICS: 311812

Top Bread Makers, 2004

The bread industry has been trying to reinvent itself in the face of Atkins and similar diets that discourage carbohydrates. Bread makers have started to push whole grain, low-carb and variety forms. Sales of white bread and private labels are expected to fair poorly (they are also the least profitable segments of the bread industry). Market shares are shown based on supermarket sales for the year ended July 18, 2004.

Interstate Bakeries	.13.9%
George Weston	.10.7
Sara Lee	.10.4
Bimbo Bakeries USA	7.1
Flowers Bakeries	5.5
Pepperidge Farm	5.3
Quality Bakers	1.9
Perfection Bakers	1.2

Lewis Bakeries	1.2%
Other	.42.8

Source: *Food Processing*, October 2004, p. 37, from Information Resources Inc.

★ 462 ★
Bread
SIC: 2051; NAICS: 311812

Top Fresh Bread Brands, 2004

Market shares are shown based on supermarket and drug store sales but exclude sales at supercenters.

Wonder	5.3%
Oroweat	4.5
Nature's Own	3.8
Arnold	3.3
Home Pride	2.8
Sunbeam	2.6
Sara Lee	2.1
Pepperidge Farm	1.6
Merita	1.5
Private label	.25.2
Other	.47.3

Source: *Snack Food & Wholesale Bakery*, August 2004, p. 14, from Information Resources Inc.

★ 463 ★
Bread
SIC: 2051; NAICS: 311812

Top Fresh Bread/Roll/Biscuit Brands, 2004

Brands are ranked by sales for the 52 weeks ended July 11, 2004.

	($ mil.)	Share
Pillsbury Home Baked Classics	$ 90.08	20.54%
New York	83.73	19.09
Pepperidge Farm	74.13	16.90
Coles	48.76	11.12
Sister Schuberts	21.63	4.93
Pillsbury	18.63	4.25
Mama Bella	17.65	4.02
Joseph Campione	7.51	1.71
Food for Life	3.69	0.84
Private label	47.06	10.73
Other	25.74	5.87

Source: *Frozen Food Age*, September 2004, p. 30, from Information Resources Inc.

★ 464 ★
Bread
SIC: 2051; NAICS: 311812

Top Frozen Bagel Brands, 2004

Brands are ranked by supermarket sales in millions of dollars for the year ended June 14, 2004.

	($ mil.)	Share
Lender's	$ 32.38	47.74%
Lender's Big 'n Crusty	16.48	24.30
Ray's Bagels	2.92	4.30
Bagels Forever	2.08	3.07
Sara Lee	0.72	1.06
Ray's New York Bagels	0.25	0.37
Other	13.00	19.17

Source: *Frozen Food Age*, August 2004, p. 53, from Information Resources Inc.

★ 465 ★
Bread
SIC: 2051; NAICS: 311812

Top Tortilla/Pocket/Pita Brands, 2004

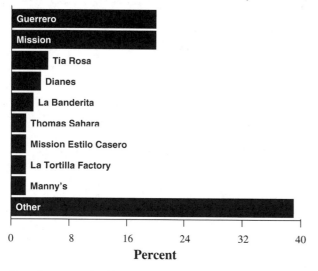

Brands are ranked by food store sales (not supercenters) in millions of dollars for the year ended May 23, 2004.

	($ mil.)	Share
Guerrero	$ 138.40	20.18%
Mission	135.68	19.78
Tia Rosa	33.93	4.95
Dianes	24.62	3.59
La Banderita	22.23	3.24
Thomas Sahara	16.72	2.44
Mission Estilo Casero	16.14	2.35
La Tortilla Factory	15.91	2.32

	($ mil.)	Share
Manny's	$ 13.65	1.99%
Other	268.64	39.16

Source: *Baking & Snack*, August 2004, p. 46, from Information Resources Inc.

★ 466 ★
Cookies
SIC: 2052; NAICS: 311821

Cookie Sales by Year

The market is expected to decline as consumers become increasingly health concious. Demographics are also influencing the industry, as fewer households have young children. As a result, manufacturers are marketing to adults with such things as ''premium'' cookies. Sales are shown in millions of dollars.

2002	$ 5,226
2003	4,988
2004	4,694
2005	4,543
2006	4,394
2007	4,248
2008	4,105

Source: *Prepared Foods*, January 2005, p. 29, from Mintel and Information Resources Inc.

★ 467 ★
Cookies
SIC: 2052; NAICS: 311821

Top Biscuit Brands in the U.K., 2004

Brands are ranked by sales in thousands of pounds sterling for the year ended October 2, 2004.

	(000)	Share
Kit Kat (two-finger variant)	£ 82,184	4.88%
McVitie's Chocolate Digestives	64,410	3.82
Quaker Snack-a-Jacks	43,421	2.58
McVitie's Jaffa Cakes	43,160	2.56
Kellogg's Nutri-Grain	36,309	2.16
Twix	31,932	1.90
Penguin	30,471	1.81
McVitie's Digestives	28,537	1.69
Rocky	27,417	1.63
Other	1,296,954	76.98

Source: *Grocer*, December 11, 2004, p. 53, from ACNielsen.

★ 468 ★
Cookies
SIC: 2052; NAICS: 311821

Top Cookie Brands, 2005

Market shares are shown based on sales at food stores, drug stores and mass merchandisers (but not Wal-Mart) for the 52 weeks ended January 23, 2005.

Nabisco Oreo	5.2%
Nabisco Chips Ahoy Original!	3.4
Nabisco Oreo Double Stuff	2.9
Pepperidge Farm Distinctive Milano	2.2
Nabisco Chips Ahoy Chewy	2.1
Little Debbie Nutty Bar	1.8
Little Debbie Oatmeal Cream Pies	1.8
Nabisco Nilla	1.7
Nabisco Fig Newton	1.4
Nabisco Chips Ahoy Chunky	1.2
Other	76.3

Source: *Grocery Headquarters*, April 2005, p. 22, from Information Resources Inc.

★ 469 ★
Cookies
SIC: 2052; NAICS: 311821

Top Cookie Makers, 2005

Market shares are shown based on sales at food stores, drug stores and mass merchandisers (but not Wal-Mart) for the 52 weeks ended January 23, 2005.

Nabisco	37.2%
Keebler	11.3
Pepperidge Farm	7.7
Little Debbie	5.8
Murray Biscuit Co.	4.7
Archway	3.1
Mother's/Bakery Wagon	2.5
Voortman	1.6
Masterfoods USA/Mars	1.0
Frito-Lay	1.0
Stella D'Oro	1.0
Other	23.1

Source: *Grocery Headquarters*, April 2005, p. 22, from Information Resources Inc.

★ 470 ★
Crackers
SIC: 2052; NAICS: 311821

Cracker Sales, 2003

Supermarket sales are shown in millions of dollars.

Flavored snack	$ 903.50
Cheese	570.43
Flaked soda	405.32
Sprayed butter	339.07
Graham	258.48
Wafers/toast/breadsticks	133.36
Sprayed flake	115.85
Matzo	26.49

Source: *Progressive Grocer*, Sept. 15, 2004, p. 26, from *2004 Progressive Grocer Consumer Expenditure Survey*.

★ 471 ★
Crackers
SIC: 2052; NAICS: 311821

Top Cracker Brands, 2004

Market shares are shown based on supermarket, drug store and mass merchandiser sales (but not Wal-Mart) for the 52 weeks ended October 3, 2004.

Nabisco Ritz Everyday	7.3%
Pepperidge Farm Goldfish	5.3
Nabisco Premium	5.0
Sunshine Cheez-It	4.4
Nabisco Wheat Thins	4.0
Nabisco Triscuit	3.4
Nabisco Honey Maid Grahams	3.0
Nabisco Wheat Thins Reduced Fat	2.8
Nabisco Ritz Chips	2.4
Keebler Club Everyday	2.4

Source: *Snack Food & Wholesale Bakery*, December 2004, p. NA, from Information Resources Inc.

★ 472 ★
Crackers
SIC: 2052; NAICS: 311821

Top Cracker Makers, 2005

Market shares are shown based on sales at food stores, drug stores and mass merchandisers (but not Wal-Mart) for the 52 weeks ended January 23, 2005.

Nabisco	47.3%
Keebler	13.3
Sunshine	10.9
Pepperidge Farm	8.7

Continued on next page.

[Continued]
Crackers

SIC: 2052; NAICS: 311821

Top Cracker Makers, 2005

Market shares are shown based on sales at food stores, drug stores and mass merchandisers (but not Wal-Mart) for the 52 weeks ended January 23, 2005.

Private label	6.7%
Other	13.1

Source: *Grocery Headquarters*, April 2005, p. 22, from Information Resources Inc.

★ 473 ★

Frozen Bakery Products

SIC: 2053; NAICS: 311813

Top Bread/Roll/Pastry Dough Brands, 2004

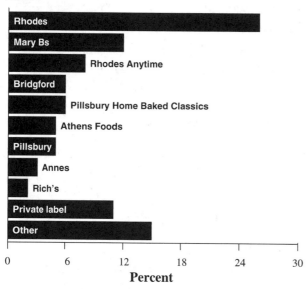

Brands are ranked by supermarket sales for the year ended July 11, 2004.

	($ mil.)	Share
Rhodes	$ 32.96	25.94%
Mary Bs	15.02	11.82
Rhodes Anytime	10.52	8.28
Bridgford	8.08	6.36
Pillsbury Home Baked Classics	7.61	5.99
Athens Foods	6.88	5.42
Pillsbury	5.83	4.59
Annes	3.23	2.54
Rich's	2.84	2.24
Private label	14.46	11.38
Other	19.62	15.44

Source: *Frozen Food Age*, September 2004, p. 30, from Information Resources Inc.

★ 474 ★

Frozen Bakery Products

SIC: 2053; NAICS: 311813

Top Frozen Pie Brands (Unit Sales), 2004

Brands are ranked by supermarket sales for the year ended August 8, 2004.

	(mil.)	Share
Mrs. Smith's	25.20	29.52%
Sara Lee	14.90	17.46
Edwards	14.50	16.99
Marie Callender's	9.60	11.25
Sara Lee Oven Fresh	3.50	4.10
Pet Ritz	2.90	3.40
Sara Lee Signature Selections	2.20	2.58
Mr. Smith's Special Recipe	2.00	2.34
Mountain Top	1.30	1.52
Edwards Sundae Singles	1.30	1.52
Private label	1.90	2.23
Other	6.06	7.10

Source: *Progressive Grocer*, October 1, 2004, p. 58, from Information Resources Inc.

★ 475 ★

Sugar

SIC: 2061; NAICS: 311311

Largest Sugar Consumers Worldwide, 2005-2006

Consumption is shown in thousands of metric tons.

	(000)	Share
India	19,300	13.52%
China	12,000	8.41
South America	10,850	7.60
United States	9,176	6.43
Russian Federation	6,000	4.20
Mexico	5,574	3.91
Other	79,811	55.92

Source: *Sugar: World Markets and Trade*, May 2005, p. 1.

★ 476 ★

Sugar Substitutes

SIC: 2062; NAICS: 311312

Artificial Sweetner Sales, 2003

Sales are estimated at $1 billion.

Aspartame	55.0%
Sucralose	13.0
Acesulfame K	12.0

Continued on next page.

★ 476 ★

[Continued]
Sugar Substitutes
SIC: 2062; NAICS: 311312

Artificial Sweetner Sales, 2003

Sales are estimated at $1 billion.

Cyclamate	.11.0%
Saccharin	8.0
Stevia	1.0

Source: *Forbes*, January 31, 2005, p. 100, from Tate & Lyle estimates.

★ 477 ★

Sugar Substitutes
SIC: 2062; NAICS: 311312

Leading Tabletop Sweeteners, 2004

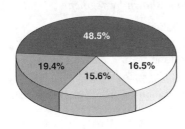

The table compares market shares for the year ended October 31, 2004 and for the previous year.

	2003	2004
Splenda	37.3%	48.5%
Equal	23.7	19.4
Sweet 'N Low	17.8	15.6
Other	21.2	16.5

Source: *New York Times*, December 22, 2004, p. C10, from Information Resources Inc.

★ 478 ★

Breath Fresheners
SIC: 2064; NAICS: 31134

Top Breath Freshener Brands, 2005

Brands are ranked by sales at supermarkets, drug stores and discount stores (excluding Wal-Mart) for the 52 weeks ended January 23, 2005.

	($ mil.)	Share
Binaca	$ 3.9	27.66%
Mint Asure	2.7	19.15
Sweet Breath	2.6	18.44

	($ mil.)	Share
Dentek Breath Remedy	$ 1.2	8.51%
Other	3.7	26.24

Source: *MMR*, March 7, 2005, p. 34, from Information Resources Inc.

★ 479 ★

Breath Fresheners
SIC: 2064; NAICS: 31134

Top Breath Freshener Makers, 2004

Market shares are shown based on sales of $223.8 million for the year ended July 11, 2004. Figures are shown based on sales of grocery, drug and mass merchandiser sales but exclude Wal-Mart.

Kraft/Callard & Bowser-Suchard	.29.7%
Ferrero USA Inc.	.27.0
Hershey Foods Corp.	.21.9
Cadbury Adams	7.8
Wm. Wrigley Jr. Co.	3.4
Chupa Chupa USA	2.0
Perfetti Van Melle	1.4
Private label	2.4
Other	4.4

Source: *The Manufacturing Confectioner*, September 2004, p. 45, from Information Resources Inc.

★ 480 ★

Confectionery Products
SIC: 2064; NAICS: 31134

Confectionery Industry

Snack bars had sales of $963.1 million and candy and individual snack sales were $4.8 billion.

Candy	.77.0%
Energy bars	.15.0
Snacks	8.0

Source: *Candy Industry*, December 2004, p. 42, from Information Resources Inc.

★ 481 ★
Confectionery Products
SIC: 2064; NAICS: 31134

Confectionery Industry Worldwide, 2003 and 2008

The total confectionery market is forecasted to increase from $112.5 billion in $122.4 billion in 2008.

	2003	2008	Share
Chocolate	$ 59.6	$ 64.3	52.53%
Sugar	38.9	41.9	34.23
Gum	14.0	16.2	13.24

Source: *Candy Industry*, July 2004, p. 42, from Euromonitor.

★ 482 ★
Confectionery Products
SIC: 2064; NAICS: 31134

Confectionery Market in France, 2003

Consumption is shown by segment.

Biscuits and baked goods	.53.0%
Chocolate	.27.0
Sugar confectionery	.21.0

Source: *The Manufacturing Confectioner*, January 2005, p. 21, from International Confectionery Association and Caobisco.

★ 483 ★
Confectionery Products
SIC: 2064; NAICS: 31134

Confectionery Market in Germany, 2003

Consumption is shown by segment.

Chocolate	.37.0%
Biscuits and baked goods	.36.0
Sugar confectionery	.27.0

Source: *The Manufacturing Confectioner*, January 2005, p. 21, from International Confectionery Association and Caobisco.

★ 484 ★
Confectionery Products
SIC: 2064; NAICS: 31134

Confectionery Market in Italy, 2003

Consumption is shown by segment.

Biscuits and baked goods	.61.0%
Chocolate	.24.0
Sugar confectionery	.15.0

Source: *The Manufacturing Confectioner*, January 2005, p. 21, from International Confectionery Association and Caobisco.

★ 485 ★
Confectionery Products
SIC: 2064; NAICS: 31134

Confectionery Market in Japan, 2003

Consumption is shown by segment.

Biscuits and baked goods	.35.0%
Chocolate	.34.0
Sugar confectionery	.32.0

Source: *The Manufacturing Confectioner*, January 2005, p. 21, from International Confectionery Association and Caobisco.

★ 486 ★
Confectionery Products
SIC: 2064; NAICS: 31134

Confectionery Market in the U.K., 2003

Consumption is shown by segment.

Biscuits and baked goods	.44.0%
Chocolate	.34.0
Sugar confectionery	.22.0

Source: *The Manufacturing Confectioner*, January 2005, p. 21, from International Confectionery Association and Caobisco.

★ 487 ★
Confectionery Products
SIC: 2064; NAICS: 31134

Confectionery Market Worldwide, 2004

Sales are shown in millions of dollars. Western Europe took 38.7% of the market for 2004, North America took 24% and Asia Pacific took 15.1%.

	2002	2003	2004
Western Europe	$ 33,539	$ 40,006	$ 46,064
North America	26,741	27,927	28,624
Asia Pacific	15,219	16,583	17,975
Latin America	8,373	8,689	9,697
Eastern Europe	8,110	9,009	9,802
Africa and Middle East . .	3,117	3,608	3,928
Australasia	1,682	2,169	2,735

Source: *The Manufacturing Confectioner*, March 2005, p. 27, from National Confectioners Association.

★ 488 ★
Confectionery Products
SIC: 2064; NAICS: 31134

Confectionery Sales, 2004

Sales are shown for food stores, drug stores and mass merchandisers (excluding Wal-Mart) for the 52 weeks ended December 26, 2004. Total sales were $10,407.4 million.

	($ mil.)	Share
Chocolate candy (boxes and bags greater than 3.5 oz)	$1,493.5	14.35%
Seasonal chocolate	1,099.8	10.57
Granola bars and other snack bars	1,059.3	10.18
Chocolate candy (less than 3.5 oz)	788.8	7.58
Sugarless gum	710.1	6.82
Non-chocolate chewy candy	700.0	6.73
Nutrition/health bars	656.3	6.31
Chocolate candy (snack size)	576.1	5.54
Other	3,323.5	31.93

Source: *Candy Industry*, March 2005, p. 42, from Information Resources Inc.

★ 489 ★
Confectionery Products
SIC: 2064; NAICS: 31134

Iced Confectionery Market in South Korea, 2003

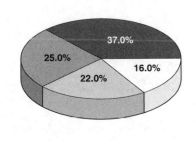

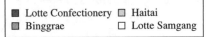

Market shares are shown in percent.

Lotte Confectionery	37.0%
Binggrae	25.0
Haitai	22.0
Lotte Samgang	16.0

Source: *Asia Africa Intelligence Wire*, January 25, 2005, p. NA.

★ 490 ★
Confectionery Products
SIC: 2064; NAICS: 31134

Largest Confectionery Firms Worldwide

Companies are ranked by net sales in millions of dollars.

Mars Inc.	$9,100
Nestle SA	8,195
Cadbury Schweppes	6,981
Ferrero Group	5,690
Hershey Foods Corp.	4,425
Wm. Wrigley Jr. Co.	4,170
Kraft Foods	2,911
Perfetti Van Melfe	1,859
Meiji Seiko Kaisha	1,746
Chocoladefabriken Lindt	1,450
Esaki Glico Co.	1,292
Haribo GmbH & Co.	1,225

Source: *Candy Industry*, January 2005, p. 42.

★ 491 ★
Confectionery Products
SIC: 2064; NAICS: 31134

Largest Confectionery Markets Worldwide, 2003

The overall market is not expected to see much growth with a compound annual growth rate of 1.7 percent through 2008. Total confectionery sales were $112.5 billion. Some impressive growth rates from 2002-2003: Brazil 17%, Indonesia 8.9% and Turkey 6.4%. Sales are shown in billions of dollars.

	($ bil.)	Share
United States	$26.0	23.1%
Germany	9.6	8.5
United Kingdom	8.7	7.7
Japan	8.0	7.1
Russia	5.2	4.6
France	4.8	4.3
Italy	4.3	3.8
China	4.3	3.9
Brazil	3.3	3.0
Mexico	2.8	2.5

Source: *Candy Industry*, July 2004, p. 42, from Euromonitor.

★ 492 ★

Confectionery Products

SIC: 2064; NAICS: 31134

Leading Confectionery Makers Worldwide

In 2003, $111 billion was spent on confectionery products, an increase of 10% over 2002. Between 1999 and 2003, gum was the fastest growing sector, increasing 13% in volume and 17% in value. Market shares are shown in percent.

Mars	.10.0%
Nestle	8.0
Hershey	6.0
Cadbury Schweppes	6.0
Kraft Foods	5.0
Wrigleys	4.0
Pfizer	4.0
Ferrero	4.0
Storck	2.0
Perfetti Van Melle	2.0
Other	.50.0

Source: *Brand Strategy*, July-August 2004, p. 44, from Euromonitor.

★ 493 ★

Confectionery Products

SIC: 2064; NAICS: 31134

Leading Fruit Snack Brands, 2004

Market shares are shown based on sales of $528.9 million at grocery stores, drug stores and mass merchandisers (excluding Wal-Mart) for the year ended July 11, 2004.

Fruit Gushers	.13.7%
Fruit by the Foot	.13.0
Fruit Roll Ups	.11.5
Scooby Doo	4.3
Kelloggs Fruit Twistables	2.6
Sunkist	2.5
Nabisco Jello Pudding Bites	1.9
Sesame Street Elmo	1.7
Dragon Tales	1.6
Private label	9.4
Other	.37.8

Source: *The Manufacturing Confectioner*, September 2004, p. 39, from Information Resources Inc.

★ 494 ★

Confectionery Products

SIC: 2064; NAICS: 31134

Leading Fruit Snack Makers, 2004

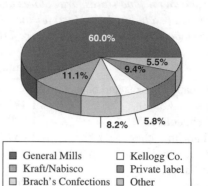

Market shares are shown based on sales of $528.9 million at grocery stores, drug stores and mass merchandisers (excluding Wal-Mart) for the year ended July 11, 2004.

General Mills	.60.0%
Kraft/Nabisco	.11.1
Brach's Confections	8.2
Kellogg Co.	5.8
Private label	9.4
Other	5.5

Source: *The Manufacturing Confectioner*, September 2004, p. 39, from Information Resources Inc.

★ 495 ★

Confectionery Products

SIC: 2064; NAICS: 31134

Leading Hard Sugar Candy Makers, 2004

Market shares are shown based on sales of $294 million at grocery stores, drug stores and mass merchandisers (excluding Wal-Mart) for the year ended July 11, 2004.

Kraft/Nabisco	.24.2%
Hershey Foods Corp.	.13.9
Kraft/Callard & Bowser-Suchard	.12.4
Tootsie Roll Industries	9.7
Storck USA	8.0
Charms Inc.	6.6
Nestle USA Inc.	6.2
Spangler Candy Co.	3.2
Private label	4.2
Other	.11.6

Source: *The Manufacturing Confectioner*, September 2004, p. 39, from Information Resources Inc.

★ **496** ★
Confectionery Products
SIC: 2064; NAICS: 31134

Leading Kashi Suppliers in Japan

The pastries segment was the top sector of the kashi market followed by chocolates. Shares are shown based on sales in millions of yen for the top 50 companies.

	(mil.)	Share
Meiji Seika	¥ 2,582	16.50%
Lotte Shoji	1,700	10.87
Morinaga & Co.	1,494	9.55
Ezaki Glico	1,355	8.66
Calbee	930	5.94
Borbon	819	5.24
Fujiya	795	5.08
Kameda Seika	635	4.06
Kanebo Foods	565	3.61
Yamazaki Nabisco	331	2.12
Imuraya Seika	292	1.87
Koikeya G	237	1.51
Other	3,909	24.99

Source: *The Manufacturing Confectioner*, March 2005, p. 23, from All Nippon Kashi Association.

★ **497** ★
Confectionery Products
SIC: 2064; NAICS: 31134

Leading Licorice Boxed/Bagged > 3.5 oz Brands, 2004

Market shares are shown based on sales of $150.5 million at grocery stores, drug stores and mass merchandisers (excluding Wal-Mart) for the year ended July 11, 2004.

Y&S Twizzler	.60.9%
American Licorice	.21.3
Good & Plenty	7.9
Bassetts	1.8
Twizzler	1.7
Kenny's	1.3
Panda	0.8
Lucky Country	0.8
Other	3.5

Source: *The Manufacturing Confectioner*, September 2004, p. 39, from Information Resources Inc.

★ **498** ★
Confectionery Products
SIC: 2064; NAICS: 31134

Leading Licorice Boxed/Bagged > 3.5 oz Makers, 2004

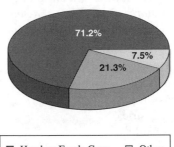

Legend: ■ Hershey Foods Corp. □ Other ■ American Licorice Co.

Market shares are shown based on sales of $150.5 million at grocery stores, drug stores and mass merchandisers (excluding Wal-Mart) for the year ended July 11, 2004.

Hershey Foods Corp.	.71.2%
American Licorice Co.	.21.3
Other	7.5

Source: *The Manufacturing Confectioner*, September 2004, p. 39, from Information Resources Inc.

★ **499** ★
Confectionery Products
SIC: 2064; NAICS: 31134

Leading Nonchocolate Chewy Candies, 2004

Market shares are shown based on sales of $647.4 million at grocery stores, drug stores and mass merchandisers (excluding Wal-Mart) for the year ended July 11, 2004.

Starburst	.13.4%
Skittles	8.2
Tootsie Roll	3.7
Life Savers Gummi Savers	3.5
Jelly Belly	3.3
Jaret Swedish Fish	2.4
Reese's Pieces	2.3
Air Heads	2.3
Private label	8.2
Other	.52.7

Source: *The Manufacturing Confectioner*, September 2004, p. 39, from Information Resources Inc.

★ 500 ★

Confectionery Products

SIC: 2064; NAICS: 31134

Leading Nonchocolate Chewy Candy Makers, 2004

Market shares are shown based on sales of $647.4 million at grocery stores, drug stores and mass merchandisers (excluding Wal-Mart) for the year ended July 11, 2004.

Masterfoods USA	22.4%
Kraft/Nabisco	10.4
Hershey Foods Corp.	7.0
Tootsie Roll Industries	5.9
Jaret International Inc.	4.9
Just Born Inc.	4.5
Farley's & Sathers Candy	4.4
Perfetti Van Melle	4.3
Private label	8.2
Other	28.0

Source: *The Manufacturing Confectioner*, September 2004, p. 39, from Information Resources Inc.

★ 501 ★

Confectionery Products

SIC: 2064; NAICS: 31134

Leading Novelty Nonchocolate Candies, 2004

Market shares are shown based on sales of $251.6 million at grocery stores, drug stores and mass merchandisers (excluding Wal-Mart) for the year ended July 11, 2004.

Sweetarts	7.5%
Tootsie Roll Childs Play	6.8
Wonka Nerds	6.2
Topps Baby Bottle Pop	5.9
Pez	3.8
Spree	3.4
Topps Ring Pop	3.3
Ce De Smarties	3.3
Private label	3.8
Other	56.3

Source: *The Manufacturing Confectioner*, September 2004, p. 39, from Information Resources Inc.

★ 502 ★

Confectionery Products

SIC: 2064; NAICS: 31134

Leading Novelty Nonchocolate Candy Makers, 2004

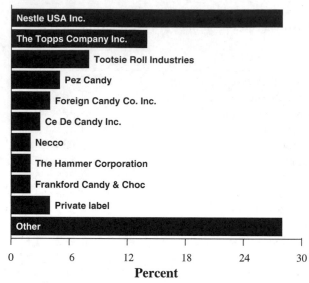

Market shares are shown based on sales of $251.6 million at grocery stores, drug stores and mass merchandisers (excluding Wal-Mart) for the year ended July 11, 2004.

Nestle USA Inc.	28.0%
The Topps Company Inc.	14.2
Tootsie Roll Industries	7.6
Pez Candy	4.5
Foreign Candy Co. Inc.	3.8
Ce De Candy Inc.	3.3
Necco	2.2
The Hammer Corporation	2.1
Frankford Candy & Choc	2.1
Private label	3.8
Other	28.4

Source: *The Manufacturing Confectioner*, September 2004, p. 39, from Information Resources Inc.

★ 503 ★
Confectionery Products
SIC: 2064; NAICS: 31134

Leading Specialty Nut/Coconut Candies, 2004

Market shares are shown based on sales of $73.9 million at grocery stores, drug stores and mass merchandisers (excluding Wal-Mart) for the year ended July 11, 2004.

Leaf Pay Day	27.3%
Brach's Maple Nut Goodies	6.7
Pearsons Salted Nut Roll	6.2
Sophie Mae	4.8
Brach's	2.9
Lance	2.6
Confetteria Raffaello	2.2
Planters	2.0
Annabelle Big Hunk	2.0
Private label	9.2
Other	34.1

Source: *The Manufacturing Confectioner*, September 2004, p. 39, from Information Resources Inc.

★ 504 ★
Confectionery Products
SIC: 2064; NAICS: 31134

Leading Specialty Nut/Coconut Candy Makers, 2004

Market shares are shown based on sales of $73.9 million at grocery stores, drug stores and mass merchandisers (excluding Wal-Mart) for the year ended July 11, 2004.

Hershey Foods Corp.	27.8%
Brach's Confections	9.6
Pearson Candy Co.	6.2
Sophie Mae Candy Corp.	4.8
Lance Inc.	2.6
Ferrero USA Inc.	2.2
Kraft/Nabisco	2.0
Annabelle Candy Co. Inc.	2.0
Private label	9.2
Other	33.6

Source: *The Manufacturing Confectioner*, September 2004, p. 39, from Information Resources Inc.

★ 505 ★
Confectionery Products
SIC: 2064; NAICS: 31134

Leading Sugarless Candy Brands, 2004

Market shares are shown based on sales of $248.7 million at grocery stores, drug stores and mass merchandisers (excluding Wal-Mart) for the year ended July 11, 2004.

Russell Stover	37.5%
Hershey's	8.0
Carborite	6.5
Carbolite	6.1
Reese's	3.9
Creme Savers	3.7
Sweet 'N Low	3.5
Whitman's Sampler	2.9
Pure Delite	2.0
Private label	3.6
Other	22.3

Source: *The Manufacturing Confectioner*, September 2004, p. 39, from Information Resources Inc.

★ 506 ★
Confectionery Products
SIC: 2064; NAICS: 31134

Leading Sugarless Candy Makers, 2004

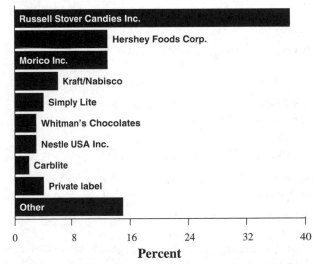

Market shares are shown based on sales of $248.7 million at grocery stores, drug stores and mass merchandisers (excluding Wal-Mart) for the year ended July 11, 2004.

Russell Stover Candies Inc.	37.5%
Hershey Foods Corp.	13.3

Continued on next page.

★ 506 ★

[Continued]
Confectionery Products
SIC: 2064; NAICS: 31134

Leading Sugarless Candy Makers, 2004

Market shares are shown based on sales of $248.7 million at grocery stores, drug stores and mass merchandisers (excluding Wal-Mart) for the year ended July 11, 2004.

Morico Inc.	13.0%
Kraft/Nabisco	5.7
Simply Lite	3.9
Whitman's Chocolates	2.9
Nestle USA Inc.	2.7
Carblite	2.0
Private label	3.6
Other	15.4

Source: *The Manufacturing Confectioner*, September 2004, p. 39, from Information Resources Inc.

★ 507 ★

Confectionery Products
SIC: 2064; NAICS: 31134

Organic Confectionery Industry

Sales in the organic candy and individual snack market grew to $19.9 million.

Candy	47.0%
Snacks	34.0
Energy bars	19.0

Source: *Candy Industry*, December 2004, p. 42, from SPINS.

★ 508 ★

Confectionery Products
SIC: 2064; NAICS: 31134

Seasonal Candy Sales, 2004

Holiday candy sales are expected to climb slightly to $6.3 billion.

Halloween	32.1%
Easter	28.2
Winter holidays	23.4
Valentine's Day	16.3

Source: *Convenience Store News*, August 2, 2004, p. 67, from Business Trend Analysts.

★ 509 ★

Confectionery Products
SIC: 2064; NAICS: 31134

Top Caramel/Taffy Apple/Kits/Dip Makers, 2004

Market shares are shown based on supermarket, drug store and discount store sales (excluding Wal-Mart) for the 52 weeks ended December 26, 2004.

T. Marzetti Co.	49.5%
Tastee Caramel Apple Co. Inc.	11.0
Concord Foods Inc.	8.6
Affy Tapple Inc.	8.2
Happy Apple Co.	5.1
Litehouse Inc.	3.1
Horton Fruit Co. Inc.	2.7
Other	11.8

Source: *The Manufacturing Confectioner*, April 2005, p. 41, from Information Resources Inc.

★ 510 ★

Confectionery Products
SIC: 2064; NAICS: 31134

Top Caramel/Taffy Apple/Kits/Dips, 2004

Market shares are shown based on supermarket, drug store and discount store sales (excluding Wal-Mart) for the 52 weeks ended December 26, 2004.

T. Marzetti	49.5%
Tastee	10.7
Concord	8.6
Affy Tapple	8.2
Happy Apples	5.1
Litehouse	3.1
Peak	2.6
Other	12.2

Source: *The Manufacturing Confectioner*, April 2005, p. 41, from Information Resources Inc.

★ 511 ★

Confectionery Products
SIC: 2064; NAICS: 31134

Top Diet Candy Vendors, 2004

Companies are ranked by sales at supermarkets, drug stores and mass merchandisers (excluding Wal-Mart) for the year ended May 16, 2004.

	($ mil.)	Share
Russell Stover Candies Inc.	$ 85.56	35.70%
Morico Inc.	34.85	14.54
Hershey Foods Corp.	31.40	13.10

Continued on next page.

★ 511 ★

[Continued]
Confectionery Products
SIC: 2064; NAICS: 31134

Top Diet Candy Vendors, 2004

Companies are ranked by sales at supermarkets, drug stores and mass merchandisers (excluding Wal-Mart) for the year ended May 16, 2004.

	($ mil.)	Share
Kraft/Nabisco	$ 12.51	5.22%
Simply Lite	9.67	4.04
Whitman's Chocolates	7.25	3.03
Nestle USA Inc.	5.84	2.44
Carbolite	5.46	2.28
William Wrigley	3.89	1.62
Other	43.21	18.03

Source: *Professional Candy Buyer*, July-August 2004, p. 36, from Information Resources Inc.

★ 512 ★

Confectionery Products
SIC: 2064; NAICS: 31134

Top Halloween Candy Makers (Non-Chocolate), 2004

Companies are ranked by supermarket, drug store and mass merchandiser sales (excluding Wal-Mart) for the 52 weeks ended November 28, 2004.

Brach's Confections Inc.	41.0%
Nestle USA Inc.	9.3
Just Born Inc.	6.2
Tootsie Roll Industries	5.9
Kraft/Nabisco	4.0
Farley's & Sathers Candy Co.	3.5
Zachary Confections Ijnc.	3.4
Pez Candy	1.7
Tzetzo Bros.	1.4
Hershey Foods	1.4
Ce De Candy Inc.	1.4
Other	20.8

Source: *Professional Candy Buyer*, January - February 2005, p. 14, from Information Resources Inc.

★ 513 ★

Confectionery Products
SIC: 2064; NAICS: 31134

Top Hard Sugar Candies, 2004

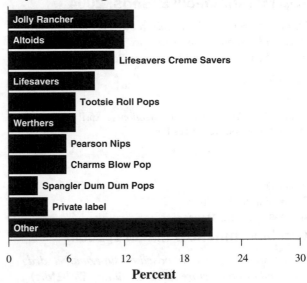

Percent

Market shares are ranked by supermarket, drug store and mass merchandiser sales (excluding Wal-Mart) for the year ended July 11, 2004.

Jolly Rancher	13.1%
Altoids	12.4
Lifesavers Creme Savers	11.4
Lifesavers	8.5
Tootsie Roll Pops	7.4
Werthers	7.3
Pearson Nips	6.2
Charms Blow Pop	5.7
Spangler Dum Dum Pops	2.8
Private label	4.2
Other	21.0

Source: *Candy Industry*, September 2004, p. 34, from Information Resources Inc.

★ 514 ★

Confectionery Products
SIC: 2064; NAICS: 31134

Top Marshmallow Brands, 2004

Market shares are shown based on supermarket, drug store and discount store sales (excluding Wal-Mart) for the 52 weeks ended December 26, 2004.

Jet Puffed	47.2%
Jet Puffed Funmallows	3.7
Campfire	2.1
De La Rosa	1.0
Jet Puffed Holiday Mallows	0.5

Continued on next page.

[Continued]
Confectionery Products
SIC: 2064; NAICS: 31134

Top Marshmallow Brands, 2004

Market shares are shown based on supermarket, drug store and discount store sales (excluding Wal-Mart) for the 52 weeks ended December 26, 2004.

Fireside	0.4%
Other	45.1

Source: *The Manufacturing Confectioner*, April 2005, p. 41, from Information Resources Inc.

★ 515 ★
Confectionery Products
SIC: 2064; NAICS: 31134

Top Marshmallow Makers, 2004

Market shares are shown based on supermarket, drug store and discount store sales (excluding Wal-Mart) for the 52 weeks ended December 26, 2004.

Kraft/Nabisco	51.7%
Campfire Inc.	2.1
Mazapan De La Rosa S.A.	1.0
Private label	44.2

Source: *The Manufacturing Confectioner*, April 2005, p. 41, from Information Resources Inc.

★ 516 ★
Confectionery Products
SIC: 2064; NAICS: 31134

Top Non-Chocolate Candies

Brands are ranked by sales in millions of dollars. Figures are from the most recent reporting period.

	($ mil.)	Share
Sweetarts Novelty	$ 18.9	7.51%
Tootsie Roll Child's Play	17.0	6.76
Wonka Nerds	15.5	6.16
Topps Baby Bottle Pop	14.8	5.88
Pez Novelty	9.4	3.74
Spree Novelty	8.4	3.34
Topps Ring Pop	8.3	3.30
Ce De Smarties	8.3	3.30
Topps Push Pop	7.7	3.06
Other	143.3	56.96

Source: *Brand Packaging*, August 2004, p. 48.

★ 517 ★
Confectionery Products
SIC: 2064; NAICS: 31134

Top Non-Chocolate Brands in the U.K., 2003

Market shares are shown in percent.

Cadbury's Dairy Milk	30.9%
Galaxy	9.8
Cadbury's Fruit and Nut	9.4
Terry's Chocolate Orange	7.9
Milky Bar	7.6
Cadbury's Whole Nut	5.9
Cadbury's Dream	4.4
Lindt	3.8
Toblerone	3.7
Double Cream	2.9
Other	13.7

Source: *Marketing*, June 9, 2004, p. 40, from Euromonitor.

★ 518 ★
Confectionery Products
SIC: 2064; NAICS: 31134

Top Sugar Confectionery Brands in the U.K., 2004

Brands are ranked by sales in thousands of pounds for the 52 weeks ended October 2, 2004. Bassett's excludes Allsorts, Beyond and Jelly Bs.

	(mil.)	Share
Wrigley's Extra	£ 162,877	13.53%
Haribo Gums & Jellies	63,691	5.29
Rowntrees Fruit Pastilles & Gums	52,097	4.33
Maynards	44,539	3.70
Wrigley's Airwaves	42,957	3.57
Wrigley's Orbit	40,742	3.38
Bassett's	37,774	3.14
Starburst	36,585	3.04
Other	722,677	60.03

Source: *The Manufacturing Confectioner*, February 2005, p. 22, from ACNielsen and *The Grocer*.

★ 519 ★
Cough Drops
SIC: 2064; NAICS: 31134

Leading Cough Drop Brands, 2004

Percent

Market shares are shown based on sales of $361.9 million at grocery stores, drug stores and mass merchandisers (excluding Wal-Mart) for the year ended July 11, 2004.

Halls	.26.6%
Ricola	9.4
Cold Eeze	7.3
Halls Fruit Breezers	7.1
Ludens	6.2
Halls Defense	5.9
Cepacol	4.2
Chloraseptic	3.7
Halls Plus	2.8
Private label	.11.7
Other	.15.1

Source: *The Manufacturing Confectioner*, September 2004, p. 39, from Information Resources Inc.

★ 520 ★
Cough Drops
SIC: 2064; NAICS: 31134

Leading Cough Drop Makers, 2004

Market shares are shown based on sales of $361.9 million at grocery stores, drug stores and mass merchandisers (excluding Wal-Mart) for the year ended July 11, 2004.

Cadbury Adams	.42.4%
Ricola Inc.	.10.2
Quigley Corporation	7.3

Pfizer Inc.	6.2%
Wyeth Labs Inc.	5.8
Combe Inc.	4.2
Prestige Brands International	3.7
Heritage Products	3.4
Private label	.11.7
Other	5.1

Source: *The Manufacturing Confectioner*, September 2004, p. 39, from Information Resources Inc.

★ 521 ★
Snack Bars
SIC: 2064; NAICS: 31134

Leading Breakfast/Cereal/Snack Makers, 2004

Market shares are shown based on sales of $528.9 million at grocery stores, drug stores and mass merchandisers (excluding Wal-Mart) for the year ended July 11, 2004.

Kellogg Co.	.43.1%
Quaker Oats Company	.19.4
General Mills	.15.6
Slim Fast Foods Co.	5.3
Atkins Nutritional	5.0
McKee Foods Corporation	2.1
Private label	4.8
Other	4.7

Source: *The Manufacturing Confectioner*, September 2004, p. 39, from Information Resources Inc.

★ 522 ★
Snack Bars
SIC: 2064; NAICS: 31134

Top Breakfast/Cereal/Snack Bar Makers, 2004

Market shares are shown based on supermarket sales of $513.2 million for the year ended December 26, 2004.

Kellogg Co.	.44.6%
Quaker Oats Co.	.18.1
General Mills	.13.7
Atkina Nutritionals	5.5
Slim Fast Foods	3.9
Kraft/Nabisco	3.1
McKee Foods Corp.	2.1
Bimbo Bakeries	1.3
Health Valley Natural	0.9

Continued on next page.

★ 522 ★

[Continued]
Snack Bars
SIC: 2064; NAICS: 31134

Top Breakfast/Cereal/Snack Bar Makers, 2004

Market shares are shown based on supermarket sales of $513.2 million for the year ended December 26, 2004.

Private label	4.7%
Other	2.1

Source: *Food Processing*, March 2005, p. 37, from Information Resources Inc.

★ 523 ★

Snack Bars
SIC: 2064; NAICS: 31134

Top Energy Bars, 2004

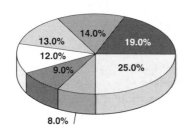

Legend:
- PowerBar
- Clif Bar
- Balance Bar
- Next Proteins
- MLO/GeniSoy
- Rexall Sundown
- Other

Market shares are shown based on revenues.

PowerBar	19.0%
Clif Bar	14.0
Balance Bar	13.0
Next Proteins	12.0
MLO/GeniSoy	9.0
Rexall Sundown	8.0
Other	25.0

Source: *USA TODAY*, March 14, 2005, p. 11B, from Frost & Sullivan.

★ 524 ★

Snack Bars
SIC: 2064; NAICS: 31134

Top Granola Bar Makers, 2004

Brands are ranked by supermarket, drug store and discount store sales (excluding Wal-Mart) for the 52 weeks ended October 3, 2004.

Quaker Oats Company	.34.3%
General Mills	.33.3
McKee Foods Corporation	8.7
Masterfoods USA	8.2
Kellogg Co.	4.5
Bestfoods	2.3
Health Valley Natural Foods	0.6
Small Planet Foods	0.2
Other	7.9

Source: *The Manufacturing Confectioner*, January 2005, p. 41, from Information Resources Inc.

★ 525 ★

Snack Bars
SIC: 2064; NAICS: 31134

Top Granola Bars, 2005

Brands are ranked by supermarket, drug store and discount store sales (excluding Wal-Mart) for the 52 weeks ended October 3, 2004.

Quaker Chewy	.23.2%
Nature Valley	.19.6
Sunbelt	8.7
Kudos	8.2
Nature Valley Chewy Trail Mix	7.0
Nature Valley Chewy Granola	6.8
Quaker Wholesome Favorites	4.5
Quaker Chewy Trail Mix	3.4
Nutri Grain Chewy Bars	2.4
Other	.16.2

Source: *The Manufacturing Confectioner*, January 2005, p. 41, from Information Resources Inc.

★ 526 ★

Snack Bars
SIC: 2064; NAICS: 31134

Top Nutritional Health Bars, 2004

Brands are ranked by supermarket, drug store and discount store sales (excluding Wal-Mart) for the 52 weeks ended October 3, 2004.

Atkins Advantage	.11.7%
Atkins Endulge	8.2
Zone Perfect	7.1
Slim Fast Meal on the Go	5.2

Continued on next page.

★ 526 ★

[Continued]
Snack Bars
SIC: 2064; NAICS: 31134

Top Nutritional Health Bars, 2004

Brands are ranked by supermarket, drug store and discount store sales (excluding Wal-Mart) for the 52 weeks ended October 3, 2004.

Clif Luna	5.2%
Balance Gold	4.8
Power Bar	4.1
Slim Fast Meal Options	3.5
Carb Solutions	3.5
EAS Advant Edge Carb Control	3.3
Other	43.4

Source: *The Manufacturing Confectioner*, January 2005, p. 41, from Information Resources Inc.

★ 527 ★

Snack Bars
SIC: 2064; NAICS: 31134

Top Nutritional Health Makers, 2004

Brands are ranked by supermarket, drug store and discount store sales (excluding Wal-Mart) for the 52 weeks ended October 3, 2004.

Atkins Nutritional	19.9%
Power Bar Inc.	12.4
Slim Fast Foods Co.	11.9
Clif Bar	8.9
Kraft Foods Inc.	8.2
Eicotech Corporation	7.1
Kellogg Co.	5.0
Exp. & Applied Sciences	4.3
Richardson Labs	3.5
Other	18.8

Source: *The Manufacturing Confectioner*, January 2005, p. 41, from Information Resources Inc.

★ 528 ★

Chocolate
SIC: 2066; NAICS: 31132, 31133

Leading Chocolate Boxed/Bagged < 3.5 oz Brands

Market shares are shown based on sales of $769.2 million at grocery stores, drug stores and mass merchandisers (excluding Wal-Mart) for the year ended July 11, 2004.

M&Ms	10.6%
Hershey's	10.3
Reese's	9.2
Snickers	8.7
Kit Kat	4.3%
Nestle Crunch	3.6
Twix	3.1
Nestle Butterfinger	3.0
Three Musketeers	2.9
York Peppermint Patty	2.7
Other	41.6

Source: *The Manufacturing Confectioner*, September 2004, p. 39, from Information Resources Inc.

★ 529 ★

Chocolate
SIC: 2066; NAICS: 31132, 31133

Leading Chocolate Boxed/Bagged < 3.5 oz Makers

Market shares are shown based on sales of $769.2 million at grocery stores, drug stores and mass merchandisers (excluding Wal-Mart) for the year ended July 11, 2004.

Hershey Foods Corp.	46.6%
Masterfoods USA	31.9
Nestle USA Inc.	13.3
Other	8.2

Source: *The Manufacturing Confectioner*, September 2004, p. 39, from Information Resources Inc.

★ 530 ★

Chocolate
SIC: 2066; NAICS: 31132, 31133

Leading Chocolate Boxed/Bagged > 3.5 oz Makers

Market shares are shown based on sales of $1.39 billion at grocery stores, drug stores and mass merchandisers (excluding Wal-Mart) for the year ended July 11, 2004.

Hershey Foods Corp.	46.2%
Masterfoods USA	26.1
Nestle USA Inc.	7.2
Ferrero USA Inc.	2.1
Lindt & Sprungli AG	1.9
Brach's Confections	1.5

Continued on next page.

★ 530 ★

[Continued]
Chocolate
SIC: 2066; NAICS: 31132, 31133

Leading Chocolate Boxed/Bagged > 3.5 oz Makers

Market shares are shown based on sales of $1.39 billion at grocery stores, drug stores and mass merchandisers (excluding Wal-Mart) for the year ended July 11, 2004.

Storck USA	1.3%
Private label	2.3
Other	11.4

Source: *The Manufacturing Confectioner*, September 2004, p. 39, from Information Resources Inc.

★ 531 ★

Chocolate
SIC: 2066; NAICS: 31132, 31133

Leading Chocolate Boxed/Bagged Brands > 3.5 oz

Market shares are shown based on sales of $1.39 billion at grocery stores, drug stores and mass merchandisers (excluding Wal-Mart) for the year ended July 11, 2004.

M&Ms	13.7%
Hershey's	11.7
Hershey's Kisses	7.6
Hershey's Nuggets	4.6
Reese's	4.1
Snickers	3.5
York Peppermint Patty	2.1
Nestle Treasures	2.0
Cadbury	2.0
Private label	2.3
Other	46.4

Source: *The Manufacturing Confectioner*, September 2004, p. 39, from Information Resources Inc.

★ 532 ★

Chocolate
SIC: 2066; NAICS: 31132, 31133

Leading Chocolate Candy Snack/Fun Size Brands, 2004

Market shares are shown based on sales of $603.7 million at grocery stores, drug stores and mass merchandisers (excluding Wal-Mart) for the year ended July 11, 2004.

Snickers	14.7%
Reese's	14.3

Kit Kat	9.8%
Milky Way	6.5
M&Ms	6.3
Nestle Butterfinger	5.8
Hershey's	5.7
Three Musketeers	4.9
Nestle Crunch	3.9
Peter Paul Almond Joy	3.6
Other	24.5

Source: *The Manufacturing Confectioner*, September 2004, p. 39, from Information Resources Inc.

★ 533 ★

Chocolate
SIC: 2066; NAICS: 31132, 31133

Leading Chocolate Candy Snack/Fun Size Makers, 2004

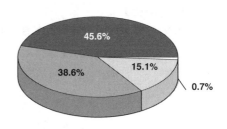

Market shares are shown based on sales of $603.7 million at grocery stores, drug stores and mass merchandisers (excluding Wal-Mart) for the year ended July 11, 2004.*

Hershey Foods Corp.	45.6%
Masterfoods USA	38.6
Nestle USA Inc.	15.1
Other	0.7

Source: *The Manufacturing Confectioner*, September 2004, p. 39, from Information Resources Inc.

★ 534 ★

Chocolate

SIC: 2066; NAICS: 31132, 31133

Leading Gift Box Chocolate Firms, 2004

Sales are shown for food stores, drug stores and mass merchandisers (excluding Wal-Mart) for the 52 weeks ended December 26, 2004.

	($ mil.)	Share
Russell Stover	$ 96.6	40.69%
Whitman's Sampler	43.2	18.20
Hershey's Pot of Gold	41.6	17.52
Queen Anne	15.4	6.49
Fannie May	12.8	5.39
Whitman's	5.4	2.27
Esther Price	3.6	1.52
Maxfields	3.0	1.26
Mrs. Fields	2.1	0.88
Nestle Turtles	1.7	0.72
Other	12.0	5.05

Source: *Candy Industry*, March 2005, p. 42, from Information Resources Inc.

★ 535 ★

Chocolate

SIC: 2066; NAICS: 31132, 31133

Leading Gift Box Chocolates (Unit Sales), 2004

Shares are shown based on food, drug store and mass merchandiser sales (excluding Wal-Mart) for the 52 weeks ended November 28, 2004.

Russell Stover	.35.8%
Whitman's Sampler	.18.3
Queen Anne	.16.7
Hershey's Pot of Gold	.16.0
Fannie May	1.9
Other	.11.3

Source: *Grocery Headquarters*, February 2005, p. 41, from Information Resources Inc.

★ 536 ★

Chocolate

SIC: 2066; NAICS: 31132, 31133

Retail Chocolate Market Worldwide, 2002-2004

Sales are shown in millions of dollars. Based on the top 52 countries the United States has 24.16% of market, 10.92% in Germany and 11.03% in United Kingdom.

	2002	2003	2004
United States	$ 13,840	$ 14,665	$ 14,974
United Kingdom	5,334	5,904	6,771
Germany	5,129	6,073	6,835
Russia	3,099	3,379	3,672
France	2,896	3,609	4,164
Japan	2,562	2,733	2,950
Italy	1,705	2,149	2,535
Canada	1,050	1,241	1,425
Australia	1,003	1,285	1,624
Switzerland	919	1,022	1,147

Source: *The Manufacturing Confectioner*, March 2005, p. 27, from National Confectioners Association.

★ 537 ★

Chocolate

SIC: 2066; NAICS: 31132, 31133

Top Chocolate Candy Snack Sizes (Unit Share), 2004

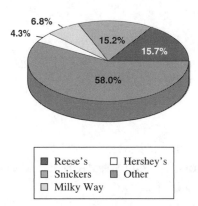

Shares are shown based on food, drug store and mass merchandiser sales (excluding Wal-Mart) for the 52 weeks ended November 28, 2004.

Reese's	.15.7%
Snickers	.15.2
Milky Way	6.8

Continued on next page.

★ 537 ★

[Continued]

Chocolate

SIC: 2066; NAICS: 31132, 31133

Top Chocolate Candy Snack Sizes (Unit Share), 2004

Shares are shown based on food, drug store and mass merchandiser sales (excluding Wal-Mart) for the 52 weeks ended November 28, 2004.

Hershey's	4.3%
Other	58.0

Source: *Grocery Headquarters*, February 2005, p. 41, from Information Resources Inc.

★ 538 ★

Chocolate

SIC: 2066; NAICS: 31132, 31133

Top Chocolate Christmas Candies, 2004

Market shares are shown based on supermarket, drug store and discount store sales (excluding Wal-Mart) for the 52 weeks ended December 26, 2004.

Hershey's Kisses	19.5%
M&M's	16.3
Reese's	9.5
Hershey's	6.5
Snickers	3.9
Palmer	2.9
York Peppermint Patty	2.8
Russell Stover	2.8
Dove	2.7
Other	33.1

Source: *The Manufacturing Confectioner*, April 2005, p. 41, from Information Resources Inc.

★ 539 ★

Chocolate

SIC: 2066; NAICS: 31132, 31133

Top Chocolate Confectionery Makers in China, 2001

Market shares are shown in percent.

Effem Foods	27.3%
Cadbury Foods	13.9
Nestle	7.7
Shenzhen La Conte	7.5
Ferrero	6.5
Hershey Foods	6.1
Shanghai Shenfeng	2.5
Chocoladefabriken Lindt	2.5

Source: *Candy Business*, July-August 2004, p. 26, from Euromonitor.

★ 540 ★

Chocolate

SIC: 2066; NAICS: 31132, 31133

Top Chocolate Easter Candies, 2004

Market shares are shown based on supermarket, drug store and discount store sales (excluding Wal-Mart) for the 52 weeks ended December 26, 2004.

Reese's	11.5%
M&M's	10.8
Hershey's	7.0
Russell Stover	6.7
Palmer	6.1
Hershey's Kisses	5.2
Cadbury Crème Egg	5.1
Leaf Robin Eggs	3.8
Other	43.8

Source: *The Manufacturing Confectioner*, April 2005, p. 41, from Information Resources Inc.

★ 541 ★

Chocolate

SIC: 2066; NAICS: 31132, 31133

Top Chocolate Firms, 2004

Market shares are shown based on supermarket, drug store and mass merchandiser sales (excluding Wal-Mart) for the year ended October 3, 2004.

Hershey's	47.1%
Masterfoods	31.7
Nestle	13.1
Ferrero	1.4
Russell Stover	0.8
Tootsie Roll	0.7
Ghirardelli	0.6
Lindt & Sprungli	0.4
Other	4.2

Source: *Candy Industry*, November 2004, p. 40, from Information Resources Inc.

★ 542 ★

Chocolate

SIC: 2066; NAICS: 31132, 31133

Top Chocolate Makers in Brazil

Market shares are shown in percent.

Kraft	33.1%
Nestle	28.4
Garoto	21.4
Other	17.1

Source: *South American Business Information*, November 17, 2004, p. NA, from ACNielsen.

★ 543 ★
Chocolate
SIC: 2066; NAICS: 31132, 31133
Top Chocolate Valentine's Day Candies, 2004

Market shares are shown based on supermarket, drug store and discount store sales (excluding Wal-Mart) for the 52 weeks ended December 26, 2004.

Russell Stover	17.6%
Hershey's Kisses	8.9
M&M's	7.1
Reese's	6.9
Dove	6.5
Elmers	5.5
Hershey's Pot of Gold	4.0
Hershey's	3.9
Palmer	3.3
Other	36.3

Source: *The Manufacturing Confectioner*, April 2005, p. 41, from Information Resources Inc.

★ 544 ★
Chocolate
SIC: 2066; NAICS: 31132, 31133
Top Easter Candy Brands, 2004

Brands are ranked by sales at food stores, drug stores and mass merchandisers (excluding Wal-Mart) for the year ended May 16, 2004. Data are for seasonally wrapped products only.

	($ mil.)	Share
Reese's	$ 49.17	4.78%
M&M's	46.28	4.50
Hershey's	30.21	2.94
Russell Stover	28.85	2.80
Palmer	26.13	2.54
Hershey's Kisses	22.71	2.21
Cadbury Creme Egg	22.00	2.14
Robin Eggs	16.45	1.60
Dove	14.81	1.44
Other	772.44	75.06

Source: *Professional Candy Buyer*, September-October 2004, p. 22, from Information Resources Inc.

★ 545 ★
Chocolate
SIC: 2066; NAICS: 31132, 31133
Top Luxury Chocolate Brands in the U.K., 2003

The average British consumer eats 8.5 kg each year, putting it above the consumption level for the United States and all of Europe. Total luxury chocolate sales were 599 million pounds.

Kraft Jacobs Suchard	17.1%
Thorntons	14.4
Nestle	10.9
Lindt	10.7
Bendicks	8.6
Ferrero Rocher	8.1
Green & Black's	3.9
Elizabeth Shaw	2.6
Masterfoods	1.3
Other	23.4

Source: *Marketing*, December 22, 2004, p. 26, from Mintel.

★ 546 ★
Cocoa
SIC: 2066; NAICS: 31132, 31133
Global Cocoa Production, 2002-2003

Roughly 70% of the world's cocoa is grown in West Africa. Data are in thousands of tons.

	(000)	Share
Ivory Coast	1,294	41.96%
Ghana	498	16.15
Indonesia	430	13.94
Other America	170	5.51
Brazil	163	5.29
Nigeria	160	5.19
Cameroon	155	5.03
Other Asia	61	1.98
Other Africa	35	1.13
Malaysia	33	1.07
Other	85	2.76

Source: *Candy Business*, May-June 2004, p. 13, from LMC International, International Cocoa Organization, and ED&F.

★ 547 ★

Gum

SIC: 2067; NAICS: 31134

Gum Market Worldwide, 2002-2004

The gum market sales by year: $12,572 million in 2002, $14,004 million in 2003 and $15,572 million in 2004. This total gives the United States a 19.54% of the market in 2004, followed by Japan with 11.8% .

	2002	2003	2004
United States	$ 2,903	$ 2,963	$ 3,037
Japan	1,325	1,599	1,841
Mexico	844	801	838
Gemany	535	634	726
United Kingdom	522	600	709
China	513	565	610
Brazil	501	535	677
Italy	456	592	736
France	410	550	680
Russia	407	428	447
Spain	238	308	371

Source: *The Manufacturing Confectioner*, March 2005, p. 27, from National Confectioners Association.

★ 548 ★

Gum

SIC: 2067; NAICS: 31134

Leading Gum Makers, 2004

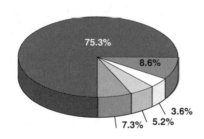

- ■ Wm. Wrigley Jr. Co. □ Farley's & Sathers Candy
- ▨ Cadbury Adams ■ Other
- ▨ Hershey Foods Corp.

Market shares are shown based on sales of $299.2 million at grocery stores, drug stores and mass merchandisers (excluding Wal-Mart) for the year ended July 11, 2004.

Wm. Wrigley Jr. Co.	.75.3%
Cadbury Adams	7.3
Hershey Foods Corp.	5.2

Farley's & Sathers Candy	3.6%
Other	8.6

Source: *The Manufacturing Confectioner*, September 2004, p. 39, from Information Resources Inc.

★ 549 ★

Gum

SIC: 2067; NAICS: 31134

Leading Regular Gum Brands, 2004

Market shares are shown based on sales of $299.2 million at grocery stores, drug stores and mass merchandisers (excluding Wal-Mart) for the year ended July 11, 2004.

Wrigley's Juicy Fruit	.15.0%
Wrigley's Winterfresh	.13.6
Wrigley's Double Mint	.12.6
Wrigley's Big Red	. 8.4
Wrigley's Spearmint	. 7.8
Freedent	. 7.1
Hubba Bubba Bubble Tape	. 6.9
Bubble Yum	. 5.1
Bubblicious	. 4.4
Other	.19.1

Source: *The Manufacturing Confectioner*, September 2004, p. 39, from Information Resources Inc.

★ 550 ★

Gum

SIC: 2067; NAICS: 31134

Leading Sugarless Gum Brands, 2004

Market shares are shown based on sales of $299.2 million at grocery stores, drug stores and mass merchandisers (excluding Wal-Mart) for the year ended July 11, 2004.

Wrigley's Extra	.23.9%
Orbit	.15.9
Wrigley's Eclipse	.15.5
Trident	.13.5
Dentyne Ice	.11.7
Ice Breakers	. 4.4
Carefree Koolerz	. 3.6
Ice Breakers Unleashed	. 1.8
Other	. 9.7

Source: *The Manufacturing Confectioner*, September 2004, p. 45, from Information Resources Inc.

★ 551 ★
Gum
SIC: 2067; NAICS: 31134

Leading Sugarless Gum Makers, 2004

Market shares are shown based on sales of $299.2 million at grocery stores, drug stores and mass merchandisers (excluding Wal-Mart) for the year ended July 11, 2004.

Wm. Wrigley Jr. Co. 55.5%
Cadbury Adams 29.9
Hershey Foods Corp. 12.0
Other 2.6

Source: *The Manufacturing Confectioner*, September 2004, p. 39, from Information Resources Inc.

★ 552 ★
Gum
SIC: 2067; NAICS: 31134

Sugarless Gum Market in Thailand

Lotte Xylitol has 91% of the decay-prevention gum market and 4% of the overall 1.64 billion baht industry.

Lotte Xylitol 91.0%
Other 9.0

Source: *Bangkok Post*, November 3, 2004, p. NA.

★ 553 ★
Gum
SIC: 2067; NAICS: 31134

Top Gum Brands, 2005

Market shares are shown based on drug store sales for the 52 weeks ended February 20, 2005.

Trident 13.5%
Wrigley's Orbit 12.8
Wrigley's Extra 11.9
Wrigley's Eclipse 10.8
Dentyne 9.6
Wrigley's Winterfresh 3.9
Wrigley's Double Mint 3.9
Wrigley's Juicy Fruit 3.8
Ice Breakers 3.3
Wrigley's Big Red 2.4
Other 24.1

Source: *Chain Drug Review*, May 23, 2005, p. 69, from Information Resources Inc.

★ 554 ★
Nuts
SIC: 2068; NAICS: 311911

Leading Sunflower/Pumpkin Seed Brands

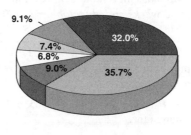

David ☐ Good Sense
Planters ■ Private label
Frito Lay ■ Other

Brands are ranked by sales in millions of dollars.

	($ mil.)	Share
David	$ 34.69	32.04%
Planters	9.83	9.08
Frito Lay	8.03	7.42
Good Sense	7.34	6.78
Private label	9.77	9.02
Other	38.60	35.65

Source: *National Petroleum News*, July 15, 2004, p. 93, from Snack Food Association and Information Resources Inc.

★ 555 ★
Nuts
SIC: 2068; NAICS: 311911

Packaged In-Shell Nut Market

Market shares are shown in percent.

Diamond 88.0%
Other 12.0

Source: *Packaging Digest*, June 2004, p. 40.

★ 556 ★
Nuts
SIC: 2068; NAICS: 311911
Snack Nut Sales, 2004

Market shares are shown based on sales at food stores, drug stores and mass merchandisers (excluding Wal-Mart) for the 52 weeks ended October 31, 2004.

	($ mil.)	Share
Snack nuts	$ 1,383.5	92.2%
Sunflower/pumpkin seeds	109.4	3.7
Toasted corn nut snacks	7.5	0.5

Source: *Grocery Headquarters*, January 2005, p. 71, from Information Resources Inc.

★ 557 ★
Nuts
SIC: 2068; NAICS: 311911
Top Snack Nut Brands, 2005

Market shares are shown based on drug store sales for the 52 weeks ended February 20, 2005.

Planters	29.6%
Blue Diamond	5.1
Mauna Loa	3.6
Sunkist	2.2
Terri Lynn	1.9
Frito-Lay	0.9
Other	56.7

Source: *Chain Drug Review*, May 23, 2005, p. 69, from Information Resources Inc.

★ 558 ★
Peanut Oil
SIC: 2076; NAICS: 311225
Peanut Oil Market

Market shares are shown in percent.

Ventura	70.0%
Other	30.0

Source: *San Diego Business Journal*, April 18, 2005, p. 26.

★ 559 ★
Olive Oil
SIC: 2079; NAICS: 311225
Olive Oil Sales, 2004

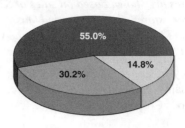

Sales are shown for the 52 weeks ended May 30, 2004.

Extra virgin	55.0%
Pure	30.2
Extra light	14.8

Source: ''North American Retail Olive Oil Market.'' from http://nacoo.mytradeassociation.org/bm~doc/chairman-repeat-for-2004.ppt [Published June 25, 2004], from Information Resources Inc.

★ 560 ★
Olive Oil
SIC: 2079; NAICS: 311225
Olive Oil Sales in Canada, 2004

Sales are shown in millions of Canadian dollars for the 52 weeks ended February 21, 2004.

2002	$ 61.9
2003	67.9
2004	77.5

Source: ''North American Retail Olive Oil Market.'' from http://nacoo.mytradeassociation.org/bm~doc/chairman-repeat-for-2004.ppt [Published June 25, 2004], from ACNielsen Market Track.

★ 561 ★
Olive Oil
SIC: 2079; NAICS: 311225
Retail Olive Oil Sales, 2000-2004

Retail sales are shown in millions to dollars. Data for 2004 are for the 52 weeks ended May 30, 2004.

2000	$ 370
2001	392

Continued on next page.

★ 561 ★
[Continued]
Olive Oil
SIC: 2079; NAICS: 311225

Retail Olive Oil Sales, 2000-2004

Retail sales are shown in millions to dollars. Data for 2004 are for the 52 weeks ended May 30, 2004.

2002	$ 414
2003	437
2004	443

Source: "North American Retail Olive Oil Market." from http://nacoo.mytradeassociation.org/bm~doc/chairman-re-peat-for-2004.ppt [Published June 25, 2004], from Information Resources Inc.

★ 562 ★
Beverages
SIC: 2080; NAICS: 31212, 31213, 31214

Alcoholic Beverage Market, 2004

Supermarket sales are shown for the year-to-date December 26, 2004.

Beer & ale	55.4%
Wine	29.5
Liquor	13.6
Pre-mixed cocktails	1.5

Source: "Supermarket Channel Overview." [online] from http://www.progressivegrocer.com [Published February 2005], from Information Resources Inc.

★ 563 ★
Beverages
SIC: 2080; NAICS: 311411, 31211, 312112

Beverage Market in Latin America, 2003

Market shares are shown in percent.

Carbonated soft drinks	10.7%
Bottled water	7.7
Milk	7.6
Coffee	7.5
Beer	5.5
Fruit beverages	2.4
Tea	1.3
Other	57.2

Source: *Beverage World*, May 15, 2005, p. 22, from Beverage Marketing Corp.

★ 564 ★
Beverages
SIC: 2080; NAICS: 311411, 312111, 312112

Beverage Market Segments, 2003

Retail sales are shown in billions of dollars.

	($ bil.)	Share
Beer	$ 58.97	27.0%
Soft drinks	55.97	25.7
Spirits	42.63	19.6
Wine	21.64	10.0
Fruit beverages	21.39	9.8
Bottled water	9.91	4.6
Sports drinks	4.08	1.9
RTD tea	2.97	1.4

Source: *Beverage Aisle*, July 15, 2004, p. 6, from Beverage Marketing Corp. and Adams Business Media.

★ 565 ★
Beverages
SIC: 2080; NAICS: 31192

Hot Drink Industry Worldwide, 2002

Total retail sales were $53.3 billion in 2002. From 1998 to 2002 the industry delined 3.4%. Green tea saw sales rise 21%, the biggest change in the sector.

	($ mil.)	Share
Coffee	$ 31,100.0	58.35%
Green tea	3.2	0.01
Other	22,196.8	41.65

Source: *PR Newswire*, October 1, 2004, p. NA.

★ 566 ★
Beverages
SIC: 2080; NAICS: 311411, 312111, 312112

Largest Beverage Firms in North America, 2003

Firms headquartered abroad are ranked by North America sales in millions of dollars.

Coca-Cola Company	$ 210,044.0
Coca-Cola Enterprises	17,330.0
Anheuser-Busch Inc.	14,146.7
Pepsi Bottling Group	10,265.0
PepsiCo. Inc.	9,962.2
FEMSA	6,755.0
Southern Wine & Spirits of America	4,400.0
Adolph Coors Co.	4,000.1
Grupo Modelo	3,561.7

Continued on next page.

★ 566 ★

[Continued]
Beverages
SIC: 2080; NAICS: 311411, 312111, 312112

Largest Beverage Firms in North America, 2003

Firms headquartered abroad are ranked by North America sales in millions of dollars.

Constellation Brands	$ 3,552.4
Miller Brewing Co.	3,473.0

Source: *Beverage Aisle*, August 15, 2004, p. 20.

★ 567 ★

Beverages
SIC: 2080; NAICS: 311411, 312111, 312112

Largest Beverage Firms Worldwide, 2003

Firms are ranked by sales in millions of dollars.

Coca-Cola Company	$ 21,044.0
Nestle	18,982.2
Coca-Cola Enterprises	17,330.0
Diageo	15,603.4
Anheuser-Busch	14,147.0
SABMiller	12,265.7
Heineken	11,621.5
Asahi	11,379.1
InBev	11,030.4
Pepsi Bottling Group	10,650.0
PepsiCo	9,890.5
Suntory	9,085.2

Source: *Beverage Industry*, October 15, 2004, p. 42.

★ 568 ★

Beverages
SIC: 2080; NAICS: 311411, 312111

Top Kid's Beverage Makers

Companies are ranked by sales in millions of dollars. Children's beverage generate $2.6 billion in sales and take 9% of the overall food and beverage market aimed at children. Aseptic juices and blends take 37% of kid's beverage sales, shelf-stable fruit juices take 24% of sales, packaged dry drink mixes took 11%.

	($ mil.)	Share
Kraft Foods Inc.	$ 779	29.96%
Nestle USA	570	21.92
Coca-Cola Co.	411	15.81

	($ mil.)	Share
Procter & Gamble	$ 247	9.50%
Cadbury Schweppes	212	8.15
Hershey Foods	47	1.81
Jel Sert	44	1.69
Other	290	11.15

Source: *Food Processing*, July 2004, p. 35, from Packaged Facts.

★ 569 ★

Beer
SIC: 2082; NAICS: 31212

Beer Industry in Thailand

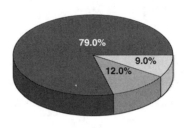

The industry is valued at 81 billion baht.

Low priced	79.0%
Standard	12.0
Premium	9.0

Source: *Bangkok Post*, November 29, 2004, p. NA.

★ 570 ★

Beer
SIC: 2082; NAICS: 31212

Beer Sales, 2001 and 2006

The light beer segment is expected to increase 6.9% in this period. Analysts expect light beer and imports to continue to drive growth in the beer industry. Figures for 2006 are forecasted.

	2001	2006
Light	43.0%	49.6%
Premium	22.7	17.8
Popular	13.2	8.8
Imports	11.0	14.8
Superpremium	4.3	4.1
Malt liquor	2.8	2.0
Other	2.9	2.9

Source: *Beverage Aisle*, May 15, 2004, p. 26, from Beverage Marketing Corp.

★ 571 ★
Beer
SIC: 2082; NAICS: 31212
Beer Sales by Packaging, 2003

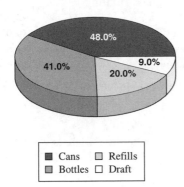

Market shares are shown in percent.

Cans	.48.0%
Bottles	.41.0
Refills	.20.0
Draft	.9.0

Source: *Restaurants & Institutions*, February 15, 2005, p. 31, from Beer Institute.

★ 572 ★
Beer
SIC: 2082; NAICS: 31212
Beer Sales Worldwide, 2003 and 2008

Sales increased from $376,637.7 million (148,359.7 million liters) in 2003 to $411,868 million in 2008 (169,976.9 million liters).

	2003	2008	Share
Standard lager . .	$ 203,392.9	$ 208,479.1	50.62%
Premium lager . .	89,806.0	111,815.6	27.15
Economy lager . .	47,013.9	53,850.7	13.07
Dark beer	23,180.1	23,436.8	5.69
Stout	8,167.6	8,295.3	2.01
Non-/low-alcohol . .	5,077.2	5,990.4	1.45

Source: *Beverage Industry*, May 2004, p. 20, from Euromonitor.

★ 573 ★
Beer
SIC: 2082; NAICS: 31212
Beer Sales Worldwide, 2004

The industry saw total sales of $412.6 billion with volume sales of 150,555 million liters. Top brewers worldwide are InBev, SABMiller and Anheuser-Busch.

	($ mil.)	Share
Western Europe	$ 134,247.0	32.54%
Asia Pacific	98,533.3	23.88
North America	86,392.1	20.94
Latin America	32,988.1	8.00
Eastern Europe	26,931.1	6.53
Africa and Middle East	21,861.1	5.30
Australasia	11,643.8	2.82

Source: *Beverage Industry*, May 2005, p. 18, from Euromonitor.

★ 574 ★
Beer
SIC: 2082; NAICS: 31212
Largest Beer Consumers in Eastern Europe

Consumption is estimated in millions of hectoliters.

	(mil.)	Share
Poland	29.50	44.68%
Czech Republic	16.30	24.69
Hungary	7.90	11.97
Slovakia	4.70	7.12
Lithuania	2.60	3.94
Slovenia	2.20	3.33
Latvia	1.50	2.27
Estonia	0.96	1.45
Cyprus	0.23	0.35
Malta	0.13	0.20

Source: *just-drinks.com (Management Briefing)*, November 2004, p. 4, from Canadean, Datamonitor, and Eurmonitor.

★ 575 ★
Beer
SIC: 2082; NAICS: 31212
Largest Beer Wholesalers, 2004

Companies are ranked by millions of cases distributed.

The Reyes Family	41.0
Ben E. Keith Beers	33.7
Silver Eagle Distributors	26.0

Continued on next page.

★ 575 ★

[Continued]

Beer

SIC: 2082; NAICS: 31212

Largest Beer Wholesalers, 2004

Companies are ranked by millions of cases distributed.

Manhattan Beer Distributors	25.6
Topa Equities	23.5
JJ Taylor Companies Inc.	23.0
The Sheehan Family	22.5
Hensley	22.4
Gold Coast Beverage Distributors	20.7
The Banko Family	20.0

Source: *Beverage World*, August 15, 2004, p. 32.

★ 576 ★

Beer

SIC: 2082; NAICS: 31212

Largest Microbreweries, 2004

Companies are ranked by number of barrels produced.

Clipper City Brewing Co.	13,200
Saint Louis Brewery Inc./Schlafy Bottleworks	13,172
Capital Brewery Co. Inc.	12,007
Karl Strauss Breweries	11,850
Wachusett Brewing Co.	10,848
Yakima Brewing	10,766
Berkshire Brewing Co. Inc.	10,661
Smuttynose Brewing Co.	10,654
Sprecher Brewing Co.	10,442
Stoudt's Brewing Co.	10,000
Harpoon Brewery - Vermont	10,000
Brooklyn Brewery	10,000

Source: *New Brewer*, May/June 2005, p. 54, from Brewers Association.

★ 577 ★

Beer

SIC: 2082; NAICS: 31212

Largest Specialty Brewers, 2004

Companies are ranked by number of barrels produced.

	Barrels	Share
Boston Beer Co.	1,267,000	18.93%
Sierra Nevada Brewing Co.	589,937	8.81
New Belgium Brewing Co.	331,000	4.95
F.X. Matt Brewing Co.	233,200	3.48
Redhook Ale Brewery	216,400	3.23

	Barrels	Share
Widmer Brothers Brewing Co.	199,000	2.97%
Pyramid Breweries	142,533	2.13
Deschutes Brewery	133,913	2.00
Alaskan Brewing and Bottling Co.	90,400	1.35
Boulevard Brewing Co.	89,083	1.33
Harpoon Brewery	86,681	1.30
Anchor Brewing Co.	83,599	1.25

Source: *New Brewer*, May/June 2005, p. 54, from Brewers Association.

★ 578 ★

Beer

SIC: 2082; NAICS: 31212

Leading Ales/Stout Brands in the U.K., 2003

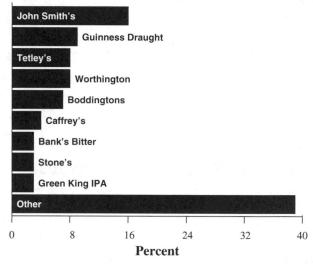

Ale is the second most common type of beer consumed in the country, with 24.8% of sales while stout follows with 5.2% (lager leads with 69.9%). Scottish & Newcastle is expected to take 36.1% of the industry in 2004, followed by Carlsberg-Tetley with 15.5%. Shares are shown based on on-trade sales in liters.

John Smith's	16.0%
Guinness Draught	9.4
Tetley's	8.0
Worthington	7.6
Boddingtons	7.3
Caffrey's	3.7
Bank's Bitter	3.2
Stone's	3.0
Green King IPA	2.7
Other	39.1

Source: *Marketing*, July 21, 2004, p. 36, from Mintel.

★ 579 ★

Beer

SIC: 2082; NAICS: 31212

Leading Beer Brands in Northeast China

Market shares are shown in percent.

Hapi/Snow 90.0%
Other 10.0

Source: *China Daily*, January 24, 2005, p. NA.

★ 580 ★

Beer

SIC: 2082; NAICS: 31212

Leading Beer Makers in Japan, 2003

Market shares are estimated based on domestic shipments.

Asahi Breweries 39.9%
Kirin Brewery 35.7
Sapporo Breweries 13.2
Suntory 10.4
Orion Breweries 0.8

Source: "Market Share Survey Report 2003." [online] from http://www.nni.nikkei.co.jp [Published July 26, 2004], from company reports.

★ 581 ★

Beer

SIC: 2082; NAICS: 31212

Leading Ice Brands, 2003

Consumption is shown in thousands of 2.25 gallon cases.

	(000)	Share
Natural Ice	2,431	36.81%
Icehouse	1,669	25.27
Milwaukee's Best Ice	1,016	15.38
Bud Ice	856	12.96
Keystone Ice	261	3.95
Bud Ice Light	123	1.86
Busch Ice	47	0.71
Schmidt Ice	44	0.67
Pabst Ice	33	0.50
Other	125	1.89

Source: *Beer Handbook*, Annual 2004, p. 36.

★ 582 ★

Beer

SIC: 2082; NAICS: 31212

Leading Light Beer Brands, 2003

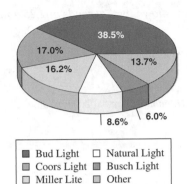

Total shipments were 97.4 million 2.25 gallon cases.

Bud Light 38.5%
Coors Light 17.0
Miller Lite 16.2
Natural Light 8.6
Busch Light 6.0
Other 13.7

Source: *Beer Handbook*, Annual 2004, p. 36.

★ 583 ★

Beer

SIC: 2082; NAICS: 31212

Leading Malt Liquor Brands, 2003

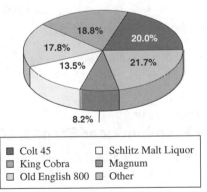

Shipments are shown by thousands of 2.25 gallon cases.

Colt 45 . . . . .20.0%
King Cobra 18.8
Old English 800 . . . . .17.8

Continued on next page.

★ 583 ★
[Continued]
Beer
SIC: 2082; NAICS: 31212
Leading Malt Liquor Brands, 2003

Shipments are shown by thousands of 2.25 gallon cases.

Schlitz Malt Liquor	.13.5%
Magnum	8.2
Other	.21.7

Source: *Beer Handbook*, Annual 2004, p. 36.

★ 584 ★
Beer
SIC: 2082; NAICS: 31212
Leading Non-Alcoholic Beer Brands, 2003

Total shipments were 17.75 million 2.25 gallon cases. The market has been on the decline since its high point of 24,500 cases in 1998.

	(000)	Share
O'Doul's	8,700	49.01%
Sharp's	1,800	10.14
Old Milwaukee	1,610	9.07
Busch	1,500	8.45
Malta Goya	770	4.34
Coors	560	3.15
Clausthaler	410	2.31
Haake Beck	375	2.11
St. Pauli Girl	360	2.03
Other	1,665	9.38

Source: *Beer Handbook*, Annual 2004, p. 36.

★ 585 ★
Beer
SIC: 2082; NAICS: 31212
Leading Premium Beer Brands, 2003

Total shipments were 1.3 billion 2.25 gallon cases.

Budweiser	.80.2%
Miller Genuine Draft	.11.8
Coors Original	4.3
Rolling Rock	2.4
Coors Extra Gold	0.3
Other	1.1

Source: *Beer Handbook*, Annual 2004, p. 36.

★ 586 ★
Beer
SIC: 2082; NAICS: 31212
Specialty Beer Sales by State, 2003

Consumption of super premium, micro/specialty and flavored malt beverages is shown by thousands of 2.25 gallon cases.

	(000)	Share
California	24,500	11.89%
Texas	14,710	7.14
New York	14,500	7.04
Florida	10,600	5.15
Illinois	8,000	3.88
Washington	6,600	3.20
Michigan	6,600	3.20
Massachusetts	6,500	3.16
New Jersey	5,780	2.81
Wisconsin	4,800	2.33
Other	103,410	50.20

Source: *Beer Handbook*, Annual 2004, p. 36.

★ 587 ★
Beer
SIC: 2082; NAICS: 31212
Top Beer Brands, 2004

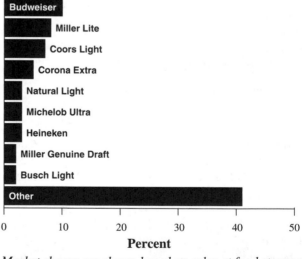

Market shares are shown based on sales at food stores, drug stores and mass merchandisers (excluding Wal-Mart) for the 52 weeks ended October 31, 2004.

Bud Light	.15.5%
Budweiser	.10.3
Miller Lite	8.0
Coors Light	6.7

Continued on next page.

★ 587 ★
[Continued]
Beer
SIC: 2082; NAICS: 31212
Top Beer Brands, 2004

Market shares are shown based on sales at food stores, drug stores and mass merchandisers (excluding Wal-Mart) for the 52 weeks ended October 31, 2004.

Corona Extra	4.8%
Natural Light	3.4
Michelob Ultra	3.2
Heineken	3.0
Miller Genuine Draft	2.3
Busch Light	2.3
Other	40.5

Source: *Grocery Headquarters*, January 2005, p. 71, from Information Resources Inc.

★ 588 ★
Beer
SIC: 2082; NAICS: 31212
Top Beer Brands (Gallons), 2004

The market was flat overall with only about 1% growth. Miller Lite saw strong growth (up 11.1%) building on a turnaround in 2003. Coors Light saw the biggest drop, down 13.6%. Market shares are shown based on a total of 199.4 million gallons.

Bud Light	20.1%
Budweiser	14.7
Miller Lite	8.9
Coors Light	7.2
Natural Light	4.2
Busch	3.7
Corona Extra	3.5
Busch Light Draft	2.7
Miller High Life	2.5
Heineken	2.3
Other	30.2

Source: *Beverage World*, April 15, 2005, p. 40, from Beverage Marketing Corp.

★ 589 ★
Beer
SIC: 2082; NAICS: 31212
Top Beer Brands (Imported), 2004

Shares are shown for the import market.

Corona Extra	29.4%
Heineken	19.5
Tecate	4.5
LaBatt Blue	4.4
Amstel Light	3.1%
Guinness	2.9
Corona Light	2.9
Beck's	2.8
Molson	2.5
Foster's	2.3
Other	25.7

Source: *Beverage World*, April 15, 2005, p. 40, from Beverage Marketing Corp.

★ 590 ★
Beer
SIC: 2082; NAICS: 31212
Top Beer Brands in Chile

At 21.9 litres per capita, beer consumption in the country is among the lowest in South America.

Heineken	38.0%
Royal	17.0
Austral	16.0
Budweiser	10.0
Kunstmann	4.5
Paulaner	3.0
Other	11.5

Source: *just-drinks.com*, November 10, 2004, p. NA.

★ 591 ★
Beer
SIC: 2082; NAICS: 31212
Top Beer Brands in China, 2003

Beer sales grew 1001.7% between 1996 and 2003, driven by overall investment in the market. Market shares are shown based on 34.3 billion liters.

Qingdao (Tsingtao)	12.8%
Yanjing	10.8
Blue Ribbon	6.4
Beck's	2.4
Heineken	2.1

Continued on next page.

★ 591 ★
[Continued]
Beer
SIC: 2082; NAICS: 31212
Top Beer Brands in China, 2003

Beer sales grew 1001.7% between 1996 and 2003, driven by overall investment in the market. Market shares are shown based on 34.3 billion liters.

Budweiser	2.1%
Reeb	1.8
San Miguel	1.1
Other	60.5

Source: *Brand Strategy*, September 2004, p. 36, from X-tribes China and Xtreme Information, 2004.

★ 592 ★
Beer
SIC: 2082; NAICS: 31212
Top Beer Makers, 2004

Market shares are shown in percent.

Anheuser-Busch	51.6%
Miller Brewing	19.0
Adolph Coors	10.2
Modelo	4.4
Pabst Brewing	3.4
Heineken	2.8
Labatt USA/Inbev USA	2.6
Diageo	1.5
DG Yuengling & Son	0.7
Boston Beer	0.6
Other	3.2

Source: *Beverage World*, April 15, 2005, p. 40, from Beverage Marketing Corp.

★ 593 ★
Beer
SIC: 2082; NAICS: 31212
Top Beer Makers in Brazil, 2004

Shares are for May - June 2004.

	May	June
Ambev	66.0%	66.3%
Schincariol	13.1	13.1
Molson	11.1	10.9
Other	3.9	3.7

Source: *America's Intelligence Wire*, July 15, 2004, p. NA.

★ 594 ★
Beer
SIC: 2082; NAICS: 31212
Top Beer Makers in China

Market shares are shown in percent.

Tsingtao Brewery	12.9%
China Resources Breweries	10.0
Beijing Yanjing Beer Group	9.4
Harbin Brewery Group	4.3
Zhujiang Brewery Group	3.4
Other	60.0

Source: *Time International (Asia Edition)*, May 17, 2004, p. 40.

★ 595 ★
Beer
SIC: 2082; NAICS: 31212
Top Beer Makers in Estonia, 2003

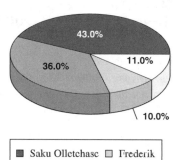

The market was valued at 960,000 hectoliters in 2003.

Saku Olletehase	43.0%
le Coq	36.0
Frederik	10.0
Other	11.0

Source: *just-drinks.com (Management Briefing)*, November 2004, p. 12, from Canadean.

★ 596 ★
Beer
SIC: 2082; NAICS: 31212
Top Beer Makers in India

Market shares are shown in percent.

UB Group	45.0%
SABMiller-Shaw Wallace	35.0
Other	20.0

Source: *Economic Times*, May 27, 2005, p. NA.

★ 597 ★

Beer

SIC: 2082; NAICS: 31212

Top Beer Makers in Mexico, 2003-2004

Mexico tied with Holland as the world's largest beer exporter. It ranked sixth in output worldwide.

	2003	2004
Grupo Modelo	57.1%	56.1%
Femsa Cervesa	42.9	43.9

Source: *Business Mexico*, Special Edition 2005, p. 20.

★ 598 ★

Beer

SIC: 2082; NAICS: 31212

Top Beer Makers in the Czech Republic

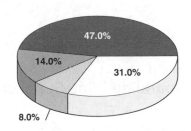

■ Plzensky Prazdroj   □ Budejovicky Budvar
■ Plzensky Pivovary   □ Other

Market shares are shown in percent.

Plzensky Prazdroj	47.0%
Plzensky Pivovary	14.0
Budejovicky Budvar	8.0
Other	31.0

Source: *Brand Strategy*, September 2004, p. 28, from *Czech Republic and Slovakia Business Report*.

★ 599 ★

Beer

SIC: 2082; NAICS: 31212

Top Lager Brands in the U.K., 2004

Brands are ranked by sales in thousands of pounds sterling for the year ended October 2, 2004.

	(000)	Share
Stella Artois	£ 591,846	37.59%
Carling	317,984	20.20
Foster's	256,853	16.31
Budweiser	£ 150,926	9.59%
Carlsberg	126,291	8.02
Other	130,603	8.29

Source: *Grocer*, December 11, 2004, p. 53, from ACNielsen.

★ 600 ★

Wine

SIC: 2084; NAICS: 31213

Largest Grape Crushers in Australia

Imports grew from 3.5 to 12 million cases from 1998 to 2002. Egged on by the the low Australian dollar, Australian wines surpasssed France to become the second largest importer to the United States (Italy is number one). Companies are ranked by grapes crushed in tons.

Hardy Wine	329,500
Southcorp	277,749
McGuigan Simeon Wines	245,000
Orlando Wyndham	200,000
Beringer Blass	106,572

Source: *USA TODAY*, October 22, 2004, p. 2B, from U.S. Department of Agriculture, Foreign Agricultural Service.

★ 601 ★

Wine

SIC: 2084; NAICS: 31213

Largest Wine Consumers in Eastern Europe

Consumption is estimated in millions of hectoliters.

	(mil.)	Share
Poland	321.0	38.74%
Czech Republic	170.0	20.51
Hungary	98.0	11.83
Slovakia	96.5	11.64
Slovenia	63.0	7.60
Lithuania	24.0	2.90
Latvia	23.5	2.84
Cyprus	14.0	1.69
Estonia	10.7	1.29
Malta	8.0	0.97

Source: *just-drinks.com (Management Briefing)*, November 2004, p. 4, from Canadean, Datamonitor, and Eurmonitor.

★ 602 ★
Wine
SIC: 2084; NAICS: 31213

Largest Wineries

Companies are ranked by production in thousands of gallons. Shares are shown for the top 50 firms.

	(000)	Share
E&J Gallo	443,000	0.71%
Constellation Wines	143,956	0.23
The Wine Group	141,700	0.23
Bronco Wine Co./JFJ Bronco Inc.	104,040	0.17
Korbel & Bros.	52,200	0.08
Robert Mondavi	50,100	0.08
Vie-Del Co.	50,000	0.08
Trinchero Family Estates	46,000	0.07
Delicato Vyds.	45,800	0.07
Jackson Wine Estates	20,000	0.03
Diageo Chateau & Estates Wines Co.	19,800	0.03
Beringer Blass Wine Estates	17,500	0.03
Other	61,045,216	98.18

Source: *Wines & Vines*, July 2004, p. 48.

★ 603 ★
Wine
SIC: 2084; NAICS: 31213

Leading Dessert Wine Makers, 2004

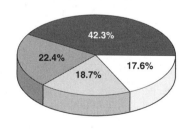

- Canandaigua Wine
- The Wine Group
- E&J Gallo Winery
- Other

Market shares are shown in percent.

Canandaigua Wine	42.3%
E&J Gallo Winery	22.4
The Wine Group	18.7
Other	17.6

Source: *Handbook Advance*, Annual 2005, p. 7.

★ 604 ★
Wine
SIC: 2084; NAICS: 31213

Leading Sparkling Wine Brands, 2004

Brands are ranked by thousands of 9-liter cases. Champagne and sparkling wine cases totaled to 12.6 million cases.

Andre/Wycliff	2,000
Cook's	1,408
Korbel	1,194
Ballatore	600
J. Roget	579
Domaine Chandon	345
Domaine St. Michelle	247
Tott's	155
Mumm Cuvee Napa	153
Gloria Ferrer	110

Source: *Handbook Advance*, Annual 2005, p. 7.

★ 605 ★
Wine
SIC: 2084; NAICS: 31213

Leading Sparkling Wine Suppliers, 2004

Market shares are shown in percent.

E&J Gallo	33.7%
Canandaigua Wine	27.7
Brown-Forman Beverages	15.2
Schieffelin & Co.	4.2
Weibel Vineyards	3.5
Other	15.7

Source: *Handbook Advance*, Annual 2005, p. 7.

★ 606 ★
Wine
SIC: 2084; NAICS: 31213

Leading Table Wine Brands, 2005

Market shares are shown based on drug store sales for the 52 weeks ended February 20, 2005.

Franzia	7.1%
Carlo Rossi	7.0
Almaden	4.6
Sutter Home	4.5
Livingston Cellars	4.1
Woodbridge by Robert Mondavi	3.9
K-J Vintners Reserve	3.5
Beringer	3.4
Yellow Tall	3.1

Continued on next page.

★ 606 ★

[Continued]

Wine

SIC: 2084; NAICS: 31213

Leading Table Wine Brands, 2005

Market shares are shown based on drug store sales for the 52 weeks ended February 20, 2005.

E&J Gallo Twin Valley	3.1%
Other	55.7

Source: *Chain Drug Review*, May 23, 2005, p. 69, from Information Resources Inc.

★ 607 ★

Wine

SIC: 2084; NAICS: 31213

Leading Wine Brands in the U.K., 2004

Brands are ranked by sales in thounds of pounds sterling for the year ended October 2, 2004.

	(000)	Share
Hardys	£ 221,079	5.93%
Blossom Hill	171,972	4.61
Jacob's Creek	145,915	3.91
E&J Gallo	144,215	3.87
Stowells	87,938	2.36
Other	2,957,448	79.32

Source: *Grocer*, December 11, 2004, p. 53, from ACNielsen.

★ 608 ★

Wine

SIC: 2084; NAICS: 31213

Leading Wine Companies, 2004

Companies are ranked by annual sales in millions of cases. Shares are shown based on sales by the top 30 companies.

	(mil.)	Share
E&J Gallo Winery	75.00	30.05%
Constellation Brands	56.00	22.44
The Wine Group	40.00	16.03
Bronco Wine Company	20.00	8.01
Beringer Blass Wine Estates	12.00	4.81
Trinchero Family Estates	9.00	3.61
Brown-Forman Wines	7.20	2.89
Kendall-Jackson	5.00	2.00
Ste. Michelle Wine Estate Wines	3.70	1.48
Diageo Chateau & Estates	3.25	1.30
Allied Domecq Wines	2.50	1.00
Other	15.91	6.38

Source: *Wine Business Monthly*, February 2005, p. NA, from ACNielsen.

★ 609 ★

Wine

SIC: 2084; NAICS: 31213

Leading Wine Makers in China

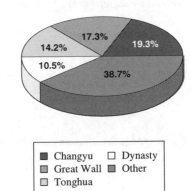

There are thought to be 8 million wine drinkers in the country, compared to 33.29 million beer drinkers and 13.58 million white spirits drinkers. Market shares are shown in percent.

Changyu	19.30%
Great Wall	17.34
Tonghua	14.17
Dynasty	10.51
Other	38.68

Source: *China Daily*, June 25, 2004, p. NA.

★ 610 ★

Wine

SIC: 2084; NAICS: 31213

Top Markets for California Wine

California represents 95% of domestic wine exports, which totaled $794 million in revenues in 2004.

United Kingdom	$ 299.1
Canada	123.8
Netherlands	85.6
Japan	82.1
Germany	26.8
Mexico	14.5
Switzerland	14.0
Denmark	14.0
Ireland	13.9
Belgium/Luxembourg	13.4

Source: *PR Newswire*, February 18, 2005, p. NA, from U.S. Department of Commerce.

★ 611 ★
Wine
SIC: 2084; NAICS: 31213

Top Wine Markets

Markets are ranked by supermarket sales in millions of dollars.

San Francisco, CA	$ 243.6
Los Angeles, CA	228.0
Miami, FL	193.7
Tampa, FL	157.4
Seattle, WA	139.1
Chicago, IL	137.2

Source: *Wine Business Monthly*, February 2005, p. NA, from ACNielsen.

★ 612 ★
Wine
SIC: 2084; NAICS: 31213

Wine Consumption by Type, 2003

Data are based on 257,500 cases.

Table	90.2%
Champagne & sparkling	4.7
Dessert & fortified	3.9
Vermouth/aperitif	0.7

Source: *Wine & Spirit Industry Marketing*, April 2004, p. 11.

★ 613 ★
Wine
SIC: 2084; NAICS: 31213

Wine Sales by Type

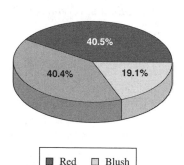

Red 40.5%
White 40.4%
Blush 19.1%

Legend: Red, Blush, White

Distribution is shown based on volume. Red recently surpassed white for the first time.

Red	40.5%
White	40.4
Blush	19.1

Source: *just-drinks.com*, April 6, 2005, p. NA, from ACNielsen.

★ 614 ★
Wine
SIC: 2084; NAICS: 31213

Wine Sales by Variety, 2004

Volume shares are shown based on supermarket sales for the weeks ended June 5, 2004.

Chardonnay	25.9%
Merlot	14.9
Cabernet Sauvignon	12.2
Other	47.0

Source: *Beverage Aisle*, September 15, 2004, p. 35, from ACNielsen Scantrack.

★ 615 ★
Liquor
SIC: 2085; NAICS: 31214

Champagne Industry in Europe, 2003

France remains the largest market in Europe but it now thought to be saturated; sales remained the same from 1998 to 2003. A push has been made in other countries to make the drink appealing to younger consumers. The industry was valued at 5.6 billion euros.

France	63.0%
U.K.	24.0
Germany	9.0
Italy	4.0
Other	10.0

Source: *Catering Update*, June 1, 2004, p. 8, from Mintel.

★ 616 ★
Liquor
SIC: 2085; NAICS: 31214

Largest Champagne Markets in Europe

Figures are in millions of British pounds.

France	£ 3.50
U.K.	1.30
Germany	0.50
Italy	0.25
Spain	0.08

Source: *Food Engineering & Ingredients*, September 2004, p. 4, from Mintel.

★ 617 ★

Liquor

SIC: 2085; NAICS: 31214

Largest Spirits Consumers in Eastern Europe

Smaller markets will probably remain small because of lack of purchasing power and the big multinationals are still developing a presence. Consumption is estimated in millions of hectoliters.

	(mil.)	Share
Poland	243.0	52.34%
Czech Republic	74.8	16.11
Hungary	59.0	12.71
Slovakia	27.6	5.94
Latvia	20.9	4.50
Lithuania	17.5	3.77
Slovenia	8.6	1.85
Estonia	8.2	1.77
Cyprus	3.0	0.65
Malta	1.7	0.37

Source: *just-drinks.com (Management Briefing)*, November 2004, p. 4, from Canadean, Datamonitor, and Euromonitor.

★ 618 ★

Liquor

SIC: 2085; NAICS: 31214

Leading Canadian Whiskey Brands, 2003

The industry continued its recovery from 2002 with sales up .4% to 15.4 million 9 liter cases. Brands are ranked by sales in thousand of 9-liter cases.

	(000)	Share
Canadian Mist	2,158	24.23%
Black Velvet	1,828	20.52
Windsor Supreme	1,155	12.97
Canadian LTD	626	7.03
Lord Calvert	590	6.62
Other	2,550	28.63

Source: *Beverage Dynamics*, January - February 2005, p. 26, from *Adams Liquor Handbook 2004*.

★ 619 ★

Liquor

SIC: 2085; NAICS: 31214

Leading Cider Brands, 2004

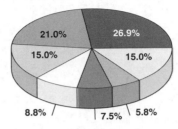

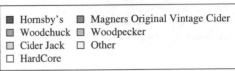

Brands are ranked by sales of thousands of 9 liter cases.

	(000)	Share
Hornsby's	1,150	26.90%
Woodchuck	900	21.05
Cider Jack	640	14.97
HardCore	375	8.77
Magners Original Vintage Cider . . .	320	7.49
Woodpecker	250	5.85
Other	640	14.97

Source: *Handbook Advance*, Annual 2005, p. 7.

★ 620 ★

Liquor

SIC: 2085; NAICS: 31214

Leading Cider Makers, 2004

Market shares are shown in percent.

Green Mountain Cidery	42.5%
E&J Gallo	27.1
HardCore Cider/Boston Beer	8.8
Other	21.6

Source: *Handbook Advance*, Annual 2005, p. 7.

★ 621 ★

Liquor

SIC: 2085; NAICS: 31214

Leading Cognac Brands, 2003

Brands are ranked by sales in thousands of 9-liter cases.

	(000)	Share
Hennessy	1,880	55.23%
Remy Martin	620	18.21
Courvoisier	535	15.72
Martell	201	5.90
Salignac	77	2.26
Other	91	2.67

Source: *Beverage Dynamics*, November - December 2004, p. 18, from Adams Beverage Group.

★ 622 ★

Liquor

SIC: 2085; NAICS: 31214

Leading Malt Beverage Brands, 2004

Brands are ranked by sales of thousands of 9 liter cases.

Smirnoff Ice	11,500
Smirnoff Twisted V	9,025
Mike's Hard Lemonade	8,500
Bartles & Jaymes	6,800
Seagram's Coolers	5,415
Smirnoff Ice Triple Black	4,845
Skyy Blue	3,300
Bacardi Silver	2,500
Bacardi Silver 03	2,300
Zima	1,900

Source: *Handbook Advance*, Annual 2005, p. 7.

★ 623 ★

Liquor

SIC: 2085; NAICS: 31214

Leading Malt Beverage Makers, 2004

Brands are ranked by sales of thousands of 9 liter cases.

Diageo-Guinness	39.7%
Anheuser-Busch/Bacardi	13.5
Mike's Hard Beverage	13.2
E&J Gallo Winery	10.6
United States Beverage	10.2
Other	12.8

Source: *Handbook Advance*, Annual 2005, p. 7.

★ 624 ★

Liquor

SIC: 2085; NAICS: 31214

Ready-to-Drink Liquor Industry in India

Market shares are shown in percent.

Bacardi Breezer	90.0%
Other	10.0

Source: *Asia Africa Intelligence Wire*, November 8, 2004, p. NA.

★ 625 ★

Liquor

SIC: 2085; NAICS: 31214

Spirits Industry in Lithuania, 2002

The total spirits market was valued at 1.94 million liter cases in 2002.

Vodka	59.0%
Liquers/specialties	35.0
Brandy	4.0
Whisky	1.0

Source: *just-drinks.com (Management Briefing)*, November 2004, p. 12, from Canadean.

★ 626 ★

Liquor

SIC: 2085; NAICS: 31214

Spirits Industry in Slovenia, 2002

The total spirits market was valued at 959,000 cases in 2002.

Brandy	19.0%
Rum/cane spirits	18.0
Fruit brandy	17.0
Vodka	15.0
Whisky	12.0
Other	19.0

Source: *just-drinks.com (Management Briefing)*, November 2004, p. 12, from Canadean.

★ 627 ★
Liquor

SIC: 2085; NAICS: 31214

Spirits Sales, 2004

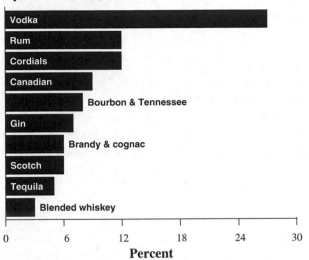

Percent

According to the source, liquor sales grew 3.1% by volume and 5.9% in dollars in 2004. Distillers and importers sold 164.2 million cases worth $14.7 billion. Irish whiskey saw the biggest jump, increasing over 11% during this period. Data show estimated figures in thousands of 9-liter cases.

	2003	2004	Share
Vodka	41,855	43,511	26.50%
Rum	19,435	20,323	12.38
Cordials	18,929	19,669	11.98
Canadian	15,281	15,543	9.47
Bourbon & Tennessee	13,405	13,874	8.45
Gin	10,997	10,934	6.66
Brandy & cognac	10,203	10,310	6.28
Scotch	9,320	9,304	5.67
Tequila	8,009	8,471	5.16
Blended whiskey	5,358	5,329	3.25

Source: *Research Alert*, March 18, 2005, p. 1, from Distilled Spirits Council of the United States.

★ 628 ★
Liquor

SIC: 2085; NAICS: 31214

Top Brandy Brands, 2003

Brands are ranked by sales in thousands of 9-liter cases.

	(000)	Share
E & J	2,420	37.11%
Paul Masson Brandy	1,230	18.86
Christian Brothers	1,150	17.63

	(000)	Share
Korbel	380	5.83%
Raynal	250	3.83
Presidente	205	3.14
Coronet Brandy	170	2.61
St. Remy	97	1.49
Other	620	9.51

Source: *Beverage Dynamics*, November - December 2004, p. 18, from *Adams Liquor Handbook 2004*.

★ 629 ★
Liquor

SIC: 2085; NAICS: 31214

Top Gin Brands, 2004

Brands are ranked by sales in thousands of 9-liter cases. Washington D.C. had 12.2% of consumption, followed by Georgia with 12.1% and Alabama with 11.1% .

	(000)	Share
Seagram's Gin	2,762	25.19%
Tanqueray	1,440	13.13
Gordon's Gin	885	8.07
Bombay Sapphire	705	6.43
Beefeater	620	5.65
Gilbey's Gin	560	5.11
Burnett's White Satin Gin	380	3.47
Barton Gin	357	3.26
Fleischmann's Gin	342	3.12
McCormick Gin	217	1.98
Other	2,698	24.60

Source: *Handbook Advance*, Annual 2005, p. 5.

★ 630 ★
Liquor

SIC: 2085; NAICS: 31213

Top Mixables Brands in North America, 2003

Market shares are shown in percent.

Martini	16.0%
Southern Comfort	12.0
Pimm's no. 1	12.0
Archers	10.0
Malibu	8.0
Taboo	7.0
Cinzano	4.0
Other	17.0

Source: *Financial Times*, Sept. 1, 2004, p. 22, from Thomson Datastream, Mintel, NABCA, and Lehman Brothers.

★ 631 ★

Liquor

SIC: 2085; NAICS: 31214

Top Rum Brands, 2004

Brands are ranked by estimated sales in thousands of 9-liter cases. Rum had its 10th straight year of growth. Hawaii took 24.2% of sales, North Dakota 18.1% and New York 17.1%.

	(000)	Share
Bacardi	8,450	40.63%
Captain Morgan	4,795	23.05
Malibu	1,300	6.25
Castillo	1,200	5.77
Ronrico	540	2.60
Cruzan Rum	435	2.09
Myers's	300	1.44
Barton Rum	200	0.96
Mount Gay	190	0.91
Monarch Rum	178	0.86
Other	3,212	15.44

Source: *Handbook Advance*, Annual 2005, p. 5.

★ 632 ★

Liquor

SIC: 2085; NAICS: 31214

Top Scotch Brands, 2004 (Bottled)

Brands are ranked by estimated sales in thousands of 9-liter cases.

Clan MacGregor	720
Scoresby	391
Cluny	290
InverHouse	220
Old Smugger	206

Source: *Beverage Dynamics*, March - April 2005, p. 48, from Adams Beverage Group Database.

★ 633 ★

Liquor

SIC: 2085; NAICS: 31214

Top Scotch Brands, 2004 (Foreign Bottled)

Brands are ranked by estimated sales in thousands of 9-liter cases.

Dewar's	1,400
Johnnie Walker Black	715
Johnnie Walker Red	685
Chivas Regal	487
J & B	370

Source: *Beverage Dynamics*, March - April 2005, p. 48, from Adams Beverage Group Database.

★ 634 ★

Liquor

SIC: 2085; NAICS: 31214

Top Scotch Whiskey Brands, 2004

Brands are ranked by sales in thousands of 9-liter cases.

	(000)	Share
Dewar's	1,400	15.59%
Johnnie Walker Black	715	7.96
Johnnie Walker Red	685	7.63
Chivas Regal	487	5.42
J&B	370	4.12
Other	5,324	59.28

Source: *Beverage Dynamics*, March - April 2005, p. 59, from Adams Beverage Group Database.

★ 635 ★

Liquor

SIC: 2085; NAICS: 31214

Top Spirits Brands in the U.K., 2005

Sales are shown in thousands of British pounds for the year ended January 22, 2005.

Smirnoff Diageo	154,438
Bell's Diageo	114,959
The Famouse Grouse Maximum UK	102,640
Glen's VodkaGlen Catrine	83,554
Bacardi Bacardi-Martin	83,329
Teacher's Allied Domecq	63,116
Jack Daniel's Bacardi Brown-Forman	48,958
William Grant's First Drinks Brands	44,346
Courvoisier Allied Domecq	29,458

Source: *Europe Intelligence Wire*, March 4, 2005, p. NA, from ACNielsen and *Off License News*.

★ 636 ★

Liquor

SIC: 2085; NAICS: 31214

Top Spirits Brands Worldwide, 2002

Market shares are shown in percent.

Bacardi	5.3%
Smirnoff	4.7
Absolut Vodka	3.1
Jack Daniel's	2.5
Captain Morgan	2.3
Jose Cuervo	2.2
Jim Beam	2.1
Crown Royal	2.0

Continued on next page.

★ 636 ★

[Continued]
Liquor
SIC: 2085; NAICS: 31214

Top Spirits Brands Worldwide, 2002

Market shares are shown in percent.

Seagram's Gin	1.9%
Seagram's 7 Crown	1.7
De Kuyper	1.7
Other	70.5

Source: *Beverage Industry*, June 2004, p. 22, from Euromonitor.

★ 637 ★

Liquor
SIC: 2085; NAICS: 31214

Top Spirits Firms Worldwide, 2004

Companies are ranked by estimated sales in billions of dollars.

Diageo	$ 12.27
Pernod Ricard	4.88
Allied Domecq	4.64
Bacardi	3.96
Soyuzplodimport	3.59

Source: *Wall Street Journal*, April 6, 2005, p. B1, from Impact Databank.

★ 638 ★

Liquor
SIC: 2085; NAICS: 31214

Top Spirits Makers, 2004

Market shares are shown based on the $16.3 billion industry.

Diageo	24.6%
Bacardi USA	9.8
Allied Domecq	8.8
Brown-Forman Beverages	6.9
Jim Beam Brands	6.2
Constellation Brands	5.0
Pernod Ricard	4.2
Absolut Spirits	4.1
Heaven Hill Distilleries	3.3
Schieffelin & Co.	3.1
Other	24.2

Source: *Handbook Advance*, Annual 2005, p. 7.

★ 639 ★

Liquor
SIC: 2085; NAICS: 31213

Top Spirits Makers in India

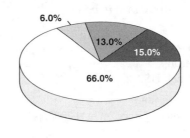

Market shares are shown in percent.

McDowell	15.0%
Shaw Wallace	13.0
Herbertson's	6.0
Other	66.0

Source: *Business India*, March 28, 2005, p. 113.

★ 640 ★

Liquor
SIC: 2085; NAICS: 31214

Top Tequila Brands, 2004

Brands are ranked by preliminary sales in thousands of 9 liter cases.

	(000)	Share
Jose Cuervo	3,408	41.20%
Sauza	1,225	14.81
Montezuma Tequila	600	7.25
Juarez	420	5.08
Patron	347	4.19
1800	345	4.17
Margaritaville	205	2.48
Cazadores	195	2.36
Rio Grande Tequila	172	2.08
Other	1,355	16.38

Source: *Beverage Dynamics*, March - April 2005, p. 59, from Adams Beverage Group Database.

★ 641 ★
Liquor
SIC: 2085; NAICS: 31214
Top Vermouth/Aperitif Makers, 2004

Market shares are shown in percent.

Bacardi USA	.31.8%
E & J Gallo Winery	.20.6
The Wine Group	.12.6
Distillerie Stock USA	.10.1
Other	.24.9

Source: *Handbook Advance*, Annual 2005, p. 7.

★ 642 ★
Liquor
SIC: 2085; NAICS: 31214
Top Vermouth Brands, 2004

Brands are ranked by sales of thousands of 9-liter cases. Consumption increased 1.6% to nearly 2 million cases.

Martini & Rossi Vermouth	570
Gallo Vermouth	400
Tribuno	245
Stock Vermouth	196
Dubonnet	75
Cinzano	65
Noilley Prat	49

Source: *Handbook Advance*, Annual 2005, p. 7.

★ 643 ★
Liquor
SIC: 2085; NAICS: 31214
Top Vodka Brands, 2004

Brands are ranked by sales in thousands of 9-liter cases. California, Florida and New York are the top consuming markets.

	(000)	Share
Smirnoff	7,257	16.46%
Absolut	4,640	10.52
Stolichnaya	1,935	4.39
McCormick	1,931	4.38
Skyy	1,880	4.26
Popov	1,850	4.20
Grey Goose	1,760	3.99
Barton	1,532	3.47
Gordon's	1,500	3.40
Ketel One	1,331	3.02
Other	18,479	41.91

Source: *Handbook Advance*, Annual 2005, p. 5.

★ 644 ★
Liquor
SIC: 2085; NAICS: 31214
Top Vodka Brands in China

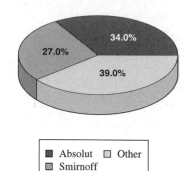

■ Absolut   □ Other
■ Smirnoff

Vodka sales were $19.5 million and 134,200 gallons in sales. As a comparison, the United States saw sales of $10.9 billion and 107.8 million gallons.

Absolut	.34.0%
Smirnoff	.27.0
Other	.39.0

Source: *Wall Street Journal*, February 14, 2005, p. B6, from Euromonitor.

★ 645 ★
Liquor
SIC: 2085; NAICS: 31214
Top Vodka Brands in Hungary, 2003

Vodka has 15% of the 2.18 million case spirits market in 2003 (fruit brandy was number one with 33% and regular brandy with 20%). Market shares are shown based on volume.

Royal	9.0%
Kalinka	9.0
Finlandia	2.0
Other	.80.0

Source: *just-drinks.com (Management Briefing)*, November 2004, p. 12, from Canadean.

★ 646 ★
Liquor
SIC: 2085; NAICS: 31214

Top Whiskey (Blended) Brands, 2004

Brands are ranked by estimated sales in thousands of 9-liter cases.

	(000)	Share
7 Crown	2,460	45.88%
Beam's 8 Star	150	2.80
Calvert Extra	155	2.89
Fleischmann's Preferred	150	2.80
Heaven Hill Blended Whiskey	160	2.98
Kentucky Deluxe	210	3.92
Kessler	785	14.64
McCormick Blend	220	4.10
Old Thompson	140	2.61
Other	822	15.33
Philadelphia	110	2.05

Source: *Handbook Advance*, Annual 2005, p. 5.

★ 647 ★
Liquor
SIC: 2085; NAICS: 31214

Top Whiskey (Bottled) Brands, 2003

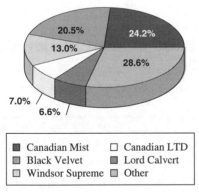

Legend:
- ■ Canadian Mist
- □ Canadian LTD
- ▨ Black Velvet
- ▨ Lord Calvert
- ▧ Windsor Supreme
- ▨ Other

Brands are ranked by sales in thousands of 9-liter cases.

	(000)	Share
Canadian Mist	2,158	24.23%
Black Velvet	1,828	20.52
Windsor Supreme	1,155	12.97
Canadian LTD	626	7.03
Lord Calvert	590	6.62
Other	2,550	28.63

Source: *Beverage Dynamics*, January - February 2005, p. 40, from *Adams Liquor Handbook 2004*.

★ 648 ★
Liquor
SIC: 2085; NAICS: 31214

Top Whiskey (Canadian) Brands, 2003

Brands are ranked by sales in thousands of 9-liter cases.

	(000)	Share
Crown Royal	3,137	48.22%
Canadian Club	1,375	21.13
Seagram's V.O.	1,293	19.87
MacNaughton	189	2.91
Royal Canadian	112	1.72
Other	400	6.15

Source: *Beverage Dynamics*, January - February 2005, p. 40, from *Adams Liquor Handbook 2004*.

★ 649 ★
Liquor
SIC: 2085; NAICS: 31214

Top Whiskey (Irish) Brands, 2003

Brands are ranked by sales in thousands of 9-liter cases.

	(000)	Share
Jameson (inc. 1780)	262	53.04%
Bushmills	130	26.32
Tullamore Dew	35	7.09
John Power	20	4.05
Kilbeggan Irish Whiskey	11	2.23
Black Bush	11	2.23
Other	25	5.06

Source: *Beverage Dynamics*, January - February 2005, p. 40, from *Adams Liquor Handbook 2004*.

★ 650 ★
Liquor
SIC: 2085; NAICS: 31214

Top Whiskey (Straight) Brands, 2003

Brands are ranked by sales in thousands of 9-liter cases.

	(000)	Share
Jack Daniel's	3,935	29.32%
Jim Beam	3,100	23.10
Evan Williams	925	6.89
Early Times	817	6.09
Wild Turkey	511	3.81
Ten High	502	3.74
Old Crow	500	3.73

Continued on next page.

★ 650 ★
[Continued]
Liquor
SIC: 2085; NAICS: 31214

Top Whiskey (Straight) Brands, 2003

Brands are ranked by sales in thousands of 9-liter cases.

	(000)	Share
Maker's Mark	490	3.65%
Heaven Hill Bourbon	250	1.86
George Dickel	180	1.34
Other	2,211	16.47

Source: *Beverage Dynamics*, September-October 2004, p. 40, from Adams Beverage Group.

★ 651 ★
Liquor
SIC: 2085; NAICS: 31214

Top Whisky Producers in Czech Republic, 2002

Market shares are shown based on volume.

Pernod Ricard	9.0%
V&S Group	5.2
Allied Domecq	1.4
Diageo	1.2
Other	83.2

Source: *just-drinks.com (Management Briefing)*, November 2004, p. 12, from Canadean.

★ 652 ★
Liquor
SIC: 2085; NAICS: 31214

U.S. Bourbon Exports, 2003

Countries are ranked by value of exports in millions of dollars.

United Kingdom	$ 87.0
Germany	64.9
Australia	49.4
Japan	36.7
Spain	24.8
France	23.7
Italy	20.2
Canada	11.4
New Zealand	8.3

Source: *American Shipper*, November 2004, p. 12, from Distilled Spirits Council of the United States.

★ 653 ★
Bottled Water
SIC: 2086; NAICS: 312112

Bottled Water Industry in Chile

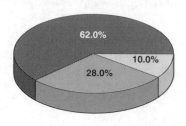

Bottled water represents roughly 7.5% of all beverage sales in the local market. Cachantum is manufactured CCU and Vital is marketed by Embotelladora Andina.

Cachantum	62.0%
Vital	28.0
Other	10.0

Source: *America's Intelligence Wire*, December 27, 2004, p. NA.

★ 654 ★
Bottled Water
SIC: 2086; NAICS: 312112

Bottled Water Industry Worldwide, 2003-2004

Retail sales are shown in millions of dollars.

	2003	2004	Share
Still	$ 34,483.8	$ 36,967.4	74.84%
Carbonated	10,040.9	10,358.0	20.97
Flavored	1,829.9	2,067.8	4.19

Source: *Beverage Industry*, July 2004, p. 22, from Euromonitor.

★ 655 ★
Bottled Water
SIC: 2086; NAICS: 312112

Enhanced Water Market

Market shares are shown in percent.

Propel Fitness Water	50.0%
Other	50.0

Source: *Wall Street Journal*, March 21, 2005, p. B6.

★ 656 ★

Bottled Water

SIC: 2086; NAICS: 312112

Largest Bottled Water Firms in China, 2003

Market shares are estimated by share of volume.

Wahaha Group	.25.0%
Guangdong Robust Group	6.0
Farmer Spring Co. Ltd.	5.0
Other	.65.0

Source: *just-drinks.com*, March 2005, p. 29, from China Beverage Industry Association.

★ 657 ★

Bottled Water

SIC: 2086; NAICS: 312112

Top Bottled Water Brands, 2004

Market shares are shown based on wholesale gallon sales of $9.16 billion.

Aquafina	.11.3%
Dasani	.10.0
Poland Spring	6.8
Arrowhead	5.8
Crystal Geyser	4.7
Deer Park	4.1
Ozarka	2.6
Ice Mountain	2.4
Zephyrhills	2.3
Deja Blue	2.0
Other	.48.0

Source: *Beverage World*, May 15, 2005, p. 34, from Beverage Marketing Corp.

★ 658 ★

Bottled Water

SIC: 2086; NAICS: 312112

Top Bottled Water Brands in France, 2003

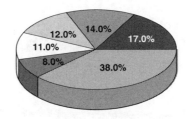

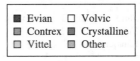

Market shares are estimated by share of volume.

Evian	.17.0%
Contrex	.14.0
Vittel	.12.0
Volvic	.11.0
Crystalline	8.0
Other	.38.0

Source: *just-drinks.com*, March 2005, p. 29, from just-drinks.com published sources.

★ 659 ★

Bottled Water

SIC: 2086; NAICS: 312112

Top Bottled Water Brands in India

Market shares are shown in percent.

Aquafina	.35.0%
Bisleri	.30.0
Other	.35.0

Source: *just-drinks.com*, December 7, 2004, p. NA.

★ 660 ★
Bottled Water
SIC: 2086; NAICS: 312112

Top Bottled Water Brands in Italy, 2003

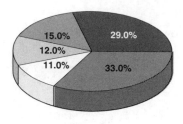

■ San Pellegrino **□** San Benetto
■ CoGeDi   **■** Other
□ Italaquae

Market shares are estimated by share of volume.

San Pellegrino	.29.0%
CoGeDi	.15.0
Italaquae	.12.0
San Benetto	.11.0
Other	.33.0

Source: *just-drinks.com*, March 2005, p. 29, from just-drinks.com published sources.

★ 661 ★
Bottled Water
SIC: 2086; NAICS: 312112

Top Bottled Water Makers, 2004

Market shares are shown based on wholesale gallon sales of $9.16 billion.

Nestle Waters	.29.9%
PepsiCo.	.11.3
Coca-Cola	.10.0
DS Waters	. 8.5
Crystal Geyser	. 4.7
Coke/Danone	. 4.4
Glacier Water	. 2.1
DPSUBG	. 2.0
Culligan	. 1.3
Vermont Pure	. 0.8
Other	.25.0

Source: *Beverage World*, May 15, 2005, p. 34, from Beverage Marketing Corp.

★ 662 ★
Bottled Water
SIC: 2086; NAICS: 312112

Top Packaged Water Markets Worldwide, 2003

Countries are ranked by sales in billions of liters.

	(bil.)	Share
Mexico	21.57	12.7%
United States	21.55	12.6
France	12.61	7.4
Italy	11.88	7.0
China	11.76	6.9
Germany	11.54	6.8
Indonesia	8.79	5.2
Spain	6.76	4.0
Turkey	5.46	3.2

Source: *just-drinks.com*, March 2005, p. 29, from just-drinks.com published sources.

★ 663 ★
Energy Drinks
SIC: 2086; NAICS: 312111

Energy Drink Market in Australia

Market shares are shown in percent.

V	.45.6%
Red Bull	.31.4
Lift Plus/Red Eye/Lucozade	.25.0

Source: *Nutraceuticals International*, December 2004, p. NA, from ACNielsen.

★ 664 ★
Energy Drinks
SIC: 2086; NAICS: 312111

Top Energy Drink Brands, 2005

Market shares are shown based on drug store sales for the 52 weeks ended February 20, 2005.

Red Bull	.71.1%
Monster	. 6.3
Amp	. 4.6
Sobe Adrenaline Rush	. 3.9
Rockstar	. 3.3
Sobe No Fear	. 2.1
Hype	. 1.9
Rush Energy	. 1.5
Hansens	. 1.5
Other	. 3.8

Source: *Chain Drug Review*, May 23, 2005, p. 69, from Information Resources Inc.

★ 665 ★

Soft Drinks

SIC: 2086; NAICS: 312111

Beverage Case Sales, 2004

Total sales were 13.9 billion cases, up from 11.9 billion in 1999.

	(bil.)	Share
Carbonated soft drinks	10.20	73.28%
Bottled water	1.80	12.93
Juice drinks	0.79	5.68
Sports drinks	0.68	4.89
Ready-to-drink teas	0.39	2.80
Energy drinks	0.06	0.43

Source: *Investor's Business Daily*, May 23, 2005, p. A11, from Beverage Marketing Corp.

★ 666 ★

Soft Drinks

SIC: 2086; NAICS: 312111

Fountain Drink Industry, 2003

Market shares are shown in percent.

Coca-Cola	.68.0%
PepsiCo.	.22.0
Cadbury Schweppes	.10.0

Source: *Atlanta Journal-Constitution*, August 26, 2004, p. E1, from *Beverage Digest*.

★ 667 ★

Soft Drinks

SIC: 2086; NAICS: 312111

Functional Soft Drink Market in Western Europe, 2003

By segment, enriched drinks take 76% of the market, followed by sports with 13%, energy with 8% and nutraceuticals with 3%. The total market stood at 3,780 million litres.

United Kingdom	.36.0%
Germany	.33.0
Italy	8.0
Spain	5.0
France	4.0
Other	.14.0

Source: *International Food Ingredients*, December 2004, p. 14, from Zenith International.

★ 668 ★

Soft Drinks

SIC: 2086; NAICS: 312111

Leading Soft Drink Firms in Japan, 2003

Market shares are estimated based on domestic sales.

Coca-Cola Group	.31.0%
Suntory	.17.9
Kirin Beverage	.10.7
Ito En	6.9
Asahi Soft Drinks	6.2
Other	.27.3

Source: "Market Share Survey Report 2003." [online] from http://www.nni.nikkei.co.jp [Published July 26, 2004], from Nikkei estimates.

★ 669 ★

Soft Drinks

SIC: 2086; NAICS: 312111

New Age Beverage Sales

The term New Age refers to beverages that are perceived as healthy alternatives to carbonated soft drinks. Such drinks are often higher priced than carbonated drinks and have attractive packaging. Data show wholesale sales of new age beverages in millions of dollars.

	2003	2008	Share
Retail PET waters	.$ 4.89	$ 9.03	45.54%
Sports beverages	2.69	3.77	19.01
Regular single-serve fruit beverages	2.57	2.90	14.62
Regular RTD teas	1.45	1.60	8.07
Energy drinks	0.65	1.17	5.90
Sparkling water	0.49	0.52	2.62
Premium soda	0.32	0.37	1.87
RTD coffee	0.31	0.47	2.37

Source: *Beverage Aisle*, September 15, 2004, p. 26, from Beverage Marketing Corp.

★ 670 ★

Soft Drinks

SIC: 2086; NAICS: 312111

New Age Beverage Sales by Year

Data show wholesale sales in millions of dollars. Growth was 8.7% in 2003, the first time in three years that growth was not double digit (11.2% in 2002 and 13% in 2001).

1999	$ 9,954.5
2000	10,825.7

Continued on next page.

★ 670 ★

[Continued]
Soft Drinks

SIC: 2086; NAICS: 312111

New Age Beverage Sales by Year

Data show wholesale sales in millions of dollars. Growth was 8.7% in 2003, the first time in three years that growth was not double digit (11.2% in 2002 and 13% in 2001).

2001	$ 12,228.4
2002	13,598.6
2003	14,777.4

Source: *Beverage World*, March 15, 2005, p. 18, from Beverage Marketing Corp.

★ 671 ★

Soft Drinks

SIC: 2086; NAICS: 312111

Soft Drink Market in Dallas, TX

Market shares are shown based on supermarket sales.

Coke	19.3%
Dr. Pepper	14.7
Pepsi	5.4
Other	59.6

Source: *Dallas Morning News*, May 25, 2004, p. NA.

★ 672 ★

Soft Drinks

SIC: 2086; NAICS: 312111

Soft Drink Market in the Philippines

The non-alcoholic beverage market is worth P45 billion.

Coca-Cola Bottlers Philippines	80.0%
Other	20.0

Source: *Asia Africa Intelligence Wire*, December 21, 2004, p. NA, from University of Asia and Pacific School of Economics.

★ 673 ★

Soft Drinks

SIC: 2086; NAICS: 312111

Top Diet Soft Drink Brands, 2004

Diet consumption stood at 4,640.4 million cases, up 6.25 from the previous year.

	Market Share	Diet Share
Diet Coke	9.8%	32.5%
Diet Pepsi	5.8	19.3
Caffeine Free Diet Coke	1.7%	5.6%
Diet Dr. Pepper	1.4	4.5
Diet Mountain Dew	1.2	4.1
Caffeine Free Diet Pepsi	1.0	3.3
Diet Sprite	0.6	2.0
Diet & Up	0.5	1.5
Diet Rite	0.4	1.2
Diet Sierra Mist	0.3	0.9

Source: *Beverage World*, April 15, 2005, p. 28, from Beverage Marketing Corp.

★ 674 ★

Soft Drinks

SIC: 2086; NAICS: 312111

Top Soft Drink Brands, 2004

Market shares are shown based on total volume of 10,239.4 million cases.

Coke Classic	17.9%
Pepsi-Cola	11.5
Diet Coke	9.7
Mountain Dew	6.3
Diet Pepsi	6.1
Sprite	5.7
Dr. Pepper	5.6
Caffeine Free Diet Coke	1.7
Sierra Mist	1.4
Diet Dr. Pepper	1.4
Other	32.7

Source: "Beverage Digest/Maxwell Ranks U.S. Soft Drink Industry." [online] from http://www.beveragedigest.com [Press release March 4, 2005], from Beverage Digest/Maxwell.

★ 675 ★

Soft Drinks

SIC: 2086; NAICS: 312111

Top Soft Drink Firms, 2004

Market shares are shown based on total volume of 10,239.4 million cases.

Coca-Cola Co.	43.1%
Pepsi-Cola Co.	31.7
Cadbury Schweppes	14.5
Cott Corp.	5.5
National Beverage	2.4
Big Red	0.4
Red Bull	0.3
Hansen Natural	0.2
Rockstar	0.1

Continued on next page.

★ 675 ★

[Continued]
Soft Drinks
SIC: 2086; NAICS: 312111

Top Soft Drink Firms, 2004

Market shares are shown based on total volume of 10,239.4 million cases.

Monarch Co.	0.1%
Other	1.7

Source: "Beverage Digest/Maxwell Ranks U.S. Soft Drink Industry." [online] from http://www.beveragedigest.com [Press release March 4, 2005], from Beverage Digest/Maxwell.

★ 676 ★

Soft Drinks
SIC: 2086; NAICS: 312111

Top Soft Drink Firms in Western Europe

Market shares are for October 2004. Germany took 26% of the market in 2003, followed by the United Kingdom 24% and Italy 11%.

Coca-Cola	21.1%
PepsiCo.	7.1
Nestle	5.0
Cadbury Schweppes	3.9
Danone	3.5
Britvic	2.5
Eckes	2.1
GSK	1.9
Cott	1.7
Other	51.2

Source: "Canned Product Markets." [online] from http://www.fft.com [Market Synopsis dated September 2004], from *Food for Thought's 2004 West European Food & Drink Database.*

★ 677 ★

Soft Drinks
SIC: 2086; NAICS: 312111

Top Soft Drink Makers in Brazil

Market shares are shown in percent.

Jugos Del Valle	25.6%
Sucos Mais	14.5
Kapo	9.6
Tampico	7.8
Coca Cola	7.8
Sufresh of WOW!	6.0
Other	28.7

Source: *America's Intelligence Wire*, September 9, 2004, p. NA, from Jugos del Valle.

★ 678 ★

Sports Drinks
SIC: 2086; NAICS: 312111

Sports Drink Market in Western Europe, 2003

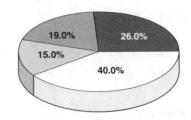

■ Germany □ U.K.
■ Italy □ Other

The sports drink market grew to $1.24 billion in 2003, representing a 477 million liter industry.

Germany	26.0%
Italy	19.0
U.K.	15.0
Other	40.0

Source: *Nutraceuticals International*, September 2004, p. NA, from Zenith International.

★ 679 ★

Sports Drinks
SIC: 2086; NAICS: 312111

Top Functional Drink Brands in the U.K., 2002

Market shares are shown in percent.

Lucozade	68.7%
Red Bull	10.6
Powerade	7.0
Isostar	1.2
Ame	1.1
Purdey's	1.0
Aqua Libra	0.6
V	0.5
Solstis	0.3
Red Rooster	0.3
Other	8.7

Source: *Marketing*, August 11, 2004, p. 38, from Euromonitor.

★ 680 ★
Sports Drinks
SIC: 2086; NAICS: 312111
Top Sports Drink Brands, 2004

Market shares are shown based on sales at food stores, drug stores and mass merchandisers (excluding Wal-Mart) for the year ended June 13, 2004.

Gatorade	45.27%
Powerade	12.73
Gatorade Frost	10.83
Gatorade Fierce	8.27
Gatorade Ice	6.20
Gatorade All Stars	4.80
Capri Sun Sport Aseptic	2.91
Gatorade X Factor	2.06
Gatorade Drink MIx	1.95
Gatorade Xtremo	1.62
Other	3.36

Source: *Beverage Industry*, July 2004, p. 20, from Information Resources Inc.

★ 681 ★
Sports Drinks
SIC: 2086; NAICS: 312111
Top Sports Drinks Worldwide

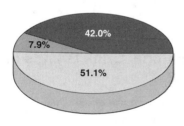

Market shares are shown in percent.

Gatorade	42.0%
Powerade	7.9
Other	51.1

Source: *Marketing*, October 20, 2004, p. 28.

★ 682 ★
Seafood
SIC: 2091; NAICS: 311711
Canned Seafood Market in Chile

Canned seafood is a $9 million market.

Robinson Crusoe	54.0%
Angelmo	25.0
Stores own label	12.0
Geomar	1.0
Other	18.0

Source: *America's Intelligence Wire*, August 16, 2004, p. NA, from ACNielsen.

★ 683 ★
Seafood
SIC: 2091; NAICS: 311711
Canned Seafood Sales, 2003

Supermarket sales are shown in millions of dollars.

Tuna	$ 1,057.00
Salmon	145.36
Sardines	73.80
Oysters	42.74
Clams	39.49
Crab	35.43
Shrimp	24.27
Anchovies	13.53

Source: *Progressive Grocer*, Sept. 15, 2004, p. 26, from *2004 Progressive Grocer Consumer Expenditure Survey*.

★ 684 ★
Seafood
SIC: 2091; NAICS: 311711
Canned Seafood Sales in the U.K., 2003

The canned fish industry is on the decline, falling 3.6% from 1999 to 2004. The entire seafood industry, however, has seen growth in terms of both volume and value.

Tuna	54.0%
Red salmon	18.0
Pink salmon	8.0
Sardines	6.0
Mackerel	5.0
Medium red salmon	2.0
Other	4.0

Source: "United Kingdom Fishery Products." [online] from http://ffas.usda.gov [Published December 17, 2004], from Foreign Agricultural Service, U.S. Department of Agriculture.

★ 685 ★

Seafood

SIC: 2091; NAICS: 311711

Canned Tuna Sales

Sales are shown in millions of dollars.

2000	$ 1,096.2
2001	1,068.6
2002	1,111.0
2003	1,062.6
2004	980.2

Source: *Food Institute Report*, January 24, 2005, p. 17, from Information Resources Inc. InfoScan.

★ 686 ★

Seafood

SIC: 2091; NAICS: 311711

Pink Salmon Market

Market shares are shown in percent.

	1996	2002
Canned	83.0%	73.0%
Frozen	14.0	17.0
Other	3.0	10.0

Source: *National Fisherman*, December 2004, p. 18, from *ADF&G Commercial Operators Annual Report*.

★ 687 ★

Seafood

SIC: 2091; NAICS: 311711

Seafood Industry in the U.K.

Market shares are shown in percent.

Fresh or frozen seafood	81.5%
Canned fish	12.0
Smoked fish	3.5
Fish meal or oil	3.0

Source: *Food (UK)*, November 26, 2004, p. NA, from IBISWorld.

★ 688 ★

Seafood

SIC: 2092; NAICS: 311712

Fish Consumption in Germany

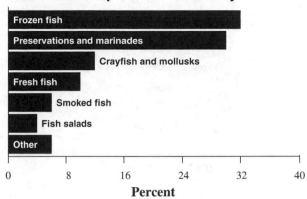

Percent

Total volume of fish produced was 439,637 metric tons in 2003.

	2000	2003
Frozen fish	25.0%	32.0%
Preservations and marinades	30.0	30.0
Crayfish and mollusks	13.0	12.0
Fresh fish	14.0	10.0
Smoked fish	7.0	6.0
Fish salads	4.0	4.0
Other	7.0	6.0

Source: "Germany Fishery Products Annual 2004." [online] from http://www.export.gov [accessed October 21, 2004], from Fish Information Center: Daten and Fakten 2004 and U.S. Department of Agriculture.

★ 689 ★

Seafood

SIC: 2092; NAICS: 311712

Frozen Salmon Imports in Japan

Data are for the first seven months of the year.

	Tons	Share
Pacific Coho	63,572	49.90%
Pink/Chum salmon	39,552	31.05
Pacific Sockeye	15,480	12.15
Atlantic salmon	2,583	2.03
Other Pacific salmon	5,836	4.58
Other salmon	379	0.30

Source: *Quick Frozen Foods International*, October 2004, p. 104.

★ 690 ★
Seafood
SIC: 2092; NAICS: 311712
Shrimp Market in Japan

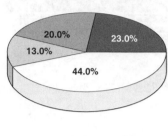

Vietnam ☐ India
☐ Indonesia ☐ Other

Vietnam recently surpassed Indonesia as the leading shrimp supplier to Japan. The major reason for this was prices 5-10% lower than those offered by Indonesia.

Vietnam	.23.0%
Indonesia	.20.0
India	.13.0
Other	.44.0

Source: *Vietnam News Briefs*, March 17, 2005, p. NA, from Japan's market research companies.

★ 691 ★
Seafood
SIC: 2092; NAICS: 311712
Top Frozen Fish in the U.K., 2004

Brands are ranked by sales in thousands of pounds sterling for the year ended October 2, 2004.

Birds Eye Cod Fillet Fish	£ 42,816
Birds Eye Simply Fish Cod	23,807
Young's Chip Shop	19,056
Young's Peeled Prawns	16,926
Young's Scottish Island	15,577

Source: *Grocer*, December 11, 2004, p. 53, from ACNielsen.

★ 692 ★
Seafood
SIC: 2092; NAICS: 311712
Top Frozen Seafood Brands, 2004

Brands are ranked by supermarket sales in millions of dollars for the year ended June 13, 2004.

	($ mil.)	Share
Gorton's	$ 159.93	10.36%
Van de Kamps	73.13	4.74
Aqua Star	53.25	3.45
SeaPak	45.89	2.97
Mrs. Paul's	39.68	2.57
Singleton	37.89	2.45
Contessa	30.30	1.96
Gorton's Grilled Fillets	24.26	1.57
Great Fish Company	21.12	1.37
Private label	592.35	38.36
Other	466.57	30.21

Source: *Frozen Food Age*, August 2004, p. 53, from Information Resources Inc.

★ 693 ★
Seafood
SIC: 2092; NAICS: 311712
Top Frozen Seafood Makers (Unit Shares), 2004

Companies are ranked by sales at supermarkets, drug stores and mass merchandisers (excluding Wal-Mart) for the 52 weeks ended October 2004.

Gorton's	.14.7%
Van de Kamp's	5.5
Aqua Star Inc.	3.6
Sea-Pak	3.2
Mrs. Paul's	3.2
Gorton's Grilled Fillets	2.8
Singleton	2.4
Trans Ocean	1.9
Contessa	1.4
Sea Best	1.1
Schooner	1.1
Private label	.25.7
Other	.33.4

Source: *Quick Frozen Foods International*, January 2005, p. 53, from Information Resources Inc.

★ 694 ★

Seafood

SIC: 2092; NAICS: 311712

Top Seafood Brands, 2004

Brands are ranked by sales in millions of dollars for the year ended June 13, 2004.

	($ mil.)	Share
Gorton's	$ 159.93	10.35%
Van de Kamps	73.13	4.73
Aqua Star	53.25	3.45
SeaPak	45.89	2.97
Mrs. Paul's	39.68	2.57
Singleton	37.89	2.45
Contessa	30.30	1.96
Gorton's Grilled Fillets	24.26	1.57
Great Fish Company	21.12	1.37
Private label	592.35	38.35
Other	466.77	30.22

Source: *Frozen Food Age*, August 2004, p. 29, from Information Resources Inc.

★ 695 ★

Seafood

SIC: 2092; NAICS: 311712

U.S. Shrimp Imports

The Department of Commerce recently recommended anti-dumping duties on those countries it deemed to have dumped shrimp onto the U.S. market. China received the highest duty of 112.81%. The dumping duties were calculated by averaging the price of shrimp imports they found below market prices. They ignored shrimp sold at or above market price.

Thailand	27.0%
China	13.0
Vietnam	9.0
Ecuador	9.0
Indonesia	8.0
India	8.0
Other	26.0

Source: *Quick Frozen Foods International*, January 2005, p. 33, from U.S. Department of Commerce.

★ 696 ★

Coffee

SIC: 2095; NAICS: 31192

Coffee Market in Germany, 2003

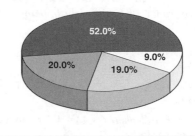

Nondecaffeinated | Natural milds
Mildly treated roasted | Decaffeinated

Germany is the eighth largest coffee consuming nation (Finland is number one). Roasted lost 8,000 tons to fall to 413,000 tons in 2003.

Nondecaffeinated	52.0%
Mildly treated roasted	20.0
Natural milds	19.0
Decaffeinated	9.0

Source: *Tea & Coffee Trade Journal*, November 20, 2004, p. 40.

★ 697 ★

Coffee

SIC: 2095; NAICS: 31192

Coffee Market in New Zealand

Sales are shown as of April 18, 2004.

Soluble	71.4%
Roast and ground	21.2
Specialty	7.2
Coffee essences	0.2

Source: *Grocer's Review*, August 2004, p. NA, from ACNielsen.

★ 698 ★
Coffee
SIC: 2095; NAICS: 31192

Coffee Sales, 2004

Consumption has been increasing rather slowly in recent years, up from 6,097 million gallons in 2001 to 6,291.8 million gallons in 2003.

Ground	86.2%
Whole bean	8.1
Instant	5.2
Ready-to-drink	0.4

Source: *National Petroleum News*, March 2005, p. 14, from Beverage Marketing Corp.

★ 699 ★
Coffee
SIC: 2095; NAICS: 31192

Fair Trade Coffee Industry

Fair trade coffee firms buy their beans from small family farm cooperatives as opposed to large plantations. The minimum price is guaranteed through the fair trade industry and this is roughly double what Central and South American growers would get from conventional coffee importers. In short, farmers get the money directly - not corporate middlemen. The company's share is eroding as the industry develops.

Equal Exchange	66.0%
Other	34.0

Source: *The Dispatch*, August 26, 2004, p. NA.

★ 700 ★
Coffee
SIC: 2095; NAICS: 31192

Premium Coffee Market in Ireland

Market shares are shown in percent.

Nescafe Gold Blend	57.0%
Other	43.0

Source: *Checkout*, December 2004, p. NA, from ACNielsen.

★ 701 ★
Coffee
SIC: 2095; NAICS: 31192

Single-Cup Brewer Placements, 2003

The office coffee service industry saw revenues of $3.39 billion from 2003-2004. Regular coffee has 65% of all coffee sales, followed by varietal with 14%, decaffeinated with 10%, flavored with 4%. Data show the number of single-cup brewer placements as of February 2003.

	Placements	Share
G.P. Rossi	50,000	25.45%
Flavia	40,000	20.36
Keurig	33,000	16.79
Filterfresh	30,000	15.27
Cafection	16,000	8.14
Crane	12,000	6.11
Zanussi	10,000	5.09
Unibrew	3,200	1.63
Newco	1,300	0.66
Rheavendors	1,000	0.51

Source: *Automatic Merchandiser*, July 2004, p. 26, from *Automatic Merchandiser 2004 State of the Coffee Service Industry Report*.

★ 702 ★
Coffee
SIC: 2095; NAICS: 31192

Top Coffee Brands, 2004

Brands are ranked by sales at supermarkets, drug stores and discount stores (but not Wal-Mart) for the year ended September 5, 2004.

	($ mil.)	Share
Folgers Ground	$ 379.6	13.64%
Maxwell House Ground	254.4	9.14
Starbuck's Ground	134.8	4.84
Folgers Instant	92.5	3.32
Maxwell House Master Blend	86.1	3.09
Folgers Coffee House Ground	82.8	2.98
General Foods Intl. Coffee Instant	81.8	2.94
Eight O'Clock Whole	73.0	2.62
Starbuck's Whole	72.8	2.62
Folgers Ground Decaffeinated	69.4	2.49
Private label	112.7	4.05
Other	1,342.8	48.26

Source: *MMR*, November 29, 2004, p. 21, from Information Resources Inc.

★ 703 ★

Coffee

SIC: 2095; NAICS: 31192

Top Coffee Makers, 2005

Market shares are shown based on sales at food stores, drug stores and mass merchandisers (but not Wal-Mart) for the 52 weeks ended January 23, 2005.

Procter & Gamble	33.7%
Kraft Foods Inc.	32.7
Millstone Coffee Inc.	2.7
Sara Lee Corp.	2.6
Chock Full O Nuts Corp.	2.1
Rowland Coffee Roasters	1.9
F. Gavina & Sons Inc.	1.9
Community Coffee Co. Inc.	1.6
Eight O'Clock Coffee Co.	1.4
Starbucks	1.2
Seattle's Best Coffee	1.0
Melitta USA	0.8
MJB Co.	0.8
Mother Parker's Tea & Coffee USA	0.8
Peet's Coffee & Tea	0.8
Reily Foods	0.8
Other	14.0

Source: *Grocery Headquarters*, April 2005, p. 22, from Information Resources Inc.

★ 704 ★

Coffee

SIC: 2095; NAICS: 31192

Top Coffee Makers in China, 2002

The coffee market is expected to grow 70% in total volume between 2003 and 2008, according to estimates from Euromonitor. Market shares are shown based on retail value sales.

Nestle	46.0%
Kraft	20.0
Other	34.0

Source: *just-drinks.com*, August 10, 2004, p. NA.

★ 705 ★

Coffee

SIC: 2095; NAICS: 31192

Top Instant Coffee Brands in the U.K., 2003

Regular coffee took 45.8% of sales and premium freeze dried took 25.6%. Market shares are shown in percent.

	(mil.)	Share
Nescafe Original	£ 221	34.80%
Nescafe Gold Blend	100	15.75
Kenco Really Smooth	47	7.40
Kimco Really Rich	35	5.51
Douwe Egberts	20	3.15
Kenco Decaffeinated	18	2.83
Carte Noir	16	2.52
Maxwell House Granules	14	2.20
Kencoi Rappor	13	2.05
Nescafe Decaffeinated	12	1.89
Other	139	21.89

Source: *Marketing*, June 3, 2004, p. 40, from Mintel.

★ 706 ★

Coffee Drinks

SIC: 2095; NAICS: 31192

Ready-to-Drink Coffee Sales

Ready-to-drink coffees are very popular outside of the United States and represent about one-fifth of the beverage market. Frappucino leads with a 81% share. Wholesale sales are shown in millions of dollars.

1998	$ 200.0
1999	193.0
2000	229.0
2001	239.7
2002	272.5
2003	308.0

Source: *Atlanta Journal-Constitution*, January 22, 2005, p. F1, from Beverage Marketing Corp.

★ 707 ★
Coffee Drinks
SIC: 2095; NAICS: 31192

Top RTD Coffee Drink Brands, 2004

Market shares are shown based on sales at food stores, drug stores and mass merchandisers (excluding Wal-Mart) for the year ended June 13, 2004. RTD stands for ready-to-drink.

Frappuccino	87.46%
Doubleshot	10.36
Kahlua	0.56
Arizona	0.46
Havana	0.28
Nescafe	0.21
Main St. Cafe	0.12
Wolfgang Puck	0.10
Mr. Brown	0.10
Gaffe D Vita	0.09
Other	0.26

Source: *Beverage Industry*, July 2004, p. 20, from Information Resources Inc.

★ 708 ★
Snacks
SIC: 2096; NAICS: 311919

Leading RTE Popcorn/Caramel Brands

Brands are ranked by supermarket, drug store and mass merchandiser sales (but not Wal-Mart) for the year ended April 18, 2004.

	($ mil.)	Share
Smart Food	$ 33.09	17.11%
Poppycock	20.46	10.58
Crunch N Munch	18.05	9.33
Cracker Jack	17.12	8.85
Houston Harvest	14.33	7.41
Other	90.34	46.71

Source: *National Petroleum News*, July 15, 2004, p. 93, from Information Resources Inc.

★ 709 ★
Snacks
SIC: 2096; NAICS: 311919

Top Chocolate-Covered Salted Snack Brands, 2004

Market shares are shown based on supermarket, drug store and discount store sales (excluding Wal-Mart) for the 52 weeks ended December 26, 2004.

Flipz	25.1%
Hershey's Bites	13.1

Sarris	8.8%
Snyders of Hanover	8.5
Private label	6.9
Other	37.6

Source: *The Manufacturing Confectioner*, April 2005, p. 41, from Information Resources Inc.

★ 710 ★
Snacks
SIC: 2096; NAICS: 311919

Top Chocolate-Covered Salted Snack Makers, 2004

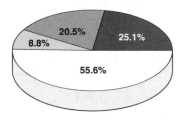

■ Lincoln Snacks Co.	□ Sarris Candies Inc.
■ Hershey Foods Corp.	□ Other

Market shares are shown based on supermarket, drug store and discount store sales (excluding Wal-Mart) for the 52 weeks ended December 26, 2004.

Lincoln Snacks Co.	25.1%
Hershey Foods Corp.	20.5
Sarris Candies Inc.	8.8
Other	55.6

Source: *The Manufacturing Confectioner*, April 2005, p. 41, from Information Resources Inc.

★ 711 ★
Snacks
SIC: 2096; NAICS: 311919

Top Potato Chip Makers, 2005

Market shares are shown based on sales at food stores, drug stores and mass merchandisers (but not Wal-Mart) for the 52 weeks ended January 23, 2005.

Frito-Lay	58.9%
Procter & Gamble	12.4
Utz Quality Foods	3.4
Wise Foods	2.9
Private label	4.7
Other	17.7

Source: *Grocery Headquarters*, April 2005, p. 22, from Information Resources Inc.

★ 712 ★
Snacks
SIC: 2096; NAICS: 311919
Top Pretzel Brands, 2004

Brands are ranked by supermarket, drug store and mass merchandiser sales (but not Wal-Mart) for the 52 weeks ended October 3, 2004.

Snyders of Hanover	$ 41.1
Rold Gold	38.8
Utz	7.3
Combos	4.7
Bachman	3.4
Herr's	3.3
Anderson	2.9
Old Dutch	2.3
Pepperidge Farm Goldfish Pretzels	2.1
Private label	14.4

Source: *Snack Food & Wholesale Bakery*, December 2004, p. NA, from Information Resources Inc.

★ 713 ★
Snacks
SIC: 2096; NAICS: 311919
Top Salty Snack Brands, 2005

Market shares are shown based on drug store sales for the 52 weeks ended February 20, 2005.

Pringles potato chips	10.8%
Doritos tortilla chips	10.8
Lay's potato chips	9.8
Chee-tos cheese snacks	7.4
General Mills Chex Mix	3.7
Ruffles potato chips	2.7
Poppycock popcorn	2.7
Tostitos tortilla chips	2.5
Fritos corn snacks	2.3
Houston harvest popcorn	2.0
Other	45.3

Source: *Chain Drug Review*, May 23, 2005, p. 69, from Information Resources Inc.

★ 714 ★
Snacks
SIC: 2096; NAICS: 311919
Top Tortilla/Tostado Chip Brands, 2005

Market shares are shown based on sales at food stores, drug stores and mass merchandisers (but not Wal-Mart) for the 52 weeks ended January 23, 2005.

Doritos	35.6%
Tostidos	22.7
Tostidos Scoops	8.1
Santitas	3.6
Mission	2.5
Tostidos Gold	2.2
Baked Doritos	1.6
Doritos Rollitos	1.2
Tostitos Natural	1.0
Private label	4.2
Other	17.3

Source: *Grocery Headquarters*, April 2005, p. 22, from Information Resources Inc.

★ 715 ★
Snacks
SIC: 2096; NAICS: 311919
Top Tortilla/Tostado Chip Makers, 2005

Market shares are shown based on sales at food stores, drug stores and mass merchandisers (but not Wal-Mart) for the 52 weeks ended January 23, 2005.

Frito-Lay	79.5%
Mission Foods Inc.	2.5
The Hain Celestial Group Inc.	1.9
Old Dutch Foods Inc.	0.9
Private label	4.2
Other	11.0

Source: *Grocery Headquarters*, April 2005, p. 22, from Information Resources Inc.

★ 716 ★
Pasta
SIC: 2098; NAICS: 311823
Leading Pasta Makers in Japan, 2003

Market shares are estimated based on domestic sales.

Nissin Foods Co.	29.8%
Nippon Flour Mills Co.	23.3

Continued on next page.

★ 716 ★
[Continued]
Pasta
SIC: 2098; NAICS: 311823

Leading Pasta Makers in Japan, 2003

Market shares are estimated based on domestic sales.

Showa Sangyo Co.	7.4%
Hagoromo Foods Corp.	6.6
Okumoto Flour Milling Co.	2.9
Other	30.0

Source: "Market Share Survey Report 2003." [online] from http://www.nni.nikkei.co.jp [Published July 26, 2004], from Nikkei estimates.

★ 717 ★
Pasta
SIC: 2098; NAICS: 311823

Macaroni and Cheese Sales

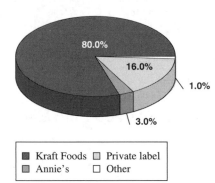

■ Kraft Foods	□ Private label
■ Annie's	□ Other

Market shares are shown in percent.

Kraft Foods	80.0%
Annie's	3.0
Private label	16.0
Other	1.0

Source: *Wall Street Journal*, March 29, 2005, p. B3.

★ 718 ★
Pasta
SIC: 2098; NAICS: 311823

Top Dry Packaged Dinner Brands, 2004

Brands are ranked by sales at supermarkets, drug stores and discount stores (but not Wal-Mart) for the year ended September 5, 2004.

	($ mil.)	Share
Betty Crocker Hamburger Helper	$ 210.2	14.40%
Kraft	169.5	11.61

	($ mil.)	Share
Kraft Velveeta	$ 132.3	9.06%
Kraft Deluxe	82.5	5.65
Rice A Roni Pasta Roni	72.7	4.98
Kraft Easy Mac	68.4	4.68
Banquet Homestyle Bakes	67.2	4.60
Lipton Noodles & Sauce	43.1	2.95
Other	614.1	42.06

Source: *MMR*, November 29, 2004, p. 21, from Information Resources Inc.

★ 719 ★
Pasta
SIC: 2098; NAICS: 311823

Top Pasta Brands, 2004

Brands are ranked by supermarket, drug store and mass merchandiser sales (excluding Wal-Mart) for the year ended October 3, 2004.

	($ mil.)	Share
Barilla	$ 182.13	15.48%
Ronzoni	70.93	6.03
Mueller's	69.64	5.92
Creamette	56.15	4.77
San Giorgio	46.89	3.99
American Beauty	38.23	3.25
Golden Grain Mission	24.58	2.09
Skinner	22.52	1.91
Prince	20.41	1.73
Private label	197.00	16.74
Other	448.16	38.09

Source: *Milling & Baking News*, December 7, 2004, p. NA, from Information Resources Inc.

★ 720 ★
Pasta
SIC: 2098; NAICS: 311823

Top Pasta Makers, 2004

Brands are ranked by supermarket, drug store and mass merchandiser sales (excluding Wal-Mart) for the year ended October 3, 2004.

	($ mil.)	Share
New World Pasta Co.	$ 285.53	29.15%
Barilla Group	182.13	18.59
American Italian Pasta Co.	127.22	12.99
Golden Grain Macaroni	25.24	2.58
Molino e Pastif/De Cecco	19.85	2.03
World Finer Foods	18.35	1.87
Hodgson Mill Inc.	12.11	1.24

Continued on next page.

★ 720 ★

[Continued]

Pasta

SIC: 2098; NAICS: 311823

Top Pasta Makers, 2004

Brands are ranked by supermarket, drug store and mass merchandiser sales (excluding Wal-Mart) for the year ended October 3, 2004.

	($ mil.)	Share
Interamerican Corp.	$ 9.75	1.00%
John Zidian Co.	5.84	0.60
Private label	197.00	20.11
Other	96.62	9.86

Source: *Milling & Baking News*, December 7, 2004, p. NA, from Information Resources Inc.

★ 721 ★

Hummus

SIC: 2099; NAICS: 311991

Hummus Industry in Israel

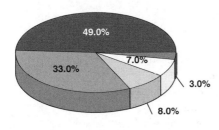

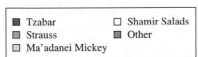

According to a survey by Tzabar, a container of hummus is in more than 95% of the homes in Israel. ACNielsen reports that 14,360 tons of industrial hummus is produced in the country each year.

Tzabar	49.0%
Strauss	33.0
Ma'adanei Mickey	8.0
Shamir Salads	7.0
Other	3.0

Source: *Haaretz*, November 5, 2005, p. NA, from ACNielsen.

★ 722 ★

Lunch Kits

SIC: 2099; NAICS: 311999

Top Refrigerated Lunch Kits, 2003

The industry saw supermarket sales of $641.66 million.

	($ mil.)	Share
Oscar Mayer Lunchables	$ 508.35	79.2%
Eckrich	38.45	6.0
Oscar Mayer Lunchables (Fun Fuel)	27.56	4.3
Hormel	20.55	3.2
Armour (Cracker Crunches)	10.24	1.6
Oscar Mayer Lunchables Cracker Stackers	8.22	1.3
Armour (meat/cheese/crackers)	7.74	1.2

Source: *National Provisioner*, November 2004, p. 26, from Information Resources Inc.

★ 723 ★

Meal Kits

SIC: 2099; NAICS: 311423

Leading Meal Kit Makers

Market shares are shown in percent.

General Mills	64.0%
ConAgra	19.0
Other	17.0

Source: *Prepared Foods*, September 2004, p. 11.

★ 724 ★

Salad

SIC: 2099; NAICS: 311991

Bagged Salad Market, 2005

Market shares in the $2.5 billion industry are shown based on food store, drug store and mass merchandiser sales (excluding Wal-Mart) for the year ended March 25, 2005.

Dole	37.0%
Chiquita	37.0
Other	26.0

Source: *Advertising Age*, April 11, 2005, p. 30, from Information Resources Inc.

★ 725 ★

Salad

SIC: 2099; NAICS: 111219

Lettuce/Packaged Salad Market Shares, 2004

Packaged salad and lettuce sales averaged $3,880 per week per store. They are the largest contributor to the produce category. Dollar shares are shown for July 2003 - June 2004.

Blend	.43.0%
Leaf	.16.0
Head	.16.0
Base salad	.16.0
Kit	8.0
Single serve	1.0

Source: *Produce Merchandising*, February 2005, p. 1, from Efficient Marketing Services and ACNielsen.

★ 726 ★

Salad

SIC: 2099; NAICS: 311999

Packaged Salad Market in Israel

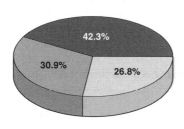

Tsabar ■ □ Other
Achla ■

Total sales of packaged salads are thought to be NIS 676 million annually. Shares are for September 2004.

Tsabar	.42.3%
Achla	.30.9
Other	.26.8

Source: *Haaretz*, November 10, 2004, p. NA, from ACNielsen.

★ 727 ★

Spices

SIC: 2099; NAICS: 311942

Pepper Exports by Vietnam, 2004

Vietnam is the largest pepper exporter by both value and volume. For the year to date, Vietnam earned $133 million from 98,000 tons of exported pepper.

Europe	.38.0%
ASEAN countries	.30.0
United States	.19.0
Middle East	7.7
Other	5.3

Source: *Asia Pulse*, November 18, 2004, p. NA.

★ 728 ★

Spices

SIC: 2099; NAICS: 311942

Seasoning Sales, 2003

Supermarket sales are shown in millions of dollars.

Spices & herbs, dry	$ 820.82
Pepper	203.34
Marinades & tendeerizers	191.29
Extracts	158.30
Salt/cooking/seasoned	141.91
Salt, table	89.83
Seasoning, liquid & remaining	75.15
Salt substitutes	31.49
Vegetables, onion, instant	23.10

Source: *Progressive Grocer*, Sept. 15, 2004, p. 26, from *2004 Progressive Grocer Consumer Expenditure Survey*.

★ 729 ★

Spices

SIC: 2099; NAICS: 311942

Spice Market in Thailand

Market shares are shown in percent.

C.M. van Sillevoldt	.63.0%
Other	.37.0

Source: *Baltimore Sun*, November 3, 2004, p. NA.

★ 730 ★

Spices

SIC: 2099; NAICS: 311942

Top Spice Brands

Brands are ranked by sales in millions of dollars.

McCormick	$ 314.83
Spice Islands	31.09
A&A Spice World	30.59
Mrs. Dash	28.23
Sazon Goya	21.98
McCormick Grill Mate	19.04
Badia	17.98
Mojave	17.91
McCormick Spice Classics	16.49
Private label	131.95

Source: *Supermarket News*, October 18, 2004, p. 70.

★ 731 ★

Spinach

SIC: 2099; NAICS: 311999

Top Spinach Brands, 2004

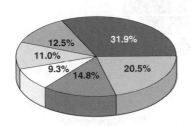

12.5%
11.0%
9.3%
14.8%
31.9%
20.5%

■ Fresh Express □ Earthbound Farms
■ Dole ■ Private label
□ Ready Pac ■ Other

Sales are shown based on sales at food stores, drug stores and mass merchandisers (excluding Wal-Mart) for the 12 weeks ended June 13, 2004.

	Sales	Share
Fresh Express	$ 22,530,392	31.95%
Dole	8,803,715	12.48
Ready Pac	7,746,449	10.98
Earthbound Farms	6,523,375	9.25
Private label	10,451,381	14.82
Other	14,473,232	20.52

Source: *Frozen Food Age*, July 2004, p. 22, from Information Resources Inc.

★ 732 ★

Syrup

SIC: 2099; NAICS: 311999

Maple Syrup Production Worldwide

Maple syrup production has tripled since the 1970s.

United States	80.0%
Canada	20.0

Source: *Christian Science Monitor*, April 6, 2005, p. 11.

★ 733 ★

Taco Kits

SIC: 2099; NAICS: 31183

Top Tortilla/Taco Kit Brands, 2004

Market shares are shown based on supermarket, drug store and mass merchandiser sales (excluding Wal-Mart) for the year ended June 13, 2004.

Guerrero	19.3%
Old El Paso	16.2
Tia Rosa	4.8
La Tortilla Factory	3.8
Taco Bell Home Originals	3.6
Ortega	3.6
Diane's	3.3
La Banderita	3.0
Mission Estilo Casero	2.1
Other	40.3

Source: *Snack Food & Wholesale Bakery*, August 2004, p. 18, from Information Resources Inc.

★ 734 ★

Taco Kits

SIC: 2099; NAICS: 31183

Top Tortilla/Taco Kit Makers, 2004

Market shares are shown based on supermarket, drug store and mass merchandiser sales (But not Wal-Mart) for the year ended June 13, 2004.

Guerrero	19.3%
General Mills	16.2
Kraft Food Inc.	5.3
Bimbo Bakeries	4.9
La Tortilla Factory	3.9
Ole Mexican Foods	3.8
Nestle USA	3.6
Other	43.0

Source: *Snack Food & Wholesale Bakery*, August 2004, p. 18, from Information Resources Inc.

★ 735 ★
Tea
SIC: 2099; NAICS: 31192

Green Tea Market in Thailand

Market shares are shown in percent.

Uni-President 40.4%
Oishi 38.0
Lipton 8.0
Sencha 5.0
Tipco 2.0
Other 6.6

Source: *Asia Africa Intelligence Wire*, February 16, 2005, p. NA, from Uni-President.

★ 736 ★
Tea
SIC: 2099; NAICS: 31192

Largest Tea Producers Worldwide, 2003

Production stood at 3.15 million tons in 2003.

India 27.40%
China 24.60
Sri Lanka 9.75
Kenya 9.40
Other 28.85

Source: *just-drinks.com*, December 8, 2004, p. NA, from Food and Agriculture Organization.

★ 737 ★
Tea
SIC: 2099; NAICS: 31192

Tea Sales, 2003

Supermarket sales are shown in millions of dollars.

	($ mil.)	Share
Tea, liquid	$ 661.21	40.89%
Tea bags	531.38	32.86
Tea, mixes	231.35	14.31
Tea, herbal bags	159.74	9.88
Tea, instant	25.67	1.59
Tea, packaged	6.62	0.41
Tea, herbal packaged	0.72	0.04
Tea, herbal instant	0.36	0.02

Source: *Progressive Grocer*, Sept. 15, 2004, p. 26, from *2004 Progressive Grocer Consumer Expenditure Survey*.

★ 738 ★
Tea
SIC: 2099; NAICS: 31192

Tea Sales in Natural Food Stores

Sales are shown in millions of dollars for the year ended November 2003. Specialty tea is forecasted to become a major part of the $10 billion tea market by 2010.

Medicinal blends 26.3%
Green tea 21.2
Herbal beverage 12.7

Source: *Gourmet Retailer*, November 2004, p. 62.

★ 739 ★
Tea
SIC: 2099; NAICS: 31192

Top Canned/Bottled Tea Brands, 2004

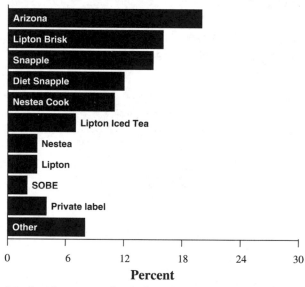

Market shares are shown based on sales at food stores, drug stores and mass merchandisers (excluding Wal-Mart) for the year ended June 13, 2004.

Arizona 19.68%
Lipton Brisk 15.50
Snapple 15.01
Diet Snapple 12.34
Nestea Cook 11.20
Lipton Iced Tea 6.86
Nestea 2.89
Lipton 2.71
SOBE 2.04
Private label 3.57
Other 8.20

Source: *Beverage Industry*, July 2004, p. 20, from Information Resources Inc.

★ 740 ★
Tea
SIC: 2099; NAICS: 31192
Top Refrigerated Tea Brands, 2004

Market shares are shown based on supermarket, drug store and mass merchandiser sales (excluding Wal-Mart) for the year ended May 16, 2004.

Turkey Hill	.28.3%
Red Diamond	. 9.5
Nestea	. 7.0
Arizona	. 6.3
Milos	. 6.1
Clover Farms	. 4.1
Minute Maid Premium	. 3.4
Swiss Premium	. 2.6
Galliker	. 2.5
Private label	.12.6
Other	.17.6

Source: *Dairy Field*, August 2004, p. 14, from Information Resources Inc.

★ 741 ★
Tea
SIC: 2099; NAICS: 31192
Top Refrigerated Tea Makers, 2004

Market shares are shown based on supermarket, drug store and mass merchandiser sales (excluding Wal-Mart) for the year ended May 16, 2004.

Turkey Hill Dairy	.28.3%
Donovan Coffee Co. Inc.	. 9.5
Coca Cola Co.	. 7.0
Ferolito Vultaggio & Sons	. 6.3
Milos Tea Co.	. 6.1
Wengerts Dairy	. 4.9
The Minute Maid Co.	. 3.4
Galliker Dairy Co.	. 2.6
Private label	.12.6
Other	.15.2

Source: *Dairy Field*, August 2004, p. 14, from Information Resources Inc.

★ 742 ★
Tea
SIC: 2099; NAICS: 31192
Top Tea Brands in Australia, 2004

Total tea sales were $56.2 million for the 52 weeks ended June 13, 2004.

Dilmah	.20.4%
Bell	.20.0
Twinings	.19.6

Choysa	.11.7%
Healtheries	. 9.1
Red Seal	. 4.2
BTC Regionals	. 4.0
PG Tips	. 2.6
Lipton	. 1.5
Other	. 6.9

Source: "World of Tea in Australia." [online] from http://www.tea.org.au/cuppa [accessed March 1, 2005], from ACNielsen.

★ 743 ★
Tea
SIC: 2099; NAICS: 31192
Top Tea Brands in the U.K., 2001 and 2004

Market shares are estimated in percent. Unilever makes PG Tips.

	2001	2004
PG Tips	21.3%	25.0%
Tetley	17.5	25.0
Other	62.2	50.0

Source: *Sunday Telegraph*, December 5, 2004, p. NA, from Euromonitor.

★ 744 ★
Whey
SIC: 2099; NAICS: 311999

Whey Production in Eastern Europe, 2003

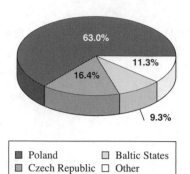

98,200 tons were produced during the year.

Poland	.63.0%
Czech Republic	.16.4
Baltic States	. 9.3
Other	.11.3

Source: *International Food Ingredients*, August-September 2004, p. 24, from Zenith International.

SIC 21 - Tobacco Products

★ 745 ★
Tobacco
SIC: 2100; NAICS: 312221, 312229

Largest Tobacco Firms, 2003

The recent tobacco agreement required the major tobacco companies to pay states over $246 billion over the next 25 years. Tobacco trade associations have been forced to disband. Tobacco firms must also restrict youths' access to tobacco. Pro-tobacco lobbying is also restricted. Tobacco research must also be open to the public. Market shares are shown in percent.

Philip Morris	.50.4%
R.J. Reynolds	.21.5
Brown & Williamson	.10.5
Lorillard	9.3
Commonwealth	3.1
Liggett & Myers	2.6
Other	2.6

Source: *USA TODAY*, September 21, 2004, p. 2B, from Tobacco Merchants Association.

★ 746 ★
Tobacco
SIC: 2100; NAICS: 312229

Non-Cigarette Tobacco Sales

The category of other tobacco products is the eighth largest convenience store category representing 2.8% of store sales.

Smokeless tobacco	.69.0%
Cigars	.28.0
Other	3.0

Source: *NACS Magazine*, December 2004, p. 67, from *NACS 2004 State of the Industry Report.*

★ 747 ★
Cigarettes
SIC: 2111; NAICS: 312221

Largest Cigarette Firms, 2004

Market shares are shown in percent.

Philip Morris	.49.80%
R.J. Reynolds	.30.82
Other	.19.38

Source: *World Tobacco*, March 2005, p. 9.

★ 748 ★
Cigarettes
SIC: 2111; NAICS: 312221

Leading Cigarette Producing Nations, 2003

Data are in billions of cigarettes.

China	1,735
United States	580
Russia	380
Japan	224
Germany	211

Source: *USA TODAY*, March 9, 2005, p. A1, from World Health Organization.

★ 749 ★
Cigarettes
SIC: 2111; NAICS: 312221

Roll-Your-Own Cigarette Market in the U.K.

Market shares are shown in percent.

Lambert & Butler	.65.9%
Other	.34.1

Source: *Daily Post*, February 2, 2005, p. 4.

★ 750 ★

Cigarettes

SIC: 2111; NAICS: 312221

Top Cigarette Brands at Convience Stores

Market shares are shown based on sales at convenience stores. Cigarettes represent 32.6% of in-store sales.

Marlboro	.48.28%
Newport	8.56
Camel	6.31
Doral	5.74
Winston	4.32
Basic	3.61
Kool	3.02
Virginia Slim	2.46
Salem	2.03
Pall Mall	1.61
Other	.20.06

Source: *Convenience Store News*, May 9, 2005, p. 18, from McIlvane Co. Inc.

★ 751 ★

Cigarettes

SIC: 2111; NAICS: 312221

Top Cigarette Brands at Drug Stores, 2005

Market shares are shown based on drug store sales for the 52 weeks ended February 20, 2005.

Marlboro Lights single pack	.16.8%
Marlboro single pack	.10.0
Marlboro Lights multi pk/cart.	6.1
Newport single pack	5.7
Marlboro Ultra Lights single pack	4.5
Parliament Light single pack	3.0
Kool single pack	2.1
Marlboro Medium single pack	1.6
Basic Lights single pack	1.6
Other	.48.6

Source: *Chain Drug Review*, May 23, 2005, p. 69, from Information Resources Inc.

★ 752 ★

Cigarettes

SIC: 2111; NAICS: 312221

Top Cigarette Brands in Egypt, 2003

Market shares are shown in percent.

Cleopatra	.58.3%
New Box	.20.4

New Cleopatra	.4.1%
Marlboro	3.6
L&M	2.0
Other	.12.6

Source: *World Tobacco*, May 2005, p. 4.

★ 753 ★

Cigarettes

SIC: 2111; NAICS: 312221

Top Cigarette Brands in Iran, 2003

Market shares are shown in percent.

57	.31.4%
Bahman	.19.8
Kent	6.4
Montana	6.4
Other	.27.3
Winston	8.7

Source: *World Tobacco*, May 2005, p. 4.

★ 754 ★

Cigarettes

SIC: 2111; NAICS: 312221

Top Cigarette Brands in Israel, 2003

Market shares are shown in percent.

Marlboro	.20.5%
Time	.17.1
L&M	8.0
Golf	6.5
Parliament	6.3
Other	.41.6

Source: *World Tobacco*, May 2005, p. 4.

★ 755 ★

Cigarettes

SIC: 2111; NAICS: 312221

Top Cigarette Brands in Japan, 2005

Market shares are shown for the year ended March 31, 2005.

Mild Seven Super Lights	8.0%
Mild Seven Lights	8.0
Mild Seven	6.9
Seven Stars	5.7
Caster Mild	3.5
Marlboro Lights Menthol Box	3.5
Mild Seven Extra Lights	3.1
Cabin Mild Box	2.1
Mild Seven One 100's Box	2.0

Continued on next page.

★ 755 ★

[Continued]
Cigarettes
SIC: 2111; NAICS: 312221

Top Cigarette Brands in Japan, 2005

Market shares are shown for the year ended March 31, 2005.

Lark Milds KS Box	2.0%
Other	55.2

Source: "Japan Tobacco Annual Report 2005." [online] from http://www.jti.co.jp/jti_e/IR/05/annual2005 [Accessed July 7, 2005], from Tobacco Institute of Japan.

★ 756 ★

Cigarettes
SIC: 2111; NAICS: 312221

Top Cigarette Brands in Syria, 2003

Market shares are shown in percent.

Orient	11.7%
Al-Hamra	9.8
Coast (Al-Shate)	8.5
Gauloises	5.2
Other	64.8

Source: *World Tobacco*, May 2005, p. 4.

★ 757 ★

Cigarettes
SIC: 2111; NAICS: 312221

Top Cigarette Brands in Turkey, 2003

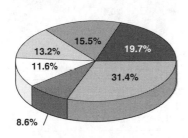

■ Tekel 2000	□ Samsun
■ Marlboro	■ Parliament
□ Maltepe	▨ Other

Market shares are shown in percent.

Tekel 2000	19.7%
Marlboro	15.5
Maltepe	13.2
Samsun	11.6
Parliament	8.6
Other	31.4

Source: *World Tobacco*, May 2005, p. 4.

★ 758 ★

Cigarettes
SIC: 2111; NAICS: 312221

Top Cigarette Makers in France, 2003

According to the source, slightly over 30% of adults smoke. Consumption has been falling since 2001. There was a slight increase in smokeless tobacco and cigars. Market shares are shown in percent.

Philip Morris	39.2%
Altadis	28.8
BAT	15.9
JTI	9.5
Imperial	3.4
Gallaher	3.0
Other	0.2

Source: *World Tobacco*, July 2004, p. 42, from Altadis.

★ 759 ★

Cigarettes
SIC: 2111; NAICS: 312221

Top Cigarette Makers in Korea

The company exported 31 billion cigarettes in 2003, a 16-fold increase from 1996.

KT&G	77.0%
Other	23.0

Source: *Institutional Investor*, November 2004, p. NA.

★ 760 ★

Cigarettes
SIC: 2111; NAICS: 312221

Top Cigarette Makers in Russia

Shares are shown based on sales volume.

Philip Morris	26.3%
Gallher	17.1
BAT	16.7
JTI	16.2
Other	23.7

Source: *Kommersant*, January 24, 2005, p. NA.

★ 761 ★
Cigarettes
SIC: 2111; NAICS: 312221

Top Cigarette Makers in Switzerland

Market shares are shown in percent.

Philip Morris	.46.8%
British American Tobacco	.43.7
Japan Tobacco International	.9.5

Source: *World Tobacco*, March 2005, p. 15.

★ 762 ★
Cigarettes
SIC: 2111; NAICS: 312221

Top Tobacco Brands Worldwide, 2004

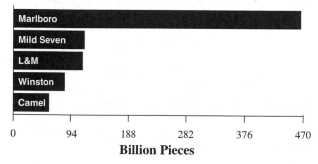

Billion Pieces

Brands are ranked by sales volume in billions of cigarettes for the year ended December 31, 2004.

Marlboro (Philip Morris)	466.4
Mild Seven (Japan Tobacco)	115.6
L&M (Philip Morris)	113.4
Winston	85.0
Camel	58.8

Source: "Japan Tobacco Annual Report 2005." [online] from http://www.jti.co.jp/jti_e/IR/05/annual2005 [Accessed July 7, 2005], from The Maxwell Report *The World Cigarette Market Leaders.*

★ 763 ★
Cigars
SIC: 2121; NAICS: 312229

Cigar Market Worldwide

The company's share does not include the United States.

Habanos	.70.0%
Other	.30.0

Source: *Forbes*, December 27, 2004, p. 51.

★ 764 ★
Cigars
SIC: 2121; NAICS: 312229

Cigar Production, 2004

Data show estimated production for selected cigar brands.

Montecristo No. 2	2,000,000
H. Upmann Magnuim 46	500,000
Cohiba Siglo VI	500,000
San Cristobel de la Habana El Morro . . .	300,000
Davidoff Millennium Blend Robusto . . .	250,000
Rocky Patel Vintage 1990 Robusto	200,000
Arturo Fuents Don Carlos No. 2	108,000
Sancho Panza Extra Fuerte Madrid	100,000
Montecristo Platinum Series Belicoso Tube	100,000
H. Upmann Vintage Cameroon Belicoso . .	100,000
C.A.O. L'Anniversaire Cameroon Robusto	100,000
Trinidad Robusto	95,000

Source: *Cigar Afficianda*, January - February 2005, p. 59.

★ 765 ★
Cigars
SIC: 2121; NAICS: 312229

Leading Cigar Producers, 2004

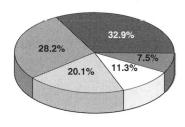

Market shares are shown for the second and third quarter of 2004. By channel, convenience stores take 74% of sales, drug stores 14% and food stores 12%.

	Q2	Q3
Altadis	.34.2%	32.9%
Swisher	.28.0	28.2
John Middleton	.19.3	20.1

Continued on next page.

★ 765 ★
[Continued]
Cigars
SIC: 2121; NAICS: 312229

Leading Cigar Producers, 2004

Market shares are shown for the second and third quarter of 2004. By channel, convenience stores take 74% of sales, drug stores 14% and food stores 12%.

	Q2	Q3
Swedish Match	10.9%	11.3%
Other	7.6	7.5

Source: *Convenience Store Decisions*, January 2005, p. 34, from ACNielsen.

★ 766 ★
Cigars
SIC: 2121; NAICS: 312229

Local Cigar Market in Lebanon

Market shares are shown in percent.

Habanos	95.0%
Other	5.0

Source: *Travel Retailer International*, August-September 2004, p. 47.

SIC 22 - Textile Mill Products

★ 767 ★
Textiles
SIC: 2200; NAICS: 31321, 315211, 315212

Largest Clothing/Textile Exporters Worldwide

The value of exports is shown in billions of dollars. Shares are shown for the top 25 countries.

	($ mil.)	Share
China	$ 98.7	31.12%
Italy	26.5	8.35
Germany	19.7	6.21
United States	16.7	5.26
Korea	14.9	4.70
Turkey	12.4	3.91
France	12.4	3.91
India	12.1	3.81
Taiwan	11.7	3.69
Belgium	10.9	3.44
Other	81.2	25.60

Source: *New York Times*, December 14, 2004, p. C7, from World Trade Organization, Organization of Economic Cooperation and Development, and Economy.com.

★ 768 ★
Upholstery
SIC: 2200; NAICS: 31321

Upholstery Industry in the U.K.

Total production increased from 683.6 million pounds in 1999 to 888.8 million pounds in 2002.

	1999	2002
Fabric	82.4%	80.1%
Leather	15.5	17.6
Microfibre	2.1	2.3

Source: *Cabinet Maker*, November 26, 2004, p. 36, from CSIL.

★ 769 ★
Upholstery
SIC: 2211; NAICS: 31321

Top Upholstery Makers

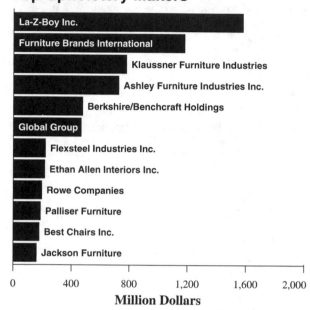

Million Dollars

Firms are ranked by sales in millions of dollars.

La-Z-Boy Inc.	$ 1,580.0
Furniture Brands International	1,180.0
Klaussner Furniture Industries	778.0
Ashley Furniture Industries Inc.	725.0
Berkshire/Benchcraft Holdings	475.0
Global Group	465.0
Flexsteel Industries Inc.	219.0
Ethan Allen Interiors Inc.	215.0
Rowe Companies	195.2
Palliser Furniture	185.8
Best Chairs Inc.	178.0
Jackson Furniture	160.0

Source: "A Year of Transition." [online] from http://www.udm.com [Accessed July 5, 2005].

★ 770 ★
Hosiery
SIC: 2251; NAICS: 315111

Stocking Market in Thailand

Market shares are shown in percent.

Cherilon 80.0%
Other 20.0

Source: *Finance Wire*, December 1, 2004, p. NA.

★ 771 ★
Hosiery
SIC: 2251; NAICS: 325611

Top Hosiery Brands, 2004

Market shares are shown based on sales at food stores, drug stores and mass merchandisers (excluding Wal-Mart) for the 52 weeks ended June 13, 2004.

L'Eggs Sheer Energy 15.3%
No Nonsense 12.2
L'Eggs Silken Mist 8.5
Everyday by L'Eggs 5.4
Just My Size 4.0
No Nonsense Great Shapes 3.8
No Nonsense Sheer Endurance 3.7
No Nonsense Almost Bare 3.1
Other 44.0

Source: *Grocery Headquarters*, August 2004, p. S88, from Information Resources Inc.

★ 772 ★
Hosiery
SIC: 2251; NAICS: 315111

Top Hosiery Makers, 2004

Market shares are shown based on sales at food stores, drug stores and mass merchandisers (excluding Wal-Mart) for the 52 weeks ended June 13, 2004.

L'Eggs Products 53.9%
Kayser-Roth 24.8
Private label 13.9
Other 7.4

Source: *Grocery Headquarters*, August 2004, p. S88, from Information Resources Inc.

★ 773 ★
Hosiery
SIC: 2251; NAICS: 315111

Top Panty Hose Brands, 2004

Market shares are shown based on drug store sales for the year ended October 31, 2004.

L'eggs Sheer Energy 15.6%
L'eggs Silken Mist 9.2
No Nonsense 7.9
Everyday by L'eggs 4.5
Just My Size 3.6
No Nonsense Figure Enhancement 3.5
L'eggs Sheer Control 3.5
Brown Sugar 3.4
Other 48.8

Source: *Chain Drug Review*, September 27, 2004, p. 36, from Information Resources Inc.

★ 774 ★
Hosiery
SIC: 2252; NAICS: 315111

Support Hosiery Market in the U.K.

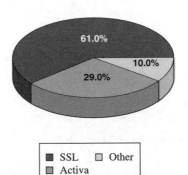

The industry was valued at 10.1 million pounds over the previous 12 months.

SSL 61.0%
Activa 29.0
Other 10.0

Source: *Community Pharmacy*, August 12, 2004, p. 28, from IMS PAC report.

★ 775 ★
Carpets and Rugs
SIC: 2273; NAICS: 31411
Leading Carpet/Rug Makers, 2003

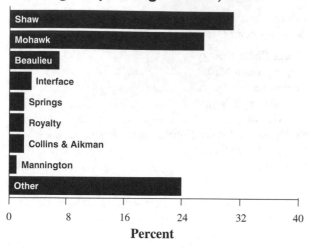

Percent

Market shares are shown based on the $13.1 billion industry. The total flooring industry saw a 5% growth, while broadloom carpets saw 3% growth and area rugs saw 8% growth.

Shaw	31.0%
Mohawk	27.0
Beaulieu	7.0
Interface	3.0
Springs	2.0
Royalty	2.0
Collins & Aikman	2.0
Mannington	1.0
Other	24.0

Source: *Floor Focus*, May 2004, p. NA.

★ 776 ★
Nonwovens
SIC: 2297; NAICS: 31323
Disposable Products Industry in India

The value of nonwovens consumed in India was estimated at $200 million in 2002. Total nonwovens consumption was 78,000 tons.

Absorbent hygiene	85.0%
Medical	6.0
Wipes	2.0
Other	7.0

Source: *Nonwovens Industry*, February 2005, p. 55.

★ 777 ★
Nonwovens
SIC: 2297; NAICS: 31323
Largest Nonwoven Goods Makers Worldwide

Companies are ranked by sales in millions of dollars.

Freudenberg Nonwovens	$ 1,400
DuPont Nonwovens	1,200
BBA FiberWeb	900
PGI Nonwovens	730
Ahlstrom FiberComposites	728
Johns Manville	500
Kimberly Clark	295
Colbond	250
Buckeye Technologies	217
Japan Vilene	185
Asahi Kasei	167
Hollingsworth & Vose	165

Source: *Nonwovens Industry*, September 2004, p. 36.

★ 778 ★
Nonwovens
SIC: 2297; NAICS: 31323
Nonwoven Fabric Production Worldwide

The nonwoven goods industry got its start about 50 years ago. Total production was 4.5 million tons or 110 billion square meters.

Carded	47.0%
Spunlaid	41.0
Airlaid	8.0
Wetlaid	4.0

Source: *Nonwovens Industry*, October 2004, p. 44, from Association of the Nonwoven Fabrics Industry.

★ 779 ★
Nonwovens
SIC: 2297; NAICS: 31323
Nonwoven Fabric Sales Worldwide

The global recession affected some end markets. East Asia development led the market in increased capacity. The overall market is forecasted to increase to 11.5 billion in 2009. North America, Western Europe and Japan represent 60% of the market.

2000	7,456
2001	7,925

Continued on next page.

★ 779 ★

[Continued]
Nonwovens
SIC: 2297; NAICS: 31323

Nonwoven Fabric Sales Worldwide

The global recession affected some end markets. East Asia development led the market in increased capacity. The overall market is forecasted to increase to 11.5 billion in 2009. North America, Western Europe and Japan represent 60% of the market.

2002	8,298
2003	8,617
2004	9,111

Source: *Research Studies - Business Communications Inc.*, September 15, 2004, p. NA, from Business Communications Co.

★ 780 ★

Nonwovens
SIC: 2297; NAICS: 31323

Nonwoven Fabrics Industry Worldwide, 2004

Nonwoven fabric production in 4.4 million metric tons worth $16 billion. North America's leading wipe segments are consumer wipes and cleaning products.

North America/Europe	57.0%
Asia	27.0
Other	16.0

Source: *Chemical Market Reporter*, January 31, 2005, p. 8, from Association of the Nonwoven Fabrics Industry.

★ 781 ★

Wipes
SIC: 2297; NAICS: 31323

Household Wipe Sales Worldwide

The industry has seen growth exceeding 20% between 1998-2003. New markets are developing in the medical, feminine hygiene, face and cosmetic wipes.

	2000	2002	Share
Electrostatic wipes	$ 647.4	$ 709.4	48.33%
Antibacterial wipes	222.1	334.6	22.79
Other	130.6	423.9	28.88

Source: *Global Cosmetic Industry*, November 2004, p. 20, from Euromonitor.

★ 782 ★

Wipes
SIC: 2297; NAICS: 31323

Leading Wipes Brands, 2004

Market shares are shown based on supermarket, drug store and mass merchandiser sales (excluding Wal-Mart).

Clorox	46.3%
Lysol	22.2
Mr. Clean	19.1
Fantastik	3.1
Formula 409	2.1
Scotch Brite	0.7
Mr. Clean Magic	0.6
Eraser Duo	0.5
Orange Clean	0.4
Private label	3.2
Other	1.8

Source: *Nonwovens Industry*, February 2005, p. 28, from Information Resources Inc.

★ 783 ★

Wipes
SIC: 2297; NAICS: 31323

Leading Wipes Producers, 2004

Market shares are shown based on supermarket, drug store and mass merchandiser sales (excluding Wal-Mart) for the 52 weeks ended December 26, 2004.

Clorox	48.4%
Reckitt Benckiser	22.2
Procter & Gamble	19.7
S.C. Johnson	3.1
3M Cloth	0.7
Method	0.5
Orange Glo	0.4
Pegasus International	0.3
Chicopee	0.3
Private label	3.2
Other	1.2

Source: *Chemical Market Reporter*, January 24, 2005, p. FR8, from Information Resources Inc.

★ 784 ★
Wipes
SIC: 2297; NAICS: 31323

Leading Wipes Sectors, 2004 and 2008

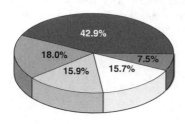

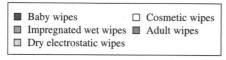

■ Baby wipes   □ Cosmetic wipes
■ Impregnated wet wipes   ■ Adult wipes
□ Dry electrostatic wipes

Total sales are forecasted to increase from $1.72 billion in 2004 to $1.81 billion in 2008.

	2004	2008	Share
Baby wipes	$ 752.3	$ 777.3	42.90%
Impregnated wet wipes . . .	305.9	326.1	18.00
Dry electrostatic wipes . . .	288.6	288.2	15.91
Cosmetic wipes	247.3	284.9	15.72
Adult wipes	134.6	135.5	7.48

Source: *Nonwovens Industry*, February 2005, p. 28, from Euromonitor.

★ 785 ★
Wipes
SIC: 2297; NAICS: 31323

Top Wipes Makers Worldwide, 2003

The world market was valued at $5.2 billion in 2003. Western Europe took $2.3 billion of sales, or 44.3% of the total. North America followed with $1.79 billion or 34.4%. By segment, personal wipes was the top sector, followed by baby wipes and then household cleaners.

Procter & Gamble Co.	.23.9%
Kimberly-Clark Corp.	9.6
Kao Corp.	5.8
Johnson & Johnson	5.6
SC Johnson & Son	5.2
Unilever	3.6
Reckitt Benckiser	3.6
Beiersdorf	2.1
Playtex Products	1.9
Clorox Co.	1.7
Other	.37.0

Source: *Global Cosmetic Industry*, April 2004, p. 40.

SIC 23 - Apparel and Other Textile Products

★ 786 ★
Apparel
SIC: 2300; NAICS: 315211, 315212, 315223
Apparel Market in Australia

The $1.86 billion market is very well developed and reflects current trends. China is the largest supplier.

Women 52.3%
Men 28.4
Infant 8.9
Girls 5.9
Boys 4.5

Source: "Apparel in Australia." [online] from http://www.export.gov [accessed September 23, 2004].

★ 787 ★
Apparel
SIC: 2300; NAICS: 315211, 315212, 315223
Apparel Market in France, 2003

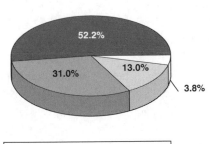

| ■ Womenswear | □ Childrenswear |
| ■ Menswear | □ Babywear |

Women's apparel takes slightly over half of the 13.5 billion euro market.

Womenswear 52.2%
Menswear 31.0
Childrenswear 13.0
Babywear 3.8

Source: "French Clothing Market." [online] from http://www.fco.gov.uk [Published February 2005], from UK Trade & Investment.

★ 788 ★
Apparel
SIC: 2300; NAICS: 315211, 315239
Jeans Market in India

The market is expected to exceed Rs 1900 crore.

Men 76.0%
Women 17.0
Children 7.0

Source: *just-style.com*, December 6, 2004, p. NA, from Images-KSA Technopak India Jeanswear Research.

★ 789 ★
Apparel
SIC: 2300; NAICS: 315211, 315239
Jeans Market in the U.K., 2003

Jeans have done well since their low point in 1997 when combat and casual pants sold well. Total market sales were 1.66 billion pounds sterling. Women were the main contributor to the growth in sales. Women's jeans sales were 713 million pounds, surpassing sales in the men's category for the first time.

Levi's 15.0%
Marks & Spencer 9.0
Other 76.0

Source: *Marketing Week*, April 1, 2004, p. 24, from TNS FashionTrak.

★ 790 ★

Apparel

SIC: 2300; NAICS: 315211, 315239

Largest Jeans Makers, 2004

Firms are ranked by sales in millions of euros. Diesel and Mustang's figures are from 2003. VF Corp. makes Lee, Wrangler and H.I.S.

Levi's	3,006
VF Corp.	1,952
Diesel	750
Replay	230
Mustang	121

Source: *Wirtschaftswoche*, May 19, 2005, p. 70, from BTE.

★ 791 ★

Apparel

SIC: 2300; NAICS: 315211, 315212, 315223

Leading Apparel Firms, 2003

The leading public firms are ranked by sales in millions of dollars.

Gap Inc.	$ 15,854.0
Nike Inc.	10,697.0
Limited Brands Inc.	8,934.0
VF Corp.	5,207.5
Jones Apparel Group	4,375.3
Liz Claiborne	4,241.1
Reebok International	3,485.3
Kellwood Co.	2,346.5
Abercrombie & Fitch	1,707.8
American Eagle Outfitters	1,520.0

Source: *Apparel*, July 2004, p. 23.

★ 792 ★

Apparel

SIC: 2300; NAICS: 315211, 315212, 315223

Leading Children's Apparel Brands, 2004

Data show respondent answers to this survey question: "If you were shopping for children's apparel in a discount store or superstore, which brand would you want?"

Hanes	14.0%
Gap	8.0
Levi's	7.0
Carter's	7.0
Osh-Kosh	6.0
Nike	6.0
Wrangler	4.0

Old Navy	4.0%
Fruit of the Loom	4.0
Dockers	4.0

Source: *DSN Retailing Today*, October 25, 2004, p. 48, from Leo J. Shapiro for *DSN Retailing Today*.

★ 793 ★

Apparel

SIC: 2300; NAICS: 315211, 315212, 315223

Leading Fleece Makers

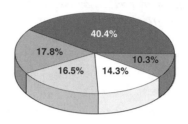

Legend: Jerzees, Fruit of the Loom, Hanes, Lee, Gildan

Market shares are shown for the first quarter of fiscal year 2003. Data reflect sales from U.S. distributors to screenprinters based on ACNielsen S.T.A.R.S. report.

Jerzees (Russell)	40.4%
Fruit of the Loom	17.8
Hanes	16.5
Lee (VF Corp.)	14.3
Gildan	10.3

Source: "Gildan Activewear." [online] from http://www.gildan.com [Accessed March 22, 2004], from Gildan.

★ 794 ★

Apparel

SIC: 2300; NAICS: 315211, 315212, 315223

Leading Golf Shirt Makers, 2004

Market shares are shown in percent.

Nike	37.16%
Ashworth	28.36
Adidas	4.83
Other	29.65

Source: "2004 SportScanInfo Year in Review." [online] from http://sportstrendinfo.com/pdf/SportScanINFO.2004.pdf [Accessed May 9, 2005], from SportScanInfo.

★ 795 ★
Apparel
SIC: 2300; NAICS: 315211, 315212, 315223
Leading Performance Apparel Makers

Market shares are shown in percent.

Under Armour	.74.0%
Nike	.11.0
Other	.15.0

Source: *Baltimore Business Journal*, December 6, 2004, p. NA.

★ 796 ★
Apparel
SIC: 2300; NAICS: 315211, 315212, 315223
Leading Sport Shirt Makers

Market shares are shown for the first quarter of fiscal year 2003. Data reflect sales from U.S. distributors to screenprinters based on ACNielsen S.T.A.R.S. report.

Jerzees (Russell)	.21.0%
Outer Banks (Hanes)	.20.8
Anvil	.16.3
Gildan	.14.7
Stedman (Hanes)	.12.2
Other	.15.0

Source: ''Gildan Activewear.'' [online] from http:// www.gildan.com [Accessed March 22, 2004], from Gildan.

★ 797 ★
Apparel
SIC: 2300; NAICS: 315211, 315212, 315223
Leading Sports Apparel Firms

Companies are ranked by sales in billions of dollars.

VF Corp.	$ 5.88
Jones Apparel Group	4.65
Liz Claiborne	4.47
Levi Strauss & Co.	4.07
Polo Ralph Lauren Corp.	3.18
Kellwood Co.	2.48
Tommy Hilfiger Corp.	1.84
Philips-Van Heusen Corp.	1.60

Source: *WWD*, March 2, 2005, p. 1.

★ 798 ★
Apparel
SIC: 2300; NAICS: 315211, 315212, 315223
Leading Sports Apparel Makers

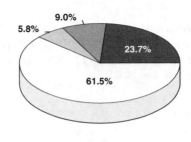

Market shares are shown in percent.

	2003	2004
Nike	25.0%	23.7%
Adidas	9.6	9.0
Under Armour	4.8	5.8
Other	60.6	61.5

Source: *USA TODAY*, December 13, 2004, p. 2B, from SportsScan.

★ 799 ★
Apparel
SIC: 2300; NAICS: 315211, 315212, 315223
Leading T-Shirt Makers, 2003

Market shares are shown for the first quarter of fiscal year 2003. Data reflect sales from U.S. distribuitors to screenprinters based on ACNielsen S.T.A.R.S. report.

Gildan	.31.4%
Hanes	.24.3
Fruit of the Loom	.17.9
Jerzees (Russell)	.12.4
Anvil	.10.7
Other	3.3

Source: ''Gildan Activewear.'' [online] from http:// www.gildan.com [Accessed March 22, 2004], from Gildan.

★ 800 ★
Apparel

SIC: 2300; NAICS: 315211, 315212, 315223

Leading Technical T-Shirt Makers, 2004

Market shares are shown for the end of 2004. Data for the week of February 25, 2005 put Under Armour at 46.18%, Nike 28.06%, Adidas 11.88% and New Balance 8.31%.

Nike	.41.16%
Under Armour	.28.29
Adidas	.11.34
New Balance	.11.33
Other	7.88

Source: "New Balance Readying for Major Euro Growth." [online] from http://www.healthandfitnessbiz.com [Accessed March 7, 2005], from SportScanInfo.

★ 801 ★
Apparel

SIC: 2300; NAICS: 315228, 315239

Public School Uniform Market in Miami, FL

The company has a market share in excess of 90%.

Ibiley	.90.0%
Other	.10.0

Source: "Board of Directors." [online] from http://www.mfha.net.bodbios.htm [Accessed May 2, 2005].

★ 802 ★
Apparel

SIC: 2300; NAICS: 315211, 315212, 315223

Sports Apparel Sales, 1999 and 2003

Distribution is shown based on units sold.

	1999	2003
Women's	38.5%	44.5%
Men's	38.5	36.3
Children's	23.0	19.2

Source: *Sporting Goods Business*, May 2004, p. 14, from Sporting Goods Manufacturers Association.

★ 803 ★
Apparel

SIC: 2300; NAICS: 315211, 315212, 315223

Top Exporters of Apparel, 2004

The top exporters to the United States are shown for the year ended May 2004.

China	.13.1%
Mexico	.10.2
Honduras	.6.0
El Salvador	.4.5
Bangladesh	.4.5
Hong Kong	.4.1
Dominican Republic	.3.9
Vietnam	.3.7
Indonesia	.3.4
Korea	.3.2
Other	.43.4

Source: *Wall Street Journal*, August 13, 2004, p. B1, from U.S. Bureau of the Census via International Development Systems.

★ 804 ★
Apparel

SIC: 2300; NAICS: 315211, 315212, 315223

U.S. Apparel Imports

The table shows the changes in market share on January 1, 2005 when the quota system governing the imports from developing countries comes to an end. Less developed countries are expected to suffer when up against the more sophisticated operations in India and China. The global trade is worth $450 billion.

	Current	After
Rest of Americas	16.0%	5.0%
China	16.0	50.0
Mexico	10.0	3.0
Hong Kong	9.0	6.0
Philippines	4.0	2.0
Indonesia	4.0	2.0
India	4.0	15.0
Bangladesh	4.0	2.0

Source: *Financial Times*, October 22, 2004, p. 7, from World Trade Organization.

★ 805 ★
Apparel

SIC: 2300; NAICS: 315211, 315212, 315223

Western Apparel Market

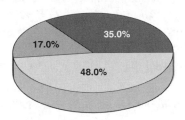

Market shares are shown in percent.

Justin Brands	.35.0%
Ariat	.17.0
Other	.48.0

Source: *Business 2.0*, October 2004, p. 72, from Ariat and *Business 2.0* estimates.

★ 806 ★
Apparel

SIC: 2311; NAICS: 315211, 315223, 315228

Leading Men's Italian Tailored Clothing Firms

Firms are ranked by sales in millions of dollars.

Ermenegildo Zegna	$ 828
Canali	180
Brioni	177
Forall (Pal Zileri)	152
Corneliani	129
Vestimenta (Hilton)	58
Sanremo (Inghirami)	55
Urbis (Tombolini)	50
Cantarelli	48
Belvest	45

Source: *WWD*, December 13, 2004, p. 36S, from Pambianco Strategie Di Impresa.

★ 807 ★
Apparel

SIC: 2320; NAICS: 315211, 315223, 315228

Leading Men's Apparel Brands, 2004

Data show respondent answers to this survey question: "If you were shopping for men's apparel in a discount store or superstore, which brand would you want?"

Hanes	.20.0%
Levi's	.14.0
Wrangler	.11.0
Fruit of the Loom	.11.0
Dockers	.10.0
Polo/Ralph Lauren	8.0
Nike	3.0
Lee	3.0
Tommy Hilfiger	2.0
Jockey	2.0

Source: *DSN Retailing Today*, October 25, 2004, p. 48, from Leo J. Shapiro for *DSN Retailing Today*.

★ 808 ★
Apparel

SIC: 2320; NAICS: 315211, 315223, 315228

Leading Men's Apparel Firms in Japan, 2003

Market shares are estimated based on domestic sales of 2.8 trillion yen.

Onward Kashiyama	2.7%
Sanyo Shokai	2.3
Five Foxes	1.4
World	1.0
D'urban	0.8
Other	.91.8

Source: "Market Share Survey Report 2003." [online] from http://www.nni.nikkei.co.jp [Published July 26, 2004], from Nikkei estimates.

★ 809 ★
Apparel
SIC: 2320; NAICS: 315211, 315223, 315228
Men's Dress Apparel

Top brands of dress slacks based on dollar sales were: Haggar, Polo/Ralph Lauren, Kenenth Cole, Savane and Dockers. Top brands of sport coats were Polo/ Ralph Lauren. Chaps, Haggar, Oscar de la Renta and Calvin Klein. Figures are in thousands of dollars.

Dress slacks	$ 1,325,085
Sports coats and jackets	1,043,366

Source: *Daily News Record*, December 6, 2004, p. 21, from NPD Fashionworld.

★ 810 ★
Apparel
SIC: 2320; NAICS: 315211, 315223, 315228
Men's Sportswear Sales, 2003

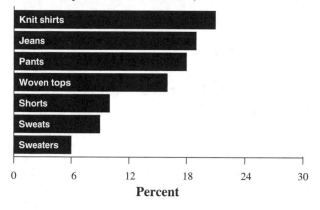

Total men's sportswear sales was $28.5 billion.

Knit shirts	21.0%
Jeans	19.0
Pants	18.0
Woven tops	16.0
Shorts	10.0
Sweats	9.0
Sweaters	6.0

Source: *Daily News Record*, June 14, 2004, p. 6B, from STS Market Research.

★ 811 ★
Apparel
SIC: 2325; NAICS: 315224
Men's Dress Pants Industry

Analysts have speculated that Haggar Corp. may be a company interested in purchasing Levi's Dockers brand. The two companies have more than two-thirds of the dress pants industry.

Haggar/Dockers	66.0%
Other	34.0

Source: *Dallas Morning News*, November 11, 2004, p. NA.

★ 812 ★
Apparel
SIC: 2325; NAICS: 315224
Men's Jeans Market, 2003

Market shares are shown in percent.

Levi Strauss	23.9%
Wrangler	9.4
Old Navy	4.3
Gap	4.3
Lee	3.3
Polo Ralph Lauren	3.0
Tommy Hilfiger	2.5
Rustler	2.1
Calvin Klein	2.0
Express	1.8
Other	43.4

Source: *WWD*, December 13, 2004, p. 52S, from Markethink Inc., STS Market Research, and *DNR*.

★ 813 ★
Apparel
SIC: 2325; NAICS: 315224
Men's Jeans Sales, 2003

Men's jeans sales totalled $5.56 billion in 2003, taking 19% of the entire men's sportswear market.

$20-$29.99	36.6%
$10-$19.99	25.3
$30-$39.99	17.3
$40-$49.99	8.0
$50-$59.99	6.2
$60-$69.99	3.8
$0-$9.99	1.4

Source: *Daily News Record*, June 14, 2004, p. 6B, from STS Market Research.

★ 814 ★
Apparel
SIC: 2330; NAICS: 315212, 315232, 315239

Leading Women's Apparel Brands, 2004

Data show respondent answers to this survey question: "If you were shopping for women's apparel in a discount store or superstore, which brand would you want?"

Lee	.12.0%
Hanes	.12.0
Levi's	.10.0
Faded Glory (Wal-Mart)	4.0
Basic Addition	4.0
Liz Claiborne	3.0
L'Eggs	2.0
Fruit of the Loom	2.0
Cherokee	2.0
Alfred Dunner	2.0

Source: *DSN Retailing Today*, October 25, 2004, p. 48, from Leo J. Shapiro for *DSN Retailing Today*.

★ 815 ★
Apparel
SIC: 2330; NAICS: 315212, 315232, 315239

Leading Women's Apparel Firms in Japan, 2003

Market shares are estimated based on domestic sales.

World	2.6%
Onward Kashiyama	2.3
Itokin	1.9
Sanyo Shokai	1.8
Sanei Intl.	1.4
Other	.89.0

Source: "Market Share Survey Report 2003." [online] from http://www.nni.nikkei.co.jp [Published July 26, 2004], from Nikkei estimates.

★ 816 ★
Apparel
SIC: 2330; NAICS: 315212, 315232, 315239

Women's Apparel Market by Age

Sales at plus-sized apparel were 1.46 million pieces in 2004, up from 1.42 million in 2003. The value of sales fell however — from $17.2 billion to $16.9 billion. Part of the fall comes from a decline in purchases at discount outlets, where many large-sized women shop.

Misses' (sizes 2-14)	.30.0%
Plus sizes	.22.0
Misses' petite (sizes 2-14)	.18.0
Misses' (sizes 16-20)	.18.0
Juniors' (sizes 1-15)	7.0
Misses' tall (sizes 2-14)	6.0

Source: *WWD*, March 9, 2005, p. 10, from Retail Forward Shopperscape.

★ 817 ★
Apparel
SIC: 2330; NAICS: 315212, 315232, 315239

Women's Apparel Market in France, 2003

Sales of womenswear represented 13.5 billion euros in 2003.

Ready-to-wear	.48.0%
Shirts, blouses and other tops	.28.0
Lingerie and other underwear	.24.0

Source: "French Clothing Market." [online] from http://www.fco.gov.uk [Published February 2005].

★ 818 ★
Apparel
SIC: 2330; NAICS: 315212, 315232, 315239

Women's Softball Apparel Market

Market shares are shown in percent.

BIKE	.55.0%
Other	.45.0

Source: "Team Apparel." [online] from http://www.bikeathletic.com/TeamApparel.aspx [Accessed April 6, 2005].

★ 819 ★
Cheerleader Uniforms
SIC: 2339; NAICS: 315212

Cheerleader Shorts Market

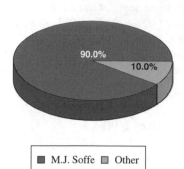

The company is the leading maker of knit shorts for cheerleading outfits.

M.J. Soffe 90.0%
Other 10.0

Source: *Fayetteville Observer*, April 16, 2005, p. NA.

★ 820 ★
Cheerleader Uniforms
SIC: 2339; NAICS: 315239

Cheerleader Uniform Market

The company has 90% of the market for clothing the country's roughly 3.5 million cheerleaders. Through its subsidiaries the company also controls the largest cheerleader camps and competitions.

Varsity Brands 90.0%
Other 10.0

Source: *New York Times*, August 15, 2004, p. 8.

★ 821 ★
Lingerie
SIC: 2341; NAICS: 315231

Leading Women's Lingerie Brands, 2004

Data show respondent answers to this survey question: "If you were shopping for women's lingerie in a discount store or superstore, which brand would you want?"

Hanes 32.0%
Playtex .17.0
Victoria's Secret 10.0
Jockey 9.0
Maidenform 7.0
L'eggs 6.0

Fruit of the Loom 4.0%
Bali 4.0
Vanity Fair 3.0
Secret Treasures 3.0

Source: *DSN Retailing Today*, October 25, 2004, p. 48, from Leo J. Shapiro for *DSN Retailing Today*.

★ 822 ★
Lingerie
SIC: 2341; NAICS: 315231

Leading Women's Underwear Firms in Japan, 2003

Market shares are estimated based on domestic sales.

Wacoal 23.3%
Triumph International 11.5
Gunze 5.1
Charle 5.0
Cecile 4.2
Other .50.9

Source: "Market Share Survey Report 2003." [online] from http://www.nni.nikkei.co.jp [Published July 26, 2004], from Nikkei estimates.

★ 823 ★
Lingerie
SIC: 2341; NAICS: 315231

Lingerie Market in France

The market, which includes bras, corsets, panties, petticoats and nightwear, was valued at 2.5 billion pounds in 2002. About 60 million units are sold each year, with 40% of bras being white, 26% printed, 7% in black and 6% flesh colored. About 122 million briefs and panties are sold annually.

Bras .45.0%
Briefs and panties 30.0
Other .25.0

Source: "French Market for Lingerie." [online] from http://www.tradepartners.go.uk/files/french_lingerie_jun03.pdf, from British Embassy Paris, Trade and Investment.

★ 824 ★
Lingerie
SIC: 2341; NAICS: 315231

Top Bra Brands in the U.K., 2003

Total spending was 725 million pounds in 2003, up from 620 million in 2001.

M&S	31.0%
Playtex	7.0
Triumph/Sloggi	7.0
Gossard	3.0
Berlei	2.0
Warner	1.0
Charnos	1.0
Pretty Polly	1.0
Other own label	32.0
Other	15.0

Source: *Marketing*, December 8, 2004, p. 32, from Mintel.

★ 825 ★
Lingerie
SIC: 2341; NAICS: 315231

Women's Nightwear Market in the U.K.

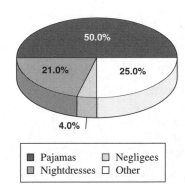

Negligees grew by 18% in past five years while pajamas only 7%. Price is seldom an issue in the purchase of nightwear, with only one in ten making a purchase in a discount store, according to a survey quoted in the source. Pajamas take nearly half of the 425 million pounds nightwear market.

Pajamas	50.0%
Nightdresses	21.0
Negligees	4.0
Other	25.0

Source: *just-style.com*, December 10, 2004, p. NA.

★ 826 ★
Carpet Underlays
SIC: 2392; NAICS: 314129

Carpet Underlay Business in Australia

Market shares are estimated in percent.

Pacific Brands	30.0%
Joyce Corporation	30.0
Other	40.0

Source: *Australian Business Intelligence*, December 2, 2004, p. NA.

★ 827 ★
Homefurnishings
SIC: 2392; NAICS: 314129

Bath Product Sales

The bath category was worth $3.7 billion.

	($ mil.)	Share
Bath towels	$ 1,887	51.0%
Bath/scatter rugs	851	23.0
Shower curtains	518	14.0
Bath accessories	407	11.0
Tank sets	37	1.0

Source: *Home Textiles Today*, March 28, 2005, p. 12, from Home Textiles Today annual bath report.

★ 828 ★
Homefurnishings
SIC: 2392; NAICS: 314129

Homefurnishing Sales, 2003

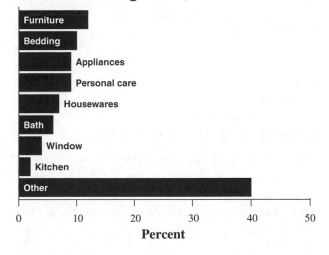

Data show retail sales in billions of dollars.

	($ bil.)	Share
Furniture	$ 8.63	11.81%
Bedding	7.59	10.38
Appliances	6.90	9.44

Continued on next page.

★ 828 ★

[Continued]
Homefurnishings
SIC: 2392; NAICS: 314129

Homefurnishing Sales, 2003

Data show retail sales in billions of dollars.

	($ bil.)	Share
Personal care	$ 6.37	8.72%
Housewares	5.42	7.42
Bath	4.34	5.94
Window	2.85	3.90
Kitchen	1.55	2.12
Other	29.44	40.28

Source: *DSN Retailing Today*, August 2, 2004, p. 29, from International Housewares Association.

★ 829 ★

Homefurnishings
SIC: 2392; NAICS: 314129

Kitchen Textile Market, 2004

Kitchen textile sales totaled $560 million. Discount department stores represented 58% all sales by channel. Home textile chains and mid-tier department stores tied with 15% market shares each.

	($ mil.)	Share
Kitchen towels	$ 280.0	50.0%
Potholders/mitts	123.2	22.0
Dishcloths	100.8	18.0
Chairpads	50.4	9.0
Other	5.6	1.0

Source: *Home Textiles Today*, March 7, 2005, p. 8, from research by the source.

★ 830 ★

Homefurnishings
SIC: 2392; NAICS: 314129

Leading Bath Rug Makers, 2004

Firms are ranked by sales in millions of dollars.

Mohawk Home	$ 187
Springs Industries	145
Maples Ind.	100
Shaw Living	50
Lacey Mills	24

Source: *Home Textiles Today*, January 10, 2005, p. 20.

★ 831 ★

Homefurnishings
SIC: 2392; NAICS: 314129

Leading Bath Towel Makers, 2004

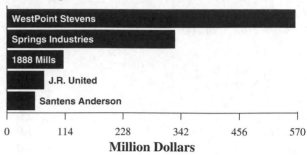

Firms are ranked by sales in millions of dollars.

WestPoint Stevens	$ 565
Springs Industries	330
1888 Mills	110
J.R. United	72
Santens Anderson	54

Source: *Home Textiles Today*, January 10, 2005, p. 20.

★ 832 ★

Homefurnishings
SIC: 2392; NAICS: 314129

Leading Blanket Makers, 2004

Firms are ranked by sales in millions of dollars.

WestPoint Stevens	$ 115
Sunbeam	115
Charles D. Owen	101
Berkshire Blankets	33
Pendleton Woolen Mills	17

Source: *Home Textiles Today*, January 10, 2005, p. 20.

★ 833 ★

Homefurnishings
SIC: 2392; NAICS: 314129

Leading Comforter Makers, 2004

Firms are ranked by sales in millions of dollars.

Springs Industries	$ 405
WestPoint Stevens	230
American Pacific	138
Dan River	116
Croscill Home	113

Source: *Home Textiles Today*, January 10, 2005, p. 20.

★ 834 ★

Homefurnishings

SIC: 2392; NAICS: 314129

Leading Curtain/Drapery Makers, 2004

Firms are ranked by sales in millions of dollars.

CHF Industries	$ 142
S. Lichtenberg	140
Springs Industries	96
Croscill Home	81
Miller Curtain	70

Source: *Home Textiles Today*, January 10, 2005, p. 20.

★ 835 ★

Homefurnishings

SIC: 2392; NAICS: 314129

Leading Decorative Pillow Makers, 2004

Brentwood Originals
The Arlee Group
Mohawk Home
Newport
Fashion Industries

0   32   64   96   128   160

Million Dollars

Firms are ranked by sales in millions of dollars.

Brentwood Originals	$ 157
The Arlee Group	74
Mohawk Home	28
Newport	25
Fashion Industries	20

Source: *Home Textiles Today*, January 10, 2005, p. 20.

★ 836 ★

Homefurnishings

SIC: 2392; NAICS: 314129

Leading Down Comforter Makers, 2004

Firms are ranked by sales in millions of dollars.

Pacific Coast Feather	$ 102
Phoenix Down	65
Down Lite International	64

Hollander Home Fashions	$ 60
WestPoint Stevens	46

Source: *Home Textiles Today*, January 10, 2005, p. 20.

★ 837 ★

Homefurnishings

SIC: 2392; NAICS: 314129

Leading Foam Pillow/Topper Makers, 2004

Firms are ranked by sales in millions of dollars.

Sleep Innovations	$ 228
Carpenter	69
Louisville Bedding	35
Laggett & Platt	31
Hudson Industries	22

Source: *Home Textiles Today*, January 10, 2005, p. 20.

★ 838 ★

Homefurnishings

SIC: 2392; NAICS: 314129

Leading Kitchen Textile Makers, 2004

Firms are ranked by sales in millions of dollars.

Barth & Dreyfuss	$ 65
Franco Mfg.	59
The John Ritzenthaler Co.	37
Town & Country	35
Cecil Saydah Co.	28

Source: *Home Textiles Today*, January 10, 2005, p. 20.

★ 839 ★

Homefurnishings

SIC: 2392; NAICS: 314129

Leading Mattress Pad Makers, 2004

Firms are ranked by sales in millions of dollars.

Louisville Bedding	$ 112
Perfect Fit	80
Pacific Coast Feather	44
Springs Industries	34
Hollander Home Fashions	20

Source: *Home Textiles Today*, January 10, 2005, p. 20.

★ 840 ★
Homefurnishings
SIC: 2392; NAICS: 314129

Leading Quilt Makers, 2004

Firms are ranked by sales in millions of dollars.

Keeco	$ 85
Sunham Home Fashions	70
PHI	66
Britannica Home Fashions	50
American Pacific	48

Source: *Home Textiles Today*, January 10, 2005, p. 20.

★ 841 ★
Homefurnishings
SIC: 2392; NAICS: 314129

Leading Rug Makers, 2004

Firms are ranked by sales in millions of dollars.

Mohawk Home	$ 340
Shaw Living	150
Maples Rugs	150
Oriental Weavers Holdings	147
Springs Industries	102

Source: *Home Textiles Today*, January 10, 2005, p. 20.

★ 842 ★
Homefurnishings
SIC: 2392; NAICS: 314129

Leading Sheet/Pillowcase Makers, 2004

Firms are ranked by sales in millions of dollars.

Springs Industries	$ 685
WestPoint Stevens	520
Dan River	136
Divatex Home Fashions	120
Franco Manufacturing	103

Source: *Home Textiles Today*, January 10, 2005, p. 20.

★ 843 ★
Homefurnishings
SIC: 2392; NAICS: 314129

Leading Shower Curtain Makers, 2004

Firms are ranked by sales in millions of dollars.

Allure Home Creation	$ 75
Ex-Cell Home Fashions	71
Springs Industries	70
Maytex Mills	41
Creative Bath	31

Source: *Home Textiles Today*, January 10, 2005, p. 20.

★ 844 ★
Homefurnishings
SIC: 2392; NAICS: 314129

Leading Sleep Pillow Makers, 2004

Firms are ranked by sales in millions of dollars.

Hollander Home Fashions	$ 134
Pacific Coast Feather	123
Springs Industries	98
WestPoint Stevens	82
Louisville Bedding	44

Source: *Home Textiles Today*, January 10, 2005, p. 20.

★ 845 ★
Slip Covers
SIC: 2392; NAICS: 314129

Slip Cover Market

Market shares are shown in percent.

Sure Fit	80.0%
Other	20.0

Source: *Morning Call*, August 4, 2004, p. NA.

★ **846** ★
Computer Bags
SIC: 2393; NAICS: 314911

Computer Bag Sales

*The share shown in several years old. The company
has lost share now that the market has grown more
competitive.*

Targus 65.0%
Other 35.0

Source: *Orange Country Register*, March 1, 2005, p. NA,
from Venture Development Corp.

★ **847** ★
Fishing Nets
SIC: 2399; NAICS: 314999

Fishing Net Market in India

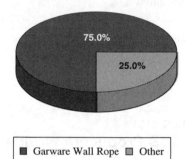

■ Garware Wall Rope ▨ Other

Market shares are shown in percent.

Garware Wall Rope 75.0%
Other 25.0

Source: *Asia Africa Intelligence Wire*, January 23, 2005,
p. NA.

★ **848** ★
Seatbelts
SIC: 2399; NAICS: 314999

Leading Seatbelt Makers in Asia

Market shares are shown in percent.

Autoliv 39.0%
TRW 10.0
Delphi 10.0
Takata 5.0
Other 36.0

Source: "Autoliv the Worldwide Leader in Automotive
Safety Systems." [online] from http://www.autoliv.com
[Accessed June 14, 2005], from Autoliv.

SIC 24 - Lumber and Wood Products

★ 849 ★

Logging

SIC: 2411; NAICS: 11331

Largest Logging Contractors in Saskatchewan

Contractors are ranked by cut to length volume in cubic meters.

John Lay & Sons Logging Ltd.	250,000
A & A Logging	200,000
Waterhen Forestry Products	180,000
Cyr Contracting Ltd.	165,000
Del Lake Enterprises Ltd.	150,000

Source: *Logging & Sawmilling Journal*, June 2004, p. NA.

★ 850 ★

Logging

SIC: 2411; NAICS: 11331

Largest Softwood Producers in Canada

Companies are ranked by production in millions of board feet.

	(mil.)	Share
Canfor	2,893	8.77%
West Fraser Timber	2,293	6.95
Weyerhaeuser Canada	2,229	6.75
Abitibi-Consolidated	2,000	6.06
Slocan Group	1,693	5.13
Tembec	1,335	4.05
Weldwood	1,181	3.58
Buchanan Lumber	1,100	3.33
Tolko	1,038	3.15
Domtar	994	3.01
JD Irving	726	2.20
Other	15,518	47.02

Source: *Logging & Sawmilling Journal*, March 2004, p. NA.

★ 851 ★

Lumber

SIC: 2421; NAICS: 11331

Leading Lumber Producers in North America, 2003

Market shares are shown in percent.

Weyerhaeuser	7.1%
Canfor	4.6
International Paper	3.4
West Fraser Timber	2.6
Abitibi-Consolidated	2.0
Other	80.3

Source: *Wood Markets*, June - July 2004, p. 2.

★ 852 ★

Lumber

SIC: 2421; NAICS: 11331

Leading OSB Producers Worldwide

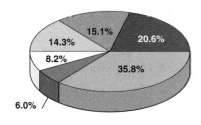

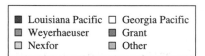

Market shares are shown in percent. OSB stands for oriented strand board.

Louisiana Pacific	20.6%
Weyerhaeuser	15.1
Nexfor	14.3
Georgia Pacific	8.2
Grant	6.0
Other	35.8

Source: *Wood Markets*, August 2004, p. 2.

★ 853 ★
Lumber
SIC: 2421; NAICS: 321113
Plastic/Composite Lumber Demand

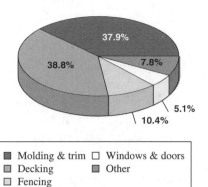

The market at the producer level for decking and railing was about $4 billion in 2003. Pressure treated wood represents about 60% of that total. Extruded wood/plastic composites have 15% of the market. Demand is shown in millions of dollars. Figures exclude residential, vinyl siding and vinyl profile for windows and doors.

	2003	2008	Share
Molding & trim	$ 840	$ 1,185	37.86%
Decking	560	1,215	38.82
Fencing	190	325	10.38
Windows & doors	75	160	5.11
Other	125	245	7.83

Source: *C&EN*, August 9, 2004, p. 15, from Freedonia Group.

★ 854 ★
Railroad Ties
SIC: 2421; NAICS: 321999
Railroad Tie Market

Wood still comprises more than 95% of the market.

Wood	.95.0%
Other	5.0

Source: *Railway Track and Structures*, April 2005, p. 43.

★ 855 ★
Hardwood
SIC: 2426; NAICS: 321918
Leading Hardwood Flooring Brands

The top brands are ranked based on a survey of consumer perceptions.

Bruce	.25.0%
Mannington	.12.0
Mohawk	. 8.0
Mirage	. 7.0
Kahrs	. 7.0
Anderson	. 7.0
Hartco	. 6.0
Other	.28.0

Source: *National Floor Trends*, February 2005, p. 14, from *Market Trends Survey*.

★ 856 ★
Cabinets
SIC: 2431; NAICS: 321918
Cabinet Shipments

Shipments are forecast to grow 5.4% per year through 2008 to $15.6 billion.

	2003	2008	Share
Kitchen	$ 9,510	$ 12,790	81.83%
Bath	1,485	2,005	12.83
Other	615	835	5.34

Source: *Wood & Wood Products*, October 2004, p. 16, from Freedonia Group.

★ 857 ★
Wood Doors
SIC: 2431; NAICS: 321911
Interior Fire Door Sales in the U.K.

The table compares the sale of doors by manufacturers and merchants. Sales are up 35% for timber fire door manufacturers.

	Manu-facturers	Mer-chants
Flush doors	88.0%	72.0%
Panel doors	3.0	15.0
Die formed doors	3.0	5.0
Laminated/timber cored/flush doors	0.0	6.0
Other	6.0	2.0

Source: *Timber Industry Magazine*, May 29, 2020, p. 33, from British Woodworking Federation.

★ 858 ★
Hardwood
SIC: 2435; NAICS: 321211

Leading Bleached Hardwood Makers Worldwide

Total production was 21.3 million tons.

Aracruz Celulose 11.0%
APRIL 8.0
Grupo Empresarial ENCE 5.0
Votorantim Group 4.0
Stora Enso 4.0
Cenibra 4.0
Portucel Group 3.0
Persons & Whittemore 3.0
International Paper 3.0
Domtar 3.0
Other 52.0

Source: *Solutions - for People, Processes and Paper*, August 2004, p. 64.

★ 859 ★
Hardwood
SIC: 2435; NAICS: 321211

Popular Types of Hardwood

Distribution is shown based on a survey conducted by the source.

Red oak 48.0%
White oak 20.0
Maple 10.0
Brazilian cherry 6.0
Other 13.0

Source: *Hardwood Floors*, April/May 2005, p. NA.

★ 860 ★
Pallets
SIC: 2448; NAICS: 32192

Global Pallet Market

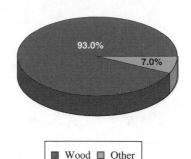

■ Wood ■ Other

Market shares are shown in percent.

Wood 93.0%
Other 7.0

Source: "Welcome Pallet Users." [online] from http://www.nwpcs.com/palletUser/PalletUsers.htm [Accessed June 17, 2005], from National Wood Pallet & Container Association.

★ 861 ★
Manufactured Homes
SIC: 2451; NAICS: 321991

Largest Manufactured Home Builders, 2003

Companies are ranked by home shipments.

Champion Enterprises 21,968
Fleetwood Enterrprises 19,982
Clayton Homes 16,898
Oakwood Home Corp. 9,212
Palm Harbor Homes 8,007
Skyline Corp. 7,922
Cavalier Homes 6,642
Patriot Homes 4,084
Horton Homes 3,660
SE Homes 3,606
Cavco 2,743
Giles Industries 1,783

Source: *Builder*, May 2004, p. 200.

★ 862 ★
Manufactured Homes
SIC: 2451; NAICS: 321991

Largest Manufactured Home Makers, 2003

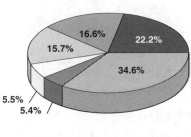

Market shares are shown in percent.

Clayton	.22.2%
Champion	.16.6
Fleetwood	.15.7
Palm Harbor	5.5
Cavalier	5.4
Other	.34.6

Source: "Fleetwood Enterprises Annual Report 2004" [online] from http://www.fleetwood.com [Accessed July 5, 2005], from Statistical Surveys Inc.

★ 863 ★
Manufactured Homes
SIC: 2451; NAICS: 321991

Largest Manufactured Home Makers (Multi-Section), 2003

Market shares are shown in percent.

Clayton	.18.3%
Fleetwood	.16.6
Champion	.16.6
Pam Harbor	6.9
Cavalier	5.6
Other	.36.0

Source: "Fleetwood Enterprises Annual Report 2004" [online] from http://www.fleetwood.com [Accessed July 5, 2005], from Statistical Surveys Inc.

★ 864 ★
Manufactured Homes
SIC: 2451; NAICS: 321991

Leading Modular Home Makers in North America, 2003

Firms are ranked by gross sales in millions of dollars.

New Era Building Systems	. $ 126.1
Ritz-Craft Corp.	92.1
Liberty Homes	84.4
R-Anell Housing Group	45.4
Penn Lyon Homes	36.0
Guerdon Enterprises	32.5
Professional Bldg. Systems	30.0
Genesis Homes	29.9
Deluxe Homes of PA	27.8
Unibilt Industries	26.8

Source: *Automated Builder*, May 2004, p. NA.

★ 865 ★
Particleboard
SIC: 2493; NAICS: 321219

Top Particleboard Makers in Colombia

Market shares are shown in percent.

Tablemac	.42.0%
Pizano	.34.0
Other	.24.0

Source: *Wood Based Panels International*, June-July 2004, p. 28.

★ 866 ★
Wood Products
SIC: 2493; NAICS: 321219

Engineered Wood Products, 2004

Production was valued at $29.5 billion in 2004. About 150 companies participate in the industry.

Reconstituted wood products	.27.0%
Softwood veneer and plywood	.25.0
Trusses	.23.0
Hardwood veneer and plywood	.16.0
Engineered wood	9.0

Source: "Veneer, Plywood and Engineered Wood Products." [online] from http://www.globalwood.org/market1/news20050501.htm [Accessed July 7, 2005.

★ 867 ★

Firelogs

SIC: 2499; NAICS: 321999

Artificial Fire Log Market in Canada

The company increased its share over the last decade from a 2% share.

Conros Corp.	.60.0%
Other	.40.0

Source: *America's Intelligence Wire*, August 16, 2004, p. NA.

★ 868 ★

Firelogs

SIC: 2499; NAICS: 321999

Top Firelog Brands, 2004

Market shares are shown based on sales at food stores, drug stores and mass merchandisers (but not Wal-Mart) for the 52 weeks ended June 13, 2004.

Duraflame	.29.9%
Pine Mountain	.10.1
Pine Mountain Superlog	9.1
Duraflame Crackleflame	6.3
Pine Mountain Cracklelog	4.5
Duraflame Colorlog	4.3
Chimney Sweeping Log	3.5
Northland	2.2
Duraflame Open Air	0.4
Private label	.28.9
Other	0.8

Source: *Grocery Headquarters*, August 2004, p. S88, from Information Resources Inc.

★ 869 ★

Firelogs

SIC: 2499; NAICS: 321999

Top Firelog Makers, 2004

Market shares are shown based on sales at food stores, drug stores and mass merchandisers (but not Wal-Mart) for the 52 weeks ended June 13, 2004.

Duraflame	.40.9%
Conros	.26.1
Jospeh Enterprises	3.5
Canadian Firelog	0.2
Private label	.26.1
Other	3.2

Source: *Grocery Headquarters*, August 2004, p. S88, from Information Resources Inc.

★ 870 ★

Floral Picks

SIC: 2499; NAICS: 321999

Floral Pick Market

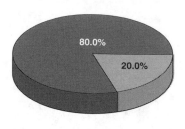

■ W.J. Cowee ■ Other

Floral picks are green woodens ticks wrapped in wire and used to hold flower arrangements.

W.J. Cowee	.80.0%
Other	.20.0

Source: *Times Union*, June 21, 2005, p. NA.

SIC 25 - Furniture and Fixtures

★ 871 ★
Furniture
SIC: 2500; NAICS: 337122, 337124, 337211
Furniture Industry in Palestine

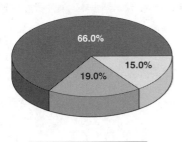

The $103 million industry is estimated for 2000, the most recent year for which data are available.

Household	.66.0%
Office	.19.0
Other	.15.0

Source: "US & FCS Market Research Reports." [online] from http://www.stat-usa.gov [Published March 28, 2004].

★ 872 ★
Furniture
SIC: 2500; NAICS: 337122, 337124, 337211
Furniture Industry in the U.K., 2003

The mature furniture market is worth 5 billion pounds. Ikea and MFI are the top furniture retailers. Need is still the major reason for furniture purchases, but interest in style and new fashions are major reasons as well.

	2003	Share
Living and dining	£ 2.3	46.0%
Kitchen	1.0	20.0
Mattresses	0.9	18.0
Bedroom	0.8	16.0

Source: *Marketing Week*, October 14, 2004, p. 34, from Mintel.

★ 873 ★
Furniture
SIC: 2500; NAICS: 337122, 337124, 337211
Furniture Production Worldwide, 2002

Market shares are shown in percent.

Wood	.39.0%
Metal	.13.0
Parts	. 5.0
Plastic	. 2.0
Mattress	. 1.0
Other	.40.0

Source: *Forest Products Journal*, November 2004, p. 14, from CSIL.

★ 874 ★
Furniture
SIC: 2500; NAICS: 337122, 337124, 337211
Global Furniture Production, 2002

Production is shown by country.

United States	.25.0%
Italy	.10.0
China	. 9.0
Germany	. 7.0
Japan	. 6.0
United Kingdom	. 5.0
France	. 4.0
Canada	. 4.0
Other	.30.0

Source: *Forest Products Journal*, November 2004, p. 14, from CSIL.

★ 875 ★
Furniture
SIC: 2500; NAICS: 337122, 337124, 337211
Household Furniture Imports

Retail sales of furniture are expected to climb to $70 billion in 2004. Imports represent about 40% of the industry.

Metal	.56.5%
Wood	.51.8
Upholstered	.16.4
Bedding	. 4.8

Source: *Wood & Wood Products*, June 2004, p. 47, from American Furniture Manufacturers Association, International Sleep Products Association, and International Trade Administration.

★ 876 ★
Furniture
SIC: 2514; NAICS: 337124
Garden Furniture Industry in the U.K.

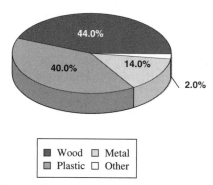

Legend: ■ Wood □ Metal ■ Plastic □ Other

The value of the industry is forecasted to be 1.1 billion pounds in 2009.

Wood	.44.0%
Plastic	.40.0
Metal	.14.0
Other	. 2.0

Source: *Cabinet Maker*, November 19, 2004, p. 18, from Focus Wickes Gardening Monitor.

★ 877 ★
Bedding
SIC: 2515; NAICS: 33791
Top Bedding Makers, 2003

Companies are ranked by wholesale shipments in millions of dollars.

	($ mil.)	Share
Sealy	$ 1,075	21.32%
Simmons	790	15.67
Serta	742	14.71
Spring Air	354	7.02
Select Comfort	197	3.91
Tempur-Pedic	188	3.73
King Koil	120	2.38
Therapedic	116	2.30
Kingsdown	100	1.98
Englander	98	1.94
Restonic	86	1.71
Lady Americana	68	1.35
IBC	68	1.35
Other	1,041	20.64

Source: *Furniture Today*, May 31, 2004, p. 16, from *Furniture Today* research.

★ 878 ★
Mattresses
SIC: 2515; NAICS: 33791
Air Chamber Beds

Market shares are estimated in percent.

Select Comfort	.80.0%
Other	.20.0

Source: *Pioneer Press*, August 4, 2004, p. NA.

★ 879 ★
Mattresses
SIC: 2515; NAICS: 33791
Mattress Market in Buffalo, NY

Market shares are forecasts.

Serta	.20.0%
Lockport Mattress	.20.0
Other	.60.0

Source: *Buffalo News*, March 7, 2005, p. B8.

★ 880 ★
Office Furniture
SIC: 2520; NAICS: 337214

Leading Office Furniture Producers

Market shares are shown for the fiscal year ended March 2004.

Steelcase	16.0%
HNI	14.0
HMI	12.0
Haworth	9.0
Knoll	7.0
Other	42.0

Source: ''Corporate Overview.'' [online] from http://www.hermanmiller.com [Accessed July 7, 2005].

★ 881 ★
Office Furniture
SIC: 2520; NAICS: 337214

Office Furniture Consumption

Figures are in millions of dollars.

1995	$ 9,888
1996	10,648
1997	12,253
1998	13,428
1999	13,591
2000	14,883
2001	12,351
2002	10,328
2003	10,068
2004	10,585
2005	11,569

Source: *Wood & Wood Products*, December 2004, p. 59, from Business and Institutional Manufacturers Association International.

★ 882 ★
Office Furniture
SIC: 2520; NAICS: 337214

Office Furniture in the U.K.

Sales are forecasts to increase to 742 million pounds in 2008. This figure is below the sector's peak of 911 million pounds in 2000.

Desks	£ 301
Seats	229
Storage products	140

Source: *Cabinet Maker*, December 17, 2004, p. 6, from *AMA's Office Furniture Market*.

★ 883 ★
Office Furniture
SIC: 2520; NAICS: 337214

Office Furniture Production, 2003-2004

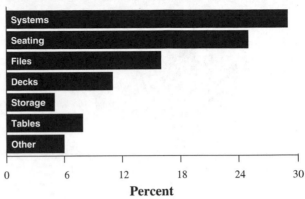

the industry is shown by segment.

	2003	2004
Systems	30.5%	28.6%
Seating	26.6	25.3
Files	13.5	16.1
Decks	11.0	10.7
Storage	8.0	5.0
Tables	6.8	8.0
Other	3.6	6.3

Source: ''Statistics.'' [online] from http://wwwbifma.com/statistics [Accessed July 7, 2005], p. 59, from Business and Institutional Manufacturers Association International.

★ 884 ★
Automotive Seating
SIC: 2531; NAICS: 33636

Heated Seat Market in North America

Market shares are shown in percent.

W.E.T. Automotive Systems Ltd.	64.0%
Other	36.0

Source: *Automotive Design & Production*, April 2005, p. 44.

★ 885 ★
Automotive Seating
SIC: 2531; NAICS: 33636

Offroad Seat Market in Europe

Market shares are shown in percent.

Grammer	65.0%
Other	35.0

Source: *Construction Contractor*, September 10, 2004, p. NA.

★ 886 ★
Fixtures
SIC: 2541; NAICS: 337212
Preferred Fixture Types, 2005

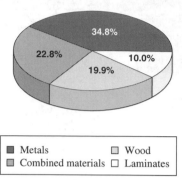

Data show the types of fixtures planned to be used by retailers.

Metals 34.8%
Combined materials 22.8
Wood 19.9
Laminates 10.0

Source: *Display & Design Ideas*, November 2004, p. 36.

SIC 26 - Paper and Allied Products

★ 887 ★
Pulp & Paper
SIC: 2611; NAICS: 322121

Leading Paper and Paperboard Firms in China

Companies are ranked by capacity in kilotons.

Chenming Paper Group	1,270
Golden East	1,214
Dongguan Nine Dragons Ltd.	913
Sun Paper Ltd.	597
Hautai Paper Group	585
Dongguan Lee & Man Paper Ltd.	568
Ningbo Zhonghua Paper	472
Bohui Paper Group	410
Guangzhou Paper Group	397

Source: *Paperboard Packaging*, February 2005, p. 40H, from Jaakko Poyry Consulting.

★ 888 ★
Pulp & Paper
SIC: 2611; NAICS: 322121

Leading Pulp/Paper Firms in Russia

The industry benefited from a rapidly growing domestic packaging sector. In 2003, Russia produced 6.3 million tons of paper and cardboard products.

Kotklassky PPM	16.0%
Arkhangelsky	13.0
Bratsky PPM	13.0
Ust-Illimsky LPK	9.0
Neusiedler Syktyvkar	9.0
Other	40.0

Source: "US & FCS Market Research Reports." [online] from http://www.stat-usa.gov [Published August 17, 2004].

★ 889 ★
Paper
SIC: 2621; NAICS: 322121

Cigarette Paper Market in the Philippines

Market shares are shown in percent.

KCPI	60.0%
Other	40.0

Source: *Solutions - for People, Processes and Paper*, January 2005, p. 10.

★ 890 ★
Paper
SIC: 2621; NAICS: 322121

Largest Tissue Paper Makers Worldwide, 2003

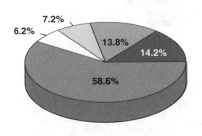

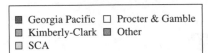

Market shares are shown in percent.

Georgia Pacific	14.2%
Kimberly-Clark	13.8
SCA	7.2
Procter & Gamble	6.2
Other	58.6

Source: "At Home Tissue Markets." [online] from http://www.conservatree.com/paper/Per/types/tissueconsumer.html [Accessed June 16, 2005], from *Pulp & Paper Paperloop Global Fact and Price Book, 2003*.

★ 891 ★
Paper
SIC: 2621; NAICS: 322121

Leading Printing Paper Makers in Japan, 2003

Market shares are estimated based on domestic production.

Nippon Paper	27.9%
Oji Paper	24.8
Daio Paper	8.9
Hokuetsu Paper Mills	8.3
Mitsubishi Paper Mills	7.9
Other	22.0

Source: "Market Share Survey Report 2003." [online] from http://www.nni.nikkei.co.jp [Published July 26, 2004], from *Nihon Keizai Shimbun.*

★ 892 ★
Paper
SIC: 2621; NAICS: 322121

Leading Tissue Paper Makers in North America

Percent

Market shares are shown based on capacity. The retail and away-from-home markets account for 95% of tissue production: toilet tissue 47%, toweling 35%, napkins 11% and facial 7%.

Georgia-Pacific	33.1%
Kimberly-Clark	17.8
Procter & Gamble	15.4
SCA	5.7
Cascades	5.1
Kruger	4.0
Irving Tissue	2.7

Cellu Tissue	2.4%
Potlatch	2.3
Marcal Paper	1.9
Other	9.7

Source: *Pulp & Paper*, February 2005, p. 19, from RISI.

★ 893 ★
Paper
SIC: 2621; NAICS: 322121

Paper Market in Australia, 2003

The paper, pulp and paperboard market was worth $3.4 billion.

General printing and stationery	34.0%
Paper packaging and containers	24.0
Pulp, paper and paperboard	10.0
Book and newspaper printing/publishing	10.0
Banking	5.0
Other	8.0

Source: "US & FCS Market Research Reports." [online] from http://www.stat-usa.gov [Published November 2004].

★ 894 ★
Paper
SIC: 2621; NAICS: 322121

Top Paper Firms in Brazil, 2002

Market shares are shown in percent.

Klabin	19.5%
Suzano Bahia Sul	12.1
International Paper	9.5
VCP	9.2
Ripasa	6.3
Other	43.4

Source: *South American Business Information*, September 27, 2004, p. NA, from Bracelpa.

★ 895 ★
Paperboard
SIC: 2631; NAICS: 32213

Corrugated Board Market, 2003

World corrugated production was 139.48 million square inches, up 2.5% from 2002.

Asia	33.0%
Europe	29.0
Other	38.0

Source: *Official Board Markets*, July 31, 2004, p. 12, from International Corrugated Case Association.

★ 896 ★
Paperboard
SIC: 2631; NAICS: 32213

Leading Linerboard Makers in North America

Market shares are shown based on capacity.

Smurfit-Stone 16.5%
International Paper 14.5
Weyerhaeuser 13.0
Inland Paperboard 10.7
Georgia Pacific 10.2
Packaging Corp. of America 5.1
Norampac 2.5
Green Bay Packaging 2.3
Longview Fibre 2.2
Boise Cascade 1.9
Other 21.1

Source: *Pulp & Paper*, January 2005, p. 19, from RISI.

★ 897 ★
Paperboard
SIC: 2652; NAICS: 32213

Cartonboard Market Worldwide

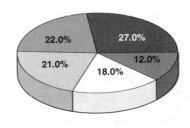

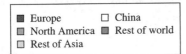

Demand is shown based on 46 million tons.

Europe .27.0%
North America 22.0
Rest of Asia 21.0
China 18.0
Rest of world 12.0

Source: *Paperboard Packaging*, February 2005, p. 40H, from Jaakko Poyry Consulting.

★ 898 ★
Coated Paper
SIC: 2671; NAICS: 322222

Coated Freesheet Demand in North America, 2004

Total demand was 5.3 million tons. The industry will benefit from the increase in direct mail volume and a rebound in commercial printing. The source notes that coated freesheet is expected to lose market share in catalogs and magazines to coated mechanical.

Commercial printing (misc) 41.0%
Direct mail 11.0
Book publishing 10.0
Magazines 9.0
Labels & wraps 9.0
Catalogs 9.0
Other 11.0

Source: *Solutions - for People, Processes and Paper*, October 2004, p. 64, from Jaakko Poyry Consulting.

★ 899 ★
Coated Paper
SIC: 2671; NAICS: 322221

Leading Coated Paper Makers in North America

Market shares are shown based on capacity. Roughly 65% of shipments go to commercial printers, magazines take 9% and books 7%.

SAPPI 23.7%
MeadWestvaco 23.5
Stora Enso N.A. 19.6
International Paper 13.0
Appleton Coated Paper 6.9
West Linn/Pasadena 6.3
Domtar 4.3
Smart Papers 1.3
Glatfelter 1.2
Cascades 1.1

Source: *Pulp & Paper*, March 2005, p. 19, from RISI.

★ 900 ★

Tape

SIC: 2672; NAICS: 322222

P-S Tape Market Worldwide, 2003

Marekt shares are shown in percent.

Asia/Pacific	36.0%
North America	30.0
Western Europe	23.0
Other	12.0

Source: *Converting Magazine*, November 2004, p. 2, from Freedonia Group.

★ 901 ★

Tape

SIC: 2672; NAICS: 322222

Top Tape Brands, 2004

Market shares are shown based on sales at food stores, drug stores and mass merchandisers (but not Wal-Mart) for the 52 weeks ended June 13, 2004.

Scotch	51.3%
Scotch Magic	23.7
Manco	5.2
Quickstik	1.5
Tartan	1.3
Scotch Long Mask	1.0
3M	0.9
Le Pages	0.5
Action	0.5
Private label	11.0
Other	3.1

Source: *Grocery Headquarters*, August 2004, p. S88, from Information Resources Inc.

★ 902 ★

Tape

SIC: 2672; NAICS: 322222

Top Tape Makers, 2004

Market shares are shown based on sales at food stores, drug stores and mass merchandisers (but not Wal-Mart) for the 52 weeks ended June 13, 2004.

3M	78.8%
Le Pages Inc.	0.9
Manco	5.7
Other	1.9
Private label	11.0
Tri-Pak	1.7

Source: *Grocery Headquarters*, August 2004, p. S88, from Information Resources Inc.

★ 903 ★

Plastic Bags

SIC: 2673; NAICS: 322223, 326111

Plastic Bag Market, 2003

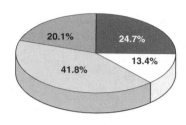

Glad □ Private label
Hefty □ Other

Consumers spent $870 million on garbage bags, lawn bags and leaf bags in 2003. Market shares are shown based on dollar and unit sales.

	Dollars	Units
Glad	30.5%	24.7%
Hefty	27.2	20.1
Private label	32.3	41.8
Other	10.0	13.4

Source: *Advertising Age*, August 30, 2004, p. 4, from Information Resources Inc.

★ 904 ★

Plastic Bags

SIC: 2673; NAICS: 322223, 326111

Top Food/Trash Bag Brands, 2005

Brands are ranked by supermarket, drug store and discount outlet sales (but not Wal-Mart) for the 52 weeks ended February 20, 2005.

	($ mil.)	Share
Ziploc food bags	$ 227.6	13.79%
Glad trash bags	172.4	10.45
Hefty Cinch Sak trash bags	143.1	8.67
Hefty One Zip food bags	100.8	6.11
Glad Lock food bags	73.4	4.45
Glad Force Flex trash bags	32.5	1.97
Glad Quick Tie trash bags	29.2	1.77
Glad Odor Shield trash bags	28.7	1.74
Glad Handle Tie trash bags	27.9	1.69
Hefty trash bags	22.0	1.33
Private label	521.8	31.62
Other	270.6	16.40

Source: *MMR*, May 30, 2005, p. 33, from Information Resources Inc.

★ 905 ★

Feminine Hygiene Products

SIC: 2676; NAICS: 322291

Top Sanitary Napkin/Liner Brands, 2004

Market shares are shown based on drug stores for the 52 weeks ended October 31, 2004.

Always	.36.3%
Stayfree	.15.7
Kotex	.13.6
Carefree	6.9
Kotex Lightdays	5.5
Always All Days	1.8
Kotex Overnights	1.6
Always Cleanweave	1.1
Carefree To Go	1.0
Always All Days Cleanweave	0.7
Private label	.12.6
Other	3.2

Source: *Chain Drug Review*, January 3, 2005, p. 95, from Information Resources Inc.

★ 906 ★

Feminine Hygiene Products

SIC: 2676; NAICS: 322291

Top Sanitary Napkins/Liner Makers, 2005

Market shares are shown based on sales at food stores, drug stores and mass merchandisers (excluding Wal-Mart) for the 52 weeks ended January 23, 2005.

Procter & Gamble	.40.6%
Kimberly-Clark	.26.2
Johnson & Johnson	.22.9
Ultrafem	0.3
Private label	.10.0

Source: *Grocery Headquarters*, April 2005, p. 113, from Information Resources Inc.

★ 907 ★

Feminine Hygiene Products

SIC: 2676; NAICS: 322291

Top Tampon Brands, 2004

Market shares are shown based on drug stores for the 52 weeks ended October 31, 2004.

Tampax	.23.1%
Playtex Gentle Glide	.16.9
Tampax Pearl	.16.8
Kotex Security	9.9

O.B.	9.3%
Tampax Compak	4.5
Playtex	3.5
Playtex Beyond	2.1
Playtex Slimfits	1.5
Tampax Satin	1.4
Private label	9.0
Other	2.0

Source: *Chain Drug Review*, January 3, 2005, p. 95, from Information Resources Inc.

★ 908 ★

Feminine Hygiene Products

SIC: 2676; NAICS: 322291

Top Tampon Makers, 2005

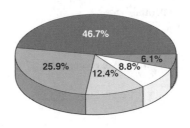

Market shares are shown based on sales at food stores, drug stores and mass merchandisers (excluding Wal-Mart) for the 52 weeks ended January 23, 2005.

Procter & Gamble	.46.7%
Playtex Products	.25.9
Kimberly-Clark Corp.	.12.4
Johnson & Johnson	8.8
Private label	6.1

Source: *Grocery Headquarters*, April 2005, p. 113, from Information Resources Inc.

★ 909 ★
Sanitary Paper Products
SIC: 2676; NAICS: 322291

Largest Hygiene Product Makers Worldwide

The global hygiene market was valued at $44.2 billion in 2003. Diapers took 46% of the market with sanitary protection taking 34%, wipes 12%, incontinence products 5% and cotton wool/buds 3%.

Procter & Gamble	.30.7%
Kimberly-Clark	.19.6
Johnson & Johnson	. 5.5
Unicharm	. 5.1
SCA Hygiene	. 4.2
Kao	. 2.6
Unilever	. 0.8
Playtex Products	. 0.8
Hengan International	. 0.8
Georgia Pacific	. 0.8
Other	.29.1

Source: *Medical Textiles*, November 2004, p. 7, from Euromonitor.

★ 910 ★
Sanitary Paper Products
SIC: 2676; NAICS: 322291

Largest Hygiene Product Markets Worldwide

The global hygiene market was valued at $44.2 billion in 2003. Western Europe and North America are mature markets with high penetration rates for hygiene products. Declining birth rates and aging populations will, the source points out, have an influence on future consumption.

Western Europe	.28.0%
North America	.24.0
Asia Pacific	.22.0
Other	.26.0

Source: *Medical Textiles*, November 2004, p. 7, from Euromonitor.

★ 911 ★
Sanitary Paper Products
SIC: 2676; NAICS: 322291

Leading AFH Tissue Makers in Europe

AFH stands for away from home.

SCA	.18.0%
Kimberly-Clark	.18.0
Georgia Pacific	.12.0
Other	.52.0

Source: "Hygiene Products." [online] from http://www.sca.com/business/hygiene.asp [Accessed July 4, 2005], from SCA.

★ 912 ★
Sanitary Paper Products
SIC: 2676; NAICS: 322291

Leading AFH Tissue Makers in North America

AFH stands for away from home. Market shares are shown in percent.

Georgia-Pacific	.35.0%
Kimberly-Clark	.23.0
SCA	.22.0
Other	.20.0

Source: "Hygiene Products." [online] from http://www.sca.com/business/hygiene.asp [Accessed July 4, 2005], from SCA.

★ 913 ★
Sanitary Paper Products
SIC: 2676; NAICS: 322291

Leading AFH Tissue Makers Worldwide

AFH stands for away from home.

Kimberly-Clark	.20.0%
Georgia Pacific	.19.0
SCA	.16.0
Other	.45.0

Source: "Svenska Cellulosa Aktiebolaget." [online] from http://www.domain-b.com/industry/general/20050531_sea.html [Accessed July 4, 2005], from SCA.

★ 914 ★
Sanitary Paper Products
SIC: 2676; NAICS: 322291

Leading Incontinence Product Makers in Europe

Market shares are shown in percent.

SCA 39.0%
Hartmann 18.0
Ontex 9.0
Tyco/Kendall 3.0
Kimberly-Clark 2.0
Other 29.0

Source: "Hygiene Products." [online] from http://www.sca.com/business/hygiene.asp [Accessed July 4, 2005], from SCA.

★ 915 ★
Sanitary Paper Products
SIC: 2676; NAICS: 322291

Leading Paper Sectors in the U.K., 2004

Total sales were 1,956 million pounds sterling for the 52 weeks ended November 7, 2004.

Soft toilet rolls 41.4%
Kitchen rolls 13.4
Boxed-flowpack 9.7
Household cleaners 9.5
Dishwash 8.7
Washing-up liquids 8.1
Dry dust removers 1.3
Sponge-backed scourers 1.0
Moist toilet tissue 1.0
Other 5.9

Source: *Grocer*, January 29, 2005, p. 44, from Taylor Nelson Sofres.

★ 916 ★
Sanitary Paper Products
SIC: 2676; NAICS: 322291

Leading Sanitary Paper Product Makers in Japan, 2003

Market shares are estimated based on domestic output.

Daio Paper 13.6%
Crecia 12.3
Oji Paper 11.1
Tokai Pulp & Paper 1.8

Mitsubishi Paper Mills 0.6%
Other 60.6

Source: "Market Share Survey Report 2003." [online] from http://www.nni.nikkei.co.jp [Published July 26, 2004], from Nikkei estimates.

★ 917 ★
Sanitary Paper Products
SIC: 2676; NAICS: 322291

Leading Tissue Makers (Consumer) in Europe

Market shares are shown in percent.

SCA 21.0%
Kimberly-Clark 17.0
Georgia-Pacific 14.0
Procter & Gamble 8.0
Sofidel 6.0
Metsa Tissue 5.0
Other 31.0

Source: "Hygiene Products." [online] from http://www.sca.com/business/hygiene.asp [Accessed July 4, 2005], from SCA.

★ 918 ★
Sanitary Paper Products
SIC: 2676; NAICS: 322291

Leading Wipes Brands Worldwide, 2004

Western Europe took $2,766.3 million out of $6,078.5 million. North America was second with $1,871.1 million. Baby wipes led the category with $2,529.4 million.

Pampers 8.6%
Swiffer 8.2

Continued on next page.

★ 918 ★

[Continued]
Sanitary Paper Products
SIC: 2676; NAICS: 322291

Leading Wipes Brands Worldwide, 2004

Wetsern Europe took $2,766.3 million out of $6,078.5 million. North America was second with $1,871.1 million. Baby wipes led the category with $2,529.4 million.

Huggies	7.8%
Quickle	4.0
Johnson's Baby	3.5
Pledge/Pronto	3.4
Clorox	2.2
Olay	1.8
Wet Ones	1.5
Dodot	1.5
Nivea Visage	1.3
Biore	1.3
Other	54.9

Source: *Global Cosmetic Industry*, April 2005, p. 38, from Euromonitor.

★ 919 ★

Sanitary Paper Products
SIC: 2676; NAICS: 322291

Paper Product Sales, 2003

Supermarket sales are shown in millions of dollars.

Toilet tissue	$ 2,669.29
Paper towels, regular	1,018.26
Disposable dishes	788.78
Facial tissue	763.81
Paper towels, jumbo	694.22
Paper napkins	419.59
Premoistened towelettes	369.25
Disposable cups	329.38

Source: *Progressive Grocer*, September 15, 2004, p. 26, from *2004 Progressive Grocer Consumer Expenditure Survey*.

★ 920 ★

Sanitary Paper Products
SIC: 2676; NAICS: 322291

Top Adult Incontinence Brands, 2004

Market shares are shown based on drug store sales for the year ended October 31, 2004.

Depend	30.9%
Depend Poise	16.0

Serenity	7.8%
Serenity Night and Day	3.0
Entrust Plus	1.1
Serenity Dri Active Plus	0.7
Sure Care slip-on	0.5
Prevail	0.5
Serenity Dri Active	0.4
Attends	0.4
Other	38.7

Source: *Chain Drug Review*, January 3, 2005, p. 91, from Information Resources Inc.

★ 921 ★

Sanitary Paper Products
SIC: 2676; NAICS: 322291

Top Adult Incontinence Markets Worldwide, 2008

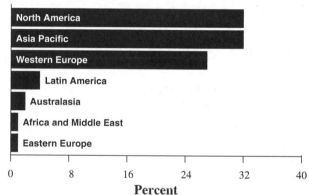

Retail sales are forecast in millions of dollars. In North America the market divides this way: $1.1 billion in retail sales and $900 million in institutional sales. From 2003-2008 Australasia saw 16.1% growth, with Eastern Europe having the second highest growth rate at 9.3%.

	($ mil.)	Share
North America	$ 1,038.6	32.24%
Asia Pacific	1,037.0	32.19
Western Europe	865.6	26.87
Latin America	140.9	4.37
Australasia	56.5	1.75
Africa and Middle East	46.2	1.43
Eastern Europe	36.7	1.14

Source: *Nonwovens Industry*, March 2005, p. 36, from Euromonitor.

★ 922 ★

Sanitary Paper Products

SIC: 2676; NAICS: 322291

Top Baby Wipe Brands

Market shares are shown based on sales at food stores, drug stores and mass merchandisers (but not Wal-Mart).

	($ mil.)	Share
Huggies Natural Care	$ 114.3	28.88%
Pampers Natural Aloe Touch	66.0	16.68
Huggies Supreme Care	23.4	5.91
Pampers Sensitive Touch	18.7	4.72
Pampers Original Cotton Care . . .	17.7	4.47
Luvs Natural	8.8	2.22
Huggies Newborn	8.6	2.17
Pampers	5.6	1.41
Huggies	5.5	1.39
Huggies Original	3.0	0.76
Private label	111.8	28.25
Other	12.4	3.13

Source: *MMR*, April 25, 2005, p. 67, from Information Resources Inc.

★ 923 ★

Sanitary Paper Products

SIC: 2676; NAICS: 322291

Top Baby Wipe Brands at Drug Stores, 2004

Market shares are shown based on drug stores for the 52 weeks ended October 31, 2004.

Huggies Natural Care	.27.2%
Pampers Natural Aloe Touch	.16.9
Pampers Original Cotton Care	4.7
Huggies Supreme Care	4.4
Pampers Sensitive Touch	3.8
Huggies Newborn	2.6
Huggies	1.4
Luvs	1.2
Huggies Original	1.1
Private label	.32.6
Other	4.1

Source: *Chain Drug Review*, January 3, 2005, p. 95, from Information Resources Inc.

★ 924 ★

Sanitary Paper Products

SIC: 2676; NAICS: 322291

Top Baby Wipe Brands in the U.K., 2003

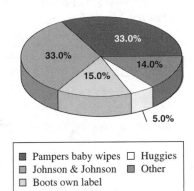

Market shares are shown in percent.

Pampers baby wipes	.33.0%
Johnson & Johnson	.33.0
Boots own label	.15.0
Huggies	5.0
Other	.14.0

Source: *Marketing*, August 18, 2004, p. 34, from Mintel.

★ 925 ★

Sanitary Paper Products

SIC: 2676; NAICS: 322291

Top Baby Wipe Makers, 2004

Market shares are shown based on sales at food stores, drug stores and mass merchandisers (excluding Wal-Mart) for the 52 weeks ended October 31, 2004.

Kimberly-Clark	.40.2%
Procter & Gamble	.30.4
Playtex Products	0.5
Aid-Pack	0.2
Rockline	0.1
American Premier Products	0.1
Private label	.28.1
Other	0.4

Source: *Grocery Headquarters*, January 2005, p. 71, from Information Resources Inc.

★ 926 ★
Sanitary Paper Products
SIC: 2676; NAICS: 322291

Top Cleaning Cloth Brands, 2005

Brands are ranked by supermarket, drug store and discount outlet sales (excluding Wal-Mart) for the 52 weeks ended February 20, 2005.

	($ mil.)	Share
Clorox	$ 84.9	35.39%
Lysol	40.9	17.05
Mr. Clean	32.7	13.63
Windex	18.1	7.54
Pledge	17.3	7.21
Glass Plus	5.7	2.38
Fantastik	5.6	2.33
Old English	3.8	1.58
Formula 409	3.0	1.25
Murphy's Oil	2.0	0.83
Other	25.9	10.80

Source: *MMR*, May 30, 2005, p. 33, from Information Resources Inc.

★ 927 ★
Sanitary Paper Products
SIC: 2676; NAICS: 322291

Top Diaper Brands, 2004

Market shares are shown based on sales at food stores, drug stores and mass merchandisers (but not Wal-Mart) for the 52 weeks ended June 13, 2004.

Huggies Ultratrim	24.7%
Pampers Baby Dry	16.3
Pampers Cruisers	12.3
Luvs Ultra Leakguards	11.8
Huggies Supreme	10.2
Pampers Swaddlers	3.5
Pampers	1.3
Luvs	1.3
Huggies Overnites	1.3
Private label	14.5
Other	2.8

Source: *Grocery Headquarters*, August 2004, p. S88, from Information Resources Inc.

★ 928 ★
Sanitary Paper Products
SIC: 2676; NAICS: 322291

Top Diaper Brands in the U.K.

Disposable diaper sales fell from 419 million pounds in 1999 to 344 million pounds in 2003.

	1999	2003
Pampers	62.0%	61.0%
Huggies	26.0	30.0
Own label	11.0	8.0
Other	1.0	1.0

Source: *Marketing*, August 18, 2004, p. 34, from Mintel.

★ 929 ★
Sanitary Paper Products
SIC: 2676; NAICS: 322291

Top Diaper Brands Worldwide

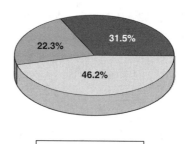

■ Pampers □ Other
■ Huggies

The global diaper industry was valued at $20 billion.

Pampers	31.5%
Huggies	22.3
Other	46.2

Source: *Brand Strategy*, May 10, 2005, p. 20, from Euromonitor.

★ 930 ★
Sanitary Paper Products
SIC: 2676; NAICS: 322291

Top Diaper Makers, 2004

Market shares are shown based on sales at food stores, drug stores and mass merchandisers (but not Wal-Mart) for the 52 weeks ended June 13, 2004.

Procter & Gamble	47.1%
Kimberly-Clark	37.4
Ass. Hygienic Products	0.9

Continued on next page.

★ 933 ★
Sanitary Paper Products
SIC: 2676; NAICS: 322291

★ 930 ★
[Continued]
Sanitary Paper Products
SIC: 2676; NAICS: 322291

Top Diaper Makers, 2004

Market shares are shown based on sales at food stores, drug stores and mass merchandisers (but not Wal-Mart) for the 52 weeks ended June 13, 2004.

Lambi S.A. de C.V.	0.1%
Private label	14.5

Source: *Grocery Headquarters*, August 2004, p. S88, from Information Resources Inc.

★ 931 ★
Sanitary Paper Products
SIC: 2676; NAICS: 322291

Top Diaper Markets Worldwide, 2003

Asia and Latin America are the key markets due to high birth rates and increasing disposable incomes. Market sizes in millions of dollars: $20,299 in 2003, $20,808 in 2004 and $23,103 in 2005.

	($ mil.)	Share
Western Europe	$ 5,139	25.32%
North America	5,093	25.09
Asia Pacific	3,386	16.68
Latin America	2,835	13.97
Africa/Middle East	2,519	12.41
Eastern Europe	990	4.88
Australasia	335	1.65

Source: *Nonwovens Industry*, January 2005, p. 34, from Euromonitor.

★ 932 ★
Sanitary Paper Products
SIC: 2676; NAICS: 322291

Top Disposable Cup Brands, 2004

Shares are shown based on food, drug store and mass merchandiser sales (excluding Wal-Mart) for the 52 weeks ended October 31, 2004.

Dixie	20.2%
Solo	17.6
Jack Frost	2.7
Dart	2.3
Dixie Coca-Cola	1.5
Sensations	1.1
Styro Cup	0.8
Partytime	0.6
The Big Cool	0.4
Private label	47.7
Other	5.1

Source: *Grocery Headquarters*, February 2005, p. 41, from Information Resources Inc.

★ 933 ★
Sanitary Paper Products
SIC: 2676; NAICS: 322291

Top Disposable Plate Brands, 2004

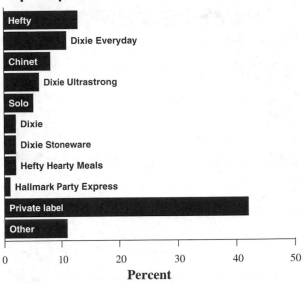

Shares are shown based on food, drug store and mass merchandiser sales (excluding Wal-Mart) for the 52 weeks ended October 31, 2004.

Hefty	12.8%
Dixie Everyday	10.8
Chinet	7.9
Dixie Ultrastrong	5.5
Solo	4.6
Dixie	2.0
Dixie Stoneware	1.7
Hefty Hearty Meals	1.5
Hallmark Party Express	0.9
Private label	41.5
Other	10.8

Source: *Grocery Headquarters*, February 2005, p. 41, from Information Resources Inc.

★ 934 ★

Sanitary Paper Products

SIC: 2676; NAICS: 322291

Top Facial Tissue Brands, 2005

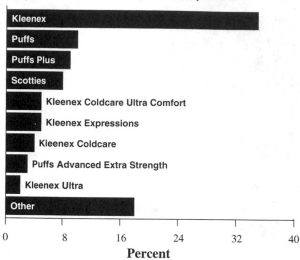

Percent

Brands are ranked by supermarket, drug store and discount outlet sales (but not Wal-Mart) for the 52 weeks ended February 20, 2005.

	($ mil.)	Share
Kleenex	$ 335.5	35.29%
Puffs	92.2	9.70
Puffs Plus	89.0	9.36
Scotties	79.4	8.35
Kleenex Coldcare Ultra Comfort	48.0	5.05
Kleenex Expressions	43.4	4.57
Kleenex Coldcare	37.7	3.97
Puffs Advanced Extra Strength	27.5	2.89
Kleenex Ultra	22.9	2.41
Other	175.0	18.41

Source: *MMR*, May 30, 2005, p. 33, from Information Resources Inc.

★ 935 ★

Sanitary Paper Products

SIC: 2676; NAICS: 322291

Top Moist Towelette Brands, 2004

Brands are ranked by sales at food stores, drug stores and mass merchandisers (but not Wal-Mart).

	($ mil.)	Share
Kleenex Cottonelle	$ 46.5	26.89%
Wet Ones	43.7	25.27
Kleenex Cottonelle Fresh	17.6	10.18
Pull-Ups Just for Kids	11.3	6.54
Charmin Fresh Mates	7.5	4.34
Pampers Tidy Tykes	5.1	2.95
Splash 'n Go	4.4	2.54

	($ mil.)	Share
Nice 'n Clean	$ 3.7	2.14%
Quilted Northern	2.3	1.33
Scott	2.2	1.27
Private label	22.0	12.72
Other	6.6	3.82

Source: *MMR*, April 25, 2005, p. 67, from Information Resources Inc.

★ 936 ★

Sanitary Paper Products

SIC: 2676; NAICS: 322291

Top Moist Towelette Makers, 2004

Market shares are shown based on sales at food stores, drug stores and mass merchandisers (excluding Wal-Mart) for the 52 weeks ended October 31, 2004.

Kimberly-Clark	46.2%
Playtex Products	25.6
Procter & Gamble	7.8
Georgia-Pacific	2.2
Nice-Pak Products	2.1
Sage Products	1.5
Lever Brothers	0.7
Rockline	0.4
Private label	12.6
Other	0.9

Source: *Grocery Headquarters*, January 2005, p. 71, from Information Resources Inc.

★ 937 ★

Sanitary Paper Products

SIC: 2676; NAICS: 322291

Top Paper Napkin Brands, 2005

Brands are ranked by supermarket, drug store and discount outlet sales (excluding Wal-Mart) for the 52 weeks ended February 20, 2005.

	($ mil.)	Share
Mardi Gras	$ 48.2	10.86%
Vanity Fair	46.5	10.48
Bounty	36.9	8.31
Marcal	23.6	5.32
Brawny	22.3	5.02
Scott	19.6	4.42
Sensations	12.3	2.77
Hallmark Party Express	12.1	2.73
Zee	11.8	2.66
Kleenex	10.9	2.46
Other	199.7	44.99

Source: *MMR*, May 30, 2005, p. 33, from Information Resources Inc.

★ 938 ★
Sanitary Paper Products
SIC: 2676; NAICS: 322291

Top Paper Towel Brands, 2005

Market shares are shown based on sales at food stores, drug stores and mass merchandisers (but not Wal-Mart) for the 52 weeks ended January 23, 2005.

Bounty	.40.4%
Brawny	.11.2
Scott	.10.3
Kleenex Viva	8.2
Sparkle	6.4
Marcal	2.1
Mardi Gras	1.0
So Dri	0.8
Bounty Double Quilted	0.3
Private label	.17.9
Other	1.4

Source: *Grocery Headquarters*, April 2005, p. 22, from Information Resources Inc.

★ 939 ★
Sanitary Paper Products
SIC: 2676; NAICS: 322291

Top Paper Towel Makers, 2005

Market shares are shown based on sales at food stores, drug stores and mass merchandisers (but not Wal-Mart) for the 52 weeks ended January 23, 2005.

Procter & Gamble	.40.8%
Georgia-Pacific	.19.7
Kimberly-Clark	.18.7
Marcal Paper Mills	2.1
Private label	.17.9
Other	0.8

Source: *Grocery Headquarters*, April 2005, p. 22, from Information Resources Inc.

★ 940 ★
Sanitary Paper Products
SIC: 2676; NAICS: 322291

Top Toilet Tissue Brands, 2005

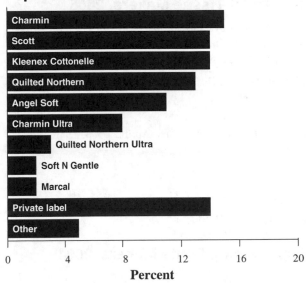

Market shares are shown based on sales at food stores, drug stores and mass merchandisers (but not Wal-Mart) for the 52 weeks ended January 23, 2005.

Charmin	.14.6%
Scott	.14.4
Kleenex Cottonelle	.14.4
Quilted Northern	.12.8
Angel Soft	.11.2
Charmin Ultra	7.9
Quilted Northern Ultra	3.2
Soft N Gentle	1.7
Marcal	1.5
Private label	.13.5
Other	4.8

Source: *Grocery Headquarters*, April 2005, p. 22, from Information Resources Inc.

★ 941 ★
Sanitary Paper Products
SIC: 2676; NAICS: 322291

Top Toilet Tissue Makers, 2005

Market shares are shown based on sales at food stores, drug stores and mass merchandisers (but not Wal-Mart) for the 52 weeks ended January 23, 2005.

Georgia Pacific	.29.1%
Kimberly-Clark Corp.	.28.9
Procter & Gamble	.26.1

Continued on next page.

★ 941 ★
[Continued]
Sanitary Paper Products
SIC: 2676; NAICS: 322291

Top Toilet Tissue Makers, 2005

Market shares are shown based on sales at food stores, drug stores and mass merchandisers (but not Wal-Mart) for the 52 weeks ended January 23, 2005.

Marcal Paper Mills Inc.	1.8%
Private label	13.5
Other	0.6

Source: *Grocery Headquarters*, April 2005, p. 22, from Information Resources Inc.

★ 942 ★
Sanitary Paper Products
SIC: 2676; NAICS: 322291

Top Training Pants Makers, 2004

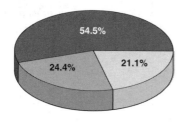

■ Kimberly-Clark	□ Other
■ Procter & Gamble	

Market shares are shown for the 24 weeks ended November 13, 2004.

Kimberly-Clark	54.5%
Procter & Gamble	24.4
Other	21.1

Source: *FWN Select*, December 1, 2004, p. NA, from ACNielsen.

★ 943 ★
Sanitary Paper Products
SIC: 2676; NAICS: 322291

Top Traning Pants Brands, 2004

Market shares are shown based on sales at food stores, drug stores and mass merchandisers (but not Wal-Mart) for the 52 weeks ended June 13, 2004.

Huggies Pull Ups	44.1%
Huggies Goodnites	17.5
Pampers Easy Ups	14.8
Huggies Little Swimmers	5.6

Fitti	0.3%
Drypers	0.3
Snuggems	0.2
Private label	17.0
Other	0.2

Source: *Grocery Headquarters*, August 2004, p. S88, from Information Resources Inc.

★ 944 ★
Office Products
SIC: 2678; NAICS: 322233

Top Office Product Brands, 2004

Market shares are shown based on drug store sales for the year ended October 31, 2004.

Scotch household tape	30.9%
Scotch Magic household tape	13.8
Krazy Glue (all types)	8.6
Elmer's (all types)	4.2
Manco household tape	4.1
Bic White Out Plus	2.1
Avery (all types)	2.0
Elmer's Glue (all types)	1.5
Private label	9.8
Other	23.0

Source: *Chain Drug Review*, September 27, 2004, p. 36, from Information Resources Inc.

★ 945 ★
Coffee Filters
SIC: 2679; NAICS: 322299

Top Coffee Filter Brands, 2003

Brands are ranked by supermarket, drug store and discount outlet sales for the year ended December 28, 2003.

	(mil.)	Share
Melitta	21.2	25.92%
Mr. Coffee	9.5	11.61
Brew Rite	1.2	1.47
Bunn	0.9	1.10
Private label	46.7	57.09
Other	2.3	2.81

Source: *MMR*, May 31, 2004, p. 33, from Information Resources Inc.

★ 946 ★
Gift Wrap
SIC: 2679; NAICS: 322299

Gift Wrap and Accessory Sales

Wrapping paper is thought to represent 58.2% of manufacturers sales in 2005 with gift bags (the fastest growing segment) taking 12.5%. Those 45-54 years of age spend the most on wrapping materials. The market should benefit from this growing segment of the population.

1999	$ 3,590.7
2000	3,770.8
2001	3,922.6
2002	4,086.4
2003	4,295.3
2004	4,510.8
2005	4,735.4
2006	5,718.5

Source: *Souvenirs, Gifts and Novelties*, November - December 2004, p. 102, from Leading Edge Reports.

SIC 27 - Printing and Publishing

★ 947 ★
Publishing
SIC: 2700; NAICS: 51111, 51112, 51113

Leading Publishing Firms in Japan, 2003

Market shares are estimated based on sales and magazine/Internet revenues of 2.74 trillion yen.

Recruit	.13.2%
Benesse	7.2
Kodansha	6.1
Shogakukan	5.4
Shueisha	5.2
Other	.62.9

Source: ''Market Share Survey Report 2003.'' [online] from http://www.nni.nikkei.co.jp [Published July 26, 2004], from Nikkei estimates.

★ 948 ★
Newspapers
SIC: 2711; NAICS: 51111

Largest Newspaper Publishers

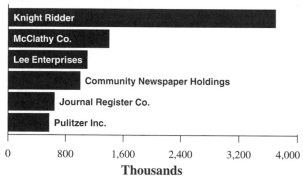

Thousands

Companies are ranked by estimated daily circulation, in thousands. Lee and Pulitzer recently announced plans for a merger valued at $1.5 billion.

Knight Ridder	3,700.0
McClathy Co.	1,400.0
Lee Enterprises	1,100.0
Community Newspaper Holdings	1,000.0
Journal Register Co.	650.0
Pulitzer Inc.	578.4

Source: *Advertising Age*, April 18, 2005, pp. S-5, from company reports.

★ 949 ★
Newspapers
SIC: 2711; NAICS: 51111

Largest Newspapers, 2005

Newspapers are ranked by circulation for the six months ended March 31, 2005. Circulation fell 1.9% which was the biggest decline since 1995-1996 circulation fell nearly 21%. Los Angeles Times, Houston Chronicle and San Francisco Chronicle include Saturday figures.

USA Today	2,281,831
The Wall Street Journal	2,070,498
New York Times	1,136,433
Los Angeles Times	907,997
Washington Post	751,871
New York Daily News	735,536
New York Post	678,086
Chicago Tribune	573,744
Houston Chronicle	527,744
San Francisco Chronicle	468,739

Source: *Wall Street Journal*, May 3, 2005, p. B4, from Audit Bureau of Circulations.

★ 950 ★
Newspapers
SIC: 2711; NAICS: 51111

Leading Daily Newspaper Markets, 2004

Newspapers in the top 50 markets are reaching nearly 8 out of 10 adults over the course of a week. The top markets for adult readership are shown. For Sunday papers, Cleveland had 73.2% of adult readers, Providence/New Bedford 72.3%.

Hartford/New Haven, CT	.64.4%
Providence/New Bedford	.63.4
Boston	.62.3
Cleveland	.61.4
New York	.61.3
Philadelphia	.60.7
Pittsburgh	.60.6
West Palm Beach	.60.0

Continued on next page.

★ 950 ★
[Continued]
Newspapers
SIC: 2711; NAICS: 51111

Leading Daily Newspaper Markets, 2004

Newspapers in the top 50 markets are reaching nearly 8 out of 10 adults over the course of a week. The top markets for adult readership are shown. For Sunday papers, Cleveland had 73.2% of adult readers, Providence/New Bedford 72.3%.

Harrisburg/Lancaster/Lebanon/York, PA . . .58.6%
Tampa/St. Petersburg/Sarasota 58.5

Source: *PR Newswire*, April 19, 2005, p. NA, from Newspaper Audience Measurement Index.

★ 951 ★
Comic Books
SIC: 2721; NAICS: 51112

Graphic Novel Sales

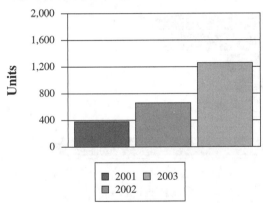

Data show number of titles. The graphic novel market will climb to $105 million in 2004 from $90 million in 2003.

2001 373
2002 668
2003 1,257

Source: *BP Report*, October 18, 2004, p. NA, from *R.R. Bowker's Books in Print.*

★ 952 ★
Comic Books
SIC: 2721; NAICS: 51112

Top Anime Comics Publishers

Viz is the leading publisher and distributor of anime comics in North America. The company estimates 15 million readers of manga for English speaking audiences. The market share is for the United States.

Viz 50.0%
Other 50.0

Source: ''Shonen Jump Teams With AOL to Offer Dragin Ball Flash Manga.'' [online] from http://www.animenewsnetwork.com [October 22, 2004].

★ 953 ★
Comic Books
SIC: 2721; NAICS: 51112

Top Comic Book Publishers, 2004

Market shares are shown based on sales of comics, magazines and graphic novels. The top comics were Superman #604, New Avengers #1 and Superman Batman #8. The top trades were Batman Hush Vol 1, Superman Red Son, and Spawn Simony One Shot.

Marvel Comics 36.54%
DC Comics 30.63
Dark Horse Comics 5.58
Image Comics 3.90
TokyoPop 3.00
Viz LLC 2.01
Wizard Entertainment 1.91
Devils Due Publishing 1.80
Dreamwave Publishing 1.43
IDW Publishing 1.19
Fantagraphics Books/Eros Comix 0.68
A.D. Vision 0.67
Gemstone Publishing 0.63
Other 10.21

Source: ''2004, By the Numbers.'' [online] from http://newsarama.com/pages/2004Numbers.htm [Accessed Febuary 18, 2005], from Diamond Comics.

★ 954 ★

Magazines

SIC: 2721; NAICS: 51112

Leading Video Game Magazines, 2004

Paid circulation is shown for January - June 2004. Figures were up slightly over 2003 figures, suggesting that consumers turn to sources other than the Internet for game information. Paid circulation for Official Xbox Magazine was up 13.6% and single copy purchases was up 27%.

Game Informer	1,647,350
Electronic Gaming Monthly	514,058
Official Xbox Magazine	406,176
PSM	400,318
PC Gamer	304,110
Official U.S. Playstation Magazine	264,432
Computer Gaming World	202,359
Tips and Tricks	146,566

Source: *Electronic Gaming Business*, September 8, 2004, p. NA, from Audit Bureau of Circulation.

★ 955 ★

Magazines

SIC: 2721; NAICS: 51112

Popular TV Guides in France, 2003

France recently lifted its ban on television advertising by the press titles. Publishers quickly rushed into the market and spent 60 million euros during the first eight months of 2004. Television listings are big business in the country as screen guides and supplements from tabloids are not widely used. Such titles account for a fifth of consumer magazine revenues. Circulation is in thousands.

TV Magazine	4,826
Tele 7 Jours	2,211
Tele Z	2,114
Tele Loisirs	1,968
TV Hebdo	1,823
Tele Star	1,789
Tele Poche	980

Source: *Financial Times*, October 26, 2004, p. 10, from *World Magazine Trends 2004-2005*.

★ 956 ★

Magazines

SIC: 2721; NAICS: 51112

Top Magazine Publishers in Australia, 2004

Australian consumers purchased 227.1 million magazines during the year. This was a 3.1% increase over 2003. Mass women's titles took 55% of the market. Youth, women's lifestyle and music magazines also performed well.

ACP	.48.0%
Pacific Magazines	.22.2
Other	.29.8

Source: *Australasian Business Intelligence*, February 17, 2005, p. NA, from Audit Bureau of Circulations.

★ 957 ★

Magazines

SIC: 2721; NAICS: 51112

Top Magazine Publishers in the U.K.

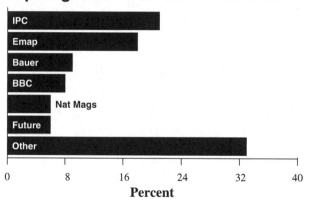

Market shares are shown in percent.

	Jan - June 2004	July - Dec. 2004
IPC	20.9%	21.1%
Emap	17.7	17.7
Bauer	9.1	8.6
BBC	8.7	8.2
Nat Mags (Hearst)	5.6	5.6
Future	4.6	5.6
Other	33.4	33.2

Source: *The Times*, February 25, 2005, p. 63, from Emap calculations and Audit Bureau of Circulations.

★ 958 ★

Magazines

SIC: 2721; NAICS: 51112

Top Magazines by Circulation, 2004

Magazines are ranked by average circulation.

AARP the Magazine	22,617,093
Reader's Digest	10,081,577
TV Guide	9,015,544
Better Homes and Gardens	7,626,088
National Geographic	5,475,135
Good Housekeeping	4,639,941
Family Circle	4,267,535
Woman's Day	4,209,130
Ladies' Home Journal	4,120,087
Time	4,034,061

Source: *Mediaweek*, March 21, 2005, p. 38, from Publishers Information Bureau and Competitive Media Reporting.

★ 959 ★

Magazines

SIC: 2721; NAICS: 51112

Top Magazines in the U.K., 2004

Magazines are ranked by circulation for December 2004.

Sky	6,709,861
Asda Magazine	2,584,693
Boots Health & Beauty Redwood	1,766,893
National Trust Magazine	1,655,088
What's on TV	1,587,578
Saga Magazine	1,247,180
Take A Break	1,222,774
The Somerfield Magazine	1,115,588
Radio Times	1,108,718

Source: *Campaign*, February 25, 2005, p. 28, from Audit Bureau of Circulations.

★ 960 ★

Magazines

SIC: 2721; NAICS: 51112

Top Men's Magazine Titles in the U.K.

The men's market saw an almost 25% surge in sales. Titles are ranked by circulation.

FHM	580,027
Nuts	275,459
Zoo	240,215
Maxim	234,183
Men's Health	229,116
Loaded	220,057
GQ	125,016

Bizarre	85,852
Front	84,093
Stuff	74,570

Source: *Campaign*, February 25, 2005, p. 30, from Audit Bureau of Circulations.

★ 961 ★

Magazines

SIC: 2721; NAICS: 51112

Top Women's Magazine Titles in the U.K.

Titles are ranked by circulation.

Take a Break	1,222,774
Chat	636,310
Now	619,186
That's Life	601,806
Heat	552,215
OK! Magazine	529,492
Woman	527,764
Closer	504,350
Woman's Own	449,688

Source: *Campaign*, February 25, 2005, p. 30, from Audit Bureau of Circulations.

★ 962 ★

Magazines

SIC: 2721; NAICS: 51112

Video Game Magazines in the U.K.

Future's share is based on a proposed acquisition of Highbury House.

Future	95.0%
Other	5.0

Source: *Sunday Times*, March 6, 2005, p. 17.

★ 963 ★

Magazines

SIC: 2721; NAICS: 51112

Women's Service Magazines and Ad Pages, 2004

Data show the number of ad pages for January - November 2004.

Better Homes & Gardens	1,913
Good Housekeeping	1,558
Woman's Day	1,499

Continued on next page.

★ 963 ★

[Continued]
Magazines
SIC: 2721; NAICS: 51112

Women's Service Magazines and Ad Pages, 2004

Data show the number of ad pages for January - November 2004.

O - The Oprah Magazine	1,435
Ladies' Home Journal	1,342
Real Simple	1,306
Family Circle	1,293
Redbook	1,178
More	771
Martha Stewart Living	609

Source: *HFN*, February 14, 2005, p. 8, from Publishers Information Bureau.

★ 964 ★

Books
SIC: 2731; NAICS: 51113

Adult Book Purchases, 2003

Market shares are shown in percent.

Romance	27.0%
General fiction	18.8
Espionage/thriller	7.6
Mystery/detective	6.3
Western fiction	4.9
Children's books	3.5
Suspense/psychology	3.3
Diet/health/fitness	2.0
Other	26.6

Source: *Supermarket News*, January 3, 2005, p. 30, from Ipsos Booktrends.

★ 965 ★

Books
SIC: 2731; NAICS: 51113

Book Industry, 2003

Americans purchased 1.176 billion books, worth $11 billion in 2003. Used book sales have grown 5% in previous years.

New	86.0%
Used	14.0

Source: *Christian Science Monitor*, May 25, 2004, p. 16, from Ipsos BookTrends.

★ 966 ★

Books
SIC: 2731; NAICS: 51113

Book Industry in Albania, 2002

The value of the market is estimated at 6 million pounds.

Publishers' receipts	£ 33.3
Academic/STM	25.0
Supplementary education	16.8
State education	8.3
Importers receipts	5.0
Textbooks	1.7
Schoolbooks	1.6
Other children's	8.3

Source: *Bookseller*, June 25, 2004, p. 28, from British Council Publisher's Association Global Publishing Information.

★ 967 ★

Books
SIC: 2731; NAICS: 51113

Book Industry in Switzerland

The Swiss book market was valued at $600 million in 2003. Bookshops take 65% of book sales.

General literature	50.0%
Scientific/professional	25.0
Art book/photographic	5.0
Comic books	4.5
Other	25.5

Source: "US & FCS Market Research Reports." [online] from http://www.stat-usa.gov [Published July 29, 2004].

★ 968 ★

Books
SIC: 2731; NAICS: 51113

Book Sales by Sector, 2003-2004

Data show net sales in thousands of dollars. From 1992-2004 some compound growth rates: religious books 14.5%, standardized tests 13.1%, juvenile paperbound 12.9%. The industry itself grew 8% overall.

	2003	2004	Share
Trade (total) . . .	$ 5,063,813	$ 5,159,791	17.87%
El-Hi (K-12 education)	4,290,361	4,294,651	14.87
Professional	3,978,696	4,058,269	14.05
Higher education . .	3,390,947	3,451,984	11.95
Adult hardbound . .	2,451,844	2,606,310	9.03
Adult paperbound . .	1,465,374	1,506,404	5.22

Continued on next page.

★ 968 ★
[Continued]
Books
SIC: 2731; NAICS: 51113

Book Sales by Sector, 2003-2004

Data show net sales in thousands of dollars. From 1992-2004 some compound growth rates: religious books 14.5%, standardized tests 13.1%, juvenile paperbound 12.9%. The industry itself grew 8% overall.

	2003	2004	Share
Book clubs & mail order	$ 1,294,767	$ 1,179,533	4.08%
Religious	1,261,848	1,332,511	4.61
Mass market paperback	1,218,035	1,109,630	3.84
Standardized tests	821,967	923,891	3.20
Juvenile hardbound	697,999	581,433	2.01
Juvenile paperbound	448,597	465,644	1.61
Other	2,100,142	2,205,150	7.64

Source: ''''Estimated Book Industry Net Sales.'' [online] from http://www.publishers.org/industry/index.cfm [Accessed April 11, 2005], from Association of American Publishers.

★ 969 ★
Books
SIC: 2731; NAICS: 51113

Harry Potter Sales

Harry Potter and the Half Blood Prince was released in July 2005. It sold an estimated 6.9 million copies during its first 24 hours. There are 102 million Harry Potter titles in print in the United States. The series has been translated into 62 languages worldwide. Data show sales of hardcover and paperback sales, in millions.

Harry Potter and the Sorcerer's Stone (1998)	26
Harry Potter and the Chamber of Secrets (1999)	24
Harry Potter and the Prisoner of Azbakan (1999)	19
Harry Potter and the Goblet of Fire (2000)	18
Harry Potter and the Order of the Phoenix (2003)	16

Source: *Wall Street Journal*, July 18, 2005, p. B3, from Scholastic.

★ 970 ★
Books
SIC: 2731; NAICS: 51113

Largest Book Publishers in Canada, 2002

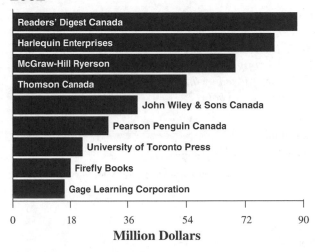

Million Dollars

The book industry has seen significant changes since 1991. General Publishing, the country's largest distributor, collapsed. Indigo and Chapters, two large book chains, merged. Amazon.com developed. These factors all contributed to book store closings. The total book market was valued at C$2.1 billion, with general consumer books taking a $1.3 billion slice. Companies are ranked by turnover in millions of dollars.

Readers' Digest Canada	$ 88.1
Harlequin Enterprises	80.7
McGraw-Hill Ryerson	68.7
Thomson Canada	53.7
John Wiley & Sons Canada	38.5
Pearson Penguin Canada	29.9
University of Toronto Press	21.5
Firefly Books	17.7
Gage Learning Corporation	15.8

Source: *The Bookseller*, November 12, 2004, p. 24, from Orbis Company Information.

★ 971 ★

Books

SIC: 2731; NAICS: 51113

Leading Spanish-Language Book Publishers

The number of Spanish-language titles is fairly small, with the the number of titles reaching its high point in 2003. The industry has been placed at $350 million, although that figure has been called into question. Companies are ranked by the number of imports of sports-language adult books.

Planeta	6,000
Santillana	216
Random House Mondadori	120

Source: *Publishers Weekly*, January 17, 2005, p. 28.

★ 972 ★

Books

SIC: 2731; NAICS: 51113

Top Book Publishers, 2004

Companies are ranked by estimated revenues in millions of dollars.

Random House	$ 2,200
Penguin	1,400
Harper Collins	1,300
Simon & Schuster	800
Time Warner Book Group	400

Source: "Media, Entertainment & Broadcasting." [online] from http://www.mind-advertising.com/sectors/sector_media.htm [Accessed July 8, 2005].

★ 973 ★

Books

SIC: 2731; NAICS: 51113

Top Book Publishers (Hardcover), 2004

Data show share of the 1,530 hardcover positions on the best seller list. Dan Brown's The DaVinci Code was at the top of the fiction charts in 31 or out of the 51 weeks. More first novels made the bestseller list in 2004, the third year of such a trend. Politics was the top nonfiction category.

Random House	28.4%
Simon & Schuster	14.8
Penguin USA	13.3
HarperCollins	12.8
Time Warner	10.0
Hyperion	6.1

Rodale	5.2%
Von Holtzbrinck	3.3
Houghton Mifflin	0.9
Other	5.2

Source: *Publishers Weekly*, January 10, 2005, p. 27.

★ 974 ★

Books

SIC: 2731; NAICS: 51113

Top Book Publishers in the U.K.

Market shares are shown in percent. Other includes Oxford University Press, BBC and Lonely Planet.

Bertesmann	16.8%
Hachette	12.5
Pearson	10.2
New Corporation	9.5
Holtzbrinck	4.5
Time Warner	4.0
Bloomsbury	2.0
Simon & Shuster	1.8
Other	38.6

Source: *Printing World*, September 30, 2004, p. 20, from Booksellers Association.

★ 975 ★

Books

SIC: 2731; NAICS: 51113

Top Book Publishers (Mass Market), 2004

Data show number of imprints.

Bantam	19
Jove	16
Berkley	16
Warner	10

Continued on next page.

★ 975 ★

[Continued]
Books
SIC: 2731; NAICS: 51113

Top Book Publishers (Mass Market), 2004

Data show number of imprints.

Pocket	10
Avon	10
St. Martin's	9
Dell	9
Pocket Star	8

Source: *Publishers Weekly*, January 10, 2005, p. 27.

★ 976 ★

Books
SIC: 2731; NAICS: 51113

Top Book Publishers (Paperback), 2004

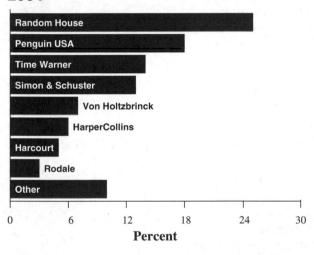

Percent

Data show share of the 1,530 paperback positions on the best seller list. About half of the new trade paperback slots were nonfiction - politics, diet and memoirs.

Random House	25.1%
Penguin USA	17.6
Time Warner	13.9
Simon & Schuster	12.7
Von Holtzbrinck	7.0
HarperCollins	5.9
Harcourt	4.6
Rodale	3.0
Other	10.2

Source: *Publishers Weekly*, January 10, 2005, p. 27.

★ 977 ★

Books
SIC: 2731; NAICS: 51113

Top Garden Title Publishers in the U.K.

Total sales in the sector were 1.1 million worth about 11.5 million pounds sterling. The best-selling title was Della's Kitchen Garden by Gay Search.

Penguin	28.2%
BBC	16.6
Hachette Livre	13.1
Random House	10.1
HarperCollins	5.2
Frances Lincoln	3.5
North American Import Group	2.8
Other	20.4

Source: *The Bookseller*, April 15, 2005, p. 31, from BookScan.

★ 978 ★

Books
SIC: 2731; NAICS: 51113

Top History Publishers in the U.K., 2004

Sales hit an all time high breaking 50 million pounds sterling for the first time. Top seller was the Bookseller of Kabul by Asne Seierstad.

Penguin	14.1%
Hachette Livre	12.4
Random House	11.0
HarperCollins	9.0
Time Warner	7.8
Pan Macmillan	4.8
Simon & Schuster	4.1
BBC	2.8
Haynes Sutton	2.2
OUP	1.9
Other	29.9

Source: *The Bookseller*, April 8, 2005, p. 27, from Nilesen Bookscan.

★ 979 ★
Books
SIC: 2731; NAICS: 51113

Top Publishers in Ecuador

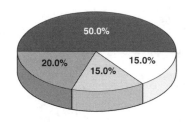

■ LNS Don Bosco/Editorial Norma **□** Santillana
▨ Poligrafica **□** Other

The publishing sector is estimated at 4 million books.

LNS Don Bosco/Editorial Norma	.50.0%
Poligrafica	.20.0
Santillana	.15.0
Other	.15.0

Source: *South American Business Information*, October 25, 2004, p. NA.

★ 980 ★
Textbooks
SIC: 2731; NAICS: 51113

K-5 Social Studies Textbooks in Texas

Social studies textbooks was the largest adoption opportunity during the previous year, according to the source. Figures are for the K-5 segment.

Scott Foresman Social Studies	.30.3%
Horizons	.28.5
Other	.41.2

Source: *Educational Marketer*, May 10, 2004, p. NA.

★ 981 ★
Textbooks
SIC: 2731; NAICS: 51113

Leading College Economics Textbook Publishers

Including micro- and macro-economics, the three major economics textbook courses saw estimated sales of $83.2 million. Thomson Learning took a 36.4% share of these sales.

McGraw-Hill	.47.4%
Thomson Learning	.34.3

Pearson Education	.10.5%
Houghton Mifflin	. 2.4
WW Norton	. 2.2
BFW	. 1.1
Other	. 1.1

Source: *Educational Marketer*, October 11, 2004, p. NA, from Monument Information Resource and Simba Information.

★ 982 ★
Textbooks
SIC: 2731; NAICS: 51113

Leading College Psychology Book Publishers

The new and used college and psychology textbook trade represents a $304.6 million industry in 2003. Used books take about 35% of this total.

Pearson Education	.26.9%
Thomson Learning	.25.0
McGraw-Hill	.16.3
BFW	.13.5
John Wiley & Sons	. 4.6
Houghton Mifflin	. 4.2
American Psych. Assoc.	. 1.8
W.W. Norton	. 1.6
Other	. 6.1

Source: *Educational Marketer*, September 13, 2004, p. NA, from Simba Information.

★ 983 ★
Textbooks
SIC: 2731; NAICS: 51113

Math Adoption Textbooks in North Carolina

North Carolina math adoptions totaled $51 million.

McGraw-Hill	.29.7%
Pearson Education	.24.9
Harcourt	.23.0
Houghton Mifflin	.19.8
Thomson Learning	. 1.5
Bedford, Freeman, Worth	. 0.7
People's Publishing	. 0.3
Other	.10.1

Source: *Educational Marketer*, November 1, 2004, p. NA, from North Carolina Textbook Warehouse and Simba Information Inc.

★ 984 ★
Textbooks
SIC: 2731; NAICS: 51113

Math Textbook Industry in Alabama, 2004

Sales of math textbooks in the state totalled $14.4 million in 2004.

Pearson Education 40.7%
Harcourt 29.3
McGraw-Hill 21.4
Houghton Mifflin 7.8
Thomson Learning 0.9

Source: *Educational Marketer*, November 8, 2004, p. NA, from Simba Information.

★ 985 ★
Textbooks
SIC: 2731; NAICS: 51113

Textbook Adoption in Tennessee

The Tennessee K-12 composition and grammar textbook market was valued at $29.5 million. Sales of foreign languages textbooks were noticeably low for the year. Some districts adopted textbooks but did not actually purchase the textbooks because of budget problems.

McGraw-Hill 40.6%
Harcourt 29.8
Houghton Mifflin 14.8
Pearson Eduation 13.5
Other 1.3

Source: *Educational Marketer*, October 18, 2004, p. NA, from Tennessee Book Co.

★ 986 ★
Textbooks
SIC: 2731; NAICS: 51113

Top Developmental/Remedial English Textbook Publishers, 2003

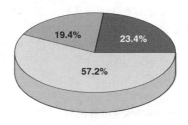

The market for developmental/remedial English textbooks on college campuses stood at $49.1 million.

McGraw-Hill 23.4%
Houghton 19.4
Other 57.2

Source: *Educational Marketer*, November 8, 2004, p. NA, from Monument Information Resource.

★ 987 ★
Book Printing
SIC: 2732; NAICS: 323117

Largest Book Printers

Firms are ranked by sales in millions of dollars.

Quebecor World . . . .$ 704
RR Donnelley 656
Banta Corp. 383
Von Hoffmann Corp. 323
Courier Corp. 202
Phoenix Color 136
Taylor Publishing 114
Walsworth Publishing 97
Cenveo 86
Maple-Vail Book Mfg. 79

Source: *Printing Impressions*, December 1, 2004, p. NA, from *Printing Impressions Top 400*.

★ 988 ★
Book Printing
SIC: 2732; NAICS: 323117

Leading Book Producers in the U.K.

Companies are ranked by turnover derived from bookprinting and binding in millions of pounds. The industry is thought to be about 1.9 - 3.7 billion pounds, depending on how the industry is defined. The U.K. has about 1.2 million titles in print at any one time.

Clays	£ 70.0
CPI	58.6
Butler and Tanner	30.0
Bookmarque and White Quill Press	15.0
Antony Rowe Group	15.0
Polestar Wheatons	13.0
Scotprint	12.0
Cambridge Printing	12.0
William Clowes	11.7
Biddles	10.7

Source: *Print Week*, August 26, 2004, p. 22.

★ 989 ★
Directories
SIC: 2741; NAICS: 51114

Largest Independent Yellow Pages Publishers

The top 3 control 57% of independent yellow pages revenues. Independent yellow pages represent 18.2% of the total market, up from 6.4% in 1996. In that year, the top 3 firms (R.H. Donnelley, TransWestern and Yellow Book) had 41% of the industry.

Yellow Book	$ 1,100
TransWestern	363
White/Associates	145

Source: *Yellow Pages & Directory Report*, September 24, 2004, p. NA, from Simba.

★ 990 ★
Directories
SIC: 2741; NAICS: 51114

Yellow Pages Industry in Canada

Yellow Pages Group is hoping to increase its share of the industry to 90% with its acquisition of SuperPages.

Yellow Pages Group	60.0%
Other	40.0

Source: *America's Intelligence Wire*, August 9, 2004, p. NA.

★ 991 ★
Instructional Materials
SIC: 2741; NAICS: 51113

Leading Instructional Material Publishers, 2003

The college market saw double digit growth in 2002 but saw only a 3.6% increase in 2003. The reason was that with troubled economies, states cut aid to colleges. Colleges in turn cut course offerings, raised tuitions and enforced enrollment caps. In the K-12 segment, cash strapped school districts experienced similar difficulties.

Pearson	22.7%
McGraw-Hill	17.5
Harcourt	10.6
Houghton Mifflin	10.3
Other	38.9

Source: *Educational Marketer*, August 2, 2004, p. NA, from Simba Information.

★ 992 ★
Trading Cards
SIC: 2741; NAICS: 511199

Trading Card Market

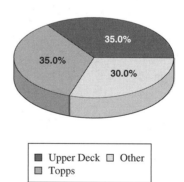

The industry hit its high point in 1991 with a wholesale market worth $1.1 billion. Annual sales are now estimated at $350 to $400 million. Market shares are shown in percent.

Upper Deck	35.0%
Topps	35.0
Other	30.0

Source: *San Diego Union Tribune*, April 3, 2004, p. NA.

★ 993 ★
Yearbooks
SIC: 2741; NAICS: 511199

Leading Yearbook Publishers in North America

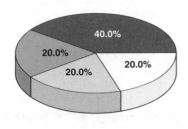

Legend:
■ Jostens □ American Achievement
■ Herff Jones □ Other

The college and high school yearbook market was valued at $685 million.

Jostens	40.0%
Herff Jones	20.0
American Achievement	20.0
Other	20.0

Source: ''Troubled Company Reporter.'' [online] from http://www.bankrupt.com/TCR_Public/040303 [Published March 3, 2004].

★ 994 ★
Printing
SIC: 2750; NAICS: 323110

Largest Catalog Printers

Firms are ranked by sales in millions of dollars.

RR Donnelley	$ 1,887
Quad/Graphics	1,040
Qubecor World	1,024
Arandell Corp.	224
Banta Corp.	156
Perry Judd's	98
Cenveo	86
Brown Printing	80
Spencer Press	75
Consolidated Graphics	70

Source: *Printing Impressions*, December 1, 2004, p. NA, from *Printing Impressions Top 400*.

★ 995 ★
Printing
SIC: 2750; NAICS: 323110

Largest Direct Mail Printers

Firms are ranked by sales in millions of dollars.

Quebecor World	$ 640
RR Donnelley	492
Vertis Inc.	317
Banta Corp.	184
IWCO Direct	118
Japs-Olson Co.	85
Von Hoffmann Corp.	79
Consolidated Graphics	70
Holden Communications	50
Berlin Industries	42

Source: *Printing Impressions*, December 1, 2004, p. NA, from *Printing Impressions Top 400*.

★ 996 ★
Printing
SIC: 2750; NAICS: 323110

Largest Government Printers, 2004

Companies are ranked by printing for the Government Printing Office in millions of dollars. The fiscal year covers October 1, 2003 - September 30, 2004. Shares are shown based on the top 50 firms.

	($ mil.)	Share
Monarch Litho	$ 22.46	9.70%
Gateway Press	21.75	9.39
Cenveo	19.71	8.51
NPC	19.17	8.28
Von Hoffman Graphics	16.02	6.92
CDCI- Sourcelink	12.23	5.28
Intelligencer Printing	9.73	4.20
Fry Communications	9.09	3.93
McDonald & Eudy Printers	8.26	3.57
Banta Corporation	5.76	2.49
Gray Graphics	5.00	2.16
R.R. Donnelley	4.33	1.87
Other	78.07	33.71

Source: *Printing News*, November 29, 2004, p. 7, from ABC Advisors.

★ 997 ★
Printing
SIC: 2750; NAICS: 323110
Largest Printers

Firms are ranked by sales in millions of dollars.

RR Donnelley	$ 8,204.50
Quebecor World	6,400.00
Quad/Graphics	2,000.00
Cenveo Inc.	1,728.00
Vertis Inc.	1,585.90
Transcontinental Inc.	1,446.00
Banta Corp.	1,418.50
Deluxe Corp.	1,240.00
Bowne & Co.	1,064.82
Valassis Communications	917.00

Source: *Printing Impressions*, December 1, 2004, p. NA, from *Printing Impressions Top 400*.

★ 998 ★
Printing
SIC: 2750; NAICS: 323110
Largest Printers in North America

Companies are ranked by most recent fiscal year sales in millions of dollars.

R.R. Donnelley & Sons	$ 8,204.50
Quebecor World Inc.	6,390.00
Quad/Graphics	2,000.00
FedEx Kinko's	2,000.00
Cenveo Inc.	1,672.66
Transcontinental Inc.	1,610.56
Vertis	1,585.90
Banta Corp.	1,418.49
Jostens Holding Corp.	1,400.00
Deluxe Corp.	1,242.10
Bowne & Co.	1,000.00

Source: *Graphic Arts Monthly*, November 2004, p. 23, from *Graphics Arts Monthly 101*.

★ 999 ★
Printing
SIC: 2750; NAICS: 323110
Largest Publication Printers

Firms are ranked by sales in millions of dollars.

RR Donnelley	$ 1,887
Quebecor World	1,664
Quad/Graphics	740
Brown Printing	320
Cadmus Communications	302

Perry Judd's	$ 184
Banta Corp.	184
Publishers Printing/Publishers Press	160
Vertis Inc.	158
The Sheridan Group	149

Source: *Printing Impressions*, December 1, 2004, p. NA, from *Printing Impressions Top 400*.

★ 1000 ★
Printing
SIC: 2750; NAICS: 323110
Leading Consumables Printers in the U.K.

Firms are ranked by sales in thousands of pounds.

Coates Brothers	£ 114,580
Sericol	66,379
Gibbon Inks & Coatings	51,227
Flint Ink	35,992
Stehlin Hostag Ink	26,267
Usher Walker	23,670
Duco International	18,327
Conitech UK	16,874
BASF Coatings	15,777
Varn Products	14,997

Source: *Printing World*, November 18, 2004, p. 47.

★ 1001 ★
Printing
SIC: 2750; NAICS: 323110
Leading Prepress Printers in the U.K.

Firms are ranked by sales in millions of pounds.

KPG	£ 105,039
Agfa	53,383
Fujifilm Electronic Imaging	46,492
Dainippon Screen	21,591
Creo UK	20,036
ECRM Inc.	14,220
Highwater Designs	4,402
X-Rite	4,184
Esko-Graphics	2,204
Gretag Macbeth	1,685

Source: *Printing World*, November 18, 2004, p. 47.

★ 1002 ★
Labels
SIC: 2752; NAICS: 323110

Label Shipments, 2003

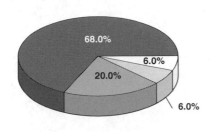

By 2008, label shipments are forecasted to reach $15.2 billion. The industry is epected to increase 5.7% annually. Pressure-sensitive, stretch-sleeve and in-mold labels are forecast to see the strongest growth.

Pressure-sensitive 68.0%
Glue-applied 20.0
Sleeve & heat-shrink 6.0
Other 6.0

Source: *Converting Magazine*, September 2004, p. 8, from Freedonia Group.

★ 1003 ★
Labels
SIC: 2752; NAICS: 323110

Release Liner Market Worldwide

By 2008 the industry will stand at 30 billion square meters. The industry is shown by region.

North America 40.0%
Europe 31.0
Asia Pacific 22.0
Other 7.0

Source: *Paper Foil Film Converter*, September 2004, p. NA, from Alexander Watson Associates.

★ 1004 ★
Check Printing
SIC: 2759; NAICS: 323119

Leading Check Printers

Consumers are writing fewer checks. Checks were used to pay for 44% of all transactions in 2003, down from 57% in 2000. Credit and debit cards represent growing methods of payment (debit cards grew from 11% to 20% in the same period) which some analysts think may mean the eventual end of the $1.8 billion check writing industry. Deluxe Corp. has more than half of the market. Harland's share is also estimated.

Deluxe Corp. 50.0%
Harland 25.0
Other 25.0

Source: *Atlanta Journal-Constitution*, January 2, 2005, p. B1.

★ 1005 ★
Greeting Cards
SIC: 2771; NAICS: 511191

Everyday Greeting Card Sales

The industry was valued at $7.3 billion in 2003 and is forecast to stay there until 2007. Much of this has to do with pricing, which has not increased in recent years. Mass retailers such as discount and dollar stores are the fastest growing channel. Trends in the sector include more urban cards, spiritual cards, humorous cards and "no fluff" cards.

Birthday 60.0%
Anniversary 8.0
Get well 7.0
Sympathy 6.0
Friendship 6.0

Source: *USA TODAY*, June 17, 2005, p. 5B, from Greeting Card Association.

★ 1006 ★
Greeting Cards
SIC: 2771; NAICS: 511191

Greeting Card Market

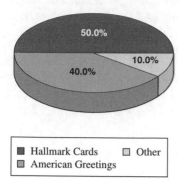

Market shares are shown in percent.

Hallmark Cards 50.0%
American Greetings 40.0
Other 10.0

Source: "American Greetings: Happy Shopping." [online]
from http://yahoo.businessweek.com/magazine/content
[Accessed May 23, 2005].

★ 1007 ★
Greeting Cards
SIC: 2771; NAICS: 511191

Greeting Card Market in India

The greeting card market was worth Rs 190 crore.

Archies Greetings and Gifts 50.0%
Other 50.0

Source: *Asia Africa Intelligence Wire*, November 30, 2004,
p. NA.

★ 1008 ★
Greeting Cards
SIC: 2771; NAICS: 511191

Seasonal Greeting Card Sales

*In the category of everyday cards, anniversary takes
8% of the total, get well cards take 7% while sympathy
and friendship/encouragement takes 6%.*

Christmas 61.0%
Valentine's Day 25.0
Mother's Day 4.0
Father's Day 3.0
Easter 3.0
Other 5.0

Source: *License*, June 2004, p. S38.

SIC 28 - Chemicals and Allied Products

★ 1009 ★
Chemicals
SIC: 2800; NAICS: 325132
Anti-Aging Product Chemicals, 2002 and 2007

Demand for formulated products that enhance appearance is thought to increase 12% a year through 2007. Figures are shown in millions of dollars.

	2002	2007	Share
Pharmaceutical active ingredients	$ 1,495	$ 2,665	56.82%
Hormones	305	348	7.42
Vitamins & antioxidants	270	390	8.32
Herbal extracts	177	300	6.40
Glucosamine	86	113	2.41
Botulinum toxin	85	190	4.05
Minerals	75	92	1.96
Proteins	73	110	2.35
Other	199	482	10.28

Source: *Nutraceuticals World*, May 2004, p. 74, from Freedonia Group.

★ 1010 ★
Chemicals
SIC: 2800; NAICS: 325132
Chemical Industry in Finland

The chemical industry is Finland's third largest industrial sector. The 12 billion euro chemical industries are geared towards forestry.

Petroleum and coal products	3.9
Basic chemicals	3.7
Plastics products	2.0
Medical products	0.8
Rubber products	0.5
Paints and inks	0.4
Other	0.7

Source: *European Chemical News*, October 4, 2004, p. 22, from Statistics Finland.

★ 1011 ★
Chemicals
SIC: 2800; NAICS: 325132
Chemical Industry in France, 2004

The industry is valued at 93.7 billion euros.

Pharmaceuticals	38.6%
Organic chemicals	21.6
Perfumes, soaps, detergents	18.6
Specialty chemicals	14.8
Inorganic chemicals	6.4

Source: *Chemical Week*, March 23, 2005, p. 19, from Ministry of Industry.

★ 1012 ★
Chemicals
SIC: 2800; NAICS: 325132
Chemical Industry in Germany

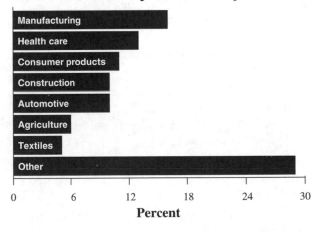

Germany is the largest chemical market in the European Union.

Manufacturing	16.0%
Health care	13.0
Consumer products	11.0
Construction	10.0
Automotive	10.0
Agriculture	6.0
Textiles	5.0
Other	29.0

Source: ''German Chemical Market.'' [online] from http://www.export.gov [Published March 2005].

★ 1013 ★
Chemicals
SIC: 2800; NAICS: 325132

Chemical Industry in India

The industry is valued at $30 billion.

Fertilizers	18.0%
Man-made fibers	16.0
Organic chemicals	15.0
Drugs and pharmacueticals	15.0
Soaps & toiletries	11.0
Inorganic chemicals	8.0
Other	13.0

Source: *Asian Chemical News*, August 2, 2004, p. 10, from Deepak Nitrate.

★ 1014 ★
Chemicals
SIC: 2800; NAICS: 325132

Chemical Industry in Spain

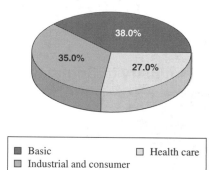

Value of chemicals in 2003 was 32,335 million euros. Under half of Spanish chemical production (47%) takes place in Catalina.

Basic	38.0%
Industrial and consumer	35.0
Health care	27.0

Source: *Asia Africa Intelligence Wire*, November 30, 2004, p. NA, from FERIQUE.

★ 1015 ★
Chemicals
SIC: 2800; NAICS: 325132

Chemicals Industry in Colombia

The industry has many small and mid-sized producers but is dominated by large multinationals such as Du-Pont, Bayer and Shell.

Oil & mining	21.4%
Pharmaceuticals	16.3

Agriculture	15.1%
Textiles	10.1
Consumer goods	8.2
Plastics	7.4
Manufacturing	6.2
Other	15.3

Source: "US & FCS Market Research Reports." [online] from http://www.stat-usa.gov [Published July 14, 2004].

★ 1016 ★
Chemicals
SIC: 2800; NAICS: 325132

Electronic Chemicals Demand, 2008

Market shares are shown in percent.

Substrate and packaging polymers	28.0%
Gases	23.0
Photoresists	21.0
Other	28.0

Source: *Chemical Week*, January 19, 2005, p. 35.

★ 1017 ★
Chemicals
SIC: 2800; NAICS: 325132

Global Catalyst Demand

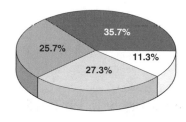

Demand is forecast to reach $1.3 billion in 2008. Gains will largely be generated from increased production of refined petroleum products, plastics and chemicals.

	2003	2008	Share
North America	$ 3,248	$ 4,040	35.69%
Western Europe	2,362	2,910	25.71
Asia Pacific	2,319	3,095	27.34
Other	918	1,275	11.26

Source: *European Chemical News*, October 25, 2004, p. 20, from Freedonia Group.

★ 1018 ★
Chemicals
SIC: 2800; NAICS: 325132

Paper Coating Chemicals and Minerals Market in Europe

The industry is valued at $2.3 billion.

Pigments	45.3%
Binders	42.7
Disperants	7.3
Modifiers	2.1
Other	2.6

Source: *Polymers Paint Colour Journal*, July 2004, p. 32.

★ 1019 ★
Chemicals
SIC: 2800; NAICS: 325132

Specialty Raw Materials for the Home/Fabric Industry

Distribution is shown based on $1 billion in value.

Specialty surfactants	37.0%
Specialty bleaches, activators, enzymes, optical brighteners	33.0
Functional polymers and organic sequestrants	12.0
Rheology control agents	8.0
Specialty silicones	6.0
Antibacterial and odor-control agents	4.0

Source: *Chemical Market Reporter*, January 24, 2005, p. FR8, from Kline & Co.

★ 1020 ★
Chemicals
SIC: 2800; NAICS: 325132

Surfactant Consumption Worldwide, 2003

Data are in millions of metric tons.

	(mil.)	Share
Soap	9.0	49.45%
Anionics	4.5	24.73
Nonionics	1.7	9.34
Quats	0.5	2.75
Amphoterics	0.1	0.55
Other	2.4	13.19

Source: *Chemical Market Reporter*, September 13, 2004, p. 18, from Cognis Corp, 6th World Surfactants Congress.

★ 1021 ★
Chemicals
SIC: 2800; NAICS: 325132

Top Chemical Firms in Europe

Firms are ranked by sales in millions of dollars.

BASF	$ 42,025
Bayer	35,986
Dow Chemical	32,632
DuPont	26,996
Atofina	22,486
Shell Chemicals	20,817
ExxonMobil Chemical	20,190
Mitsubishi Chemical	18,481
BP	15,483
Akzo Nobel	15,483
Degussa	14,395
Sabic	12,475

Source: *European Chemical News*, September 6, 2004, p. 22.

★ 1022 ★
Chemicals
SIC: 2800; NAICS: 325132

Top Chemical Firms in Japan

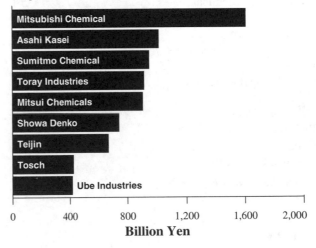

Billion Yen

Companies are ranked by sales in billions of yen.

Mitsubishi Chemical	¥ 1,606.220
Asahi Kasei	1,011.787
Sumitmo Chemical	948.020
Toray Industries	911.910
Mitsui Chemicals	902.990
Showa Denko	740.700
Teijin	667.090

Continued on next page.

★ 1022 ★
[Continued]
Chemicals
SIC: 2800; NAICS: 325132

Top Chemical Firms in Japan

Companies are ranked by sales in billions of yen.

Tosch	¥ 424.760
Ube Industries	417.110

Source: *Asian Chemical News*, February 21, 2005, p. 10, from companies.

★ 1023 ★
Chemicals
SIC: 2800; NAICS: 325132

Top Chemical Firms in North America, 2004

Nearly every producer saw double digit growth with the exception of DuPont, which sold its Invista fibre/textile business to Koch Industries. The firms involved in petrochemical production did particularly well. Firms are ranked by turnover in billions of dollars.

Dow Chemical	$ 40.2
ExxonMobil Chemical	35.1
DuPont	27.3
Huntsman Corp.	11.5
ChevronPhillips Chemicals	9.6
Equistar	9.3
GE Advanced Materials	8.3
Air Products	7.4
Rohm and Haas	7.3
PPG Industries	7.3
Praxair	6.6
Eastman Chemicals	6.6

Source: *European Chemical News*, March 28, 2005, p. 23.

★ 1024 ★
Chemicals
SIC: 2800; NAICS: 325132

Top Chemical Firms Worldwide

Companies are ranked by chemical sales in billions of dollars.

Dow Chemical	$ 32.63
BASF	30.76
DuPont	30.24
Bayer	21.56
Total	20.19
ExxonMobil	20.19
BP	16.07

Royal Dutch/Shell	$ 15.18
Mitsubishi Chemical	13.21
Degussa	12.92
Akzo Nobel	10.75
SABIC	10.31

Source: *C&EN*, July 19, 2004, p. 12.

★ 1025 ★
Chemicals
SIC: 2800; NAICS: 325132

Water Chemicals Demand, 2003

The municipal water market is experiencing severe price pressures and low volume growth, according to the source. By type of market, coagulants and flocculants take over half of the market. Demand is shown based on revenues.

Industrial water	23.4%
Municipal	22.8
Paper and pulp	20.7
Portable water treat	8.6
Recreational	3.6
Other industrial	20.9

Source: *Water World*, October 2004, p. 30, from Frost & Sullivan.

★ 1026 ★
Chemicals
SIC: 2800; NAICS: 325132

Wet Chemicals Market, 2003

The water treatment chemicals sector is likely to develop further as populations increase and continue to put demands on the water supply. Figures show distribution of revenues.

Industrial water treatment	23.4%
Municipal water treatment	22.8
Paper and pulp water treatment	20.7
Portable water treatment	8.6
Recreational water treatment	3.6
Other industrial applications	20.9

Source: *Water World*, October 2004, p. 30, from Frost & Sullivan.

★ 1027 ★
Alkalies and Chlorine
SIC: 2812; NAICS: 325181

Chlorine Market in Western Europe, 2003

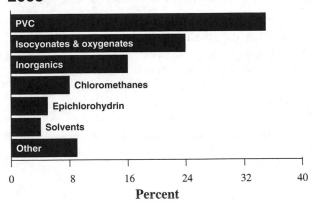

The industry is based on 9.39 billion tons.

PVC	.35.0%
Isocyonates & oxygenates	.24.0
Inorganics	.16.0
Chloromethanes	8.0
Epichlorohydrin	5.0
Solvents	4.0
Other	9.0

Source: *European Chemical News*, February 21, 2005, p. 18, from Euro Chlor.

★ 1028 ★
Alkalies and Chlorine
SIC: 2812; NAICS: 325181

Chloro-Alkali Capacity, 2003

The chloro-alkali industry is expected to see a shortfall of chlorine in coming years.

North America	.26.0%
Northeast Asia	.23.0
Western Europe	.20.0
Southeast Asia	8.0
Japan	8.0
Eastern Europe	7.0
South America	4.0
Middle East and Africa	4.0

Source: *Asian Chemical News*, July 19, 2004, p. 22, from Tecnon Orbichem.

★ 1029 ★
Alkalies and Chlorine
SIC: 2812; NAICS: 325181

Largest Soda Ash Producing Nations, 2004

Countries are ranked by estimated production in thousands of metric tons.

	(000)	Share
United States	10,800	94.49%
Kenya	350	3.06
Botswana	280	2.45

Source: *Mineral Commodities Summaries 2005*, January 2005, p. 20, from U.S. Geological Survey, U.S. Department of the Interior.

★ 1030 ★
Alkalies and Chlorine
SIC: 2812; NAICS: 325181

Leading Chlorine Makers in Brazil

Companies are ranked by production in thousands of metric tons.

	(000)	Share
Trikem	524	35.31%
Dow Chemical	385	25.94
OxyChem-Carboclora	278	18.73
Other	297	20.01

Source: *Chemical Week*, February 9, 2005, p. 28, from CMAI.

★ 1031 ★
Alkalies and Chlorine
SIC: 2812; NAICS: 325181

Leading Chlorine Makers in North America

Companies are ranked by production in thousands of metric tons.

Dow Chemical	4,292
OxyChem	2,449
PPG Industries	1,695
Olin	1,695
Formosa Plastics	878
Vulcan Chemicals	643
OxyVinyls	580
Georgia Gulf	470

Source: *Chemical Week*, February 9, 2005, p. 28, from CMAI.

★ 1032 ★
Alkalies and Chlorine
SIC: 2812; NAICS: 325181
Leading Chlorine Markets Worldwide

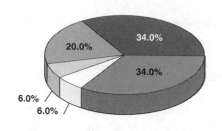

- ■ Vinyls
- ■ Organics
- □ Water treatment
- □ Chlorinated intermediates
- ■ Other

The market is valued at 48.4 million metric tons.

Vinyls	.34.0%
Organics	.20.0
Water treatment	. 6.0
Chlorinated intermediates	. 6.0
Other	.34.0

Source: *Chemical Week*, February 9, 2005, p. 28, from CMAI.

★ 1033 ★
Alkalies and Chlorine
SIC: 2812; NAICS: 325181
Soda Ash Consumption

Data show the top end markets.

Glass	.49.0%
Chemicals	.26.0
Soap and detergents	.11.0
Distributors	. 5.0
Flue gas desulphurization	. 2.0
Pulp and paper	. 2.0
Water treatment	. 1.0
Other	. 4.0

Source: *Chemical Market Reporter*, May 31, 2004, p. 17, from U.S. Geological Survey.

★ 1034 ★
Industrial Gases
SIC: 2813; NAICS: 32512
How Helium is Used, 2004

Domestic consumption was 77 million cubic meters.

Cryogenic applications	.28.0%
Pressurizing and purging	.26.0
Welding gas	.20.0
Controlled atmospheres	.13.0
Leak detection	. 4.0
Breathing mixtures	. 2.0
Other	. 7.0

Source: *Mineral Commodities Summaries 2005*, January 2005, p. 20, from U.S. Geological Survey, U.S. Department of the Interior.

★ 1035 ★
Industrial Gases
SIC: 2813; NAICS: 32512
Industrial Gas Demand, 2003

Total demand was $40.8 billion.

Manufacturing	.31.0%
Chemicals	.17.5
Steel	.13.5
Health care	.13.5
Food	. 7.0
Electronics	. 7.0
Other	.10.5

Source: *European Chemical News*, January 17, 2005, p. 18, from Spiritus.

★ 1036 ★
Industrial Gases
SIC: 2813; NAICS: 32512
Leading Industrial Gas Makers Worldwide

The industry saw 5% volume gains and double digit earnings growth. Manufacturing, chemicals and steel were the top end markets, taking roughly 60% of end uses. Demand was higher in the United States than expected. Shares are shown for the $44 billion market.

Air Liquide	.25.0%
Praxair	.16.0
BOC	.13.0
Linde	.11.0

Continued on next page.

★ 1036 ★

[Continued]
Industrial Gases
SIC: 2813; NAICS: 32512

Leading Industrial Gas Makers Worldwide

The industry saw 5% volume gains and double digit earnings growth. Manufacturing, chemicals and steel were the top end markets, taking roughly 60% of end uses. Demand was higher in the United States than expected. Shares are shown for the $44 billion market.

Air Products 2.0%
Other 33.0

Source: *Chemical Week*, February 23, 2005, p. 17.

★ 1037 ★

Inorganic Chemicals
SIC: 2816; NAICS: 325131

Leading Titanium Dioxide Makers Worldwide

Market shares are shown based on global capacity.

DuPont 23.0%
Millennium Chemicals 14.0
Kerr-McGee 13.0
Huntsman Tioxide 12.0
Kronos 10.0
Other 28.0

Source: *Chemical Week*, November 17, 2004, p. 9, from J.P. Morgan Securities.

★ 1038 ★

Inorganic Chemicals
SIC: 2819; NAICS: 325188

Global Catalyst Market

Chiral catalysts offer one of the strongest opportunities for catalysts firms, according to the source. Demand is shown in millions of dollars.

	2000	2003	Share
North America	$ 4,078	$ 1,498	15.97%
Western Europe	2,992	3,324	35.43
Japan	1,840	1,736	18.50
Other	2,482	2,825	30.11

Source: *Chemical Week*, August 11, 2004, p. 19, from SRI Consulting.

★ 1039 ★

Inorganic Chemicals
SIC: 2819; NAICS: 325188

Hydrofluoric Acid Demand Worldwide

Total demand in 2001 was 650,000 metric tons. Top producers include Honeywell, DuPont and Quimica Fluor.

Fluorocarbons 58.0%
Metal pickling 5.0
Petroleum allkylation 3.0
Aluminum 2.0
Other 32.0

Source: *Chemical Week*, October 20, 2004, p. 36, from SRI Consulting.

★ 1040 ★

Inorganic Chemicals
SIC: 2819; NAICS: 325188

Largest Iodine Producing Nations, 2004

Countries are ranked by estimated production in thousands of metric tons.

	(000)	Share
Chile	16,200	63.49%
Japan	6,500	25.47
United States	1,340	5.25
Indonesia	500	1.96
Turkmenistan	300	1.18
Russia	300	1.18
Azerbaijan	300	1.18
Indonesia	75	0.29
Uzbekistan	2	0.01

Source: *Mineral Commodities Summaries 2005*, January 2005, p. 20, from U.S. Geological Survey, U.S. Department of the Interior.

★ 1041 ★
Inorganic Chemicals
SIC: 2819; NAICS: 325998

Precipitated Silica Demand Worldwide, 2003

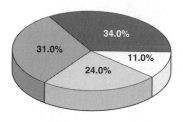

■ Asia	□ NAFTA
■ European Union	□ Other

The global industry for precipitated silica and sodium aluminum silicates is forecast to grow 4% to 1.5 million metric tons in 2010. Silica's major use is for filler in rubber and plastics.

Asia	.34.0%
European Union	.31.0
NAFTA	.24.0
Other	.11.0

Source: *Rubber World*, June 2004, p. 11, from Notch Consulting.

★ 1042 ★
Inorganic Chemicals
SIC: 2819; NAICS: 325131

Sodium Silicate Industry, 2004

Total demand was 1.2 million short tons. PQ, PPG, OxyChem and J.M. Huber are leading producers.

Detergents	.38.0%
Catalysts	.15.0
Pulp and paper	.12.0
Elastomers	. 7.0
Other	.28.0

Source: *Chemical Market Reporter*, February 7, 2005, p. 23.

★ 1043 ★
Inorganic Chemicals
SIC: 2819; NAICS: 325188

Sodium Sulfate Industry

Total demand is expected to grow from 118,000 tons in 2003 to 125,000 in 2008. Calbarian, General Chemical and Southern Ionics are leading producers.

Pulp and paper	.55.0%
Water treatment	.20.0
Photography	.10.0
Oil recovery	. 5.0
Other	.10.0

Source: *Chemical Market Reporter*, January 31, 2005, p. 23.

★ 1044 ★
Plastics
SIC: 2821; NAICS: 325211

Advanced Composites Market Worldwide, 2003-2008

Market shares are shown based on production. By application, automotive took 23% of production, followed by building/public works took 21%, aeronautics 17% and sports 11%.

North America	.40.0%
Europe	.35.0
Asia	.22.0
Other	. 3.0

Source: *Advanced Composites Bulletin*, December 2004, p. 12, from *Structure and Dynamics of the Composites Industry*.

★ 1045 ★
Plastics
SIC: 2821; NAICS: 325211

Degradable Plastics Market, 2008

The market stood at 370 million pounds, valued at $460 million.

Film	.45.0%
Ring carriers	.20.0
Foodservice	. 8.0
Other packaging	. 8.0
Other	.22.0

Source: *Converting*, March 2005, p. 2, from Freedonia Group.

★ 1046 ★
Plastics
SIC: 2821; NAICS: 325211
Epoxy Resin Market in Taiwan

The company has 10% fo the market in China.

Nan Ya	70.0%
Other	30.0

Source: *Asian Chemical News*, September 20, 2004, p. 7.

★ 1047 ★
Plastics
SIC: 2821; NAICS: 325211
Global Emulsion Polymer Demand

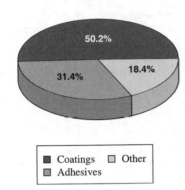

■ Coatings ☐ Other
■ Adhesives

Demand is forecast to increase to 11.4 million metric tons, representing a $24 billion market. North America and Western Europe have 65% of global demand for emulsion polymers. Figures are in millions of metric tons.

	2003	2008	Share
Coatings	4,530	5,700	50.22%
Adhesives	2,935	3,560	31.37
Other	1,655	2,090	18.41

Source: *Adhesives & Sealants Industry*, October 2004, p. 16, from Freedonia Group.

★ 1048 ★
Plastics
SIC: 2821; NAICS: 325211
Global PET Demand, 2004 and 2009

PET stands for polyethyelene terephthalate. EMEA stands for Europe, Middle East and Africa.

	2004	2009
Americas	38.0%	34.0%
EMEA	37.0	37.0
Asia	25.0	29.0

Source: *Asian Chemical News*, April 11, 2005, p. 10, from CMAI.

★ 1049 ★
Plastics
SIC: 2821; NAICS: 325211
Largest Input Plastic Material Producers Worldwide

Market shares are shown in percent.

BASF	11.0%
Basell	9.0
Dow	8.5
Exxon Mobil	8.0
BP Solvay	6.5
Other	57.0

Source: *Europe Intelligence Wire*, November 8, 2004, p. NA.

★ 1050 ★
Plastics
SIC: 2821; NAICS: 325211
Leading ABS Resin Firms in Japan, 2003

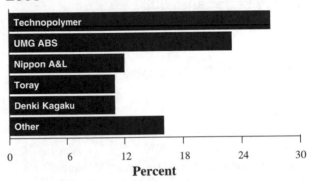

Market shares are estimated based on domestic shipments.

Technopolymer	27.0%
UMG ABS	23.0
Nippon A&L	12.0
Toray	11.4
Denki Kagaku	10.6
Other	16.0

Source: "Market Share Survey Report 2003." [online] from http://www.nni.nikkei.co.jp [Published July 26, 2004], from Japan ABS Resin Industry Association.

★ 1051 ★
Plastics
SIC: 2821; NAICS: 325211

Leading AH Salt (PA66) Makers

Shares are shown based on capacity of 3.46 million tons.

Invista/DuPont/Saband	.52.0%
Solutia	.16.5
Rhodia	.12.4
Asahi Kasei	4.3
China Shenma	3.0
Other	.11.8

Source: *Asian Chemical News*, January 17, 2005, p. 10, from Tecnon Orbichem.

★ 1052 ★
Plastics
SIC: 2821; NAICS: 325211

Leading Low-Density Polyethylene Makers in Japan, 2003

Market shares are estimated based on domestic shipments.

Japan Polyethylene	.31.1%
Mitsui Chemicals	.13.9
Sumitomo Chemical	.13.8
Nippon Unicar	.12.1
Tosoh	8.5
Other	.20.6

Source: ''Market Share Survey Report 2003.'' [online] from http://www.nni.nikkei.co.jp [Published July 26, 2004], from Nikkei estimates.

★ 1053 ★
Plastics
SIC: 2821; NAICS: 325211

Leading Polypropylene Makers, 2003

The total market was at 19.3 billion pounds annually.

Basell	.17.0%
BP	.14.0
Sunoco Chemicals	.13.0
ExxonMobil	.13.0
Total Petrochemicals	.11.0
Formosa Plastics	7.0
Dow Chemicals	7.0
Other	.18.0

Source: *Chemical Week*, March 23, 2005, p. 28.

★ 1054 ★
Plastics
SIC: 2821; NAICS: 325211

Leading Polystyrene Makers in Europe, 2003

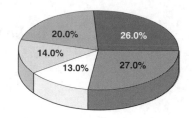
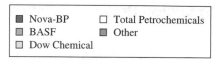

The industry is valued at $3.8 billion.

Nova-BP	.26.0%
BASF	.20.0
Dow Chemical	.14.0
Total Petrochemicals	.13.0
Other	.27.0

Source: *Chemical Week*, November 24, 2004, p. 6, from Chemical Market Associates Inc. and Nova Chemicals.

★ 1055 ★
Plastics
SIC: 2821; NAICS: 325211

Leading Urethane Makers in North America

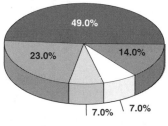
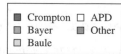

Market shares are shown in percent.

Crompton	.49.0%
Bayer	.23.0

Continued on next page.

★ **1055** ★

[Continued]

Plastics

SIC: 2821; NAICS: 325211

Leading Urethane Makers in North America

Market shares are shown in percent.

Baule	7.0%
APD	7.0
Other	14.0

Source: "Investor Presentation Slides Crompton Corp." [online] from http://www.crompston.com [published September 15, 2004].

★ **1056** ★

Plastics

SIC: 2821; NAICS: 325211

Plastic Coatings Technology Market in Western Europe

■ Polyurethanes	□ UV-curables
■ Acrylics	□ Other

The Western European market was placed at 119,930 tons in 2003. It should grow to 142,000 tons in 2008.

Polyurethanes	.58.0%
Acrylics	.21.0
UV-curables	8.0
Other	.13.0

Source: *Coatings World*, August 2004, p. 12, from Iinformation Research Ltd.

★ **1057** ★

Plastics

SIC: 2821; NAICS: 325211

Plastics Consumption in the U.K.

Market shares are shown in percent.

Packing	.36.0%
Building/construction	.21.7
Electrical	8.1
Transportation	7.3

Furniture/housewares	7.1%
Agriculture	7.0
Toys, leisure, sport	3.0
Other	9.8

Source: *Aluminum International Today*, January - February 2005, p. 34, from British Plastics Federation.

★ **1058** ★

Plastics

SIC: 2821; NAICS: 325211

Plastics Market in Canada

The market was valued at $10.6 billion in 2002.

Packaging	.34.0%
Construction	.26.0
Automotive	.18.0
Electronics	.12.0
Furniture	5.0
Other	5.0

Source: "US & FCS Market Research Reports." [online] from http://www.stat-usa.gov [Published February 23, 2004], from FENASEG.

★ **1059** ★

Plastics

SIC: 2821; NAICS: 325211

Plastics Market in Chile, 2002

The industry represents a total demand of 538,000 metric tons annually of plastic materials and resins worth $450 million in 2002.

Packing & packaging	.48.0%
Industrial applications	.13.0
Construction	9.0
Mining	8.0
Agricultural	5.0
Other	.17.0

Source: "Plastics Industry: Machinery & Resins." [online] from http://www.export.gov [accessed September 23, 2004], from ASIPLA.

★ 1060 ★

Plastics

SIC: 2821; NAICS: 325211

Polycarbonate Demand by End Use

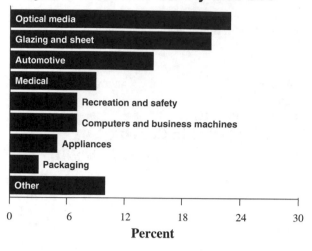

Demand is forecast to increase from 1,065 million pounds in 2004 to 1,255 million pounds in 2008. Leading producers are Bayer, Dow and GE Plastics.

Optical media 23.0%
Glazing and sheet 21.0
Automotive 15.0
Medical 9.0
Recreation and safety 7.0
Computers and business machines 7.0
Appliances 5.0
Packaging 3.0
Other 10.0

Source: *Chemical Market Reporter*, February 28, 2005, p. 23.

★ 1061 ★

Plastics

SIC: 2821; NAICS: 325211

Polypropylene Market in Egypt

Egypt consumes 300,000 tons of polypropylene each year. A single company in the private sector is producing polypropylene under the license of Union Carbide.

Fiber 58.0%
Injection molding 19.0
Films 19.0
Blow molding 1.0
Other 3.0

Source: "US & FCS Market Research Reports." [online] from http://www.stat-usa.gov [Published November 2004], from Railroads and Elaboration Lafis.

★ 1062 ★

Plastics

SIC: 2821; NAICS: 325211

Polyurethane Market in South East Asia/Australia, 2003

Market shares are shown in percent.

Australia 22.0%
Singapore 21.0
Malaysia 16.0
Indonesia 11.0
Philippines 4.0
Other 26.0

Source: *Urethanes Technology*, June - July 2004, p. 36, from Reed Business Group.

★ 1063 ★

Plastics

SIC: 2821; NAICS: 325211

Polyurethane Plastics in East Asia, 2003

The market will continue to develop in the coming five years. China and Hong Kong represent 60% of the region's total business of 3.2 million tons.

Flexible foams 28.0%
Coatings 23.0
Elastomers 22.0
Rigid foams 15.0
Adhesives & sealants 12.0

Source: *Urethanes Technology*, October - November 2004, p. 28, from IAL Consultants.

★ 1064 ★

Plastics

SIC: 2821; NAICS: 325211

Resin Sales by Type

Manufacturers have been focusing on resins for coatings with high solids content. Data show value in millions of dollars in selected markets.

	($ mil.)	Share
Acrylics	$ 1,350	28.46%
Polyvinyl acetates	992	20.92
Urethanes	600	12.65
Epoxy resins	475	10.01
Alkyds	356	7.51
Polyester	261	5.50
Polyvinyl chloride	156	3.29
Amino resin crosslinkers	94	1.98

Continued on next page.

★ 1064 ★

[Continued]

Plastics

SIC: 2821; NAICS: 325211

Resin Sales by Type

Manufacturers have been focusing on resins for coatings with high solids content. Data show value in millions of dollars in selected markets.

	($ mil.)	Share
Cellulosics	$ 59	1.24%
Other	400	8.43

Source: *JCT CoatingsTech*, February 2005, p. 54.

★ 1065 ★

Plastics

SIC: 2821; NAICS: 325211

Thermoplastic Resin Demand, 2003 and 2008

Demand is expected to increase 3.4% annually until reaching 3.4 metric tons in 2008. Construction will be the largest end-user sector for the compound resins market. Smaller applications, such as fencing, are also providing a boost to the market.

	2003	2008	Share
Engineered thermoplastics	712	883	25.71%
PVC	650	743	21.63
PP	511	641	18.66
Polyethlene	497	591	17.21
Thermoplastic elastomers	272	357	10.39
Polystyrene	188	220	6.40

Source: *High Performance Plastics*, November 2004, p. 1, from Freedonia Group.

★ 1066 ★

Plastics

SIC: 2821; NAICS: 325211

Top Polypropylene Makers, 2004

Companies are ranked by production in millions of metric tons. Capacity in the industry is forecast to rise 3% this year to 413 million metric tons.

	(mil.)	Share
Basell	4.46	10.52%
BP	2.70	6.37
Atofina	2.10	4.96
ExxonMobil Chemical	2.00	4.72
Sabic	1.67	3.94
Borealis	1.50	3.54

	(mil.)	Share
Reliance Industries	1.40	3.30%
Dow Chemical	1.20	2.83
Japan Polychem	1.10	2.60
Sunoco	1.08	2.55
Other	23.17	54.67

Source: *Chemical Week*, August 11, 2004, p. 33, from Chemical Marketing Associates International.

★ 1067 ★

Plastics

SIC: 2821; NAICS: 325211

Top PVC Makers

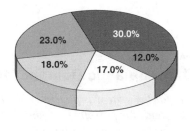

■ Shintech □ Formosa Plastics
■ OxyVinyls ■ Other
□ Georgia Gulf

Total annual capacity is 15.7 billion pounds.

Shintech	30.0%
OxyVinyls	23.0
Georgia Gulf	18.0
Formosa Plastics	17.0
Other	12.0

Source: *C&EN*, December 13, 2004, p. 7, from SRI Consulting.

★ 1068 ★

Plastics

SIC: 2821; NAICS: 325211

TPU End Markets

Demand is forecast to increase 5.6% annually to 70.3 kilotonnes in 2007. TPUs (thermoplastic polyurethane elastomers) were the first thermoplastic elastomers introduced commercially in the 1950s.

Motor vehicles	27.0%
Consumer products	13.0
Adhesives & sealants	13.0
Industrial products	12.0

Continued on next page.

★ 1068 ★

[Continued]
Plastics
SIC: 2821; NAICS: 325211

TPU End Markets

Demand is forecast to increase 5.6% annually to 70.3 kilotonnes in 2007. TPUs (thermoplastic polyurethane elastomers) were the first thermoplastic elastomers introduced commercially in the 1950s.

Construction	12.0%
Other	23.0

Source: *Urethanes Technology*, February/March 2004, p. 32, from Freedonia Group.

★ 1069 ★

Plastics
SIC: 2821; NAICS: 325211

World Thermoplastic Demand, 2003

Total demand for the year was placed at 320 billion pounds. PVC stands for polyethylene vinyl chloride. HDPE stands for high-density polyethylene, LLDPE stands for linear low-density polyethylene.

PP	24.0%
PVC	20.0
HDPE	17.0
LLDPE	11.0
LDPE	11.0
PS	8.0
Other	9.0

Source: *Converting*, July 2004, p. 10, from Chemical Market Associates Inc.

★ 1070 ★

Rubber
SIC: 2822; NAICS: 325212

Industrial Rubber Demand, 2003 and 2008

Demand increased from $13.6 billion in 2003 to $17.4 billion in 2008.

	2003	2008	Share
Motor vehicles	$ 5,115	$ 6,245	35.81%
Industrial machinery/ equipment	4,325	5,945	34.09
Construction	1,620	1,995	11.44
Aerospace/other transportation	1,580	2,080	11.93
Other	975	1,175	6.74

Source: *Rubber World*, August 2004, p. 11, from Freedonia Group.

★ 1071 ★

Rubber
SIC: 2822; NAICS: 325212

Leading Rubber Makers in North America, 2003

Companies are ranked by sales in millions of dollars.

Goodyear Tire & Rubber Co.	$ 7,425.0
Michelin North America Inc.	6,090.0
Bridgestone America Holding	5,250.0
Cooper Tire & Rubber Co.	2,836.8
Continental Tire North America Inc.	1,640.5
Tomkins	1,420.0
Parker Hannifin Corp.	1,250.0
New Balance Athletic Shoe	918.0
Carlisle Companies Inc.	900.0
Freudenberg--NOK	816.0

Source: *Rubber & Plastics News*, July 12, 2004, p. 12.

★ 1072 ★

Rubber
SIC: 2822; NAICS: 325212

Leading Synthetic Rubber Makers in Japan, 2003

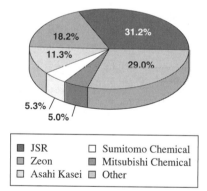

JSR — Sumitomo Chemical
Zeon — Mitsubishi Chemical
Asahi Kasei — Other

Market shares are estimated based on domestic shipments.

JSR	31.2%
Zeon	18.2
Asahi Kasei	11.3
Sumitomo Chemical	5.3
Mitsubishi Chemical	5.0
Other	29.0

Source: "Market Share Survey Report 2003." [online] from http://www.nni.nikkei.co.jp [Published July 26, 2004], from Nikkei estimates.

★ 1073 ★
Fibers
SIC: 2823; NAICS: 325221

Global Man-Made Fiber Production

Data are in billions of pounds.

	2005	2010	Share
Polyester	53,000	64,000	62.64%
Olefin	15,000	20,000	19.57
Nylon	8,500	8,150	7.98
Acylic	5,500	5,000	4.89
Cellulosic	4,450	3,900	3.82
Other	900	1,125	1.10

Source: *Textile World*, September 2004, p. 71, from Fiber Economics Bureau and author's estimates.

★ 1074 ★
Fibers
SIC: 2823; NAICS: 325221

Largest Synthetic Fiber Producers Worldwide

Companies are ranked by capacity in thousands of tons.

Invista	1,500
Formosa Plastics Corp.	1,400
Reliance Industries Ltd.	1,100
Tuntex Thailand PLC	910
Sinopec Corp.	760
Yizheng Chemical Fiber	745
Hualon Corp.	715
Far Eastern Textile	710
Teijin Ltd.	665
Huvis Corp.	660

Source: *WWD*, December 13, 2004, p. 26S, from PCI Fibres.

★ 1075 ★
Fibers
SIC: 2823; NAICS: 325221

Nonwoven Fiber Shipments, 2002-2003

Total shipments of manufactured staple fiber to non-woven roll goods producers were 717 million pounds. This figure is 13% below 2002 statistics. Home uses represented 43.5% of the end market, followed by in-dustrial uses with 37.4%. Apparel held the rest of the market.

	2002	2003	Share
O/P	765	683	48.79%
Olefin	459	369	26.36
Polyester	306	294	21.00
Rayon	62	54	3.86

Source: *Nonwovens Industry*, June 2004, p. 26, from Fiber Economics Bureau.

★ 1076 ★
Fibers
SIC: 2824; NAICS: 325222

Leading Nylon Fiber Makers in North America

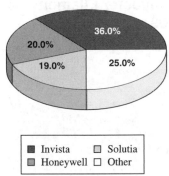

The industry is challenged by costs in energy and ma-terials. Also, the industry is going to be affected by the shift in the global apparel industry to Asia Pacific countries.

Invista	.36.0%
Honeywell	.20.0
Solutia	.19.0
Other	.25.0

Source: *Chemical Market Reporter*, May 24, 2004, p. 15, from PCI Fibres.

★ 1077 ★

Fibers

SIC: 2824; NAICS: 325222

Leading Nylon Producers in India, 2002-2003

The nylon market slowed between 1995 and 1998. Demand for nylon might have fallen because of the fall in polyester and duty prices. Companies are ranked by production in metric tons.

	MT	Share
Modipon	7,942	22.50%
JCT	6,995	19.82
Century Enka	5,713	16.19
GSFC	5,134	14.55
Shree Synthetics	4,214	11.94
SRF	2,160	6.12
Imports	1,270	3.60
Other	1,865	5.28

Source: *Chemical Business*, January - March 2004, p. 11, from ASFI and industry estimates.

★ 1078 ★

Fibers

SIC: 2824; NAICS: 325222

Leading Polyester Filament Makers in Japan, 2003

Market shares are estimated based on domestic shipments.

Toray Ind.	32.7%
Teijin	22.0
Toyobo	16.4
Unitika	10.0
Kanebo Gohsen	7.9
Other	22.2

Source: "Market Share Survey Report 2003." [online] from http://www.nni.nikkei.co.jp [Published July 26, 2004], from Nikkei estimates.

★ 1079 ★

Nutraceuticals

SIC: 2833; NAICS: 325411

Global Nutraceutical Demand

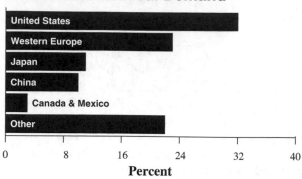

Demand is forecast to increase 6.1% annually to $9.6 billion in 2008. Herbal and nonherbal extracts will be the the major forces for growth. The market will also be affected by consumers and their increased knowledge of healthy products.

	2003	2008	Share
United States	$ 2,365	$ 3,028	31.66%
Western Europe	1,692	2,200	23.00
Japan	826	1,017	10.63
China	557	935	9.78
Canada & Mexico	229	307	3.21
Other	1,434	2,078	21.73

Source: *Manufacturing Chemist*, November 2004, p. 54, from Freedonia Group.

★ 1080 ★

Nutraceuticals

SIC: 2833; NAICS: 325411

Global Nutraceutical Market, 2003

The industry was valued at $60.9 billion in 2003.

Dairy products	38.9%
Soft drinks	24.9
Bakery and cereal products	24.6
Other	11.6

Source: *Nutraceuticals International*, January 2005, p. NA, from Datamonitor.

★ 1081 ★
Nutraceuticals
SIC: 2833; NAICS: 325411

Nutraceuticals Demand in the Czech Republic, 2003

Sales of vitamins and dietary supplements grew 9% over the previous year to $175 million in 2003.

Dietary supplements	.39.0%
Tonics/bottled drinks	.36.0
Child-specific products	.25.0

Source: *Nutraceuticals International*, September 2004, p. NA.

★ 1082 ★
Supplements
SIC: 2833; NAICS: 325411

Ethical Nutrition Market

The ethical nutrition market was dominated by the infant nutrition market at 38.8% in 2003. The adult nutrition segment saw the fastest growth.

	2003	2008	Share
Infant nutrition products	$ 3,985.6	$ 5,011.3	36.87%
Ethical nutrition supplies and equipment	3,039.8	3,999.1	29.43
Parenteral nutrition	1,758.2	2,294.8	16.89
Adult nutrition products	1,489.7	2,285.5	16.82

Source: *Research Studies - Business Communications Inc.*, August 20, 2004, p. NA, from BCC Inc.

★ 1083 ★
Supplements
SIC: 2833; NAICS: 325411

Natural Health Products in Canada, 2003

The market for natural health products at $2 billion in retail sales in 2004.

Multi-vitamins	.22.5%
Herbal supplements	.17.9
Glucosamine	.13.9
Calcium	.12.6
Vitamin C	9.3
Vitamin B	8.8
Vitamin E	8.4
Child multi-vitamins	4.2
Other	2.4

Source: "US & FCS Market Research Reports." [online] from http://www.stat-usa.gov [Published October 2004], from FENASEG.

★ 1084 ★
Supplements
SIC: 2833; NAICS: 325411

Supplements Industry in Indonesia

Indonesia imported $141 million in food supplements.

Vitamins, amino acids & minerals	.41.0%
Diet and aesthetics	.22.0
Vitality and stamina	.19.0
Degenerative prevention	.18.0

Source: "Health Food Supplements Market in Indonesia." [online] from http://www.export.gov [Accessed March 2005].

★ 1085 ★
Supplements
SIC: 2833; NAICS: 325411

Top Fiber Supplements, 2005

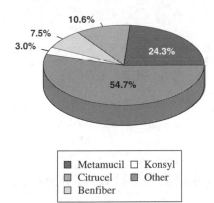

Metamucil	□ Konsyl
Citrucel	■ Other
Benfiber	

Brands are ranked by drug store sales in millions of dollars for the 52 weeks ended January 23, 2005.

	($ mil.)	Share
Metamucil	$ 27.8	24.28%
Citrucel	12.1	10.57
Benfiber	8.6	7.51
Konsyl	3.4	2.97
Other	62.6	54.67

Source: *Drug Store News*, March 21, 2005, p. 34, from Information Resources Inc.

★ 1086 ★
Supplements
SIC: 2833; NAICS: 325411
Top Herbal Supplements, 2005

Herbs are ranked by supplement sales in food stores, drug stores and mass market channels for the 52 weeks ended January 2, 2005.

	($ mil.)	Share
Garlic	$ 27.01	10.49%
Echinacea	23.78	9.23
Saw Palmetto	20.33	7.89
Ginkgo	19.33	7.51
Soy	17.41	6.76
Cranberry	13.44	5.22
Ginseng	12.16	4.72
Black Cohosh	11.98	4.65
St. John's wort	9.08	3.53
Milk thistle	7.77	3.02
Evening primose	6.08	2.36
Valerian	3.44	1.34
Other	85.70	33.28

Source: "Herbal Sales Down 7.4% in Mainstream Market." [online] from http://www.herbalgram.org [Accessed May 25, 2005], from Information Resources Inc.

★ 1087 ★
Vitamins
SIC: 2833; NAICS: 325411
Leading Vitamin Makers Worldwide

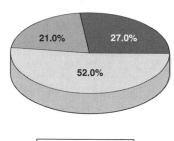

Chinese firms take about a quarter of the global market. They dominate in the vitamin C market where 60% of trade exports come from this country. Market shares are shown in percent.

Roche	.27.0%
BASF	.21.0
Other	.52.0

Source: *Chemical Market Reporter*, February 28, 2005, p. 6.

★ 1088 ★
Vitamins
SIC: 2833; NAICS: 325411
Top Mineral Supplement Brands, 2005

Brands are ranked by supermarket, drug store and discount store sales (excluding Wal-Mart) for the 52 weeks ended January 23, 2005.

	($ mil.)	Share
Nature Made	$ 80.6	6.89%
Nature's Beauty	67.4	5.76
Osteo Bi Flex	60.7	5.19
Sundown	38.6	3.30
Nature's Resource	33.0	2.82
Viactiv	31.0	2.65
Caltrate 600	28.3	2.42
Citracal	27.9	2.38
Os Cal	27.4	2.34
Private label	352.2	30.10
Other	422.9	36.15

Source: *MMR*, March 7, 2005, p. 32, from Information Resources Inc.

★ 1089 ★
Vitamins
SIC: 2833; NAICS: 325411
Top Multivitamin Brands, 2005

Brands are ranked by supermarket, drug store and discount store sales (excluding Wal-Mart) for the 52 weeks ended January 23, 2005.

	($ mil.)	Share
Centrum Silver	$ 99.5	14.13%
Centrum	83.1	11.80
One-A-Day	38.0	5.40
One-A-Day Weight Smart	26.9	3.82
Flintstones	24.7	3.51
Centrum Performance	22.2	3.15
Airborne	20.8	2.95
Bausch & Lomb Ocuvite	19.3	2.74
One-A-Day Men's Health Formula .	18.5	2.63
Private label	156.0	22.16
Other	195.0	27.70

Source: *MMR*, March 7, 2005, p. 32, from Information Resources Inc.

★ 1090 ★
Vitamins
SIC: 2833; NAICS: 325411

Top Vitamin Brands (Mineral Supplements), 2004

Market shares are shown based on drug stores for the 52 weeks ended October 31, 2004.

Nature Made	6.4%
Nature's Bounty	6.0
Osteo-Bi-Flex	4.5
Nature's Resource	3.1
Sundown	2.5
Natrol	2.4
Os-Cal	2.3
Citracal	2.1
Caltrate 600	2.0
Viactiv	1.9
Private label	31.7
Other	35.1

Source: *Chain Drug Review*, January 3, 2005, p. 95, from Information Resources Inc.

★ 1091 ★
Vitamins
SIC: 2833; NAICS: 325411

Vitamin Consumption, 2003

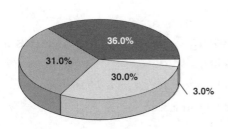

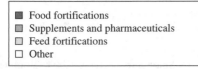

■ Food fortifications
■ Supplements and pharmaceuticals
□ Feed fortifications
□ Other

Total consumption was 55,194 metric tons.

Food fortifications	36.0%
Supplements and pharmaceuticals	31.0
Feed fortifications	30.0
Other	3.0

Source: *Chemical Market Reporter*, February 28, 2005, p. 6, from CEH.

★ 1092 ★
Vitamins
SIC: 2833; NAICS: 325411

Vitamin Industry Worldwide, 2002 and 2007

Sales are shown in millions of dollars.

	2002	2007	Share
Vitamin E	$ 694	$ 725	31.91%
B- group	683	765	33.67
Vitamin C	496	459	20.20
Other	336	323	14.22

Source: *Chemical Market Reporter*, October 18, 2004, p. FR8, from Business Communications Co.

★ 1093 ★
Weight Control Products
SIC: 2833; NAICS: 325411

Leading Diet Aid Products, 2004

Brands are ranked by drug store sales in millions of dollars for the 13 weeks ended September 5, 2004.

Trim Spa	$ 8.0
Ensure	6.9
Hydroxycut	5.2
Slim Fast Meal Options	5.0
Zantrex 3	4.7
Atkins Advantage	3.9
Ensure Plus	3.7
Boost	3.5
Xenadrine EFX	3.3
Metabolite Ultra	2.9

Source: *Drug Store News*, October 11, 2004, p. 31, from Information Resources Inc.

★ 1094 ★
Weight Control Products
SIC: 2833; NAICS: 325411

Top Weight Control Products (Candy/Tablet), 2004

Market shares are shown based on drug stores for the 52 weeks ended October 31, 2004.

Trim Spa	16.5%
Zantrex 3	10.0
Hydroxycut	9.5
Xenadrine EFX	7.7
Metabolife Ultra	6.4
Stacker 2	4.2
Cortislim	2.9
Relacore	2.2

Continued on next page.

★ 1094 ★
[Continued]
Weight Control Products
SIC: 2833; NAICS: 325411

Top Weight Control Products (Candy/ Tablet), 2004

Market shares are shown based on drug stores for the 52 weeks ended October 31, 2004.

Metabolife 356	2.2%
Dexatrim Natural	2.2
Private label	6.5
Other	29.7

Source: *Chain Drug Review*, January 3, 2005, p. 95, from Information Resources Inc.

★ 1095 ★
Weight Control Products
SIC: 2833; NAICS: 325411

Top Weight Control Products (Liquid/ Powder), 2004

Market shares are shown based on drug stores for the 52 weeks ended October 31, 2004.

Ensure	16.0%
Slim-Fast Meal Options	11.2
Ensure Plus	9.1
Boost	7.4
Ensure Glucerna	6.2
PediaSure	5.9
Atkins Diet	5.5
Hollywood Celebrity Diet	3.7
Ultra Slim-Fast	2.1
Other	32.9

Source: *Chain Drug Review*, January 3, 2005, p. 95, from Information Resources Inc.

★ 1096 ★
Weight Control Products
SIC: 2833; NAICS: 325411

Top Weight Loss Product Makers (Candy/Tablet), 2004

Market shares are shown based on sales at food stores, drug stores and mass merchandisers (but not Wal-Mart) for the 52 weeks ended June 13, 2004.

Metabolife	16.1%
Nutramerica	11.4
Cytodine Technologies	9.2
Muscle Tech Research	7.9
Other	55.4

Source: *Grocery Headquarters*, August 2004, p. S88, from Information Resources Inc.

★ 1097 ★
Analgesics
SIC: 2834; NAICS: 325412

Leading Cold/Flu Products in the U.K.

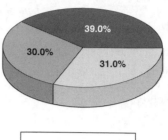

Lemsip □ Other
■ Beechams

Cold and flu products take 30.5% of the winter remedies market (cough brands take 26.1%, sore throat medicines 23.7% and decongestants 19.7%). Market shares are estimated in percent.

Lemsip	39.0%
Beechams	30.0
Other	31.0

Source: *Chemist & Druggist*, October 9, 2004, p. 10, from Information Resources Inc.

★ 1098 ★
Analgesics
SIC: 2834; NAICS: 325412

Leading Cold Medicine Makers in Japan, 2003

Market shares are estimated based on domestic sales.

Taisho Pharmaceutical	33.2%
Sankyo	11.8
SSP	8.5
Zenyaku Kogyu	7.7
Takeda Pharmaceutical	6.0
Other	32.8

Source: ''Market Share Survey Report 2003.'' [online] from http://www.nni.nikkei.co.jp [Published July 26, 2004], from Nikkei estimates.

★ 1099 ★
Analgesics
SIC: 2834; NAICS: 325412
Leading Dry Mouth Treatments in the U.K.

The value of the market was 142,300 pounds sterling. Spending at Superdrug and Boots is not included.

Salivix	.29.6%
Biotene Oralbalance	.27.6
Glandosane	.24.7
Other	.18.1

Source: *Community Pharmacy*, February 8, 2005, p. NA, from IMS Pharmatrend.

★ 1100 ★
Analgesics
SIC: 2834; NAICS: 325412
Pain Reliever Sales

People may take the same drugs for multiple kinds of pain. Figures ae in millions of dollars.

Headache	$ 2,000.0
Children's liquid	217.1
Arthritis	80.0
Alkalizing effervescents	51.9
Premenstrual	51.6
Urinary tract	25.2
Back and leg	17.4
Tranquilizers/calmatives	1.4

Source: *USA TODAY*, December 22, 2004, p. 3B, from ACNielsen.

★ 1101 ★
Analgesics
SIC: 2834; NAICS: 325412
Popular Analgesics for Children in the U.K.

The value of the pediatric analgesics industry was placed at 32.2 million pounds. Sales are based on shop prices and exclude Boots and Superdrug.

Calpol	.61.0%
Nurofen for Children	.27.0
Medised	6.0
Other	6.0

Source: *Community Pharmacy*, January 12, 2005, p. 22, from Pharmatrend.

★ 1102 ★
Analgesics
SIC: 2834; NAICS: 325412
Popular Hay Fever Brands in Germany

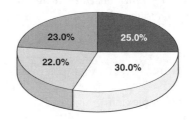

About 6% of adults take hay fever treatments.

Zyrtec	.25.0%
Vividrin	.23.0
Lisino Zyrtec	.22.0
Other	.30.0

Source: *Brand Strategy*, July - August 2004, p. 50, from TGI Europa.

★ 1103 ★
Analgesics
SIC: 2834; NAICS: 325412
Popular Hay Fever Brands in Spain

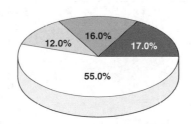

Market shares are shown in percent.

Ebastel	.17.0%
Polarmine	.16.0
Clarityn	.12.0
Other	.55.0

Source: *Brand Strategy*, July - August 2004, p. 50, from TGI Europa.

★ 1104 ★
Analgesics
SIC: 2834; NAICS: 325412

Top Acne Treatment Brands, 2004

Market shares are shown based on drug store sales for the year ended October 31, 2004.

Clearasil	9.6%
Clean & Clear	7.1
Neutrogena oil-free	6.7
Oxy	5.4
Aveeno Clear Complexion	4.7
Klear Action	4.0
Dermo Expertise Pure Zone	3.8
Neutrogena On the Spot	3.5
Neutrogena Clear Pore	3.5
Clean & Clear blackhead clearing	3.5
Other	48.2

Source: *Chain Drug Review*, January 3, 2005, p. 91, from Information Resources Inc.

★ 1105 ★
Analgesics
SIC: 2834; NAICS: 325412

Top Analgesic Brands (External), 2005

Market shares are shown based on sales at food stores, drug stores and mass merchandisers (but not Wal-Mart) for the 52 weeks ended January 23, 2005.

	($ mil.)	Share
Icy Hot	$ 48.3	19.55%
Bengay	46.5	18.82
Aspercreme	14.0	5.67
Salonpas	11.6	4.69
Joint Ritis	8.9	3.60
Well Patch	7.6	3.08
Absorbine Jr.	7.3	2.95
Super Strength Blue Emu	7.1	2.87
Tiger Balm	5.9	2.39
Capzasin HP	5.9	2.39
Private label	15.8	6.39
Other	68.2	27.60

Source: *MMR*, April 25, 2005, p. 67, from Information Resources Inc.

★ 1106 ★
Analgesics
SIC: 2834; NAICS: 325412

Top Analgesic Makers (Internal), 2004

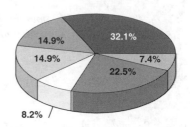

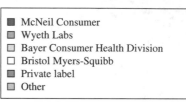

- McNeil Consumer
- Wyeth Labs
- Bayer Consumer Health Division
- Bristol Myers-Squibb
- Private label
- Other

Market shares are shown based on sales at food stores, drug stores and mass merchandisers (but not Wal-Mart) for the 52 weeks ended June 13, 2004.

McNeil Consumer	32.1%
Wyeth Labs	14.9
Bayer Consumer Health Division	14.9
Bristol Myers-Squibb	8.2
Private label	22.5
Other	7.4

Source: *Grocery Headquarters*, August 2004, p. S88, from Information Resources Inc.

★ 1107 ★
Analgesics
SIC: 2834; NAICS: 325412

Top Analgesics (Internal), 2004

Market shares are shown based on drug stores for the 52 weeks ended October 31, 2004.

Tylenol	13.3%
Advil	13.1
Aleve	7.6
Bayer	5.5
Tylenol PM	5.2
Motrin IB	4.2
Tylenol Arthritis	2.8
Excedrin	2.6
Ecotrin	2.2
Excedrin Migraine	2.1

Continued on next page.

★ 1107 ★

[Continued]
Analgesics
SIC: 2834; NAICS: 325412

Top Analgesics (Internal), 2004

Market shares are shown based on drug stores for the 52 weeks ended October 31, 2004.

Private label 24.5%
Other 16.9

Source: *Chain Drug Review*, January 3, 2005, p. 95, from Information Resources Inc.

★ 1108 ★

Analgesics
SIC: 2834; NAICS: 325412

Top Antacid Brands (Liquid/Powder), 2004

Market shares are shown based on drug store sales for the year ended October 31, 2004.

Mylanta 23.6%
Mylicon 17.5
Maalox Max 17.5
Mylanta Supreme 5.8
Gaviscon 5.2
Maalox 5.0
Gerber 2.8
Beano 2.4
Little Tummy's 1.4
Brioschi 1.1
Private label 14.4
Other 17.7

Source: *Chain Drug Review*, January 3, 2005, p. 91, from Information Resources Inc.

★ 1109 ★

Analgesics
SIC: 2834; NAICS: 325412

Top Antacid Brands (Tablet), 2004

Market shares are shown based on drug store sales for the year ended October 31, 2004.

Prilosec 30.4%
Pepcid AC 9.2
Zantac 75 . . . . 7.6
Tums Extra 5.0
Pepcid Complete 4.5
Gas X 4.4
Rolaids 3.0

Tums Ultra 1.9%
Lactaid Ultra 1.6
Beano 1.6
Private label 14.8
Other 30.8

Source: *Chain Drug Review*, January 3, 2005, p. 91, from Information Resources Inc.

★ 1110 ★

Analgesics
SIC: 2834; NAICS: 325412

Top Antacid Makers (Tablet), 2004

Market shares are shown based on sales at food stores, drug stores and mass merchandisers (but not Wal-Mart) for the 52 weeks ended June 13, 2004.

Procter & Gamble 21.7%
Glaxosmithkline 21.1
Johnson & Johnson 16.4
Pfizer 12.6
Private label 15.2
Other 13.0

Source: *Grocery Headquarters*, August 2004, p. S88, from Information Resources Inc.

★ 1111 ★

Analgesics
SIC: 2834; NAICS: 325412

Top Anti-Itch Treatments, 2004

Market shares are shown based on drug store sales for the year ended October 31, 2004.

Benadryl 8.0%
Cortizone 10 . . . . 7.3
Aveeno 6.1
Cortaid 4.7
Zanfel 4.4
Lamisil AT 3.5

Continued on next page.

★ 1111 ★
[Continued]
Analgesics
SIC: 2834; NAICS: 325412

Top Anti-Itch Treatments, 2004

Market shares are shown based on drug store sales for the year ended October 31, 2004.

Lotrimin AF	3.2%
Cortizone 10 Plus	3.1
Lanacane	2.7
Sarna	2.1
Private label	22.7
Other	32.2

Source: *Chain Drug Review*, January 3, 2005, p. 91, from Information Resources Inc.

★ 1112 ★
Analgesics
SIC: 2834; NAICS: 325412

Top Anti-Smoking Gums, 2004

Market shares are shown based on drug store sales for the year ended October 31, 2004.

Nicorette	61.8%
Rugby	0.1
Private label	38.1

Source: *Chain Drug Review*, January 3, 2005, p. 91, from Information Resources Inc.

★ 1113 ★
Analgesics
SIC: 2834; NAICS: 325412

Top Chest Rub Brands

Market shares are shown based on sales at food stores, drug stores and mass merchandisers (but not Wal-Mart).

	($ mil.)	Share
Vicks VapoRub	$ 36.6	62.46%
Triaminic Vapor Patch	8.2	13.99
Mentholatum	4.4	7.51
Vicks Baby Rub	1.7	2.90
Johnson's Baby	1.0	1.71
Lander	0.2	0.34
TheraPatch	0.1	0.17
Private label	5.9	10.07
Other	0.5	0.85

Source: *MMR*, April 25, 2005, p. 67, from Information Resources Inc.

★ 1114 ★
Analgesics
SIC: 2834; NAICS: 325412

Top Cold/Allergy/Sinus Remedies (Liquid/Powder) Brands, 2004

Market shares are shown based on drug store sales for the 52 weeks ended October 31, 2004.

Vicks Nyquil	12.5%
Tylenol Plus	8.1
Triaminic	5.9
Benadryl	5.6
Dimetapp	5.4
Robitussin CF	5.3
Pediacre	4.5
Robitussin	4.3
Motrin	3.9
Vicks Dayquil	3.4
Private label	32.6
Other	20.5

Source: *Chain Drug Review*, January 3, 2005, p. 95, from Information Resources Inc.

★ 1115 ★
Analgesics
SIC: 2834; NAICS: 325412

Top Cold/Allergy/Sinus Treatment Makers, 2004

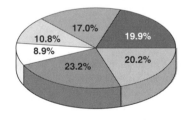

Market shares are shown based on sales at food stores, drug stores and mass merchandisers (but not Wal-Mart) for the 52 weeks ended June 13, 2004.

Schering-Plough	19.9%
Pfizer	17.0
McNeil Consumer Products	10.8
Wyeth Labs	8.9
Private label	23.2
Other	20.2

Source: *Grocery Headquarters*, August 2004, p. S88, from Information Resources Inc.

★ **1116** ★

Analgesics

SIC: 2834; NAICS: 325412

Top Cold/Flu Remedy Brands in the U.K., 2004

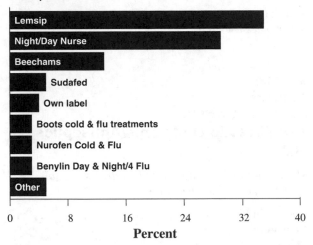

Percent

Total sales were 119 million pounds in 2004.

Lemsip	.35.0%
Night/Day Nurse	.29.0
Beechams	.13.0
Sudafed	5.0
Own label	4.0
Boots cold & flu treatments	3.0
Nurofen Cold & Flu	3.0
Benylin Day & Night/4 Flu	3.0
Other	5.0

Source: *Marketing*, February 2, 2005, p. 36, from Mintel.

★ **1117** ★

Analgesics

SIC: 2834; NAICS: 325412

Top Cold/Remedy/Sinus (Tablets) Brands

Market shares are shown based on sales at food stores, drug stores and mass merchandisers (but not Wal-Mart).

	($ mil.)	Share
Claritin D	$ 117.6	6.92%
Benadryl	114.0	6.71
Claritin	113.1	6.65
Alavert	54.4	3.20
Mucinex	54.2	3.19
Tylenol Sinus	53.9	3.17
Sudafed	53.6	3.15
Tylenol Cold	49.7	2.92
Theraflu	47.4	2.79

	($ mil.)	Share
Alka-Seltzer Plus	$ 47.1	2.77%
Private label	419.5	24.68
Other	575.5	33.85

Source: *MMR*, April 25, 2005, p. 67, from Information Resources Inc.

★ **1118** ★

Analgesics

SIC: 2834; NAICS: 325412

Top Cough Syrup Brands, 2004

Market shares are shown based on drug store sales for the 52 weeks ended October 31, 2004.

Robitussin DM	.25.9%
Delsym	.15.6
Robitussin	.12.8
Vicks Nyquil	4.3
Diabetic Tussin	2.6
Vicks Formula 44	1.9
Vicks Formula 44E	1.6
Robitussin Pediatric	1.4
Robitussin Honey	1.2
Simply Cough	1.1
Private label	.26.2

Source: *Chain Drug Review*, January 3, 2005, p. 95, from Information Resources Inc.

★ **1119** ★

Analgesics

SIC: 2834; NAICS: 325412

Top Diarrhea Tablet Brands

Market shares are shown based on sales at food stores, drug stores and mass merchandisers (but not Wal-Mart).

	($ mil.)	Share
Imodium AD	$ 53.0	38.27%
Imodium Advanced	50.4	36.39
Kaopectate	2.9	2.09
Private label	32.0	23.10
Other	0.2	0.14

Source: *MMR*, April 25, 2005, p. 67, from Information Resources Inc.

★ 1120 ★

Analgesics

SIC: 2834; NAICS: 325412

Top Ear Drop Brands

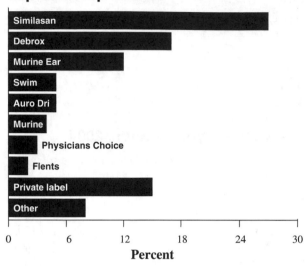

Percent

Market shares are shown based on sales at food stores, drug stores and mass merchandisers (but not Wal-Mart).

	($ mil.)	Share
Similasan	$ 11.90	26.80%
Debrox	7.70	17.34
Murine Ear	5.50	12.39
Swim	2.40	5.41
Auro Dri	2.30	5.18
Murine	1.90	4.28
Physicians Choice	1.40	3.15
Flents	1.09	2.45
Private label	6.60	14.86
Other	3.61	8.13

Source: *MMR*, April 25, 2005, p. 67, from Information Resources Inc.

★ 1121 ★

Analgesics

SIC: 2834; NAICS: 325412

Top External Analgesic Rub Brands, 2004

Market shares are shown based on drug store sales for the 52 weeks ended October 31, 2004.

Bengay	16.0%
Icy Hot	15.9
Salonpas	6.5
Joint-Ritis	4.6
Aspercreme	4.3
Asborbine Jr.	3.5
Super Strength Blue Emu	3.3

Tiger Balm	3.0%
Jointflex	2.5
Stopain	2.4
Private label	6.9
Other	31.1

Source: *Chain Drug Review*, January 3, 2005, p. 95, from Information Resources Inc.

★ 1122 ★

Analgesics

SIC: 2834; NAICS: 325412

Top First Aid Ointments/Antiseptics, 2004

Market shares are shown based on drug store sales for the 52 weeks ended October 31, 2004.

Neosporin Plus	10.9%
Neosporin	8.5
Medera	6.8
Aquaphor	3.2
Polysporin	2.5
Solarcaine	2.4
Bactine	2.2
Neosporin Scar Solution	2.1
Betadine	1.9
BD	1.8
Private label	35.7
Other	22.0

Source: *Chain Drug Review*, January 3, 2005, p. 95, from Information Resources Inc.

★ 1123 ★

Analgesics

SIC: 2834; NAICS: 325412

Top Hemorrhoidal Treatments, 2004

Brands are ranked by sales at food stores, drug stores and mass merchandisers (but not Wal-Mart).

	($ mil.)	Share
Preparation H	$ 43.2	63.53%
Anusol	3.6	5.29
Nupercainal	3.0	4.41
Anusol HC 1	2.6	3.82
Balneol	1.3	1.91
Hemorid	1.0	1.47
Private label	10.3	15.15
Other	3.0	4.41

Source: *MMR*, April 25, 2005, p. 67, from Information Resources Inc.

★ 1124 ★
Analgesics
SIC: 2834; NAICS: 325412
Top Insect Bite Treatments, 2004

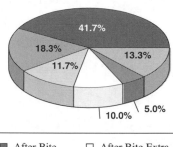

Brands are ranked by sales at food stores, drug stores and mass merchandisers (but not Wal-Mart).

	($ mil.)	Share
After Bite	$ 2.5	41.67%
After Bite Kids	1.1	18.33
Chigarid	0.7	11.67
After Bite Extra	0.6	10.00
Chiggerex	0.3	5.00
Other	0.8	13.33

Source: *MMR*, April 25, 2005, p. 67, from Information Resources Inc.

★ 1125 ★
Analgesics
SIC: 2834; NAICS: 325412
Top Laxatives (Liquid/Powder/Oil), 2004

Market shares are shown based on drug store sales for the 52 weeks ended October 31, 2004.

Metamucil	24.1%
Fleet	11.0
Citrucel	10.6
Fleet Phospho Soda	8.2
Benfiber	7.4
Konsyl	2.8
Fletcher's Castoria	2.1
Fleet Babylax	1.7
Lactinex	0.6
Kondremul	0.6
Private label	27.1
Other	3.8

Source: *Chain Drug Review*, January 3, 2005, p. 95, from Information Resources Inc.

★ 1126 ★
Analgesics
SIC: 2834; NAICS: 325412
Top Laxatives (Tablets), 2004

Market shares are shown based on drug store sales for the 52 weeks ended October 31, 2004.

Dulcolax	11.9%
Metamucil	6.5
Ex-Lax	6.3
Colace	5.3
Fibercon	4.0
Fleet	3.5
Correctol	3.0
Citrucel	3.0
Surfak	2.0
Fiber Choice	1.5
Private label	42.1
Other	10.9

Source: *Chain Drug Review*, January 3, 2005, p. 95, from Information Resources Inc.

★ 1127 ★
Analgesics
SIC: 2834; NAICS: 325412
Top Lice Treatments, 2004

Market shares are shown based on drug store sales for the 52 weeks ended October 31, 2004.

Rid	31.8%
Nix	15.3
Pronto Plus	4.5
Lice Freee	3.3
Lice Guard Robi Comb	2.1
Acu-Life	2.0
Pronto	1.8
Pin X	1.6
Lice Guard	0.9
Clear	0.9
Private label	30.9
Other	4.9

Source: *Chain Drug Review*, January 3, 2005, p. 95, from Information Resources Inc.

★ 1128 ★
Analgesics
SIC: 2834; NAICS: 325412
Top Oral Pain Relief Brands, 2004

Market shares are shown based on drug store sales for the 52 weeks ended October 31, 2004.

Orajel	15.5%
Anbesol	15.2

Continued on next page.

★ 1128 ★

[Continued]

Analgesics

SIC: 2834; NAICS: 325412

Top Oral Pain Relief Brands, 2004

Market shares are shown based on drug store sales for the 52 weeks ended October 31, 2004.

Baby Orajel	7.8%
Colgate Peroxyl	5.7
Kanka	4.4
Glyoxide	3.6
Dentek Temparin	3.4
Dentemp	3.2
Zilactin	3.1
Hyland's	2.7
Private label	5.5
Other	29.9

Source: *Chain Drug Review*, January 3, 2005, p. 95, from Information Resources Inc.

★ 1129 ★

Analgesics

SIC: 2834; NAICS: 325412

Top Oral Pain Remedies, 2004

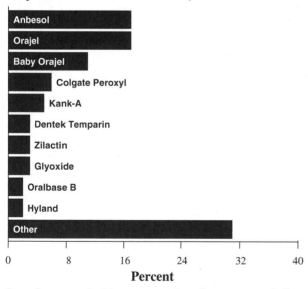

Percent

Brands are ranked by supermarket, drug store and discount stores (excluding Wal-Mart) sales in millions of dollars for the 52 weeks ended August 8, 2004.

	($ mil.)	Share
Anbesol	$ 27.5	17.34%
Orajel	27.2	17.15
Baby Orajel	17.2	10.84
Colgate Peroxyl	9.6	6.05
Kank-A	7.6	4.79

	($ mil.)	Share
Dentek Temparin	$ 4.8	3.03%
Zilactin	4.1	2.59
Glyoxide	4.1	2.59
Oralbase B	3.8	2.40
Hyland	3.7	2.33
Other	49.0	30.90

Source: *MMR*, October 4, 2004, p. 30, from Information Resources Inc.

★ 1130 ★

Analgesics

SIC: 2834; NAICS: 325412

Top Stomach Pain Treatments (Tablets), 2004

Brands are ranked by sales at food stores, drug stores and mass merchandisers (but not Wal-Mart).

	($ mil.)	Share
Pepto Bismol	$ 22.0	75.34%
Phillips	1.4	4.79
Equalactini	1.1	3.77
Private label	4.6	15.75
Other	0.1	0.34

Source: *MMR*, April 25, 2005, p. 67, from Information Resources Inc.

★ 1131 ★

Drugs

SIC: 2834; NAICS: 325412

Animal Drug Purchases, 2004

Veternarians represent 63% of animal drug sales by channel, followed by drug stores with 11%. Data are for the first three months of the year.

External parasites	21.0%
Heartworm	10.0
Arthritis and pain	8.0
Ear conditions	6.0
Skin and coat	5.0
Antibiotics	5.0
Gastrointestinal	4.0
Other	41.0

Source: *Feedstuffs*, August 2, 2004, p. 5, from Ipsos PetTrends.

★ 1132 ★
Drugs
SIC: 2834; NAICS: 325412
Arthritis Treatment Remedies, 2004 and 2005

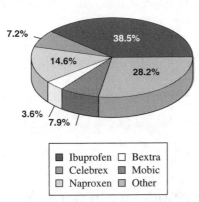

Vioxx, Celebrex and Bextra came under fire for offering cardiovascular risks. Vioxx was withdrawn on September 30. Market shares are for the weeks ended October 15, 2004 and March 11, 2005.

	Oct. 15	March 11
Ibuprofen	27.2%	38.5%
Celebrex	16.4	7.2
Naproxen	16.0	14.6
Bextra	13.6	3.6
Mobic	6.3	7.9
Other	20.5	28.2

Source: *USA TODAY*, March 24, 2005, p. B1, from Verispan.

★ 1133 ★
Drugs
SIC: 2834; NAICS: 325412
Drug Industry in India

Market shares are shown in percent

Anti-biotics	.70.0%
Cardiac	6.9
CNS and psychiatric	6.5
Vitamins	6.1
NSAID	6.0
Other	4.4

Source: *Asia Pulse*, March 10, 2005, p. NA.

★ 1134 ★
Drugs
SIC: 2834; NAICS: 325412
Drug Industry in Portugal

There are 35 authorized drug manufacturers in Portugal. National laboratories held 24% of the market authorizations issued by the National Institute for Pharamacy and Medicine. Foreign nationals held the balance. Companies are shown by share of market authorizations of the National Health Service market.

Merck Sharp & Dohme	8.07%
Novartis Farma	5.62
Pfizer Laboratories	4.56
Servier Portugal	4.35
Pharmacia Corp.	3.99
AstraZeneca	3.75
Other	.69.66

Source: "US & FCS Market Research Reports." [online] from http://www.stat-usa.gov [Published May 14, 2004].

★ 1135 ★
Drugs
SIC: 2834; NAICS: 325412
Drug Outsourcing Industry, 2004

There has been a slowdown in the bulk active pharmaceutical intermediates (API) field and some firms have moved into the area of custom research and process development. The industry is valued at $30 billion in 2004.

	($ mil.)	Share
Dosage form production	$ 7,000	23.33%
API & intermediate production . . .	7,000	23.33
Clinical development	5,000	16.67
Formulation development	4,000	13.33
Other	7,000	23.33

Source: *Chemical Week*, September 29, 2004, p. 48, from A.D. Little Benelux.

★ 1136 ★
Drugs
SIC: 2834; NAICS: 325412

Drug Spending in the Middle East, 2003

Those in the Middle East continue to have difficulty getting access to quality health care. Multinationals have been pushing for more liberalized markets but also for the development of the legal systems in the region so the companies have some sense of copyright protection against counterfeit drug manufacturers. Spending is shown in millions of dollars.

Saudi Arabia	$ 1,300
Egypt	1,150
UAE	425
Iran	400
Lebanon	380
Kuwait	330
Iraq	300
Syria	250
Jordan	150
Oman	75
Qatar	55
Bahrain	45

Source: *Middle East Economic Digest*, November 12, 2004, p. 4, from Pfizer, World Health Organization, and 2003 World Development Indicators.

★ 1137 ★
Drugs
SIC: 2834; NAICS: 325412

ED Drug Sales by Year

Sales are shown in millions of dollars. Data for 2004 are through November. For the week ended January 21, 2005 Viagra commanded 63.4% of all new prescriptions, while Cialis had 21.8% and Levitra 13.4%. ED stands for erectile dysfunction.

2000	$ 874
2001	970
2002	1,100
2003	1,300
2004	1,200

Source: *USA TODAY*, February 3, 2005, p. 3B, from IMS Health.

★ 1138 ★
Drugs
SIC: 2834; NAICS: 325412

ED Market Leaders, 2004

Cialis was launched in November 2003 to compete with Viagra, the leader in the erectile dysfunction market.

Viagra	69.0%
Cialis	20.0
Other	11.0

Source: *Seattle Times*, January 27, 2005, p. NA.

★ 1139 ★
Drugs
SIC: 2834; NAICS: 325412

Flu Vaccine Industry in Canada

ID Biomedical is trying to earn regulatory approval to distribute the flu vaccine in the United States (where there are only two makers of the vaccine).

ID Biomedical	75.0%
Other	25.0

Source: *The Washington Times*, October 11, 2004, p. A16.

★ 1140 ★
Drugs
SIC: 2834; NAICS: 325412

Flu Vaccine Production Worldwide

Flu vaccines generated about $1 billion in worldwide sales last year. Of the 292 million doses delivered last year, 29.2% were delivered to the United States, 26.3% in Western Europe and 10.1% in Japan. Companies are shown by headquarters and millions of doses produced.

Aventis (France)	70
Aventis (U.S.)	58
Chiron (U.K.)	48
Denka Seiken/Kaketsuken/Biken/Kitsato Institute	40
Chiron (Germany/Italy)	37
GlaxoSmithKline (Germany)	30
CSL Limited (Australia)	20

Source: *USA TODAY*, November 17, 2004, p. 3B, from World Health Organization and companies.

★ 1141 ★
Drugs
SIC: 2834; NAICS: 325412

Insulin Market Leaders

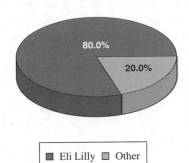

80.0%

20.0%

■ Eli Lilly ☐ Other

Market shares are shown in percent.

Eli Lilly	.80.0%
Other	.20.0

Source: *Indianapolis Star*, August 11, 2004, p. NA.

★ 1142 ★
Drugs
SIC: 2834; NAICS: 325412

Largest Drug Markets Worldwide, 2004

Sales are shown for the year ended June 2004. The figures cover direct and indirect pharmaceutical purchases from pharmaceutical wholesalers and manufacturers; they include prescription and certain over-the-counter data and present manufacturer's prices.

	($ mil.)	Share
United States	$ 228.7	46.0%
Japan	55.4	11.1
Germany	27.8	5.6
France	26.4	5.3
U.K.	18.4	3.7
Italy	17.9	3.6
Spain	12.8	2.6
Canada	10.5	2.1
China	6.6	1.3
Mexico	6.3	1.3

Source: *C&EN*, December 6, 2004, p. 18, from IMS Health.

★ 1143 ★
Drugs
SIC: 2834; NAICS: 325412

Leading Drug Firms in Japan, 2003

Market shares are estimated based on domestic sales.

Takeda Pharmaceutical	7.3%
Yamanouchi Pharmaceutical	5.0
Sankyo	4.3
Chugai Pharmaceutical	4.2
Pfizer Japan	4.0
Other	.75.2

Source: "Market Share Survey Report 2003." [online] from http://www.nni.nikkei.co.jp [Published July 26, 2004], from Nikkei estimates.

★ 1144 ★
Drugs
SIC: 2834; NAICS: 325412

Leading DTC Spenders

Spending exceeded $3 billion. DTC stands for direct to consumer.

Pfizer	.19.6%
GlaxoSmithKline	.14.8
Merck & Co.	.10.8
Johnson & Johnson	8.0
AstraZeneca	7.8
Novartis	5.4
Aventis	5.4
Bristol-Myers Squibb	4.7
Tap Pharma	3.7
Schering-Plough	3.5
Other	.16.3

Source: *Medical Marketing & Media*, April 2004, p. 36, from Verispan/TNSMI and Competitive Media Reporting.

★ 1145 ★
Drugs
SIC: 2834; NAICS: 325412

Nonsurgical Injectable Wrinkle Treatments, 2002

Market shares are shown in percent.

Botulinum type A & B	.67.0%
Dermal fillers	.33.0

Source: *Skin & Allergy News*, February 2005, p. 43, from Kalorama Information.

★ 1146 ★
Drugs
SIC: 2834; NAICS: 325412

Nonsurgical Injectable Wrinkle Treatments Worldwide, 2002

Market shares are shown in percent.

Dermal fillers	.62.0%
Botulinum type A & B	.38.0

Source: *Skin & Allergy News*, February 2005, p. 43, from Kalorama Information.

★ 1147 ★
Drugs
SIC: 2834; NAICS: 325412

OTC Drug Market Worldwide, 2002

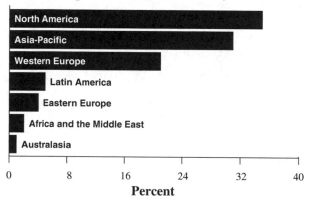

The value of the over-the-counter market is expected to grow 13% from 2002-2007.

North America	.35.4%
Asia-Pacific	.31.2
Western Europe	.21.3
Latin America	5.2
Eastern Europe	3.5
Africa and the Middle East	2.2
Australasia	1.2

Source: *Brand Strategy*, June 2004, p. 24, from Euromonitor.

★ 1148 ★
Drugs
SIC: 2834; NAICS: 325412

Prescription Drug Distribution, 2004

Total sales were $235.36 billion. Sales represents total dispensed prescriptions, including insulin dispensed through chain stores, food stores, independent long term care and mail service pharmacies.

	($ mil.)	Share
Chain stores	.$ 84,132	35.7%
Mail service	33,877	14.4
Independent	33,410	14.2
Non-federal facilities	24,768	10.5
Clinics	21,887	9.3
Food stores	20,755	8.8
Long-term care	8,160	3.5
Federal facilities	3,608	1.5
Home health	2,445	1.0

Source: "2004 Year-End U.S. Prescription and Sales." [online] from http://www.imshealth.com [Accessed March 3, 2005], from IMS Health, National Sales Perspectives.

★ 1149 ★
Drugs
SIC: 2834; NAICS: 325412

Top Anti-Seizure Drugs, 2004

Anti-seizure medications are the fifth largest drug category in the United States. They are commonly used to treat conditions other than just epilepsy.

	($ bil.)	Share
Neurontin	$ 2.6	30.95%
Topamax	1.3	15.48
Lamictal	1.0	11.90
Depakote	0.8	9.52
Trileptal	0.5	5.95
Gabapentin	0.2	2.38
Other	2.0	23.81

Source: *USA TODAY*, April 21, 2005, p. 3B, from IMS Health.

★ 1150 ★
Drugs
SIC: 2834; NAICS: 325412

Top Cholesterol Reducing Drugs

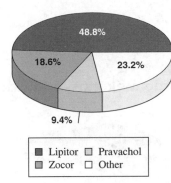

48.8%

18.6%   23.2%

9.4%

■ Lipitor   □ Pravachol
■ Zocor   □ Other

Market shares are shown in percent.

Lipitor	.48.8%
Zocor	.18.6
Pravachol	.9.4
Other	.23.2

Source: *New York Times*, January 13, 2005, p. C10, from Verispan.

★ 1151 ★
Drugs
SIC: 2834; NAICS: 325412

Top Drug Firms by Dispensed Descriptions, 2004

Market shares are shown based on total prescriptions.

Pfizer	.10.2%
Novartis	6.4
Teva	6.3
Mylan Labs	6.1
Watson	5.0
GlaxoSmithKline	3.9
Merck & Co.	3.7
AstraZeneca	2.9
Johnson & Johnson	2.7
Abbott	2.6
Sanofi-Aventis	2.4
Ivax Corp.	2.4
Barr Labs	2.4
Other	.43.0

Source: "Leading 20 Therapeutic Classes by US Sales 2004." [online] from http://www.imshealth.com [Accessed March 3, 2005], from IMS Health, National Sales Perspectives.

★ 1152 ★
Drugs
SIC: 2834; NAICS: 325412

Top Drugs, 2004

Total sales were $235.36 billion. Sales represent total dispensed prescriptions, including insulin dispensed through chain stores, food stores, independent long term care and mail service pharmacies.

Lipitor	3.3%
Zocor	1.9
Prevacid	1.6
Nexium	1.6
Procrit	1.4
Zoloft	1.3
Plavix	1.3
Epogen	1.3
Zyprexa	1.2
Celebrex	1.2
Advair Diskus	1.2
Other	.82.7

Source: "2004 Year-End U.S. Prescription and Sales." [online] from http://www.imshealth.com [Accessed March 3, 2005], from IMS Health, National Sales Perspectives.

★ 1153 ★
Drugs
SIC: 2834; NAICS: 325412

Top Drugs Classes, 2004

Total sales were $235.36 billion. Sales represent total dispensed prescriptions, including insulin dispensed through chain stores, food stores, independent long term care and mail service pharmacies.

HMG-COA reductase inhibitors	6.6%
Proton pump inhibitors	5.3
SSRI/SNRI	4.7
Antipsychotics, other	3.8
Seizure disorders	3.5
Erythropoitins	3.4
Antiarth, COX-2 inhibitors	2.3
Calcium blockers	1.9
Angiotensin II Antag	1.9
Ace inhibitors	1.7
Other	.64.9

Source: "Leading 20 Therapeutic Classes by US Sales 2004." [online] from http://www.imshealth.com [Accessed March 3, 2005], from IMS Health, National Sales Perspectives.

★ 1154 ★
Drugs
SIC: 2834; NAICS: 325412

Top Drugs Firms, 2004

Total sales were $235.36 billion.

Pfizer	.13.1%
GlaxoSmithKline	8.0
Johnson & Johnson	6.9
Merck & Co.	6.4
AstraZeneca	4.8
Sanofi-Aventis	4.3
Novartis	4.3
Amgen	4.1
Bristol-Myers Squibb	3.9
Wyeth	3.5
Other	.40.7

Source: *Financial Times*, March 10, 2005, p. 21, from IMS Health, National Sales Perspectives.

★ 1155 ★
Drugs
SIC: 2834; NAICS: 325412

Top Generic Drug Firms

Generic sales totaled $18.1 billion (name brands saw $216.4 billion). Generic drugs are, of course, less expensive than name brand drugs. Analysts expect sales of generic drugs to grow as pressures to cut health care costs increase. Just over half (53%) of all new drug prescriptions written are for generics. Companies are ranked by sales in millions of dollars.

Teva	$ 213
Mylan	203
Watson	148
Novartis units	133
Ivax	84

Source: *Investor's Business Daily*, June 13, 2005, p. A20, from IMS Health, Generic Pharmaceutical Association, and Bloomberg, Reuters.

★ 1156 ★
Drugs
SIC: 2834; NAICS: 325412

Top Generic Drug Makers, 2004

Market shares are shown based on sales from January 2003 to August 2004.

Teva	.11.3%
Mylan	9.0
Watson	7.7
Sandoz	6.5

Ivax	4.9%
Other	.60.6

Source: *Drug Store News*, November 22, 2004, p. 28, from IMS Health and IMS National Sales Perspectives.

★ 1157 ★
Drugs
SIC: 2834; NAICS: 325412

Top HIV Drug Makers Worldwide

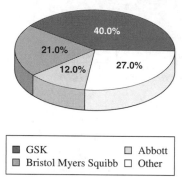

■ GSK ☐ Abbott
■ Bristol Myers Squibb ☐ Other

Protease inhibitors present some problems as a treatment option: patients must take a number of pills and often with complex restrictions. Patients often face unpleasant side effects also. The global market for HIV treatments is forecast to be $12 billion in 2012.

GSK	.40.0%
Bristol Myers Squibb	.21.0
Abbott	.12.0
Other	.27.0

Source: *M2 Presswire*, May 24, 2004, p. NA, from Datamonitor.

★ 1158 ★
Drugs
SIC: 2834; NAICS: 325412

Top HIV Drugs, 2003

Worldwide, 40 million people are infected with the virus that causes AIDS. Treating AIDS with medications can be more difficult than other diseases because patients often have to take multiple drugs at multiple times of the day.

Combivir	.15.2%
Trizivir	.10.6
Kaletra	.10.6
Viread	9.8

Continued on next page.

★ 1158 ★

[Continued]
Drugs
SIC: 2834; NAICS: 325412

Top HIV Drugs, 2003

Worldwide, 40 million people are infected with the virus that causes AIDS. Treating AIDS with medications can be more difficult than other diseases because patients often have to take multiple drugs at multiple times of the day.

Sustiva	9.7%
Other	44.1

Source: *Pharmaceutical Executive*, June 2004, p. 68, from IMS Health.

★ 1159 ★

Drugs
SIC: 2834; NAICS: 325412

Top Kids' OTC Remedies in Drug Stores

Brands are ranked by sales in millions of dollars. OTC stands for over the counter.

Children's Motrin	$ 26.4
Triaminic	18.5
Pediacare	14.0
Infant's Motrin	11.8
Children's Motrin (tablet)	8.5
Similasan	8.4
Children's Tylenol	8.3

Source: *Drug Store News*, December 13, 2004, p. 41, from Information Resources Inc.

★ 1160 ★

Drugs
SIC: 2834; NAICS: 325412

Top Multiple Schlerosis Drugs

Market shares are shown in percent.

Copaxone	33.0%
Rebif	17.6
Betaseron	16.6
Other	32.8

Source: *Boston Globe*, April 14, 2005, p. NA, from IMS Health.

★ 1161 ★

Drugs
SIC: 2834; NAICS: 325412

Top Therapeutic Classes by Dispensed Descriptions, 2004

Market shares are shown based on total prescriptions. Sales represent total dispensed prescriptions, including insulin dispensed through chain stores, food stores, independent long term care and mail service pharmacies.

Codeine	4.5%
SSRI/SNRI	4.2
Ace inhibitors	4.1
HMG-COA reductase inhibitors	4.0
Beta blockers	3.4
Thyroid hormone, synthetic	2.6
Proton pump inhibitors	2.6
Calcium blockers	2.5
Seizure disorders	2.4
Oral contraceptives	2.3
Other	67.4

Source: "Leading 20 Therapeutic Classes by US Sales 2004." [online] from http://www.imshealth.com [Accessed March 3, 2005], from IMS Health, National Sales Perspectives.

★ 1162 ★

Feminine Hygiene Products
SIC: 2834; NAICS: 325412

Top Douche Brands

Market shares are shown based on sales at food stores, drug stores and mass merchandisers (but not Wal-Mart).

	($ mil.)	Share
Summer's Eve	$ 16.5	41.35%
Massengill	10.7	26.82
Summer's Eve Ultra	2.4	6.02
Vagi-Gard	1.2	3.01
Private label	8.7	21.80
Other	0.4	1.00

Source: *MMR*, April 25, 2005, p. 67, from Information Resources Inc.

★ 1163 ★
Feminine Hygiene Products
SIC: 2834; NAICS: 325412

Top Douche Makers, 2005

Market shares are shown based on sales at food stores, drug stores and mass merchandisers (excluding Wal-Mart) for the 52 weeks ended January 23, 2005.

C.B. Fleet Co.	47.9%
Glaxosmithkline	26.6
Lake Pharmaceuticals	3.1
Laboratorios Rysell	0.4
Private label	21.8

Source: *Grocery Headquarters*, April 2005, p. 113, from Information Resources Inc.

★ 1164 ★
Feminine Hygiene Products
SIC: 2834; NAICS: 325412

Top Feminine Pain Relievers, 2004

Market shares are shown based on sales at food stores, drug stores and mass merchandisers (but not Wal-Mart).

	($ mil.)	Share
Midol	$ 31.1	60.62%
Pamprin	9.8	19.10
Women's Tylenol	2.9	5.65
Premsyn PMS	2.8	5.46
Diurex PMS	0.2	0.39
Private label	4.3	8.38
Other	0.2	0.39

Source: *MMR*, April 25, 2005, p. 67, from Information Resources Inc.

★ 1165 ★
Feminine Hygiene Products
SIC: 2834; NAICS: 325412

Top Vaginal Treatment Brands, 2004

Brands are ranked by supermarket, drug store and discount stores sales (excluding Wal-Mart) in millions of dollars for the year ended August 8, 2004.

	($ mil.)	Share
Monistat 3	$ 50.0	23.01%
Monistat 1	36.3	16.71
Monistat 7	28.2	12.98
1 Day	14.9	6.86
Vagistat 1	10.8	4.97
Combined Replens	5.8	2.67
Vagistat 3	3.5	1.61

	($ mil.)	Share
Vagisil	$ 2.6	1.20%
Vagi-Gard	2.6	1.20
Gyne Lotrimin 3	2.1	0.97
Other	60.5	27.84

Source: *MMR*, September 20, 2004, p. 17, from Information Resources Inc.

★ 1166 ★
Smoking Cessation Products
SIC: 2834; NAICS: 325412

Smoking Cessation Aids in the U.K.

Total spending increased from 72 million pounds in 2002 to 89 million pounds in 2004.

Nicorette	43.0%
NiQuitin CQ	26.0
Nicotinell	21.0
Own-label	9.0
Nicobrevin	1.0

Source: *Marketing*, January 12, 2005, p. 14, from Mintel.

★ 1167 ★
Smoking Cessation Products
SIC: 2834; NAICS: 325412

Top Smoking Cessation Products (Gum), 2004

Brands are ranked by sales at food stores, drug stores and mass merchandisers (but not Wal-Mart).

	($ mil.)	Share
Nicorette	$ 179.7	64.76%
Rugby	0.3	0.11
Private label	97.5	35.14

Source: *MMR*, April 25, 2005, p. 67, from Information Resources Inc.

★ 1168 ★
Smoking Cessation Products
SIC: 2834; NAICS: 325412

Top Smoking Cessation Products (Patch), 2004

Brands are ranked by sales at food stores, drug stores and mass merchandisers (but not Wal-Mart).

	($ mil.)	Share
Nicoderm	$ 85.4	63.21%
Nicotrol	2.6	1.92
Private label	47.1	34.86

Source: *MMR*, April 25, 2005, p. 67, from Information Resources Inc.

★ 1169 ★
Smoking Cessation Products
SIC: 2834; NAICS: 325412

Top Smoking Cessation Products (Tablet), 2004

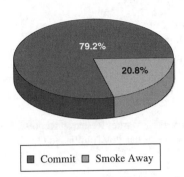

Brands are ranked by sales at food stores, drug stores and mass merchandisers (but not Wal-Mart).

	($ mil.)	Share
Commit	$ 52.3	79.24%
Smoke Away	13.7	20.76

Source: *MMR*, April 25, 2005, p. 67, from Information Resources Inc.

★ 1170 ★
Blood Testing Equipment
SIC: 2835; NAICS: 325413

Blood Bank Screening Industry

The company has most of the market for the screening of HIV and hepatitis C.

Gen-Probe 80.0%
Other 20.0

Source: *Investor's Business Daily*, March 7, 2005, p. A9.

★ 1171 ★
Blood Testing Equipment
SIC: 2835; NAICS: 325414

Hematology Reference Controls Worldwide

The company has 35% of the hematology reference controls used in the blood testing industry.

Sterck 65.0%
Other 35.0

Source: *Omaha World-Herald*, October 13, 2004, p. NA.

★ 1172 ★
Blood Testing Equipment
SIC: 2835; NAICS: 325414

Leading Blood Type Analyzer Makers Worldwide

Market shares are shown for the automated industry.

Ortho's ProVue 34.0%
Ummucor 31.0
Diamed 29.0
Other 6.0

Source: *Investor's Business Daily*, June 27, 2005, p. A6, from Piper Jaffray.

★ 1173 ★
Diagnostics
SIC: 2835; NAICS: 325414

Cervical Cancer Screening

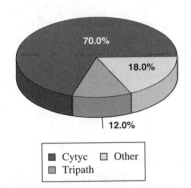

Tripath has between 10-12% of the market.

Cytyc 70.0%
Tripath 12.0
Other 18.0

Source: *Investor's Business Daily*, October 27, 2004, p. A8.

★ 1174 ★
Diagnostics
SIC: 2835; NAICS: 325414

Chemistry/Immunochemistry Testing Industry Worldwide

The industry is estimated at $11 billion.

Roche 17.0%
Abbott 13.0
Dade Behring 10.0
Beckman Coulter 10.0
Bayer 7.0

Continued on next page.

★ 1174 ★

[Continued]
Diagnostics
SIC: 2835; NAICS: 325414

Chemistry/Immunochemistry Testing Industry Worldwide

The industry is estimated at $11 billion.

J&J	5.0%
Other	38.0

Source: *Investor's Business Daily*, March 17, 2005, p. A6, from RBC Capital Markets.

★ 1175 ★

Diagnostics
SIC: 2835; NAICS: 325414

IVD Market Shares in Europe

The intravenous diagnostics market will grow at 5% each year.

Germany	24.0%
Italy	18.0
Other	58.0

Source: *PR Newswire*, October 4, 2004, p. NA.

★ 1176 ★

Test Kits
SIC: 2835; NAICS: 325414

Top Pregnancy Test Kits, 2004

Market shares are shown based on drug stores for the 52 weeks ended October 31, 2004.

e.p.t.	21.2%
First Response	17.6
Clearblue Easy	12.0
Accu-Clear	6.6
e.p.t. Certainty	5.8
Answer Quick & Easy	5.2
Fact Plus Select	3.9
Answer	1.4
SelfCare	0.4
Clear Choice	0.3
Private label	24.6

Source: *Chain Drug Review*, January 3, 2005, p. 95, from Information Resources Inc.

★ 1177 ★

Biotechnology
SIC: 2836; NAICS: 325414

Biotech Sector in Germany

The number of biotech firms in Germany fell from 360 in 2002 to 350 in 2003.

Therapeutics	52.0%
Molecular diagnostics	28.0
Tissue engineering	8.0
Drug delivery	8.0
Fine chemicals	5.0
Other	11.0

Source: "US & FCS Market Research Reports." [online] from http://www.stat-usa.gov [Published October 2004].

★ 1178 ★

Biotechnology
SIC: 2836; NAICS: 325414

Biotechnology Industry Worldwide, 2003

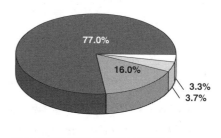

Global biotechnology revenues totalled $47 billion. This represented 13% increase over 2002. The industry also saw losses of $6.4 billion. Foreign investors have become more interested in the field according to the creation of the biotech hub in San Francisco, according to the source. Indeed, states have become more competitive with each other for investment dollars (and the jobs that come with them).

United States	77.0%
Europe	16.0
Canada	3.7
Asia Pacific	3.3

Source: *USA TODAY*, June 7, 2004, p. B1, from Ernst & Young.

★ 1179 ★
Biotechnology
SIC: 2836; NAICS: 325414

Leading Biotech Firms

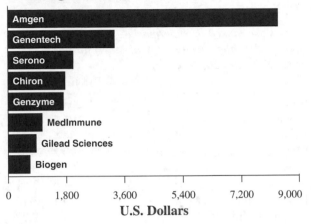

U.S. Dollars

Firms are ranked by revenues in millions of dollars.

Amgen	$ 8,356
Genentech	3,300
Serono	2,019
Chiron	1,766
Genzyme	1,714
MedImmune	1,054
Gilead Sciences	868
Biogen	679

Source: *Technology Review*, January 2005, p. 86, from Reverse Research.

★ 1180 ★
Detergents
SIC: 2841; NAICS: 325611

Detergent Market in New Zealand

Sales are shown as of June 13, 2004.

Total heavy duty detergents powder	$ 87.50
Total prewash stain removers	14.90
Total heavy duty detergents	9.40
Total fabric softeners/antistatic pads	7.03
Total laundry soaps	0.97
Total ironing aids/laundry starch	0.44

Source: *Grocer's Review*, August 2004, p. NA, from ACNielsen.

★ 1181 ★
Detergents
SIC: 2841; NAICS: 325611

Household Care Industry Worldwide, 2003

Market sizes are shown based on retail sales in millions of dollars.

Laundry care	$ 42,543.2
Surface care	12,939.1
Dishwashing products	8,829.0
Air fresheners	5,423.6
Insecticides	4,779.3
Chlorine bleach	3,013.9
Polishes	2,946.2
Toilet care	2,798.6

Source: *Household & Personal Products Industry*, July 2004, p. 76, from Euromonitor.

★ 1182 ★
Detergents
SIC: 2841; NAICS: 325611

Leading Bleaching Powder Concentrate Makers in China, 2003

Bleaching powder is used in wool washing and in the carpet and paper making sectors. In the early 1990s, bleaching agents were produced for export. In recent years, however, domestic consumption has increased. Companies are ranked by capacity in tons each year.

	Tons	Share
Tianjin Zhenjiang Sopo Chemical Industrial Co.	80,000	60.84%
SINOPEC Jianghan Oilfield Salt Chemicla Complex	15,000	11.41
Shanghai Chlor-Alkali Co. LTd.	10,000	7.60
Jiangsu Zhenjiang Sopo Chemical Industrial Co.	10,000	7.60
Other	16,500	12.55

Source: *China Chemical Reporter*, November 16, 2004, p. 19, from CNCIC Chemdata.

★ 1183 ★
Detergents
SIC: 2841; NAICS: 325611

Leading Detergent (Kitchen Use) Firms in Japan, 2003

Market shares are estimated based on domestic shipments of 48.76 billion yen.

Procter & Gamble	.34.7%
Kao	.30.9
Lion	.25.2
Other	. 9.2

Source: "Market Share Survey Report 2003." [online] from http://www.nni.nikkei.co.jp [Published July 26, 2004], from Nikkei estimates and Japan Soap and Detergent Association.

★ 1184 ★
Detergents
SIC: 2841; NAICS: 325611

Leading Dishwashing Liquid Makers in Poland, 2004

Market shares are shown based on sales of ZL 282 million.

Inco-Veritas	.40.5%
Henkel	.11.3
Cussons	. 9.4
Colgate-Palmolive	. 5.9
Beckiser	. 4.0
Private label	. 4.5
Other	.24.4

Source: *Europe Intelligence Wire*, March 25, 2005, p. NA, from Gazeta Prawna and MEMBR.

★ 1185 ★
Detergents
SIC: 2841; NAICS: 325611

Top Detergent Brands in the U.K.

The laundry aids market is worth more than 1.2 billion pounds, which includes detergents, fabric conditioners and stain removers.

Persil	.29.0%
Ariel	.21.0
Bold	.13.0
Daz	. 8.0
Surf	. 7.0
Fairy	. 7.0
Other	.15.0

Source: *Marketing*, March 16, 2005, p. 34, from Mintel.

★ 1186 ★
Detergents
SIC: 2841; NAICS: 325611

Top Dishwashing Detergent Brands, 2005

Brands are ranked by supermarket, drug store and discount outlet sales (excluding Wal-Mart) for the year ended February 20, 2005.

	($ mil.)	Share
Cascade	$ 205.7	13.23%
Dawn	106.6	6.86
Palmolive	84.4	5.43
Electrasol	70.2	4.52
Ajax	61.7	3.97
Joy	54.6	3.51
Dawn Fresh Escapes	49.1	3.16
Cascade Complete	45.4	2.92
Palmolive	36.0	2.32
Jet Dry	31.4	2.02
Other	809.5	52.07

Source: *MMR*, May 30, 2005, p. 33, from Information Resources Inc.

★ 1187 ★
Detergents
SIC: 2841; NAICS: 325611

Top Laundry Detergent Brands, 2005

Brands are ranked by supermarket, drug store and discount outlet sales (excluding Wal-Mart) for the year ended February 20, 2005.

	($ mil.)	Share
Tide liquid	$ 955.3	28.86%
Tide powder	392.1	11.85
All liquid	245.6	7.42
Purex liquid	237.0	7.16
Gain liquid	175.1	5.29
Xtra liquid	135.9	4.11
Wisk liquid	127.3	3.85
Gain powder	124.1	3.75
Cheer liquid	120.2	3.63
Arm & Hammer liquid	105.8	3.20
Other	691.6	20.89

Source: *MMR*, May 30, 2005, p. 33, from Information Resources Inc.

★ 1188 ★
Detergents
SIC: 2841; NAICS: 325611

Top Liquid Detergent Brands, 2004

Market shares are shown for the year ended October 31, 2004. Figures exclude Wal-Mart.

Tide 38.2%
Purex 10.1
All 10.1
Gain 6.9
Xtra 5.7
Wisk 5.1
Cheer 4.9
Arm & Hammer 4.4
Era 3.5
Private label 2.2
Other 8.9

Source: *Household & Personal Products Industry*, January 2005, p. 75, from Information Resources Inc.

★ 1189 ★
Detergents
SIC: 2841; NAICS: 325611

Top Liquid Detergent Makers, 2004

Market shares are shown for the year ended October 31, 2004. Figures exclude Wal-Mart.

Procter & Gamble 55.4%
Lever Brothers 16.6
The Dial Corp. 10.3
Church & Dwight 10.3
Colgate-Palmolive 3.1
Huish 1.1
Reckitt Benckiser 0.3

Redox 0.1%
Laundry Aids 0.1
Private label 2.2

Source: *Household & Personal Products Industry*, January 2005, p. 75, from Information Resources Inc.

★ 1190 ★
Detergents
SIC: 2841; NAICS: 325611

Top Powder Detergent Brands, 2004

Market shares are shown for the year ended October 31, 2004. Figures exclude Wal-Mart.

Tide 47.8%
Gain 14.9
Cheer 6.8
Arm & Hammer 6.5
Surf 4.8
Sun 2.2
Ariel 2.0
Purex 1.8
All 1.8
Private label 2.4
Other 9.0

Source: *Household & Personal Products Industry*, January 2005, p. 75, from Information Resources Inc.

★ 1191 ★
Detergents
SIC: 2841; NAICS: 325611

Top Powder Detergent Makers, 2004

Market shares are shown for the year ended October 31, 2004. Figures exclude sales at Wal-Mart.

Procter & Gamble 74.1%
Church & Dwight 8.0
Lever Brothers 7.0
The Dial Corp. 2.4
Huish 2.4
Fabrica De Jabon 2.0
Colgate-Palmolive 1.4
Redox 0.3
Private label 2.4

Source: *Household & Personal Products Industry*, January 2005, p. 75, from Information Resources Inc.

★ 1192 ★
Laundry Aids
SIC: 2841; NAICS: 325611

Top Fabric Care Makers Worldwide, 2003

Market shares are shown in percent.

Procter & Gamble	27.0%
Unilever	21.0
Henkel	10.0
Other	42.0

Source: ''Household Care.'' [online] from http://www.mind-advertising.com/sectors/sector_food.htm [Accessed July 8, 2005], from Datamonitor.

★ 1193 ★
Laundry Aids
SIC: 2841; NAICS: 325611

Top Fabric Softener Sheet Brands, 2005

Brands are ranked by supermarket, drug store and discount outlet sales (but not Wal-Mart) for the year ended February 20, 2005.

	($ mil.)	Share
Bounce	$ 136.5	40.70%
Snuggle	34.2	10.20
Downy	32.5	9.69
Bounce Free	18.6	5.55
Arm & Hammer Fresh & Soft	17.3	5.16
All Fabric Softener Sheets	13.4	4.00
Cling Free	10.0	2.98
Gain	7.5	2.24
Purex Soft	4.9	1.46
Xtra Nice 'n Fluffy	2.4	0.72
Private label	53.3	15.89
Other	4.8	1.43

Source: *MMR*, May 30, 2005, p. 33, from Information Resources Inc.

★ 1194 ★
Laundry Aids
SIC: 2841; NAICS: 325611

Top Laundry Aid Brands, 2005

Brands are ranked by supermarket, drug store and discount outlet sales (excluding Wal-Mart) for the 52 weeks ended February 20, 2005.

	($ mil.)	Share
Shout	$ 50.7	0.0%
Oxi Clean	49.5	0.0
Woolite	46.4	0.0
Spray & Wash	44.3	0.0
Clorox Oxi Magic	12.7	0.0
Zout	12.6	0.0
20 Mule Team	10.9	0.0
Faultless	10.7	0.0
Niagara Professional	9.4	0.0
Other	103.7	0.0

Source: *MMR*, May 30, 2005, p. 33, from Information Resources Inc.

★ 1195 ★
Soap
SIC: 2841; NAICS: 325611

Bath Product Market in France, 2003

The market grew 4.4% in 2003 to reach 693.7 million euros. Growth slowed slightly over 2002 levels.

	(mil.)	Share
Bath & shower	559.78	80.69%
Bar soap	89.09	12.84
Liquid soap	42.30	6.10
Talcs/powder	2.60	0.37

Source: *European Cosmetic Markets*, January 2005, p. 11, from Federation des Industries de la Parfumerie.

★ 1196 ★
Soap
SIC: 2841; NAICS: 325611

Bath Product Market in Germany, 2004

Figures are in millions of euros for January - October 2004.

	(mil.)	Share
Shower additives	376.77	65.95%
Bath additives	121.27	21.23
Liquid soaps	73.28	12.83

Source: *European Cosmetic Markets*, January 2005, p. 11, from Information Resources Inc.

★ 1197 ★
Soap
SIC: 2841; NAICS: 325611

Global Soap Sales

Sales reached $14.3 billion in 2003. The increase in sales came in part from the move from bar soaps to the higher priced body washes and shower gels. Bar and liquid soaps added to their products — moisturizers, for example — which also helped the market.

	2001	2002	2003
Bar soap	$ 8,919.9	$ 8,778.2	$ 9,197.5
Body wash/shower gel	4,186.7	4,471.2	5,197.9

Source: *Global Cosmetic Industry*, January 2005, p. 40, from Euromonitor.

★ 1198 ★
Soap
SIC: 2841; NAICS: 325611

Largest Soap Makers in India

Market shares are shown in percent.

Hindustan Lever	.57.0%
Nirma	.10.0
Godrej	. 8.0
Other	.25.0

Source: *Asia Africa Intelligence Wire*, November 30, 2004, p. NA.

★ 1199 ★
Soap
SIC: 2841; NAICS: 325611

Leading Bath/Shower Soap Brands Worldwide, 2003

The market was worth $20.5 billion in 2003.

Dove	7.1%
Lux	5.6
Palmolive	3.1

Nivea Bath Care	2.0%
Bath & Body Works	1.9
Fa	1.7
Dial	1.7
Avon	1.7
Zest	1.5
Safeguard	1.5
Private label	4.7
Other	.67.5

Source: *Global Cosmetic Industry*, January 2005, p. 36, from Euromonitor.

★ 1200 ★
Soap
SIC: 2841; NAICS: 325611

Leading Liquid Hand Soap Brands, 2004

Market shares are shown based on $225 million in sales for the year ended August 8, 2004.

Traditional Softsoap	.20.7%
Dial	.20.6
Softsoap Aquarium Series	. 9.2
Softsoap Fruit Essential	. 4.7
Softsoap Naturals	. 4.6
Dial Complete	. 4.2
Clean & Smooth	. 3.9
Softsoap 2 in 1 Moisturizing	. 2.1
Softsoap Country Designs	. 2.0
Private label	.14.5
Other	.13.5

Source: *European Cosmetic Markets*, January 2005, p. 11, from Information Resources Inc.

★ 1201 ★
Soap
SIC: 2841; NAICS: 325611

Leading Non-Deodorant Bar Soap Brands, 2004

Market shares are shown based on $464 million in sales for the year ended August 8, 2004.

Dove	.44.7%
Caress	. 9.5
Ivory	. 8.1
Olay	. 7.3
Irish Spring	. 3.4
Dial	. 2.9
Dove Nutrium	. 2.4

Continued on next page.

★ 1201 ★
[Continued]
Soap
SIC: 2841; NAICS: 325611

Leading Non-Deodorant Bar Soap Brands, 2004

Market shares are shown based on $464 million in sales for the year ended August 8, 2004.

Lever 2000	1.6%
Jergens	1.6
Tone Island Mist	1.5
Other	17.0

Source: *European Cosmetic Markets*, January 2005, p. 11, from Information Resources Inc.

★ 1202 ★
Soap
SIC: 2841; NAICS: 325611

Leading Soap Brands (All Others), 2004

Market shares are shown based on $460 million in sales for the year ended August 8, 2004. The category excludes liquid hand soap.

Dove	13.0%
Olay Complete	6.8
Softsoap Liquid	5.3
Suave Naturals	5.1
St. Ives Swiss Formula	4.8
Caress Liquid	4.8
Lever 2000	4.6
Other	55.6

Source: *European Cosmetic Markets*, January 2005, p. 11, from Information Resources Inc.

★ 1203 ★
Soap
SIC: 2841; NAICS: 325611

Leading Soap Brands in Spain, 2004

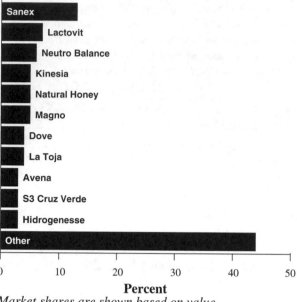

Market shares are shown based on value.

Sanex	13.2%
Lactovit	6.6
Neutro Balance	5.7
Kinesia	5.2
Natural Honey	4.7
Magno	4.5
Dove	3.9
La Toja	3.5
Avena	3.1
S3 Cruz Verde	2.8
Hidrogenesse	2.8
Other	44.0

Source: *European Cosmetic Markets*, January 2005, p. 11, from Fragrancias y Cosmetica.

★ 1204 ★
Soap
SIC: 2841; NAICS: 325611

Top Bath/Shower Brands in Western Europe, 2003

Total market sizes: bath wash/shower gels $2,628.8 million, bath additives $1,069.7 million, bar soaps $1,115.1 million and liquid soaps $22.2 million.

Dove	8.4%
Palmolive	5.7
Nivea Bath Care	5.5

Continued on next page.

★ 1204 ★

[Continued]

Soap

SIC: 2841; NAICS: 325611

Top Bath/Shower Brands in Western Europe, 2003

Total market sizes: bath wash/shower gels $2,628.8 million, bath additives $1,069.7 million, bar soaps $1,115.1 million and liquid soaps $22.2 million.

Fa	3.3%
Sanex	2.9
Radox	2.5
Imperial Leather	2.0
Le Petit Marseillais	1.9
Neutro Roberts	1.7
Johnson's pH5.5	1.7
Private label	10.4
Other	54.0

Source: *Soap, Perfumery & Cosmetics*, February 2005, p. 24, from Euromonitor.

★ 1205 ★

Soap

SIC: 2841; NAICS: 325611

Top Bubble Bath Brands

Market shares are shown based on sales at food stores, drug stores and mass merchandisers (but not Wal-Mart).

	($ mil.)	Share
Mr. Bubbles	$ 6.4	10.68%
Vaseline Intensive Care	6.2	10.35
Village Naturals	4.2	7.01
Batherapy	3.9	6.51
Calgon	3.5	5.84
Aveeno	3.0	5.01
Lander	2.7	4.51
Coty Healing Garden	2.7	4.51
Sesame Street	2.3	3.84
Village Naturals Spa	2.1	3.51
Private label	17.7	29.55
Other	5.2	8.68

Source: *MMR*, April 25, 2005, p. 67, from Information Resources Inc.

★ 1206 ★

Soap

SIC: 2841; NAICS: 325611

Top Hand Sanitizers, 2004

Brands are ranked by sales at food stores, drug stores and mass merchandisers (but not Wal-Mart).

	($ mil.)	Share
Purell	$ 28.0	63.93%
Dial	2.0	4.57
Germ X	1.3	2.97
Purell Senses	0.5	1.14
Hand Clens	0.2	0.46
Private label	11.1	25.34
Other	0.7	1.60

Source: *MMR*, April 25, 2005, p. 67, from Information Resources Inc.

★ 1207 ★

Soap

SIC: 2841; NAICS: 325611

Top Liquid Soap Brands, 2004

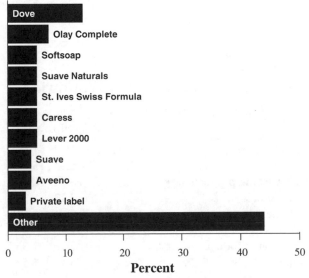

Market shares are shown based on mass market sales (but not Wal-Mart) for the year ended August 8, 2004.

Dove	13.0%
Olay Complete	6.8
Softsoap	5.3
Suave Naturals	5.1
St. Ives Swiss Formula	4.8
Caress	4.8
Lever 2000	4.6
Suave	4.4
Aveeno	3.7

Continued on next page.

★ 1207 ★
[Continued]
Soap
SIC: 2841; NAICS: 325611

Top Liquid Soap Brands, 2004

Market shares are shown based on mass market sales (but not Wal-Mart) for the year ended August 8, 2004.

Private label 3.3%
Other 44.2

Source: *Household & Personal Products Industry*, November 2004, p. 65, from Information Resources Inc.

★ 1208 ★
Cleaning Products
SIC: 2842; NAICS: 325612

Bleach Market

Market shares are shown in percent.

Clorox 69.0%
Other 31.0

Source: *Wall Street Journal*, January 31, 2005, p. C3.

★ 1209 ★
Cleaning Products
SIC: 2842; NAICS: 325612

Cleaning Product Industry Worldwide

The total market size was placed at $83.27 billion.

	($ bil.)	Share
Laundry care	$ 42.54	51.09%
Surface care	12.93	15.53
Dishwashing products	8.82	10.59
Insecticides	4.77	5.73
Chlorine bleach	3.01	3.61
Polishes	2.94	3.53
Toilet care products	2.79	3.35
Other	5.47	6.57

Source: *Household and Personal Products Industry*, July 2004, p. 76, from Euromonitor.

★ 1210 ★
Cleaning Products
SIC: 2842; NAICS: 325612

Industrial & Institutional Cleanser Demand, 2003 and 2008

Demand for industial and institutional cleaning chemicals is forecast to increase 4% annually until it reaches $9.3 billion in 2008. Figures are in millions of dollars.

	2003	2008	Share
General purpose I&I cleaners	$ 2,035	$ 2,385	25.62%
Floor care products	1,300	1,525	16.38
Warehousing detergents . . .	1,105	1,295	13.91
Disinfectants & sanitizers . .	845	1,155	12.41
Hand cleansers	445	580	6.23
Other	1,910	2,370	25.46

Source: *Cleanroom Technology*, January 2005, p. 3, from Freedonia Group.

★ 1211 ★
Cleaning Products
SIC: 2842; NAICS: 325612

Leading Cleaning Product Makers in Poland, 2004

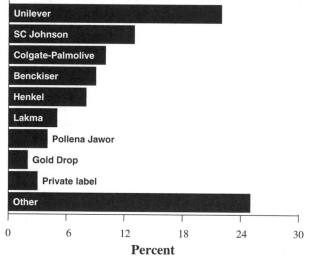

Market shares are shown based on value.

Unilever 21.9%
SC Johnson 12.9
Colgate-Palmolive 10.1
Benckiser 9.0
Henkel 7.6
Lakma 5.0
Pollena Jawor 3.7
Gold Drop 2.2

Continued on next page.

★ 1211 ★
[Continued]
Cleaning Products
SIC: 2842; NAICS: 325612

Leading Cleaning Product Makers in Poland, 2004

Market shares are shown based on value.

Private label 2.7%
Other 24.9

Source: *Europe Intelligence Wire*, March 25, 2005, p. NA, from Gazeta Prawna and MEMBR.

★ 1212 ★
Cleaning Products
SIC: 2842; NAICS: 325612

Leading Household Cleaner Makers in the U.K.

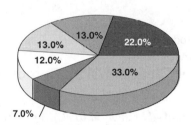

■ Lever Faberge	□ Procter & Gamble
■ SC Johnson	■ Jeyes
□ Reckitt Benckiser	■ Other

Reckitt Benckiser's main brands are Dettol, Windolene and Mr. Sheen. SC Johnson makes Mr. Muscle, Toilet Duck and Pledge. Top segments in order of sales are all purpose cleaners, toilet care and liquid bleach disinfectants.

Lever Faberge 22.0%
SC Johnson 13.0
Reckitt Benckiser 13.0
Procter & Gamble 12.0
Jeyes 7.0
Other 33.0

Source: *Marketing Week*, July 7, 2004, p. 20, from Mintel.

★ 1213 ★
Cleaning Products
SIC: 2842; NAICS: 325612

Shoe Care Industry

The company is the best known shoe care brand in the world. Shares are for the U.S. market.

Kiwi 65.0%
Other 35.0

Source: *New York Times*, December 14, 2004, p. C4.

★ 1214 ★
Cleaning Products
SIC: 2842; NAICS: 325612

Top Bathroom Cleansers, 2004

Brands are ranked by sales at supermarkets, drug stores and mass merchandisers (but not Wal-Mart) for the year ended August 8, 2004.

	($ mil.)	Share
Clorox	$ 47.3	16.01%
Lysol Cling	33.0	11.17
2000 Flushes	24.4	8.26
Lysol	22.5	7.61
Rid X	16.9	5.72
Scrubbing Bubbles Fresh Brush . . .	15.6	5.28
Lysol Plus Bleach	12.8	4.33
Scrubbing Bubbles	11.7	3.96
Clorox Toilet Wand	10.6	3.59
Vanish Drop Ins	9.6	3.25
Other	91.1	30.83

Source: *MMR*, October 4, 2004, p. 18, from Information Resources Inc.

★ 1215 ★
Cleaning Products
SIC: 2842; NAICS: 325612

Top Cleaner/Disinfectant Brands, 2004

Brands are ranked by sales at drug stores, supermarkets and mass merchandisers (excluding Wal-Mart) for the year ended October 3, 2004.

	($ mil.)	Share
Pine Sol	$ 65.2	15.64%
Lysol	64.1	15.37
Clorox Clean Up	42.4	10.17
Mr. Clean	41.3	9.90
Formula 409	36.9	8.85
Fantastik	26.0	6.24

Continued on next page.

★ 1215 ★
[Continued]
Cleaning Products
SIC: 2842; NAICS: 325612

Top Cleaner/Disinfectant Brands, 2004

Brands are ranked by sales at drug stores, supermarkets and mass merchandisers (excluding Wal-Mart) for the year ended October 3, 2004.

	($ mil.)	Share
Murphy's Oil Soap	$ 16.6	3.98%
Fabuloso	13.3	3.19
Spic & Span	10.8	2.59
Private label	18.0	4.32
Other	82.4	19.76

Source: *Household & Personal Products Industry*, December 2004, p. 96, from Information Resources Inc.

★ 1216 ★
Cleaning Products
SIC: 2842; NAICS: 325612

Top Floor Cleaners/Wax Remover Makers, 2004

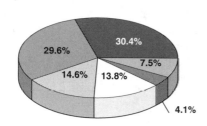

■ S.C. Johnson & Son □ Clorox
■ Procter & Gamble ■ Colgate Palmolive
□ Reckitt Benckiser ■ Other

Market shares are shown based on sales at food stores, drug stores and mass merchandisers (excluding Wal-Mart) for the 52 weeks ended June 13, 2004.

S.C. Johnson & Son	30.4%
Procter & Gamble	29.6
Reckitt Benckiser	14.6
Clorox	13.8
Colgate Palmolive	4.1
Other	7.5

Source: *Grocery Headquarters*, August 2004, p. S88, from Information Resources Inc.

★ 1217 ★
Cleaning Products
SIC: 2842; NAICS: 325612

Top Floor Cleaners/Wax Removers, 2004

Market shares are shown based on sales at food stores, drug stores and mass merchandisers (excluding Wal-Mart) for the 52 weeks ended June 13, 2004.

Swiffer Wet Jet	29.6%
Clorox Ready Mop	12.9
Mop & Glo Triple Action	10.8
Armstong	9.6
Pledge	8.1
Future	8.1
Murphys Oil Soap	5.1
Other	15.8

Source: *Grocery Headquarters*, August 2004, p. S88, from Information Resources Inc.

★ 1218 ★
Cleaning Products
SIC: 2842; NAICS: 325612

Top Floor Cleanser/Wax Removers, 2003

Brands are ranked by supermarket, drug store and discount outlet sales (but not Wal-Mart) for the year ended December 28, 2003.

	($ mil.)	Share
Swiffer Wet Jet	$ 20.9	23.91%
Clorox Ready Mop	12.4	14.19
Mop & Glo Triple Action	10.2	11.67
Armstong	9.1	10.41
Future	7.4	8.47
Pledge	4.8	5.49
Murphy's Oil Soap	3.8	4.35
Pledge Grab It Go Mop	3.5	4.00
Brite	3.2	3.66
Lysol	3.0	3.43
Other	9.1	10.41

Source: *MMR*, May 31, 2004, p. 33, from Information Resources Inc.

★ 1219 ★
Cleaning Products
SIC: 2842; NAICS: 325612

Top Shoe Polish Brands, 2005

Brands are ranked by supermarket, drug store and discount outlet sales (excluding Wal-Mart) for the 52 weeks ended February 20, 2005.

	($ mil.)	Share
Kiwi polish	$ 27.8	28.02%
Kiwi laces/accessories	14.0	14.11
Griffin laces/accessories	5.0	5.04
Lynk laces/accessories	4.3	4.33
Stay Ty laces/accessories	3.5	3.53
Kiwi Scuff Magic polish	3.5	3.53
Sterilite laces/accessories	3.3	3.33
Adcor laces/accessories	1.9	1.92
Kiwi Suede & Nubuck polish	1.7	1.71
Kiwi Shoe White polish	1.6	1.61
Other	32.6	32.86

Source: *MMR*, May 30, 2005, p. 33, from Information Resources Inc.

★ 1220 ★
Baby Care
SIC: 2844; NAICS: 32562

Baby Care Industry, 2004

Total baby sales were $375.5 million for the year ended April 18, 2004 (excluding Wal-Mart). Baby product sales are connected to the birth rate, a rate that has only recently begun to climb out of a record low period.

	($ mil.)	Share
Baby soaps	$ 80.6	21.49%
Baby ointments/creams	75.9	20.23
Baby powder	56.4	15.04
Baby lotions	47.9	12.77
Petroleum jelly	43.8	11.68
Baby oils	38.2	10.18
Baby shampoo	32.3	8.61

Source: *Household and Personal Products Industry*, August 2004, p. 49, from Information Resources Inc.

★ 1221 ★
Baby Care
SIC: 2844; NAICS: 32562

Baby Care Industry Worldwide

The market is seeing strong growth and competition is increasing. More products are coming to the market, such as baby liquid soap and disposable washcloths. Figures include children up 11 years of age.

	($ mil.)	Share
Baby toiletries	$ 1,281.6	37.08%
Baby skin care	1,106.0	32.00
Baby hair care	763.7	22.09
Baby sun care	305.3	8.83

Source: *Soap, Perfumery & Cosmetics*, March 2005, p. 18, from Euromonitor.

★ 1222 ★
Baby Care
SIC: 2844; NAICS: 32562

Top Baby Lotion Brands, 2004

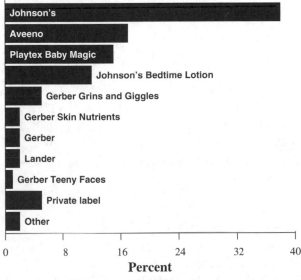

Market shares are shown based on sales at food stores, drug stores and mass merchandisers (excluding Wal-Mart) for the 52 weeks ended October 31, 2004.

Johnson's	37.5%
Aveeno	16.6
Playtex Baby Magic	15.3
Johnson's Bedtime Lotion	12.4
Gerber Grins and Giggles	4.5
Gerber Skin Nutrients	2.2
Gerber	1.8
Lander	1.6

Continued on next page.

★ 1222 ★
[Continued]
Baby Care
SIC: 2844; NAICS: 32562

Top Baby Lotion Brands, 2004

Market shares are shown based on sales at food stores, drug stores and mass merchandisers (excluding Wal-Mart) for the 52 weeks ended October 31, 2004.

Gerber Teeny Faces	1.1%
Private label	5.1
Other	1.9

Source: *Grocery Headquarters*, January 2005, p. 71, from Information Resources Inc.

★ 1223 ★
Baby Care
SIC: 2844; NAICS: 32562

Top Baby Needs (Petroleum Jelly), 2005

Market shares are shown based on sales at food stores, drug stores and mass merchandisers (but not Wal-Mart).

	($ mil.)	Share
Vaseline	$ 25.6	60.52%
Lander	0.3	0.71
Soft and Precious	0.1	0.24
Eboline	0.1	0.24
Private label	15.8	37.35
Other	0.4	0.95

Source: *MMR*, April 25, 2005, p. 67, from Information Resources Inc.

★ 1224 ★
Baby Care
SIC: 2844; NAICS: 32562

Top Baby Ointment/Cream Brands, 2004

Market shares are shown based on drug stores for the 52 weeks ended October 31, 2004.

Desitin	30.5%
A and D	28.7
Balmex	12.4
Aquaphor Baby	4.5
Triple Paste	4.4
Dr. Smith's	3.6
Aveeno	2.9
Boudreaux's Butt Paste	2.1
Johnson's No More Rash	1.5

Dermacloud	0.8%
Other	8.6

Source: *Chain Drug Review*, January 3, 2005, p. 95, from Information Resources Inc.

★ 1225 ★
Baby Care
SIC: 2844; NAICS: 32562

Top Baby Powder Brands, 2004

Market shares are shown based on sales at drug stores for the 52 weeks ended October 31, 2004.

Johnson's	61.5%
Caldesene	6.7
Gold Bond	4.7
Burt's Bees	0.7
Gerber	0.6
Valet	0.5
Johnson & Johnson	0.3
Healing Garden ZZZ	0.1
Burt's Bees Baby Bee	0.1
Private label	23.9
Other	0.9

Source: *Chain Drug Review*, January 3, 2005, p. 95, from Information Resources Inc.

★ 1226 ★
Cosmetics
SIC: 2844; NAICS: 32562

Cosmetics Industry in France

Market shares are shown in percent.

Beauty products	12.9%
Shampoo	9.6
Bath & shower	9.1
Blades and razors	7.3
Make-up	7.0
Toothpaste	6.7
Other	47.4

Source: "US & FCS Market Research Reports." [online] from http://www.stat-usa.gov [Published July 15, 2004], from *Cosmetique Trade*.

★ 1227 ★
Cosmetics
SIC: 2844; NAICS: 32562

Cosmetics Industry Worldwide

The industry is valued at $180 billion.

Hygiene	36.0%
Hair care	21.0
Skin care	18.0

Continued on next page.

★ 1227 ★
[Continued]
Cosmetics
SIC: 2844; NAICS: 32562
Cosmetics Industry Worldwide

The industry is valued at $180 billion.

Make-up	.13.0%
Perfume	.12.0

Source: *Chemical Market Reporter*, March 7, 2005, p. 3, from Deutsche Bank Securities Inc.

★ 1228 ★
Cosmetics
SIC: 2844; NAICS: 32562
Largest Cosmetics Firms Worldwide, 2003

Firms are ranked by estimated sales in billions of dollars.

L'Oreal	$ 15.50
Procter & Gamble	13.00
Unilever	8.00
Shiseido	5.20
Estee Lauder	5.10
Avon Products	4.40
Beiersdorf	3.79
Johnson & Johnson	3.75
Kao Corp.	2.80
Alberto-Culver	2.70

Source: *WWD*, December 13, 2004, p. 22S.

★ 1229 ★
Cosmetics
SIC: 2844; NAICS: 32562
Leading Cosmetics Brands in France, 2003

Market shares are shown in percent.

Gemey	.18.6%
L'Oreal Paris	.12.1
Yves Rocher	.10.4
Lancome	7.7
Agnes B	7.1
Nivea	6.3
Bourjois	5.9
Dior	5.1
Other	.26.8

Source: *Soap, Perfumery & Cosmetics*, December 2004, p. 20, from Euromonitor.

★ 1230 ★
Cosmetics
SIC: 2844; NAICS: 32562
Leading Cosmetics Firms in Malaysia

Market shares are shown based on sales.

Colgate-Palmolive	9.2%
Unilever Holdings	8.4
L'Oreal Malaysia	5.7
Unza	5.6
Procter & Gamble	5.5
Avon Cosmetics	4.5
Estee Lauder	4.1
Gillette	3.5
Amway	3.4
Kao Malaysia	2.8
Other	.47.3

Source: "US & FCS Market Research Reports." [online] from http://www.stat-usa.gov [Published August 4, 2004], from Euromonitor.

★ 1231 ★
Cosmetics
SIC: 2844; NAICS: 32562
Leading Cosmetics Firms in Western Europe, 2003

Market shares are shown in percent.

L'Oreal Groupe	.31.5%
Cory Inc.	.10.6
Procter & Gamble Co.	8.5
Estee Lauder	5.0
Chanel SA	4.4
LVMH	4.3
Beiersdorf	4.0
The Boots Co	3.5

Continued on next page.

289

★ 1231 ★

[Continued]
Cosmetics
SIC: 2844; NAICS: 32562

Leading Cosmetics Firms in Western Europe, 2003

Market shares are shown in percent.

Private label	2.5%
Other	.25.7

Source: *Soap Perfumery & Cosmetics*, January 2005, p. 16, from Euromonitor.

★ 1232 ★

Cosmetics
SIC: 2844; NAICS: 32562

Premium Cosmetics Market Worldwide, 2003

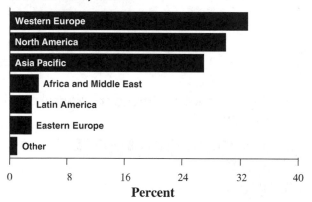

Percent

Market sizes are shown in millions of dollars. Fragrances take $14.6 billion and skin care takes $14.4 billion.

	($ bil.)	Share
Western Europe	$ 15.47	32.94%
North America	13.97	29.75
Asia Pacific	12.84	27.34
Africa and Middle East	1.69	3.60
Latin America	1.28	2.73
Eastern Europe	1.18	2.51
Other	0.53	1.13

Source: *Global Cosmetic Industry*, September 2004, p. 35.

★ 1233 ★

Cosmetics
SIC: 2844; NAICS: 32562

Prestige Eye Market

The top prestige makeup brands are Clinique, Lancome, Estee Lauder, MAC and Chanel.

Eye shadow	.37.0%
Mascara	.31.0
Eye liner	.21.0
Other	.11.0

Source: *Soap Perfumery & Cosmetics*, September 2004, p. 20.

★ 1234 ★

Cosmetics
SIC: 2844; NAICS: 32562

Prestige Face Makeup Market, 2004

Market shares are shown for the 52 weeks ended December 26, 2004. Figures exclude Wal-Mart.

Foundation	.55.0%
Powder	.16.0
Blush	.15.0
Concealer	9.0
Applicators	3.0
Other	2.0

Source: *Beauty Biz*, February 1, 2005, p. 21, from Information Resources Inc.

★ 1235 ★

Cosmetics
SIC: 2844; NAICS: 32562

Prestige Lip Makeup Market

Market shares are shown for the 52 weeks ended December 26, 2004. Figures exclude Wal-Mart.

Lip color	.50.0%
Lip gloss	.29.0
Lipliner	.19.0
Other	2.0

Source: *Beauty Biz*, February 1, 2005, p. 21, from Information Resources Inc.

★ 1236 ★
Cosmetics
SIC: 2844; NAICS: 32562

Top Cosmetics Brands in China, 2003

Market shares are shown in percent.

Aupres	.16.3%
Yue-Sai	.14.8
Kose	.11.1
Maybelline	.10.1
Ludanian	7.3
Christian Dior	5.3
Cheng Mingming	3.1
L'Oreal Perfection	2.4
Clinique	2.2
Qing Fei	1.4
Other	.26.0

Source: *Brand Strategy*, September 2004, p. 36, from *X-tribes China* and Xtreme Information, 2004.

★ 1237 ★
Cosmetics
SIC: 2844; NAICS: 32562

Top Cosmetics Brands in Germany, 2003

Market size was placed at 1,191.4 million euros.

Jade	.23.38%
L'Oreal Paris	.11.83
Manhattan	9.29
Ellen Betrix	8.28
Nivea Beauty	7.33
Astor	7.21
ArtDeco	3.73
Chicago	3.38
Lancome	2.18
Other	.18.49

Source: *Soap Perfumery & Cosmetics*, October 2004, p. 18, from Beiersdorf.

★ 1238 ★
Cosmetics
SIC: 2844; NAICS: 32562

Top Eye Makeup Brands, 2004

Market shares are shown based on drug store sales for the year ended October 31, 2004.

Great Lash	5.4%
Voluminous	3.8
CoverGirl Eye Enhancers	3.2

Wear Infinite	2.9%
ColorStay	2.8
Double Extend	2.7
Volum' Express	2.6
Sky High Curves	2.5
Expert Eyes	2.4
Almay One Coat	2.4
Other	.69.3

Source: *Chain Drug Review*, January 31, 2005, p. 36, from Information Resources Inc.

★ 1239 ★
Cosmetics
SIC: 2844; NAICS: 32562

Top Face Makeup Brands, 2004

Market shares are shown based on drug store sales for the year ended October 31, 2004.

CoverGirl Clean Powder	2.7%
ColorStay	2.6
True Match	2.5
Age Defying	2.4
Visible Lift	2.2
New Complexion	2.1
CoverGirl Clean Foundation	2.1
CoverGirl Tru Blend	1.7
CoverGirl Aquasmooth	1.6
Age Defying All Day Lifting	1.5
Other	.78.6

Source: *Chain Drug Review*, January 31, 2005, p. 36, from Information Resources Inc.

★ 1240 ★
Cosmetics
SIC: 2844; NAICS: 32562

Top Face Makeup Producers, 2004

Market shares are shown based on sales at food stores, drug stores and mass merchandisers (but not Wal-Mart) for the 52 weeks ended June 13, 2004.

Noxell	.31.9%
Revlon	.21.1
L'Oreal	.15.3
Maybelline	.11.6
Other	.20.1

Source: *Grocery Headquarters*, August 2004, p. S88, from Information Resources Inc.

★ 1241 ★
Cosmetics
SIC: 2844; NAICS: 32562

Top Face Makeup Removers (Gels/ Moisturizers), 2004

Market shares are shown based on sales at food stores, drug stores and mass merchandisers (but not Wal-Mart).

	($ mil.)	Share
Maybelline Expert Eyes	$ 7.7	31.17%
L'Oreal Plenitude	5.5	22.27
Almay	2.3	9.31
L'Oreal	1.7	6.88
Almay Dual Phase	1.6	6.48
Neutrogena	1.4	5.67
Nivea Visage	1.3	5.26
Cover Girl Clear Eyes	1.2	4.86
Revlon ColorStay	0.6	2.43
Physicians Formula	0.3	1.21
Private label	0.3	1.21
Other	0.8	3.24

Source: MMR, April 25, 2005, p. 67, from Information Resources Inc.

★ 1242 ★
Cosmetics
SIC: 2844; NAICS: 32562

Top Face Makeup Removers (Implements), 2004

Market shares are shown based on sales at food stores, drug stores and mass merchandisers (but not Wal-Mart).

	($ mil.)	Share
Almay	$ 10.9	45.80%
Andrea EyeQ's	2.2	9.24
Buf Puf	1.2	5.04
Body Benefits	0.6	2.52
Almay Gently Clean	0.6	2.52
Body Image	0.4	1.68
Mon Image	0.3	1.26
Compac	0.3	1.26
Youthful Face	0.2	0.84
Swab Plus	0.2	0.84
Other	6.9	28.99

Source: MMR, April 25, 2005, p. 67, from Information Resources Inc.

★ 1243 ★
Cosmetics
SIC: 2844; NAICS: 32562

Top Lip Makeup Brands, 2004

Market shares are shown based on drug store sales for the year ended October 31, 2004.

Super Lustrous	5.7%
CoverGirl Outlast	5.5
Endless	4.3
ColorStay Overtime	4.0
Colour Riche	3.6
Lipglide	3.2
Max Factor Lipfinity	2.9
CoverGirl Continuous Color	2.8
Moon Drops	2.7
Moisture Whip	2.4
Other	62.9

Source: Chain Drug Review, January 31, 2005, p. 36, from Information Resources Inc.

★ 1244 ★
Cosmetics
SIC: 2844; NAICS: 32562

Top Mascara Brands, 2005

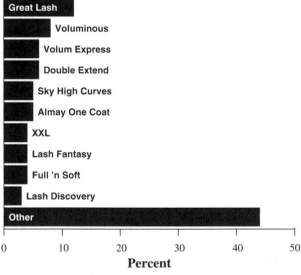

Market shares are shown based on sales for drug stores for the 52 weeks ended February 20, 2005.

Great Lash	11.6%
Voluminous	8.3
Volum Express	6.0
Double Extend	5.9
Sky High Curves	5.1
Almay One Coat	4.9
XXL	4.0

Continued on next page.

★ 1244 ★

[Continued]

Cosmetics

SIC: 2844; NAICS: 32562

Top Mascara Brands, 2005

Market shares are shown based on sales for drug stores for the 52 weeks ended February 20, 2005.

Lash Fantasy	3.6%
Full 'n Soft	3.6
Lash Discovery	2.7
Other	44.3

Source: *Chain Drug Review*, March 28, 2005, p. 24, from Information Resources Inc.

★ 1245 ★

Denture Care

SIC: 2844; NAICS: 32562

Top Denture Adhesive Brands, 2004

Market shares are shown based on sales at drug stores for the 52 weeks ended October 31, 2004.

Fixodent	35.1%
Super Poligrip	13.1
Sea-Bond	9.7
Fixodent Complete	9.1
Fixodent Free	8.0
Poligrip Free	5.6
Poligrip Ultra Fresh	3.9
Super Wernets	3.2
Cushion Grip	2.4
Dentu Grip	2.1
Private label	3.0
Other	4.8

Source: *Chain Drug Review*, January 3, 2005, p. 95, from Information Resources Inc.

★ 1246 ★

Denture Care

SIC: 2844; NAICS: 32562

Top Denture Cleanser Brands, 2004

Market shares are shown based on sales at drug stores for the 52 weeks ended October 31, 2004.

Polident	25.2%
Efferdent	24.3
Efferdent Plus	14.1
Polident Overnight	11.5
Smoker's Polident	4.2
Polident for Partials	1.0
Fixodent	0.2
Other	19.5

Source: *Chain Drug Review*, January 3, 2005, p. 95, from Information Resources Inc.

★ 1247 ★

Denture Care

SIC: 2844; NAICS: 32562

Top Denture Cleanser Brands (Tablets)

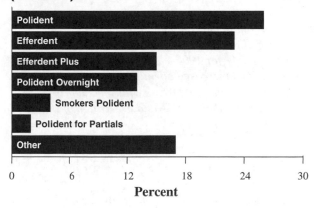

Market shares are shown based on sales at food stores, drug stores and mass merchandisers (but not Wal-Mart).

	($ mil.)	Share
Polident	$ 21.8	26.08%
Efferdent	19.3	23.09
Efferdent Plus	12.5	14.95
Polident Overnight	10.6	12.68
Smokers Polident	3.4	4.07
Polident for Partials	1.8	2.15
Other	14.2	16.99

Source: *MMR*, April 25, 2005, p. 67, from Information Resources Inc.

★ 1248 ★

Deodorants

SIC: 2844; NAICS: 32562

Deodorant Market Sizes Worldwide, 2003

The global antiperspirant deodorant market is worth $9,242.8 million in 2003 and has seen year on year growth of 38.3% for 1997-2003. The industry has benefitted from increased attention on men's deodorants and antiperspirants with special properties, such as conditioning and prevention of skin irritation during shaving.

	($ mil.)	Share
Sprays	$ 3,845.4	41.60%
Sticks	2,278.6	24.65
Roll-ons	1,944.6	21.04
Pumps	575.9	6.23

Continued on next page.

★ 1248 ★
[Continued]
Deodorants
SIC: 2844; NAICS: 32562

Deodorant Market Sizes Worldwide, 2003

The global antiperspirant deodorant market is worth $9,242.8 million in 2003 and has seen year on year growth of 38.3% for 1997-2003. The industry has benefitted from increased attention on men's deodorants and antiperspirants with special properties, such as conditioning and prevention of skin irritation during shaving.

	($ mil.)	Share
Creams	$ 511.0	5.53%
Wipes	87.2	0.94

Source: *Soap, Perfumery & Cosmetics*, July 2004, p. 33, from Euromonitor.

★ 1249 ★
Deodorants
SIC: 2844; NAICS: 32562

Top Antiperspirant Makers, 2004

Market shares are shown based on sales at food stores, drug stores and mass merchandisers (excluding Wal-Mart) for the 52 weeks ended December 26, 2004.

Degree	6.4%
Secret Platinum	6.1
Mennen Speed Stick	5.9
Right Guard Sport	5.5
Old Spice High Endurance	5.2
Dove	5.1
Secret Sheer Dry	3.7
Secret	3.6
Mitchum	3.3
Ban	3.1
Other	52.1

Source: *Household and Personal Products Industry*, March 2005, p. 82, from Information Resources Inc.

★ 1250 ★
Deodorants
SIC: 2844; NAICS: 32562

Top Deodorant Brands Worldwide

The industry saw sales of nearly $9.5 billion in 2004.

Rexona	11.3%
Axe	7.4
Nivea	6.1

Dove	4.4%
Secret	3.6
Right Guard	3.5
Old Spice	3.1
Fa	2.8
Gillette Touch	2.7
Other	55.1

Source: *Global Cosmetics Industry*, April 2005, p. 62, from Euromonitor.

★ 1251 ★
Deodorants
SIC: 2844; NAICS: 32562

Top Deodorants, 2005

Brands are ranked by supermarket, drug store and discount store sales (excluding Wal-Mart) for the 52 weeks ended January 23, 2005.

	($ mil.)	Share
Degree	$ 70.4	6.40%
Secret Platinum	67.3	6.12
Mennen Speed Stick	63.6	5.78
Right Guard Sport	60.2	5.47
Old Spice High Endurance	56.4	5.13
Dove	56.3	5.12
Secret	40.2	3.65
Secret Sheer Dry	38.9	3.54
Mitchum	35.5	3.23
Ban	34.4	3.13
Other	576.8	52.44

Source: *MMR*, March 21, 2005, p. 21, from Information Resources Inc.

★ 1252 ★
Depilatories
SIC: 2844; NAICS: 32562

Leading Wax Brands in the U.K., 2004

Market shares are shown in percent.

Alberto VO5	18.6%
ShockWaves	14.8
Brylcreem	11.3
Studio Line	6.4
Imperial Dax	4.2
Fructis	2.7
Other	42.0

Source: *European Cosmetic Markets*, October 2004, p. 378, from industry sources.

★ 1253 ★
Depilatories
SIC: 2844; NAICS: 32562

Top Depilatories, 2005

Brands are ranked by supermarket, drug store and discount store sales (excluding Wal-Mart) for the 52 weeks ended January 23, 2005.

	($ mil.)	Share
Nair	$ 25.7	24.55%
Sally Hansen	25.3	24.16
Veet	14.6	13.94
Nad's	6.9	6.59
Magic	5.2	4.97
Bikini Zone	3.9	3.72
Hair Off	3.3	3.15
Nair for Men	3.2	3.06
Veet Neet	2.6	2.48
Ardell Surgi Cream	2.3	2.20
Other	11.7	11.17

Source: *MMR*, March 21, 2005, p. 21, from Information Resources Inc.

★ 1254 ★
Eye Care
SIC: 2844; NAICS: 32562

Prestige Eye Care Market

Market shares are shown in percent.

Eye shadow	37.0%
Mascara	31.0
Eye liner	21.0
Eye brow	6.0
Eye applicator	3.0
Other	2.0

Source: *Soap Perfumery & Cosmetics*, September 2004, p. 20, from NPD.

★ 1255 ★
Eye Care
SIC: 2844; NAICS: 32562

Top Eye/Lens Care Solution Brands, 2004

Market shares are shown based on drug stores for the 52 weeks ended October 31, 2004.

Renu Multiplus	7.3%
Opti-Free Express	6.7
Refresh Tears	3.4
Renu	3.0
Refresh Plus	2.5

Genteal	2.5%
Visine	2.4
Clear Eyes	2.3
Opti-Free	2.1
Systane	2.0
Private label	12.7
Other	53.1

Source: *Chain Drug Review*, January 3, 2005, p. 95, from Information Resources Inc.

★ 1256 ★
Eye Care
SIC: 2844; NAICS: 32562

Top Eye/Lens Care Solution Makers, 2004

Market shares are shown based on sales at food stores, drug stores and mass merchandisers (but not Wal-Mart) for the 52 weeks ended June 13, 2004.

Bausch & Lomb	32.0%
Alcon/Nestle	21.0
Pfizer	15.4
Allergan Pharm.	7.0
Private label	15.6
Other	9.0

Source: *Grocery Headquarters*, August 2004, p. S88, from Information Resources Inc.

★ 1257 ★
Eye Care
SIC: 2844; NAICS: 325412

Top Eye/Lens Care Tablets/ Accessories, 2004

Market shares are shown based on drug stores for the 52 weeks ended October 31, 2004.

Ocusoft	7.3%
Magnivision	6.8
Optic Shop	5.7
Aosept	5.0
Amo Ultrazyme	4.7
Eye Scrub	3.9
Coverlet	3.9
Flents Wipe 'n Clear	3.8
Lami	3.4
Renu	3.1
Private label	25.1
Other	27.3

Source: *Chain Drug Review*, January 3, 2005, p. 95, from Information Resources Inc.

★ 1258 ★
Foot Care
SIC: 2844; NAICS: 325412

Top Foot Care/Athlete's Foot Medications, 2004

Market shares are shown based on drug stores for the 52 weeks ended October 31, 2004.

Lamisil AT	13.9%
Lotrimin AF	10.4
Tinactin	8.5
Lotrimin Ultra	4.2
Kerasal	4.0
Dr. Scholl's	3.6
Flexitol	3.5
Reclaim AF	3.0
Desenex	2.8
Gold Bond	2.7
Private label	25.3
Other	18.1

Source: *Chain Drug Review*, January 3, 2005, p. 95, from Information Resources Inc.

★ 1259 ★
Foot Care
SIC: 2844; NAICS: 325412

Top Foot Care Devices, 2004

Market shares are shown based on drug stores for the 52 weeks ended October 31, 2004.

Dr. Scholl's	29.7%
Dr. Scholl's Advantage	5.7
Dr. Scholl's Tri Comfort	5.0
ProFoot	4.2
Airplus	4.2
ProFoot Triad	2.6
PediFix	2.2
Dr. Scholl's One Step	2.0
Dr. Scholl's Air Pillo	2.0
PediFex Visco Gel	1.9
Private label	13.6
Other	26.9

Source: *Chain Drug Review*, January 3, 2005, p. 95, from Information Resources Inc.

★ 1260 ★
Fragrances
SIC: 2844; NAICS: 32562

Global Fragrances Market, 2003

Market sizes in selected countries: The United States was $5,858.2 million, France $1,978.1 million and Germany $11,488.5 million.

	($ mil.)	Share
Premium women's fragrance	$9,673.7	43.22%
Premium men's fragrance	4,724.0	21.11
Mass women's fragrance	4,595.7	20.53
Mass men's fragrance	2,897.6	12.95
Premium unisex fragrance	292.1	1.31
Mass unisex fragrance	198.5	0.89

Source: *Soap Perfumery & Cosmetics*, October 2004, p. 28, from Euromonitor.

★ 1261 ★
Fragrances
SIC: 2844; NAICS: 32562

Leading Fragrance Brands in the Eastern Europe, 2003

Premium and mass fragrances represented markets worth $682.5 million and $701.5 million respectively.

Avon	9.8%
Oriflame	4.6
Adidas	2.6
Gillette Aftershave Splash	1.7
J'adore	1.2
Charlie	1.1
Chanel N	1.1
Other	77.9

Source: *Global Cosmetic Industry*, October 2004, p. 30, from Euromonitor.

★ 1262 ★
Fragrances
SIC: 2844; NAICS: 32562

Leading Fragrance Brands in the U.K., 2003

Data refer to mass market fragrances. Joop!Our Homme leads the fine fragrance industry with a 3.8% share. By channel, Boots took 33% of the industry with department stores with 25%.

Lynx	16.7%
Old Spice	13.2
Brut	9.4
Gillette Aftershave Splash	6.7

Continued on next page.

★ 1262 ★

[Continued]
Fragrances
SIC: 2844; NAICS: 32562

Leading Fragrance Brands in the U.K., 2003

Data refer to mass market fragrances. Joop!Our Homme leads the fine fragrance industry with a 3.8% share. By channel, Boots took 33% of the industry with department stores with 25%.

Adidas	6.7%
Insignia	4.4
Addiction	4.0
Legendary Harley-Davidson	0.3
Rapport	0.2
Private label	6.2
Other	29.7

Source: *Marketing*, September 15, 2004, p. 20, from Euromonitor.

★ 1263 ★

Fragrances
SIC: 2844; NAICS: 32562

Leading Fragrance Brands in Western Europe, 2003

Premium and mass fragrances represented markets worth $6,869.1 million and $2,033.3 million respectively.

Chanel No. 5	1.8%
Avon	1.1
Allure	1.1
J'adore	1.0
cK one	1.0
Angel	1.0
Adidas	1.0
Other	92.0

Source: *Global Cosmetic Industry*, October 2004, p. 30, from Euromonitor.

★ 1264 ★

Fragrances
SIC: 2844; NAICS: 32562

Leading Men's Fragrance Brands (Prestige), 2004

The industry is valued at $1.2 billion.

Acqua dio Gio Pour Homme (Giorgio Armani) .	6.8%
Polo Blue (Ralph Lauren)	5.3
Eternity for Men (Calvin Klein)	3.6
Tommy	3.5
Very Sexy for Him (Limited Brands)	3.4

Cool Water (Davidoff)	3.3%
Curve for Men (Liz Claiborne)	3.2
Polo (Ralph Lauren)	3.0
Obsession for Men (Calvin Klein)	2.9
Romance for Men (Ralph Lauren)	2.8
Other	62.2

Source: *Daily News Record*, April 4, 2005, p. 28, from Euromonitor.

★ 1265 ★

Fragrances
SIC: 2844; NAICS: 32562

Leading Men's Fragrances in France, 2003

Market shares are shown in percent.

Le Male	3.9%
Eau Sauvage	3.5
Boss Bottled	3.5
Azzaro pour Homme	3.5
Brut de Faberge	3.3
Allure Homme	3.1
Fahrenheit	3.0
Habit Rouge	2.8
Hugo	2.4
Chrome	2.1
Other	68.9

Source: *Soap, Perfumery & Cosmetics*, December 2004, p. 20, from Euromonitor.

★ 1266 ★

Fragrances
SIC: 2844; NAICS: 32562

Leading Men's Shaving/Cologne/Talc Brands, 2005

Brands are ranked by supermarket, drug store and discount store sales (excluding Wal-Mart) for the 52 weeks ended January 23, 2005.

	($ mil.)	Share
Axe	$ 61.0	18.56%
Old Spice	17.8	5.42
Nivea for Men	10.5	3.19
Brut	10.5	3.19
Gillette Series	9.7	2.95
Coty Stetson	9.7	2.95
Drakkar Noir	8.9	2.71
Davidoff Cool Water	7.1	2.16
Curve for Men	6.9	2.10

Continued on next page.

★ 1266 ★
[Continued]
Fragrances
SIC: 2844; NAICS: 32562

Leading Men's Shaving/Cologne/Talc Brands, 2005

Brands are ranked by supermarket, drug store and discount store sales (excluding Wal-Mart) for the 52 weeks ended January 23, 2005.

	($ mil.)	Share
Private label	$ 7.1	2.16%
Other	179.5	54.61

Source: *MMR*, March 21, 2005, p. 21, from Information Resources Inc.

★ 1267 ★
Fragrances
SIC: 2844; NAICS: 32562

Leading Women's Fragrance Brands, 2005

Market shares are shown based on sales for drug stores for the 52 weeks ended February 20, 2005.

Healing Garden	7.3%
Body & Earth	5.5
Calgon	4.9
Celine Dion	2.7
Elizabeth Taylor White Diamonds	2.6
Red Door	2.4
Burt's Bees	2.3
Body Fantasy	2.3
Tommy Girl	1.7
Liz Claiborne	1.7
Other	66.6

Source: *Chain Drug Review*, March 28, 2005, p. 24, from Information Resources Inc.

★ 1268 ★
Fragrances
SIC: 2844; NAICS: 32562

Leading Women's Fragrances in France, 2003

Market shares are shown in percent.

Angel	4.3%
Chanel No. 5	3.8
J'adore	3.0
Lolita Lempicka	2.7

Flower	2.6%
Shalimar	2.1
Opium	2.0
Paris	1.9
Coco Mademoiselle	1.9
Allure	1.9
Other	26.2

Source: *Soap, Perfumery & Cosmetics*, December 2004, p. 20, from Euromonitor.

★ 1269 ★
Hair Care
SIC: 2844; NAICS: 32562

African American Hair Care Market, 2004

Sales are shown in millions of dollars and exclude Wal-Mart.

Chemicals	$ 41.27
Styling	35.51
Hair dressing	25.58
Conditioners	25.58
Hair coloring	20.41
Shampoo	9.91
Curl/wave styling	8.13
Men's styling	4.67
Children's hair care	2.41

Source: *Household & Personal Products Industry*, April 2005, p. 78, from Information Resources Inc.

★ 1270 ★
Hair Care
SIC: 2844; NAICS: 32562

Hair Care Market in France, 2003

France represents the largest hair care market among the top five European markets (France, Germany, Italy, Spain and the United Kingdom). Sales rose 4.5% for the year to 1.9 billion euros.

	(mil.)	Share
Shampoos	786.7	41.37%
Colorants	725.9	38.18
Conditioners	171.3	9.01
Treatments	155.9	8.20
Lotions	61.7	3.24

Source: *European Cosmetic Markets*, September 2004, p. 20, from FIP statistics.

★ 1271 ★
Hair Care
SIC: 2844; NAICS: 32562
Hair Care Market in Russia

Roughly a quarter of Russians use hair dye. Russians have recently shown interest in making their hair care purchases in expensive specialty stores. Open markets fell from 41% to 35% in 2002 to 2003.

	2005	2007	Share
Shampoo	$ 459.4	$ 499.3	35.43%
Colorants	320.5	394.8	28.01
2-in-1 products	206.2	236.1	16.75
Styling agents	127.0	140.7	9.98
Conditioners	104.0	114.5	8.12
Perms and relaxants	22.6	23.9	1.70

Source: *Global Cosmetic Industry*, December 2004, p. 40, from Euromonitor.

★ 1272 ★
Hair Care
SIC: 2844; NAICS: 32562
Hair Care Sales in Germany

Drug stores were the outlet of choice with 246.3 million euros in sales. Supermarkets followed with 153.42 million in sales. Distribution is shown based on sales for July 2003 - June 2004.

Anti-dandruff	19.0%
Normal	17.4
Colored	12.0
Dry	11.9
Oily	8.2
Fine	7.8
Damaged	5.4
Children's	4.4
Other	8.1

Source: *European Cosmetic Markets*, September 2004, p. NA, from Information Resources Inc.

★ 1273 ★
Hair Care
SIC: 2844; NAICS: 32562
Hair Dye Market in Turkey

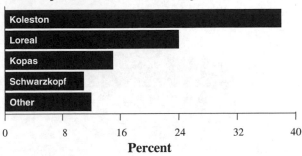

The hair dye market was valued at 31 million euros, up from 25 million in the previous year.

Koleston	37.5%
Loreal	23.8
Kopas	15.4
Schwarzkopf	11.0
Other	12.3

Source: "Hair Dye Market in Turkey." [online] from http://www.export.gov [Accessed March 2005].

★ 1274 ★
Hair Care
SIC: 2844; NAICS: 32562
Largest Shampoo Makers in India

Market shares are shown in percent.

HLL	50.0%
Calvinkare	22.0
Procter & Gamble	10.0
Other	18.0

Source: *Asia Africa Intelligence Wire*, November 30, 2004, p. NA.

★ 1275 ★

Hair Care

SIC: 2844; NAICS: 32562

Leading Antidandruff Shampoo Makers in the U.K.

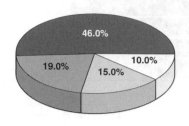

■ Johnson & Johnson   □ Procter & Gamble
■ Abbott   □ Other

The antidandruff shampoo market is valued at 6.5 million pounds.

Johnson & Johnson	.46.0%
Abbott	.19.0
Procter & Gamble	.15.0
Other	.10.0

Source: *Community Pharmacy*, August 12, 2004, p. 24.

★ 1276 ★

Hair Care

SIC: 2844; NAICS: 32562

Leading Hair Care Brands Worldwide, 2003

The leading segments: shampoo $11,248.3 million, colorants $8,336.8 million, styling agents $7,689.6 million and conditioners $7,066.8 million.

Pantene Pro-V	6.7%
Elseve/Elvive	3.2
Sunsilk	2.8
Fructis	2.3
Studio Line	1.8
Head & Shoulders	1.8
Clairol Herbal Essences	1.7
Kanebo	1.6
Excellence	1.6
Other	.74.1

Source: *Soap Perfumery & Cosmetics*, November 2004, p. 19, from Euromonitor.

★ 1277 ★

Hair Care

SIC: 2844; NAICS: 32562

Leading Hair Growth Tonic Makers in Japan, 2003

Market shares are estimated based on domestic shipments.

Taisho Pharm	.38.7%
Kao	.19.6
Daiichi Pharm	.10.5
Lion	. 9.7
Shiseido	. 9.5
Other	.12.0

Source: "Market Share Survey Report 2003." [online] from http://www.nni.nikkei.co.jp [Published July 26, 2004], from Nikkei estimates.

★ 1278 ★

Hair Care

SIC: 2844; NAICS: 32562

Leading Hair Spray Brands in the U.K., 2004

Market shares are shown in percent.

Elnett	.24.1%
Silvikrin	.23.6
Pantene Pro-V	. 8.8
Alberto VO5	. 3.3
Harmony	. 3.0
Bristows	. 3.0
Supersoft	. 1.7
Other	.32.5

Source: *European Cosmetic Markets*, October 2004, p. 378, from industry sources.

★ 1279 ★

Hair Care

SIC: 2844; NAICS: 32562

Leading Styling Brands in the U.K., 2004

During an average week, 46% of women and 21% of men use a styling product. Market shares are shown in percent.

ShockWaves	.14.5%
VO5	.13.5
Brylcreem	. 9.8
Studio Line	. 9.4
Fructis	. 4.4

Continued on next page.

★ 1279 ★

[Continued]
Hair Care
SIC: 2844; NAICS: 32562

Leading Styling Brands in the U.K., 2004

During an average week, 46% of women and 21% of men use a styling product. Market shares are shown in percent.

Silvikrin	1.3%
Other	47.1

Source: *European Cosmetic Markets*, October 2004, p. 378, from industry sources.

★ 1280 ★

Hair Care
SIC: 2844; NAICS: 32562

Leading Styling Product Makers in the U.K.

Percent

Shares are shown based on total sales of 275 million British pounds.

L'Oreal	33.5%
Procter & Gamble	14.7
Alberto Culver	10.5
Sara Lee	6.5
Schwarzkopt	2.8
Other	32.0

Source: *Marketing Week*, July 22, 2004, p. 26.

★ 1281 ★

Hair Care
SIC: 2844; NAICS: 32562

Top Baby Shampoo Brands, 2004

Market shares are shown based on sales at food stores, drug stores and mass merchandisers (excluding Wal-Mart) for the 52 weeks ended October 31, 2004.

Johnson's Baby	68.6%
Johnson's Softwash	5.8
Playtex Baby Magic	3.2

Gerber	1.9%
Gerber Grins and Giggles	1.6
Lander	1.3
Grisi	1.0
Paul Mitchell Baby Don't Cry	0.4
Vera Para Mi Bebe	0.3
Private label	14.8
Other	1.1

Source: *Grocery Headquarters*, January 2005, p. 71, from Information Resources Inc.

★ 1282 ★

Hair Care
SIC: 2844; NAICS: 32562

Top Dandruff Shampoos, 2004

Market shares are shown based on drug store sales for the 52 weeks ended October 31, 2004.

T/Gel	12.5%
Head & Shoulders Classic Clean	11.8
Selsun Blue	10.2
Nizoral	8.9
Head & Shoulders Dry Scalp Care	8.6
Denorex	4.7
Head & Shoulders Classic din. 2 in 1	4.0
Head & Shoulders Refresh	3.6
Head & Shoulders Smooth & Silky 2 in 1	2.4
Head & Shoulders Extra Fullness	2.4
Private label	6.5
Other	24.4

Source: *Chain Drug Review*, January 31, 2005, p. 24, from Information Resources Inc.

★ 1283 ★

Hair Care
SIC: 2844; NAICS: 32562

Top Hair Care Brands in Germany, 2003

Market size was placed at 2,365.7 million euros for the year.

Elvital	12.48%
Schauma	11.66
Nivea Hair Care	8.82
Pantene	8.15
Fliss Kur	7.20
Guhl	7.06
Fructis	6.14
Head & Shoulders	4.67

Continued on next page.

★ 1283 ★
[Continued]
Hair Care
SIC: 2844; NAICS: 32562

Top Hair Care Brands in Germany, 2003

Market size was placed at 2,365.7 million euros for the year.

Herbal Essences	3.39%
Other	.26.25

Source: *Soap Perfumery & Cosmetics*, October 2004, p. 18, from Beiersdorf.

★ 1284 ★
Hair Care
SIC: 2844; NAICS: 32562

Top Hair Care Brands Worldwide, 2003

Shampoo is the largest sector of the market. In mature markets, manufacturers have begun to target shampoo to men, women and children and specific hair types. In emerging markets, disposable income remains an influential factor in shampoo selection. Market shares are shown in percent.

Pantene	6.7%
Elseve/Elvive	3.2
Sunsilk	2.8
Fructis	2.4
Head & Shoulders	2.3
Studio Line	1.8
Clairol Herbal Essences	1.8
Excellence	1.7
Kanebo	1.6
Dove	1.6
Private label	2.1
Other	.72.0

Source: *Global Cosmetic Industry*, December 2004, p. 60, from Euromonitor.

★ 1285 ★
Hair Care
SIC: 2844; NAICS: 32562

Top Hair Care Makers in Latin America, 2003

Hair care sales in Latin America reached nearly $4.5 billion for the year.

Procter & Gamble	.20.6%
Unilever Groupe	.14.4
Colgate-Palmolive	8.4

Revlon Inc.	2.9%
Alberto-Culver	2.0
Avon Products Inc.	1.6
Nisai SA	1.3
Cia Distribuidora del Centro	1.2
L'Oreal Groupe	1.0
Other	.31.1

Source: *Global Cosmetic Industry*, December 2004, p. 42, from Euromonitor.

★ 1286 ★
Hair Care
SIC: 2844; NAICS: 32562

Top Hair Care Makers Worldwide, 2003

Global sales were $42.4 billion. Hair care was the top segment of the cosmetics and toiletries sector. Market shares are shown in percent.

Procter & Gamble	.22.0%
L'Oreal Groupe	.18.6
Unilever Group	.11.9
Henkel	5.5
Kao Corp.	2.7
Shiseido Co.	2.6
Albeto-Culver	2.0
Colgate-Palmolive	1.9
Kanebo	1.8
Mandom Corp.	1.4
Other	.29.6

Source: *Global Cosmetic Industry*, December 2004, p. 60, from Euromonitor.

★ 1287 ★

Hair Care

SIC: 2844; NAICS: 32562

Top Hair Colorant Brands, 2005

Market shares are shown based on sales for drug stores for the 52 weeks ended February 20, 2005.

Preference	11.5%
Clairol Nice 'n Easy	8.5
Excellence	8.4
Just For Men	7.7
Feria	7.5
Clairol Natural Instincts	6.8
Gamier Nutrisse	5.0
Couleur Experts	4.9
Colorsilk	3.8
Clairol Hydrience	3.2
Other	32.7

Source: *Chain Drug Review*, March 28, 2005, p. 24, from Information Resources Inc.

★ 1288 ★

Hair Care

SIC: 2844; NAICS: 32562

Top Hair Colorant Brands in the U.K., 2003

The industry is valued at 185 million pounds.

Clairol Nice 'n' Easy	13.1%
Excellence	8.6
Preference	8.3
Belle Color	6.6
Feria Color	6.0
Clairol Hydrience	5.8
Alberto VO5	5.5
Clairol Loving Care	5.3
Casting	4.1
Viva Color	4.0
Movida	4.0
Other	28.7

Source: *Marketing*, October 13, 2004, p. 32, from Euromonitor.

★ 1289 ★

Hair Care

SIC: 2844; NAICS: 32562

Top Hair Colorant Makers in the U.K., 2003

The industry is valued at 185 million pounds.

L'Oreal Paris	31.0%
Clairol	27.0

Laboratoires Garnier	18.0%
Wella	5.0
Schwarzkopf & Henkel	4.0
Other	15.0

Source: *Marketing*, October 13, 2004, p. 32, from Mintel.

★ 1290 ★

Hair Care

SIC: 2844; NAICS: 32562

Top Hair Conditioner Brands in Poland, 2004

Market shares are shown in percent.

Avon	18.5%
Ziaja	11.4
Timotei	10.0
Pantene Pro-V	7.5
Joanna	6.8
Dove	6.1
Other	39.7

Source: "Hair Care Cosmetics Market." [online] from http://www.export.gov [Published January 31, 2005], from SMG/KRC and ACNielsen.

★ 1291 ★

Hair Care

SIC: 2844; NAICS: 32562

Top Hair Conditioner/Cream Rinse Brands, 2004

Market shares are shown based on drug store sales for the year ended October 31, 2004.

Garnier Fructis	4.6%
Infusium23	4.2
Alberto VO5	4.1
Vive	3.8
Dove	3.3
Pantene Pro V	3.0

Continued on next page.

★ 1291 ★
[Continued]
Hair Care
SIC: 2844; NAICS: 32562

Top Hair Conditioner/Cream Rinse Brands, 2004

Market shares are shown based on drug store sales for the year ended October 31, 2004.

Thermasilk	2.4%
Pantene Smooth and Sleek	2.3
Clairol Herbal Essences	2.2
Other	73.1

Source: *Chain Drug Review*, January 31, 2005, p. 36, from Information Resources Inc.

★ 1292 ★
Hair Care
SIC: 2844; NAICS: 32562

Top Hair Conditioner Makers, 2004

Market shares are shown based on sales at food stores, drug stores and mass merchandisers (but not Wal-Mart) for the 52 weeks ended June 13, 2004.

Procter & Gamble	21.0%
Clairol	13.7
Helene Curtis	13.4
Alberto Culver	9.9
L'Oreal	5.3
Other	36.7

Source: *Grocery Headquarters*, August 2004, p. S88, from Information Resources Inc.

★ 1293 ★
Hair Care
SIC: 2844; NAICS: 32562

Top Hair Relaxer Kits, 2004

Market shares are shown based on sales at food stores, drug stores and mass merchandisers (but not Wal-Mart).

	($ mil.)	Share
Soft Sheen Optimum Care	$ 5.1	11.62%
Dark & Lovely	3.7	8.43
Proline Soft & Beautiful	3.2	7.29
Just for Me	3.1	7.06
Gentle Treatment	2.3	5.24
Dark & Lovely Plus	2.3	5.24
Lusters Scurl	2.2	5.01
African Pride	2.1	4.78
Easy Straight	1.9	4.33

	($ mil.)	Share
Ogilvie Straightener	$ 1.7	3.87%
Other	16.3	37.13

Source: *MMR*, April 25, 2005, p. 67, from Information Resources Inc.

★ 1294 ★
Hair Care
SIC: 2844; NAICS: 32562

Top Hair Spray/Spritz Brands, 2004

Market shares are shown based on drug store sales for the year ended October 31, 2004.

Sebastian Shaper Plus	6.1%
Pantene Classic Care	5.5
Rave	5.4
Sebastian Shaper	5.2
Salon Grafix	4.2
Suave	4.0
Clairol Herbal Essences	3.6
Tresemme Tres Two	3.5
Aqua Net	3.1
Finesse Touchable	2.9
Other	56.5

Source: *Chain Drug Review*, January 31, 2005, p. 36, from Information Resources Inc.

★ 1295 ★
Hair Care
SIC: 2844; NAICS: 32562

Top Hair Styling Brands in Spain, 2003

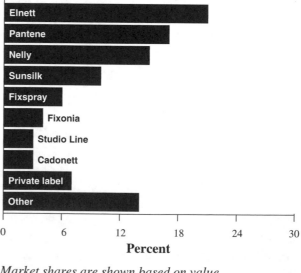

Market shares are shown based on value.

Elnett	21.0%
Pantene	17.0
Nelly	15.0

Continued on next page.

★ 1295 ★

[Continued]
Hair Care
SIC: 2844; NAICS: 32562

Top Hair Styling Brands in Spain, 2003

Market shares are shown based on value.

Sunsilk	10.0%
Fixspray	6.0
Fixonia	4.0
Studio Line	3.0
Cadonett	3.0
Private label	7.0
Other	14.0

Source: *European Cosmetic Markets*, October 2004, p. 376, from ACNielsen.

★ 1296 ★

Hair Care
SIC: 2844; NAICS: 32562

Top Hair Styling Product Brands in Germany, 2003

The hair styling market was worth 496.11 million pounds, with hair sprays taking 54.2% of the total, followed by gels and waxes with 22.4% and styling foam with 20.2%.

Drei Wetter	23.2%
Wellaflex	12.0
Gard	9.7
Nivea Hair Care	8.7
Studio Line	8.5
Other	37.9

Source: *European Cosmetic Markets*, October 2004, p. 372, from Industrie Gesellschaft Aerosole.

★ 1297 ★

Hair Care
SIC: 2844; NAICS: 32562

Top Men's Hair Care Brands Worldwide, 2003

Total market size was $2,383.5 million in 2003. Japan takes about half of the market.

Shiseido	8.9%
Lucido	7.8
Gatsby	6.9
Just for Men	6.4
Kanebo	6.0
American Crew	5.6

Auslese	4.6%
Nivea for Men	3.0
Brylcreem	2.4
Elseve/Elvive	2.3
Private label	2.9
Other	43.2

Source: *Global Cosmetic Industry*, June 2004, p. 60, from Euromonitor.

★ 1298 ★

Hair Care
SIC: 2844; NAICS: 32562

Top Men's Hair Care Makers Worldwide, 2003

Market shares are shown in percent.

Mandom Corp.	18.6%
Shiseido Co. Ltd.	11.9
Kanebo Ltd.	8.6
Combe Inc.	8.3
The Colomer Group	5.8
L'Oreal Groupe	5.2
Beiersdorf AG	3.0
Procter & Gamble	2.6
Kao Corp.	2.6
Other	33.4

Source: *Global Cosmetic Industry*, June 2004, p. 60, from Euromonitor.

★ 1299 ★

Hair Care
SIC: 2844; NAICS: 32562

Top Shampoo Brands, 2004

Brands are ranked by sales at food stores, drug stores and mass merchandisers (but not Wal-Mart).

	($ mil.)	Share
Clairol Herbal Essences	$ 53.1	5.76%
Garnier Fructis	50.7	5.50
Dove	50.3	5.45
L'Oreal Vive	36.1	3.91
Pantene Classically Clean	33.7	3.65
Suave Naturals	33.5	3.63
Pantene Smooth and Sleek	33.2	3.60
Pantene Sheer Volume	31.5	3.41
Pantene Daily Moisture Renewal	29.7	3.22
Pantene Color Revival	26.1	2.83
Other	544.6	59.04

Source: *MMR*, April 25, 2005, p. 67, from Information Resources Inc.

★ 1300 ★
Hair Care
SIC: 2844; NAICS: 32562
Top Shampoo Brands in Poland, 2004

Market shares are shown based on $1.15 billion in spending.

Familijny/Pollena Savona 14.8%
Timotei 13.8
Palmolive 13.4
Schauma 9.6
Avon 8.3
Other 40.1

Source: "Hair Care Cosmetics Market." [online] from http://www.export.gov [Published January 31, 2005], from SMG/KRC and ACNielsen.

★ 1301 ★
Hair Care
SIC: 2844; NAICS: 32562
Top Shampoo Brands in Spain, 2003

Market shares are shown in percent.

Pantene 16.6%
Head & Shoulders 12.8
Fructis 9.0
Elvive 8.9
Timotei 6.8
Herbal Essences 5.0
Johnson's 4.2
Ultrasuave 3.4
Flex 3.4
Other 29.9

Source: *European Cosmetic Markets*, September 2004, p. NA, from Fragrances y Cosmetics.

★ 1302 ★
Hair Care
SIC: 2844; NAICS: 32562
Top Shampoo Brands in the U.K., 2003

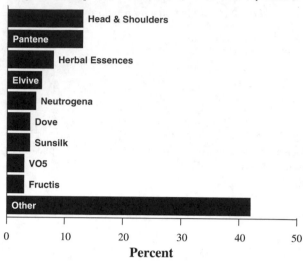

The overall hair care market is thought to be saturated and saw just 1.3% growth from 2003 to 2004. Market shares are shown in percent.

Head & Shoulders 12.6%
Pantene 12.5
Herbal Essences 7.5
Elvive 6.1
Neutrogena 5.1
Dove 4.3
Sunsilk 3.9
VO5 . . . . 3.4
Fructis 3.0
Other 41.6

Source: *European Cosmetic Markets*, September 2004, p. NA, from industry estimates.

★ 1303 ★
Hair Care
SIC: 2844; NAICS: 32562
Top Styling Brands in China, 2002

The industry is valued at $640.3 million.

Arch 10.0%
Alkai 5.5
Pantene 4.5
Maestro 4.5
Elseve 4.5
Sifone 2.5
Vidal Sassoon 2.0
Ador 1.5
Wella 1.2

Continued on next page.

★ 1303 ★

[Continued]
Hair Care
SIC: 2844; NAICS: 32562

Top Styling Brands in China, 2002

The industry is valued at $640.3 million.

Dep	1.0%
Other	.62.8

Source: *European Cosmetic Markets*, June 2004, p. 237, from Euromonitor.

★ 1304 ★

Lip Care
SIC: 2844; NAICS: 32562

Top Lip Balm/Cold Sore Makers, 2004

Market shares are shown based on sales at food stores, drug stores and mass merchandisers (but not Wal-Mart) for the 52 weeks ended June 13, 2004.

Wyeth Labs	.28.6%
Blistex	.19.7
Glaxosmithkline	.18.5
Carma Labs	6.1
Other	.29.1

Source: *Grocery Headquarters*, August 2004, p. S88, from Information Resources Inc.

★ 1305 ★

Lip Care
SIC: 2844; NAICS: 32562

Top Lip Balms, 2004

Brands are ranked by sales at food stores, drug stores and mass merchandisers (but not Wal-Mart).

	($ mil.)	Share
Abreva	$ 53.0	18.56%
Chapstick	35.6	12.46
Blistex	23.0	8.05
Carmex	17.5	6.13
Chapstick Lip Moisturizer	17.3	6.06
Mentholatum Soft Lips	9.4	3.29
Campho Phenique	8.4	2.94
Chapstick Medicated	7.5	2.63
Herpecin L	5.3	1.86
Blistex Complete Moisture	5.3	1.86
Other	103.3	36.17

Source: *MMR*, April 25, 2005, p. 67, from Information Resources Inc.

★ 1306 ★

Lip Care
SIC: 2844; NAICS: 32562

Top Lip Gloss Brands, 2004

Market shares are shown based on drug stores for the 52 weeks ended October 31, 2004.

Lipglide	6.7%
Super Lustrous	4.5
Colour Juice	3.6
Wet Shine	3.2
Cover Girl Wetslicks	3.2
MoistureShine	2.7
Almay Whipped Gloss	2.3
Cover Girl Lipsticks	2.0
Lip Smackers	1.7
Milani	1.4
Other	.68.7

Source: *Chain Drug Review*, March 28, 2005, p. 95, from Information Resources Inc.

★ 1307 ★

Nail Care
SIC: 2844; NAICS: 32562

Largest Nail Care Markets Worldwide, 2003

Retail sales are shown in millions of dollars.

United States	$ 674.1
France	183.1
Germany	118.9
United Kingdom	113.8
Italy	106.2
Spain	49.2

Source: *Soap Perfumery & Cosmetics*, January 2005, p. 16, from Datamonitor.

★ 1308 ★

Nail Care
SIC: 2844; NAICS: 32562

Nail Care Market Worldwide, 2003

The nail care industry was worth about $3.1 billion worldwide. Sales are shown in millions of dollars.

	($ mil.)	Share
Western Europe	$ 952.1	31.02%
North America	783.5	25.53
Latin America	512.6	16.70
Asia Pacific	285.4	9.30
Africa and Middle East	253.3	8.25

Continued on next page.

★ 1308 ★

[Continued]
Nail Care
SIC: 2844; NAICS: 32562

Nail Care Market Worldwide, 2003

The nail care industry was worth about $3.1 billion worldwide. Sales are shown in millions of dollars.

	($ mil.)	Share
Eastern Europe	$ 253.1	8.25%
Australasia	28.9	0.94

Source: *Global Cosmetic Industry*, March 2005, p. 32, from Euromonitor.

★ 1309 ★

Nail Care
SIC: 2844; NAICS: 32562

Nail Care Sales, 2006-2008

Retail sales are shown in millions of dollars.

	2006	2007	2008
Nail polish	$ 457.8	$ 456.0	$ 456.0
Nail treatments	129.7	130.5	130.6
Polish remover	73.8	71.6	69.0

Source: *DSN Retailing Today*, January 24, 2005, p. 12, from Euromonitor.

★ 1310 ★

Nail Care
SIC: 2844; NAICS: 32562

Top Nail Care Brands, 2005

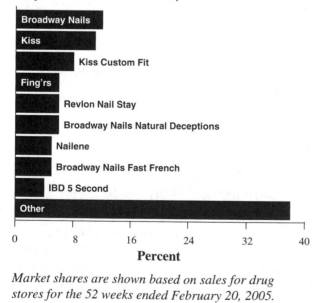

Percent

Market shares are shown based on sales for drug stores for the 52 weeks ended February 20, 2005.

Broadway Nails	12.0%
Kiss	10.9
Kiss Custom Fit	7.5

Fing'rs	6.0%
Revlon Nail Stay	5.6
Broadway Nails Natural Deceptions	5.5
Nailene	5.4
Broadway Nails Fast French	4.8
IBD 5 Second	4.0
Other	.38.3

Source: *Chain Drug Review*, March 28, 2005, p. 24, from Information Resources Inc.

★ 1311 ★

Nail Care
SIC: 2844; NAICS: 32562

Top Nail Polish Brands, 2004

Brands are ranked by sales at food stores, drug stores and mass merchandisers (but not Wal-Mart).

	($ mil.)	Share
Sally Hansen Hard as Nails	$ 21.8	9.04%
Revlon	18.8	7.80
Sally Hansen Maximum Growth . .	12.1	5.02
L'Oreal Jet Set Shine	8.7	3.61
L'Oreal Steel Colour	8.5	3.53
Maybelline Express Finish	8.4	3.48
New York Color	8.3	3.44
Maybelline Forever Stong	7.1	2.94
Sally Hansen Nail Prisms	6.9	2.86
Revlon Crystalline	6.4	2.65
Other	134.1	55.62

Source: *MMR*, April 25, 2005, p. 67, from Information Resources Inc.

★ 1312 ★

Nail Care
SIC: 2844; NAICS: 32562

Top Nail Polish Removers, 2004

Brands are ranked by sales at food stores, drug stores and mass merchandisers (but not Wal-Mart).

	($ mil.)	Share
Cutex Quick & Gentle	$ 8.9	17.18%
Cutex Essential Care	4.0	7.72
Pretty Nails	2.8	5.41
Sally Hansen	2.7	5.21
Cutex	1.4	2.70
Revlon	1.2	2.32
Calico	0.9	1.74
Sally Hansen Kwik Off	0.7	1.35
Polish Off	0.6	1.16
Onyx Professional	0.5	0.97

Continued on next page.

★ 1312 ★

[Continued]
Nail Care
SIC: 2844; NAICS: 32562

Top Nail Polish Removers, 2004

Brands are ranked by sales at food stores, drug stores and mass merchandisers (but not Wal-Mart).

	($ mil.)	Share
Private label	$ 26.2	50.58%
Other	1.9	3.67

Source: *MMR*, April 25, 2005, p. 67, from Information Resources Inc.

★ 1313 ★

Nasal Care
SIC: 2844; NAICS: 32562

Top Nasal Spray/Drop/Inhalers, 2004

Market shares are shown based on drug stores for the 52 weeks ended October 31, 2004.

Primatene Mist	13.3%
Zicam	12.5
Afrin	10.1
Afrin No Drip	5.2
Vicks Sinex	4.9
NasalCrom	3.2
Neo-Synephrine	3.0
Vicks	2.7
4-Way	2.7
Breathe Right	2.5
Private label	17.8
Other	22.1

Source: *Chain Drug Review*, January 3, 2005, p. 95, from Information Resources Inc.

★ 1314 ★

Nasal Care
SIC: 2844; NAICS: 32562

Top Nasal Strips, 2004

Brands are ranked by sales at food stores, drug stores and mass merchandisers (but not Wal-Mart).

	($ mil.)	Share
Breathe Right	$ 46.60	89.44%
Clear Passage	0.04	0.08
Breathe Right Near Clear	0.01	0.02
Private label	2.70	5.18
Other	2.75	5.28

Source: *MMR*, April 25, 2005, p. 67, from Information Resources Inc.

★ 1315 ★

Oral Care
SIC: 2844; NAICS: 32562

Top Dental Care Brands, 2005

Brands are ranked by sales at supermarkets, drug stores and discount stores (excluding Wal-Mart) for the 52 weeks ended January 23, 2005.

	($ mil.)	Share
Johnson & Johnson Reach	$ 24.2	20.84%
Glide	17.1	14.73
Crest	6.2	5.34
J&J Reach Dentotap	5.5	4.74
Oral B Satinfloss	5.3	4.57
J&J Reach Gentle Gum Care	4.8	4.13
J&J Reach Easy Glide	4.7	4.05
J&J Reach Clean Burst	4.5	3.88
Glide Comfort Plus	3.8	3.27
Private label	21.0	18.09
Other	19.0	16.37

Source: *MMR*, March 7, 2005, p. 34, from Information Resources Inc.

★ 1316 ★

Oral Care
SIC: 2844; NAICS: 32562

Top Dental Floss Brands

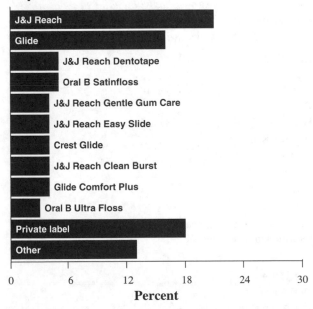

Market shares are shown based on sales at food stores, drug stores and mass merchandisers (but not Wal-Mart).

	($ mil.)	Share
J&J Reach	$ 24.2	20.83%
Glide	18.9	16.27

Continued on next page.

★ 1316 ★

[Continued]
Oral Care

SIC: 2844; NAICS: 32562

Top Dental Floss Brands

Market shares are shown based on sales at food stores, drug stores and mass merchandisers (but not Wal-Mart).

	($ mil.)	Share
J&J Reach Dentotape	$ 5.6	4.82%
Oral B Satinfloss	5.3	4.56
J&J Reach Gentle Gum Care	4.8	4.13
J&J Reach Easy Slide	4.7	4.04
Crest Glide	4.7	4.04
J&J Reach Clean Burst	4.4	3.79
Glide Comfort Plus	4.2	3.61
Oral B Ultra Floss	3.3	2.84
Private label	21.1	18.16
Other	15.0	12.91

Source: *MMR*, April 25, 2005, p. 67, from Information Resources Inc.

★ 1317 ★

Oral Care

SIC: 2844; NAICS: 32562

Top Mouthwash/Dental Rinses, 2004

Market shares are shown based on sales at food stores, drug stores and mass merchandisers (but not Wal-Mart) for the 52 weeks ended June 13, 2004.

Listerine	51.7%
Scope	13.7
Act	4.4
Plac	3.2
Biotene	1.8
Act for Kids	1.2
Cepacol	1.1
Targon	0.7
Therabreath	0.5
Other	21.7

Source: *Grocery Headquarters*, August 2004, p. S88, from Information Resources Inc.

★ 1318 ★

Oral Care

SIC: 2844; NAICS: 32562

Top Oral Care Brands (Portable), 2004

Brands are ranked by sales at food stores, drug stores and mass merchandisers (but not Wal-Mart).

	($ mil.)	Share
Listerine Pocketpaks	$ 53.9	32.95%
Trident White	53.7	32.82

	($ mil.)	Share
Wrigley's Eclipse Flash Strips	$ 17.0	10.39%
Orbit White	8.3	5.07
Altoids	6.3	3.85
Wrigley's Eclipse Flash Strips	6.1	3.73
Arm & Hammer Dental Care	2.6	1.59
Arm & Hammer Advance White	1.8	1.10
Wrigley's Winterfresh Thin Ice	1.6	0.98
Biotene Oral Balance	1.6	0.98
Private label	3.1	1.89
Other	7.6	4.65

Source: *MMR*, April 25, 2005, p. 67, from Information Resources Inc.

★ 1319 ★

Oral Care

SIC: 2844; NAICS: 32562

Top Oral Care Markets in New Zealand

Sales are shown as of March 21, 2004.

Toothpaste	$ 47.1
Toothbrushes	23.8
Mouthwashes	9.2
Denture care	3.9
Lip salves	3.4
Dental floss/flossers	2.8

Source: *Grocer's Review*, May 2004, p. NA, from ACNielsen.

★ 1320 ★

Oral Care

SIC: 2844; NAICS: 32562

Top Tooth Bleaching/Whitening Brands, 2004

Market shares are shown based on drug stores for the 52 weeks ended October 31, 2004.

Crest Whitestrips Premium	29.9%
Crest Whitestrips	29.0
Crest Night Effects	7.8
Rembrandt	5.5
Colgate Simply White Night	5.1
Colgate Simply White	4.6
Rembrandt Dazzling White	2.4
Rembrandt Plus	2.1
Plus-White	1.1
Dr. George's Dental White	0.8
Other	11.7

Source: *Chain Drug Review*, January 3, 2005, p. 95, from Information Resources Inc.

★ 1321 ★
Oral Care
SIC: 2844; NAICS: 32562

Top Toothpaste Makers, 2004

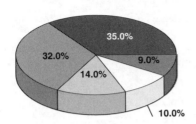

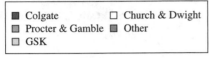

Market shares are shown in percent.

Colgate	.35.0%
Procter & Gamble	.32.0
GSK	.14.0
Church & Dwight	.10.0
Other	9.0

Source: *Chemical Market Reporter*, May 9, 2005, p. NA, from ACNielsen.

★ 1322 ★
Oral Care
SIC: 2844; NAICS: 32562

Top Toothpaste Makers in the U.K., 2003

The industry saw sales of 294 million British pounds. By type, complete protection took 30% of the total, with family taking 20%.

Colgate-Palmolive	.41.0%
GlaxoSmithKline	.36.0
Procter & Gamble	5.0
Own brands	5.0
Lever Faberge	5.0
Other	7.0

Source: *Marketing*, September 22, 2004, p. 36, from Mintel.

★ 1323 ★
Personal Care Products
SIC: 2844; NAICS: 325611, 32562

Best-Selling Health & Beauty Items

Sales are shown in millions of dollars.

Vitamins	. $ 2,360.0
Analgesics	. 2,200.0
Cold/allergy/sinus tablets	1,740.0
Skin care	. 1,570.0
Toothpastes	. 1,470.0
Gastrointestinal tablets	. 1,460.0
Sanitary napkins/tampons	1,400.0
Toothbrushes/dental accessories	. 1,320.0
Hair shampoos	1,230.0
Deodorants	. 1,080.0
Hair colorings	. 1,020.0
Diet aids (liquid/powder)	892.4

Source: *MMR*, September 6, 2004, p. 25, from Information Resources Inc.

★ 1324 ★
Personal Care Products
SIC: 2844; NAICS: 325611, 32562

Body Spray Industry

Body sprays are deodorant and light colognes used in addition to antiperspirants. The industry is valued at $180 million.

Axe	.83.0%
Other	.17.0

Source: *Time Inside Business*, March 2005, p. B22.

★ 1325 ★
Personal Care Products
SIC: 2844; NAICS: 325611, 32562

Health & Beauty Care Sales, 2004

Sales are shown in thousands of dollars at food stores, drug stores and mass merchandiser outlets for the year ended June 12, 2004. Figures exclude Wal-Mart. Total sales were $40,632,018,569.

Cold remedies, adult	. $ 1,936,255
Nutritional supplements	1,425,200
Face cleansers & creams & lotions	1,091,585
Antacids	964,906
Adult incontinence	582,290
Cough syrups & tablets	387,236
First aid treatments	372,945
Cold remedies, children	314,267

Continued on next page.

★ 1325 ★
[Continued]
Personal Care Products
SIC: 2844; NAICS: 325611, 32562

Health & Beauty Care Sales, 2004

Sales are shown in thousands of dollars at food stores, drug stores and mass merchandiser outlets for the year ended June 12, 2004. Figures exclude Wal-Mart. Total sales were $40,632,018,569.

Suntan preparations, suncreens & sunblocks	$ 314,086
Cosmetics, foundation liquid	304,009

Source: *Retail Merchandiser*, September 2004, p. 40, from ACNielsen Strategic Planner.

★ 1326 ★
Personal Care Products
SIC: 2844; NAICS: 325611, 32562

Leading Cosmetics/Toiletries Brands in Japan, 2003

The market was valued at 2,542.5 billion yen for the year, with skin care taking in 861.4 billion yen, hair care with 594.1 billion and cosmetics with 422 million.

Kanebo	6.7%
Sofina	3.9
Shiseido FITIT	3.6
Shiseido	2.2
Kose	1.8
FT Shiseido	1.6
Pola	1.5
Lux	1.4
Biore	1.4
Private label	1.7
Other	71.9

Source: *Soap, Perfumery & Cosmetics Asia*, May 2004, p. 16, from Euromonitor.

★ 1327 ★
Personal Care Products
SIC: 2844; NAICS: 325611, 32562

Leading Cosmetics/Toiletries Brands in Korea, 2003

The total industry was valued at 5,322.5 KTW billion. Skin care led with 2,497.3 million, color cosmetics with 867.2 million and hair care 652.6 million.

Amore	6.7%
Hera	6.0
LacVert	4.1

Isa Knox	3.5%
Sulwhasoo	3.3
Dove	1.5
Hercyna	1.3
Man With Flower	1.2
Pantene Pro-V	1.1
Other	71.3

Source: *Soap, Perfumery & Cosmetics Asia*, March 2005, p. 11, from Euromonitor.

★ 1328 ★
Personal Care Products
SIC: 2844; NAICS: 325611, 32562

Leading Cosmetics/Toiletries Brands in South Africa, 2004

Fragrances led the sector with sales of $3,527.3 million, followed by hair care $3,258.2 million and cosmetics $2,616.3 million. Market shares are shown in percent.

Revlon	3.9%
Charlie	3.3
Collate	3.0
Aquafresh	2.1
Cutex	1.8
Rexona	1.7
Dark & Lovely	1.6
Almay	1.6
Wilkinson Sword/Schick	1.5
Vaseline Intensive Care	1.5
Private label	2.0
Other	76.0

Source: *Global Cosmetic Industry*, April 2005, p. 55, from Euromonitor.

★ 1329 ★
Personal Care Products
SIC: 2844; NAICS: 325611, 32562

Leading Cosmetics/Toiletries Brands in Thailand, 2003

The total industry was valued at 57,377.40 million baht. Bath and shower was the largest sector with sales of 12,865.60 million, followed by skin care 11,296.20 million and hair care at 10,674.90 million. Unilever Thai Holdings led with a 20.4% share followed by Colgate-Palmolive Thailand with a 11.2% share.

Sunsilk	5.7%
Colgate	4.1
Lux	4.0

Continued on next page.

★ 1329 ★

[Continued]
Personal Care Products
SIC: 2844; NAICS: 325611, 32562

Leading Cosmetics/Toiletries Brands in Thailand, 2003

The total industry was valued at 57,377.40 million baht. Bath and shower was the largest sector with sales of 12,865.60 million, followed by skin care 11,296.20 million and hair care at 10,674.90 million. Unilever Thai Holdings led with a 20.4% share followed by Colgate-Palmolive Thailand with a 11.2% share.

Care	3.2%
Johnson's Baby	2.4
Pantene Pro-V	2.3
Close-Up	1.9
Avon	1.8
Dove	1.7
Nivea Body	1.7
Other	71.2

Source: *Soap, Perfumery & Cosmetics Asia*, March 2005, p. 11, from Euromonitor.

★ 1330 ★

Personal Care Products
SIC: 2844; NAICS: 325611, 32562

Leading Cosmetics/Toiletries Brands in the U.K., 2003

Cosmetics and toiletry sales stood at 6,164.2 million pounds sterling for the year. Hair care leads with 1,206.3 million, followed by skin care at 863.7 million and color cosmetics at 932 million. Market shares are shown in percent.

Avon	3.5%
Boots No 7	2.2
Lynx	2.0
Dove	1.9
Oil of Olay	1.6
Pantene Pro-V	1.5
Estee Lauder	1.5
Sure	1.4
Rimmel	1.4
Max Factor	1.4
Other	81.6

Source: *Soap Perfumery & Cosmetics*, July 2004, p. 18, from Euromonitor.

★ 1331 ★

Personal Care Products
SIC: 2844; NAICS: 325611, 32562

Leading Cosmetics/Toiletries Makers in Eastern Europe, 2003

Skin care increased 29% from 2002 - 2003. Total market size was $12,446.7 million.

Procter & Gamble	9.4%
Avon Products	6.5
Beiersdorf	5.7
L'Oreal Groupe	5.6
Unilever	5.4
Henkel	5.2
Oriflame International	4.6
Colgate-Palmolive	3.2
Gillette	3.0
Other	51.4

Source: *Soap Perfumery & Cosmetics*, November 2004, p. 19, from Euromonitor.

★ 1332 ★

Personal Care Products
SIC: 2844; NAICS: 325611, 32562

Leading Cosmetics/Toiletries Makers in Indonesia, 2003

Sales grew about 17% in 2003 to bring the cosmetics and toiletries sector to Rp 9.6 trillion. However, much of the value growth comes from price increases because of the country's 9% inflation rate. Market shares are estimated.

	($ mil.)	Share
Unilever	$ 41	41.0%
Procter & Gamble	10	10.0
Ultra Prima Abadi PT	5	5.0
Sayap Mas Utama PT	4	4.0
Other	40	40.0

Source: *Soap, Perfumery & Cosmetics Asia*, August 2004, p. 10, from Euromonitor.

★ 1333 ★
Personal Care Products
SIC: 2844; NAICS: 325611, 32562

Leading Cosmetics/Toiletries Makers in Japan, 2003

The market was valued at 2,542.5 billion yen for the year, with skin care taking in 861.4 billion yen, hair care with 594.1 billion and cosmetics with 422 million.

Shiseido	15.9%
Kanebo Ltd.	12.6
Kao Corp.	11.7
Kose Corp.	6.4
Lion Corp.	5.3
Procter & Gamble	4.4
Unilever	4.0
Mandom Corp.	2.6
Other	37.1

Source: *Soap, Perfumery & Cosmetics Asia*, May 2004, p. 16, from Euromonitor.

★ 1334 ★
Personal Care Products
SIC: 2844; NAICS: 325611, 32562

Leading Cosmetics/Toiletries Makers Worldwide, 2004

The United States has the largest market size at $45.6 billion, followed by Japan $30.7 billion and France $14 billion.

L'Oreal	10.0%
Procter & Gamble	8.8
Unilever	8.2
Estee Lauder	4.4
Colgate-Palmolive	4.0
Gillette	3.8
Beiersdorf	3.1
Avon Products	3.1
Shiseido	3.0
J&J	2.1
Private label	2.2
Other	47.3

Source: *Chemical Market Reporter*, May 9, 2005, p. 15, from Euromonitor.

★ 1335 ★
Personal Care Products
SIC: 2844; NAICS: 325611, 32562

Leading Cosmetics/Toiletries Markets in Belgium, 2003

The industry is expected to grow from $709.1 million in 2003 to $819 million in 2008.

Fragrances	23.8%
Make-up	23.3
Personal hygiene	20.7
Hair care	19.0
Skin care	13.2

Source: *Datamonitor Industry Market Research*, November 1, 2004, p. NA, from Datamonitor.

★ 1336 ★
Personal Care Products
SIC: 2844; NAICS: 325611, 32562

Leading Cosmetics/Toiletries Markets in France, 2003

The cosmetics and toiletries market slowed down in 2003, with the 3.5% growth down from the 4.9% the previous year. Sales are in millions of euros.

	(mil.)	Share
Facial skin care	1,985.36	18.54%
Hair care	1,901.49	17.76
Women's fragrance	1,459.11	13.63
Color cosmetics	1,151.02	10.75
Men's lines	904.30	8.45
Bathroom products	693.77	6.48
Hair styling	595.58	5.56
Deodorants	588.14	5.49
Oral hygiene	517.04	4.83
Other	910.20	8.50

Source: *Soap Perfumery & Cosmetics*, December 2004, p. 18, from source calculations based on the Federation des Industries de la Parfumerie.

★ 1337 ★

Personal Care Products

SIC: 2844; NAICS: 325611, 32562

Leading Cosmetics/Toiletries Markets in Italy, 2003

Leading channels of the cosmetics industry in Italy: mass distribution with 2,552.4 million euros, perfumeries with 1288.6 million, chemists 560.2 million.

	(mil.)	Share
Hair products	1,189.4	16.8%
Body care products	1,152.7	16.3
Facial skin care	1,039.6	14.7
Personal hygiene products	1,028.1	14.5
Alcoholic perfumery	816.1	14.1
Lip products	293.3	7.5
Facial make-up	278.5	6.9
Eye make-up	227.9	4.6
Hand care products	156.2	3.6

Source: *Soap Perfumery & Cosmetics*, May 2004, p. 34, from Euromonitor and Unipro.

★ 1338 ★

Personal Care Products

SIC: 2844; NAICS: 325611, 32562

Leading Cosmetics/Toiletries Markets in Spain, 2003

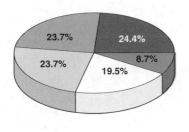

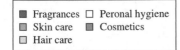

Total sales were 3.9 billion euros in 2003 up from 3.7 billion in 2002. By distribution channel: mass market 49.2%, select 27.8%, Pharmacy 9.4%, hair salons 8.0% and direct sales 5.6%.

Fragrances	24.4%
Skin care	23.7
Hair care	23.7
Peronal hygiene	19.5
Cosmetics	8.7

Source: *Soap Perfumery & Cosmetics*, June 2004, p. 18, from Stanpa.

★ 1339 ★

Personal Care Products

SIC: 2844; NAICS: 325611, 32562

Leading Cosmetics/Toiletries Markets in Western Europe

Market shares are shown in percent.

Germany	19.4%
France	17.9
United Kingdom	14.7
Other	48.0

Source: *Cosmetics International*, January 14, 2005, p. 1, from Industrial Association for Body Care Products and Detergents.

★ 1340 ★

Personal Care Products

SIC: 2844; NAICS: 325611, 32562

Leading Cosmetics/Toiletries Markets Worldwide

In 2003, spending on cosmetics & toiletries reached $201 billion. The United States and Japan represent 33% of the market. Both countries have high per capita spending. Luxury items still sold well in spite of tough economic conditions. Brazil increased 114% obetween 2002 and 2003.

	($ bil.)	Share
United States	$ 45.4	22.59%
Japan	21.9	10.90
France	12.1	6.02
Germany	11.3	5.62
United Kingdom	10.1	5.02
Italy	8.5	4.23
Brazil	7.3	3.63
China	6.0	2.99
Spain	5.7	2.84
Russia	5.3	2.64
Other	67.4	33.53

Source: *Global Cosmetic Industry*, December 2004, p. 52, from Euromonitor.

★ 1341 ★

Personal Care Products

SIC: 2844; NAICS: 325611, 32562

Men's Care Market in the U.K., 2004

Men's care products have grown from $288 million in August 2002 to $330 million in August 2004.

Deodorants	33.0%
Shaving preps	11.0
Post-shave	3.3

Continued on next page.

★ 1341 ★

[Continued]
Personal Care Products
SIC: 2844; NAICS: 325611, 32562

Men's Care Market in the U.K., 2004

Men's care products have grown from $288 million in August 2002 to $330 million in August 2004.

Skin care	0.7%
Other	.52.0

Source: *B&T Weekly*, September 20, 2004, p. NA, from ACNielsen.

★ 1342 ★

Personal Care Products
SIC: 2844; NAICS: 325611, 32562

Men's Care Market in Western Europe, 2003

Retail sales are shown in millions of dollars.

	($ mil.)	Share
Razors and blades	$ 2,303.9	42.94%
Deodorants	1,168.3	21.77
Pre-shave	751.1	14.00
Hair care	369.6	6.89
Bath & shower	323.5	6.03
Post-shave	301.8	5.62
Skin care	147.2	2.74

Source: *Global Cosmetic Industry*, February 2005, p. 42, from Euromonitor.

★ 1343 ★

Personal Care Products
SIC: 2844; NAICS: 325611, 32562

Personal Care Industry in Argentina, 2003 and 2005

With a population of 40 million, Argentina offers a significant opportunity for growth.

	2003	2005
Hair care	$ 752.0	$ 803.6
Cosmetic coloring	355.2	423.1
Deodorants	344.1	372.1
Fragrances	333.1	344.7
Skin care	327.2	357.1
Bath and shower products	236.0	247.4
Men's shygiene	218.8	240.6
Oral hygiene	208.9	233.8
Baby care	28.6	29.4
Solar care	27.5	29.5

Source: "US & FCS Market Research Reports." [online] from http://www.stat-usa.gov [Published September 30, 2003], from Euromonitor.

★ 1344 ★

Personal Care Products
SIC: 2844; NAICS: 325611, 32562

Personal Care Industry Worldwide, 2003

Market sizes are shown based on retail sales in millions of dollars.

Hair care	$ 42,491.8
Skin care	38,481.4
Color cosmetics	28,055.0
Fragrances	22,408.9
Bath and shower	20,701.2
Oral hygiene	20,335.9
Men's grooming	16,221.2
Deodorants	9,242.8
Sun care	4,302.5

Source: *Household & Personal Products Industry*, July 2004, p. 76, from Euromonitor.

★ 1345 ★

Personal Care Products
SIC: 2844; NAICS: 325611, 32562

Top Body Care Brands Worldwide, 2003

The world market is worth $7.2 billion.

Nivea Body	.14.9%
Vaseline Intensive Care	5.5
Avon	5.2
Dove	3.3
Clarins	2.9
Jergens	2.2
Bath & Body Works	2.2
Neutrogena	1.6
Lubriderm	1.5
Private label	3.2
Other	.57.5

Source: *Global Cosmetic Industry*, August 2004, p. 41, from Freedonia Group.

★ 1346 ★

Personal Care Products
SIC: 2844; NAICS: 325611, 32562

Top Body Care Firms Worldwide, 2003

The world market is worth $201.4 billion.

L'Oreal Groupe	.10.0%
Procter & Gamble Co.	9.0
Unilever	8.7
Colgate-Palmolive	4.1
Gillette Co.	3.9

Continued on next page.

★ 1346 ★

[Continued]
Personal Care Products
SIC: 2844; NAICS: 325611, 32562

Top Body Care Firms Worldwide, 2003

The world market is worth $201.4 billion.

Estee Lauder	3.2%
Beiersdorf	3.2
Shiseido Co Ltd.	2.5
Avon Products	2.5
Kao Corp.	2.4
Johnson & Johnson	2.1
Private label	2.4
Other	45.3

Source: *Global Cosmetic Industry*, August 2004, p. 41, from Eurmonitor.

★ 1347 ★

Personal Care Products
SIC: 2844; NAICS: 325611, 32562

Top Men's Grooming Brands Worldwide, 2003

Market shares are shown in percent.

Gillette Mach 3	8.5%
Wilkinson Sword/Schick	6.7
Axe/Lynx/Ego	4.7
Gillette Series	3.9
Gillette Prestobarba	3.6
Nivea for Men	3.5
Gillette Sensor Excel	3.5
Gillette Sensor	2.6
Gillette	2.3
Old Spice	2.1
Bic	2.1
Other	56.5

Source: *Soap, Perfumery & Cosmetics*, December 2004, p. 26, from Euromonitor.

★ 1348 ★

Personal Care Products
SIC: 2844; NAICS: 325611, 32562

Top Men's Grooming Categories Worldwide, 2003

Market shares are shown in percent.

Men's razors and blades	42.4%
Men's deodorants	20.7
Men's hair care	13.6
Men's pre-shave	11.0
Men's post shave	4.6%
Other	7.7

Source: *Soap, Perfumery & Cosmetics*, December 2004, p. 26, from Euromonitor.

★ 1349 ★

Personal Care Products
SIC: 2844; NAICS: 325611, 32562

Top Men's Grooming Product Makers Worldwide

Fragrances took 20.7% of sales, followed by personal cleansing products 19.9%, hair care 19.5%, deodorants and antiperspirants with 15.9%.

Gillette	35.0%
Unilever	8.0
Energizer Holdings	7.0
Beiersdorf	4.0
Procter & Gamble	3.0
Shiseido	2.0
Mandom	2.0
L'Oreal	2.0
Colgate-Palmolive	2.0
Bic SA	2.0
Private label	3.0
Other	30.0

Source: *Chemical Market Reporter*, May 9, 2005, p. 22, from Euromonitor.

★ 1350 ★

Personal Care Products
SIC: 2844; NAICS: 325611, 32562

Top Personal Lubricant Brands, 2005

Market shares are shown based on sales at food stores, drug stores and mass merchandisers (excluding Wal-Mart) for the 52 weeks ended January 23, 2005.

KY Warming Liquid	23.1%
KY	15.6
KY Liquid	10.9
Astroglide	10.6
Private label	11.3
Other	28.5

Source: *Grocery Headquarters*, April 2005, p. 113, from Information Resources Inc.

★ 1351 ★
Personal Care Products
SIC: 2844; NAICS: 325611, 32562

Top Personal Lubricant Makers, 2005

Market shares are shown based on sales at food stores, drug stores and mass merchandisers (excluding Wal-Mart) for the 52 weeks ended January 23, 2005.

Johnson & Johnson	.71.4%
Biofilm	.12.0
Trigg Labs	2.0
Upsher-Smith Labs	0.6
Private label	.11.3
Other	2.7

Source: *Grocery Headquarters*, April 2005, p. 113, from Information Resources Inc.

★ 1352 ★
Shaving Needs
SIC: 2844; NAICS: 325611, 32562

Men's Shaving Market in the U.K.

Market shares are shown in percent for shaving and men's skin care industry.

Gillette	.60.0%
King of Shaves	.11.6
Nivea for Men	7.3
Other	.21.1

Source: *Market Europe*, April 1, 2005, p. NA, from Information Resources Inc.

★ 1353 ★
Shaving Needs
SIC: 2844; NAICS: 325611, 32562

Top Shaving Cream Brands, 2004

Brands are ranked by sales at food stores, drug stores and mass merchandisers (but not Wal-Mart).

	($ mil.)	Share
Skintimate	$ 53.4	19.78%
Edge	45.8	16.96
Gillette Series	29.1	10.78
Gillette Satin Care	19.0	7.04
Gillette Foamy	18.7	6.93
Barbasol	13.1	4.85
Edge Active Care	11.9	4.41
Colgate	11.6	4.30
Aveeno	8.2	3.04
Private label	13.6	5.04
Other	45.6	16.89

Source: *MMR*, April 25, 2005, p. 67, from Information Resources Inc.

★ 1354 ★
Shaving Needs
SIC: 2844; NAICS: 325611, 32562

Top Shaving Cream Makers, 2004

Market shares are shown for the food, drug and mass merchandisers (excluding Wal-Mart) for the 52 weeks ended October 31, 2004.

S.C. Johnson	.43.7%
Gillette	.27.5
Ferio	5.4
Colgate	4.5
Private label	5.2
Other	.13.7

Source: *Grocery Headquarters*, December 2004, p. 54, from Information Resources Inc.

★ 1355 ★
Shaving Needs
SIC: 2844; NAICS: 325611, 32562

Top Shaving Lotions/Cologne/Talc Brands, 2005

Market shares are shown based on sales for drug stores for the 52 weeks ended February 20, 2005.

Axe	.11.4%
Old Spice	4.7
Drakkar Noir	3.7
Stetson	3.5
Brut	3.0
Eternity for Men	2.8
Jovan Musk for Men	2.7
Cool Water	2.6
Nivea for Men	2.5
Obsession for Men	2.4
Private label	2.8
Other	.57.9

Source: *Chain Drug Review*, March 28, 2005, p. 24, from Information Resources Inc.

★ 1356 ★
Skin Care
SIC: 2844; NAICS: 32562

Anti-Aging Skin Care Sales Worldwide

Sales are shown in billions of dollars.

2000	.$ 5.8
2001	6.2
2002	6.9
2003	8.5
2004	9.9

Source: *Time Inside Business*, May 2005, p. A17, from Euromonitor.

★ 1357 ★
Skin Care
SIC: 2844; NAICS: 32562

Largest Premium Face Care Makers in the U.K., 2003

The premium facial skin care market is worth 153 million pounds. The overall market was worth 531 million pounds, up 37% from 1999. An aging population has helped the market developed.

Lauder Group	.35.0%
Clarins	.21.0
L'Oreal	.15.0
Elizabeth Arden	.13.0
Other	.16.0

Source: *Marketing*, September 2, 2004, p. 32, from Mintel.

★ 1358 ★
Skin Care
SIC: 2844; NAICS: 32562

Men's Prestige Face Care Sales, 2004

Sales are shown in millions of dollars.

	($ mil.)	Share
Facial skin care	$ 47.6	50.21%
Treatment/shave	14.7	15.51
Moisturizers	12.8	13.50
Exfoliators	7.0	7.38
Cleansers	5.8	6.12
Eye products	3.1	3.27
Anti-aging	2.6	2.74
Other	1.2	1.27

Source: *Beauty Biz*, April 1, 2005, p. 16, from NPD Beauty Care.

★ 1359 ★
Skin Care
SIC: 2844; NAICS: 32562

Top Face Care Brands in France, 2003

Market shares are shown in percent.

Nivea Visage	.11.5%
Demo Expertise	.8.7
Yves Rocher	.7.5
Diademine	.7.3
Clarins	.6.4
Lancome	.3.9
Avene	.3.6
Vichy	.2.9
Other	.48.2

Source: *Soap, Perfumery & Cosmetics*, December 2004, p. 20, from Euromonitor.

★ 1360 ★
Skin Care
SIC: 2844; NAICS: 32562

Top Face Care Brands in Germany, 2003

Market shares are shown in percent.

Nivea Visage	.18.1%
Dermo Expertise	.9.2
Oil of Olay	.6.2
Nivea Vital	.5.2
Jade	.3.8
Aok	.3.7
Bebe	.3.6
Diadermine	.3.2
Lancome	.2.9
Other	.44.1

Source: *Soap Perfumery & Cosmetics*, October 2004, p. 18, from Beiersdorf.

★ 1361 ★
Skin Care
SIC: 2844; NAICS: 32562

Top Face Cleanser Brands, 2004

Market shares are shown based on drug store sales for the year ended October 31, 2004.

Pond's	.7.7%
Olay Daily Facials	.7.1
Cetaphil	.6.6
Olay	.4.4
Neutrogena Deep Clean	.4.4
Clean & Clear	.4.2
Biore	.3.3
St. Ives Swiss Formula	.3.2
Neutrogena	.3.2
Noxzema	.2.9
Private label	.5.3
Other	.47.7

Source: *Chain Drug Review*, January 31, 2005, p. 36, from Information Resources Inc.

★ 1362 ★
Skin Care
SIC: 2844; NAICS: 32562

Top Face Moisturizer Brands, 2005

Brands are ranked by supermarket, drug store and discount store sales (excluding Wal-Mart) for the 52 weeks ended December 26, 2004.

	($ mil.)	Share
Olay	$ 43.4	16.51%
Olay Complete	33.1	12.60

Continued on next page.

★ 1362 ★
[Continued]
Skin Care
SIC: 2844; NAICS: 32562

Top Face Moisturizer Brands, 2005

Brands are ranked by supermarket, drug store and discount store sales (excluding Wal-Mart) for the 52 weeks ended December 26, 2004.

	($ mil.)	Share
Ponds Facial	$ 18.6	7.08%
Neutrogena	15.9	6.05
Aveeno	13.0	4.95
Neutrogena Healthy Skin	10.5	4.00
Neutrogena Healthy Defense	9.7	3.69
Dove Essential Nutrients	9.5	3.61
L'Oreal Dermo Expertise Refinish . .	8.3	3.16
Olay Complete Defense	6.4	2.44
Other	94.4	35.92

Source: *MMR*, March 7, 2005, p. 21, from Information Resources Inc.

★ 1363 ★
Skin Care
SIC: 2844; NAICS: 32562

Top Face Moisturizers, 2004

Market shares are shown based on sales at food stores, drug stores and mass merchandisers (but not Wal-Mart).

	($ mil.)	Share
Olay	$ 43.4	16.51%
Olay Complete	33.1	12.60
Pond's	18.6	7.08
Neutrogena Moisture	15.9	6.05
Aveeno	13.0	4.95
Nuetrogena Healthy Skin	10.5	4.00
Neutrogena Healthy Defense	9.7	3.69
Dove Essentials Nutrients	9.5	3.61
L'Oreal Dermo Expertise	8.3	3.16
Olay Complete Defense	6.4	2.44
Other	94.4	35.92

Source: *MMR*, April 25, 2005, p. 67, from Information Resources Inc.

★ 1364 ★
Skin Care
SIC: 2844; NAICS: 32562

Top Hand and Body Lotions, 2004

Brands are ranked by sales at food stores, drug stores and mass merchandisers (but not Wal-Mart).

	($ mil.)	Share
Vaseline Intensive Care	$ 57.7	7.77%
Nivea	51.2	6.89
Aveeno	47.3	6.37
Lubriderm	36.4	4.90
Eucerin	27.4	3.69
Cetaphil	26.9	3.62
Curel	25.9	3.49
Jergens	24.1	3.24
St. Ives Swiss Formula	23.6	3.18
Jergens Ultra	22.6	3.04
Private label	45.7	6.15
Other	354.2	47.67

Source: *MMR*, April 25, 2005, p. 67, from Information Resources Inc.

★ 1365 ★
Skin Care
SIC: 2844; NAICS: 32562

Top Hand/Lotion Makers, 2004

Market shares are shown based on sales at food stores, drug stores and mass merchandisers (but not Wal-Mart) for the 52 weeks ended June 13, 2004.

Andrew Jergens	14.0%
Beiersdorf	13.3
Chesebrough-Pond's	10.6
Johnson & Johnson	8.4
Pfizer	7.7
Other	46.0

Source: *Grocery Headquarters*, August 2004, p. S88, from Information Resources Inc.

★ 1366 ★
Skin Care
SIC: 2844; NAICS: 32562

Top Skin Care Brands Worldwide

Market sizes of various sectors based on sales: skin care was $38,481.4 million, facial care $29,903.6 million, body care $7,216.3 million and hand care with $1,361.5 milion.

Nivea Visage	4.0%
Avon	3.9
L'Oreal Dermo-Expertise	3.2
Nive Body	3.0

Continued on next page.

★ 1366 ★

[Continued]
Skin Care
SIC: 2844; NAICS: 32562

Top Skin Care Brands Worldwide

Market sizes of various sectors based on sales: skin care was $38,481.4 million, facial care $29,903.6 million, body care $7,216.3 million and hand care with $1,361.5 milion.

Olay	2.8%
Estee Lauder	2.5
Lancome	2.4
Clinique	2.4
Shiseido	2.0
Pond's	2.0
Other	71.8

Source: *Soap Perfumery & Cosmetics*, June 2004, p. 22, from Euromonitor.

★ 1367 ★

Skin Care
SIC: 2844; NAICS: 32562

Top Suncreen/Insect Repellants, 2004

Brands are ranked by sales at food stores, drug stores and mass merchandisers (but not Wal-Mart).

	($ mil.)	Share
Coppertone Bug & Sun	$ 1.8	47.37%
Off Skintastic	1.6	42.11
Sun & Bug Stuff	0.3	7.89
Other	0.1	2.63

Source: *MMR*, April 25, 2005, p. 67, from Information Resources Inc.

★ 1368 ★

Sun Care
SIC: 2844; NAICS: 32562

Top Sun Care Brands, 2004

Market shares are shown in percent. Sun protection products saw $823.3 million in sales, aftersun products totalled $24.3 million and self-tanning products saw $244 million in sales.

Coppertone	16.4%
Banana Boat	13.3
Neutrogena	12.8
Hawaiian Tropic	6.5
No-Ad	5.0
Estee-Lauder	2.6
Ombrelle	1.6
Lancome	1.5
Clinique	1.5
Bain de Soleil	1.4

Private label	6.8%
Other	30.6

Source: *Soap, Perfumery & Cosmetics*, April 2005, p. 32, from Euromonitor.

★ 1369 ★

Sun Care
SIC: 2844; NAICS: 32562

Top Sun Care Brands in Africa/Middle East, 2003

Market shares are shown in percent.

Piz Buin	24.6%
Estee Lauder	12.0
Suncelle	10.2
Tropitone	9.6
Nivea Sun	4.1
Other	39.5

Source: *Global Cosmetic Industry*, November 2004, p. 32, from Euromonitor.

★ 1370 ★

Sun Care
SIC: 2844; NAICS: 32562

Top Sun Care Brands in Australasia, 2003

Market shares are shown in percent.

Ambre Solaire	33.2%
Le Tan	31.6
Clarins	9.8
Estee Lauder	5.2
Coppertone	4.1
Other	16.1

Source: *Global Cosmetic Industry*, November 2004, p. 32, from Euromonitor.

★ 1371 ★

Sun Care
SIC: 2844; NAICS: 32562

Top Sun Care Brands in Eastern Europe, 2003

Market shares are shown in percent.

Nivea Sun	15.8%
Ambre Solaire	13.9
Dr Trena Eris	12.2
Soraya	6.2
Nature Sun	3.5
Other	48.4

Source: *Global Cosmetic Industry*, November 2004, p. 32, from Euromonitor.

★ 1372 ★
Sun Care
SIC: 2844; NAICS: 32562

Top Sun Care Brands in Latin America, 2003

Market shares are shown in percent.

Nivea Sun	9.6%
Avon	9.4
Australian Gold	6.8
Sundown	4.6
Banana Boat	4.0
Other	65.6

Source: *Global Cosmetic Industry*, November 2004, p. 32, from Euromonitor.

★ 1373 ★
Sun Care
SIC: 2844; NAICS: 32562

Top Sun Care Brands in Russia, 2003

Of the $48.6 million market, mass market brands took $23.5 million, sun protection $15.6 million, aftersun products took $8.7 million and premium $0.8 million. Department stores took nearly half (48%) of sales.

Nivea Sun	28.7%
Ambre Solaire	18.1
Johnson's	7.7
Green Mama	6.7
Molochko Posle Zagara	2.9
Linda	1.0
Other	34.9

Source: *European Cosmetic Markets*, April 2004, p. 237, from Euromonitor.

★ 1374 ★
Sun Care
SIC: 2844; NAICS: 32562

Top Sun Care Brands in the U.K., 2003

Sun protection products take about 80% of the sun care market, aftersun took 13% and self tanning took 8%.

Boots	23.0%
Garnier Ambre Solaire	19.0
Beiersdorf Nivea Sun	16.0
Johnson & Johnson	8.0
Avon Bronze	8.0
Other	26.0

Source: *Marketing*, February 23, 2005, p. 38, from Mintel.

★ 1375 ★
Sun Care
SIC: 2844; NAICS: 32562

Top Sun Care Brands Worldwide, 2003

The global industry was worth 4.3 billion euros in 2003. Sun protection took 3.5 billion of the total, followed by self tanning with 462.5 million.

Nivea Sun	11.7%
Ambre Solaire	7.2
Coppertone	6.1
Banana Boat	4.0
Neutrogena	3.1
Delial	2.3
Hawaiian Tropic	2.1
Piz Buin	1.8
Soltan	1.6
Clarins	1.5
Private label	5.3
Other	53.4

Source: *Soap Perfumery & Cosmetics*, April 2004, p. 64, from Euromonitor.

★ 1376 ★
Sun Care
SIC: 2844; NAICS: 32562

Top Sun Tan Lotion Makers, 2004

Companies are ranked by sales in millions of dollars at food stores, drug stores and mass merchandisers (excluding Wal-Mart) for the 52 weeks ended December 26, 2004.

	($ mil.)	Share
Schering-Plough	$ 122.79	29.37%
Playtex	87.64	20.96
Tanning Research Labs	70.66	16.90
L'Oreal	13.32	3.19
Solar Cosmetics Lab	10.26	2.45
Chattem Inc.	8.54	2.04
European Tanning System	5.42	1.30
Sun & Skin Care Research	4.04	0.97
Other	95.43	22.82

Source: *Household and Personal Products Industry*, March 2005, p. 82, from Information Resources Inc.

★ 1377 ★
Paints and Coatings
SIC: 2851; NAICS: 32551

Architectural Coatings Segments, 2003

Industry shipments were the highest ever with 1,316.6 million gallons having a value of $16,932.9 million. Architectual coatings shipments were 772.8 million gallons, representing 58.7% of the total paint and coating industry.

	(mil.)	Share
Flat	315.9	40.68%
Semigloss	201.9	26.00
Primers	100.6	12.95
Stains/sealers	38.9	5.01
Gloss/enamel	19.5	2.51
Clears/sealers/varnish	13.0	1.67
Decks & floors	3.7	0.48
Other	83.1	10.70

Source: *Paint & Coatings Industry*, February 2005, p. 60, from U.S. Census Bureau.

★ 1378 ★
Paints and Coatings
SIC: 2851; NAICS: 32551

Automotive Coatings Industry in North America, 2003

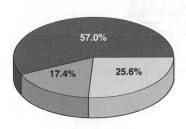

The revenues from this market are expected to reach $2 billion by 2010.

Body	.57.0%
Components	.17.4
Other	.25.6

Source: *Advanced Coatings & Surface Technology*, November 2004, p. 12, from Frost & Sullivan.

★ 1379 ★
Paints and Coatings
SIC: 2851; NAICS: 32551

Automotive Interior Coatings in Europe, 2002

Total revenue for the year was 256 million euros, reflecting 78,000 tons.

Molded skins	.41.0%
Synthetic leather	.22.0
Other	.37.0

Source: *Advanced Coatings & Surface Technology*, November 2004, p. 12, from Frost & Sullivan.

★ 1380 ★
Paints and Coatings
SIC: 2851; NAICS: 32551

Paint Industry, 2002-2003

The United States experienced rather lackluster sales in 2003. Analysts claim the global market saw much better results however. The U.S. represents about $18 billion of the $70 billion global market. Sales are shown in billions of dollars.

	2002	2003	Share
Architectural	$ 7.12	$ 7.63	47.30%
Product coatings	5.55	5.26	32.61
Special-purpose coatings	3.35	3.24	20.09

Source: *Chemical & Engineering News*, October 18, 2004, p. 26, from U.S. Bureau of the Census.

★ 1381 ★
Paints and Coatings
SIC: 2851; NAICS: 32551

Paint Industry in Mexico

Market shares are shown in percent.

Comex	.54.0%
Other	.46.0

Source: *Denver Post*, September 29, 2004, p. NA.

★ 1382 ★
Paints and Coatings
SIC: 2851; NAICS: 32551

Paints and Coatings Industry Worldwide

The architectural segment is shown by region.

	($ bil.)	Share
Europe	$ 9.83	32.20%
Asia Pacific	8.00	26.20
North America	6.50	21.29
Other	6.20	20.31

Source: *Chemical Market Reporter*, April 18, 2005, p. 18, from Chemark Consulting Group.

★ 1383 ★
Paints and Coatings
SIC: 2851; NAICS: 32551

Special Coatings Demand, 2003

The segment represents roughly a third of the overall $16.1 billion coatings market. Top players include PPG, DuPont, Azko, RPM and BASF.

Auto refinishing	50.0%
Industrial, exterior	19.0
Traffic marking	8.0
Marine/offshore	8.0
Aerosol	7.0
Industrial, interior	7.0
Other	1.0

Source: *Chemical Market Reporter*, October 25, 2004, p. FR3.

★ 1384 ★
Paints and Coatings
SIC: 2851; NAICS: 32551

Top Auto Colors in Asia, 2004

Data show percent of vehicles manufactured for the 2004 model year.

Silver/gray	37.0%
White	16.0
Blue	13.0
Black	13.0
Red	9.0
Green	4.0
Light brown	2.0
Other	6.0

Source: *PR Newswire*, December 9, 2004, p. NA, from *2004 DuPont Automotive International Color Popularity Survey*.

★ 1385 ★
Paints and Coatings
SIC: 2851; NAICS: 32551

Top Auto Colors in Europe, 2004

Data show percent of vehicles manufactured for the 2004 model year.

Silver	30.0%
Black	17.0
Blue	16.0
Gray	11.0
White/White pearl	8.0
Red	7.0
Brown	6.0
Other	5.0

Source: *PR Newswire*, December 9, 2004, p. NA, from *2004 DuPont Automotive International Color Popularity Survey*.

★ 1386 ★
Paints and Coatings
SIC: 2851; NAICS: 32551

Top Auto Colors in North America, 2004

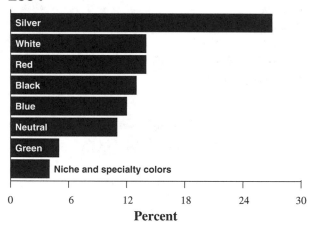

Figures are based on a survey.

Silver	27.0%
White	14.0
Red	14.0
Black	13.0
Blue	12.0
Neutral	11.0
Green	5.0
Niche and specialty colors	4.0

Source: *Detroit News*, November 4, 2004, p. 8C, from PPG Automotive.

★ 1387 ★
Paints and Coatings
SIC: 2851; NAICS: 32551
Top Auto Colors in South America, 2004

Data show percent of vehicles manufactured for the 2004 model year.

Silver	31.0%
White	16.0
Gray	15.0
Black	15.0
Red	8.0
Blue	7.0
Beige	4.0
Green	3.0
Yellow	1.0

Source: *PR Newswire*, December 9, 2004, p. NA, from *2004 DuPont Automotive International Color Popularity Survey*.

★ 1388 ★
Paints and Coatings
SIC: 2851; NAICS: 32551
Top Coatings Firms Worldwide

Firms are ranked by sales in millions of dollars.

Akzo Nobel	$ 5,900
PPG	4,830
ICI Group	4,780
Henkel	4,610
Sherwin-Williams	4,360
DuPont	3,500
BASF Coatings	2,280
Valspar	2,240
RPM	2,080
SigmaKalon	1,920
Nippon Paint	1,610
Kansai Paint	1,500

Source: *Coatings World*, July 2004, p. 24, from *Coatings World 2004 Top Companies Report*.

★ 1389 ★
Paints and Coatings
SIC: 2851; NAICS: 32551
Top Paint Makers, 2003

The architectural segment has been in the top spot for the last three years. Firms are ranked by sales in billions of dollars.

Akzo Nobel	$ 6.32
Sherwin-Williams	5.41
PPG Industries	$ 4.84
DuPont	3.73
ICI	3.68
BASF	2.44
Valspar	2.25
RPM	2.08
Sigma-Kalon	1.99
Nippon	1.87

Source: *Chemical Week*, October 20, 2004, p. 25, from The ChemQuest Group.

★ 1390 ★
Paints and Coatings
SIC: 2851; NAICS: 32551
Top Paint Makers in Europe

Companies are ranked by sales in millions of litres.

Akzo Nobel	1,280
ICI	1,100
Valspar	886
PPG	874
SigmaKalon	739
DuPont	615
BASF	500
RPM	379
DAW	330
Ostendorf	221

Source: *Polymers Paint Colour Journal*, November 2004, p. 41, from *PPCJ Yearbook 2005*.

★ 1391 ★
Paints and Coatings
SIC: 2851; NAICS: 32551
Top Paint Makers in Thailand

Market shares are shown in percent.

ICI Paints	50.0%
TOA	45.0
Other	5.0

Source: *Bangkok Post*, December 16, 2004, p. NA.

★ 1392 ★
Charcoal
SIC: 2861; NAICS: 325191
Charcoal Market

Market shares are shown in percent.

Kingsford	70.0%
Other	30.0

Source: *Knight Ridder/Tribune Business News*, December 10, 2004, p. NA.

★ 1393 ★
Organic Chemicals
SIC: 2865; NAICS: 32511

Global Phenol Market, 2007 and 2010

Demand is shown in thousands of tons.

	2007	2010	Share
Asia	3,300	3,690	39.17%
North America	2,370	2,450	26.01
Europe	2,360	2,500	26.54
Other	770	780	8.28

Source: *European Chemical News*, January 31, 2005, p. 10, from Ineos Phenol.

★ 1394 ★
Organic Chemicals
SIC: 2865; NAICS: 32511

Leading Adipic Acid Makers

Market shares are shown in percent.

Invista	.37.0%
Rhodia	.18.5
Solutia	.14.0
BASF	9.0
Raici Chinica	5.0
Other	.16.5

Source: *Chemical Week*, May 4, 2005, p. 31.

★ 1395 ★
Organic Chemicals
SIC: 2865; NAICS: 32511

Leading Ethylene Firms in Japan, 2003

Market shares are estimated based on domestic production.

Mitsubishi Chemical	.18.2%
Mitsui Chemicals	.15.5
Idemitsu Petrochemical	.13.4
Maruzen Petrochemical	.11.9
Showa Denko	8.7
Other	.32.3

Source: ''Market Share Survey Report 2003.'' [online] from http://www.nni.nikkei.co.jp [Published July 26, 2004], from Nikkei estimates.

★ 1396 ★
Organic Chemicals
SIC: 2865; NAICS: 32511

Leading Ethylene Glycol Makers

Companies are ranked by capacity in millions of pounds.

Dow Chemical	2,610
Shell	880
PD Glycol	800
Formosa Plastics	660

Source: *Chemical Market Reporter*, October 18, 2004, p. 31.

★ 1397 ★
Organic Chemicals
SIC: 2865; NAICS: 32511

Leading Ethylene Oxide Makers

Companies are ranked by capacity in millions of pounds.

Dow Chemical	2,005
Shell	1,260
Huntsman	1,015
Old World Industries	780
PD Glycol	640

Source: *Chemical Market Reporter*, October 11, 2004, p. 31.

★ 1398 ★
Organic Chemicals
SIC: 2869; NAICS: 325188

Adipic Acid Market Worldwide, 2004

Adipic acid is used in nylon66 salt, lubricants and food additives. Total capacity was 2.74 million tons with DuPont taking 38% of the market.

North America	.43.2%
West Europe	.34.3
South Korea	4.7
China	4.7
Japan	4.4
South Asia	3.6
Latin America	2.4
Other	0.6

Source: *China Chemical Reporter*, March 26, 2005, p. 18.

★ 1399 ★

Organic Chemicals

SIC: 2869; NAICS: 325188

Amino Acid Market Worldwide by Application

The worldwide value of amino acids is shown in synthesis applications. Data are in millions of dollars. Amino acids for the synthetic market is a segment of $45-75 fine chemicals industry. Amino acids are used in the formation of proteins.

	2004	2009	Share
Biotechnology and pharmaceutical applications	$ 358.3	$ 571.0	57.23%
High intensity sweeteners	354.4	426.8	42.77

Source: *Research Studies - Business Communications Inc.*, March 8, 2005, p. NA, from BCC.

★ 1400 ★

Organic Chemicals

SIC: 2869; NAICS: 325188

Diethylene Glycol Market

Demand is forecast to increase from 746 million pounds in 2003 to 800 million pounds in 2004.

Polyurethane	.22.7%
Unsaturated polyester resins	.20.2
Triethylene glycol and tetraethylene glycol	.10.0
Antifreeze blending	8.5
Solvents	8.0
Morpholine	7.0
Other	.23.6

Source: *Chemical Market Reporter*, November 8, 2004, p. 31.

★ 1401 ★

Organic Chemicals

SIC: 2869; NAICS: 325188

Ethanolamine Consumption Worldwide

MEA stands for monoethanolamine, DEA stands for diethanolamine, and TEA stands for triethanolamine.

MEA	.41.0%
DEA	.34.0
TEA and residues	.25.0

Source: *European Chemical News*, November 1, 2004, p. 18.

★ 1402 ★

Organic Chemicals

SIC: 2869; NAICS: 325188

Fatty Ester Market

There are more than 200 significant types of fatty esters. According to the source: "Fatty esters are reaction products of natural fatty carboxylix acids with alcohol, and are produced using an esterification reaction that involves elimination of water."

Food	.38.4%
Functional fluids	.21.6
Plastics	.17.6
Personal Care & cosmetics	.14.0
Other	9.1

Source: *Soap Perfumery & Cosmetics*, May 2004, p. 30, from Frost & Sullivan.

★ 1403 ★

Organic Chemicals

SIC: 2869; NAICS: 325188

FCC Market Shares

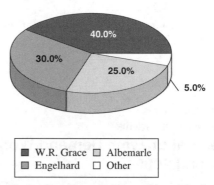

FCC stands for fluidized catalytic cracking. The industry is valued at 237,000 metric tons in 2003 and is forecast to climb to 249,000 metric tons in 2008. This will translate into a $426 million market. FCC demand is driven by EPA regulations requiring lower emissions in transportation fuels, according to the source.

W.R. Grace	.40.0%
Engelhard	.30.0
Albemarle	.25.0
Other	5.0

Source: *Chemical Week*, March 30, 2005, p. 37, from SRI Consulting.

★ 1404 ★
Organic Chemicals
SIC: 2869; NAICS: 325188
Flame Retardant Market, 2005

The industry is valued at $1.3 billion, with brominated compounds seeing the strongest growth rates.

Bromine compounds 45.0%
Phosphorous compounds 27.0
Antimony oxide 8.0
Other 20.0

Source: *Chemical Week*, March 16, 2005, p. 29, from Freedonia Group.

★ 1405 ★
Organic Chemicals
SIC: 2869; NAICS: 325188
Global Aroma Chemicals Market, 2003

The industry is valued at $1.9 billion.

Western Europe 37.0%
Asia Pacific 33.0
North America 26.0
Other 4.0

Source: *Chemical Market Reporter*, March 14, 2005, p. 8, from Information Resources Inc.

★ 1406 ★
Organic Chemicals
SIC: 2869; NAICS: 325188
Industrial Enzyme Demand Worldwide, 2004 and 2009

The global market was estimated to be worth $2 billion in 2004. The average annual growth rate is forecast to slip 3% in the next five years because of the increased number of small companies that have entered the market.

	2004	2009	Share
Technical enymes . . .	$ 1,040	$ 1,222	51.96%
Food enzymes	740	863	36.69
Animal feed enymes	220	267	11.35

Source: *Research Studies - Business Communications Inc.*, December 8, 2004, p. NA, from Business Communications Co. Inc.

★ 1407 ★
Organic Chemicals
SIC: 2869; NAICS: 325188
Leading Acetone Makers

Companies are ranked by production in thousands of tons per year.

	(000)	Share
Sunoco Chemicals	555	29.35%
Shell Chemicals	352	18.61
Ineos Phenol	273	14.44
Dow Chemical	260	13.75
Mount Vernon Phenol	211	11.16
Georgia Gulf	186	9.84
JLM Industries	31	1.64
Other	23	1.22

Source: *Chemical Week*, November 17, 2004, p. 28, from Tecnon Orbichem.

★ 1408 ★
Organic Chemicals
SIC: 2869; NAICS: 325188
Leading Formaldehyde Makers

Firms are ranked by capacity in thouands of tons per year.

Dynea 720
BASF 650
Degussa 519
Borden 380
Total 371
Formol y Derivados 280
Bayer 271

Source: *European Chemical News*, January 10, 2005, p. 17, from Nexant Chemsystems.

★ 1409 ★
Organic Chemicals
SIC: 2869; NAICS: 325188
Leading Neopentyl Glycol Makers Worldwide

Market shares are shown based on capacity.

BASF 36.0%
Eastman 23.0
Mitsubishi Gas Chemical 9.0
LG Chem 8.0
Other 24.0

Source: *Chemical Week*, July 21, 2004, p. 12, from LG Chem.

★ 1410 ★
Organic Chemicals
SIC: 2869; NAICS: 325188

Leading Paper Chemicals Makers Worldwide, 2003

The overall pulp and paper market has not performed well because of a weak economy and industry over-capacity. Hercules was the leader in the $7.1 billion industry.

Hercules	11.0%
Nalco Holding	9.0
Ciba Specialty Gifts	8.0
Kemira	6.0
Eka Chemicals	3.0
Other	63.0

Source: *Chemical Week*, February 3, 2005, p. 25.

★ 1411 ★
Organic Chemicals
SIC: 2869; NAICS: 325188

Leading Titanium Dioxide Makers Worldwide

Distribution is shown based on 4.75 million metric tons.

DuPont	23.0%
Millennium Chemicals	14.0
Kerr McGee	14.0
Huntsman Tioxide	12.0
ISK	4.0
Kemira	3.0
Other	20.0

Source: *Chemical Week*, May 26, 2004, p. 33, from Millennium Chemicals.

★ 1412 ★
Organic Chemicals
SIC: 2869; NAICS: 325188

Leading Toulene Producers in Western Europe

Companies are ranked by capacity in thousands of tons. Toulene is used as an octane booster in gasoline.

Shell	435
Huntsman	330
ExxonMobil	260
Cepsa	200
BASF	155

BP	130
FinaAntwerp-Olefins	100

Source: *European Chemical News*, December 6, 2004, p. 17, from Dewitt.

★ 1413 ★
Organic Chemicals
SIC: 2869; NAICS: 325188

Paper Chemical Market, 2003

Market shares are shown by application.

Sizing	24.0%
Wet strength	15.0
Retention & drainage	13.0
Defoaming	13.0
Biocides	12.0
Other	23.0

Source: *European Chemical News*, November 22, 2004, p. 17.

★ 1414 ★
Organic Chemicals
SIC: 2869; NAICS: 325188

SBS Consumption Worldwide

Consumption is shown in thousands of tons. SBS stands for styrene butadiene styrene.

	(000)	Share
United States	274	30.89%
West Europe	228	25.70
Japan	96	10.82
Other	289	32.58

Source: *China Chemical Reporter*, January 26, 2005, p. 23, from CNCIC Chemdata.

★ 1415 ★
Organic Chemicals
SIC: 2869; NAICS: 325199

Top End Markets Worldwide for Acylonitrile, 2002

The average annual growth rate between 1995 and 2002 was around 4.3%. Capacity in the United States and Western Europe has remained unchanged in recent years. China is expected to see strong demand in recent years, with capacity up 230,000 tons in 2003 from 500,000 tons annually in 2002.

Acylic fibers	.50.0%
ABS/AS resins	.24.0
Adipic dinitrile	.10.0
Other	.20.0

Source: *China Chemical Reporter*, November 6, 2004, p. 15, from CNCIC Chemicals.

★ 1416 ★
Organic Chemicals
SIC: 2869; NAICS: 325199

Water/Wastewater Treatment Worldwide, 2010

Suppliers of water and wastewater treatment products and services and suppliers of filtration and services will climb to $183 billion in 2010. The outsourcing of municipal and industrial treatment operations represents the largest growth market. Spending is shown in billions of dollars.

	($ bil.)	Share
Municipal wastewater	$ 50	27.32%
Municipal drinking water	50	27.32
Industrial water	47	25.68
Industrial wastewater	30	16.39
Other	6	3.28

Source: *National Driller*, January 2005, p. 10S, from McIlvaine Co.

★ 1417 ★
Insecticides
SIC: 2879; NAICS: 32532

Insecticide Sales, 2003

Supermarket sales are shown in millions of dollars.

Ant & roach, reg. Aerosol	$ 61.72
Insect repellants	45.90
Indoor foggers	19.83
Wasp & hornet	17.52
Rodenticides	16.16

Flying insect, aerosol	$ 12.83
Mouse & rat & mole traps	12.23
Flea & tick, aerosol	6.40
Outdoor foggers	6.05
House & garden, aerosol	4.61

Source: *Progressive Grocer*, Sept. 15, 2004, p. 26, from *2004 Progressive Grocer Consumer Expenditure Survey.*

★ 1418 ★
Insecticides
SIC: 2879; NAICS: 32532

Maize Insecticide Industry in India

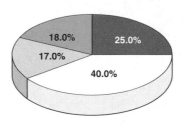

Market shares are shown in percent.

Syngenta	.25.0%
Bayer CropScience	.18.0
BASF	.17.0
Other	.40.0

Source: *Asia Africa Intelligence Wire*, July 1, 2004, p. NA, from Chemical Business NewsBase.

★ 1419 ★
Insecticides
SIC: 2879; NAICS: 32532

Top Pest Control Brands, 2005

Brands are ranked by supermarket, drug store and discount outlet sales (excluding Wal-Mart) for the 52 weeks ended February 20, 2005.

	($ mil.)	Share
Raid Multipurpose	$ 50.7	10.92%
Raid Indoor	30.1	6.48
Deepwoods Off Outdoor	28.9	6.22
Off Outdoor	26.1	5.62
Raid Outdoor	19.5	4.20
Hot Shot Indoor	16.4	3.53
Enoz Indoor	11.4	2.45
D Con	10.7	2.30

Continued on next page.

★ 1419 ★

[Continued]
Insecticides
SIC: 2879; NAICS: 32532

Top Pest Control Brands, 2005

Brands are ranked by supermarket, drug store and discount outlet sales (excluding Wal-Mart) for the 52 weeks ended February 20, 2005.

	($ mil.)	Share
Combat Quick Kill	$ 10.7	2.30%
Raid	10.5	2.26
Other	249.4	53.70

Source: *MMR*, May 30, 2005, p. 33, from Information Resources Inc.

★ 1420 ★

Adhesives & Sealants
SIC: 2891; NAICS: 32552

Adhesives Market in Western and Central Europe, 2004

The market has been estimated at 1,280 kilotons (dry resin weight basis) in 2004.

Packaging	40.0%
Building and construcion	23.0
Various non-rigid bonding	15.0
Other	22.0

Source: *European Adhesives & Sealants*, September 2004, p. 15.

★ 1421 ★

Adhesives & Sealants
SIC: 2891; NAICS: 32552

Global Adhesives Market

The market is worth $28.4 billion. The industry has seen several important consolidations. Henkel, the global leader, recently purchased Lucky Silicone Industry Co. and plans to acquire Sovereigh Specialty Chemicals.

North America	34.1%
Western Europe	28.1
Asia Pacific	26.5
Other	11.3

Source: *Chemical Market Reporter*, October 18, 2004, p. 8, from Adhesives & Sealants Council.

★ 1422 ★

Adhesives & Sealants
SIC: 2891; NAICS: 32552

Leading Adhesive/Sealant Firms, 2004

Firms are ranked by sales in millions of dollars.

Henkel	$ 770
National Starch	575
H.B. Fuller	525
3M	310
Bostik Findley	285

Source: *Chemical Market Reporter*, March 7, 2005, p. 12, from Impact Marketing Consultants.

★ 1423 ★

Adhesives & Sealants
SIC: 2891; NAICS: 32552

Sealant Demand by Industry, 2004

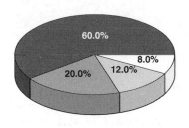

■ Construction □ Consumer
■ Transportation □ Assembly/other

Demand is valued at $1,240 million with an average growth rate placed at 2% for 2003 - 2005.

Construction	60.0%
Transportation	20.0
Consumer	12.0
Assembly/other	8.0

Source: *Adhesives & Sealants Industry*, January 2005, p. 13, from DPNA International.

★ 1424 ★

Adhesives & Sealants
SIC: 2891; NAICS: 32552

Sealant Demand by Product, 2004

Total demand was 520 million pounds.

Silicones	46.0%
Urethanes	23.2
Latex acrylic sealants	7.6
Butyl sealants	4.4

Continued on next page.

★ 1424 ★

[Continued]
Adhesives & Sealants
SIC: 2891; NAICS: 32552

Sealant Demand by Product, 2004

Total demand was 520 million pounds.

Oil based caulks	3.9%
Other	14.9

Source: *Adhesives & Sealants Industry*, January 2005, p. 13, from DPNA International and ASC.

★ 1425 ★

Adhesives & Sealants
SIC: 2891; NAICS: 32552

Top Adhesive Markets, 2004

The industry is estimated at sales of $11 billion in 2004. Distribution is shown based on revenues.

Packaging	20.0%
Construction	19.0
Rigid bonding	17.0
Transportation	15.0
Tape	13.0
Non-rigid bonding	9.0
Consumer	7.0

Source: *Chemical Market Reporter*, May 31, 2004, p. 13, from ChemQuest Group.

★ 1426 ★

Adhesives & Sealants
SIC: 2891; NAICS: 32552

Vehicular Sealant Industry Worldwide

The global industry is valued at $4.7 billion.

Cooper Standard Automotive	22.0%
Gencorp's GDX Automotive	17.0
Other	61.0

Source: *Rubber & Plastics News*, December 13, 2004, p. 15.

★ 1427 ★

Ink
SIC: 2893; NAICS: 32591

Leading Ink Firms in Europe

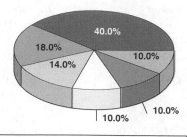

Market shares are estimated in percent. Sun's share has been placed at 35-40%. SICPA, Huber and Siegwerk all have shares between 8-10%.

Sun	40.0%
BASF/ANI Printing Inks	18.0
Flint Schmidt	14.0
Siegwerk	10.0
SICPA	10.0
Huber	10.0

Source: *Ink World*, November 2004, p. 18.

★ 1428 ★

Ink
SIC: 2893; NAICS: 32591

Ultraviolet Printing Inks, 2002

The ultraviolet ink market was estimated at $360 million in 2002.

Screen UV printing	40.0%
Sheetfed litho/letterpress	38.0
Other	22.0

Source: *Ink World*, November 2004, p. 24, from Thor Jondahl.

★ 1429 ★

Carbon Black

SIC: 2895; NAICS: 325182

Carbon Black Demand Worldwide, 2004

Demand is forecast to grow from 3.5% until 2010 when it is forecasted to reach 10.1 million tons. In 2003, demand stood at 7.9 million tons.

Europe	.25.0%
NAFTA	.23.0
China	.15.0
Japan	.11.0
Other	.26.0

Source: *European Chemical News*, February 7, 2005, p. 12, from Notch Consulting Group.

★ 1430 ★

Carbon Black

SIC: 2895; NAICS: 325182

Largest Carbon Black Producers in China

Companies are ranked by output in kilotons.

Shanghai Cabot Chemical Industrial	87.6
Chinese Rubber (Ma'anshan) Chemical	58.6
Tianjin Dolphin Carbon Black	57.2
Suzhou Baohua Carbon Black	50.1
Qingdao Degussa Chemical	41.6
Zhuzhou Xinglong Chemical Industrial Co.	33.2
Liaoning Dashiqiao Liaobin Carbon Black	31.9

Source: *China Chemical Reporter*, August 16, 2004, p. 21, from CNCIC Chemdata.

★ 1431 ★

Aerosols

SIC: 2899; NAICS: 325998

Aerosol Production in Germany, 2003

Figures are in millions of units. Output fell to 970 million tons.

	(mil.)	Share
Deodorants/antiperspirants	259	38.48%
Hairsprays	208	30.91
Hair mousse	102	15.16
Shaving foam	56	8.32
Shaving gel	15	2.23
Other personal care	33	4.90

Source: *Soap Perfumery & Cosmetics*, September 2004, p. 27, from Industrie Gemeinschaft Aerosol.

★ 1432 ★

Air Fresheners

SIC: 2899; NAICS: 325998

Auto Freshener Market

Market shares are shown in percent.

Auto Expressions	.70.0%
Other	.30.0

Source: *San Jose Mercury News*, August 27, 2004, p. NA.

★ 1433 ★

Air Fresheners

SIC: 2899; NAICS: 325998

Top Air Freshener Brands, 2005

Market shares are shown based on supermarket sales for the year ended January 23, 2005.

	($ mil.)	Share
Glade Plugins	$ 135.32	25.61%
Air Wick	84.51	15.99
Oust	56.68	10.73
Glade	43.08	8.15
Renuzit Longlast Adjustable	31.08	5.88
Lysol Neutra Air	22.22	4.21
Renuzit	20.74	3.92
Glade Wisp	16.10	3.05
Air Wick Decosphere	13.76	2.60
Febreze Air Effects	12.77	2.42
Other	92.15	17.44

Source: *Chemical Market Reporter*, March 14, 2005, p. 8, from Information Resources Inc.

★ 1434 ★

Air Fresheners

SIC: 2899; NAICS: 325998

Top Air Freshener Makers, 2004

Home fragrance sales increased to $2.6 billion in 2004. Companies are ranked by sales for the year ended July 11, 2004. Wal-Mart sales are excluded.

S.C. Johnson	.49.7%
Reckitt Benckiser	.28.6
Dial Corp.	.13.1
Vapor Products	. 0.7
California Scents	. 0.7
Beaumont Products	. 0.6
New Ideas	. 0.4
Medo Industries	. 0.4
Labs Ltd.	. 0.3

Continued on next page.

★ 1434 ★

[Continued]
Air Fresheners
SIC: 2899; NAICS: 325998

Top Air Freshener Makers, 2004

Home fragrance sales increased to $2.6 billion in 2004. Companies are ranked by sales for the year ended July 11, 2004. Wal-Mart sales are excluded.

Private label	2.4%
Other	3.1

Source: Household & Personal Products Industry, September 2004, p. 85, from Information Resources Inc.

★ 1435 ★

Air Fresheners
SIC: 2899; NAICS: 325998

Top Air Freshener Makers Worldwide, 2003

Candles take 55% of the market, followed by diffusers with 25%.

SC Johnson & Son Inc.	33.5%
Reckitt Benckiser	14.7
Sara Lee Corp.	9.0
Kobayshi Pharmaceutical	5.0
ST Chemical Co Ltd.	4.3
Dial Corp.	3.1
Koninklijke Shell Group/Royal Dutch Shell Group	2.2
Car-Freshener Corp.	2.2
Alticor Inc.	1.2
Other	24.8

Source: Global Cosmetic Industry, March 2005, p. 47, from Euromonitor.

★ 1436 ★

Air Fresheners
SIC: 2899; NAICS: 325998

Top Air Freshener Markets Worldwide, 2003

The top category of air fresheners was spray/aerosols with sales of $1,474.9 million, electric air fresheners followed with sales of $1,255.1 million, gels with $655 million, candles with $424.3 million, car air fresheners with $842.4 million.

	($ mil.)	Share
Western Europe	$ 2,001.4	36.88%
North America	1,767.6	32.57
Asia Pacific	1,012.9	18.66
Eastern Europe	208.6	3.84
Latin America	$ 185.3	3.41%
Africa and Middle East	142.2	2.62
Australasia	109.1	2.01

Source: Global Cosmetic Industry, March 2005, p. 32, from Euromonitor.

★ 1437 ★

Firestarters
SIC: 2899; NAICS: 325998

Top Firestarter Brands, 2004

Market shares are shown based on sales at food stores, drug stores and mass merchandisers (but not Wal-Mart) for the 52 weeks ended June 13, 2004.

Starter Logg	31.6%
Quick Start	21.3
Diamond Super Match	7.8
Duraflame Firestart	7.6
Pine Mountain	4.6
Fatwood	2.4
Coleman	1.5
Lightning Nugget	1.0
Village Candle	0.4
Private label	19.6
Other	2.2

Source: Grocery Headquarters, August 2004, p. S88, from Information Resources Inc.

★ 1438 ★

Firestarters
SIC: 2899; NAICS: 325998

Top Firestarter Makers, 2004

Market shares are shown based on sales at food stores, drug stores and mass merchandisers (but not Wal-Mart) for the 52 weeks ended June 13, 2004.

Conros	36.5%
Duraflame	28.9
Diamond Brands	7.8
Wood Products	2.4
Private label	19.6
Other	4.8

Source: Grocery Headquarters, August 2004, p. S88, from Information Resources Inc.

★ 1439 ★

Flavors and Fragrance
SIC: 2899; NAICS: 311942, 325199

Flavor and Fragrance Market Worldwide, 2008

Estimated demand is valued at $14.8 billion. Developing markets, especially Japan, will be the major drivers for the market.

Western Europe	.29.0%
Asia Pacific	.27.0
United States	.24.0
Other	.20.0

Source: *Chemical Week*, February 16, 2005, p. 24, from Freedonia Group.

★ 1440 ★

Pool Chemicals
SIC: 2899; NAICS: 325998

Pool/Spa Chemical Market

Market shares are shown in percent.

Clearon/Occidental/BioLab	.74.0%
Other	.26.0

Source: *Pool & Spa News*, August 20, 2004, p. 12.

★ 1441 ★

Salt
SIC: 2899; NAICS: 325199

Global Salt Consumption, 2003

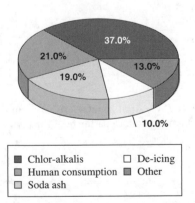

Salt production is expected to rise 20 million tons over the next five year. In 2003, total production was 223 million tons.

Chlor-alkalis	.37.0%
Human consumption	.21.0
Soda ash	.19.0

De-icing	.10.0%
Other	.13.0

Source: *European Chemical News*, August 23, 2004, p. 11, from Roskill.

★ 1442 ★

Salt
SIC: 2899; NAICS: 325199

How Salt is Used, 2004

Total value of salt produced $1.2 billion. The 29 companies involved in the industry operated 64 facilities in 15 states.

Highway deicing	.37.0%
Distributors	.8.0
Industrial	.6.0
Food	.4.0
Agricultural	.3.0
Water treatment	.2.0
Other	.40.0

Source: *Mineral Commodities Summaries 2005*, January 2005, p. 20, from U.S. Geological Survey, U.S. Department of the Interior.

★ 1443 ★

Salt
SIC: 2899; NAICS: 325199

Largest Salt Producing Nations, 2004

The surge of industrial projects in China caused demand to outpace domestic capacity. In the United States, demand is expected to be lower in 2005 than in 2004.

	(000)	Share
United States	45,100	22.82%
China	34,000	17.21
Germany	16,000	8.10
India	15,000	7.59
Canada	13,300	6.73
Mexico	8,000	4.05
Brazil	6,100	3.09
United Kingdom	5,800	2.94
Other	54,300	27.48

Source: *Mineral Commodities Summaries 2005*, January 2005, p. 20, from U.S. Geological Survey, U.S. Department of the Interior.

SIC 29 - Petroleum and Coal Products

★ 1444 ★

Gasoline

SIC: 2911; NAICS: 32411

Gasoline Industry in Russia, 2001 and 2003

Gasoline consumption has been on the increase since 2000 after the country began to show recovery from the 1998 economic census. Also, consumption has increased as car ownership increases in the country.

	2001	2003
Cars	51.0%	63.0%
Buses	21.0	17.0
Trucks	15.0	13.0
Other	13.0	7.0

Source: *FSU Energy*, November 5, 2004, p. 6.

★ 1445 ★

Gasoline

SIC: 2911; NAICS: 32411

Leading Gasoline Firms in Japan, 2003

Market shares are estimated based on domestic sales.

Nippon Oil	22.7%
Exxon Mobil	19.2
Showa Shell Seikyu	14.1
Idemitsu Kosan	13.8
Cosmo Oil	11.0
Other	19.2

Source: "Market Share Survey Report 2003." [online] from http://www.nni.nikkei.co.jp [Published July 26, 2004], from Nikkei estimates.

★ 1446 ★

Gasoline

SIC: 2911; NAICS: 32411

Leading Gasoline Refiners, 2003

Market shares are shown based on sales of 138.6 billion gallons.

ConocoPhillips	15.14%
ExxonMobil	12.94

BP	12.35%
Shell	11.93
Citgo	11.01
MarathonAshland Petroleum	8.54
Chevron Texaco	7.40
Amerada Hess	5.12
Sunoco	4.59
Valero	4.40
Other	7.05

Source: *National Petroleum News*, July 15, 2004, p. 106, from company reports.

★ 1447 ★

Petroleum Refining

SIC: 2911; NAICS: 32411

Largest Refiners, 2004

Valero Energy and Premcor announced plans recently to merge creating the world's largest crude oil company, assuming it passes anti-trust hurdles. The 149 refineries can handle nearly 17 million barrels of crude oil a year. Demand is increasing. Companies are ranked by capacity in millions of barrels a day.

	(mil.)	Share
Valero/Premcor	3.3	19.53%
ConocoPhillips	2.2	13.02
ExxonMobil	1.8	10.65
BP	1.5	8.88
ChevronTexaco	1.0	5.92
Other	7.1	42.01

Source: *USA TODAY*, April 26, 2005, p. 3B, from Energy Information Administration, Department of Energy.

★ 1448 ★

Petroleum Refining

SIC: 2911; NAICS: 32411

Leading Petroleum Additive Makers in North America

Market shares are shown in percent.

Crompton 12.0%
Ciba 6.0
Oronite 4.0
Uniqema 3.0
ExxonMobil 2.0
Other 73.0

Source: "Investor Presentation Slides Crompton Corp." [online] from http://www.crompston.com [published September 15, 2004].

★ 1449 ★

Petroleum Refining

SIC: 2911; NAICS: 32411

Leading Refined Products, 2003-2004

Data are in thousands of barrels.

	2003	2004	Share
Gasoline	208,167	211,491	31.23%
Distillate	136,542	118,985	17.57
Natural gas liquids & LRG	100,889	111,621	16.48
Unfinished oils	75,904	92,581	13.67
Kerosine jet fuel	38,767	39,976	5.90
Residual	37,800	36,818	5.44
Kerosine	5,584	3,539	0.52
Special naphthas	2,006	1,638	0.24
Naphtha jet fuel	17	152	0.02
Other	55,364	60,371	8.92

Source: *Oil & Gas Journal*, January 17, 2005, p. 30.

★ 1450 ★

Petroleum Refining

SIC: 2911; NAICS: 32411

Leading Refinery Catalyst Players

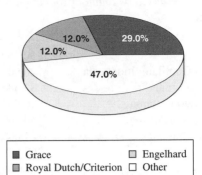

| ■ Grace | □ Engelhard |
| ▨ Royal Dutch/Criterion | □ Other |

The industry is valued at $2 billion.

Grace 29.0%
Royal Dutch/Criterion 12.0
Engelhard 12.0
Other 47.0

Source: *Chemical Week*, August 11, 2004, p. 23.

★ 1451 ★

Lubricants

SIC: 2992; NAICS: 324191

Finished Lubricant Demand Worldwide, 2003

Automotive lubricants took 57% of demand, followed by process oils and metalworking fluids each with 10% shares.

North America 30.0%
Asia Pacific 29.0
Western Pacific 14.0
Central and Eastern Europe 13.0
Central and South America 7.0
Near and Middle East 4.0
Africa 3.0

Source: *European Chemical News*, February 14, 2005, p. 18, from Kline & Co.

★ 1452 ★

Lubricants

SIC: 2992; NAICS: 324191

Leading Lubricant Makers in Indonesia

Companies are ranked by annual production capacity in kiloliters.

	K.L.	Share
Pertamina	550,160	45.47%
Wiraswasta Gemilang Indonesia	120,000	9.92
Nusaraya Putramandiri	83,300	6.88
Agip Lubrindo Pratama	40,000	3.31
Castrol Indonesia	30,000	2.48
Dirga Buana Sarana	24,000	1.98
Other	362,540	29.96

Source: "Synthetic Lubricant Market in Indonesia." [online] from http://www.export.gov [Published March 2005].

★ 1453 ★

Motor Oil

SIC: 2992; NAICS: 324191

Top Motor Oil Brands, 2003-2004

Market shares are shown based on a survey of quick lube owners with fewer than 30 chains.

	2003	2004
Pennzoil	31.0%	28.0%
Valvoline	12.0	20.0
Quaker State	11.0	12.0
Mobil	10.0	7.0
Castrol	10.0	7.0
Other	26.0	26.0

Source: *Lube Report*, September 21, 2004, p. NA, from *National Oil and Lube News*.

SIC 30 - Rubber and Misc. Plastics Products

★ 1454 ★

Tires

SIC: 3011; NAICS: 326211

Highway Truck Tire Market in North America, 2004

Market shares are shown for passenger tires for the United States and Canada.

Goodyear	19.0%
Michelin	18.0
Bridgestone	16.0
Firestone	6.0
Yokohama	4.5
General	4.5
Toyo	4.0
Sumitomo	3.0
Other	25.0

Source: *Tire Business*, January 31, 2005, p. 8.

★ 1455 ★

Tires

SIC: 3011; NAICS: 326211

Leading Tire Makers in Japan, 2003

Market shares are estimated based on domestic production of 1.24 million tons.

Bridgestone	49.1%
Sumitomo Rubber	21.6
Yokohama Rubber	16.0
Toyo Tire & Rubber	11.6
Other	1.7

Source: "Market Share Survey Report 2003." [online] from http://www.nni.nikkei.co.jp [Published July 26, 2004], from Nikkei estimates and Japan Automobile Tire Manufacturers Association.

★ 1456 ★

Tires

SIC: 3011; NAICS: 326211

Leading Tire Makers in Poland

Consumers are now paying more attention to premium tire segments, high performance tires and 4X4 tires. Market shares are shown for the car and van segment.

Goodyear	49.0%
Michelin	33.0
Other	18.0

Source: *Europe Intelligence Wire*, March 15, 2005, p. NA, from *Gazeta Prawna*.

★ 1457 ★

Tires

SIC: 3011; NAICS: 326211

Light Tire Market in North America, 2004

Market shares are shown for passenger tires for the United States and Canada.

Goodyear	11.0%
Michelin	8.0
BFGoodrich	8.0
Cooper	6.5
Firestone	6.0
Bridgestone	6.0
General	4.5
Kumho	3.5
Toyo	3.0
MasterCraft	3.0
Kelly-Springfield	3.0
Continental	3.0
Other	34.5

Source: *Tire Business*, January 31, 2005, p. 8.

★ 1458 ★

Tires

SIC: 3011; NAICS: 326211

Passenger Car Tire Market in Europe, 2004

The replacement tire market is shown by company.

Michelin	.24.0%
Goodyear	.22.0
Continental	.18.0
Bridgestone	.10.0
Pirelli	.9.0
Other	.17.0

Source: *just-auto.com*, September 2004, p. 5.

★ 1459 ★

Tires

SIC: 3011; NAICS: 326211

Passenger Tire Market in North America, 2004

Market shares are shown for passenger tires for the United States and Canada.

Goodyear	.14.0%
Michelin	8.5
Firestone	6.5
Cooper	6.0
Bridgestone	5.5
BFGoodrich	5.5
General	3.5
Uniroyal	3.5
Kumho/Marshal	3.0
Yokohama	2.5
Kelly-Springfield	2.5
Dunlop	2.5
Dayton	2.5
Toyo	2.5
Hankook/Aurora	2.5
Other	.29.0

Source: *Tire Business*, January 31, 2005, p. 8.

★ 1460 ★

Tires

SIC: 3011; NAICS: 326211

Replacement Light Tire Market in Canada, 2004

Market shares are shown based on 2.4 million replacement tires shipped during the year.

Goodyear	.15.0%
Motomaster	.13.0
Michelin	.10.5

Bridgestone	. 8.0%
BFGoodrich	. 7.5
Hankook	. 5.5
Firestone	. 5.0
Toyo	. 4.0
Dayton	. 4.0
Yokohama	. 3.5
President	. 3.5
Kumho	. 3.0
Other	.17.0

Source: *Modern Tire Dealer*, January 2005, p. 15, from *Modern Tire Dealer* estimates.

★ 1461 ★

Tires

SIC: 3011; NAICS: 326211

Replacement Light Tire Market in Mexico, 2004

Market shares are shown based on 5 million tires shipped during the year.

Goodyear	.22.0%
Tornel	.18.0
Firestone	.18.0
Euzkadi	. 8.0
Uniroyal	. 6.0
BFGoodrich	. 6.0
TBC	. 4.0
Bridgestone	. 3.0
General	. 2.5
Continental	. 2.0
Other	. 9.5

Source: *Modern Tire Dealer*, January 2005, p. 15, from *Modern Tire Dealer* estimates.

★ 1462 ★

Tires

SIC: 3011; NAICS: 326211

Replacement Tire Market in Canada (Passenger), 2004

Market shares are shown based on 16.5 million replacement tires shipped during the year.

Motomaster	.18.0%
Goodyear	.15.0
Michelin	. 9.5
Bridgestone	. 6.5
BFGoodrich	. 5.5
Hankook	. 4.5
Toyo	. 4.0
Uniroyal	. 3.5

Continued on next page.

★ 1462 ★

[Continued]

Tires

SIC: 3011; NAICS: 326211

Replacement Tire Market in Canada (Passenger), 2004

Market shares are shown based on 16.5 million replacement tires shipped during the year.

President	3.5%
Firestone	3.5
Dayton	3.5
Cooper	3.5
Other	21.5

Source: *Modern Tire Dealer*, January 2005, p. 15, from *Modern Tire Dealer* estimates.

★ 1463 ★

Tires

SIC: 3011; NAICS: 326211

Replacement Tire Market in Mexico, 2004

Market shares are shown based on 12.8 million tires shipped during the year.

Goodyear	20.0%
Firestone	16.0
Tornel	13.0
Euzkadi	11.0
Uniroyal	7.0
Bridgestone	6.0
BFGoodrich	6.0
TBC	4.0
General	3.5
Michelin	2.0
Other	10.0

Source: *Modern Tire Dealer*, January 2005, p. 15, from *Modern Tire Dealer* estimates.

★ 1464 ★

Tires

SIC: 3011; NAICS: 326211

Tire Market Shares in North America, 2004

Market shares are shown for the orginal equipment consumer market for the United States and Canada. Data exclude imports.

Goodyear	33.9%
Bridgestone	15.5
General	13.4
Michelin	12.2
Continental	6.1

Firestone	5.7%
BFGoodrich	5.0
Dunlop	4.2
Pirelli	1.7
Uniroyal	1.4
Hankook	1.0

Source: *Modern Tire Dealer*, January 2005, p. 15, from *Modern Tire Dealer* estimates.

★ 1465 ★

Tires

SIC: 3011; NAICS: 326211

Tire Market Worldwide, 2003

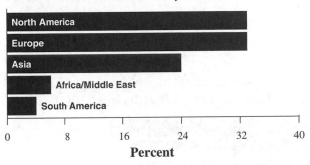

Market shares are shown based on units.

North America	33.0%
Europe	33.0
Asia	24.0
Africa/Middle East	6.0
South America	4.0

Source: *just-auto.com*, September 2004, p. 18, from Michelin.

★ 1466 ★

Tires

SIC: 3011; NAICS: 326211

Tire Shipments, 2004

Shipments are shown in thousands of units for the year-to-date October 2004.

	Oct. 2003	Oct. 2004	Share
Replacement (passenger)	230,965.0	232,158.0	51.35%
OE (passenger)	163,305.0	164,999.0	36.49
Replacement (light truck)	28,687.0	30,038.0	6.64
Replacement (medium truck)	13,052.0	13,489.0	2.98
OE (light truck)	6,914.0	6,340.0	1.40
OE (medium truck)	3,488.0	4,800.0	1.06
Heavy trucks	278.8	310.7	0.07

Source: *Rubber & Plastics News*, January 24, 2005, p. 19, from Rubber Manufacturers Association.

★ 1467 ★
Tires
SIC: 3011; NAICS: 326211
Top Tire Makers in Europe, 2003

Shares are shown for the original equipment market.

Michelin 28.0%
Continental 27.0
Goodyear 17.0
Bridgestone 13.0
Pirelli 11.0
Other 4.0

Source: *just-auto.com*, September 2004, p. 18, from Michelin.

★ 1468 ★
Tires
SIC: 3011; NAICS: 326211
Top Tire Makers Worldwide, 2003

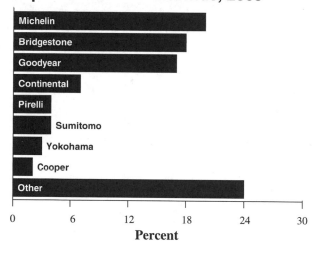

Market shares are shown in percent.

Michelin 20.1%
Bridgestone 18.4
Goodyear 16.9
Continental 7.0
Pirelli 4.1
Sumitomo 3.6
Yokohama 3.2
Cooper 2.3
Other 24.4

Source: *Tire Business*, January 31, 2005, p. 8.

★ 1469 ★
Tires
SIC: 3011; NAICS: 326211
Truck Tire Market, 2004

Market shares are shown based on 16.06 million tires (medium/heavy) shipped during the year.

Goodyear 21.5%
Michelin 18.0
Bridgestone 17.5
Firestone 7.0
General 5.0
Yokohama 4.5
Toyo 3.5
Kelly 3.5
Sumitomo 3.0
Kumho 2.5
Hankook 2.5
Continental 2.5
BFGoodrich 2.5
Other 10.5

Source: *Modern Tire Dealer*, January 2005, p. 15, from *Modern Tire Dealer* estimates.

★ 1470 ★
Footwear
SIC: 3021; NAICS: 316213
Army Boot Market in Iraq

Market shares are shown in percent.

State Company for Leather Industries 90.0%
Other 10.0

Source: "SOE Overview." [online] from http://www.cpa-iraq.org/business/industries/leather%20.co.xls [Accessed March 23, 2005].

★ 1471 ★
Footwear
SIC: 3021; NAICS: 316211

Casual Shoe Market

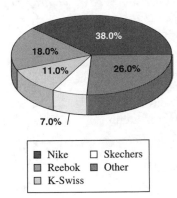

Market shares are estimated as of June 27, 2004.

Nike	.38.0%
Reebok	.18.0
K-Swiss	.11.0
Skechers	. 7.0
Other	.26.0

Source: *Sporting Goods Business*, August 2004, p. S4, from SportScanInfo.

★ 1472 ★
Footwear
SIC: 3021; NAICS: 316211

Top Footwear Firms in France, 2002

Footwear production fell 14% to 1.4 billion euros in 2003. Firms produced 60.9 million pairs, down from 75.5 million pairs. Market shares are shown in percent.

Vivarte	.16.0%
Eram SA	.14.0
Adidas AG	. 6.0
Mephisto SA	. 2.0
Bata France SA	. 2.0
Bally SA	. 2.0
Other	.58.0

Source: "French Market for Footwear." [online] from http://www.fco.gov.uk [Published October 2004].

★ 1473 ★
Footwear
SIC: 3021; NAICS: 316211

Water Sandal Market

Market shares are shown as of June 27, 2004.

Teva	.20.0%
Columbia	. 6.0
Keen	. 5.0
Wolverine	. 3.0
Other	.66.0

Source: *Sporting Goods Business*, August 2004, p. S4, from SportScanInfo.

★ 1474 ★
Condoms
SIC: 3069; NAICS: 326299

Condom Market in New Zealand

Sales are shown as of April 18, 2004.

Durex	.71.0%
Other	.29.0

Source: *Grocer's Review*, June 2004, p. NA, from ACNielsen Scantrack.

★ 1475 ★
Condoms
SIC: 3069; NAICS: 326299

Top Condom Brands

Market shares are shown based on sales at food stores, drug stores and mass merchandisers (but not Wal-Mart).

	($ mil.)	Share
Trojan	$ 58.6	25.48%
Trojan Enz	37.8	16.43
Lifestyles	20.9	9.09
Trojan Magnum	16.9	7.35
Durex Extra Sensitive	13.1	5.70
Trojan Her Pleasure	9.5	4.13
Trojan Ultra Pleasure	8.2	3.57
Durex	6.5	2.83
Kling Tite Naturalamb	6.5	2.83
Trojan Extended Pleasure . .	6.5	2.83
Other	45.5	19.78

Source: *MMR*, April 25, 2005, p. 67, from Information Resources Inc.

★ 1476 ★

Condoms

SIC: 3069; NAICS: 326299

Top Condom Brands in the U.K.

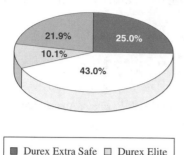

21.9%   25.0%

10.1%

43.0%

■ Durex Extra Safe   □ Durex Elite
■ Durex Featherlite   □ Other

The value of the market was 24.5 million pounds sterling. Spending at Superdrugs and Boots is not included.

Durex Extra Safe	25.0%
Durex Featherlite	21.9
Durex Elite	10.1
Other	43.0

Source: *Community Pharmacy*, February 8, 2005, p. NA, from IMS Pharmatrend.

★ 1477 ★

Condoms

SIC: 3069; NAICS: 326299

Top Condom Makers, 2004

Market shares are shown based on sales at food stores, drug stores and mass merchandisers (but not Wal-Mart) for the 52 weeks ended June 13, 2004.

Church & Dwight	70.0%
Durex Consumer Prods	14.3
Ansell	12.8
Okamoto USA	0.5
Gain	0.5
Other	1.8

Source: *Grocery Headquarters*, August 2004, p. S88, from Information Resources Inc.

★ 1478 ★

Condoms

SIC: 3069; NAICS: 326199

Top Contraceptive Brands, 2004

Market shares are shown based on drug stores for the 52 weeks ended October 31, 2004.

Trojan	24.1%
Trojan Enz	16.4
LifeStyles	7.7
Trojan Magnum	7.3
Durex Extra Sensitive	6.7
Kling Tite Natural Lamb	4.2
Trojan Her Pleasure	3.9
Trojan Ultra Pleasure	3.6
Trojan Extended Pleasure	3.0
Durex	2.5
Other	4.1

Source: *Chain Drug Review*, January 3, 2005, p. 95, from Information Resources Inc.

★ 1479 ★

Cosmetic Storage

SIC: 3069; NAICS: 326299

Top Cosmetic Storage Brands

Market shares are shown based on sales at food stores, drug stores and mass merchandisers (but not Wal-Mart).

	($ mil.)	Share
Living Things	$ 8.0	19.85%
Caboodles	6.5	16.13
Modella	4.1	10.17
Basics	2.7	6.70
Studio Basics	2.0	4.96
Studio Collection	1.7	4.22
Allegro Pacific	1.7	4.22
Revlon	1.4	3.47
Private label	6.9	17.12
Other	5.3	13.15

Source: *MMR*, April 25, 2005, p. 67, from Information Resources Inc.

★ 1480 ★

Plastic Pipe

SIC: 3084; NAICS: 326122

Corrugated HDPE Pipe Market in North America

HDPE stands for high density polyethylene.

ADS/Hancor	70.0%
Other	30.0

Source: *Plastics News*, April 11, 2005, p. 1.

★ **1481** ★
Coolers
SIC: 3089; NAICS: 326199

Leading Cooler Makers, 2004

Market shares are shown in percent.

Coleman	38.89%
Igloo	23.74
Other	37.37

Source: "2004 SportScanInfo Year in Review." [online] from http://sportstrendinfo.com/pdf/ SportScanINFO.2004.pdf [Accessed May 9, 2005], from SportScanInfo.

★ **1482** ★
Plastic Containers
SIC: 3089; NAICS: 326199

Top Household Plastic Brands, 2005

Brands are ranked by supermarket, drug store and discount outlet sales (excluding Wal-Mart) for the 52 weeks ended February 20, 2005.

	($ mil.)	Share
Sterilite supply containers	$ 15.8	9.61%
Sterilite trash receptacles	11.0	6.69
Rubbermaid trash receptacles	7.6	4.62
Cornerstone trash receptacles	6.5	3.95
Rubbermaid Roughneck trash	5.7	3.47
Rubbermaid supply containers	4.5	2.74
United Plastics trash receptacles	4.3	2.62
Sterilite Ultra supply containers	3.4	2.07
United Plastics supply containers	3.4	2.07
Homz supply containers	3.1	1.89
Private label	58.8	35.77
Other	40.3	24.51

Source: *MMR*, May 30, 2005, p. 33, from Information Resources Inc.

★ **1483** ★
Plastic Containers
SIC: 3089; NAICS: 326199

Top Kitchen Storage Brands, 2005

Brands are ranked by supermarket, drug store and discount outlet sales (excluding Wal-Mart) for the 52 weeks ended February 20, 2005.

	($ mil.)	Share
Sterilite	$ 97.3	13.87%
Ziploc	51.5	7.34
Homz	50.3	7.17
Gladware	45.6	6.50

	($ mil.)	Share
Sterilite Clearview	$ 36.4	5.19%
Sterilite Ultra	33.8	4.82
Rubbermaid Servin' Saver	24.4	3.48
Rubbermaid	24.1	3.44
Rubbermaid Roughneck	19.4	2.77
Private label	33.3	4.75
Other	285.2	40.67

Source: *MMR*, May 30, 2005, p. 33, from Information Resources Inc.

★ **1484** ★
Plastic Molding
SIC: 3089; NAICS: 326199

Plastic Molding and Trim Demand

Plastic moulding & trim will take 12.7% in 2008 and 14.7% in 2012 of the overall moulding & trim market.

	2008	2013	Share
Polyvinyl chloride	460	645	41.21%
Polyurethane	315	440	28.12
Other	380	480	30.67

Source: *Urethanes Technology*, June/July 2004, p. 5, from Freedonia Group.

★ **1485** ★
Transparencies
SIC: 3089; NAICS: 326122

Transparency Market for F-16 Aircraft

The company has 90% of the market for polycarbonate and acrylic based anti ballistic window panels called transparencies.

Texstars	90.0%
Other	10.0

Source: *Plastics News*, November 1, 2004, p. 1.

SIC 31 - Leather and Leather Products

★ 1486 ★
Footwear
SIC: 3140; NAICS: 316219

Leading Licensed Footwear Brands, 2003

Brands are ranked by sales in millions of dollars.

Mary-Kate and Ashley	$ 12.80
Barbie	9.08
Spider-Man	5.61
Hello Kitty	4.01
Winnie the Pooh	2.68

Source: *License!*, October 2004, p. 54, from NPD Fashionworld Consumer Panel.

★ 1487 ★
Footwear
SIC: 3143; NAICS: 316213

Comfort Footwear Sales, 2002-2003

Those 55 years of age and older have the largest share of the market (38.1% of dollar sales and 36.9% of unit sales).

	2002	2003	Share
Women's	$ 3,161	$ 3,489	75.44%
Men's	1,104	1,078	23.31
Children's	72	58	1.25

Source: *Footwear News*, April 26, 2004, p. 1, from NPD Group, NPD Fashionworld, and Consumer Data Estimates.

★ 1488 ★
Footwear
SIC: 3143; NAICS: 316999

Leading Outdoor Shoe Makers, 2003

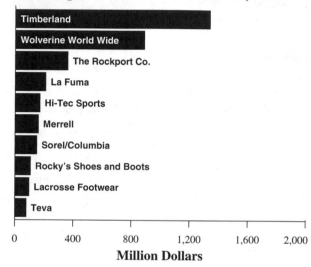

Firms are ranked by estimated footwear revenue in millions of dollars.

Timberland	$ 1,340.0
Wolverine World Wide	888.9
The Rockport Co.	361.0
La Fuma	210.0
Hi-Tec Sports	170.0
Merrell	160.0
Sorel/Columbia	148.6
Rocky's Shoes and Boots	106.2
Lacrosse Footwear	95.7
Teva	76.5

Source: *Sportsedge*, September 2004, p. 26.

★ 1489 ★
Footwear
SIC: 3143; NAICS: 316213

Men's Footwear Sales, 2003

Men between 35 to 54 years of age drive purchases in the $17.04 billion men's shoe market. The top dress shoe brands for the year, in order: Johnson & Murphy, Florsheim, Rockport, Cole Haan and Kenneth Cole. Overall, the top brands are Timberland, Rockport, Red Wing Boots, Nike and Skechers.

12 and under	$ 406.4
13-17	2,510.0
18-24	2,880.0
25-34	3,250.0
35-54	5,870.0
55 and older	2,130.0

Source: *Footwear News*, May 24, 2004, p. 1, from NPD Group.

★ 1490 ★
Footwear
SIC: 3144; NAICS: 316214

Women's Dress Shoe Sales, 2004

Distribution of sales is shown for July - December 2004.

Thin	19.0%
Stiletto	18.0
Block (thick)	16.0
Medium	14.0
Kitten (narrow, low)	3.0
Other	30.0

Source: *Research Alert*, May 20, 2005, p. 9, from NPD Fashionworld.

★ 1491 ★
Footwear
SIC: 3149; NAICS: 316211

Athletic Footwear Sales, 2003-2004

The average price fell from $33.71 in 2003 to $33.18 in 2004. Spending is shown in billions of dollars.

	2003	2004
Men's	$ 8.0	$ 7.8
Women's	4.6	4.8
Children's	3.3	3.7

Source: "Consumer Spending for Athletic Footwear Rises 3% in 2004." [online] from http://www.sgma.com [Press release March 2, 2005], from NPD Group/NPD Fashionworld.

★ 1492 ★
Footwear
SIC: 3149; NAICS: 316219

Cleated Footwear Market, 2004

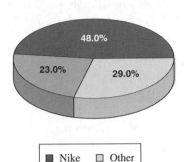

Nike ■ □ Other
Adidas ■

Market shares are estimated as of June 27, 2004.

Nike	48.0%
Adidas	23.0
Other	29.0

Source: *Sporting Goods Business*, August 2004, p. S4, from SportScanInfo.

★ 1493 ★
Footwear
SIC: 3149; NAICS: 316219

Leading Basketball Shoe Makers, 2004

Market shares are shown in percent.

Nike	65.99%
Adidas	16.71
Reebok	10.75
Other	6.55

Source: "2004 SportScanInfo Year in Review." [online] from http://sportstrendinfo.com/pdf/ SportScanINFO.2004.pdf [Accessed May 9, 2005], from SportScanInfo.

★ 1494 ★
Footwear
SIC: 3149; NAICS: 316219

Leading Cross-Trainer Makers, 2004

Market shares are shown in percent.

Nike/New Balance	83.0%
Other	17.0

Source: "2004 SportScanInfo Year in Review." [online] from http://sportstrendinfo.com/pdf/ SportScanINFO.2004.pdf [Accessed May 9, 2005], from SportScanInfo.

★ 1495 ★
Footwear
SIC: 3149; NAICS: 316211

Leading Running Shoe Brands, 2004

According to the survey, sales of men's running shoes increased 13.1% and women's shoes increased in 12.3%.

Asics	.22.0%
Brooks	.17.0
Saucony	.12.0
Nike	.12.0
Mizuno	.10.0
Adidas	.10.0
Other	.17.0

Source: *Footwear News*, February 7, 2005, p. 102, from Sports Marketing Surveys USA.

★ 1496 ★
Footwear
SIC: 3149; NAICS: 316211

Leading Sports Shoe Brands, 2004

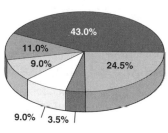

■ Nike ☐ Reebok
■ New Balance ■ K-Swiss
☐ Adidas ■ Other

Casual footwear has become the largest and fastest-growing category with a 28% share. Data are for the year through June 27, 2004.

Nike	.43.0%
New Balance	.11.0
Adidas	.9.0
Reebok	.9.0
K-Swiss	.3.5
Other	.24.5

Source: *Sporting Goods Business*, August 2004, p. S4, from SportScanInfo.

★ 1497 ★
Footwear
SIC: 3149; NAICS: 316211

Leading Sports Shoe Firms, 1993 and 2003

Market shares are shown in percent.

	1993	2003
Nike	.32.30%	36.4%
Adidas	.3.10	12.5
New Balance	.1.70	10.9
Reebok	.20.90	9.1
Other	.41.01	31.1

Source: *Time*, November 8, 2004, p. 49, from Sporting Goods Intelligence.

★ 1498 ★
Footwear
SIC: 3149; NAICS: 316219

Leading Walking Shoe Makers, 2004

The market is valued at $280 million.

New Balance	.34.14%
Nike	.31.14
Other	.34.72

Source: "2004 SportScanInfo Year in Review." [online] from http://sportstrendinfo.com/pdf/ SportScanINFO.2004.pdf [Accessed May 9, 2005], from SportScanInfo.

★ 1499 ★
Footwear
SIC: 3149; NAICS: 316211

NBA Shoe Market, 2004

Basketball shoes took about a quarter of the $7.7 billion spent on sports shoes through June 2004. Nike took over half of the market.

Nike	.50.0%
Adidas	.15.0
Reebok	.7.0
Other	.28.0

Source: *Brandweek*, October 11, 2004, p. 10.

★ 1500 ★
Footwear
SIC: 3149; NAICS: 316219

Performance Basketball Market

Market shares are shown as of June 27, 2004.

Nike 70.0%
Other 30.0

Source: *Sporting Goods Business*, August 2004, p. S4, from SportScanInfo.

★ 1501 ★
Footwear
SIC: 3149; NAICS: 316219

Soccer Footwear Market, 2004

Market shares are estimated as of June 27, 2004.

Adidas 55.0%
Nike 33.0
Other 12.0

Source: *Sporting Goods Business*, August 2004, p. S4, from SportScanInfo.

★ 1502 ★
Footwear
SIC: 3149; NAICS: 316211

Soccer Footwear Market in Europe

Market shares are shown in percent.

Nike 34.0%
Adidas 30.0
Other 36.0

Source: *America's Intelligence Wire*, November 24, 2004, p. NA.

★ 1503 ★
Footwear
SIC: 3149; NAICS: 316211

Sports Shoe Market Worldwide, 2002-2003

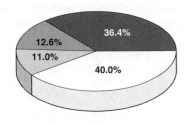

| | Nike | | New Balance |
| | Reebok | | Other |

Market shares are shown in percent.

	2002	2003
Nike	39.0%	36.4%
Reebok	11.9	12.6
New Balance	11.6	11.0
Other	37.5	40.0

Source: *Footwear News*, October 25, 2004, p. 21.

★ 1504 ★
Footwear
SIC: 3149; NAICS: 316211

Tennis Shoe Market, 2004

Market shares are estimated as of June 27, 2004.

Nike 20.0%
New Balance 20.0
Adidas 20.0
Other 40.0

Source: *Sporting Goods Business*, August 2004, p. S4, from SportScanInfo.

★ 1505 ★
Footwear
SIC: 3149; NAICS: 316211

Top Athletic Footwear Sectors, 2004

Data are based on sales reported to NPD by department stores, national chains, shoe chains, athletic footwear specialty chains and sporting goods stores.

Running 28.9%
Basketball 22.2
Low performance 12.0

Continued on next page.

★ 1505 ★
[Continued]
Footwear
SIC: 3149; NAICS: 316211

Top Athletic Footwear Sectors, 2004

Data are based on sales reported to NPD by department stores, national chains, shoe chains, athletic footwear specialty chains and sporting goods stores.

Cross-training/fitness	7.8%
Walking	4.8
Hiking	3.7
Work/occupational/safety	3.6
Infants	2.9
Recreational boots	2.2
Tennis	2.0
Sports sandals	2.0
Other	6.9

Source: "Consumer Spending for Athletic Footwear Rises 3% in 2004." [online] from http://www.sgma.com [Press release March 2, 2005], from NPD Group/NPD Fashionworld.

★ 1506 ★
Footwear
SIC: 3149; NAICS: 316211

Top Football Footwear Brands in Europe, 2004

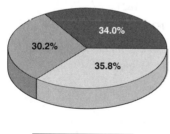

Nike ☐ **Other**
Adidas

Market shares are shown for the previous 12 months.

Nike	34.0%
Adidas	30.2
Other	35.8

Source: *Brand Strategy*, September 2004, p. 7, from NPD.

★ 1507 ★
Luggage
SIC: 3161; NAICS: 316991

Luggage Market Shares

The South East takes 20.5% of luggage sales, the Pacific 18.7% and the Mid-Atlantic 17.4%. Market shares are shown in percent.

Samsonite	35.0%
National Traveler	20.0
Hartmann	13.0
Other	32.0

Source: "National Traveler Luggage and Accessories." [online] from http://www.adbuzz/MediaBuzz/mediaplans.doc [Accessed March 22, 2004].

★ 1508 ★
Luggage
SIC: 3161; NAICS: 316991

Top Luggage Makers in India

The Rs 1,800 crore market is dominated by the unorganized sector (66% of the total) and the rest is held by organized players. Hard luggage represents 60% of the market and soft luggage represents the balance.

VIP	60.0%
Aristocrat	15.0
Safari	12.0
Samsonite	10.0
American Tourister	3.0

Source: *Business India*, April 11, 2005, p. 60.

★ 1509 ★
Handbags
SIC: 3171; NAICS: 316992

Handbag Market in Japan

Market shares are shown in percent.

LV	28.0%
Coach	8.0
Other	64.0

Source: *Time*, April 25, 2005, p. A4.

SIC 32 - Stone, Clay, and Glass Products

★ 1510 ★

Glass

SIC: 3211; NAICS: 327211

Automotive Glass Market in India

Market shares are shown in percent.

Asahi	85.0%
Other	15.0

Source: *Asia Africa Intelligence Wire*, December 25, 2004, p. NA.

★ 1511 ★

Glass

SIC: 3211; NAICS: 327211

Flat Glass Demand in North America, 2003

The market is shown for the United States and Canada.

Residential	37.0%
Automotive	27.0
Commercial	23.0
Specialty	13.0

Source: "Industry Statistics." [online] from http://www.glassmagazine.org [Accessed June 20, 2005], from AFG Industries.

★ 1512 ★

Glass

SIC: 3211; NAICS: 327211

Flat Glass Demand Worldwide, 2008 and 2013

The top four producers — Asahi Glass, Saint-Gobain, Pilkington and Guardian — represent more than 40% of the global flat glass market by value. Figures are in millions of dollars.

	2008	2013	Share
North America	$ 15,315	$ 19,320	28.62%
Western Europe	15,900	19,230	28.49
China	6,180	9,100	13.48
Japan	4,550	5,100	7.56
Other Asia Pacific	$ 6,145	$ 8,230	12.19%
Other	4,900	6,520	9.66

Source: *Glass Magazine*, January 2005, p. NA, from Freedonia Group.

★ 1513 ★

Glass

SIC: 3211; NAICS: 327211

Largest Automotive Glass Makers in North America, 2003

The top producers in the United States and Canada are ranked by share of total capacity of 6.84 million short tons.

PPG Industries	21.9%
AFG Industries	19.8
Guardian Industries	19.5
Pilkington North America	13.4
Vitro Group	8.3
Cardinal Flat Glass	8.0
Vissteon Corp.	6.7
Saint-Gobain	2.1
Other	0.3

Source: "Industry Statistics." [online] from http://www.glassmagazine.org [Accessed June 20, 2005].

★ 1514 ★
Glass
SIC: 3211; NAICS: 327211
Leading Glass Firms Worldwide

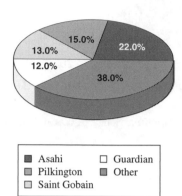

Legend: Asahi, Guardian, Pilkington, Other, Saint Gobain

Market shares are shown based on global capacity.

Asahi	22.0%
Pilkington	15.0
Saint Gobain	13.0
Guardian	12.0
Other	38.0

Source: "Flat Glass Industry - Global Players." [online] from http://www.pilkington.com [Accessed July 7, 2005].

★ 1515 ★
Glass
SIC: 3211; NAICS: 327211
Leading Glass Makers in Western Europe, 2004

The industry was valued at 1.6 billion pounds.

OI	30.0%
Rexam	25.0
St. Gobain	12.0
Ardagh	11.0
Other	22.0

Source: "Northern European Glass." [online] from http://www.rexam.com/index.asp?pageid523 [Accessed June 14, 2005], from Rexam estimates.

★ 1516 ★
Glass
SIC: 3211; NAICS: 327211
Leading Sheet Glass Makers in Japan, 2003

Market shares are estimated based on domestic shipments.

Asahi Glass	40.7%
Nippon Sheet Glass	30.0
Central Glass	17.1
PPG-CI	1.8
Guardian Japan	1.7
Other	8.7

Source: "Market Share Survey Report 2003." [online] from http://www.nni.nikkei.co.jp [Published July 26, 2004], from Nikkei estimates.

★ 1517 ★
Glass
SIC: 3211; NAICS: 327211
Mother Glass Market Worldwide

AGC is the second largest producer.

Corning	50.0%
Other	50.0

Source: *Asia Africa Intelligence Wire*, February 18, 2005, p. NA.

★ 1518 ★
Glass
SIC: 3211; NAICS: 327211
Top Flat Glass Makers in Mexico

Market shares are for the $300 million construction segment.

Vitromart	58.0%
Other	42.0

Source: *America's Intelligence Wire*, July 28, 2004, p. NA.

★ 1519 ★
Glass
SIC: 3211; NAICS: 327211

World Glass Demand by End Market, 2008 and 2013

The flat glass demand is forcast to increase from $53 billion in 2008 to $67.5 billion in 2013.

	2008	2013	Share
Construction	$ 33,650	$ 43,500	64.44%
Motor vehicles	10,500	12,500	18.52
Other	8,900	11,500	17.04

Source: *Auto Glass*, January 2005, p. NA, from Frost & Sullivan.

★ 1520 ★
Glass Containers
SIC: 3221; NAICS: 327213

Glass Container Shipments

Shipments are for the first six months of the year.

Beer	.56.4%
Food applications	.17.3
Non-alcoholic beverages	9.4
Wine	5.1
Alcoholic coolers and cocktails (ready-to-drink)	3.8
Liquor	2.9
Other	5.1

Source: *Ceramic Industry*, October 2004, p. 33, from U.S. Department of Commerce.

★ 1521 ★
Cement
SIC: 3241; NAICS: 32731

Cement Consumption, 2004-2006

Domestic production has been stretched to its limits, according to the source. Domestic supply increases by year: 2.3% in 2004, 1.8% in 2005 and 1.7% in 2006. Data are in thousands of tons of which portland takes 96% of the total.

	2004	2005	2006
Portland	112,295	115,598	118,025
Masonry	5,143	5,320	5,383

Source: *Concrete Products*, December 2004, p. 25, from Portland Cement Association.

★ 1522 ★
Cement
SIC: 3241; NAICS: 32731

Cement Market by End Use, 2003

Market shares are shown in percent.

Streets & highways	.32.0%
Residential buildings	.31.0
Commercial buildings	.10.0
Water & waste management	8.0
Public buildings	8.0
Other	.11.0

Source: "Market Research." [online] from http://www.cement.org/market, from Portland Cement Association.

★ 1523 ★
Cement
SIC: 3241; NAICS: 32731

Leading Cement Makers in Eastern India

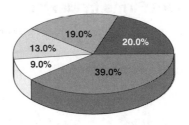

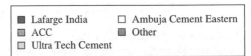

The region consumes about 18.5 metric tons each year and has been growing at approximately 14% for the current financial year.

Lafarge India	.20.0%
ACC	.19.0
Ultra Tech Cement	.13.0
Ambuja Cement Eastern	9.0
Other	.39.0

Source: *Asia Africa Intelligence Wire*, January 4, 2005, p. NA.

★ 1524 ★

Cement

SIC: 3241; NAICS: 32731

Leading Cement Makers in Japan, 2003

Market shares are estimated based on domestic shipments of 59.68 metric tons.

Taiheiyo	.36.7%
Ube-Mitsubishi	.23.8
Sumitomo Osaka	.19.3
Tokuyama	7.3
Aso	3.5
Other	9.4

Source: ''Market Share Survey Report 2003.'' [online] from http://www.nni.nikkei.co.jp [Published July 26, 2004], from Japan Cement Association and *Nihon Keizai Shimbun*.

★ 1525 ★

Cement

SIC: 3241; NAICS: 32731

Top Cement Firms in Mexico

Producers are ranked by installed capacity of 49.1 metric tons.

Cemex Mexico	.53.0%
Apasco	.20.0
Cruz Azul	.11.0
Moctezuma	9.0
GCC	6.0
La Polar	1.0

Source: ''Is Cemex Built on Sand?'' [online] from http://cement4mexico.com/docs/Cemex%20report.pdf [Published November 2004], from UBS and Morgan Stanley.

★ 1526 ★

Cement

SIC: 3241; NAICS: 32731

Top Cement Makers in Chile, 2004

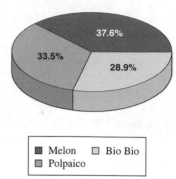

■ Melon □ Bio Bio
■ Polpaico

Shares are shown based on shipments for the first six months of the year.

Melon	.37.6%
Polpaico	.33.5
Bio Bio	.28.9

Source: *America's Intelligence Wire*, December 6, 2004, p. NA.

★ 1527 ★

Cement

SIC: 3241; NAICS: 32731

Top Cement Producing Nations, 2004

Countries are ranked by estimated production in thousands of metric tons. The United States includes Puerto Rico.

	(000)	Share
China	850,000	44.26%
India	110,000	5.73
United States	96,500	5.02
Japan	69,000	3.59
Korea	60,000	3.12
Russia	46,000	2.40
Brazil	38,000	1.98
Thailand	35,000	1.82
Mexico	35,000	1.82
Egypt	35,000	1.82
Other	546,000	28.43

Source: *Mineral Commodities Summaries 2005*, January 2005, p. 20, from U.S. Geological Survey, U.S. Department of the Interior.

★ 1528 ★
Ceramics
SIC: 3250; NAICS: 327331
Advanced Ceramics Demand, 2003

The market for advanced ceramic components is forecast to grow from $8.6 billion in 2003 to $12.8 billion in 2008.

Electronics	66.2%
Chemical & environmental	17.9
Coatings	9.9
Structural	6.0

Source: *American Ceramic Society Bulletin*, no. 8, 2004, p. 23, from Business Communications Co. Inc.

★ 1529 ★
Bricks
SIC: 3251; NAICS: 327121
Brick Shipments by Region, 2003

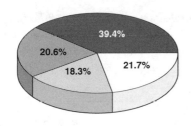

Legend	
■ South Atlantic	□ Central region
▨ East South Central	□ Other

Total shipments were 7.9 billion units.

South Atlantic	$ 39.4
East South Central	20.6
Central region	18.3
Other	21.7

Source: *Cermic Industry*, October 2004, p. 34, from Brick Industry Association.

★ 1530 ★
Tiles
SIC: 3251; NAICS: 327121
Clay Tile Market in France

Market shares are shown in percent.

Imerys	41.0%
Terreal	35.0
Lafarge	14.0
Other	10.0

Source: "Business." [online] from http://www.eurazeo.com/uk/02_invest/pe_terreal.php [Accessed July 7, 2005], from Terreal and FFTB.

★ 1531 ★
Tiles
SIC: 3253; NAICS: 327122
Ceramic Tile Sales

Data are based on a survey of 1,500 floor covering dealers. According to the source, there is a 16 percent increase projected in the first 18 months.

Floor tile	71.0%
Wall tile	14.0
Countertops & backsplashes	8.0
Trims & decorative tile	5.0
Exterior	2.0

Source: *National Floor Trends*, November 2004, p. 22, from *Ceramic Stone Tile Market Trends Study* by *National Floor Trends*.

★ 1532 ★
Tiles
SIC: 3253; NAICS: 327122
U.S. Ceramic Tile Imports

The Untied States consumed 2.87 billion square feet of tile in 2003 with imports representing 77.6% (2.27 billion). Brazil posted 23.45% gain imports.

Italy	34.0%
Spain	17.0
Brazil	12.0
Other	37.0

Source: *Ceramic Industry*, October 2004, p. 29.

★ 1533 ★
Refractories
SIC: 3255; NAICS: 327124

Refractories Market in Western Europe, 2002

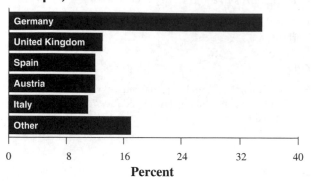

Percent

The market stood at 3.3 metric tons in 2002.

Germany	.35.0%
United Kingdom	.13.0
Spain	.12.0
Austria	.12.0
Italy	.11.0
Other	.17.0

Source: *Advanced Ceramics Report*, December 2004, p. 12, from Materials Technology Publications.

★ 1534 ★
Refractories
SIC: 3255; NAICS: 327124

Refractories Market Worldwide, 2003

Market shares are shown in percent.

RHI	.11.0%
Vesuvius	.9.0
Other	.80.0

Source: *Advanced Ceramics Report*, December 2004, p. 12, from Materials Technology Publications.

★ 1535 ★
Refractories
SIC: 3255; NAICS: 327124

Refractories Production in Western Europe, 2003

Market shares are shown in percent.

Iron and steel	.55.0%
Other	.45.0

Source: *Advanced Ceramics Report*, December 2004, p. 12, from European and International Refractories Industry.

★ 1536 ★
Plumbing Fixtures
SIC: 3261; NAICS: 327111

Leading Sanitary Ceramic Makers in Japan, 2003

Market shares are estimated based on domestic shipments of 8.65 million.

Toto	.62.2%
Inax	.28.7
Janis	.4.0
Asahi Eito	.3.8

Source: "Market Share Survey Report 2003." [online] from http://www.nni.nikkei.co.jp [Published July 26, 2004], from Nikkei estimates.

★ 1537 ★
Plumbing Fixtures
SIC: 3261; NAICS: 327111

Residential Sinks

The residential segment takes 67% of the entire market. "Other" includes countertop, undercounter, abovecounter, tile-in and console/vanity.

Drop-ins	.35.0%
Wall mounts	.30.0
Pedestal	.25.0

Source: *Plumbing & Mechanical*, August 2004, p. 104, from Catalina Research and U.S. Department of Commerce.

★ 1538 ★
Concrete
SIC: 3271; NAICS: 327331

Concrete Industry in Finland

The share of concrete in building facades is about 23% of the total building market in Finland. In multi-story residential buildings it is 70% and 35% in commercial buildings. The turnover for the concrete industry is shown below in pounds sterling.

	(mil.)	Share
Precast	258	54.0%
Ready-mix	122	26.0
Concrete products	84	20.0

Source: *Contract Journal*, January 26, 2005, p. 24.

★ 1539 ★
Concrete Planks
SIC: 3272; NAICS: 32739

Concrete Plank Market in Thailand

The company now has 35% of the market for pre-stressed planks in the Central region but additions of new machinery could give it half the industry.

DCom Products 50.0%
Other 50.0

Source: *Bangkok Post*, October 16, 2004, p. NA.

★ 1540 ★
Gypsum
SIC: 3275; NAICS: 32742

Leading Gypsum Makers in Thailand

The industry is estimated to have grown 20% over the previous year.

Siam Gypsum Industry 60.0%
BPB Thai Gypsum 38.0
Other 2.0

Source: *Bangkok Post*, December 17, 2004, p. NA, from Siam Gypsum Industry.

★ 1541 ★
Plasterboard
SIC: 3275; NAICS: 32742

Plasterboard Market in the U.K.

Figures are in metric square meters.

1998 . . . . 177.90
1999 . . . . 182.70
2000 . . . . 188.74
2001 . . . . 194.37
2002 . . . . 208.95
2003 . . . . 216.26
2004 . . . . 233.12
2005 . . . . 216.03

Source: *BMJ Supplement*, February 2005, p. 53.

★ 1542 ★
Abrasives
SIC: 3291; NAICS: 32791

Top Abrasives (Manufactured) Producing Nations, 2004

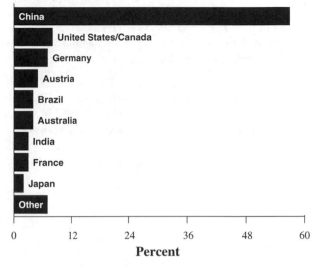

Data show estimated fused aluminum oxide capacity in thousands of metric tons.

	(000)	Share
China	700,000	57.30%
United States/Canada	96,600	7.91
Germany	80,000	6.55
Austria	60,000	4.91
Brazil	50,000	4.09
Australia	50,000	4.09
India	40,000	3.27
France	40,000	3.27
Japan	25,000	2.05
Other	80,000	6.55

Source: *Mineral Commodities Summaries 2005*, January 2005, p. 20, from U.S. Geological Survey, U.S. Department of the Interior.

★ 1543 ★
Friction Products
SIC: 3299; NAICS: 327999

Friction Product Market Worldwide, 2003 and 2008

The industry is expected to increase from $6.8 billion to $7.75 billion. Friction materials were intended as a replacement for non-asbestos organics. Semi-metallic and low-metallic are popular also.

	2003	2008	Share
Ground transport	$3,887	$3,907	53.29%
Industrial and other	2,325	2,688	36.66
Aircraft/aerospace	590	737	10.05

Source: *Advanced Materials & Composites News*, April 19, 2004, p. NA, from Business Communications Co.

SIC 33 - Primary Metal Industries

★ 1544 ★
Metals
SIC: 3300; NAICS: 331111, 331221

Leading Service Centers in North America

Service centers are the single largest customer group for North American mills, buying and selling about 25% of all the steel, aluminum, copper and brass produced annually. Firms are ranked by annual sales in millions of dollars. Shares are shown based on $27.2 billion in revenues generated by the top 50 firms.

	($ mil.)	Share
Ryerson Tull Inc.	$ 2,200.0	8.09%
ThyssenKrupp Materials North America	1,850.0	6.80
Integris Metals Inc.	1,494.0	5.49
Reliance Steel & Aluminum Co.	1,383.0	5.08
Worthington Steel Co.	1,373.0	5.05
Samuel, Son & Co. Ltd.	1,150.0	4.23
Russel Metals	1,145.0	4.21
Macsteel Service Centers	1,000.0	3.68
Carpenter Technology Corp.	1,000.0	3.68
Earle M. Jorgensen Co.	964.3	3.55
Other	13,640.7	50.15

Source: *Metal Center News*, September 2004, p. 18, from *Metal Center News Top 50 survey*.

★ 1545 ★
Steel
SIC: 3312; NAICS: 331111, 331221

Largest Steel Producers in the Ukraine, 1999-2002

The iron and steel industry covers 365 enterprises. Market shares are averages.

Kryvorizstal	17.8%
Mariupol Illich	17.3
Azovztal	12.8
Zaporizhstal	11.0
Alchevsk	6.8
Dniprodzerz hynsk	6.6%
Other	27.7

Source: *Steel Times International*, October 2004, p. 38, from Vlad Mykhnenko.

★ 1546 ★
Steel
SIC: 3312; NAICS: 331111, 331221

Largest Steel Producing Nations Worldwide

Production is shown in millions of metric tons.

	(mil.)	Share
China	220.1	22.87%
Japan	110.5	11.48
United States	91.4	9.50
Russia	61.3	6.37
South Korea	46.3	4.81
Germany	44.8	4.65
Ukraine	36.7	3.81
India	31.8	3.30
Brazil	31.1	3.23
Italy	26.7	2.77
Other	261.8	27.20

Source: *Steel Times International*, February-March 2004, p. 6, from International Iron and Steel Institute.

★ 1547 ★
Steel
SIC: 3312; NAICS: 331111, 331221

Leading Carbon Steel Plate Makers in North America

Market shares are shown based on capacity.

International Steel Group	30.0%
Ipsco	27.0
Nucor	20.0
Oregon Steel	13.0
Jindal	13.0
Citisteel	5.0
LeTourneau	4.0

Source: *Metal Center News*, August 2004, p. 28.

★ 1548 ★

Steel

SIC: 3312; NAICS: 331111, 331221

Leading Crude Steel Firms in Japan, 2003

Market shares are estimated based on domestic output.

Nippon Steel	29.5%
JFE Holdings	27.5
Sumitomo Metal	11.5
Kobe Steel	6.6
Nisshin Steel	3.5
Other	21.4

Source: "Market Share Survey Report 2003." [online] from http://www.nni.nikkei.co.jp [Published July 26, 2004], from Nikkei estimates.

★ 1549 ★

Steel

SIC: 3312; NAICS: 331111, 331221

Leading Stainless Steel Makers in Japan, 2003

Market shares are estimated based on domestic production.

Nippon Steel & Sumikin Stainless Steel	29.3%
Nisshin Steel	18.8
JFE Steel	18.1
Nippon Yakin Kogyo	10.3
Nippon Metal Industry	9.7
Other	13.8

Source: "Market Share Survey Report 2003." [online] from http://www.nni.nikkei.co.jp [Published July 26, 2004], from Nikkei estimates.

★ 1550 ★

Steel

SIC: 3312; NAICS: 331111, 331221

Leading Steel Firms in Canada

Canadian mills hold about 3 or 4 percent of the steel market in the United States.

Stelco/Dofasco	65.0%
Other	35.0

Source: *Metal Center News*, November 2004, p. 36.

★ 1551 ★

Steel

SIC: 3312; NAICS: 331111, 331221

Leading Steel Producers in Western Europe

ThyssenKrupp was unsuccessful in its recent attempt to merge withCorus, Riva, Salzgittier and Voestalpine. Companies are ranked by output in millions of tons.

	(mil.)	Share
Arcelor	43	27.74%
Corus	19	12.26
ThyssenKrupp	16	10.32
Riva	16	10.32
Voestalpine	6	3.87
Salzgitter	5	3.23
SSAB	4	2.58
Rautarruuki	4	2.58
Lucchini	4	2.58
Celsa	4	2.58
Other	34	21.94

Source: *Financial Times*, October 19, 2004, p. 26, from James King consultancy and International Iron and Steel Institute.

★ 1552 ★

Steel

SIC: 3312; NAICS: 331111, 331221

Leading Steel Producers Worldwide, 2004

Companies are ranked by annual production in millions of tons.

	(mil.)	Share
Arcelor	43	4.3%
LNM	41	4.1
Posco	32	3.2
Nippon Steel	32	3.2
JFE	30	3.0
US Steel	20	2.0
ThyssenKrupp	20	2.0
Nucor	20	2.0
Boasteel	20	2.0
Corus	19	1.9
Other	723	72.3

Source: *Financial Times*, September 29, 2004, p. 11, from *Metal Bulletin* and World Steel Dynamics.

★ 1553 ★
Steel
SIC: 3312; NAICS: 331111, 331221

Rolled Steel Market

Market shares are shown in percent.

Mittal	.40.0%
United States Steel Corp.	.25.0
Nucor Corp.	7.0
Other	.28.0

Source: *Daily Deal*, December 21, 2004, p. NA, from U.S. Department of Justice.

★ 1554 ★
Steel
SIC: 3312; NAICS: 331111, 331221

Specialty Steel Consumption, 2004

Figures are for the first nine months of the year.

	Tons	Share
Stainless teel/strip	1,348,741	64.91%
Electrical steel	288,864	13.90
Stainless plate	221,118	10.64
Stainless bar	151,761	7.30
Stainless rod	67,529	3.25

Source: *PR Newswire*, December 23, 2004, p. NA, from Specialty Steel Industries of North America.

★ 1555 ★
Steel Wiring
SIC: 3315; NAICS: 331222, 332618

PC Strand Production

PC strand is used primarily to reinforce concrete and in non-residential and government facility construction. Market share is estimated.

Insteel Industries	.50.0%
Other	.50.0

Source: *Winston-Salem Journal*, July 11, 2004, p. D1.

★ 1556 ★
Steel Wiring
SIC: 3315; NAICS: 331222, 332618

Wire and Cable Demand, 2003 and 2008

Demand for wiring and cable products is forecast to grow 4% a year through 2008. Fiber optics was the largest growth sector, up 10.7%, followed by electronics at 6%.

	2003	2008	Share
Power and telephones . . .	$ 4,325	$ 5,100	25.50%
Transportation	3,740	4,385	21.92
Building	3,230	3,835	19.17
Electronics	2,755	3,690	18.45
Fiber optics	1,800	2,990	14.95

Source: *EC&M*, October 2004, p. 10, from Freedonia Group.

★ 1557 ★
H-Beams
SIC: 3316; NAICS: 331221

Leading H-Beam Firms in Japan, 2003

Market shares are estimated based on domestic output.

Tokyo Steel Mfg.	.35.2%
Nippon Steel	.16.6
Sumikinsteel & Shapes	.11.6
Yamato Steel	.11.0
NKK Bars & Shapes	9.5
Other	.16.1

Source: "Market Share Survey Report 2003." [online] from http://www.nni.nikkei.co.jp [Published July 26, 2004], from Nikkei estimates.

★ 1558 ★
Steel Coils
SIC: 3316; NAICS: 331221

Leading Hot-Roiled Coil Makers in Japan, 2003

Market shares are estimated based on domestic production of 43.43 million tons.

Nippon Steel	.37.4%
JFE Holdings	.34.0
Sumitomo Metal Industries	.12.3
Nisshin Steel	6.7
Other	9.6

Source: "Market Share Survey Report 2003." [online] from http://www.nni.nikkei.co.jp [Published July 26, 2004], from Nikkei estimates.

★ 1559 ★
Steel Tubes
SIC: 3317; NAICS: 33121

Leading Steel Tube Makers in the Ukraine, 1999-2003

Shares are averages based on sales.

Nyzhniodniprovsk Tube-Rolling Works	.55.6%
Novomosko vsk Tube Works	9.5
Khartsyzsk Tube Works	8.8
Nikopol Niko Tube	7.6
Nikopol Stainless Tube Works	3.8
Other	.14.6

Source: *Steel Times International*, October 2004, p. 38, from *Rusting Away? Ukranian Iron and Steel Industry in Transition*.

★ 1560 ★
Castings
SIC: 3321; NAICS: 331511

Castings Capacity, 2005

Data show capacity in tons. Shipments totaled 14.27 million tons in 2005 and are expected to climb to 15.27 million tons in 2008.

	Tons	Share
Iron	11,660,000	67.24%
Aluminum	2,990,000	17.24
Steel	1,460,000	8.42
Zinc/lead	410,000	2.36
Copper base	400,000	2.31
Investment	210,000	1.21
Magnesium	140,000	0.81
Other nonferrous	70,000	0.40

Source: *Modern Casting*, January 2005, p. 22, from *AFS Metalforecasting & Trends Report*.

★ 1561 ★
Foundries
SIC: 3321; NAICS: 331511

Foundries Market Shares Worldwide, 2004

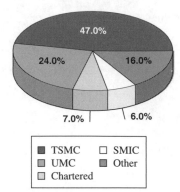

TSMC led in sales with an $8.03 billion in sales, followed by UMC at $4 billion, chartered with $1.22 billion, SMIC with $1.03 billion and Dongbu/Anam at $0.45 billion. Growth rate forecasts for 2004: SMIC 181%, chartered 67%, UMC 53%, TSMC 37% and Dongbu/Anam 36%.

TSMC	.47.0%
UMC	.24.0
Chartered	7.0
SMIC	6.0
Other	.16.0

Source: *Investor's Business Daily*, August 12, 2004, p. A4, from IC Insights.

★ 1562 ★
Copper
SIC: 3331; NAICS: 331411

Top Copper Markets, 2004

Production was valued at $3.4 billion in the United States.

Building construction	.48.0%
Electric and electronic products	.21.0
Consumer and general products	.11.0
Transportation equipment	.10.0
Industrial machinery and equipment	.10.0

Source: *Mineral Commodities Summaries 2005*, January 2005, p. 54, from U.S. Geological Survey, U.S. Department of the Interior.

★ 1563 ★

Aluminum

SIC: 3334; NAICS: 331312

Aluminum Production in Russia

The company was created by the merger of the four largest aluminum smelters in the country.

Rusal	.75.0%
Other	.25.0

Source: *Aluminum International Today*, July/August 2004, p. 14.

★ 1564 ★

Aluminum

SIC: 3334; NAICS: 331312

How Aluminum is Used, 2004

Production fell from 2.7 million metric tons in 2002 to 2.5 million metric tons in 2004.

Transportation	.38.0%
Packaging	.29.0
Building	.13.0
Electrical	6.0
Consumer durables	6.0
Other	8.0

Source: *Mineral Commodity Summaries*, 2005, p. 20, from U.S. Geological Survey, U.S. Department of the Interior.

★ 1565 ★

Aluminum

SIC: 3334; NAICS: 331312

Largest Aluminum Consumers, 2004

The industry has seen considerable consolidation in the previous decade. The number of primary aluminum producing companies has fallen by more than 50%. The top five companies (led by Alcoa) control 60% of world capacity. In the United states, the top five control 75% of capacity. Total consumption was 27.4 million tons. CIS stands for Commonwealth of Independent States.

North America	.24.0%
Western Europe	.23.0
China	.19.0
Japan	9.0
Eastern Europe	3.0
CIS	3.0
Other	.19.0

Source: *Aluminum International Today*, September - October 2004, p. 67.

★ 1566 ★

Aluminum

SIC: 3334; NAICS: 331312

Leading Aluminum Product Makers in Japan, 2003

Market shares are estimated based on domestic output of 2.3 million tons.

Furukawa-Sky Aluminum	.17.9%
Kobe Steel	.15.8
Sumitomo Light Metal	.15.7
Mitsubishi Aluminum	7.4
Showa Denko	4.2
Other	.39.0

Source: "Market Share Survey Report 2003." [online] from http://www.nni.nikkei.co.jp [Published July 26, 2004], from Nikkei estimates.

★ 1567 ★

Aluminum

SIC: 3334; NAICS: 331312

Top Aluminum Smelter Producing Nations, 2004

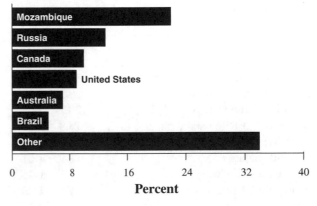

Production is estimated in thousands of tons.

	(000)	Share
Mozambique	6,100	22.17%
Russia	3,600	13.09
Canada	2,640	9.60
United States	2,500	9.09
Australia	1,880	6.83
Brazil	1,450	5.27
Other	9,340	33.95

Source: *Mineral Commodities Summaries 2005*, January 2005, p. 20, from U.S. Geological Survey, U.S. Department of the Interior.

★ 1568 ★

Cadmium

SIC: 3339; NAICS: 331419

How Cadmium is Used, 2004

Only two companies produce cadmium, one in Tennessee and Pennsylvania. The combined output of primary and secondary metal was valued at $790,000 in 2004.

Batteries	78.0%
Pigments	12.0
Coatings and plating	8.0
Stabilizers for plastics	1.5
Nonferrous alloys and other	0.5

Source: *Mineral Commodities Summaries 2005*, January 2005, p. 20, from U.S. Geological Survey, U.S. Department of the Interior.

★ 1569 ★

Aluminum Foil

SIC: 3353; NAICS: 331315

Top Aluminum Foil/Wrap Brands, 2005

Brands are ranked by supermarket, drug store and discount outlet sales (excluding Wal-Mart) for the 52 weeks ended February 20, 2005.

	($ mil.)	Share
Reynolds Wrap foil	$ 197.5	35.64%
Reynolds wrap	35.2	6.35
Glad Cling wrap	35.2	6.35
Glad Press 'n Seal wrap	29.5	5.32
Reynolds Wrap Release foil	20.2	3.64
Reynolds Cut Rite waxed paper	18.3	3.30
Saran wrap	16.6	3.00
Reynolds paper	8.9	1.61
Saran Cling Plus wrap	8.1	1.46
Saran Quick Covers wrap	6.8	1.23
Other	177.9	32.10

Source: *MMR*, May 30, 2005, p. 33, from Information Resources Inc.

★ 1570 ★

Copy Machine Wires

SIC: 3357; NAICS: 331422

Copy Machine Wires in Japan

The company has half of the market for stainless steel wires used in the drive for copying machines.

Aichi Prefecture	50.0%
Other	50.0

Source: *Asia Africa Intelligence Wire*, July 1, 2004, p. NA.

SIC 34 - Fabricated Metal Products

★ 1571 ★
Beverage Cans
SIC: 3411; NAICS: 332431

Leading Beverage Can Makers in Europe, 2004

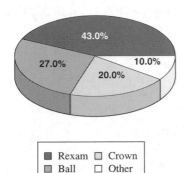

The industry was valued at 40 billion cans.

Rexam	.43.0%
Ball	.27.0
Crown	.20.0
Other	.10.0

Source: "Beverage Cans in Europe." [online] from http://www.rexam.com/index.asp?pageid523 [Accessed June 14, 2005], from Rexam estimates.

★ 1572 ★
Beverage Cans
SIC: 3411; NAICS: 332431

Leading Beverage Can Makers in South America, 2004

The industry was valued at 10 billion cans.

Rexam	.64.0%
Crown	.17.0
Ball	.15.0
Metallic	.4.0

Source: "Beverage Cans in South America." [online] from http://www.rexam.com/index.asp?pageid523 [Accessed June 14, 2005], from Rexam estimates.

★ 1573 ★
Beverage Cans
SIC: 3411; NAICS: 332431

Leading Beverage Can Makers Worldwide, 2004

Market shares are shown in percent.

Rexam	.23.0%
Ball	.20.0
Crown	.14.0
Metal Containers	.12.0
Other	.31.0

Source: "Beverage Packaging." [online] from http://www.rexam.com/index.asp?pageid523 [Accessed June 14, 2005], from Rexam estimates.

★ 1574 ★
Razor Blades
SIC: 3421; NAICS: 332211

Top Blade Brands (Cartridge), 2004

Market shares are shown for the food stores, drug stores and mass merchandisers (excluding Wal-Mart) for the 52 weeks ended October 31, 2004.

Gillette Mach3	.25.7%
Gillette Mach3 Turbo	.19.5
Gillette Venus	.10.5
Gillette Sensor	.7.3
Schick Intuition	.5.6
Gillette Sensor	.5.0
Schick Quattro	.3.5
Gillette M3 Power	.3.0
Gillette Venus Divine	.2.7
Private label	.3.3
Other	.13.9

Source: *Grocery Headquarters*, December 2004, p. 54, from Information Resources Inc.

★ 1575 ★

Razor Blades

SIC: 3421; NAICS: 332211

Top Blade Makers (Cartridge), 2004

Market shares are shown for the food stores, drug stores and mass merchandisers (excluding Wal-Mart) for the 52 weeks ended October 31, 2004.

Gillette	82.8%
Energizer	13.3
American Safety Razor	0.6
Procter & Gamble	0.1
Private label	3.3

Source: *Grocery Headquarters*, December 2004, p. 54, from Information Resources Inc.

★ 1576 ★

Razor Blades

SIC: 3421; NAICS: 332211

Top Razor Blade Makers, 2004

Market shares are shown for the food stores, drug stores and mass merchandisers (excluding Wal-Mart) for the 52 weeks ended October 31, 2004.

Gillette	63.3%
Energizer	34.5
Procter & Gamble	0.4
American Safety Razor	0.1
Private label	1.6
Other	1.0

Source: *Grocery Headquarters*, December 2004, p. 54, from Information Resources Inc.

★ 1577 ★

Razor Blades

SIC: 3421; NAICS: 332211

Top Razors, 2005

Brands are ranked by supermarket, drug store and discount store sales (excluding Wal-Mart) for the 52 weeks ended January 23, 2005.

	($ mil.)	Share
Gillette M3 Power	$ 35.9	16.85%
Schick Intuition	28.7	13.47
Schick Quattro	24.3	11.41
Gillette Venus Divine	20.5	9.62
Gillette Mach3 Turbo	12.7	5.96
Gillette Mach3	12.3	5.77
Gillette Mach3 Champion	12.3	5.77
Gillette Venus Passion	10.0	4.69
Gillette Venus	8.3	3.90

	($ mil.)	Share
Gillette Sensor 3	$ 4.8	2.25%
Other	43.2	20.28

Source: *MMR*, March 21, 2005, p. 21, from Information Resources Inc.

★ 1578 ★

Hand Tools

SIC: 3423; NAICS: 332212

Hand Tool Imports in Australia, 2003

In 2002, the $17 billion hardware industry was composed of 62% trade and 38% DIY. Hand tools were a significant part of the DIY sector. In 2003, imports stood at $674.9 million.

China	28.0%
United States	16.6
Germany	10.8
Japan	10.3
Taiwan	8.6
United Kingdom	4.8
Other	20.9

Source: "US & FCS Market Research Reports." [online] from http://www.stat-usa.gov [Published November 2004].

★ 1579 ★

Tools

SIC: 3423; NAICS: 332212

Hammer Sales by Type, 2004

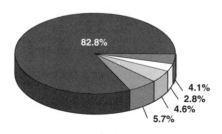

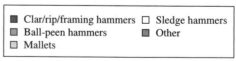

Sales are shown for October - December 2004. A total of 3,964,307 hammers were sold for a value of $45,903,610.

Clar/rip/framing hammers	82.8%
Ball-peen hammers	5.7
Mallets	4.6

Continued on next page.

[Continued]
Tools
SIC: 3423; NAICS: 332212

Hammer Sales by Type, 2004

Sales are shown for October - December 2004. A total of 3,964,307 hammers were sold for a value of $45,903,610.

Sledge hammers	2.8%
Other	4.1

Source: *Home Channel News*, March 7, 2005, p. 26, from NPD Group/NPD Houseworld — Consumer.

★ 1580 ★
Tools
SIC: 3423; NAICS: 332212

Tool Imports by Type

According to the source, the net tool market is forecast to grow from $15.4 billion in 2007 to $16.6 billion in 2012. New home construction and renovation help fuel the market growth.

Electric	.37.0%
Hand	.30.0
Pneumatic	.16.0
Gas engines	. 6.0
Other	.11.0

Source: *Tools of the Trade*, July-August 2004, p. 30, from Freedonia Group.

★ 1581 ★
Locks
SIC: 3429; NAICS: 332722

Door Lock Finishes

The 32 million units represent $737.3 million.

Polished brass	.48.0%
Antique brass	.18.0

Brushed steel/nickel	.15.0%
Chrome	6.0
Other	.13.0

Source: *Do-It-Yourself Retailing*, June 2005, p. 58, from NPD Group and NPD Houseworld.

★ 1582 ★
Faucets
SIC: 3432; NAICS: 332913

Bathroom Faucet Market, 2003

Data show the preferred types of metals.

Chrome	.59.0%
Stainless steel	.14.0
Polished brass	.13.0
Nickel	. 5.0
Solid color	. 4.0
Other	. 5.0

Source: *Kitchen & Bath Design News*, June 2004, p. NA, from National Kitchen & Bath Association 2003 research.

★ 1583 ★
Faucets
SIC: 3432; NAICS: 332913

Faucet Market Shares

Market shares are shown in percent.

Masco	.25.0%
Delta	.25.0
Other	.50.0

Source: *Indianapolis Star*, May 1, 2005, p. NA, from Bear Stearns & Co.

★ 1584 ★
Faucets
SIC: 3432; NAICS: 332913

Kitchen Faucet Market, 2003

Data show the preferred types of metals.

Chrome	.61.0%
Stainless steel	.23.0
Solid color	. 9.0
Polished brass	. 2.0
Nickel	. 2.0
Other	. 3.0

Source: *Kitchen & Bath Design News*, June 2004, p. NA, from National Kitchen & Bath Association 2003 research.

★ 1585 ★
Pool Heating Equipment
SIC: 3433; NAICS: 333414

Solar Heaters for Pools

The company claims to have 70% of the market for so-lar pool heating and hot-water heater controls.

Goldline Controls Inc. 70.0%
Other 30.0

Source: *Pool & Spa News*, July 7, 2004, p. 1.

★ 1586 ★
Solar Equipment
SIC: 3433; NAICS: 333414

Largest Solar Equipment Makers Worldwide, 2003

Companies are ranked by megawatts of capacity sold.

Sharp 198
Shell Solar 77
Kyocera 72
BPSolar 70
RWE 42
Mitsubishi 40
Sanyo 35
Isofoton 35
Q-Cells 28
Photowatt 20

Source: *BusinessWeek*, September 6, 2004, p. 95, from PV Energy Systems Inc.

★ 1587 ★
Solar Equipment
SIC: 3433; NAICS: 333414

Leading Solar Battery Makers in Japan, 2003

Market shares are estimated based on domestic ship-ments.

Sharp 54.4%
Kyocera 16.1
Sanyo Electric 13.0
Mitsubishi Electric 8.9
Kaneka 5.8
Other 1.8

Source: "Market Share Survey Report 2003." [online] from http://www.nni.nikkei.co.jp [Published July 26, 2004], from Nikkei estimates.

★ 1588 ★
Aluminum Sashes
SIC: 3442; NAICS: 332321

Leading Aluminum Sash Makers in Japan, 2003

Market shares are estimated based on domestic ship-ments of 233,602 tons.

Tostem 35.4%
YKK AP 28.5
Sankyo Aluminum 15.8
Shin Nikkei 13.2
Tateyama Aluminum 5.7
Other 1.4

Source: "Market Share Survey Report 2003." [online] from http://www.nni.nikkei.co.jp [Published July 26, 2004], from Nikkei estimates.

★ 1589 ★
Door Hardware
SIC: 3442; NAICS: 332321

Door Hardware Market Shares

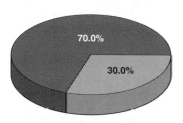

■ Bright brass ■ Alternative finishes

Four companies now account for 20% of the $25 bil-lion door and window industry. Alternative finishes in-clude copper, distressed brass, bronze and satin-nick-el.

Bright brass 70.0%
Alternative finishes 30.0

Source: *Assembly*, June 1, 2004, p. NA.

★ 1590 ★
Metal Buildings
SIC: 3448; NAICS: 332311

Metal Building Industry, 2004

Roughly 40% of non-residential low-rise buildings constructed during the year were made of metal building systems. This share has been increasing steadily since 2001 when the share was 32.9%. Manufacturing refers to plants, labs and warehouses. Community buildings include churches and educational and government establishments. Market shares are shown based on the 40.9% of low-rise buildings made of metal.

Commercial buildings 43.7%
Manufacturing 30.6
Community buildings 16.9
Other 9.8

Source: "MBMA Study Shows Increase in Market Share for Metal Building Construction." [online] from http://www.businesswire.com [Accessed June 6, 2005], from Metal Building Manufacturers Association.

★ 1591 ★
Fasteners
SIC: 3451; NAICS: 332721

Assembly Fastening Market Worldwide

The global industry is valued at $350 billion with an average growth rate placed at 4-5% for 2003 - 2006.

Weld/braze 28.0%
Rivets 20.0
Bolts & nuts 20.0
Crimps 10.0
Tabs 6.0
Adhesives 6.0
Other 10.0

Source: *Adhesives & Sealants Industry*, January 2005, p. 13, from DPNA International.

★ 1592 ★
Fasteners
SIC: 3451; NAICS: 332721

Carbon Screw Market in Canada

The industry is valued at $189 million.

China/Taiwan 55.0%
Other 45.0

Source: *American Metal Market*, January 31, 2005, p. 5.

★ 1593 ★
Fasteners
SIC: 3451; NAICS: 332721

Industrial Fastener Demand Worldwide

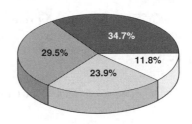

| ■ Asia/Pacific | □ Western Europe |
| ■ North America | □ Other |

Global demand is expected to increase 5% through 2008, from $3.77 billion in 2003 to $4.82 billion in 2008. The industry will be stimulated by construction activity and the manufacturing of durable goods.

	2003	2008	Share
Asia/Pacific	$ 12,150	$ 16,750	34.72%
North America	11,400	14,250	29.53
Western Europe	9,900	11,550	23.94
Other	4,300	5,700	11.81

Source: *Wire Journal International*, August 2004, p. 37, from Freedonia Group.

★ 1594 ★
Fasteners
SIC: 3451; NAICS: 332721

World Fastener Market

The industry is valued at $350 billion.

Welding and brazing 28.0%
Rivets 20.0
Bolts and nuts 20.0
Crimps 10.0
Screws and nails 7.0
Tabs 6.0
Adhesives 6.0
Tape 3.0
Other 20.0

Source: *Advanced Manufacturing Technology*, February 15, 2005, p. 11, from DPNA International.

★ 1595 ★
Rotary Bolting
SIC: 3452; NAICS: 332722

Rotary Bolting Units for Coal Mining in South Africa

The company has 85% of the market for rotary bolting units used in underground coal mining in South Africa.

Rham Equipment 85.0%
Other 15.0

Source: *World Mining Equipment*, October 2004, p. 19.

★ 1596 ★
Forging
SIC: 3462; NAICS: 332111

Impression-Die Forging Sales in North America, 2004

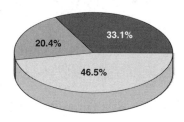

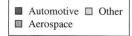

Total shipments of custom impression-die forging stood at $4.9 billion, up 26% from the $3.9 billion in shipments from 2003.

Automotive 33.1%
Aerospace 20.4
Other 46.5

Source: *Forging*, May - June 2005, p. 16, from Forging Industry Association.

★ 1597 ★
Automotive Trim
SIC: 3465; NAICS: 33637

Global Auto Interiors Market

The top 10 firms are SAS Automotive, Visteon, Johnson Controls, Faurecia, Collins & Aikman, Lear, Intier, Calsonic Kansei, Grupo Antolin and Peguform. They control $16.5 billion of the $25.7 billion interiors market.

Top 10 . . . . .64.0%
Other 36.0

Source: *PR Newswire*, May 17, 2005, p. NA, from CSM Worldwide.

★ 1598 ★
Automotive Trim
SIC: 3465; NAICS: 33637

Interior Trim Industry in North America

The top five firms are Visteon, Lear, Johnson Controls, Delphi and CalsonicLansei.

Top five firms 65.0%
Other 35.0

Source: "Automotive Trim Market Growing to $10B." [online] from http://www.csmauto.com [accessed November 15, 2004], from CSM Worldwide.

★ 1599 ★
Bakeware
SIC: 3469; NAICS: 332116

Bakeware Sales by Shape, 2004

Unit shares are shown based on shape. Figures are shown based on 18.6 billion units valued at $191.1 billion.

Rectangle 52.2%
Round 30.0
Oval 7.1
Square 6.6
Multi 1.0

Source: *DSN Retailing Today*, May 9, 2005, p. 27, from NPD Group/NPD Household/POS.

★ 1600 ★
Metal Powders
SIC: 3479; NAICS: 332812

Metal Powder Industry, 2003 and 2008

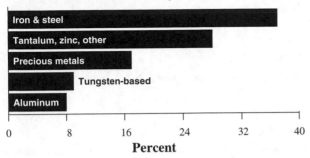

Demand increased from $1.6 billion in 2003 to $2.32 billion in 2008. The industry growth will be driven by improved outlook for the computer and electronic component markets.

	2003	2008	Share
Iron & steel	$ 603	$ 890	37.39%
Tantalum, zinc, other	452	670	28.15
Precious metals	248	400	16.81
Tungsten-based	155	225	9.45
Aluminum	152	195	8.19

Source: *Welding Design & Fabrication*, May 2004, p. 10, from Freedonia Group.

★ 1601 ★
Guns
SIC: 3484; NAICS: 332994

Air Gun Market

About 3.2 million BB guns and pellet guns are sold annually. BB guns represent about a third of the total. "Other" includes Marksman Corp., Gamo Precision and Air Guns Inc.

Daisy	60.0%
Other	40.0

Source: *Arkansas Business*, December 6, 2004, p. 1.

★ 1602 ★
Guns
SIC: 3484; NAICS: 332994

Largest Firearm Makers, 2003

There was a modest dip in production during the year, from 3.34 million to 3.27 million. This comes on the heels of the 15% increase in production that took place in 2002. Production includes pistols, revolvers, rifles, and shotguns.

	Units	Share
Remington Arms	591,272	18.04%
Sturm, Ruger & Co.	448,449	13.68
Marlin Firearms	238,542	7.28
H&R 1871	202,202	6.17
Smith & Wesson	198,634	6.06
O.F. Mossberg & Sons	181,160	5.53
U.S. Repeating Arms	168,386	5.14
Springfield	98,019	2.99
Savage Arms	96,788	2.95
Beretta U.S.A.	88,460	2.70
Other	965,514	29.46

Source: "Poised for Growth." [online] from http://www.shootingindustry.com/02pages/SpecRep1.html [Accessed July 18, 2005], from Bureau of Alcohol, Firearms & Tobacco.

★ 1603 ★
Guns
SIC: 3484; NAICS: 332994

Largest Handgun Makers, 2003

Handgun production has been on the increase in recent years: 943,213 in 2001, 1,088,584 in 2002 and 1,121,024 in 2003.

	Units	Share
Sturm, Ruger & Co.	209,316	18.67%
Smith & Wesson	198,634	17.72
Beretta	92,033	8.21
Beemiller	81,150	7.24
Springfield	78,254	6.98
Bryco Arms	59,841	5.34
Sigarms	57,501	5.13
Kimber Mfg.	48,245	4.30
Kel-Tec	47,020	4.19
Other	249,030	22.21

Source: "Poised for Growth." [online] from http://www.shootingindustry.com/02pages/SpecRep1.html [Accessed July 18, 2005], from Bureau of Alcohol, Firearms & Tobacco.

★ 1604 ★
Guns
SIC: 3484; NAICS: 332994

Largest Pistol Makers, 2003

Pistol production was 811,660 units.

	Units	Share
Sturm, Ruger & Co.	98,422	12.13%
Beretta	92,033	11.34
Beemiller	81,150	10.00
Springfield	78,254	9.64
Smith & Wesson	78,236	9.64
Bryco Arms	59,841	7.37
Sigarms	57,501	7.08
Kimber Mfg.	48,245	5.94
Kel-Tec	47,020	5.79
Other	170,958	21.06

Source: "Poised for Growth." [online] from http://
www.shootingindustry.com/02pages/SpecRep1.html
[Accessed July 18, 2005], from Bureau of Alcohol, Firearms
& Tobacco.

★ 1605 ★
Guns
SIC: 3484; NAICS: 332994

Largest Rifle Makers, 2003

*Total production was 1,284,554 units in 2001,
1,515,286 units in 2002 to 1,430,324 units in 2003.*

	Units	Share
Remington	290,873	20.34%
Ruger	234,595	16.40
Marlin	233,759	16.34
Other	671,097	46.92

Source: "Poised for Growth." [online] from http://
www.shootingindustry.com/02pages/SpecRep1.html
[Accessed July 18, 2005], from Bureau of Alcohol, Firearms
& Tobacco.

★ 1606 ★
Guns
SIC: 3484; NAICS: 332994

U.S. Gun Exports, 2003

Data include handguns, rifles and shotguns.

	Units	Share
Canada	55,091	20.37%
United Kingdom	33,847	12.51
Japan	14,789	5.47
Germany	13,469	4.98
Australia	13,050	4.82
Colombia	12,489	4.62%
Italy	12,334	4.56
Spain	8,839	3.27
Belgium	6,562	2.43
France	5,516	2.04
Ecuador	5,197	1.92
Other	89,323	33.02

Source: *Shooting Industry*, July 2004, p. 38.

★ 1607 ★
Valves
SIC: 3491; NAICS: 332911

Industrial Valve Shipments

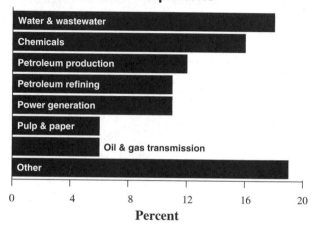

*Value of shipments is forecast to increase slightly from
$3.16 billion in 2003 to $3.18 billion in 2004.*

Water & wastewater	17.9%
Chemicals	16.2
Petroleum production	12.4
Petroleum refining	11.4
Power generation	11.0
Pulp & paper	6.3
Oil & gas transmission	5.7
Other	19.0

Source: *Supply House Times*, June 2004, p. 28, from Valve
Manufacturers Association of America.

★ 1608 ★
Valves
SIC: 3491; NAICS: 332911
World Valve Market

Companies in the eleventh through fifteenth positions have only 3% market share. The industry is forecasted to increase from $38 billion in 2003 to $44 billion in 2007.

Tyco/Flowserve/Emerson/Dresser/Kitz 12.0%
ABB/SPX/Circor/Metso/KSB 4.0
Other 84.0

Source: "World Valve Market to Exceed $44 Billion by 2007." [online] from http://www.mcilvanecompany.com [Accessed June 24, 2005], from McIlvane Company.

★ 1609 ★
Fences
SIC: 3496; NAICS: 332618
Electric Fence Market in New Zealand

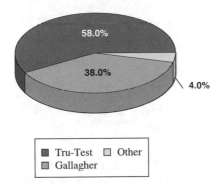

Market shares are shown in percent.

Tru-Test 58.0%
Gallagher 38.0
Other 4.0

Source: "Commission Decision Ensures Choice and Innovation for Farmers." [online] from http://www.tru-test.com [Published August 26, 2004].

★ 1610 ★
Stabilizing Bars
SIC: 3499; NAICS: 332999
Leading Stabilizer Bars in Japan

Chup Spring's share is estimated at 30-35% and Mitsubishi Steel at 5-10%.

NHK 60.0%
Chup Spring 35.0
Mitsubishi Steel Manufacturing 10.0

Source: *Automotive Industries*, March 2005, p. 8.

SIC 35 - Industry Machinery and Equipment

★ 1611 ★
Generators
SIC: 3511; NAICS: 333611

Electronic Chlorine Generator Market

The company has more than 65% of the market.

Goldline Controls 65.0%
Other 35.0

Source: *Pool & Spa News*, July 7, 2004, p. 1.

★ 1612 ★
Generators
SIC: 3511; NAICS: 333611

Largest Diesel Generator Exporters Worldwide, 2003 and 2004

China was the leading importer of diesel generating sets (about $400 million). The source points out that export records in this field are notoriously inaccurate, however. The leading exporters of diesel generating sets are shown in millions of dollars. Data are for sets 1 kVA to over 2000 kVA. The total number of units exported fell 11% over 2003 to 290,475 in 2004

	2003	2004
European Union	$ 1,161	$ 1,325
United Kingdom	892	1,108
United States	529	518
Japan	191	140

Source: *African Review of Business and Technology*, April 2005, p. 69.

★ 1613 ★
Generators
SIC: 3511; NAICS: 333611

Leading Wind Power Generators in Japan, 2003

Market shares are estimated based on domestic deliveries of 2.73 billion kilowatts.

Vestas Wind Systems 33.5%
General Electric 20.3
Nordex 10.9

Bonus Energy 8.1%
JFE Engineering 8.0
Other 19.2

Source: "Market Share Survey Report 2003." [online] from http://www.nni.nikkei.co.jp [Published July 26, 2004], from Japan Wind Power Association.

★ 1614 ★
Turbines
SIC: 3511; NAICS: 333611

Leading Turbine Makers Worldwide, 2002

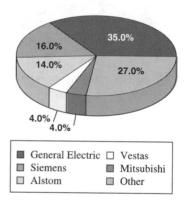

Market shares are shown in percent.

General Electric 35.0%
Siemens 16.0
Alstom 14.0
Vestas 4.0
Mitsubishi 4.0
Other 27.0

Source: *Business Economics*, July 2004, p. 60.

★ 1615 ★
Turbines
SIC: 3511; NAICS: 333618

Leading Wind Turbine Makers in Germany, 2003

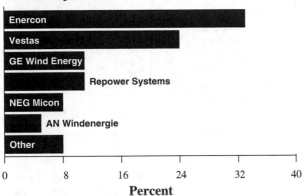

Percent

The wind industry reached 2,645 megawatts in 2003, down 18% from 3,247 megawatts in 2002.

Enercon	.33.4%
Vestas	.23.5
GE Wind Energy	.11.2
Repower Systems	.10.7
NEG Micon	8.2
AN Windenergie	5.0
Other	8.0

Source: "US & FCS Market Research Reports." [online] from http://www.stat-usa.gov [Published July 15, 2004].

★ 1616 ★
Turbines
SIC: 3511; NAICS: 333611

Wind Power Worldwide

Worldwide, global wind capacity surged 25% during 2003. Wind power is expected to increase in Europe in the next two decades. By 2020 wind power is expected to generate more than 12% of the region's electricity. Distribution is shown based on global wind turbine production.

Germany	.37.0%
United States	.16.0
Spain	.16.0
Denmark	8.0
India	5.0
Other	.18.0

Source: *Technology Review*, September 2004, p. 24.

★ 1617 ★
Turbines
SIC: 3511; NAICS: 333611

World Turbine Demand, 2002 and 2007

Figures are in billions of dollars.

	2002	2007	Share
Electric power	.$ 27.4	$ 40.0	52.22%
Aircraft	24.6	32.9	42.95
Marine & other	2.6	3.7	4.83

Source: *Business Economics*, July 2004, p. 60.

★ 1618 ★
Engines
SIC: 3519; NAICS: 333618

Largest Engine Families Worldwide

Engine manufacturers are facing pressure to increase economies of scale by using common components and modules. To belong to the same family should have common bore centres. Figures are in units produced.

Volkswagen EA827/113	1,948,784
Volkswagen EA086/153/188	1,879,576
GM GEN3/GEN4	1,808,042
Ford MOD I V8	1,411,215
Adam Opel I	1,394,927
Suzuki F	1,335,380
PSA DW	1,270,674
PSA TU	1,238,069

Source: *just-auto.com*, February 2005, p. 1, from PricewaterhouseCoopers Autofacts.

★ 1619 ★
Engines
SIC: 3519; NAICS: 333618

Leading Boat Engine Makers in North America

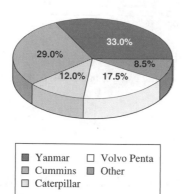

Legend: Yanmar, Cummins, Caterpillar, Volvo Penta, Other

Shares are shown based on total repower and new construction.

	2001	2003
Yanmar	31.0%	33.0%
Cummins	28.0	29.0
Caterpillar	19.5	12.0
Volvo Penta	12.5	17.5
Other	9.0	8.5

Source: *Diesel Progress North American Edition*, August 2004, p. 40, from National Marine Manufacturers Association.

★ 1620 ★
Engines
SIC: 3519; NAICS: 333618

Power Equipment Engine Industry

Market shares are shown in percent.

Cars & light trucks, on-highway	33.0%
Lawn & garden	15.0
Cars & trucks, medium & heavy	14.0
Power sports	11.0
Marine	8.0
Construction & industrial	8.0
Power generation	7.0
Agricultural	4.0

Source: *Diesel Progress North American Edition*, December 2004, p. 24.

★ 1621 ★
Farm Equipment
SIC: 3523; NAICS: 333111

Farm Tractor Sales, 2003 and 2005

Sales increases are forecast for all types of tractors sold in 2004. The largest gains will be in the 2 WD 100 PTO hp and over sector, which will increase 17.4% and 4 WD which will increase 19%. Data for 2005 are forecasted.

	2003	2005	Share
2-wheel drive, 100 PTO HP & over	14,223	14,298	3.33%
2-wheel drive, 40-100 PTO HP	60,304	59,693	13.89
2-wheel drive, under 40 PTO HP	125,333	136,315	31.73
4-wheel drive	199,860	219,316	51.05

Source: *Implement & Tractor*, July-August 2004, p. 27, from Association of Equipment Manufacturers.

★ 1622 ★
Farm Equipment
SIC: 3523; NAICS: 333111

Farm Tractor Sales in Canada, 2003 and 2005

Data for 2005 are forecast.

	2003	2005
2 wheel drive, 100 PTO IIP & over	3,794	3,495
2 wheel drive, 40-100 PTO HP	6,511	6,617
2 wheel drive, under 40 PTO HP	5,596	5,825
4 wheel drive	673	718

Source: *Implement & Tractor*, July-August 2004, p. 27, from Association of Equipment Manufacturers.

★ 1623 ★
Farm Equipment
SIC: 3523; NAICS: 333111

Herd Recording Market Worldwide

Market shares are shown in percent.

Tru-Test	95.0%
Other	5.0

Source: "Milk Meter Products." [online] from http://www.tru-test.com/milkmeter [Accessed March 9, 2005].

★ 1624 ★

Farm Equipment

SIC: 3523; NAICS: 333111

Leading Farm Equipment Makers Worldwide, 2003

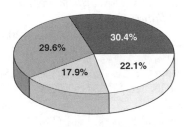

Market shares are shown in percent.

Deere	.30.4%
CNH	.29.6
Agco	.17.9
Other	.22.1

Source: *Financial Times*, January 6, 2005, p. 15, from JPMorgan estimates.

★ 1625 ★

Farm Equipment

SIC: 3523; NAICS: 333111

Leading Tractor Makers in Argentina, 2004

Sales of tractors during the first eleven months stood at 5,646 units, up 56% over the same period in 2003. In that year, the harvesting equipment sector saw its best sales in three years. Market shares are shown in percent.

John Deere	.23.0%
CNH	.17.2
Pauny	.13.0
Valtra	.12.0
Other	.34.8

Source: *America's Intelligence Wire*, December 13, 2004, p. NA, from AFAT.

★ 1626 ★

Farm Equipment

SIC: 3523; NAICS: 333111

Leading Tractor Makers in the U.K.

The market remained at its highest level ever. While 4X2 dropped by 11.6%, 3 axle units increased 4.8% (3 axles also represent 72% of the market).

	Units	Share
Daf	4,199	22.47%
Volvo	3,447	18.44
Scania	3,340	17.87
Mercedes	3,255	17.42
ERF	1,219	6.52
MAN	1,186	6.35
Renault	1,125	6.02
Iveco	552	2.95
Other	366	1.96

Source: *Motor Transport*, January 13, 2005, p. 24.

★ 1627 ★

Farm Equipment

SIC: 3523; NAICS: 333111

Top Tractor Makers in the U.K.

Data show unit shipments.

	Units	Share
CNH	4,680	31.1%
John Deere	3,939	26.2
AGCO	2,613	17.4
McCormick	1,060	7.0
Valtra	586	3.9
Renault	546	3.6
JCB	268	1.8
Other	1,351	9.0

Source: *Implement & Tractor*, March - April 2005, p. 10.

★ 1628 ★

Lawn & Garden Equipment

SIC: 3524; NAICS: 332212, 333112

Electric Garden Tool Market in Europe, 2003

Market shares are shown in percent.

Great Britain	.24.0%
Germany	.24.0
France	.13.0
Other	.39.0

Source: ''Bosch Garden Tools.'' [online] from http://www.bosch-presse.de [Published August 5, 2004].

★ 1629 ★

Lawn & Garden Equipment

SIC: 3524; NAICS: 333112, 333112

Leading Mower Makers (Walk Behind, Gas), 2003

Market shares are shown based on shipments of 5.6 million.

Electrolux Home Products	.24.0%
Murray	.18.0
MTD Products	.18.0
Toro	9.0
Snapper	2.0
Other	.29.0

Source: *Appliance*, September 2004, pp. P-3, from *Appliance Magazine's 27th Annual Portrait of the U.S. Appliance Industry.*

★ 1630 ★

Lawn & Garden Equipment

SIC: 3524; NAICS: 332212, 333112

Turf Care Products, 2003-2004

There was a 27% increase in turf care products for the model year (September 2003 - August 2004). Much of this increase came from zero-turn radio technology. Transmission steer midmount increased 44%. Shipments are shown for model year (September and runs through August).

	2003	2004	Share
Transmission steer mid-mount	129,543	186,571	62.80%
Walk-behind rotary turf mowers	48,874	49,871	16.79
Intermediate walk-behind mowers	39,457	44,205	14.88
Rear wheel steer front mount	8,065	7,999	2.69
Transmission steer front mount	7,140	7,191	2.42
3-wheel rider	1,396	1,247	0.42

Source: *Outdoor Power Equipment*, January 2005, p. 6, from Outdoor Power Equipment Institute.

★ 1631 ★

Construction Equipment

SIC: 3531; NAICS: 33312

Construction Machinery Industry in Italy, 2001-2003

Data show unit sales. The earthmoving market was valued at $1.2 billion in 2003.

	2001	2002	2003
Mini-excavators	9,638	11,441	9,761
Skid-steer loaders	4,201	4,540	3,649
AWS backhoe loaders	3,229	3,046	2,224
Wheel loaders	1,994	2,205	1,899
Rigid backhoe loaders	1,698	1,604	1,200
Telehandlers	1,688	1,930	1,901
Crawler loaders	175	166	117
Bulldozers	164	162	134

Source: "US & FCS Market Research Reports." [online] from http://www.stat-usa.gov [Published July 28, 2004], from COMAMOTER and Cantiermacchini.

★ 1632 ★

Construction Equipment

SIC: 3531; NAICS: 33312

Largest Construction Equipment Markets in Europe, 2003 and 2005

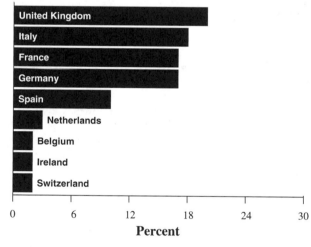

By type of equipment, mini excavator sales are forecast to be 42,105 units, crawler excavators 19,485 units and backhoe loaders 12,942 units.

	2003	2005	Share
United Kingdom	26,246	27,043	19.65%
Italy	26,687	24,480	17.79
France	22,407	23,465	17.05
Germany	21,669	23,211	16.86
Spain	13,845	13,275	9.65
Netherlands	3,310	3,591	2.61

Continued on next page.

★ 1632 ★

[Continued]
Construction Equipment
SIC: 3531; NAICS: 33312

Largest Construction Equipment Markets in Europe, 2003 and 2005

By type of equipment, mini excavator sales are forecast to be 42,105 units, crawler excavators 19,485 units and backhoe loaders 12,942 units.

	2003	2005	Share
Belgium	2,913	3,194	2.32%
Ireland	3,044	3,100	2.25
Switzerland	2,816	2,891	2.10

Source: *Diesel Progress North American Edition*, December 2004, p. 12, from Offhighway Research.

★ 1633 ★

Construction Equipment
SIC: 3531; NAICS: 33312

Leading Construction Equipment Makers in Indonesia

Total domestic demand was 4,180 units in 2004.

Komatsu	39.8%
Caterpillar	29.1
Hitachi	15.6
Other	15.5

Source: "US & FCS Market Research Reports." [online] from http://www.stat-usa.gov [Published July 15, 2004], from Association of Heavy Equipment Companies.

★ 1634 ★

Construction Equipment
SIC: 3531; NAICS: 33312

Leading Construction Equipment Makers Worldwide, 2003

The top 50 firms sold $65.84 billion.

Caterpillar	20.8%
Komatsu	9.9
Terex	5.9
Volvo Construction Equipment	4.9
Liebherr	4.7
CNH	4.5
Ingersoll-Rand	4.4
Hitachi	4.2
Deere	4.1
Metso Minerals	3.1
Sandvik Mining	3.0

JCB	2.3%
Other	28.2

Source: *International Construction*, April 15, 2004, p. NA.

★ 1635 ★

Construction Equipment
SIC: 3531; NAICS: 33312

Leading Forklift Makers in Japan, 2003

Market shares are estimated based on domestic sales.

Toyota Industries	42.6%
Komatsu Forklift	20.0
Nippon Yusoki	9.7
TCM	8.2
Nissan Motor	7.7
Other	11.8

Source: "Market Share Survey Report 2003." [online] from http://www.nni.nikkei.co.jp [Published July 26, 2004], from Nikkei estimates.

★ 1636 ★

Construction Equipment
SIC: 3531; NAICS: 33312

Leading Hydraulic Shovel Makers in Japan, 2003

Market shares are estimated based on domestic sales.

Komatsu	28.8%
Shin Caterpillar	23.6
Hitachi	21.1
Kobelco	14.4
Sumitomo	7.7
Other	4.4

Source: "Market Share Survey Report 2003." [online] from http://www.nni.nikkei.co.jp [Published July 26, 2004], from Nikkei estimates.

★ 1637 ★

Construction Equipment
SIC: 3531; NAICS: 33312

Self-Propelled Trencher Market

The market hit its peak in the late 1990s, declined 35% over a three year period and then hit bottom in 2002. Sales in 2004 exceed 11,000 turnaround.

Ditch Witch	50.0%
Vermeer	20.0
Case	20.0
Other	10.0

Source: *Diesel Progress North American Edition*, November 2004, p. 12.

★ 1638 ★
Construction Equipment
SIC: 3531; NAICS: 33312

Top Crawler Excavator Makers in North America

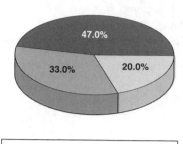

47.0%

33.0%   20.0%

■ Komatsu/Deere/Kobelco □ Other
■ Caterpillar

There are over 20 suppliers in North America. Unit sales were 17,000. The excavator line is a $3 billion industry.

Komatsu/Deere/Kobelco	.47.0%
Caterpillar	.33.0
Other	.20.0

Source: *Diesel Progress North American Edition*, October 2004, p. 12.

★ 1639 ★
Mining Trucks
SIC: 3532; NAICS: 333131

Mining Truck Shipments Worldwide, 2004

The industry saw recent orders skyrocket, with more than 1,100 units shipped worldwide. Shipments based on minerals mined: coal 43%, gold 16%, copper 15%, iron 14% and other 12%.

Asia, Australasia	.44.0%
North America	.22.0
Latin America	.17.0
Europe, Africa, Middle East	.17.0

Source: *World Mining Equipment*, March 2005, p. 12, from source.

★ 1640 ★
Oil & Gas Equipment
SIC: 3533; NAICS: 333132

Bi-Center Bits Industry

Market shares are shown in percent.

Diamond Products International	.50.0%
Other	.50.0

Source: *Oil Daily*, August 23, 2004, p. NA.

★ 1641 ★
Oil & Gas Equipment
SIC: 3533; NAICS: 333132

Deepwater Subsea Market Spending Worldwide

Infield forecasts that spending on platforms, subsea and pipeline supplies and services will increase from an aggregate of $29.2 billion from 1999-2003 to $57 billion in 2004 - 2008.

Drilling and completion	.56.0%
Pipelines	.33.0
Equipment	.8.0
Other	.3.0

Source: *Offshore*, September 2004, p. 16, from Infield Systems.

★ 1642 ★
Oil & Gas Equipment
SIC: 3533; NAICS: 333132

Pressure Control Market

Oil, gas and water wells are under high pressure. As companies drill deeper into wells, they must be careful that they release the pressure in the wells in a controlled manner. A sudden, uncontrolled release of pressure would be very dangerous.

Cooper Cameron	.35.0%
Varco International	.30.0
Hydril	.25.0
Other	.10.0

Source: *Investor's Business Daily*, January 28, 2005, p. A5.

★ 1643 ★
Oil & Gas Equipment
SIC: 3533; NAICS: 333132
Trenchless Market in China

A total of 475 drilling rigs were added to the nation's fleet during 2003, with 408 of them manufactured in China.

Small	.85.0%
Middle	.12.0
Large	. 3.0

Source: *Underground Construction*, September 2004, p. 26, from China Society for Trenchless Technology.

★ 1644 ★
Elevators
SIC: 3534; NAICS: 333921
Elevator Market in China

Market shares are shown in percent.

Otis	.80.0%
Other	.20.0

Source: *Chief Executive*, November 2004, p. 42.

★ 1645 ★
Elevators
SIC: 3534; NAICS: 333921
Largest Elevator Firms Worldwide, 2003

Market shares are shown in percent.

Otis	.23.0%
Schindler	.13.0
Thyssen	.11.0
Mitsubishi	. 9.0
Kone	. 9.0
Hitachi	. 7.0
Toshiba	. 4.0
Fujitec	. 2.0
Other	.22.0

Source: "Kone Corporation." [online] from http://www.kone.com [Published August 17, 2004], from Kone.

★ 1646 ★
Stair Lifts
SIC: 3534; NAICS: 333921
Leading Stair Lift Makers in Europe

Stair lifts are chairs or platforms that are fastened to the wall. The user is then transported from one floor to the other. They are popular medical devices for seniors or those individuals with restricted mobility.

ThysssenKrupp	.28.0%
Stannah	.25.0
Bison	.11.0
Otto Ooms	. 5.0
Hiro	. 5.0
Acorn	. 5.0
Other	.21.0

Source: *Wirtschaftswoche*, March 3, 2005, p. 52, from ThyssenKrupp.

★ 1647 ★
Cranes
SIC: 3536; NAICS: 333923
Crane Market in Italy, 2003

Market shares are shown in percent.

Terex Italia	.60.0%
Other	.40.0

Source: *Cranes Today*, October 2004, p. 37.

★ 1648 ★
Cranes
SIC: 3536; NAICS: 333923
Largest Loader Crane Makers in Italy

Companies are ranked by number of cranes produced.

	2000	2003	% of Group
Fassi	5,100	4,900	41.00%
PM	3,144	3,400	28.45
Effer	1,982	2,150	17.99
F. Ili Ferrari	1,950	1,500	12.55

Source: *Cranes Today*, June 2004, p. 39.

★ 1649 ★
Hoists and Winches
SIC: 3536; NAICS: 333923

Aerospace Hoists and Winches for the World Market

The company has over 50% of the world market for making specialized hoists and winches for the defense and aerospace industries.

TransTechnology Corp. 50.0%
Other 50.0

Source: *Home News Tribune*, August 30, 2004, p. NA.

★ 1650 ★
Hoists and Winches
SIC: 3536; NAICS: 333923

Manual Hoist and Trolley Market

Market shares are estimated in percent.

CMCO 67.0%
Other 33.0

Source: "Material Handling Products & Solutions." [online] from http://www.cmworks.com [Published June 9, 2005], from industry associations.

★ 1651 ★
Lift Trucks
SIC: 3537; NAICS: 333924

Industrial Truck Shipments

In 2003, manufacturers shipped 77,122 electric rider and motorized hand trucks and 63,365 internal combustion engine vehicles.

	2002	2003
Electric rider and motorized hand trucks	57.0%	55.0%
Internal combustion engine	43.0	45.0

Source: *Logistics Management*, November 2004, p. 65, from Industrial Truck Association.

★ 1652 ★
Lift Trucks
SIC: 3537; NAICS: 333924

Leading Electric Lift Truck Makers in North America

The top four firms have 65% of units sold.

Crown/Yale/Hyster/Raymond 65.0%
Other 35.0

Source: *Diesel Progress North American Edition*, March 2005, p. 12.

★ 1653 ★
Lift Trucks
SIC: 3537; NAICS: 333924

Leading Lift Truck Suppliers Worldwide, 2003

There were orders placed for 602,000 lift trucks worldwide. Suppliers are ranked by revenue in millions of dollars.

Toyota . . . .$ 4,230
Linde 3,860
Jungheinrich 1,850
NACCO Industries 1,780
Crown 1,100
Mitsubishi 1,040
Komatsu 938
TCM 672
Nissan 650
Nichiyu 325
Daewoo 268
Atlet 250
Clark 237

Source: *Modern Materials Handling*, August 2004, p. 37.

★ 1654 ★
Machine Tools
SIC: 3540; NAICS: 333512

Largest Machine Tool Consuming Nations, 2004

Countries are ranked by value of tools consumed in millions of dollars. The United States installed $4.9 billion in new machine tools, up 26% over 2003.

China . . . .$ 9,260.0
Japan 5,923.8
Germany 5,353.4
United States 4,932.1
Italy 3,316.4
South Korea 2,928.9
Taiwan 2,530.7
France 1,203.6
Canada 1,124.1
Spain 1,022.2
United Kingdom 862.6

Source: *Modern Machine Shop*, April 2005, p. 96, from World Machine Tool Survey.

★ 1655 ★
Machine Tools
SIC: 3540; NAICS: 333512

Largest Machine Tool Producing Nations, 2004

Countries are ranked by value of tools produced in millions of dollars.

Japan	$ 10,521.0
Germany	9,216.2
Italy	4,639.2
China	4,000.0
Taiwan	2,892.2
United States	2,812.2
Switzerland	2,360.0
South Korea	2,298.9
Spain	1,023.5
United Kingdom	877.2
France	766.4
Canada	742.2

Source: *Modern Machine Shop*, April 2005, p. 96, from *World Machine Tool Survey.*

★ 1656 ★
Machine Tools
SIC: 3541; NAICS: 333512

Christmas-tree Broaches Production in Japan

The company controls the domestic market and 25% of the world industry. Christmas tree broaches are used in manufacturing turbines for jet engines and generators and are called Christmas tree shapes because of their cross-sectional shape. They are used to carve grooves in turbine disks where turbine blades are attached.

Nachi-Fujikoshi Corp.	90.0%
Other	10.0

Source: *Asia Africa Intelligence Wire*, February 9, 2005, p. NA.

★ 1657 ★
Machine Tools
SIC: 3541; NAICS: 333512

Leading Hard Tool Makers in Japan, 2003

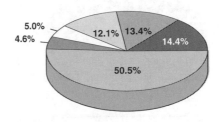

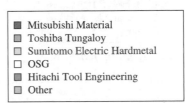

Market shares are estimated based on domestic sales.

Mitsubishi Material	14.4%
Toshiba Tungaloy	13.4
Sumitomo Electric Hardmetal	12.1
OSG	5.0
Hitachi Tool Engineering	4.6
Other	50.5

Source: ''Market Share Survey Report 2003.'' [online] from http://www.nni.nikkei.co.jp [Published July 26, 2004], from Nikkei estimates.

★ 1658 ★
Machine Tools
SIC: 3541; NAICS: 333512

Leading NC Lathe Makers in Japan, 2003

Market shares are estimated based on domestic sales.

Yamazaki Mazak	30.4%
Mori Seiki	25.1
Okuma	21.5
Citizen Watch	11.6
Miyano	6.1
Other	5.3

Source: ''Market Share Survey Report 2003.'' [online] from http://www.nni.nikkei.co.jp [Published July 26, 2004], from Ministry of Economy, Trade and Industry.

★ 1659 ★

Machine Tools

SIC: 3541; NAICS: 333512

Machine Tool Orders by Region, 2004

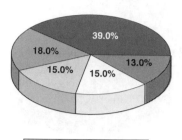

The industry saw $3 billion in orders.

Midwest	.39.0%
Central	.18.0
South	.15.0
Northeast	.15.0
West	.13.0

Source: *Metalworking Insiders' Report*, February 21, 2005, p. 6, from *U.S. Machine Tools Consumption*.

★ 1660 ★

Maching Centers

SIC: 3541; NAICS: 333512

Leading Machining Center Makers in Japan, 2003

Market shares are estimated based on domestic sales.

Yamazaki Mazak	.24.8%
Makino Milling Machine	.23.1
Mori Seiki	.21.5
Okuma	.20.6
Toyoda Machine Works	.5.3
Other	.4.7

Source: "Market Share Survey Report 2003." [online] from http://www.nni.nikkei.co.jp [Published July 26, 2004], from Nikkei estimates.

★ 1661 ★

Power Tools

SIC: 3546; NAICS: 333991

Power and Hand Tool Demand, 2002 and 2007

Demand is shown in millions of dollars.

	2002	2007	Share
Power tools	$ 7,240	$ 9,500	38.15%
Electric tools	5,435	7,200	28.92
Hand tools	4,860	5,900	23.69
Other power tools	1,805	2,300	9.24

Source: *Do-It-Yourself Retailing*, January 2005, p. 58, from Freedonia Group.

★ 1662 ★

Power Tools

SIC: 3546; NAICS: 333991

Power Saw Sales, 2004

Distribution is shown for January - June 2004.

South Atlantic	.20.5%
East North Central	.15.0
Middle Atlantic	.14.2
Pacific	.12.0
Mountain	.7.9
West North Central	.7.6
East South Central	.6.4
New England	.4.0

Source: *Do-It-Yourself Retailing*, January 2005, p. 58, from NPD Houseworld.

★ 1663 ★

Power Tools

SIC: 3546; NAICS: 333991

Power Tool Industry Worldwide, 2002

The top four companies have 27% of the industry.

Black & Decker/Bosch/Atlas Copco/Makita	.27.0%
Other	.73.0

Source: *Modern Plastics*, September 2004, p. 48, from Freedonia Group.

★ 1664 ★

Knitting Machines

SIC: 3552; NAICS: 333292

Knitting/Crocheting Equipment Market in Canada

The company has about 18% of the U.S. market.

Spinrite	.62.0%
Other	.38.0

Source: *Buyouts*, February 14, 2005, p. NA.

★ 1665 ★
Knitting Machines
SIC: 3552; NAICS: 333292

Seamless Knitting Machine Market Worldwide

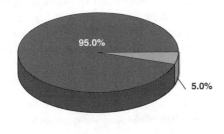

Market shares are shown in percent.

Santoni SPA	95.0%
Other	5.0

Source: *Winston-Salem Journal*, September 10, 2004, p. D1.

★ 1666 ★
Printing Equipment
SIC: 3555; NAICS: 333293

Four Up CTP Systems, 2003

The top five firms account for about three-quarters of all four-up metal CTP (computer-to-plate) unit placements.

Agfa/Creo/Heidelberg/Presstek/Screen	75.0%
Other	25.0

Source: *Graphic Arts Monthly*, October 2004, p. 34, from State Street Consultants.

★ 1667 ★
Printing Equipment
SIC: 3555; NAICS: 333293

Top Printing Equipment Firms in Germany

Sales of digital printing systems was $920 million.

Xerox	35.0%
Xeikon	15.0
Heidelberg DL	15.0
Oce	10.0
Indigo	10.0

Agfa	8.0%
Other	29.0

Source: "US & FCS Market Research Reports." [online] from http://www.stat-usa.gov [Published September 29, 2004].

★ 1668 ★
Heat Exchangers
SIC: 3556; NAICS: 333294

Heating Equipment in the North American Food Industry

In 2004, the industry will invest $2.1 billion in heat exchangers.

Plate	52.3%
Shell and tube	6.1
Scraped surface	5.3
Other	36.3

Source: *Food Engineering*, May 2004, p. 45, from Frost & Sullivan.

★ 1669 ★
Dry Film Resists
SIC: 3559; NAICS: 333295

Dry Film Resist Industry

The industry saw many consolidations between 1999 and early 2003.

Hitachi	25.0%
Eternal	24.0
DuPont	22.0
Kolon	8.0
Nichigo Morton	3.0
CCP	3.0
Other	15.0

Source: *CircuiTree*, August 2004, p. 16.

★ 1670 ★
DVD Replication Machines
SIC: 3559; NAICS: 333298

Prerecorded DVD Line Market Worldwide

Singlus' share is over 65% of the market.

Singlus	65.0%
Other	35.0

Source: *Medialine*, November 1, 2004, p. 52.

★ 1671 ★
Outdoor Safety Equipment
SIC: 3559; NAICS: 333298

Avalanche Transceiver Market Worldwide

Market shares are estimated in percent.

Orotovox 50.0%
Other 50.0

Source: "Ortovox." [online] from http://www.skisite.com/manufDetail.cfm?id5440 [Accessed May 31, 2005].

★ 1672 ★
Plastics Machinery
SIC: 3559; NAICS: 33322

All-Electric Press Market in Europe

In the United States, all-electric presses represent 20% of all molding machine sales.

Fanuc 75.0%
Other 25.0

Source: *Plastics News*, January 10, 2005, p. 4.

★ 1673 ★
Plastics Machinery
SIC: 3559; NAICS: 33322

Leading Plastic Injection Molding Machinery Makers in Japan, 2003

Market shares are estimated based on domestic production.

Sumitomo Heavy Industries 21.1%
Nissei Plastic Industrial 18.3
Fanuc 16.3
Japan Steel Works 13.1
Toshiba Machine 11.0
Other 20.2

Source: "Market Share Survey Report 2003." [online] from http://www.nni.nikkei.co.jp [Published July 26, 2004], from Nikkei estimates.

★ 1674 ★
Plastics Machinery
SIC: 3559; NAICS: 33322

PET Preform Press Market Worldwide

Market shares are shown in percent.

Husky 75.0%
Other 25.0

Source: *Plastics News*, December 6, 2004, p. 4, from Husky.

★ 1675 ★
Rubber Machinery
SIC: 3559; NAICS: 33322

Largest Rubber Machinery Makers Worldwide

The global rubber machinery business is worth about 2,000 million euros annually. Overall sales grew about 17% over 2003, with the the major part of this growth coming from the tire sector. China assumed the lead in the market for the first time with 23% of the industry. Companies are ranked by sales in millions of euros.

ThyssenKrupp 163.6
Berstorff GmbH 126.3
Kobe Steel Ltd. 100.0
Mitsubishi Heavy Industries 80.0
Klockner Desma 53.0
Guilin Rubber Mach. Factory 52.7
REP SA 49.0
Tianjin Saixiang Tech. 46.3
ITW Ride Quality 40.0
Sanming Huaxing Control Co. 39.8

Source: *European Rubber Journal*, March 1, 2005, p. 14.

★ 1676 ★
Semiconductor Equipment
SIC: 3559; NAICS: 333295

Demodulator Market Worldwide

Market shares are shown in percent.

ATI 85.0%
Other 15.0

Source: *Canadian Corporate News*, December 20, 2004, p. NA.

★ 1677 ★
Semiconductor Equipment
SIC: 3559; NAICS: 333295

Leading Chip Making Equipment Firms Worldwide, 2003-2004

Total sales increased from $22.9 billion in 2003 to $37.6 billion in 2004.

	2003	2004
Applied Materials	14.0%	16.5%
Tokyo Electron	9.5	10.5
ASML	6.3	7.0
Nikon	5.7	4.0
Advantest	4.7	5.8

Continued on next page.

★ 1677 ★
[Continued]
Semiconductor Equipment
SIC: 3559; NAICS: 333295

Leading Chip Making Equipment Firms Worldwide, 2003-2004

Total sales increased from $22.9 billion in 2003 to $37.6 billion in 2004.

	2003	2004
KLA-Tencor	4.4%	4.1%
Other	55.4	52.1

Source: *Investor's Business Daily*, April 8, 2005, p. A4, from Gartner Inc.

★ 1678 ★
Semiconductor Equipment
SIC: 3559; NAICS: 333295

Leading Photomask Merchant Makers Worldwide, 2003

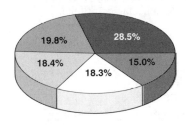

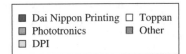

Market shares are shown in percent.

Dai Nippon Printing	28.5%
Phototronics	19.8
DPI	18.4
Toppan	18.3
Other	15.0

Source: *Semiconductor International*, November 2004, p. 32, from Information Network.

★ 1679 ★
Semiconductor Equipment
SIC: 3559; NAICS: 333295

Old-Generation Slurry Market Worldwide

Market shares are estimated in percent.

CMP	90.0%
Other	10.0

Source: *Philadelphia Inquirer*, October 25, 2004, p. NA, from Deutsche Bank.

★ 1680 ★
Semiconductor Equipment
SIC: 3559; NAICS: 333295

Semiconductor Equipment Industry Worldwide, 2005 and 2007

Wafer process equipment takes the lion's share of sales with $23.17 billion in 2005, $23.88 billion in 2006 and $27.34 billion in 2007. Taiwan is forecast to take 19.64% of the market in 2007, Japan 18.56%, North America 15.35%, South Korea 13.86% and Europe 9.29%.

	2005	2006	2007
Japan	$ 6.79	$ 6.68	$ 7.35
Taiwan	6.22	6.55	7.78
North America	5.52	5.48	6.08
South Korea	4.80	4.84	5.49
Europe	3.35	3.40	3.68
China	2.73	3.30	4.21
Other	4.08	4.27	5.02

Source: *PR Newswire*, December 1, 2004, p. NA, from Semiconductor Equipment Manufacturers Institute.

★ 1681 ★
Semiconductor Equipment
SIC: 3559; NAICS: 333295

Single-Wafer Wet Clean Tools in Asia/ Pacific, 2003

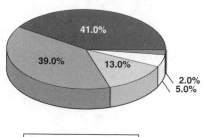

Distribution is for the installed base.

Taiwan	.41.0%
Japan	.39.0
Singapore	.13.0
Korea	.5.0
China	.2.0

Source: *Solid State Technology*, August 2004, p. S13, from SEZ.

★ 1682 ★
Tire Shredding
SIC: 3559; NAICS: 33322

Tire Shredding Equipment Market

Market shares are estimated in percent.

CMCO	.80.0%
Other	.20.0

Source: "Material Handling Products & Solutions." [online] from http://www.cmworks.com [Published June 9, 2005], from industry associations.

★ 1683 ★
Bearings
SIC: 3562; NAICS: 332991

Leading Bearing Firms in Japan, 2003

Market shares are estimated based on domestic shipments.

NSK	.35.0%
Koyo	.28.4
NTN	.25.6
Nachi-Fujikoshi	.6.1

Minebea	4.2%
Other	0.7

Source: "Market Share Survey Report 2003." [online] from http://www.nni.nikkei.co.jp [Published July 26, 2004], from Nikkei estimates.

★ 1684 ★
Packaging Machinery
SIC: 3565; NAICS: 333993

Packaging Machinery Shipments, 2002

Data show the top industries for the package machinery industry. Total spending is estimated to be $5.14 billion in 2004. Conveying, feeding and placing machinery are the most popular types of equipment, taking 21.3% of the total.

Food	.39.3%
Beverages	.20.9
Pharmaceuticals	.9.6
Other	.30.2

Source: *Packaging Digest*, May 2004, p. S14, from Packaging Machinery Manufacturers Institute.

★ 1685 ★
Packaging Machinery
SIC: 3565; NAICS: 333993

Retort Pouch Food Market

The company is the top supplier of automatic filler/ sealer for retort pouch foods and has an estimated 80% of the market.

Nabtesco	.80.0%
Other	.20.0

Source: "Nabtesco: No. 1 Products of Nabtesco." [online] from http://www.nabtesco.com/en/advantage [accessed November 9, 2004].

★ 1686 ★
Garbage Incinerators
SIC: 3567; NAICS: 333994

Leading Garbage Incinerator Makers in Japan, 2003

Market shares are estimated based on domestic sales.

Hitachi Zosen	.34.1%
Nippon Steel	.28.3
Takuma	.20.9
Mitsubishi Heavy	.7.8

Continued on next page.

★ 1686 ★

[Continued]
Garbage Incinerators
SIC: 3567; NAICS: 333994

Leading Garbage Incinerator Makers in Japan, 2003

Market shares are estimated based on domestic sales.

Kobelco-Eco Solutions	2.7%
Other	6.2

Source: "Market Share Survey Report 2003." [online] from http://www.nni.nikkei.co.jp [Published July 26, 2004], from Nikkei estimates.

★ 1687 ★

Filters
SIC: 3569; NAICS: 333999

Soot Filter Market in Europe

Market shares are shown in percent.

Faurecia	60.0%
Other	40.0

Source: *Automotive News Europe*, October 4, 2004, p. 4.

★ 1688 ★

Robots
SIC: 3569; NAICS: 333999

Leading Industrial Robot Makers in Japan, 2003

Market shares are estimated based on domestic sales.

Matsushita Electric Industrial	28.6%
Yaskawa Electric	16.5
Fanuc	12.8
Kawasaki Heavy Industries	5.9
Yamaha Motor	5.2
Other	21.2

Source: "Market Share Survey Report 2003." [online] from http://www.nni.nikkei.co.jp [Published July 26, 2004], from Nikkei estimates.

★ 1689 ★

Robots
SIC: 3569; NAICS: 333999

New Robot Orders in North America, 2004

North American firms ordered 7,852 robots valued at $473.3 million through June 2004.

Spot welding	29.0%
Material handling > 10 lbs.	26.0
Arc welding	16.0
Material handling < 10 lbs.	12.0
Dispensing/coating	8.0
Assembly < 10 lbs.	5.0
Material removal	3.0
Other	1.0

Source: *Advanced Manufacturing Technology*, September 15, 2004, p. 4, from Robotic Industries Association.

★ 1690 ★

Robots
SIC: 3569; NAICS: 333999

Robot Industry in Germany

Germany has 112,700 robots, the highest number in Europe. Fabricated metal products, machinery and e-lectrical machinery have 4-6 shares.

Automotive	56.0%
Chemicals	9.0
Machinery	6.0
Fabricated metal products	6.0
Electrical machinery	6.0
Other	17.0

Source: *Advanced Manufacturing Technology*, November 15, 2004, p. 11, from United National Economic Commission for Europe.

★ 1691 ★

Robots
SIC: 3569; NAICS: 333999

Robot Industry in Italy

Italy has 50,000 robots.

Automotive	36.0%
Chemicals	27.0
Fabricated metal products	13.0
Other	24.0

Source: *Advanced Manufacturing Technology*, November 15, 2004, p. 11, from United National Economic Commission for Europe.

★ 1692 ★
Robots
SIC: 3569; NAICS: 333999
Robot Industry in Spain

Italy has 20,000 robots.

Automotive	.69.0%
Chemicals	8.0
Fabricated metal products	5.0
Other	.18.0

Source: *Advanced Manufacturing Technology*, November 15, 2004, p. 11, from United National Economic Commission for Europe.

★ 1693 ★
Robots
SIC: 3569; NAICS: 333999
Robot Industry in the U.K.

The United Kingdom has 14,000 robots.

Welding applications	.49.0%
Plastic molding tallying	.13.0
Material handling	8.0
Other	.30.0

Source: *Advanced Manufacturing Technology*, November 15, 2004, p. 11, from United National Economic Commission for Europe.

★ 1694 ★
Water Filtration Equipment
SIC: 3569; NAICS: 333999
Top Water Filter Brands, 2005

Brands are ranked by supermarket, drug store and discount outlet sales (excluding Wal-Mart) for the 52 weeks ended February 20, 2005.

	($ mil.)	Share
Brita filters	$ 57.6	40.48%
Brita devices	25.2	17.71
Pur Ultimate filters	17.4	12.23
Brita Ultra filters	10.2	7.17
Pura Ultimate devices	9.0	6.32
Brita Ultra devices	6.8	4.78
Pur Plus filters	5.0	3.51
Pur Plus devices	3.8	2.67
Pur Advantage filters	1.9	1.34
Pur Advantage devices	1.0	0.70
Other	4.4	3.09

Source: *MMR*, May 30, 2005, p. 33, from Information Resources Inc.

★ 1695 ★
Water Filtration Equipment
SIC: 3569; NAICS: 333999
Water Filtering Equipment in France

The company has over half the market.

Eureka Forbes	.50.0%
Other	.50.0

Source: "US & FCS Market Research Reports." [online] from http://www.stat-usa.gov [Published September 29, 2004].

★ 1696 ★
Computers
SIC: 3571; NAICS: 334111
Computer Industry, 1998 and 2004

The average price of a laptop fell from $2,126 in 2000 to $1,116 in 2004 in the United States. Laptop sales are forecast to overtake desktops by 2008.

	1998	2004
Desktops	81.9%	70.4%
Laptops	18.1	29.6

Source: *USA TODAY*, April 13, 2005, p. 8D, from International Data Corp.

★ 1697 ★
Computers
SIC: 3571; NAICS: 334111
Computer Industry Shipments, 2004-2006

Portable computers are the major force driving growth in the market. Shipments are shown in millions of units.

	2004	2005	2006
Commercial	36.5	39.3	41.9
Consumer	21.8	23.6	26.2

Source: "PC Outlook is Still Strong." [online] from http://www.idc.com [Accessed June 29, 2005], from International Data Corp.

★ 1698 ★

Computers

SIC: 3571; NAICS: 334111

Computer Industry Shipments Worldwide, 2004-2006

Shipments are shown in millions of units.

	2004	2005	2006
Commercial	114.6	126.8	138.0
Consumer	64.2	72.4	79.1

Source: "PC Outlook is Still Strong." [online] from http://www.idc.com [Accessed June 29, 2005], from International Data Corp.

★ 1699 ★

Computers

SIC: 3571; NAICS: 334111

Industrialized Computer Systems Demand, 2003 and 2006

Demand for ruggedized/industrial computer systems in North America and Western Europe will increase from $1.64 billion in 2003 to $1.9 billion in 2006. The defense sector will see the largest increase in spending (5%).

	2003	2006
Defense & aerospace	$ 635	$ 735
Industrial automation controls & instrumentation	484	537
Communications	341	389
Medical, laboratory & scientific	97	110
Energy, utilities & transportation infrastructure	91	102

Source: *Electronic Design*, July 19, 2004, p. 23, from Venture Development Corp.

★ 1700 ★

Computers

SIC: 3571; NAICS: 334111

K-12 Hardware Market, 2003

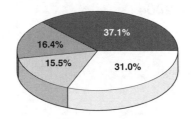

The average selling price of computer systems to the education market fell 38% between 1999 and 2003. Dell lowered its prices 46% during this period which helped propell it to the number one spot.

Dell	37.1%
Hewlett-Packard	16.4
Apple	15.5
Other	31.0

Source: *Electronic Education Report*, July 9, 2004, p. NA, from International Data Corp.

★ 1701 ★

Computers

SIC: 3571; NAICS: 334111

Laptop Production by Country

Qanta Computer is the world's largest maker of laptops. It makes a quarter of all laptops and then sells them under the Hewlett-Packard and Dell labels.

China	68.0%
Taiwan	17.0
Japan	8.0
United States	1.0
Korea	1.0
Other	5.0

Source: *Wall Street Journal*, June 9, 2005, p. B1, from International Data Corp.

★ 1702 ★
Computers
SIC: 3571; NAICS: 334111

Leading Computer Makers in Australia, 2004

Market shares are shown for the second quarter of 2004.

Hewlett-Packard	20.6%
Dell	12.5
Acer	8.6
IBM	6.6
Toshiba	5.9
Apple	3.2
Optima	2.6
Other	40.0

Source: "IDC Reports Record Figures for Australia's PC Market ." [online] from http://www.idc.com [Press release August 13, 2004], from International Data Corp.

★ 1703 ★
Computers
SIC: 3571; NAICS: 334111

Leading Electronic Dictionary Makers in Japan, 2003

Market shares are shown based on domestic shipments.

Casio Computer	48.9%
Sharp	26.5
Seiko Instruments	14.2
Canon	6.4
Sony	3.9

Source: "Market Share Survey Report 2003." [online] from http://www.nni.nikkei.co.jp [Published July 26, 2004], from Nikkei estimates.

★ 1704 ★
Computers
SIC: 3571; NAICS: 334111

Leading Handheld Device Makers in Australia, 2004

Market shares are shown for the second quarter of the smart handheld computer market.

palmOne	23.1%
Hewlett-Packard	18.9
Nokia	15.5
O2	13.4

Motorola	8.1%
Other	21.0

Source: "Q204 Sees New Leader in Total SHD Market." [online] from http://www.idc.com [Press release September 13, 2004], from International Data Corp.

★ 1705 ★
Computers
SIC: 3571; NAICS: 334111

Leading Smart Handheld Devices in Australia, 2004

Shares are shown for the third quarter.

Motorola	26.5%
Nokia	23.0
HP	20.6
PalmOne	9.7
RIM	7.3
Other	12.9

Source: "Converged Devices are the Next Big Thing." [online] from http://www.idc.com.au [Press release November 30, 2004], from International Data Corp.

★ 1706 ★
Computers
SIC: 3571; NAICS: 334111

Leading Thin Client Device Makers in Australia, 2003

Market grew 48% from 2002 to 2003.

Wyse	64.6%
Hewlett Packard	14.8
Sun	7.6
Neoware	5.2
Maxspeed	3.0
Other	4.8

Source: "Record Year for Thin Client Devices in 2003." [online] from http://www.idc.com [Press release September 13, 2004], from International Data Corp.

★ 1707 ★
Computers
SIC: 3571; NAICS: 334111

Top Computers in the Middle East/ Europe/Africa, 2004

The industry benefitted from a strong euro, the increased adoption of portable computers and increased commercial investment.

	(000)	Share
Hewlett-Packard	10,152	17.6%
Dell	6,767	11.7
Acer	4,359	7.5
Fujitsu Siemens	4,276	7.4
IBM	3,134	5.4
Other	29,154	50.4

Source: "EMEA PC Market Hits Forecasts in 4Q04." [online] from http://www.idc.com [Published January 20, 2005], from International Data Corp.

★ 1708 ★
Computers
SIC: 3571; NAICS: 334111

Top Handheld Device Makers Worldwide, 2004

Companies are ranked by estimated shipments.

	Units	Share
palmOne	3,645,399	39.6%
Hewlett-Packard	2,492,539	27.1
Dell	695,171	7.6
Sony	418,832	4.6
Medion	234,325	2.5
Other	1,716,895	18.7

Source: "Worldwide Handheld Market Experiences Third Straight Year of Decline." [online] from http://www.idc.com [Press release February 2, 2005], from International Data Corp.

★ 1709 ★
Computers
SIC: 3571; NAICS: 334111

Top Notebooks, 2004

Market shares are shown for the fourth quarter of 2004.

Dell	28.9%
Hewlett-Packard	19.0
Toshiba	12.5
IBM	7.9

Apple	5.0%
Other	26.7

Source: *Macworld*, June 2005, p. 16, from International Data Corp.

★ 1710 ★
Computers
SIC: 3571; NAICS: 334111

Top Notebooks in Australia, 2004

Market shares are shown for the third quarter of 2004.

Toshiba	17.8%
Dell	16.5
HP	14.5
Acer	12.8
IBM	8.9
Apple	5.4
Other	24.1

Source: "Australian Notebook Market Attracts One New Competitor." [online] from http://www.idc.com.au [Press release December 8, 2004], from International Data Corp.

★ 1711 ★
Computers
SIC: 3571; NAICS: 334111

Top Notebooks in Taiwan, 2004

Market shares are shown based on unit shipments for the second quarter of 2004.

Asustek	29.4%
Acer	21.5
IBM	15.2
Hewlett-Packard	9.3
Other	24.6

Source: *Taiwan Economic News*, September 16, 2004, p. NA, from International Data Corp.

★ 1712 ★
Computers
SIC: 3571; NAICS: 334111

Top PC Firms, 2003-2004

Total shipments increased from 57.51 million units in 2003 to 62.27 million in 2004. Figures include desk-based PCs, mobile PCs and x86-32 servers.

	2003	2004
Dell	27.7%	30.3%
Hewlett-Packard	18.6	18.4

Continued on next page.

★ 1712 ★

[Continued]
Computers
SIC: 3571; NAICS: 334111
Top PC Firms, 2003-2004

Total shipments increased from 57.51 million units in 2003 to 62.27 million in 2004. Figures include desk-based PCs, mobile PCs and x86-32 servers.

	2003	2004
Gateway	6.3%	5.8%
IBM	4.4	4.7
Apple	2.9	3.2
Other	39.7	37.7

Source: "Gartner Says Strong Mobile Sales Lift Worldwide." [online] from http://www.gartner.com [Published January 18, 2005], from Gartner.

★ 1713 ★

Computers
SIC: 3571; NAICS: 334111
Top PC Firms in Canada, 2004

Market shares are shown for the third quarter of 2004.

	(000)	Share
Hewlett-Packard	203	20.2%
Dell	203	24.6
IBM	107	10.6
Toshiba	58	5.7
Acer	51	5.1
Other	340	33.8

Source: *Computer Dealer News*, January 7, 2005, p. 1, from International Data Corp. Canada.

★ 1714 ★

Computers
SIC: 3571; NAICS: 334111
Top PC Firms in China, 2004

Market shares are shown for the third quarter.

Lenovo	26.4%
Founder	10.3
Tsinghua Tongfang	8.7
Dell	8.1
IBM	6.0
Other	40.5

Source: *USA TODAY*, December 8, 2004, p. B1, from Gartner.

★ 1715 ★

Computers
SIC: 3571; NAICS: 334111
Top PC Firms in Germany, 2004

Market shares are shown in percent.

Fujitsu-Siemens	17.8%
Medion	9.9
Hewlett-Packard	9.8
Acer	8.8
Dell	7.0
Other	46.7

Source: *Heise Online*, February 10, 2005, p. NA, from Gartner.

★ 1716 ★

Computers
SIC: 3571; NAICS: 334111
Top PC Firms in Hungary

Home personal computer penetration is rather low in the country, recently placed at 17%. Sales are improving however, with 290,850 PCs sold in 2003, up 18% from 2002. Market shares for the desktop market are estimated.

Dell	7.6%
DTK	6.5
Fujitsu Siemens	6.4
IBM	6.2
Hungarian Albacamp	5.9
Other	67.4

Source: "US & FCS Market Research Reports." [online] from http://www.stat-usa.gov [Published September 20, 2004], from International Data Corp.

★ 1717 ★

Computers
SIC: 3571; NAICS: 334111
Top PC Firms in Japan

Market shares are shown in percent.

Dell	10.7%
Sony	7.1
Hewlett-Packard Japan	5.7
Other	76.5

Source: *Asia Africa Intelligence Wire*, February 9, 2005, p. NA, from MM Research Institute.

★ 1718 ★
Computers
SIC: 3571; NAICS: 334111
Top PC Firms in Poland, 2003

The industry saw 1.16 million unit sales worth $1 billion in 2003. Growth was particularly strong in the laptop segment as prices fell and Wi-Fi became more popular. Companies are ranked by unit shipments.

	Units	Share
HP Polska	86,080	7.42%
NTT System	85,800	7.40
Optimus	55,300	4.77
Dell	50,800	4.38
Action	41,100	3.54
Other	840,920	72.49

Source: *Europe Intelligence Wire*, May 14, 2004, p. NA, from International Data Corp.

★ 1719 ★
Computers
SIC: 3571; NAICS: 334111
Top PC Firms in the U.K., 2004

Market shares are shown for the third quarter.

Dell	25.2%
New HP	20.0
Toshiba	5.6
NEC CI	5.6
IBM	5.2
Other	38.4

Source: "U.K. PC Market Receives Further Boost in 2004." [online] from http://www.idc.com [Press release November 4, 2004], from International Data Corp. EMEA PC Tracker.

★ 1720 ★
Computers
SIC: 3571; NAICS: 334111
Top PC Firms Worldwide, 2005

Market shares are shown based on shipments of 48.9 million for the second quarter of 2005. The industry divides roughly this way: desktop PCs 73.3%, notebooks PCs 24% and entry level servers 2.8%.

Dell	17.9%
Hewlett-Packard	14.6
Lenovo	7.2
Acer	4.3
Fujitsu-Siemens	3.6
Other	52.4

Source: *Investor's Business Daily*, July 22, 2005, p. A4, from Gartner.

★ 1721 ★
Computers
SIC: 3571; NAICS: 334111
Top PDA Makers Worldwide, 2005

Market shares are shown for the first quarter of the year. Windows CE represents 46% of shipments, RIM 20.8%, Symbian 9.9%, Linux 0.8%.

RIM	20.8%
palmOne	18.0
Hewlett-Packard	17.6
Nokia	9.9
Dell	6.3
Other	27.4

Source: *Investor's Business Daily*, May 10, 2005, p. A5, from Gartner.

★ 1722 ★
Computers
SIC: 3571; NAICS: 334111
Top PDAs Worldwide by Shipments, 2004

Shipments exceeded 2.8 million units for the third quarter of 2004. PDA stands for personal digital assistants.

Windows CE	48.1%
Palm OS	29.8
Research in Motion	19.8
Linux	0.9
Other	1.5

Source: *M2 Presswire*, November 12, 2004, p. NA, from Gartner.

★ 1723 ★
Computer Data Storage
SIC: 3572; NAICS: 334112
Compact Tape Industry Worldwide, 2003

Market shares are shown based on revenues.

Hewlett-Packard	28.0%
Quantum	27.0
IBM	17.0
Certance	13.0
Sony	10.0
Other	5.0

Source: *InfoStar*, August 2004, p. 1, from Freeman Reports.

★ 1724 ★
Computer Data Storage
SIC: 3572; NAICS: 334112

Computer Tape Storage Market

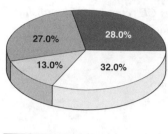

Legend: ■ Hewlett-Packard □ Certance ▨ Quantum □ Other

Market shares are shown in percent.

Hewlett-Packard 28.0%
Quantum 27.0
Certance 13.0
Other 32.0

Source: *Rethink It*, December 2004, p. 32, from Freeman Report.

★ 1725 ★
Computer Data Storage
SIC: 3572; NAICS: 334112

Disk Storage System Market Worldwide, 2004

Shares are shown based on $20.9 billion in factory revenues.

Hewlett-Packard 23.6%
IBM 20.6
EMC 14.3
Dell 7.2
Hitachi 6.0
Sun Microsystems 5.9
Other 22.4

Source: *Investor's Business Daily*, February 14, 2005, p. A4, from International Data Corp.

★ 1726 ★
Computer Data Storage
SIC: 3572; NAICS: 334112

External Data Storage Market Worldwide, 2004

Companies are ranked by third quarter revenues in millions of dollars.

	($ mil.)	Share
EMC	$ 724	21.2%
Hewlett-Packard	647	19.0
IBM	448	13.1
Hitachi	289	8.5
Dell	237	6.9
Other	1,066	31.3

Source: *Client Server News*, December 13, 2004, p. 9, from International Data Corp.

★ 1727 ★
Computer Data Storage
SIC: 3572; NAICS: 334112

External Disk Array Market Worldwide

Market shares are shown based on revenues of $13.5 billion.

EMC 22.6%
Hewlett-Packard 16.5
IBM 12.0
Hitachi/HDS 8.7
Sun Microsytems 6.3
Dell 5.8
Network Appliance 5.4
Other 22.6

Source: *Infostor*, April 2005, p. 1, from Gartner Dataquest Inc.

★ 1728 ★
Computer Data Storage
SIC: 3572; NAICS: 334112

External/Internal Storage Market in the Asia Pacific, 2004

Market shares are shown for the second quarter of 2004.

Hewlett-Packard 22.8%
EMC 15.8
Sun 9.4
HDS 6.8

Continued on next page.

★ 1728 ★

[Continued]

Computer Data Storage

SIC: 3572; NAICS: 334112

External/Internal Storage Market in the Asia Pacific, 2004

Market shares are shown for the second quarter of 2004.

IBM	0.0%
Other	18.4

Source: "Asia/Pacific Disk Storage Systems Market Grows 7.9%." [online] from http://www.idc.com [Press release September 14, 2004], from International Data Corp.

★ 1729 ★

Computer Data Storage

SIC: 3572; NAICS: 334112

Super Drive Industry Worldwide, 2003

Market shares are shown in percent.

Quantum	33.5%
Hewlett-Packard	29.0
IBM	24.8
Sony	6.5
Certance	5.4
Tandberg	0.8

Source: *InfoStar*, August 2004, p. 1.

★ 1730 ★

Computer Data Storage

SIC: 3572; NAICS: 334112

Top CD-Rewritable Disc Drive Makers, 2004

Shares are shown based on sales of $204.3 million for January - November 2004.

Sony	12.1%
Memorex	8.6
I/O Magic	7.9
Iomega	6.7
Mad Dog Multimedia	6.6
Other	58.1

Source: *New York Times*, January 17, 2005, p. C7, from NPD Group/NPD Techworld.

★ 1731 ★

Computer Data Storage

SIC: 3572; NAICS: 334112

Top Storage Makers Worldwide, 2004

Market shares are shown for the second quarter of 2004.

EMC	32.5%
Veritas	22.6
IBM	7.0
Hewlett-Packard	7.0
Computer Associates	6.6
Other	24.2

Source: "Worldwide Storagte Software Posts 3rd Consecutive Quarter of Growth." [online] from http://www.idc.com [Press release September 14, 2004], from International Data Corp.

★ 1732 ★

Computer Monitors

SIC: 3575; NAICS: 334119

Leading Computer Monitor Makers in Australia, 2004

Market shares are shown for the second quarter of 2004.

Samsung	17.5%
LG	16.0
Philips	13.7
BenQ	11.5
Acer	11.0
Other	30.3

Source: "Record Sales and a New Branded Monitor Market Leader ." [online] from http://www.idc.com [Press release September 8, 2004], from International Data Corp.

★ 1733 ★

Computer Monitors

SIC: 3575; NAICS: 334119

Leading LCD Monitor Assemblers Worldwide

Market shares are shown in percent. LCD television sets totaled $53 billion in 2004.

TPV	15.1%
Samsung	12.9
BenQ	10.3
Lite-On	9.3
LG Electronics	8.6

Continued on next page.

★ 1733 ★

[Continued]
Computer Monitors
SIC: 3575; NAICS: 334119

Leading LCD Monitor Assemblers Worldwide

Market shares are shown in percent. LCD television sets totaled $53 billion in 2004.

Philips	6.7%
Other	36.9

Source: *Wall Street Journal*, March 24, 2005, p. B4, from DisplaySearch and Market Intelligence Center.

★ 1734 ★

Computer Monitors
SIC: 3575; NAICS: 334113

Leading LCD Monitor Makers in North America, 2004

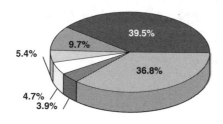

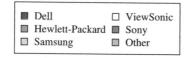

Market shares are shown for the fourth quarter 2004.

Dell	39.5%
Hewlett-Packard	9.7
Samsung	5.4
ViewSonic	4.7
Sony	3.9
Other	36.8

Source: *Investor's Business Daily*, March 31, 2005, p. A5, from DisplaySearch.

★ 1735 ★

Computer Monitors
SIC: 3575; NAICS: 334113

Leading LCD Monitor Makers in Taiwan, 2004

Market shares are shown for the fourth quarter 2004.

	Units	Share
Viewsonic	105,000	21.4%
CMO	91,000	21.0
BenQ	82,000	19.0
Acer	54,000	12.5

Source: *Taiwan Economic News*, March 15, 2005, p. NA, from International Data Corp.

★ 1736 ★

Computer Monitors
SIC: 3575; NAICS: 334113

Leading LCD Monitor Suppliers Worldwide, 2004

The top desktop LCD monitor suppliers are shown for the third quarter.

Dell	16.4%
Samsung	10.3
Hewlett-Packard	9.4
LG	5.9
BenQ	4.6
Other	52.4

Source: *Computer Reseller News*, January 10, 2005, p. 29, from DisplaySearch.

★ 1737 ★

Computer Monitors
SIC: 3575; NAICS: 334419

Leading Liquid Crystal Display Makers Worldwide

Market shares are shown in percent.

Samsung	22.1%
LG Philips	20.7
AUO	12.8
CPT	7.8
CMO	7.3
Sharp	5.3
Other	24.0

Source: *The Online Reporter*, August 14, 2004, p. NA, from DisplaySearch.

★ 1738 ★
Computer Monitors
SIC: 3575; NAICS: 334113

Top Computer Monitor Makers in Australia, 2004

Shares are shown for the third quarter.

LG 18.0%
Samsung 15.5
BenQ 12.3
Mitsubishi 10.9
Philips 10.7
Other 32.6

Source: "Australia's Total PC Monitor Falls 17% from Q2 2004." [online] from http://www.idc.com.au [Press release December 6, 2004], from International Data Corp.

★ 1739 ★
Computer Printers
SIC: 3577; NAICS: 334119

Top Inkjet Printer Firms in Japan, 2003

Market shares are estimated based on domestic shipments.

Seiko Epson 45.6%
Canon 41.6
HP Japan 6.9
Brother Industries 2.1
Other 3.8

Source: "Market Share Survey Report 2003." [online] from http://www.nni.nikkei.co.jp [Published July 26, 2004], from Gartner Japan.

★ 1740 ★
Computer Printers
SIC: 3577; NAICS: 334119

Top Inkjet Printer Makers, 2003-2004

Market shares are shown for fourth quarters of 2003 and 2004. Hewlett Packard's share is down from 57.4% in the fourth quarter 2003. Analysts quoted in the source point out that this is an unusual drop in such a mature market.

	2003	2004
Hewlett-Packard	57.4%	48.1%
Lexmark	17.5	19.3
Epson	10.2	10.3
Dell	8.5	13.8
Canon	5.2	7.3
Other	1.2	1.2

Source: *Wall Street Journal*, March 10, 2005, p. B1, from International Data Corp.

★ 1741 ★
Computer Printers
SIC: 3577; NAICS: 334119

Top Inkjet Printer Makers in Canada

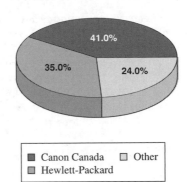

■ Canon Canada   □ Other
■ Hewlett-Packard

Unit shares are shown in percent.

Canon Canada 41.0%
Hewlett-Packard 35.0
Other 24.0

Source: *Computer Dealer News*, September 17, 2004, p. 34, from NPD Intelect.

★ 1742 ★
Computer Printers
SIC: 3577; NAICS: 334119

Top Multifunction Printer Makers, 2004

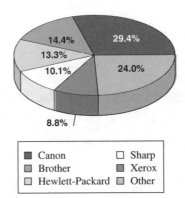

■ Canon   □ Sharp
■ Brother   ■ Xerox
□ Hewlett-Packard ■ Other

Market shares of laser multifunction printer market are shown for the first six months of the year.

Canon 29.4%
Brother 14.4
Hewlett-Packard 13.3
Sharp 10.1

Continued on next page.

★ 1742 ★
[Continued]
Computer Printers
SIC: 3577; NAICS: 334119

Top Multifunction Printer Makers, 2004

Market shares of laser multifunction printer market are shown for the first six months of the year.

Xerox	8.8%
Other	24.0

Source: *Investor's Business Daily*, November 24, 2004, p. A4, from International Data Corp.

★ 1743 ★
Computer Printers
SIC: 3577; NAICS: 334119

Top Printer Makers

Market shares are shown based on unit sales for December 2004.

Hewlett Packard	48.7%
Lexmark	14.8
Epson	14.6
Canon	9.8
Kodak	6.8
Other	5.3

Source: "Top 5 Printers." [online] from http://www.npdtechworld.com [March 2, 2005], from NPD Group/NPD Techworld.

★ 1744 ★
Computer Printers
SIC: 3577; NAICS: 334119

Top Printer Makers Worldwide, 2003-2004

Market shares are shown in percent.

	2003	2004
Hewlett-Packard	44.0%	40.5%
Epson	20.0	19.2
Lexmark	15.6	15.2
Canon	14.9	15.9
Dell	1.8	5.1
Other	3.7	4.1

Source: *USA TODAY*, July 12, 2005, p. 3B, from International Data Corp.

★ 1745 ★
Webcams
SIC: 3577; NAICS: 334119

Webcam Market Shares

The company has more than 55% of the market in Webcams, more than 33% in computer mice and more than 40% in keyboards.

Logitech	55.0%
Other	45.0

Source: *Investor's Business Daily*, February 24, 2005, p. A4.

★ 1746 ★
Automated Teller Machines
SIC: 3578; NAICS: 333313

ATM Installations Worldwide

There are about 1.3 million installations worldwide. Growth in mature markets such as Japan and the United States will come in the replacement and off-site deployment sectors.

	Units	Share
United States	380,000	28.2%
Japan	164,539	12.2
Brazil	93,865	7.0
South Korea	80,153	5.9
China	71,000	5.3

Source: *Electronic Payments International*, December 2004, p. 15, from Retail Banking Research.

★ 1747 ★
Automated Teller Machines
SIC: 3578; NAICS: 334119

Automated Teller Machine Industry Worldwide, 2003

Distribution is shown in percent.

North America	31.4%
Asia Pacific	30.2
Western Europe	22.1
Latin America	10.1
Eastern Europe	3.4
Middle East & Africa	2.1

Source: *ATM & Debit News*, December 16, 2004, p. 2, from Retail Banking Research.

★ **1748** ★
Automated Teller Machines
SIC: 3578; NAICS: 334119

Leading ATM Makers in Western Europe

Market shares are shown in percent.

NCR .47.5%
Wincor Nixdorf 21.8
Diebold 18.3
Other 12.4

Source: *Electronic Payments International*, February 2005, p. 15, from Retail Banking Research 2005.

★ **1749** ★
Automated Teller Machines
SIC: 3578; NAICS: 333313

Leading IAD Makers in the U.K.

Shares are shown based on number of ATMs. IAD stands for independent ATM deployers.

Hanco 27.0%
Cardpoint 19.0
Moneybox 15.0
Scott Todd 7.0
Bank machine 5.0
Other 27.0

Source: *Electronic Payments International*, March 2005, p. 8, from LINK, Moneybox, and Cardpoint.

★ **1750** ★
POS Terminals
SIC: 3578; NAICS: 334119

POS Terminal Shipments in North America

Spending on PC-based point of sales terminals stood at $6.5 billion. The figure includes POS hardware, software and services. Linux-based units represent only 6% of the market but grew 34% over the year. They are expected to have a larger share of the market in the future.

Windows 2000/XP 56.0%
Windows 9x/CE 15.0
Other 29.0

Source: *Business Wire*, March 9, 2005, p. NA, from IHL Consulting Group.

★ **1751** ★
Postage Meters
SIC: 3578; NAICS: 333313

Postage Meter Market

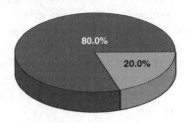

Market shares are shown in percent.

Pitney Bowes 80.0%
Other 20.0

Source: *Forbes*, February 28, 2005, p. 104.

★ **1752** ★
Self-Service Checkouts
SIC: 3578; NAICS: 334119

Self-Service Checkout Industry

The company also has 90% of the European market.

NCR .80.0%
Other 20.0

Source: *International Herald Tribune*, September 20, 2004, p. 14.

★ **1753** ★
Staplers
SIC: 3579; NAICS: 333313

Stapler Market

Market shares are shown in percent.

Swingline 65.0%
Other 35.0

Source: *Time*, March 14, 2005, p. A5.

★ 1754 ★
Vending Machines
SIC: 3581; NAICS: 45421

Vending Machine Placements, 2003

With the economy losing jobs and companies operating with fewer people, many vending machine operators found themselves pulling machines. The decline in vending machine sales in recent years further reflect this trend ($21.01 billion in 2003 after a highpoint of $24.49 billion in 1999). The South Atlantic region had 23% of operators, Pacific 16%, East North Central 14%, Middle Atlantic 12%.

Manufacturing	.30.2%
Schools, colleges	.16.3
Offices	.14.2
Retail sites	.12.2
Hospitals, nursing homes	.9.0
Restaurants, bars, clubs	.5.1
Hotels/motels	.4.8
Correctional facilities	.2.7
Military bases	.2.3
Other	.3.2

Source: *Automatic Merchandiser*, August 2004, p. 44, from *2004 Automatic Merchandiser State of the Vending Industry Report*.

★ 1755 ★
Display Cases
SIC: 3585; NAICS: 335222

Leading Refrigerated Display Case Makers, 2003

Market shares are shown based on shipments of 191,549.

Hussman	.48.0%
Tyler Refrigeration	.16.0
Hill/Phoenix	.15.0
Kysor/Warren	.6.0
Other	.15.0

Source: *Appliance*, September 2004, pp. P-2, from *Appliance Magazine's 27th Annual Portrait of the U.S. Appliance Industry*.

★ 1756 ★
Heating and Cooling
SIC: 3585; NAICS: 333415

Automotive HVAC Control Industry

HVAC stands for heating, ventillation and air conditioning. The industry refers to equipment that controls a vehicle's air flow direction and speed. Market shares are estimated.

Manual/automatic blended	.55.0%
Electronic	.45.0
Manual	.5.0

Source: *Automotive News*, September 27, 2004, p. 38.

★ 1757 ★
Heating and Cooling
SIC: 3585; NAICS: 333415

Commercial Refrigeration Equipment, 2003 and 2008

Demand is shown in millions of dollars. The products expected to see the strongest growth are cryogenic equipment, display cases and beverage refrigeration equipment.

	2003	2008	Share
Food & beverage distribution	$ 2,005	$ 2,540	29.71%
Food & beverage retail	1,625	2,165	25.32
Foodservice	1,540	2,025	23.68
Food & beverage production	400	485	5.67
Other	980	1,335	15.61

Source: *Contracting Business*, December 2004, p. 16, from Freedonia Group.

★ 1758 ★
Heating and Cooling
SIC: 3585; NAICS: 333415

Leading Air Conditioner Makers (Room), 2003

Market shares are shown based on shipments of 8.21 million.

LG Electronics (Goldstar)	.32.0%
Fedders	.20.5
Electrolux (Frigidaire)	.12.5
Whirlpool	.9.0
Haier	.8.5
Samsung	.4.5
Sharp	.3.0
Matsushita	.2.5

Continued on next page.

★ 1758 ★

[Continued]
Heating and Cooling
SIC: 3585; NAICS: 333415

Leading Air Conditioner Makers (Room), 2003

Market shares are shown based on shipments of 8.21 million.

Goodman (Amana)	2.5%
Other	5.0

Source: *Appliance*, September 2004, pp. P-2, from *Appliance Magazine's 27th Annual Portrait of the U.S. Appliance Industry.*

★ 1759 ★

Heating and Cooling
SIC: 3585; NAICS: 333415

Leading Dehumidifer Makers, 2003

Market shares are shown based on shipments of 1.31 million.

Whirlpool	30.0%
LG Electronics (Goldstar)	25.0
W.C. Wood	12.0
Electrolux (Frigidaire)	11.0
Fedders	10.0
Samsung	4.0
Ebco	2.0
Other	6.0

Source: *Appliance*, September 2004, pp. P-2, from *Appliance Magazine's 27th Annual Portrait of the U.S. Appliance Industry.*

★ 1760 ★

Heating and Cooling
SIC: 3585; NAICS: 333415

Leading Furnace Makers (Gas & Warm Air), 2003

Market shares are shown based on shipments of 3.2 million.

UTC/Carrier	31.0%
Goodman (Amana)	16.0
Lennox	14.0
American Standard (Trane)	13.0
Rheem	11.0
York	7.0
Nordyne	6.0
Other	2.0

Source: *Appliance*, September 2004, pp. P-2, from *Appliance Magazine's 27th Annual Portrait of the U.S. Appliance Industry.*

★ 1761 ★

Heating and Cooling
SIC: 3585; NAICS: 333415

Leading Home Air Conditioner Makers in Japan, 2003

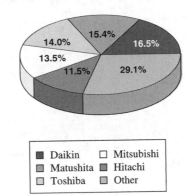

Market shares are shown based on domestic shipments.

Daikin	16.5%
Matushita	15.4
Toshiba	14.0
Mitsubishi	13.5
Hitachi	11.5
Other	29.1

Source: "Market Share Survey Report 2003." [online] from http://www.nni.nikkei.co.jp [Published July 26, 2004], from Nikkei estimates.

★ 1762 ★

Heating and Cooling
SIC: 3585; NAICS: 333415

Primary Underfloor Heating Market in the U.K., 2004

The market is estimated at 45 million pounds sterling. The market size (product sales only) was 29 million pounds sterling in 2003, 45 million in 2004, 55 million in 2005.

Water	83.0%
Electric	17.0

Source: *Contract Flooring Journal*, March 2005, p. 38, from AMA Research.

★ 1763 ★
Power Transmission Equipment
SIC: 3593; NAICS: 333999

Hydraulic Power Market Segments

Hydraulic power is generated by the use of pressurized liquid. It represents 75% of the fluid power market (or $7.8 billion).

Aerospace	.25.0%
Valves	.14.0
Pumps	.14.0
Cylinders	.11.0
Motors	.6.0
Other	.30.0

Source: *Advanced Manufacturing Technology*, January 15, 2005, p. 11, from National Fluid Power Association and U.S. Department of Commerce.

★ 1764 ★
Power Transmission Equipment
SIC: 3593; NAICS: 333999

Pneumatic Power Market Segments

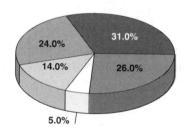

■ Aerospace □ Filters
■ Values ■ Other
□ Cylinders

Pneumatic power uses compressed air or gases. It represents 25% of the fluid power market (or $2.7 billion).

Aerospace	.31.0%
Values	.24.0
Cylinders	.14.0
Filters	.5.0
Other	.26.0

Source: *Advanced Manufacturing Technology*, January 15, 2005, p. 11, from National Fluid Power Association and U.S. Department of Commerce.

★ 1765 ★
Scales
SIC: 3596; NAICS: 333997

Livestock Scale Market

The company has a market share of over 60%.

Tru-Test	.60.0%
Other	.40.0

Source: "Tru-Test Annual General Meeting 2004." [online] from http://www.tru-test.com [Accessed March 8, 2005].

★ 1766 ★
Auto Filters
SIC: 3599; NAICS: 336399

Automotive Filter Industry in Europe

The European market is forecast to reach 663 million euros in 2006 and 1.9 billion in 2012. Market shares are shown in percent.

Faurecia	.60.0%
Other	.40.0

Source: *Automotive News Europe*, October 4, 2004, p. 4, from B&D Forecast.

★ 1767 ★
Robotic Arms
SIC: 3599; NAICS: 333999

Robotic Arm Market

The average cost of Schilling's robotic arms is $125,000. While customers can use robotic arms for a variety of purspoes - military projects and collecting rare fish, for example - most of Schilling's customers are offshore drillers. Market shares are shown in percent.

Schilling Robotics	.90.0%
Other	.10.0

Source: *Houston Chronicle*, May 4, 2005, p. 1, from Schilling.

SIC 36 - Electronic and Other Electric Equipment

★ 1768 ★

Electronics

SIC: 3600; NAICS: 334111, 33422

Electronic Assembly Industry Worldwide

Total sales were $1.21 trillion.

Japan	.21.4%
North America	.19.0
Western Europe	.18.0
Other	.41.6

Source: *CircuiTree*, November 2004, p. 58, from Custer Consulting Group.

★ 1769 ★

Electronics

SIC: 3600; NAICS: 334111, 33422

Largest Contract Manufacturers, 2003

Companies are ranked by total revenues in millions of dollars.

	($ mil.)	Share
Flextronics	$ 13,821.8	20.95%
Solectron	11,143.8	16.89
Sanmina	10,794.8	16.36
Celestica	6,735.3	10.21
Jabil Circuit	5,170.2	7.84
Elcoteq	2,807.3	4.26
Venture	1,861.2	2.82
Benchmark	1,839.8	2.79
Universal Scientific	1,200.8	1.82
Plexus Corp.	841.0	1.27
Other	9,748.5	14.78

Source: *Purchasing*, October 21, 2004, p. 38.

★ 1770 ★

Electronics

SIC: 3600; NAICS: 334111, 33422

Original Design Manufacturer Revenues in Tawain, 2003

The industry was valued at $51.7 billion.

Computer systems	.44.0%
Computer peripherals	.25.0
Consumer	.13.0
Wireless telecom	.12.0
Wired telecom	5.0
Automotive	1.0

Source: *Electronic Business*, September 2004, p. 47, from Technology Forecasters.

★ 1771 ★

Circuit Breakers

SIC: 3613; NAICS: 335313

Circuit Breaker Market in Thailand

The industry is valued at 600 million baht.

Safe-T-Cut	.88.0%
Other	.12.0

Source: *Bangkok Post*, November 4, 2004, p. NA.

★ 1772 ★

Electrostatic Products

SIC: 3629; NAICS: 335999

Electrostatic Discharge Market

The market for electrostatic discharge products is forecasted to increase from $881.7 million in 2003 to $1.47 billion in 2009.

	2003	2009	Share
Packaging	$ 249.5	$ 462.5	31.42%
Static control polymers	220.0	372.8	25.33
Furniture	130.0	240.1	16.31
Apparel	115.0	150.4	10.22
Flooring	102.2	151.4	10.29
Instruments	65.0	94.8	6.44

Source: *Research Studies - Business Communications Co.*, September 1, 2004, p. NA, from Business Communications Co.

★ 1773 ★
Fuel Cells
SIC: 3629; NAICS: 335999
Fuel Cell Vehicle Components

The market for new vehicle components is forecasted to increase from $35 million in 2004 to $208 million in 2009.

	2002	2004	2009
Tanks, battery & electric motor components	$ 10	$ 25	$ 118
Vehicle fuel cell modules	5	10	90

Source: *Research Studies - Business Communications Inc.*, September 21, 2004, p. NA, from Business Communications Co.

★ 1774 ★
Fuel Cells
SIC: 3629; NAICS: 335999
Premium Portable Power Source Industry Worldwide, 2009

The global market is forecast to reach $6.3 billion in 2009, an average annual growth rate of 7.2%.

Li-ion/polymer 93.5%
Hydrogen fuel cells 6.1
Zinc-air cells 0.4

Source: *Portable Design*, December 2004, p. 9, from Business Communications Co.

★ 1775 ★
Appliances
SIC: 3630; NAICS: 335221, 335222, 335224
Appliance Market Worldwide, 2003

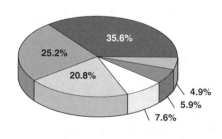

■ Cooking appliances	□ Vacuum cleaners
■ Refrigeration appliances	■ Heaters
□ Washing appliances	■ Dishwashers

Distribution is shown in percent.

Cooking appliances 35.6%
Refrigeration appliances 25.2

Washing appliances 20.8%
Vacuum cleaners 7.6
Heaters 5.9
Dishwashers 4.9

Source: *Modern Plastics*, September 2004, p. 30.

★ 1776 ★
Appliances
SIC: 3630; NAICS: 335221, 335222, 335224
Global Appliance Market, 2003

Market shares are shown in percent.

Europe 32.1%
Asia-Pacific 27.1
United States 24.7
Other 16.1

Source: *Modern Plastics*, September 2004, p. 30.

★ 1777 ★
Appliances
SIC: 3630; NAICS: 335221, 335222, 335224
Leading Appliance Makers in Europe, 2003

Market shares are shown based on shipments.

AB Electrolux 16.2%
BSH Bosch 15.2
Merloni 14.7
Whirlpool 8.6
Candy 3.5
Other 41.8

Source: *Appliance*, November 2004, pp. P-3.

★ 1778 ★
Appliances
SIC: 3630; NAICS: 335221, 335222, 335224
Leading Appliance Makers Worldwide, 2000 and 2004

Market shares are shown in percent. Figures include dishwashers, dryers, freezers, ranges, refrigerators and washers.

	2000	2004
Whirlpool	33.1%	32.3%
GE	26.6	23.7
Maytag	17.9	12.6
Electrolux (Frigidaire)	16.6	20.8
Other	3.3	10.6

Source: *Business 2.0*, May 2005, p. 75, from *Appliance Magazine* and *Business 2.0*.

★ 1779 ★
Cooking Equipment
SIC: 3631; NAICS: 335221

Leading Built-In Oven Makers in Germany, 2003

Market shares are shown based on shipments of 1.6 million units.

BSH 31.5%
Electrolux 24.3
Whirlpool 12.3
Merloni 5.4
Other 26.5

Source: *Appliance*, November 2004, pp. P-3.

★ 1780 ★
Cooking Equipment
SIC: 3631; NAICS: 335221

Leading Built-In Oven Makers in Italy, 2003

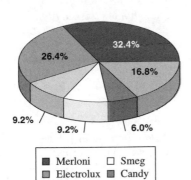

■ Merloni	□ Smeg
■ Electrolux	■ Candy
□ Whirlpool	▨ Other

Market shares are shown based on shipments of 1.4 million units.

Merloni 32.4%
Electrolux 26.4
Whirlpool 9.2
Smeg 9.2
Candy 6.0
Other 16.8

Source: *Appliance*, November 2004, pp. P-3.

★ 1781 ★
Cooking Equipment
SIC: 3631; NAICS: 335221

Leading Cooker Equipment Makers in France, 2003

Market shares are shown based on shipments of 810,000 units.

Elco Brandt 24.9%
Electrolux 19.4
Merloni 16.0
Candy 7.2
Other 32.5

Source: *Appliance*, November 2004, pp. P-3.

★ 1782 ★
Cooking Equipment
SIC: 3631; NAICS: 335221

Leading Cooker Equipment Makers in Turkey, 2003

Market shares are shown based on shipments of 400,000 units.

Arcelik 59.0%
BSH 26.1
Vestel 5.3
Other 9.6

Source: *Appliance*, November 2004, pp. P-3.

★ 1783 ★
Cooking Equipment
SIC: 3631; NAICS: 335221

Leading Microwave Makers, 2003

Market shares are shown based on shipments of 14.6 million units.

Samsung 30.0%
Sharp 27.0
LG Electronics (Goldstar) 17.0
Whirlpool 12.0
Matsushita 10.0
Sanyo 2.0
Daewoo 2.0

Source: *Appliance*, September 2004, pp. P-2, from *Appliance Magazine's 27th Annual Portrait of the U.S. Appliance Industry.*

★ 1784 ★
Cooking Equipment
SIC: 3631; NAICS: 335221

Leading Outdoor Grill Makers, 2003

Market shares are shown based on shipments of 8.3 million units. Figures include gas and full-size.

Bradley/Coleman	.40.0%
Weber-Stephen	.25.0
Sunbeam Outdoor Products	.10.0
Ducane	2.0
Other	.23.0

Source: *Appliance*, September 2004, pp. P-3, from *Appliance Magazine's 27th Annual Portrait of the U.S. Appliance Industry.*

★ 1785 ★
Cooking Equipment
SIC: 3631; NAICS: 335221

Leading Range (Electric) Makers, 2003

Market shares are shown based on shipments of 5.6 million units.

GE	.49.0%
Whirlpool	.23.0
Maytag	.13.0
Electrolux (Frigidaire)	.10.0
Peerless Premier	5.0

Source: *Appliance*, September 2004, pp. P-2, from *Appliance Magazine's 27th Annual Portrait of the U.S. Appliance Industry.*

★ 1786 ★
Cooking Equipment
SIC: 3631; NAICS: 335221

Leading Range (Gas) Makers, 2003

Market shares are shown based on shipments of 3.4 million.

GE	.36.0%
Electrolux (Frigidaire)	.27.0
Maytag	.20.0
Whirlpool	8.0
Peerless Premier	8.0
Other	1.0

Source: *Appliance*, September 2004, pp. P-2, from *Appliance Magazine's 27th Annual Portrait of the U.S. Appliance Industry.*

★ 1787 ★
Cooking Equipment
SIC: 3631; NAICS: 335221

Leading Range Hood Makers, 2003

Market shares are shown based on shipments of 3.6 million units.

Broan	.62.0%
Nutone	.22.0
GE	6.0
Ventline	5.0
Other	5.0

Source: *Appliance*, September 2004, pp. P-2, from *Appliance Magazine's 27th Annual Portrait of the U.S. Appliance Industry.*

★ 1788 ★
Cooking Equipment
SIC: 3631; NAICS: 335221

Ranges/Cooktop/Ovens Market

The table shows the preferred brands of residential remodeling and new home construction.

	Re-Modeling	New Homes
Freestanding range	53.0%	60.0%
Cooktop & wall oven combo . .	25.0	15.0
Slide-in ranges	20.0	18.0
Drop-in ranges	2.0	7.0

Source: *Kitchen & Bath Design News*, June 2004, p. NA, from National Kitchen & Bath Association 2003 research.

★ 1789 ★
Freezers
SIC: 3632; NAICS: 335222

Leading Freezer (Chest and Upright) Makers, 2003

Market shares are shown based on shipments of 2.5 million units.

Electrolux (Frigidaire)	.68.0%
W.C. Wood	.21.0
Haier	9.0
Other	2.0

Source: *Appliance*, September 2004, pp. P-2, from *Appliance Magazine's 27th Annual Portrait of the U.S. Appliance Industry.*

★ 1790 ★

Freezers

SIC: 3632; NAICS: 335222

Leading Freezer Makers in France, 2003

Market shares are shown based on shipments of 798,000 units.

Whirlpool	.25.8%
Electrolux (Frigidaire)	.13.2
Elco Brandt	8.8
Merloni	6.7
Other	.45.5

Source: *Appliance*, November 2004, pp. P-3.

★ 1791 ★

Refrigerators

SIC: 3632; NAICS: 335222

Leading Refrigerator (Built-In, Undercounter) Makers, 2003

Market shares are shown based on shipments of 153,500 units.

U-Line	.66.0%
Marvel Industries	.26.0
Sub-Zero	7.0
Other	1.0

Source: *Appliance*, September 2004, pp. P-2, from *Appliance Magazine's 27th Annual Portrait of the U.S. Appliance Industry.*

★ 1792 ★

Refrigerators

SIC: 3632; NAICS: 335222

Leading Refrigerator (Commercial) Makers, 2003

Market shares are shown based on shipments of 268,000 units.

True	.39.0%
Victory	.12.0
Traulsen	.12.0
Delfield	5.0
Other	.32.0

Source: *Appliance*, September 2004, pp. P-2, from *Appliance Magazine's 27th Annual Portrait of the U.S. Appliance Industry.*

★ 1793 ★

Refrigerators

SIC: 3632; NAICS: 335222

Leading Refrigerator Makers, 2003

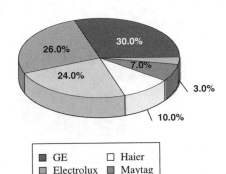

GE ■ | □ Haier
Electrolux ■ | ■ Maytag
Whirlpool ■ | ■ Other

Market shares are shown based on shipments of 10 million units.

GE	.30.0%
Electrolux (Frigidaire)	.26.0
Whirlpool	.24.0
Haier	.10.0
Maytag	7.0
Other	3.0

Source: *Appliance*, September 2004, pp. P-2, from *Appliance Magazine's 27th Annual Portrait of the U.S. Appliance Industry.*

★ 1794 ★

Refrigerators

SIC: 3632; NAICS: 335222

Leading Refrigerator Makers in Germany, 2003

Market shares are shown based on shipments.

BSH	.28.0%
Electrolux	.14.3
Liebherr	9.4
Whirlpool	7.7
Other	.40.6

Source: *Appliance*, November 2004, pp. P-3.

★ 1795 ★
Refrigerators
SIC: 3632; NAICS: 335222

Leading Refrigerator Makers in Japan, 2003

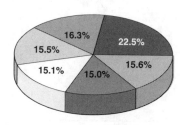

Market shares are estimated based on domestic shipments.

Matsushita Electric Industrial	.22.5%
Toshiba	.16.3
Hitachi Home & Life Solutions	.15.5
Sanyo Electric	.15.1
Sharp	.15.0
Other	.15.6

Source: "Market Share Survey Report 2003." [online] from http://www.nni.nikkei.co.jp [Published July 26, 2004], from Nikkei estimates.

★ 1796 ★
Refrigerators
SIC: 3632; NAICS: 335222

Leading Refrigerator Makers in the U.K., 2003

Market shares are shown based on shipments of 2.72 million units.

Merloni	.18.5%
Electrolux	.15.9
Arcelik	.11.7
Other	.53.9

Source: *Appliance*, November 2004, pp. P-3.

★ 1797 ★
Laundry Equipment
SIC: 3633; NAICS: 335224

Leading Dryer Makers (Electric), 2003

Market shares are shown based on shipments of 5.7 million units.

Whirlpool	.56.0%
Maytag	.18.0
GE	.15.0
Electrolux (Frigidaire)	.11.0

Source: *Appliance*, September 2004, pp. P-2, from *Appliance Magazine's 27th Annual Portrait of the U.S. Appliance Industry*.

★ 1798 ★
Laundry Equipment
SIC: 3633; NAICS: 335224

Leading Dryer Makers (Gas), 2003

Market shares are shown based on shipments of 1.6 million units.

Whirlpool	.55.0%
Maytag	.26.0
GE	.11.0
Electrolux (Frigidaire)	. 8.0

Source: *Appliance*, September 2004, pp. P-2, from *Appliance Magazine's 27th Annual Portrait of the U.S. Appliance Industry*.

★ 1799 ★
Laundry Equipment
SIC: 3633; NAICS: 335224

Leading Dryer Makers in Germany, 2003

Market shares are shown based on shipments of 935,000 units.

BSH	.25.4%
Whirlpool	.13.6
Electrolux	.13.2
Miele	.10.6
Other	.37.2

Source: *Appliance*, November 2004, pp. P-3.

★ 1800 ★
Laundry Equipment
SIC: 3633; NAICS: 335224
Leading Washer Makers in France, 2003

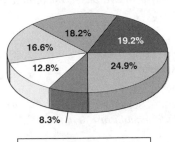

Market shares are shown based on shipments of 2.2 million units.

Elco Brandt	.19.2%
Whirlpool	.18.2
Electrolux	.16.6
Merloni	.12.8
BSH	. 8.3
Other	.24.9

Source: *Appliance*, November 2004, pp. P-3.

★ 1801 ★
Laundry Equipment
SIC: 3633; NAICS: 335224
Leading Washer Makers in the U.K., 2003

Market shares are shown based on shipments of 2.9 million units.

Merloni	.36.6%
Electrolux	.17.6
Candy	. 8.9
Other	.36.9

Source: *Appliance*, November 2004, pp. P-3.

★ 1802 ★
Laundry Equipment
SIC: 3633; NAICS: 335224
Leading Washing Machine Makers in Japan, 2003

Market shares are estimated based on domestic shipments.

Matsushita	.22.8%
Hitachi	.20.7
Toshiba	.19.1
Sanyo	.13.3
Sharp	.13.0
Other	.11.1

Source: "Market Share Survey Report 2003." [online] from http://www.nni.nikkei.co.jp [Published July 26, 2004], from Nikkei estimates.

★ 1803 ★
Personal Care Appliances
SIC: 3634; NAICS: 335211
Leading Beard/Mustache Trimmer Makers, 2003

Market shares are shown based on shipments of 9.5 million units.

Conair	.31.0%
Remington	.25.0
Wahl	.16.0
Micro Touch	.15.0
Other	.13.0

Source: *Appliance*, September 2004, pp. P-2, from *Appliance Magazine's 27th Annual Portrait of the U.S. Appliance Industry*.

★ 1804 ★
Personal Care Appliances
SIC: 3634; NAICS: 335211
Leading Curling Iron/Curling Brushes/ Hot-Air Brush Makers, 2003

Market shares are shown based on shipments of 30 million units.

Conair	.49.0%
Helen of Troy	.27.0
Other	.24.0

Source: *Appliance*, September 2004, pp. P-2, from *Appliance Magazine's 27th Annual Portrait of the U.S. Appliance Industry*.

★ 1805 ★
Personal Care Appliances
SIC: 3634; NAICS: 335211

Leading Electric Shaver Makers (Men's), 2003

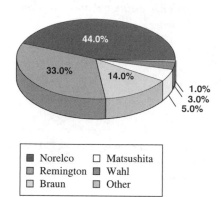

- ■ Norelco   □ Matsushita
- ■ Remington ■ Wahl
- □ Braun   ■ Other

Market shares are shown based on shipments of 6.12 million units.

Norelco	.44.0%
Remington	.33.0
Braun	.14.0
Matsushita (Panasonic)	.5.0
Wahl	.3.0
Other	.1.0

Source: *Appliance*, September 2004, pp. P-2, from *Appliance Magazine's 27th Annual Portrait of the U.S. Appliance Industry.*

★ 1806 ★
Personal Care Appliances
SIC: 3634; NAICS: 335211

Leading Electric Shaver Makers (Women's), 2003

Market shares are shown based on shipments of 2.16 million units.

Remington	.56.0%
Conair	.26.0
Matsushita (Panasonic)	.12.0
Norelco Consumer Products	.3.0
Other	.3.0

Source: *Appliance*, September 2004, pp. P-2, from *Appliance Magazine's 27th Annual Portrait of the U.S. Appliance Industry.*

★ 1807 ★
Personal Care Appliances
SIC: 3634; NAICS: 335211

Leading Hair Dryer (Hand-held) Makers, 2003

Market shares are shown based on shipments of 22.4 million.

Conair	.48.0%
Helen of Troy	.32.0
Remington/Clairol	.4.0
Other	.16.0

Source: *Appliance*, September 2004, pp. P-2, from *Appliance Magazine's 27th Annual Portrait of the U.S. Appliance Industry.*

★ 1808 ★
Personal Care Appliances
SIC: 3634; NAICS: 335211

Top Dental Accessory/Tool Brands, 2004

Market shares are shown based on drug store sales for the 52 weeks ended October 31, 2004.

Teledyne Water Pik	.7.7%
Doctor's Nightguard	.6.9
Dentek	.6.8
Reach	.4.9
Oral B Brush Ups	.4.6
Oral B	.4.4
Butler Gum	.4.2
Glide	.4.0
Oral B Hummingbird	.3.4
Butler Proxabrush	.3.2
Other	.49.9

Source: *Chain Drug Review*, January 3, 2005, p. 95, from Information Resources Inc.

★ 1809 ★
Personal Care Appliances
SIC: 3634; NAICS: 335211

Top Nasal Aspirators, 2004

Brands are ranked by sales at food stores, drug stores and mass merchandisers (but not Wal-Mart).

	($ mil.)	Share
First Years	$ 1.3	34.21%
Safety 1st	0.8	21.05
Luv 'n Care	0.6	15.79
Gerber	0.4	10.53
Little Noses	0.2	5.26
Ross	0.1	2.63

Continued on next page.

★ 1809 ★

[Continued]
Personal Care Appliances
SIC: 3634; NAICS: 335211

Top Nasal Aspirators, 2004

Brands are ranked by sales at food stores, drug stores and mass merchandisers (but not Wal-Mart).

	($ mil.)	Share
Private label	$ 0.3	7.89%
Other	0.1	2.63

Source: *MMR*, April 25, 2005, p. 67, from Information Resources Inc.

★ 1810 ★

Personal Care Appliances
SIC: 3634; NAICS: 335211

Top Power Toothbrush Brands, 2004

Brands are ranked by sales at drug stores, supermarkets and mass merchandisers (excluding Wal-Mart) for the year ended December 26, 2004.

	($ mil.)	Share
Sonicare Advance	$ 44.7	14.33%
Braun Oral-B Flexisoft	36.2	11.60
Crest Spinbrush Pro	27.7	8.88
Braun Oral-B	27.5	8.81
Sonicare Elite	26.1	8.37
Braun Oral-B Crossaction	19.0	6.09
Crest Spinbrush Pro Whitening . . .	18.8	6.03
Colgate Motion	8.0	2.56
Oral-B Professional Care	7.7	2.47
Teledyne Water Pik	7.4	2.37
Other	88.9	28.49

Source: *MMR*, February 7, 2005, p. 28, from Information Resources Inc.

★ 1811 ★

Small Appliances
SIC: 3634; NAICS: 335211

Leading Blender Makers, 2003

Market shares are shown based on shipments of 11.5 million units. Figures include hand-helds.

Hamilton Beach/Proctor-Silex	54.0%
Oster/Sunbeam	23.0
Salton/Toastermaster/Welbilt	7.0
Cuisinart	6.0
Waring	3.0
Krups	2.0
KitchenAid	2.0

Braun	2.0%
Holmes Group	1.0

Source: *Appliance*, September 2004, pp. P-2, from *Appliance Magazine's 27th Annual Portrait of the U.S. Appliance Industry*.

★ 1812 ★

Small Appliances
SIC: 3634; NAICS: 335211

Leading Breadmaker Producers, 2003

Market shares are shown based on shipments of 11.5 million units.

Oster/Sunbeam	37.0%
Salton/Toastermaster/Weltbilt/Breadman . .	35.0
West Bend	3.0
Hamilton Beach/Proctor-Silex	2.5
Zojiushi	2.0
Regal	2.0
Other	18.5

Source: *Appliance*, September 2004, pp. P-3, from *Appliance Magazine's 27th Annual Portrait of the U.S. Appliance Industry*.

★ 1813 ★

Small Appliances
SIC: 3634; NAICS: 335211

Leading Coffee Maker Producers, 2003

Market shares are shown based on shipments of 14.4 million units.

Oster/Sunbeam/Mr. Coffee	27.0%
Hamilton Beach/Proctor-Silex	17.0
Applica (Windmere/Black & Decker)	16.0
Krups	7.0
Cuisinart	6.0
Braun	6.0
Other	21.0

Source: *Appliance*, September 2004, pp. P-3, from *Appliance Magazine's 27th Annual Portrait of the U.S. Appliance Industry*.

★ 1814 ★

Small Appliances
SIC: 3634; NAICS: 335211

Leading Food Processor Makers, 2003

Market shares are shown based on shipments of 1.7 million units.

Cuisinart	26.0%
Applica (Windmere/Black & Decker)	20.0
Hamilton Beach/Proctor-Silex	13.0

Continued on next page.

★ 1814 ★

[Continued]
Small Appliances
SIC: 3634; NAICS: 335211

Leading Food Processor Makers, 2003

Market shares are shown based on shipments of 1.7 million units.

KitchenAid 9.0%
Other 32.0

Source: *Appliance*, September 2004, pp. P-3, from *Appliance Magazine's 27th Annual Portrait of the U.S. Appliance Industry.*

★ 1815 ★

Small Appliances
SIC: 3634; NAICS: 335211

Leading Iron Makers, 2003

Market shares are shown based on shipments of 17.4 million units.

Applica (Windmere/Black & Decker) 27.0%
Oster/Sunbeam 17.5
Hamilton Beach/Proctor-Silex 15.5
Rowenta 9.0
GE 7.0
The Holmes Group (Rival) 5.0
Other 19.0

Source: *Appliance*, September 2004, pp. P-3, from *Appliance Magazine's 27th Annual Portrait of the U.S. Appliance Industry.*

★ 1816 ★

Vacuum Cleaners
SIC: 3635; NAICS: 335212

Leading Vacuum Cleaner Makers (Hand-Held), 2003

Market shares are shown based on shipments of 6.4 million units.

Black & Decker 35.0%
Royal 23.0
EuroPro 20.0
Eureka 4.0
Hoover 2.0
Other 16.0

Source: *Appliance*, September 2004, pp. P-2, from *Appliance Magazine's 27th Annual Portrait of the U.S. Appliance Industry.*

★ 1817 ★

Vacuum Cleaners
SIC: 3635; NAICS: 335212

Top Vacuum Cleaners, 2004

Dyson had no share when it arrived in the $2.2 billion upright vacuum market in March 2003. The vacuum is expensive, costing generally between $399-550. Consumers seem to have responded to its ad line as the first vacuum cleaner to never lose suction. Up until first quarter of 2004, half of all devices sold cost $95-125 or less. Data are for the three months ended September 30, 2004 and refer only to upright vacuums.

Hoover 19.6%
Dyson 14.7
Other 65.7

Source: *Advertising Age*, December 6, 2004, p. 1, from NPD.

★ 1818 ★

Vacuum Cleaners
SIC: 3635; NAICS: 335212

Vacuum Cleaner Market

Market shares are estimated in percent.

Dyson 21.0%
Hoover 16.0
Kirby 14.0
Other 49.0

Source: *U.S. News & World Report*, May 23, 2005, p. EE15.

★ 1819 ★

Dishwashers
SIC: 3639; NAICS: 335228

Leading Dishwasher/Dryer Makers in Japan, 2003

Market shares are shown based on domestic shipments.

Matsushita Electric Industrial 67.7%
Toshiba 13.0
Toto 6.6
Sanyo Electric 6.1
Hitachi Home & Life Solutions 5.7
Other 0.9

Source: "Market Share Survey Report 2003." [online] from http://www.nni.nikkei.co.jp [Published July 26, 2004], from Nikkei estimates.

★ 1820 ★

Dishwashers
SIC: 3639; NAICS: 335228

Leading Dishwasher Makers in France, 2003

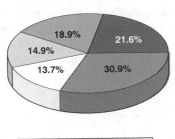

Market shares are shown based on shipments.

BSH	.21.6%
Whirlpool	.18.9
Merloni	.14.9
Electrolux	.13.7
Other	.30.9

Source: *Appliance*, November 2004, pp. P-3.

★ 1821 ★

Dishwashers
SIC: 3639; NAICS: 335228

Leading Dishwasher Makers in Germany, 2003

Market shares are shown based on shipments.

BSH	.48.3%
Electrolux	.18.0
Whirlpool	. 8.8
Miele	. 7.1
Merloni	. 3.7
Candy	. 0.5
Other	.13.6

Source: *Appliance*, November 2004, pp. P-3.

★ 1822 ★

Garbage Disposals
SIC: 3639; NAICS: 335228

Leading Garbage Disposal Makers, 2003

Market shares are shown based on shipments of 6.2 million units.

In-Sink-Erator	.80.0%
Anaheim Mfg.	.20.0

Source: *Appliance*, September 2004, pp. P-2, from *Appliance Magazine's 27th Annual Portrait of the U.S. Appliance Industry.*

★ 1823 ★

Steam Cleaners
SIC: 3639; NAICS: 335228

Leading Shampooers/Steam Cleaner Makers, 2003

Market shares are shown based on shipments of 3.02 million units.

Bissell	.52.0%
Hoover	.28.0
Royal	. 8.0
Oreck	. 1.0
Other	.11.0

Source: *Appliance*, September 2004, pp. P-2, from *Appliance Magazine's 27th Annual Portrait of the U.S. Appliance Industry.*

★ 1824 ★

Trash Compactors
SIC: 3639; NAICS: 335228

Leading Trash Compactor Makers, 2003

Market shares are shown based on shipments of 126,000 units.

Whirlpool	.91.0%
Other	. 9.0

Source: *Appliance*, September 2004, pp. P-2, from *Appliance Magazine's 27th Annual Portrait of the U.S. Appliance Industry.*

★ 1825 ★

Light Bulbs

SIC: 3641; NAICS: 33511

Top Light Bulb Brands, 2004

Market shares are shown based on drug store sales for the year ended October 31, 2004.

GE	.54.8%
Reveal	5.9
GE Long Life	4.1
GE Miser	3.7
Feit	2.3
Sylvania	1.1
GE Light Effects	1.1
GE Miser Plus	1.0
GE House and Garden	0.7
Private label	.20.4
Other	4.9

Source: *Chain Drug Review*, September 27, 2004, p. 36, from Information Resources Inc.

★ 1826 ★

Light Bulbs

SIC: 3641; NAICS: 33511

Top Light Bulb Makers, 2004

Market shares are shown based on sales at food stores, drug stores and mass merchandisers (but not Wal-Mart) for the 52 weeks ended June 13, 2004.

General Electric	.72.8%
Osram Sylvania	7.7
Philips Lighting	3.4
Feit Electric	1.0
Private label	.12.3
Other	2.8

Source: *Grocery Headquarters*, August 2004, p. S88, from Information Resources Inc.

★ 1827 ★

Automotive Lighting

SIC: 3647; NAICS: 336321

Automotive Lighting Market in North America

Market shares are shown in percent.

	2001	2004
Guide	75.0%	65.0%
Other	25.0	35.0

Source: *Automotive News*, December 20, 2004, p. 1.

★ 1828 ★

Automotive Lighting

SIC: 3647; NAICS: 336321

Vehicular Lighting in China, 2002

There are 35 auto bulb manufacturers in the country. Auto parts sales (including lighting) benefit from sales in the automotive sector. In 2005, auto sales in the country are forecast to exceed 3 million units.

Tail lights	.61.30%
H4-H7 and 900 front light	.12.58
Auto meter indicators	8.00
Motorcycle bulbs	7.01
Right front light	4.52
H1-H3	4.18
Other	2.41

Source: "US & FCS Market Research Reports." [online] from http://www.stat-usa.gov [Published February 23, 2004].

★ 1829 ★

Consumer Electronics

SIC: 3650; NAICS: 33431

Consumer Electronics Sales

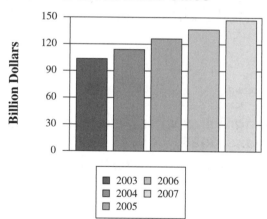

Sales are shown in billions of dollars.

2003	. $ 102.61
2004	113.54
2005	125.72
2006	135.78
2007	146.64

Source: *Electronic Design*, June 30, 2005, p. 27, from Consumer Electronics Association.

★ 1830 ★
Consumer Electronics
SIC: 3650; NAICS: 33431

Leading Consumer Electronics Firms, 2003

Market shares are shown based on retail volume.

Sony Corp.	24.5%
Matsushita	17.2
Pioneer	5.3
Toshiba	5.1
Sharp	4.4
Fujix	3.9
Kenwood	3.5
JVC	3.2
Other	32.9

Source: *Financial Times*, October 28, 2004, p. 19, from Thomson Datastream and Euromonitor.

★ 1831 ★
Consumer Electronics
SIC: 3650; NAICS: 33431

Leading Electronics Categories, 2003-2004

Sales are shown in millions of dollars.

	2003	2004
Televisions	$ 15,551.25	$ 18,623.75
Cell phones	11,453.75	13,172.50
DVD players	3,372.50	3,075.00
Audio systems	2,548.75	2,970.00
Digital camcorders	2,502.50	2,126.25
Telephones	1,905.00	1,776.25
Satellite equipment	1,845.00	2,357.50
Portable audio (boomboxes)	1,693.75	1,225.00
Home theater systems	1,201.25	1,213.75
PDAs	948.75	821.25

Source: *HFN*, February 28, 2005, p. 43, from Consumers Electronics Association.

★ 1832 ★
Audio Equipment
SIC: 3651; NAICS: 33431

Audio Music Player Market (Hard Drive), 2003-2005

Total number of hard drive units shipped: 1.15 million in 2003, 4.91 million in 2004 and 17.69 million in 2005.

	2003	2004	2005
iPod	82.0%	90.0%	92.0%
Other	18.0	10.0	8.0

Source: *Star Tribune*, January 25, 2005, p. 1D, from NPD and Piper Jaffray.

★ 1833 ★
Audio Equipment
SIC: 3651; NAICS: 33431

Digital Music Player Market in Japan

Apple's share has increased from 50% of the market.

iPod	80.0%
Other	20.0

Source: "Apple Aims 80% of Japanese Market." [online] from http://www.dvhardcxware.net/article3959.html [accessed January 24, 2005].

★ 1834 ★
Audio Equipment
SIC: 3651; NAICS: 33431

Digital Music Player Market Worldwide

Market shares are shown in percent.

iPod	50.0%
Other	50.0

Source: *Marketing Week*, October 7, 2004, p. 26.

★ 1835 ★
Audio Equipment
SIC: 3651; NAICS: 33431

Leading Audio Shelf System Brands, 2003

Market shares are shown in percent.

Panasonic	18.62%
Sony	18.28
JVC	15.92
Sharp	11.84
Jwin	3.46

Continued on next page.

★ 1835 ★

[Continued]
Audio Equipment
SIC: 3651; NAICS: 33431

Leading Audio Shelf System Brands, 2003

Market shares are shown in percent.

Teac	2.68%
Other	29.10

Source: *Dealerscope*, August 2004, p. 44, from *Dealerscope 2004 CE Stats Statistical Survey & Report.*

★ 1836 ★

Audio Equipment
SIC: 3651; NAICS: 33431

Leading Minidisc Recorder/Player Makers in Japan, 2003

Market shares are estimated based on domestic shipments.

Sony	38.8%
Matsushita Electric Industrial	24.5
Sharp	22.2
Kenwood	6.9
Victor Co. of Japan	6.3
Other	1.3

Source: "Market Share Survey Report 2003." [online] from http://www.nni.nikkei.co.jp [Published July 26, 2004], from Nikkei estimates.

★ 1837 ★

Audio Equipment
SIC: 3651; NAICS: 33431

Leading MP-3 Players in the Asia-Pacific Region, 2004

Market shares are shown for the first six months of the year.

Apple	53.0%
Creative	16.0
Archos	7.0
Other	25.0

Source: *Financial Times*, March 30, 2005, p. 19, from iSuppli and Daiwa Institute of Research.

★ 1838 ★

Audio Equipment
SIC: 3651; NAICS: 33431

Leading Receiver/Amplifier/Tuner Makers, 2004

Market shares are shown based on sales at specialty channels for the 12 months ended September 2004.

Denon, Marantz, McIntosh	32.9%
Yamaha	31.4
B&K	8.1
Sony	7.0
Pioneer	5.0
Onkyo	2.2

Source: "Creating Future Premium Audio/Visual Entertainment Solutions." [online] from http://www.dm-holdings.com [Published November 16, 2004], from NPD Intelect and Frost & Sullivan.

★ 1839 ★

Audio Equipment
SIC: 3651; NAICS: 33431

Leading Receiver/Amplifier/Tuner Makers in Japan, 2004

Market shares are shown based on sales at specialty channels for the 12 months ended September 2004.

Denon, Marantz, McIntosh	30.9%
Yamaha	28.3
Onkyo	14.7
Pioneer	11.3
Sony	3.8
Accuphase	2.1
Other	8.9

Source: "Creating Future Premium Audio/Visual Entertainment Solutions." [online] from http://www.dm-holdings.com {Published November 16, 2004], from Gfk.

★ 1840 ★

Audio Equipment
SIC: 3651; NAICS: 33431

Live Sound Business

Live sound business refers to a type of in-ear headphones.

Ultimate Ears	70.0%
Other	30.0

Source: *Stereophile*, December 2004, p. NA.

★ 1841 ★
Audio Equipment
SIC: 3651; NAICS: 33431

Movie Theater Speaker Market

Market shares are estimated in percent.

Yamaha	50.0%
Other	50.0

Source: *Knight Ridder/Tribune Business News*, September 16, 2004, p. NA.

★ 1842 ★
Audio Equipment
SIC: 3651; NAICS: 33431

Portable Digital Audio Player Market

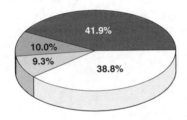

41.9%
10.0%
9.3%
38.8%

■ Apple □ Creative
■ Rio □ Other

Market shares are shown in percent.

Apple	41.9%
Rio	10.0
Creative	9.3
Other	38.8

Source: *DCD Business Report*, November 24, 2004, p. NA, from NPD Group.

★ 1843 ★
Audio Equipment
SIC: 3651; NAICS: 33431

Top Music Player Makers (Drive-based), 2004

Market shares are for September 2004.

Apple Computer	87.3%
Hewlett-Packard	4.6
Rio	2.8
Creative	2.6
iRiver	1.5
Other	1.2

Source: "Music Player Market Shares." [online] from http://www.itfacts.biz/index.php?idP1970 [accessed January 6, 2005], from NPD Group.

★ 1844 ★
Audio Equipment
SIC: 3651; NAICS: 33431

Top Music Player Makers (Flash-based), 2004

Market shares are for September 2004.

iRiver	18.8%
Rio	18.6
Digital Way	15.8
RCA	8.8
Samsung	6.2
Other	31.8

Source: "Music Player Market Shares." [online] from http://www.itfacts.biz/index.php?idP1970 [accessed January 6, 2005], from NPD Group.

★ 1845 ★
Camcorders
SIC: 3651; NAICS: 33431

Leading Camcorder Makers in Japan, 2003

Market shares are shown based on domestic shipments.

Sony	38.3%
Matsushita Electric	25.2
JVC	16.5
Canon	10.7
Sharp	9.1

Source: "Market Share Survey Report 2003." [online] from http://www.nni.nikkei.co.jp [Published July 26, 2004], from Nikkei estimates and Japan Electronics and Information Technology Industries Association.

★ 1846 ★
Camcorders
SIC: 3651; NAICS: 33431

Leading Camcorder Makers Worldwide, 2003

Market shares are shown based on domestic shipments.

Sony	38.3%
JVC	20.9
Matsushita Electric	18.9
Canon	12.5

Continued on next page.

★ 1846 ★
[Continued]
Camcorders
SIC: 3651; NAICS: 33431

Leading Camcorder Makers Worldwide, 2003

Market shares are shown based on domestic shipments.

Samsung Electronics	8.2%
Other	1.2

Source: "Market Share Survey Report 2003." [online] from http://www.nni.nikkei.co.jp [Published July 26, 2004], from Nikkei estimates and Japan Electronics and Information Technology Industries Association.

★ 1847 ★
Camcorders
SIC: 3651; NAICS: 33431

Leading Digital Video Camera Makers in Thailand

Market shares are shown in percent.

Sony	40.0%
Panasonic	25.0
Other	35.0

Source: *Bangkok Post*, February 19, 2005, p. NA.

★ 1848 ★
Camcorders
SIC: 3651; NAICS: 33431

Top Camcorder Makers, 2004

Unit shares are shown for January - November 2004.

Sony	43.2%
Panasonic	14.1
Canon	13.8
Samsung	13.2

JVC	11.8%
Other	3.9

Source: *New York Times*, January 17, 2005, p. C7, from NPD Group/NPD Techworld.

★ 1849 ★
Camcorders
SIC: 3651; NAICS: 33431

Top Camcorder Makers in Japan, 2003

Market shares are shown in percent.

Sony	38.3%
JVC	20.9
Panasonic	18.9
Canon	12.5
Other	9.4

Source: *Consumer Electronics Daily*, August 3, 2004, p. NA, from Japan Electronics & Information Technology.

★ 1850 ★
DVD Players
SIC: 3651; NAICS: 33431

Leading DVD Player Makers in Japan, 2003

Market shares are shown based on domestic shipments.

Matsushita Electric Industrial	41.5%
Toshiba	17.8
Pioneer	14.8
Sony	14.1
Sharp	9.8
Other	1.8

Source: "Market Share Survey Report 2003." [online] from http://www.nni.nikkei.co.jp [Published July 26, 2004], from Nikkei estimates.

★ 1851 ★
DVD Players
SIC: 3651; NAICS: 33431

Leading DVD Player Makers Worldwide, 2003

Market shares are shown based on domestic shipments.

Matsushita Electric Industrial	42.5%
Royal Philips Electronics	14.8
Pioneer	14.2

Continued on next page.

★ 1851 ★

[Continued]
DVD Players
SIC: 3651; NAICS: 33431

Leading DVD Player Makers Worldwide, 2003

Market shares are shown based on domestic shipments.

Sony	.12.2%
Toshiba	.11.0
Other	5.3

Source: "Market Share Survey Report 2003." [online] from http://www.nni.nikkei.co.jp [Published July 26, 2004], from Nikkei estimates.

★ 1852 ★

DVD Players
SIC: 3651; NAICS: 33431

Top DVD Player Makers, 2003

Market shares are shown in percent.

Sony	.13.13%
Panasonic	.12.97
Samsung	.10.73
Cyberhome	7.31
Philips	5.23
JVC	4.67
Other	.45.96

Source: *Dealerscope*, August 2004, p. 44, from *Dealerscope 2004 CE Stats Statistical Survey & Report*.

★ 1853 ★

DVD Players
SIC: 3651; NAICS: 33431

Top DVD Player Makers, 2004

Unit shares are shown for January - November 2004.

Cyberhome	.14.5%
Sony	.11.9
Toshiba	7.8
Samsung	6.6
Panasonic	5.1
Other	.54.1

Source: *New York Times*, January 17, 2005, p. C7, from NPD Group/NPD Techworld.

★ 1854 ★

DVD Players
SIC: 3651; NAICS: 33431

Top DVD Recorder Makers Worldwide, 2003

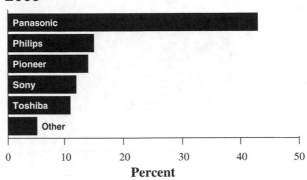

Market shares are shown in percent.

Panasonic	.42.5%
Philips	.14.8
Pioneer	.14.2
Sony	.12.2
Toshiba	.11.0
Other	5.3

Source: *Consumer Electronics Daily*, July 29, 2004, p. NA, from Japan Electronics & Information Technology.

★ 1855 ★

DVD Players
SIC: 3651; NAICS: 33431

Top DVD Recorders, 2003

Market shares are shown in percent.

Panasonic	.36.05%
goVideo	8.62
Pioneer	6.85
Toshiba	6.43
Cyberhome	5.54
Other	.36.51

Source: *Dealerscope*, August 2004, p. 44, from *Dealerscope 2004 CE Stats Statistical Survey & Report*.

★ 1856 ★

Televisions

SIC: 3651; NAICS: 33431

Big-Screen Television Market, 2004

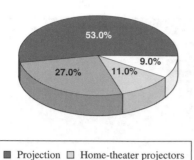

Distribution is shown based on sales of advanced 30-inch and larger displays for the second quarter.

Projection 53.0%
Plasma 27.0
Home-theater projectors 11.0
LCD 9.0

Source: *Wall Street Journal*, October 14, 2004, p. B1, from Quixel Research.

★ 1857 ★

Televisions

SIC: 3651; NAICS: 33431

Digital TV Set Industry Worldwide (40-inch and larger)

Total shipments are forecast to increase from 7.3 million units to 21.7 million units. Plasma televisions are forecast to increase in market share at the expensive of rear projection CRT sets. CRT stands for cathode ray tube. LCD stands for liquid crystal display. DLP stands for digital light processing.

	2004	2008
Rear projection CRT	57.0%	5.0%
Plasma	21.0	49.0
Rear projection LCD	10.0	15.0
DLP	10.0	13.0
Direct view LCD	2.0	16.0

Source: *Investor's Business Daily*, September 27, 2004, p. A4, from iSuppli.

★ 1858 ★

Televisions

SIC: 3651; NAICS: 33431

DLP Rear-Projection TV Market, 2004

Market shares are shown for the third quarter of 2004. DLP stands for ditial light processing.

Sharp 72.0%
RCA 8.0
LG Electronics 6.0
Mitsubishi 5.0
Panasonic 4.0
Toshiba 3.0
Optima 1.0

Source: *HFN*, January 10, 2005, p. 67, from DisplaySearch.

★ 1859 ★

Televisions

SIC: 3651; NAICS: 33431

LCD Television Shipments Worldwide, 2004

By screen size, 20-21'' is the dominant category worldwide. Sharpe led the market with a 28% share. Market shares are shown for the third quarter of 2004.

Europe 35.0%
Japan 29.0
North America 26.0
China 3.0
Other 7.0

Source: "New DisplaySearch Report Provides TV Shipments." [online] from http://www.displaysearch.com [Published January 3, 2005], from Display Search.

★ 1860 ★

Televisions

SIC: 3651; NAICS: 33431

LCD TV Market

In terms of sales of large screens (over 30 inches) flat panel TV sets, about half use micromirror based DLP chips made by T1. Other companies have entered the market and are offering prices lower than TI's cost of $350-550.

Projection TVs (including home theater) 62.2%
Technology (> 30 inch screens) 28.2
Plasma TVs 9.6

Source: *Display Development News*, November 2004, p. NA, from BCC.

★ 1861 ★
Televisions
SIC: 3651; NAICS: 33431

Leading Home Theaters (Front Projector)

Market shares are shown in percent.

InFocus 18.71%
HP 17.92
Sony 14.65
Optoma 10.88
Other 37.84

Source: *Dealerscope*, August 2004, p. 44, from *Dealerscope 2004 CE Stats Statistical Survey & Report.*

★ 1862 ★
Televisions
SIC: 3651; NAICS: 33431

Leading LCD Flat-Screen TV Makers Worldwide, 2004

Market shares are shown for the second quarter of 2004.

Sharp 30.8%
Sony 10.9
Philips Electronics 10.9
Matsushita Electric Industrial 8.3
Samsung 6.7
Other 32.4

Source: *Wall Street Journal*, September 10, 2004, p. B3, from iSuppli.

★ 1863 ★
Televisions
SIC: 3651; NAICS: 33431

Leading Plasma TV Makers, 2004

Shares are for the first quarter of 2004.

	Units	Share
Panasonic	27,366	15.6%
Gateway	21,795	12.4
LG Electronics	21,244	12.1
Hitachi	14,828	8.5

Source: *America's Intelligence Wire*, August 23, 2004, p. NA, from iSuppli.

★ 1864 ★
Televisions
SIC: 3651; NAICS: 33431

Leading Plasma TV Makers in Japan, 2003

Market shares are estimated based on domestic shipments.

Hitachi 30.8%
Matsushita Electric Industrial 29.1
Sony 16.3
Pioneer 14.6
Victor Co. of Japan 5.0
Other 4.2

Source: "Market Share Survey Report 2003." [online] from http://www.nni.nikkei.co.jp [Published July 26, 2004], from Nikkei estimates.

★ 1865 ★
Televisions
SIC: 3651; NAICS: 33431

Leading Plasma TV Makers Worldwide

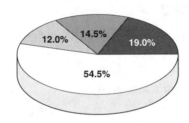

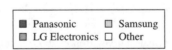

Market shares are shown for the fourth quarter 2004.

Panasonic 19.0%
LG Electronics 14.5
Samsung 12.0
Other 54.5

Source: *Investor's Business Daily*, February 28, 2005, p. A4, from DisplaySearch.

★ 1866 ★

Televisions

SIC: 3651; NAICS: 33431

Leading Television Makers in Japan (CRT), 2003

Market shares are shown based on domestic shipments. CRT stands for cathode ray tube.

Sony	.16.8%
Sharp	.16.6
Matsushita Electric Industrial	.16.2
Toshiba	.15.7
Mitsubishi Electric	.11.0
Other	.23.7

Source: "Market Share Survey Report 2003." [online] from http://www.nni.nikkei.co.jp [Published July 26, 2004], from Nikkei estimates and Japan Electronics and Information Technology Industries Association.

★ 1867 ★

Televisions

SIC: 3651; NAICS: 33431

Leading Television Makers (LCD) in Japan, 2003

Market shares are shown based on domestic shipments.

Sharp	.56.6%
Matushita Electric Industrial	.17.8
Sony	.12.9
Toshiba	.5.6
Hitachi	.2.4
Other	.4.7

Source: "Market Share Survey Report 2003." [online] from http://www.nni.nikkei.co.jp [Published July 26, 2004], from Nikkei estimates.

★ 1868 ★

Televisions

SIC: 3651; NAICS: 33431

Leading Television Makers (LCD) Worldwide, 2003

Market shares are shown based on domestic shipments.

Sharp	.48.1%
Sony	.14.9
Matsushita Electric Industrial	.13.1
Samsung Electronics	.10.1

LG Electronics	.7.2%
Other	.6.6

Source: "Market Share Survey Report 2003." [online] from http://www.nni.nikkei.co.jp [Published July 26, 2004], from Nikkei estimates.

★ 1869 ★

Televisions

SIC: 3651; NAICS: 33431

PDP Television Shipments Worldwide, 2004

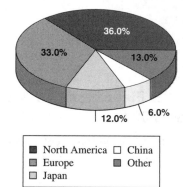

By size, 42" WVGA reached a 54% share with 42-43" XGA/SXGA followed with 21% share. Market shares are shown for the third quarter of 2004.

North America	.36.0%
Europe	.33.0
Japan	.12.0
China	.6.0
Other	.13.0

Source: "New DisplaySearch Report Provides TV Shipments." [online] from http://www.displaysearch.com [Published January 3, 2005], from Display Search.

★ 1870 ★

Televisions

SIC: 3651; NAICS: 33431

Plasma Television Shipments in Asia, 2004

Shipments are in thousands of units.

	(000)	Share
Japan	338	39.44%
China/Hong Kong	263	30.69
Korea	74	8.63
Australia	64	7.47
Taiwan	54	6.30

Continued on next page.

★ 1870 ★

[Continued]
Televisions
SIC: 3651; NAICS: 33431

Plasma Television Shipments in Asia, 2004

Shipments are in thousands of units.

	(000)	Share
Singapore	32	3.73%
Other	32	3.73

Source: *Screen Digest*, August 2004, p. 25S, from Decision Tree Consulting.

★ 1871 ★

Televisions
SIC: 3651; NAICS: 33431

Television Sales, 2004 and 2008

The number of digital televisions is expected to expand four fold. LCD stands for liquid crystal displays. CRT stands for liquid crystal displays.

	2004	2008
LCD	43.0%	36.0%
CRT	28.0	43.0
Rear-projection	19.0	8.0
Plasma displays	10.0	8.0

Source: *ExtremeTech.com*, November 18, 2004, p. NA, from iSuppli.

★ 1872 ★

Televisions
SIC: 3651; NAICS: 33431

Television Sales, 2008

Most televisions are still analog, but high definition and enhanced definition are becoming increasingly popular.

Analog	80.0%
HDTV	15.0
EDTV	5.0

Source: *Investor's Business Daily*, July 2, 2004, p. A4, from Diffusion Group.

★ 1873 ★

Televisions
SIC: 3651; NAICS: 33431

Top Color TV Makers in India, 2003-2004

The color television market was worth Rs 7500 crore. The top four firms have 69% and may take 85% in the next three to four years by some estimates. Market shares are shown in percent.

Videocon	22.1%
LG	19.0
Samsung	14.5
Onida	13.1
Other	31.3

Source: *Asia Africa Intelligence Wire*, September 20, 2004, p. NA, from India Business Insight.

★ 1874 ★

Televisions
SIC: 3651; NAICS: 33431

Top Digital Televisions, 2003

Market shares are shown in percent.

Sony	29.0%
Samsung	14.0
Toshiba	13.0
Mitsubishi	11.0
Hitachi	11.0
Other	22.0

Source: *Dealerscope*, August 2004, p. 44, from *Dealerscope 2004 CE Stats Statistical Survey & Report*.

★ 1875 ★

Televisions
SIC: 3651; NAICS: 33431

Top LCD RPTV Makers Worldwide, 2004

Market shares are shown for the third quarter 2004.

Sony	65.0%
Panasonic	14.0
Hitachi	11.0
LGE/Zenith	9.0
Other	1.0

Source: ''New DisplaySearch Report Provides TV Shipments.'' [online] from http://www.displaysearch.com [Published January 3, 2005], from Display Search.

★ 1876 ★
Televisions
SIC: 3651; NAICS: 33431

Top LCD Television Vendors Worldwide

Market shares are shown in percent for the third quarter of 2004.

Sharp	.28.0%
Philips	.11.0
Sony	.10.0
Other	.51.0

Source: "New DisplaySearch Report Provides TV Shipments." [online] from http://www.displaysearch.com [Published January 3, 2005], from Display Search.

★ 1877 ★
Televisions
SIC: 3651; NAICS: 33431

Top PDP Television Makers in China

PDP stands for homemade plasma display panels for October 2004.

Xoceco	.17.8%
Matsushita	.17.3
Samsung	.10.3
LG	.7.5
Haier	.7.0

Source: *Asia Pulse*, November 19, 2004, p. NA.

★ 1878 ★
Televisions
SIC: 3651; NAICS: 33431

Top PDP Television Makers Worldwide

Market shares are shown for the third quarter of 2004.

Panasonic	.20.0%
Sony	.13.0
LGE	.12.0
Samsung	.8.0
Hitachi	.8.0
Pioneer	.7.0
Philips	.7.0
Other	.25.0

Source: "New DisplaySearch Report Provides TV Shipments." [online] from http://www.displaysearch.com [Published January 3, 2005], from Display Search.

★ 1879 ★
Televisions
SIC: 3651; NAICS: 33431

Top Television Brands (Rear Projection), 2003

Market shares are shown in percent.

Sony	.26.53%
Hitachi	.11.92
Zenith	.10.22
Panasonic	.10.04
Toshiba	.9.95
Other	.31.34

Source: *Dealerscope*, August 2004, p. 44, from *Dealerscope 2004 CE Stats Statistical Survey & Report*.

★ 1880 ★
Televisions
SIC: 3651; NAICS: 33431

Top Television Makers, 2004

Unit shares are shown for January - November 2004.

Sony	.14.6%
Toshiba	.11.1
RCA	.8.4
Panasonic	.7.7
Sylvania	.6.6
Other	.51.6

Source: *New York Times*, January 17, 2005, p. C7, from NPD Group/NPD Techworld.

★ 1881 ★
Video Cassette Recorders
SIC: 3651; NAICS: 33431

Leading VCR Makers in Japan, 2003

Market shares are estimated based on domestic shipments.

Matsushita Electric Industrial	.24.4%
JVC	.19.6
Mitsubishi Electric	.15.7
Sony	.9.6
Funai Electric	.8.9
Other	.21.8

Source: "Market Share Survey Report 2003." [online] from http://www.nni.nikkei.co.jp [Published July 26, 2004], from Nikkei estimates.

★ 1882 ★

Music

SIC: 3652; NAICS: 334612, 51222

Album Sales by Format, 2004-2005

Sales are shown for the year-to-date. CD sales fell 8.4%, cassettes fell 74% and the other category fell 36.3%.

	2004 (000)	2005 (000)	Share
CDs	189,461	173,508	99.18%
Cassette	4,034	1,048	0.60
Other	567	380	0.22

Source: *Billboard*, May 7, 2005, p. 49, from Nielsen SoundScan.

★ 1883 ★

Music

SIC: 3652; NAICS: 334612, 51222

Best-Selling Albums, 2005

Albums are ranked by millions of units sold from January 2004 - January 2005.

Confessions by Usher	7.9
Feels Like Home by Norah Jones	3.8
Encore by Eminem	3.5
When the Sun Goes Down by Kenny Chesney . .	3.1
Here for the Party by Gretchen Wilson	2.9
Live Like You Were Dying by Tim McGraw . . .	2.8
Songs About Jane by Maroon 5	2.7
Now 16 by various artists	2.6
Fallen by Evanescence	2.6
Autobiography by Ashlee Simpson	2.6

Source: *Detroit Free Press*, January 7, 2005, p. 1H, from Nielsen SoundScan.

★ 1884 ★

Music

SIC: 3652; NAICS: 334612, 51222

Best-Selling Country Albums, 2005

Country album sales totalled 77.91 million units for January 5, 2004 - January 2, 2005.

Come On Over by Shania Twain	15,267,050
When the Sun Goes Down by Kenny Chesney	3,072,224
Here for the Party by Gretchen Wilson .	2,931,097
Live Like You Were Dying by Tim McGraw	2,786,840
Greatest Hits by Shania Twain	2,336,048
Greatest Hits Vol 2 by Toby Keith . . .	1,916,897
50 Number Ones by George Strait . . .	1,878,295

Horse of a Different Color by Big & Rich	1,778,247
Shock 'N Y'all by Toby Keith	1,649,358

Source: *PR Newswire*, January 6, 2005, p. NA, from Nielsen SoundScan.

★ 1885 ★

Music

SIC: 3652; NAICS: 334612, 51222

Best-Selling Musicians

Data show millions of units sold.

The Beatles	166.5
Elvis Presley	117.5
Led Zeppelin	106.0
Garth Brooks	105.0
The Eagles	88.0

Source: *USA TODAY*, September 20, 2004, p. 4B, from Recording Industry Association of America.

★ 1886 ★

Music

SIC: 3652; NAICS: 334612, 51222

Best-Selling Soundtracks

Unit sales are for the week ended November 7, 2004. The Cheetah Girls, Tupac: Resurrection and Lord of the Rings were released before 2004. Their figures are for the year only.

Shrek 2	708,000
The Cheetah Girls	659,000
Spider-Man 2	573,000
50 First Dates	418,000
A Cinderella Story	402,000
The Punisher: The Album	399,000
The Lord of the Rings: The Return of the Kings	356,000
Tupac: Resurrection	355,000
The Princess Diaries 2: Royal Engagement .	331,000
Garden State	324,000

Source: *Billboard*, November 20, 2004, p. 10, from Nielsen Soundscan.

★ 1887 ★
Music
SIC: 3652; NAICS: 334612, 51222

Largest Music Markets Worldwide, 2004

World shipments fell 1.3% to $33.6 billion. By units, the market fell just 0.4% to 2.75 billion units. The industry seemed to stabilize after several years of decline. Digital sales saw strong growth. In the top four markets — the United States, Untied Kingdom, France and Germany — there were more than 200 million downloads, ten times as many as in 2003.

		($ mil.)	Share
United States		$ 12,153	36.17%
Japan		5,168	15.38
United Kingdom		3,509	10.44
Germany		2,149	6.40
France		1,979	5.89
Australia		717	2.13
Canada		694	2.07
Italy		652	1.94
Spain		573	1.71
Netherlands		508	1.51
Other		5,496	16.00

Source: *Billboard*, April 2, 2005, p. 6, from International Federation of the Phonographic Industry.

★ 1888 ★
Music
SIC: 3652; NAICS: 334612, 51222

Music Sales by Year in Latin America

Latin America is the only global territory to see double digit growth (12.6%). The industry benefited from music DVDs, economic recovery in the region and successful anti-piracy campaigns. Retail value are in millions of dollars.

2000	$ 1,710
2001	1,330
2002	1,050
2003	850
2004	956

Source: *Billboard*, April 9, 2005, p. 25, from International Federation of the Phonographic Industry.

★ 1889 ★
Music
SIC: 3652; NAICS: 334612, 51222

Music Sales in India

The recorded music market was worth $230 million in 2003. Piracy is thought to account for 40% of sales. Sales are expected to climb to $270 million in 2008 because of new formats (music over the Internet, music on portable devices).

Indian film music	67.0%
Indi-pop	15.0
International (mostly U.S.)	6.0
Other	12.0

Source: "US & FCS Market Research Reports." [online] from http://www.stat-usa.gov [Published April 27, 2004], from International Data Corp.

★ 1890 ★
Music
SIC: 3652; NAICS: 334612, 51222

Popular Music Genres, 2004

Genres are ranked by millions of units sold. Country increased 12% over 2003, R&B increased 8%, Alternative 3%, Metal up 2%, Christian down 7% and Latin up 16%.

	(mil.)	Share
R&B	162.0	24.88%
Alternative	132.0	20.27
Country	78.0	11.98
Metal	75.0	11.52
Christian	43.0	6.60
Latin	32.0	4.91
Other	129.1	19.83

Source: *USA TODAY*, January 6, 2005, p. 1D, from Nielsen SoundScan.

★ 1891 ★
Music
SIC: 3652; NAICS: 334612, 51222

Top Album Distributors in Europe, 2005

Shares are shown for the first quarter of the year. UMI led the singles market with a 39.2% share, followed by Sony BMG with 26%.

UMI	35.1%
EMI	24.5
Sony BMG	18.6

Continued on next page.

★ 1891 ★

[Continued]
Music
SIC: 3652; NAICS: 334612, 51222

Top Album Distributors in Europe, 2005

Shares are shown for the first quarter of the year. UMI led the singles market with a 39.2% share, followed by Sony BMG with 26%.

Warner	.18.0%
Other	3.8

Source: *Billboard*, May 14, 2005, p. 11, from *Billboard* statistics.

★ 1892 ★

Music
SIC: 3652; NAICS: 334612, 51222

Top Music Distributors, 2004

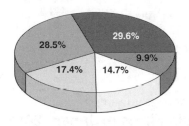

The table compares market shares for total and current album sales for the 52 week year. Album sales totaled 666.7 million units for the 52 week period, up about 1.6% over the same period in 2003. Because of an anomaly in the calendar it was actually a 53 week year which would bring the actual total to 681.4 million.

	Current	Total
UMVD	32.2%	29.6%
Sony BMG	29.8	28.5
Independents	15.8	17.4
WEA	13.0	14.7
EMM	9.3	9.9

Source: *Billboard*, January 15, 2004, p. 5, from SoundScan.

★ 1893 ★

Music
SIC: 3652; NAICS: 334612, 51222

Top Music Distributors (Latin), 2004

Sales of Spanish-language albums through December 31, 2004 totaled 32.3 million units.

UMVD	.48.1%
Sony BMG	.23.6
Indies	.13.8
EMM	8.1
WEA	6.5

Source: *Billboard*, January 22, 2005, p. 23, from Nielsen Soundscan.

★ 1894 ★

Music
SIC: 3652; NAICS: 334612, 51222

Top Music Distributors (R&B), 2004

Market shares are shown in percent.

UMVD	.40.9%
Sony BMG	.30.8
Indies	9.7
WEA	9.4
EMM	9.3

Source: *Billboard*, January 22, 2005, p. 23, from Nielsen Soundscan.

★ 1895 ★

Music
SIC: 3652; NAICS: 334612, 51222

Top Music Distributors (Rap), 2004

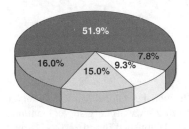

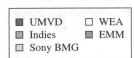

Market shares are shown in percent.

UMVD	.51.9%
Indies	.16.0
Sony BMG	.15.0

Continued on next page.

★ 1895 ★
[Continued]
Music
SIC: 3652; NAICS: 334612, 51222
Top Music Distributors (Rap), 2004

Market shares are shown in percent.

WEA 9.3%
EMM 7.8

Source: *Billboard*, January 22, 2005, p. 23, from Nielsen Soundscan.

★ 1896 ★
Music
SIC: 3652; NAICS: 334612, 51222
Top Music Firms in Africa, 2003

Market shares are shown in percent.

Indies 34.0%
EMI 21.2
Universal 19.9
Sony 13.1
BMG 11.8

Source: "IFPI Publishes Global Music Market Shares." [online] from http://www.ifpi.org/site-content/press/ 20040616a.html [Published June 16, 2004], from International Federation of the Phonographic Industry.

★ 1897 ★
Music
SIC: 3652; NAICS: 334612, 51222
Top Music Firms in Australasia, 2003

Market shares are shown in percent.

Universal 20.3%
EMI 18.4
Indies 17.5
Sony 16.9
Warner 15.1
BMG 11.7

Source: "IFPI Publishes Global Music Market Shares." [online] from http://www.ifpi.org/site-content/press/ 20040616a.html [Published June 16, 2004], from International Federation of the Phonographic Industry.

★ 1898 ★
Music
SIC: 3652; NAICS: 334612, 51222
Top Music Firms in Australia, 2003

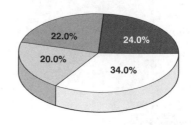

Market shares are shown in percent.

Universal Music Group 24.0%
Sony Music 22.0
Independents 20.0
Other 34.0

Source: *Billboard*, August 7, 2004, p. NA.

★ 1899 ★
Music
SIC: 3652; NAICS: 334612, 51222
Top Music Firms in Japan, 2003

Market shares are estimated based on domestic shipments.

Sony Music Entertainment 16.8%
Universal Music 13.5
Avex 13.2
Toshiba 11.5
Victor Entertainment 8.6
Other 36.4

Source: "Market Share Survey Report 2003." [online] from http://www.nni.nikkei.co.jp [Published July 26, 2004], from Recording Industry Association of Japan.

★ 1900 ★
Music
SIC: 3652; NAICS: 334612, 51222
Top Music Firms in Latin America, 2003

Market shares are shown in percent.

Indies 26.0%
Sony 19.6
Warner 15.4

Continued on next page.

★ 1900 ★

[Continued]
Music
SIC: 3652; NAICS: 334612, 51222

Top Music Firms in Latin America, 2003

Market shares are shown in percent.

Universal 14.7%
BMG 12.2
EMI 12.1

Source: "IFPI Publishes Global Music Market Shares."
[online] from http://www.ifpi.org/site-content/press/
20040616a.html [Published June 16, 2004], from International Federation of the Phonographic Industry.

★ 1901 ★

Music
SIC: 3652; NAICS: 334612, 51222

Top Music Firms in the U.K., 2004

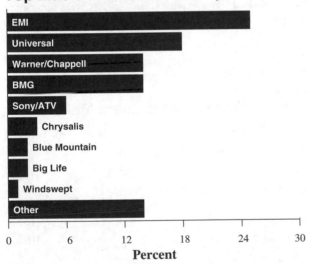

Market shares are shown in percent. Figures include both albums and singles.

EMI 25.4%
Universal 18.0
Warner/Chappell 14.4
BMG 14.4
Sony/ATV 5.5
Chrysalis 2.6
Blue Mountain 2.1
Big Life 2.0
Windswept 1.3
Other 14.3

Source: *Music Week*, March 5, 2005, p. 7.

★ 1902 ★

Music
SIC: 3652; NAICS: 334612, 51222

Top Music Firms (Independent) in the U.K., 2004

Market shares are shown in percent.

Chrysalis 11.5%
Blue Mountain 9.5
Big Life 8.9
Windswept 5.7
Catalyst 5.6
Nothing Hill 4.2
IMG 3.6
Carlin 2.2
Perfect 2.1
Bug 2.1
Other 44.6

Source: *Music Week*, March 5, 2005, p. 7.

★ 1903 ★

Music
SIC: 3652; NAICS: 334612, 51222

Top Music Firms Worldwide, 2003

Industry sales totaled $32 billion in audio and video products.

Independents 25.3%
Universal 23.5
EMI 13.4
Sony 13.2
Warner 12.7
BMG 11.9

Source: *DCD Business Report*, September 29, 2004, p. NA, from International Federation of the Phonographic Industry.

★ 1904 ★
Ring-Tones
SIC: 3652; NAICS: 334612, 51222

Ring-Tone Industry Worldwide, 2004

The ringtone market has not developed as quickly in the United States as it has in other countries. The source points out that no company has done for the industry what Apple has down for music downloading. Analysts differ on the future development of the market. By 2008, sources have estimated the U.S. market as high as $1 billion and as low as $330 million. The United States had sales of $300 million of the current $4 billion world industry.

	($ mil.)	Share
Western Europe	$ 1,500	37.5%
Japan	1,000	25.0
Korea	500	12.5
United States	300	7.5
Other	700	17.5

Source: *Billboard*, September 18, 2004, p. 3, from Consect.

★ 1905 ★
Camera Phones
SIC: 3661; NAICS: 33421

Leading Camera Phone Makers, 2004

Market shares are shown for the third quarter.

Nokia	48.0%
Sony Ericsson	12.0
Samsung	9.0
Other	31.0

Source: "3G Handsets on the Rise." [online] from http://www.canalys.com/pr/2004/r2004111.htm [published December 2, 2004], from Canalys.

★ 1906 ★
Camera Phones
SIC: 3661; NAICS: 33421

Leading Camera Phone Makers in Europe/Middle East/Africa

Shares are shown based on shipments of phones with integrated digital cameras for the second quarter of 2003.

Nokia	42.6%
Sony Ericsson	22.1
Samsung	10.5
Sharp	9.7

Panasonic	7.4%
Other	7.7

Source: "UMTS and 3G Maket Share Distribution." [Online] from http://www.umtsworld.com/industry/user_equipment.htm [accessed October 18, 2004], from Canalys.com.

★ 1907 ★
Camera Phones
SIC: 3661; NAICS: 33421

Leading Camera Phone Makers Worldwide

An estimated 257 million camera phones were shipped worldwide. This figure represents about 38% of total handset sales.

Nokia	18.0%
Motorola	17.0
Samsung	13.0
Other	52.0

Source: *Business Wire*, April 14, 2005, p. NA, from Strategy Analytics.

★ 1908 ★
Camera Phones
SIC: 3661; NAICS: 33421

Leading Cell Phone Camera Makers Worldwide

Market shares are shown in percent.

Toshiba	16.6%
Sanyo	16.6
Sharp	14.0
Samsung	10.7
Matsushita	10.7
Other	31.4

Source: *Solid State Technology*, November 2004, p. S18.

★ 1909 ★
Cellular Phones
SIC: 3661; NAICS: 33421

Display Lighting for the Global Cell Phone Market

The company has 64% of the market for lighting for color displays in cellular phones.

National Semiconductor	64.0%
Other	36.0

Source: *Product News Network*, November 19, 2004, p. NA, from DisplaySearch and International Data Corp.

★ 1910 ★

Cellular Phones

SIC: 3661; NAICS: 33421

Leading CDMA Phone Makers in North America

Market shares are shown in percent. CDMA stand for code division multiple access.

Lucent	60.0%
Nortel	25.0
Other	15.0

Source: *Telephony*, March 14, 2005, p. NA, from Cellular Telecommunications & Internet Association's *Wireless 2005*.

★ 1911 ★

Cellular Phones

SIC: 3661; NAICS: 33421

Leading CDMA Phone Makers Worldwide

CDMA stands code division multiple access.

Nokia	30.7%
Motorola	13.9
Samsung	13.6
Other	41.8

Source: *Asia Africa Intelligence Wire*, November 24, 2004, p. NA.

★ 1912 ★

Cellular Phones

SIC: 3661; NAICS: 33421

Leading Cellular Phone Makers in Brazil, 2004

Market shares are shown based on the third quarter 2004.

Vivo	42.3%
Claro	20.6
Other	37.1

Source: *America's Intelligence Wire*, November 16, 2004, p. NA, from teleco.com.br.

★ 1913 ★

Cellular Phones

SIC: 3661; NAICS: 33421

Leading Cellular Phone Makers in Philippines, 2003

Philippines has one of the highest penetration rates in Asia (35%).

Smart	45.0%
Globe Telecom	39.0
Piltel	13.0%
Digitel	3.0
Extelcom	1.0

Source: *Asia Pulse*, July 29, 2004, p. NA, from National Telecommunications Commission.

★ 1914 ★

Cellular Phones

SIC: 3661; NAICS: 33421

Leading Smart Phone Makers, 2004

Market shares are shown for the second quarter of 2004.

Nokia	41.0%
RIM	13.0
Motorola	12.0
Fujitsu	10.0
palmOne	4.0
Other	20.0

Source: *Business 2.0*, October 2004, p. 136, from Bloomberg, Canalys, PalmOne, and RIM.

★ 1915 ★

Cellular Phones

SIC: 3661; NAICS: 33421

Leading Smart Phone Makers Worldwide, 2004

Nokia doubled its shipments from 2003 in order to distinguish itself. Smart phones are still expensive and represent less than 3% of the global cell phone industry. Companies are ranked by millions of units shipped.

	(mil.)	Share
Nokia	11.54	65.98%
Fujitsu	1.27	7.26
Sony-Ericsson	1.02	5.83
palmOne	0.94	5.37
Motorola	0.90	5.15
Other	1.82	10.41

Source: *Wall Street Journal*, January 31, 2005, p. B4, from Canalys Ltd.

★ 1916 ★
Cellular Phones
SIC: 3661; NAICS: 33421

Mobile Phones in Brazil

TDMA stands for time division multiple access. CDMA stands for code division multiple access. GSM stands for global standard for mobile communications.

TDMA	.24.9%
CDMA	.16.1
GSM	.12.5

Source: *Latin America Telecom*, September 2004, p. 1, from UMTS Forum.

★ 1917 ★
Cellular Phones
SIC: 3661; NAICS: 33421

Top Cell Phone Firms in Japan, 2004

Market shares are shown based on shipments of 44.02 million units.

NEC Corp.	.17.0%
Sharp	.14.6
Panasonic Mobile	.14.5
Other	.53.9

Source: *Asia Pulse*, March 2, 2005, p. NA, from International Data Corp.

★ 1918 ★
Cellular Phones
SIC: 3661; NAICS: 33421

Top Cell Phone Makers in Latin America

Market shares are shown in percent.

Motorola	.31.0%
Nokia	.30.0
Other	.39.0

Source: *Wireless Week*, March 15, 2005, p. 28.

★ 1919 ★
Cellular Phones
SIC: 3661; NAICS: 33421

Top Cell Phone Makers in Western Europe, 2005-2006

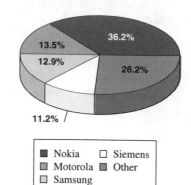

■ Nokia   □ Siemens
■ Motorola   ■ Other
■ Samsung

Market shares are shown in percent.

	2005	2006
Nokia	35.9%	36.2%
Motorola	12.5	13.5
Samsung	12.1	12.9
Siemens	11.3	11.2
Other	28.2	26.2

Source: *Wireless Week*, March 15, 2005, p. 28, from Gartner.

★ 1920 ★
Cellular Phones
SIC: 3661; NAICS: 33421

Top Cellular Phone Makers in China, 2004

Market shares are shown for the first six months of the year.

Motorola	.12.1%
Nokia	.11.9
Samsung	.9.9
Ningbo Bird	.9.6
TCL	.8.2
Konka	.5.6
Dbtel	.5.5
Amoi	.3.9
Other	.33.4

Source: *China Telecom*, November 2004, p. 1, from China Center of Information Industry Development.

★ **1921** ★
Cellular Phones
SIC: 3661; NAICS: 33421

Top Cellular Phone Makers Worldwide, 2004

Companies are ranked by estimated shipments.

	(000)	Share
Nokia	207,600	31.2%
Motorola	104,500	15.7
Samsung	86,500	13.0
Siemens	49,400	7.4
LG Electronics	44,400	6.7
Other	172,000	25.9

Source: "2004 Worldwide Mobile Phone Shipments Up 18.1%." [online] from http://www.idc.com [Press release January 27, 2005], from International Data Corp.

★ **1922** ★
Fax Machines
SIC: 3661; NAICS: 33421

Leading Fax Machine Makers in Japan

Market shares are shown in percent.

Panasonic	30.0%
Sharp	26.0
Brother	25.0
Canon	10.0
Ricoh	4.0
Other	5.0

Source: *Vietnam News Briefs*, September 16, 2004, p. NA, from Gartner Group.

★ **1923** ★
Fiber Optics
SIC: 3661; NAICS: 334418

Global Fiber Market

Total demand was 55 million fiber-kilometers.

North America	30.0%
China	25.0
Western Europe	15.0
Japan	15.0
Other Asia	10.0
Other	5.0

Source: *Fiber Optics Weekly Update*, March 18, 2005, p. 1, from Corning.

★ **1924** ★
Fiber Optics
SIC: 3661; NAICS: 334418

Optical Ground Wire Industry Worldwide, 2008

Market shares are shown in percent.

Asia Pacific	33.0%
Western Europe	20.0
North America	13.0
Eastern Europe	13.0
Other	21.0

Source: *Fiber Optics Weekly Update*, September 10, 2004, p. 1, from KMI.

★ **1925** ★
Mobile Devices
SIC: 3661; NAICS: 33421

Leading Mobile Terminal Makers Worldwide, 2004

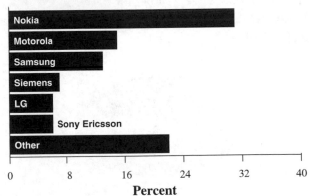

Percent

The market saw strong growth and surpassed 674 million units in 2004. The industry was driven by replacement sales, seasonal dynamics and continued growth in emerging markets.

	Units	Share
Nokia	207,231.3	30.7%
Motorola	104,124.4	15.4
Samsung	85,238.4	12.6
Siemens	48,455.8	7.2
LG	42,276.8	6.3
Sony Ericsson	42,031.7	6.2
Other	144,643.7	21.6

Source: "Gartner Says Strong 4Q Sales Led Worldwide Mobile Phone Sales." [online] from http://www.gartner.com [Press release March 2, 2004], from Gartner Dataquest.

★ 1926 ★
Modems
SIC: 3661; NAICS: 33421, 334418

Leading Cable Modem Providers Worldwide, 2004

Shares are for the second quarter.

	Units	Share
Motorola	1,720,000	41.92%
Ambit	555,403	13.54
Terayon	498,000	12.14
Thomson	365,000	8.90
S-A	360,000	8.77
Arris	129,984	3.17
Other	475,000	11.58

Source: *Screen Digest*, October 2004, p. 319, from Kinetic Strategies.

★ 1927 ★
Satellites
SIC: 3661; NAICS: 33421, 334418

Leading Satellite Makers Worldwide, 2005-2009

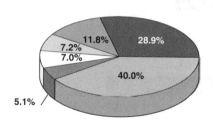

■ Boeing Satellite Systems □ Mitsubishi Electric
■ Lockheed Martin ▨ Alcatel Space
□ Astrium ▤ Other

Total value of production was $56.8 billion from 2005 - 2009. Figures are based on fiscal year 2005 dollars.

Boeing Satellite Systems	28.9%
Lockheed Martin	11.8
Astrium	7.2
Mitsubishi Electric	7.0
Alcatel Space	5.1
Other	40.0

Source: *Aviation Week & Space Technology*, January 17, 2005, p. 29, from Forecast International.

★ 1928 ★
Broadcasting Equipment
SIC: 3663; NAICS: 33422

Conditional Access Market Leaders

Conditional acess technology is used to control access to pay television services to users by encrypting the transmitted programming. Market shares are shown based on digital/pay TV subscribers.

NDS	33.0%
Kudelski/Nagra platform	27.0
Other	40.0

Source: *America's Intelligence Wire*, March 2, 2005, p. NA, from RBC Capital Markets.

★ 1929 ★
Broadcasting Equipment
SIC: 3663; NAICS: 33429

Live Video Screen Market

Market shares are shown in percent.

Barco	85.0%
Other	15.0

Source: *Lighting Dimensions*, March 1, 2005, p. NA.

★ 1930 ★
Broadcasting Equipment
SIC: 3663; NAICS: 33422

Trucks and High-Definition TV Equipment

The company has almost all of the market for broadcasting equipment in trucks needed to record high-definition live programming.

EVS	95.0%
Other	5.0

Source: *Wall Street Journal*, February 3, 2005, p. B4.

★ 1931 ★
Radio Towers
SIC: 3663; NAICS: 33422

Radio Tower Business

Companies are ranked by number of tower sites.

American Tower	13,000
Crown Castle	11,000
Spectrasite	7,500
Clear Channel's tower business	1,300

Source: *Wireless Review*, September 2004, p. 18.

★ 1932 ★
Automatic Data Capturing
SIC: 3669; NAICS: 33429

Leading ADC Suppliers Worldwide

Suppliers are ranked by revenue in millions of dollars.

Symbol Technologies	$ 1,530
Intermec	706
Danaher	550
Zebra Technologies	536
Sato Corp.	389
Imaje	287
Psion-Teklogix	211
PSC	186
Denso ID Systems	177
Hand Held Products (HHP)	145
Metrologic Instruments	138

Source: *Modern Materials Handling*, September 2004, p. 37, from Venture Development Corp.

★ 1933 ★
Fire Detection Equipment
SIC: 3669; NAICS: 33429

Aerospace Fire-Safety Systems Market

Market shares are shown in percent.

Kidde	55.0%
Other	45.0

Source: "Kidde Says $2.45B United Technologies Bid Too Low." [online] from http://www.quote.bloomberg.com [Press release October 22, 2004].

★ 1934 ★
Fire Detection Equipment
SIC: 3669; NAICS: 33429

Fire Equipment Market in France

There was virtually no growth in the oversaturated market in 2003. The industry is related to the construction market, which has been suffering as well.

Automatic detection systems	54.0%
Equipment	39.0
Maintenance	7.0

Source: "US & FCS Market Research Reports." [online] from http://www.stat-usa.gov [Published April 21, 2004].

★ 1935 ★
Military Communications
SIC: 3669; NAICS: 33429

Surface Communications Market Worldwide

The source forecasts that defense departments will spend $11.42 billion purchasing, developing and in the maintenance of 58 different surface communications systems. The market share of the top 3 firms is shown.

Boeing/General Dynamics/Thales	73.66%
Other	23.34

Source: "Forecast Study projects $11.4B Surface Communications Market." [online] from http://www.forecast1.com [accessed November 24, 2004], from Forecast International.

★ 1936 ★
Networking Equipment
SIC: 3669; NAICS: 33429

10-Gigabit Ethernet Switch Market Worldwide

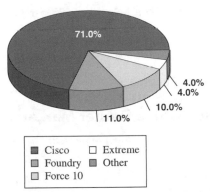

Cisco ■ Extreme □
Foundry ■ Other ■
Force 10 □

Market shares are shown in percent.

Cisco	71.0%
Foundry	11.0
Force 10	10.0
Extreme	4.0
Other	4.0

Source: *Investor's Business Daily*, August 23, 2004, p. A14, from Dell'Oro Group.

★ 1937 ★

Networking Equipment

SIC: 3669; NAICS: 33429

Application Front End Market Worldwide

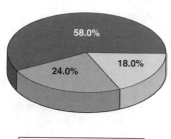

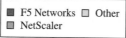

Application front end equipment is purchased to accelerate the speed of slow-performing business applications.

F5 Networks 58.0%
NetScaler 24.0
Other 18.0

Source: *Internet Wire*, March 28, 2005, p. NA.

★ 1938 ★

Networking Equipment

SIC: 3669; NAICS: 33422

Branch Office Router Market

Market shares are shown in percent.

Cisco 89.0%
Adtran Inc. 1.4
Nortel Networks 1.0
Other 8.6

Source: "VOIP to Boost Sluggish Router Market." [online] from http://www.searchnetworking.techtarget.com/originalcontent/0.289142.si, from In-Stat/MDR.

★ 1939 ★

Networking Equipment

SIC: 3669; NAICS: 33429

DSL CPE Market Worldwide

According to the source, "DSL CPE is achieving double digit growth in order to match the installed base of DSLAM and next generation DLC and DSL port deployments". Distribution is shown based on revenues.

ASDL modems 52.0%
ADSL routers 37.0
VDSL modems and routers 4.0
G.SHDSL modems and routers 3.0
DSL IADs 3.0

Source: *Worldwide Telecom*, July 2004, p. 5, from Infonetics Research.

★ 1940 ★

Networking Equipment

SIC: 3669; NAICS: 33422

Enterprise Router Market

Market shares are shown in percent.

Cisco 95.0%
Nortel 1.1
Other 3.9

Source: "VOIP to Boost Sluggish Router Market." [online] from http://www.searchnetworking.techtarget.com/originalcontent/0.289142.si, from In-Stat/MDR.

★ 1941 ★

Networking Equipment

SIC: 3669; NAICS: 33429

Enterprise WLAN Market Shares Worldwide, 2004

Market shares are shown based on revenues for the third quarter. WLAN stands for wireless local area network.

Cisco 42.8%
Symbol 15.9
Airespace 5.7
Proxim 4.4
3Com 4.4
Other 26.8

Source: *Computer Reseller News*, January 3, 2005, p. 27, from Synergy Research Group.

★ 1942 ★

Networking Equipment
SIC: 3669; NAICS: 33429

Fibre Channel HBA Market Shares

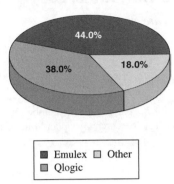

Shares are based on revenues for June 2004. HBA stands for host bus adapter.

Emulex 44.0%
Qlogic 38.0
Other 18.0

Source: *Infostar*, October 2004, p. 10, from Dell'Oro Group.

★ 1943 ★

Networking Equipment
SIC: 3669; NAICS: 33429

Fibre-Channel Switch Market

Fibre channel switching involves connecting networks storing large amounts of corporate data and making them accessible in many locations.

McData 47.0%
Brocade 24.0
Cisco 23.0
CNT 7.4

Source: *Star Tribune*, January 19, 2005, p. 1D, from Yankee Group.

★ 1944 ★

Networking Equipment
SIC: 3669; NAICS: 33429

Global Enterprise Router Market

Market shares are shown based on revenue for fourth quarter 2004. Revenues totalled $816 million in revenues.

Cisco 84.0%
Vanguard 1.0
Other 15.0

Source: *PR Newswire*, February 22, 2005, p. NA, from Infonetics Research.

★ 1945 ★

Networking Equipment
SIC: 3669; NAICS: 33429

High-End Router Market in Asia

Market shares are shown in percent.

Cisco 86.7%
Other 13.3

Source: *BusinessWeek*, February 7, 2005, p. 50, from International Data Corp. Asia Pacific.

★ 1946 ★

Networking Equipment
SIC: 3669; NAICS: 33429

High-End Router Market Worldwide, 2004

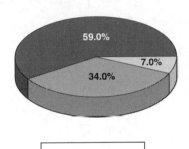

Market shares are shown for first quarter 2004.

Cisco 59.0%
Juniper 34.0
Other 7.0

Source: *Business 2.0*, September 2004, p. 105, from Dell'Oro Group.

★ 1947 ★

Networking Equipment
SIC: 3669; NAICS: 33429

Home Wireless Equipment Market, 2004

Shares are shown for the third quarter of 2004.

Cisco-Linksys 30.7%
D-Link 20.4
Netgear 4.2
Other 44.7

Source: *Business Journal of Jacksonville*, December 13, 2004, p. NA, from Synergy Research Group.

★ 1948 ★
Networking Equipment
SIC: 3669; NAICS: 33429

Internet Phone System Gear Worldwide

The market is forecast to increase from $3.5 billion in 2004 to $10.5 billion in 2008. Cisco's share was 40% in 2002.

Avaya	.25.0%
Cisco	.23.0
Other	.52.0

Source: *BusinessWeek*, February 21, 2005, p. 62.

★ 1949 ★
Networking Equipment
SIC: 3669; NAICS: 33429

IP Backbone Industry Worldwide, 2004

Market shares are shown in percent.

NTT	.33.0%
Reach	.28.0
Korea Telecom	.22.0
Asia Netcom	.18.0
China Telecom	.16.0

Source: *Total Telecom Magazine*, November 2004, p. 41, from Gartner Dataquest.

★ 1950 ★
Networking Equipment
SIC: 3669; NAICS: 33429

IP Data Network Routing/Switching Equipment Worldwide

Shares are for the the enterprise market.

Cisco	.85.0%
Other	.15.0

Source: *America's Intelligence Wire*, February 1, 2005, p. NA.

★ 1951 ★
Networking Equipment
SIC: 3669; NAICS: 33429

IP PBX Market Shares

IP PBX stands for Internet Protocol Private Branch Exchange.

Cisco	.77.0%
3Com	.15.0
Other	.8.0

Source: *Internet Week*, August 31, 2004, p. NA.

★ 1952 ★
Networking Equipment
SIC: 3669; NAICS: 33429

Leading Networking Equipment Producers Worldwide, 2004

Market shares are shown in percent.

Cisco/Linksys	.27.0%
D-Link	.20.0
Netgear	.13.0
Other	.40.0

Source: *Investor's Business Daily*, December 30, 2004, p. A6, from Synergy Research Group and First Call.

★ 1953 ★
Networking Equipment
SIC: 3669; NAICS: 33429

Leading Optical Vendors in Asia Pacific

Shares are third quarter 2003 - third quarter 2004.

Huawei	.24.0%
NEC	.19.3
Nortel	.11.5
Alcatel	.8.9
Other	.36.3

Source: *Financial Times*, January 11, 2005, p. 13, from Dell'Oro Group.

★ 1954 ★
Networking Equipment
SIC: 3669; NAICS: 33429

Leading PBX Firms Worldwide

There has been a 73% drop in private branch exchange sales over the last four years. Shares are for installed private branch exchanges.

Nortel	.29.0%
Avaya	.24.0
Siemens	.14.0
Fujitsu	.12.0
NEC	.11.0
Mitel	.3.0
EADS	.3.0

Source: *Telecom's Manager's Voice Report*, January 10, 2005, p. 9, from Synergy Research Group.

★ 1955 ★
Networking Equipment
SIC: 3669; NAICS: 33429

Leading PBX Producers, 2004

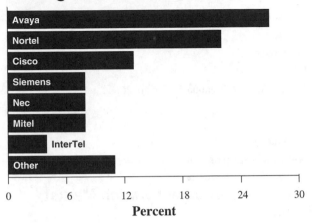

Market shares are shown based on station shipments. PBX market revenues were estimated at $4.75 billion for core system hardware/software, $2.05 billion for system installation maintenance services and $2.15 billion for pre- and post-sale vendors.

Avaya	27.00%
Nortel	22.00
Cisco	13.00
Siemens	8.25
Nec	8.00
Mitel	7.75
InterTel	3.50
Other	10.50

Source: *Business Communications Review*, January 2005, p. 38.

★ 1956 ★
Networking Equipment
SIC: 3669; NAICS: 33429

Leading SOHO Networking Equipment Vendors Worldwide, 2004

Market shares are shown in percent for the second quarter. SOHO stands for small office home office.

Netgear	11.6%
3Com	7.9
Thomson	4.9
Other	75.4

Source: *Taiwan Economic News*, September 13, 2004, p. NA.

★ 1957 ★
Networking Equipment
SIC: 3669; NAICS: 33429

Leading VoIP Firms, 2004

Data show percent of VoIP lines using each company's gear. Shares are shown for the third quarter of 2004.

Alcatel	24.0%
Avaya	20.0
Nortel	19.0
Cisco	13.0
Mitel	5.0
Other	19.0

Source: *Investor's Business Daily*, February 22, 2005, p. A7, from Infonetics Research.

★ 1958 ★
Networking Equipment
SIC: 3669; NAICS: 33429

Metro Ethernet Market Leaders Worldwide, 2003

The industry is roughly five years old but already a billion dollar industry.

Cisco	38.9%
Nortel Networks	21.3
Extreme Networks	3.6
Lucent	2.4
Other	33.8

Source: *Computer Reseller News*, May 24, 2004, p. 33, from International Data Corp.

★ 1959 ★
Networking Equipment
SIC: 3669; NAICS: 33429

Online Meetings and Web Conferencing

Market shares are shown in percent.

WebEx	67.0%
Other	33.0

Source: *On Wall Street*, November 1, 2004, p. NA.

★ 1960 ★
Networking Equipment
SIC: 3669; NAICS: 33429

Routers and Switches Market in China

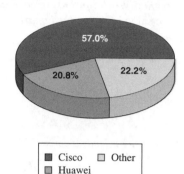

Market shares are shown in percent.

Cisco 57.0%
Huawei 20.8
Other 22.2

Source: *BusinessWeek*, February 7, 2005, p. 50.

★ 1961 ★
Networking Equipment
SIC: 3669; NAICS: 33429

Soft Switch Worldwide, 2004

Market shares are shown based on third quarter shipments.

Nortel 24.83%
Huawei Technologies 21.86
Other 53.31

Source: *Europe Intelligence Wire*, November 25, 2004, p. NA, from Dittberner's NGN Quarterly Shipments Analysis.

★ 1962 ★
Networking Equipment
SIC: 3669; NAICS: 33429

SSL VPN Industry

VPN stands for virtual protocol network. According to Frost & Sullivan, SSL VPN services are expected to take 10% of the managed security services market by 2007.

Aventail 95.0%
Other 5.0

Source: *PR Newswire*, January 6, 2005, p. NA, from Frost & Sullivan.

★ 1963 ★
Networking Equipment
SIC: 3669; NAICS: 33429

Switch/Lightweight AP Market

Market shares are shown in percent.

Symbol 43.0%
Airespace 25.0
Other 32.0

Source: *Rethink It*, January 2005, p. 26.

★ 1964 ★
Networking Equipment
SIC: 3669; NAICS: 33429

Traffic Management Switch Market, 2003

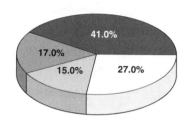

Market shares are shown in percent.

Cisco 41.0%
Nortel 17.0
F5 . . . . .15.0
Other 27.0

Source: *Investor's Business Daily*, November 16, 2004, p. A8, from Dell'Oro Group.

★ 1965 ★
Networking Equipment
SIC: 3669; NAICS: 33429

Videoconferencing Market Leaders Worldwide, 2004

Market shares are shown for the third quarter of 2004.

Polycom 44.0%
Tandberg 23.0
China-based companies 14.0
Sony 8.0

Continued on next page.

★ 1965 ★

[Continued]
Networking Equipment
SIC: 3669; NAICS: 33429

Videoconferencing Market Leaders Worldwide, 2004

Market shares are shown for the third quarter of 2004.

Aethra 7.0%
Other 4.0

Source: *Technology & Learning*, March 1, 2005, p. 13, from *Wainhouse Research Bulletin*.

★ 1966 ★

Networking Equipment
SIC: 3669; NAICS: 33429

Web Accelerator Market Worldwide

Web accelerators deliver business software through networks. They may speed up software tasks or provide enough space on a network to allow users fast access to software. Market shares are shown in percent.

Cisco 27.0%
Stratacache 13.0
F5 . . . . .12.0
Network Appliance 9.0
Packeteer 8.0
Peribit 3.0
Netscaler 3.0
Other 25.0

Source: *Investor's Business Daily*, May 17, 2005, p. A6, from Gartner.

★ 1967 ★

Networking Equipment
SIC: 3669; NAICS: 33429

Wi-Fi Equipment Industry Worldwide, 2004

Wi-Fi equipment revenue climbed to $2.8 billion in 2004, up 15% in 2003. Units reached 36.1 million, up from 51% in 2003. Distribution is shown based on revenues for the third quarter.

North America 50.0%
EMEA 25.0
Asia Pacific 20.0
Other 4.0

Source: *PR Newswire*, February 25, 2005, p. NA, from Infonetics Research.

★ 1968 ★

Networking Equipment
SIC: 3669; NAICS: 33429

WLAN Market Shares Worldwide, 2004

Market shares are shown based on revenues for the third quarter. WLAN stands for wireless local area network.

Cisco 19.2%
Linksys 16.9
D-Link 11.3
Netgear 7.8
Symbol 7.1
Other 37.7

Source: *Computer Reseller News*, January 3, 2005, p. 27, from Synergy Research Group.

★ 1969 ★

Networking Equipment
SIC: 3669; NAICS: 33429

WLAN SOHO Market Shares, 2004

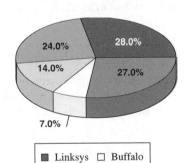

Market shares are shown in percent for the second quarter. WLAN stands for wireless local area network. SOHO stands for small office home office.

Linksys 28.0%
D-Link 24.0
NetGear 14.0
Buffalo 7.0
Other 27.0

Source: *Online Reporter*, December 11, 2004, p. 13, from JP Morgan.

★ 1970 ★
Security Equipment
SIC: 3669; NAICS: 33429

Biometrics Industry in Italy

Market shares are shown in percent.

Public	.40.0%
Private	.15.0
Banks	.15.0
Health	.10.0
Airports	.10.0
Other	.10.0

Source: "US & FCS Market Research Reports." [online] from http://www.stat-usa.gov [Published November 2004], from International Data Corp.

★ 1971 ★
Security Equipment
SIC: 3669; NAICS: 33429

Leading Biometric Surveillance Firms in Italy

Market shares are shown in percent.

Identix	.30.0%
Cognitic	.10.0
Other	.60.0

Source: "US & FCS Market Research Reports." [online] from http://www.stat-usa.gov [Published November 2004], from International Data Corp.

★ 1972 ★
Security Equipment
SIC: 3669; NAICS: 33429

Leading Security Appliance Makers Worldwide, 2004

The security server appliance market grew 57% year over year. Shares are for the second quarter of 2004.

Cisco	.29.1%
Nokia	7.3
SonicWall	5.1
Juniper	4.2
WatchGuard	3.2
Other	.41.1

Source: "Worldwide Security Appliance Market Grows 57% in 2Q04." [online] from http://www.idc.com [Press release September 13, 2004], from International Data Corp.

★ 1973 ★
Security Equipment
SIC: 3669; NAICS: 33429

Leading UTM Makers Worldwide

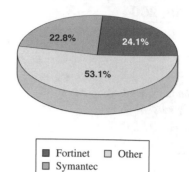

■ Fortinet □ Other
■ Symantec

This is a recently identified category of security server market, 12% of the market place (firewalls and VPNs 70%). UTM stands for unified threat management.

Fortinet	.24.1%
Symantec	.22.8
Other	.53.1

Source: "Worldwide Security Appliance Market Grows 57% in 2Q04." [online] from http://www.idc.com [Press release September 13, 2004], from International Data Corp.

★ 1974 ★
Security Equipment
SIC: 3669; NAICS: 33429

Security Equipment Industry, 2003 and 2008

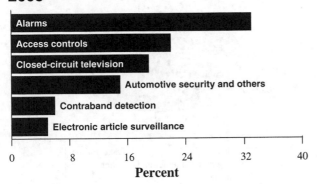

Percent

Total demand is forecast to increase from 8.7% from $10.2 billion in 2003 to $15 billion in 2008. Alarms are the major components of the industry but other categories are seeing impressive growth. Access control devices will grow 10.2% for the period shown and closed-circuit televisions will increase 12.8%. Demand is shown in millions of dollars.

	2003	2008	Share
Alarms	$ 3,760	$ 5,050	32.58%
Access controls	2,095	3,400	21.94
Closed-circuit television	1,590	2,900	18.71
Automotive security and others	1,510	2,350	15.16
Contraband detection	690	1,000	6.45
Electronic article surveillance	560	800	5.16

Source: *Security Distributing & Marketing*, July 2004, p. 15, from Freedonia Group.

★ 1975 ★
Security Equipment
SIC: 3669; NAICS: 33429

Security Hologram Industry in India

The industry is doing well in India, with growth rates of 25-30%. In the packaging sector for holographic materials, the industry is closer to 40%. Holostik has more than half of the market.

Holostik	.50.0%
Other	.50.0

Source: *Holography News*, August 2004, p. 8.

★ 1976 ★
Telematics
SIC: 3669; NAICS: 33429

Telematics Research, 2003 and 2008

Telematics revenues are expected to increase from $5.6 billion in 2003 to $6.5 billion in 2008.

	2003	2008
Consumer hardware	$ 2,965.0	$ 2,722.7
Commercial service revenues	1,801.5	2,393.7
Commercial hardware	711.1	880.5
Consumer service revenues	163.5	453.8

Source: *Research Studies - Business Communications Inc.*, Aug. 28, 2004, p. NA, from Business Communications Inc.

★ 1977 ★
Memory Cards
SIC: 3672; NAICS: 334119

Leading Memory Card Makers in Japan, 2003

Market shares are estimated based on domestic shipments.

Matsushita Electric Industrial	.17.8%
Sony	.15.1
SanDisk	.14.8
Hagiwara Sys-Com	.13.2
Buffalo	.12.8
Other	.26.3

Source: "Market Share Survey Report 2003." [online] from http://www.nni.nikkei.co.jp [Published July 26, 2004], from Nikkei estimates.

★ 1978 ★
Printed Circuit Boards
SIC: 3672; NAICS: 334412

Leading PCB Makers Worldwide, 2003

The source places the world market for printed circuit boards at $34.5 billion. Firms are ranked by sales in millions of dollars.

	($ mil.)	Share
Nippon Mektron	$ 1,175	3.41%
CMK	1,049	3.04
Ibiden	1,027	2.98
Hitachi Chemical	685	1.99
Shinko Electric Industry	636	1.84
Unimicron	609	1.77
Samsung Electro-Mechanics	545	1.58
Compeq	462	1.34
Nanya PCB	453	1.31

Continued on next page.

★ 1978 ★

[Continued]
Printed Circuit Boards
SIC: 3672; NAICS: 334412

Leading PCB Makers Worldwide, 2003

The source places the world market for printed circuit boards at $34.5 billion. Firms are ranked by sales in millions of dollars.

	($ mil.)	Share
Daeduck Group	$ 422	1.22%
Other	27,437	79.53

Source: *Circuits Assembly*, September 2004, p. 16, from N.T. Information.

★ 1979 ★

Lasers
SIC: 3674; NAICS: 334413

Commercial Laser Sales Worldwide, 2003-2005

The industry is shown by revenues. The market has a generally positive outlook, but the overall optoelectronics industry has not reaped the benefits from recent events that it could (lasers have many applications for homeland security and the military in Iraq).

	2003	2004	2005
Diode	63.0%	59.0%	61.0%
Nondiode	37.0	41.0	39.0

Source: *Laser Focus World*, January 2005, p. 83, from Strategies Unlimited.

★ 1980 ★

Lasers
SIC: 3674; NAICS: 334413

Diode Laser Sales Worldwide, 2004-2005

The market grew 18% in 2003 but just 4% in 2004. The primary reason was the drop in prices across all optical storage sectors.

	2004	2005	Share
Optical data storage	$ 1,865	$ 1,844	55.48%
Telecommunications	943	1,131	34.03
Solid-state laser pumping . . .	110	116	3.49
Medical	62	65	1.96
Image recording	52	53	1.59
Entertainment & display . . .	20	19	0.57
Other	82	96	2.89

Source: *Optoelectronics Report*, February 1, 2005, p. 1, from Strategies Unlimited and *Laser Focus Review 2005 Annual Review and Forecast of the Market*.

★ 1981 ★

Lasers
SIC: 3674; NAICS: 334413

Gallium Nitrate Laser Diode Market

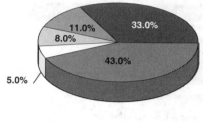

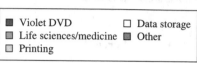

By 2008, violet DVD 97% is forecast to take 97% of the market.

Violet DVD	.33.0%
Life sciences/medicine	.11.0
Printing	. 8.0
Data storage	. 5.0
Other	.43.0

Source: *Chemical Market Reporter*, January 17, 2005, p. 15, from Strategy Analysts.

★ 1982 ★

Lasers
SIC: 3674; NAICS: 334413

High-brightness LED Market Worldwide, 2003

The market is expected to increase from $2.7 billion in 2003 to $6 billion in 2008.

Cellular phones and other devices	.50.0%
Outdoor signs	.23.0
Automotive	.18.0
Other	. 8.0

Source: *San Jose Mercury News*, December 6, 2004, p. NA, from Strategies Unlimited.

★ 1983 ★
Lasers
SIC: 3674; NAICS: 334413

Nondiode Laser Sales Worldwide, 2003 and 2005

Nondiode laser sales represent 37% of the $4.9 billion market in 2003 and 39% of the $5.9 billion laser sales. Part of the reason for the striking fall in revenues in the inspection and measurement control is that gas lasers are being phased out.

	2003	2005	Share
Materials processing	$ 1,206.0	$ 1,503.0	53.52%
Military and aerospace	326.0	433.0	15.42
Medical equipment	326.0	433.0	15.42
Entertainment and display	136.0	156.0	5.55
Basic research	136.0	155.0	5.52
Instrumentation	76.5	86.2	3.07
Inspection, measurement, control	76.5	5.3	0.19
Image recording	39.4	37.0	1.32

Source: *Optoelectronics Report*, January 1, 2005, p. 1, from Strategies Unlimited.

★ 1984 ★
Lasers
SIC: 3674; NAICS: 334413

OLED and LED Global Sales, 2006-2008

OLED displays are brighter, lighter and faster than their LCD counterparts. LCD displays are still the dominant form. The markets for organic light-emitting diodes and liquid crystal displays are shown in millions of dollars.

	2006	2007	2008
LCD	$ 73,659	$ 79,124	$ 84,104
OLED	1,369	1,829	2,258

Source: *Electronic Business*, November 2004, p. 17, from iSuppli.

★ 1985 ★
Microprocessors
SIC: 3674; NAICS: 334413

Global Market for MPEG-2 Decoder Silicon Chips

The company is the world's largest supplier of MPEG-2 decoder silicon chips for set-top boxes.

ST	77.0%
Other	23.0

Source: *Product News Network*, September 22, 2004, p. NA.

★ 1986 ★
Microprocessors
SIC: 3674; NAICS: 334413

IC Circuit Simulation Market, 2003

Market shares are shown in percent.

Synopsys	42.0%
Nassda	37.0
Other	21.0

Source: *Electronic Engineering Times*, December 6, 2004, p. 1, from Gartner Dataquest.

★ 1987 ★
Microprocessors
SIC: 3674; NAICS: 334413

IC Market Shares Worldwide

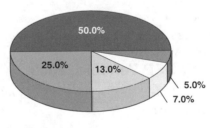

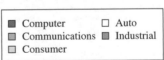

The industry is valued at $177.9 billion.

Computer	50.0%
Communications	25.0
Consumer	13.0
Auto	7.0
Industrial	5.0

Source: *Purchasing*, November 18, 2004, p. 22, from IC Insights.

★ 1988 ★

Microprocessors

SIC: 3674; NAICS: 334413

Largest Wireless LAN Chip Makers Worldwide, 2003

Market shares are shown in percent.

Conexant	29.0%
Broadcom	24.0
TI	12.0
Atheros	11.0
Agere	7.0
Marvell	6.0
RFMicro	3.0
Other	8.0

Source: *Electronic Business*, June 2004, p. 28, from iSuppli.

★ 1989 ★

Microprocessors

SIC: 3674; NAICS: 334413

Leading DRAM Chips Worldwide, 2004

Market shares are shown for the third quarter of 2004.

Samsung	31.4%
Micron Technology	15.2
Hynix Semiconductor	15.2
Other	38.2

Source: *The Economist*, January 15, 2005, p. 64, from Gartner.

★ 1990 ★

Microprocessors

SIC: 3674; NAICS: 334413

Leading DSP Vendors, 2003

Shares are shown based on sales of $6.13 billion for the calendar year.

Texas Instruments	47.7%
Agere	13.1
Motorola	10.3
Analog Devices	7.6
Other	21.6

Source: *Electronic Business*, December 2004, p. 48, from Forward Concepts.

★ 1991 ★

Microprocessors

SIC: 3674; NAICS: 334413

Leading Graphics Chips Makers Worldwide, 2005

Market shares are shown in percent for the first quarter.

Intel	43.1%
ATI Technologies	26.1
Nvidia	17.9
VIA Technologies	6.9
Silicon Integrated Systems	5.4
Other	0.6

Source: *Investor's Business Daily*, April 28, 2005, p. A4, from Jon Peddie Research.

★ 1992 ★

Microprocessors

SIC: 3674; NAICS: 334413

Leading Microprocessors Worldwide, 2003-2004

Market shares are shown in percent.

	2003	2004
Intel	80.6%	81.5%
AMD	16.5	15.7
Freescale	1.8	1.2
IBM	0.1	0.8
Other	1.1	0.9

Source: *USA TODAY*, April 19, 2005, p. 3B, from International Data Corp.

★ 1993 ★

Microprocessors

SIC: 3674; NAICS: 334413

Nonvolatile Memory Market Worldwide, 2005

NAND is forecast to surpass NOR technology in cell phone manufacturing during the second half of 2005. NAND is forecast to grow from $6.4 billion in 2004 to $8 billion in 2005.

NAND	47.4%
NOR	45.5
Other	7.1

Source: *Purchasing*, April 21, 2005, p. 17, from IC Insights.

★ 1994 ★

Microprocessors

SIC: 3674; NAICS: 334413

Programmable Logic Market Worldwide, 2004

Market shares are shown in percent.

	Q1	Q2
Xilinx	53.2%	52.5%
Altera	32.0	33.3
Lattice	7.8	7.5
Actel	5.6	5.4
Other	1.4	1.3

Source: *Electronics Weekly*, September 15, 2004, p. 22, from Gartner Dataquest Inc.

★ 1995 ★

Microprocessors

SIC: 3674; NAICS: 334413

Theater and NXT Demodulators

ATI's television unit shipped more than 5 million chips for HDTVs and HD cable and terrestrial STBs in 2004, according to the source. Market shares are shown in percent.

ATI	85.0%
Other	15.0

Source: *America's Intelligence Wire*, December 21, 2004, p. NA.

★ 1996 ★

Microprocessors

SIC: 3674; NAICS: 334413

Top Microcontroller Makers Worldwide, 2004

Market shares are shown for the first quarter.

Renesas	21.4%
Freescale	15.0

NEC	10.7%
Infineon	7.0
Matsushita	5.5
Other	40.4

Source: *Electronic Business*, November 2004, p. 47, from iSuppli.

★ 1997 ★

Semiconductors

SIC: 3674; NAICS: 334413

10 Gb/s Ethernet Semiconductors

The market is regarded as still being in its infancy.

Quake Technologies	80.0%
Other	20.0

Source: *Broadband Business Forecast*, November 2, 2004, p. NA.

★ 1998 ★

Semiconductors

SIC: 3674; NAICS: 334413

Flash Memory Market Worldwide

The flash NOR and NAND memory market is 2.4 billion units and valued at $11.6 billion.

Samsung	25.0%
Intel	15.0
AMD/Fujitsu	15.0
Toshiba	13.0
Renesas	9.0
Other	23.0

Source: *Electronic Business*, July 2004, p. 44, from Gartner.

★ 1999 ★

Semiconductors

SIC: 3674; NAICS: 334413

Global Semiconductor Market, 2005

Total sales were $21.4 billion.

PC/Computer	42.6%
Consumer	18.5
Cell phones/mobile	16.3
Industrial/military	9.2
Automotive	6.9
Wired communications	6.5

Source: *Financial Times*, February 9, 2005, p. 8, from Semiconductor Industry Association.

★ 2000 ★
Semiconductors
SIC: 3674; NAICS: 334413

Leading Analog Chip Makers Worldwide

Companies are ranked by revenues in millions of dollars.

	($ bil.)	Share
Texas Instruments	$ 3.45	12.88%
Infineon Microelectronics	3.41	12.73
STMicroelectronics	2.26	8.44
Analog Devices	1.76	6.57
National Semiconductor	1.41	5.26
Other	14.50	54.12

Source: *New York Times*, August 9, 2004, p. C4, from Databeans.

★ 2001 ★
Semiconductors
SIC: 3674; NAICS: 334413

Top Flash Memory Suppliers Worldwide, 2003

Market shares are shown based on $11,649 million.

Samsung Electronics	19.4%
Spansion	15.8
Toshiba	15.6
Intel	14.5
Renesas Technology	9.1
STMicroelectronics	8.6
Sharp Electronics	8.6
Silicon Storage Technology	2.5
Macronix International	1.9
NEC Electronics	1.6
Other	2.4

Source: *EDN*, November 11, 2004, p. S62, from iSuppli.

★ 2002 ★
Semiconductors
SIC: 3674; NAICS: 334413

Top Semiconductor Makers Worldwide, 2005

Market shares are shown in percent for the first quarter of the year.

Intel	15.2%
Samsung Electronics	7.3
Renesas Technology	4.3
Texas Instruments	4.3

Toshiba	4.0%
Infineon Technologies	3.7
STMicroelectronics	3.7
Other	57.5

Source: *Financial Times*, June 9, 2005, p. 15, from iSuppli.

★ 2003 ★
Flat Panel Displays
SIC: 3679; NAICS: 334419

Flat Panel Display Demand Worldwide, 2004 and 2009

Demand is shown in millions of dollars.

	2004	2009	Share
Mobile phones	$ 408	$ 1,383	48.90%
Industrial equipment	9	321	11.35
Cameras	61	266	9.41
Desktop monitors	0	189	6.68
Camcorders	12	156	5.52
Handheld games	19	119	4.21
Portable DVD players	0	44	1.56
Television	0	31	1.10
Other	23	319	11.28

Source: *BusinessWeek*, May 10, 2004, p. 110, from iSuppli.

★ 2004 ★
Flat Panel Displays
SIC: 3679; NAICS: 334119

Leading PDP Makers in South Korea

Pie chart: 23.1%, 33.9%, 20.5%, 22.5%

Legend: ■ Matsushita Electric □ LG Electric ■ Samsung □ Other

Shares are shown based on 790,000 panels for the quarter to June 2004.

Matsushita Electric	23.1%
Samsung	22.5
LG Electric	20.5
Other	33.9

Source: *Bangkok Post*, October 20, 2004, p. NA.

★ 2005 ★

Flat Panel Displays

SIC: 3679; NAICS: 334119

Plasma Television Display Shipments in Asia

The market in Asia is expected to increase 70%.

	2003	2004	Share
Japan	275	338	39.44%
China/Hong Kong	108	263	30.69
Korea	35	74	8.63
Australia	33	64	7.47
Taiwan	22	54	6.30
Singapore	17	32	3.73
Other	14	32	3.73

Source: *Electronic Engineering Times*, July 19, 2004, p. 30, from Decision Tree Consulting.

★ 2006 ★

Flat Panel Displays

SIC: 3679; NAICS: 334119

Top Automobile Monitor Module Firms Worldwide

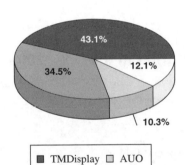

| ■ TMDisplay | ☐ AUO |
| ■ Sharp | ☐ Other |

Market shares are shown for the second quarter of 2004.

TMDisplay	.43.1%
Sharp	.34.5
AUO	.10.3
Other	.12.1

Source: "DisplaySearch Adds Portable DVD Players." [online] from http://www.displaysearch.com [Published October 25, 2004], from Display Search.

★ 2007 ★

Flat Panel Displays

SIC: 3679; NAICS: 334119

Top Digital Still Camera Module Firms Worldwide

Market shares are shown the second quarter of 2004.

Casio	.27.9%
Sanyo	.20.0
AUO	.18.9
Other	.33.2

Source: "DisplaySearch Adds Portable DVD Players." [online] from http://www.displaysearch.com [Published October 25, 2004], from Display Search.

★ 2008 ★

Flat Panel Displays

SIC: 3679; NAICS: 334119

Top Mobile Phone Display Firms Worldwide

Market shares are shown for the second quarter of 2004.

Samsung SDI	.21.3%
Phlips	.15.5
Epson	.13.1
Other	.50.1

Source: "DisplaySearch Adds Portable DVD Players." [online] from http://www.displaysearch.com [Published October 25, 2004], from Display Search.

★ 2009 ★

Flat Panel Displays

SIC: 3679; NAICS: 334119

Top Subdisplay Firms Worldwide

Market shares are shown for the third quarter of 2004.

Samsung SDI	.28.9%
Optrex	.9.8
Wintek	.7.4
Other	.53.9

Source: "DisplaySearch Reports Mobile Phone Display Shipments." [online] from http://www.displaysearch.com [Published December 14, 2004], from Display Search.

★ 2010 ★

Photonics

SIC: 3679; NAICS: 334419

Nanophotonics Market Worldwide

The industry is closely related to nanophotoelectronics or the development of electronic devices that interact with light. The global market is forecast to increase from $420.7 million in 2004 to $9,325 million in 2009.

Nanphotonic light-emitting diodes	82.0%
Near-field optics	14.4
Nanocrystalline dye-sensitized solar cells	3.3
Other	0.3

Source: *Fiber Optics Weekly Update*, January 14, 2005, p. 1, from Business Communications Co.

★ 2011 ★

Photonics

SIC: 3679; NAICS: 334419

Photonics Industry in Taiwan, 2004

Taiwan's share of the global photonics industry increased from 11 to 13 percent from 2003 to 2004. The photonics market is valued at $203 billion in production value. TN/STN stands for twisted nematic/super twisted nematic LCD panels.

TFT-LCD	$ 14.40
Recorable CD discs	1.49
TN/STNs LCD panels	1.47
Digital still cameras	1.41
Recordable DVD discs	1.22

Source: *Taiwan News*, January 19, 2005, p. NA, from Photonics Industry & Technology Development Association.

★ 2012 ★

Batteries

SIC: 3692; NAICS: 335912

Advanced Battery Industry, 2003 and 2008

Over the previous decade nickel-metal hydride, secondary lithium and zinc-air developed into commercial battery markets. Large battery market growth will develop from hybrid vehicles and portable devices. The industry is expected to reach $4.5 billion by 2008.

	2003	2008	Share
Lithium containing	$ 1,016	$ 1,574	35.07%
Nickel-containing	912	1,088	24.24
Lead-acid	881	1,163	25.91
Developmental	34	584	13.01

	2003	2008	Share
Specialty	$ 33	$ 30	0.67%
Zinc air/metal air	28	49	1.09

Source: *Research Studies - Business Communications Inc.*, August 19, 2004, p. NA, from BCC Inc.

★ 2013 ★

Batteries

SIC: 3692; NAICS: 335912

Battery Control Technology Sales, 2004 and 2009

The wholesale battery market is forecast to increase from $2.2 billion in 2004 to $4.2 billion in 2009.

	2004	2009	Share
Battery chargers & power converters	$ 1,437	$ 1,800	42.25%
Smart batteries	768	2,233	52.42
Power conditioners	121	227	5.33

Source: *Research Studies - Business Communications Inc.*, April 2, 2004, p. NA, from BCC Inc.

★ 2014 ★

Batteries

SIC: 3692; NAICS: 335912

Battery Market in the U.K., 2004

The total market was worth 245.9 million pounds sterling for the year ended June 20, 2004.

Alkaline	77.7%
Zinc carbon	10.3
Button cells/special lithium	7.5
Rechargeable	4.3

Source: *Grocer*, September 4, 2004, p. 60, from TNS Superpanel.

★ 2015 ★

Batteries

SIC: 3692; NAICS: 335912

Battery Sales by Type, 2004

Unit shares are shown by food store, drug store and mass merchandiser sales (but not Wal-Mart) for the year ended May 16, 2004.

AA	41.0%
AAA	16.0
9V	11.0
C	9.1

Continued on next page.

[Continued]
Batteries
SIC: 3692; NAICS: 335912

Battery Sales by Type, 2004

Unit shares are shown by food store, drug store and mass merchandiser sales (but not Wal-Mart) for the year ended May 16, 2004.

D	8.1%
Other	.15.3

Source: *Grocery Headquarters*, August 2004, p. 30, from Information Resources Inc.

★ 2016 ★

Batteries
SIC: 3692; NAICS: 335912

Largest Battery Makers Worldwide

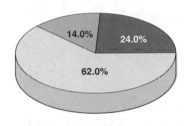

Johnson Controls ☐ **Other**
Exide

Market shares are shown in percent.

Johnson Controls	.24.0%
Exide	.14.0
Other	.62.0

Source: *Milwaukee Journal Sentinel*, July 20, 2004, p. NA.

★ 2017 ★

Batteries
SIC: 3692; NAICS: 335912

Leading Battery Brands in the U.K., 2003

Alkalines accounted for 68.5% of volume and 52.8% of value sales.

	(mil.)	Share
Duracell	241.5	34.21%
Energizer	165.6	23.46
Panasonic	157.3	22.28
Own label	71.5	10.13
Rayovac	36.4	5.16

	(mil.)	Share
Uniross	14.7	2.08%
Other	19.0	2.69

Source: *Marketing*, October 27, 2004, p. 32, from Mintel.

★ 2018 ★

Batteries
SIC: 3692; NAICS: 335912

Leading Hearing Aid Battery Brands

Brands are ranked by drug store sales in millions of dollars.

	($ mil.)	Share
Duracell EasyTab	$ 16.8	41.9%
Energizer	7.5	18.8
Energizer EZ Change	2.1	5.3
Private label	9.9	24.5

Source: *Drug Store News*, May 23, 2005, p. 37, from Information Resources Inc.

★ 2019 ★

Batteries
SIC: 3692; NAICS: 335912

Leading OEM Battery Makers in Thailand, 2002

OEM stands for original equipment manufacturer.

Siam GS Battery Company	.55.0%
Yuasa	.17.0
Siam Furukawa Company	.13.0
Siam Battery Industry	. 5.0
Matsushita Battery (Thailand) Public Company	. 5.0
Thai Storage Battery Public Company	. 5.0

Source: *Batteries International*, October 2004, p. 62.

★ 2020 ★

Batteries
SIC: 3692; NAICS: 335912

Rechargable Button Cell Market Worldwide

Market shares are shown in percent.

Varta	.65.0%
Other	.35.0

Source: *Batteries International*, October 2004, p. 61.

★ 2021 ★
Batteries
SIC: 3692; NAICS: 335912

Top Battery Brands, 2005

Market shares are shown based on drug store sales for the 52 weeks ended February 20, 2005.

Duracell alkaline	.31.3%
Energizer Max alkaline	.11.7
Duracell all other	9.5
Energizer all other	6.1
Energizer E2 lithium all other	4.2
Duracell Ultra alkaline	3.8
Duracell Easytab zinc air	2.9
Duracell Ultra all other	1.5
Energizer zinc air	1.3
Energizer E2 titanium alkaline	1.3
Other	.26.4

Source: *Chain Drug Review*, May 23, 2005, p. 69, from Information Resources Inc.

★ 2022 ★
Batteries
SIC: 3692; NAICS: 335912

Top Battery Makers, 2004

Market shares are shown based on sales at food stores, drug stores and mass merchandisers (but not Wal-Mart) for the 52 weeks ended June 13, 2004.

Duracell	.47.3%
Energizer	.32.2
Rayovac	7.0
Panasonic	0.8
Private label	.12.0
Other	0.7

Source: *Grocery Headquarters*, August 2004, p. 67, from Information Resources Inc.

★ 2023 ★
Batteries
SIC: 3692; NAICS: 335912

Top Battery Makers in Thailand

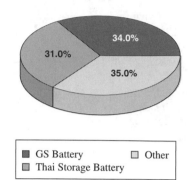

■ GS Battery	□ Other
■ Thai Storage Battery	

Market shares are shown in percent.

GS Battery	.34.0%
Thai Storage Battery	.31.0
Other	.35.0

Source: *Bangkok Post*, March 1, 2005, p. NA.

★ 2024 ★
Injection Systems
SIC: 3694; NAICS: 336322

Leading Diesel Injection System Makers in Europe

Market shares are shown in percent.

Robert Bosch	.62.5%
Siemens VDO	.24.0
Delphi	.10.0
Magnetti Marelli	1.5
Denso	1.0
Other	1.0

Source: *Automotive News Europe*, November 1, 2004, p. 3, from DRI.

★ 2025 ★

Blank CDs

SIC: 3695; NAICS: 334613

Top Blank CD Brands, 2004

Brands are ranked by 52 weeks ended based on super-markets, drug stores and discount stores (excluding Wal-Mart) for the year ended November 28, 2004.

	($ mil.)	Share
Memorex	$ 25.9	26.14%
TDK	23.3	23.51
Sony	15.5	15.64
Fuji	11.9	12.01
Maxell	10.8	10.90
Imation	7.5	7.57
Khypermedia	2.1	2.12
Napster	1.4	1.41
Other	0.7	0.71

Source: *MMR*, January 10, 2005, p. 94, from Information Resources Inc.

★ 2026 ★

Video Tape

SIC: 3695; NAICS: 334613

Leading Blank Video Cassettes, 2004

Brands are ranked by food store, drug store and mass merchandiser sales (but not Wal-Mart) in millions of dollars for the year ended November 28, 2004.

	($ mil.)	Share
Sony	$ 30.5	15.74%
Sony V	20.9	10.78
Fuji	16.6	8.57
TDK Revue	16.1	8.31
Fuji HQ	14.0	7.22
Maxell	11.4	5.88
TDK	11.0	5.68
Maxell GX Silver	9.9	5.11
Sony HMP	7.6	3.92
Maxell HGX Gold	6.5	3.35
Other	49.3	25.44

Source: *MMR*, January 10, 2005, p. 91, from Information Resources Inc.

★ 2027 ★

Video Tape

SIC: 3695; NAICS: 334613

Top Video Tape Makers, 2004

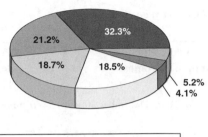

Market shares are shown based on sales at food stores, drug stores and mass merchandisers (but not Wal-Mart) for the 52 weeks ended June 13, 2004.

Sony Tape Sales	32.3%
TDK Electronics	21.2
Maxell	18.7
Fuji Photo Film	18.5
Panasonic	4.1
Other	5.2

Source: *Grocery Headquarters*, August 2004, p. S88, from Information Resources Inc.

★ 2028 ★

Automotive Electronics

SIC: 3699; NAICS: 334419

Automotive Electronics Market in North America

The industry is valued at $7 billion.

United States	81.0%
Canada	12.0
Mexico	7.0

Source: *Internet Wire*, February 8, 2005, p. NA, from Freedonia.

★ 2029 ★

Automotive Electronics

SIC: 3699; NAICS: 334419

Automotive Electronics Market Worldwide, 2002 and 2007

The industry is seen by segment.

	2002	2007
Safety and convenience	47.3%	48.8%
Powertrain electronics	34.8	31.0
Other	17.8	20.2

Source: *EDN Asia*, December 2004, p. 54, from In-Stat and MDR.

★ 2030 ★

Automotive Electronics

SIC: 3699; NAICS: 333618

Car Ignition Immobilizers Worldwide

Market shares are shown in percent.

EM Microeletronic	.40.0%
Other	.60.0

Source: *The Gazette*, December 12, 2004, p. NA.

★ 2031 ★

Automotive Electronics

SIC: 3699; NAICS: 334419

In-car Technology Installed Base Worldwide, 2004 and 2008

Data are in millions of units.

	2004	2008
GPS receivers	9.4	30.0
DVD systems	8.4	21.9
Voice recognition	5.8	30.0
In-vehicle phone options	4.5	33.0
Telematics	2.5	28.0
Satellite radio	2.2	15.1
Bluetooth	0.5	11.4

Source: *Screen Digest*, August 2004, p. 25S, from Telematics Research Group.